JE WEEK

LONGMAN HISTORY OF ITALY
General editor: Denys Hay

Italy in the Early Middle Ages 600–1200
T.S. Brown

*Italy in the Age of Dante and Petrarch 1216–1380
John Larner*

*Italy in the Age of the Renaissance 1380–1530
Denys Hay and John Law*

*Italy 1530–1630
Eric Cochrane (edited by Julius Kirshner)*

*Italy in the Seventeenth Century 1598–1713
Domenico Sella*

*Italy in the Age of Reason 1685–1789
Dino Carpanetto and Giuseppe Ricuperati*

*Italy in the Age of the Risorgimento 1790–1870
Harry Hearder*

*Modern Italy: 1871–1995. Second Edition
Martin Clark*

*already published

LONGMAN HISTORY OF ITALY

Modern Italy
1871–1995

Second Edition

MARTIN CLARK

An imprint of **Pearson Education**

Harlow, England · London · New York · Reading, Massachusetts · San Francisco
Toronto · Don Mills, Ontario · Sydney · Tokyo · Singapore · Hong Kong · Seoul
Taipei · Cape Town · Madrid · Mexico City · Amsterdam · Munich · Paris · Milan

Pearson Education Limited
Edinburgh Gate
Harlow, Essex CM20 2JE, United Kingdom
and Associated Companies throughout the world.

Visit us on the World Wide Web at:
http://www.pearsoneduc.com

©Longman Group Limited 1984
Second edition © Addison Wesley Longman Limited 1996

First published 1984
Second edition 1996

ISBN 0 582 05126 6 PPR

British Library Cataloguing-in-Publication Data
A catalogue record of this book is available from the British Library

Library of Congress Cataloging-in-Publication Data
Clark, Martin, 1938–
Modern Italy, 1871–1995 / Martin Clark. – 2nd ed.
p. cm. -- (Longman history of Italy (Unnumbered))
Rev. ed. of: Modern Italy, 1871–1982. 1984.
Includes bibliographical references and index.
ISBN 0–582–05126–6 (ppr)
1. Italy--History--1870–1915. 2. Italy--History--20th century.
I. Clark, Martin, 1938– Modern Italy, 1871–1982. II. Title.
III. Series.
DG555.C55 1996
945'.09--dc20   95–53742
                                                        CIP
                                                        AC

10 9 8 7 6 5
04 03 02 01 00

Set by 7 in 10/12 ITC Garamond
Printed in Malaysia, PP

Contents

List of maps x
Abbreviations xi
Measures and prices xii
Acknowledgements xiii

Chapter One   Introduction 1
                1.1   Themes and problems 1
                1.2   Historiography 4
                1.3   Sources 7

PART ONE
1871–87

Chapter Two   Italietta – a backward society? 12
                2.1   Agriculture 12
                2.2   The industrial economy 21
                2.3   The economic and social élite 28
                2.4   Making Italians 30
                2.5   Education and literacy 34
                2.6   Leisure 41

Chapter Three   The Liberal·State 44
                3.1   The Crown and its prerogatives 44
                3.2   Foreign policy 46
                3.3   The army 48
                3.4   The police and judiciary 51
                3.5   The civil service 55
                3.6   Local government 58
                3.7   Parliament 61
                3.8   Conclusion 66

Chapter Four   The subversives 69
                4.1   Popular disaffection and its institutions 69
                4.2   The anarchists 73

4.3	Socialism and labourism	75
4.4	The Republicans, Radicals and Garibaldini	78
4.5	The Church and her influence	81
4.6	Conclusion: strategies and counter-strategies	88

PART TWO
1887–1914

Chapter Five	The first crisis of the Liberal State, 1887–1900		92
	5.1	Crispi the reformer	92
	5.2	The 'tariff war'	93
	5.3	The banks	97
	5.4	Africa	99
	5.5	Riot and insurrection: the Sicilian *Fasci* and the riots of 1898	101
	5.6	The Catholics	105
	5.7	The Italian Socialist Party	108
	5.8	The Radicals and Republicans	112
	5.9	The debate on the State, 1896–1900	114
	5.10	Conclusion	117
Chapter Six	The first 'economic miracle': industrialization and the economy, 1896–1914		119
	6.1	Industry	119
	6.2	Agriculture	127
	6.3	The limits to growth	131
Chapter Seven	Politics in the age of Giolitti, 1900–14		136
	7.1	The 'Giolittian system'	136
	7.2	The Radicals and Socialists	140
	7.3	The Catholics	146
	7.4	The Nationalists	150
	7.5	The Libyan War	153
	7.6	The suffrage of 1912	156
	7.7	The end of the 'Giolittian system'	157
Chapter Eight	An Italian people?		161
	8.1	Population and migration	161
	8.2	The uses of leisure	167
	8.3	Education and literacy	169
	8.4	The press	172
	8.5	The revolt of the intellectuals	173
	8.6	Conclusion	177

PART THREE
1914–43

Chapter Nine	Italy and the Great War		180
	9.1	The Salandra government and 'Red Week'	180

9.2	The intervention crisis	181
9.3	The Great War: fighting and campaigns	185
9.4	The war at home: the economic impact	190
9.5	Wartime politics	194
9.6	The outsiders' politics	197
9.7	Conclusion	200

Chapter Ten — The strange death of Liberal Italy, 1919–25 ... 203

10.1	High Politics: patriotism insulted and patriotism avenged	203
10.2	Economic problems	206
10.3	Agriculture	209
10.4	Political breakdown	211
10.5	The rise of Fascism	213
10.6	Mussolini as Prime Minister (October 1922 to April 1924)	222
10.7	The Matteotti crisis	224

Chapter Eleven — The Fascist State: the new authoritarianism ... 230

11.1	The defeat of the opposition	230
11.2	The strong State	232
11.3	The defeat of the Fascists?	236
11.4	Summary	239

Chapter Twelve — The Fascist regime: the quest for consensus ... 242

12.1	Ideology and indoctrination	242
12.2	Fascist syndicates and corporations	247
12.3	Anti-Fascism	251
12.4	The Church	254
12.5	The breakdown of Fascist consensus	257
12.6	Summary	259

Chapter Thirteen — The economy and society under the Fascists ... 263

13.1	Economic policy	263
13.2	Agriculture	268
13.3	Social change and the population	271
13.4	Education	276
13.5	Conclusion	278

Chapter Fourteen — Fascist diplomacy and Fascist war ... 280

14.1	Foreign policy	280
14.2	The war: campaigns	285
14.3	The war economy	288
14.4	Propaganda and the party	290
14.5	On the fringe	292
14.6	Underground stirrings	293
14.7	The July plot	295

PART FOUR
1943–95

Chapter Fifteen   Resistance and renewal: Italy from 1943 to 1948 302
   15.1 The forty-five days 302
   15.2 The Allies and the 'Kingdom of the South' 304
   15.3 The Republic of Salò 308
   15.4 The Resistance 310
   15.5 The wind from the North 316
   15.6 The 'institutional questions' 319
   15.7 The exclusion crisis 323
   15.8 Conclusion 325

Chapter Sixteen   The triumph of 'Low Politics' 327
   16.1 Parliament and the parties 327
   16.2 Government, subterranean and local 334
   16.3 The civil service 338
   16.4 The judiciary 340
   16.5 The police 341
   16.6 The army 343
   16.7 Foreign policy 344
   16.8 Summary 346

Chapter Seventeen   The economy and society under the Republic 348
   17.1 Reconstruction and the 'economic miracle' 348
   17.2 Agriculture 354
   17.3 The battle for the South 357
   17.4 Emigration 360
   17.5 Population, health and the family 362
   17.6 Education and its uses 364
   17.7 Culture, high and low 366
   17.8 Secularization 370
   17.9 Summary 372

Chapter Eighteen   The Great Cultural Revolution: Italy in the 1970s 374
   18.1 The universities 374
   18.2 The economy 375
   18.3 Divorce and the family 380
   18.4 Terrorism 384
   18.5 The political response: the 'historic compromise' .. 387
   18.6 The rebirth of regionalism 390

Chapter Nineteen   The economy and society, 1980–95 394
   19.1 The years of 'thoughtless prosperity' 394
   19.2 Social change and the family 400
   19.3 Health and welfare 402
   19.4 The Church 404
   19.5 The press and media 405

CONTENTS

Chapter Twenty   The collapse of the 'First Republic'? 408

20.1 The established parties 408

20.2 Reform by referendum 411

20.3 The Northern leagues 412

20.4 Corruption, 'Tangentopoli' and organized crime 413

20.5 Elections, referenda and parties, 1992–94 419

20.6 Conclusion 424

Bibliography.. 427

Maps 439

Index 443

List of maps

1. Modern Italy 440
2. Italy's northern frontiers 441
3. Trieste and Venezia Giulia 442

Abbreviations

ACS	Archivio Centrale dello Stato
NRS	Nuova Rivista Storica
QS	Quaderni Storici
RSC	Rivista di Storia Contemporanea
RSI	Rivista Storica Italiana
SC	Storia Contemporanea
SS	Studi Storici

Note: For other abbreviations, referring to Italian institutions etc., please see the index

Measures and prices

The metric system has been used throughout this book.

1 centimetre = 0.39 inches
1 metre = 1.09 yards
1 kilometre = 0.62 miles
1 hectare (10,000 sq. metres) = 2.47 acres
1 litre = 1.76 pints
1 hectolitre = 22.00 gallons
1 gram = 0.035 ounces
1 kilogram = 2.20 lbs.
1 tonne (1,000 kg.) = 0.98 tons

The word 'billion' indicates 1,000 million.

PRICES

Prices are given in Italian lire. Exchange-rates always fluctuated, but the approximate rates at different times were as follows:

	£1 sterling = 25 lire; 1 US dollar =	5 lire
1871–1914		
October 1922	90	19
July 1926	150	31
Dec 1927–Sept 1931	92	19
Sept 1931–April 1933	58	19
April 1933–Oct 1936	58	12
Oct 1936–June 1940	92	19
January 1946	900	225
Dec 1947–Sept 1949	2300	575
Sept 1949–Nov 1967	1730	625
Nov 1967–Dec 1971	1500	625
1972 (average)	1400	580
1977 (average)	1540	885
1982 (average)	2400	1400
1991 (average)	2200	1250
1995 (summer)	2500	1600

Acknowledgements

I welcome this opportunity of thanking all the helpful staff of the Central State Archives in Rome, the National Libraries in Rome and Florence, the British Library, the National Library of Scotland and the Edinburgh University Library. I should also like to thank both the Carnegie Trust for the Universities of Scotland and the Travel and Research Committee of the University of Edinburgh, for generous grants enabling me to make several study visits to Italy. I am grateful to Mrs Molly Glover of M.P.G. Secretarial Services, Edinburgh, for helping to prepare the manuscript. Professor Denys Hay proved an exceptionally patient general editor, and made valuable suggestions for improving the text. Finally, I should like to thank Ruth, Adam and Ivan for their forbearance over the years this book has taken to write.

CHAPTER ONE

Introduction

1.1 THEMES AND PROBLEMS

In 1910 Vincenzo Morello looked back on fifty years of united Italy, and commented:

In Italy a really extraordinary thing has happened. There is no religious sentiment, yet a clerical party has been set up; there is no class hatred, yet a large Socialist party has been organized; but although there is a mature State, equipped with Army, Navy, Civil Service and Foreign Office, nobody has ever been able to create even the glimmering of a State party. In the struggle for existence, only the State has no membership, no ideology, no strategy, no tactics. Contemporary history is all about the State's enemies; but the State itself does not exist.[1]

Admittedly Morello was a Nationalist, and that was why he wanted a stronger State; but his views have been echoed, even in our own day, by many other people – Socialist novelists and Liberal historians, Communist critics and Fascist apologists, Italian sociologists and American anthropologists. They all deplore the weakness of the State. Some of them portray a Hobbesian scene: Italians, distrusting both official institutions and each other, are shown competing irresponsibly for wealth, status and power. The law is ignored whenever possible, evaded whenever necessary. Rulers, including party officials and deputies, are there to be bribed; they attract no respect, enjoy no legitimacy.

Here are the grand themes of post-Unification history. After 1861 the State existed at last, as a set of unified institutions; but this 'legal Italy' failed to secure the support of the Italian people. In Gramsci's famous term, 'Italy' lacked 'hegemony' – an automatic acceptance by most people of the élite's title to rule, and a general sharing of the élite's values and beliefs. Most analyses of the 'Liberal' regime (1861–1922) discuss why those Italians who took part in politics were so few, and so unpopular. Why did Italy have such a centralized, legalistic civil service, and so little local democracy? Why was parliament ineffective in defusing popular resentments? Why was there never a conservative party? – but, instead, several mass parties calling themselves revolutionary, all hostile to the political order? Do these weaknesses account for the collapse of the Liberal State and the rise of Fascism in the 1920s? How did the Fascists, in turn, seek to strengthen the State they had conquered, and to win some popular support? Did they succeed? Did the anti-Fascist Resistance manage to set up a new kind of democratic State after the Second World War, or was there simply a restoration of the old system? Was the 'regime of the parties' after 1948 simply ineffective and corrupt? And what, in any case, was meant by 'the State'? What was the relationship between the 'permanent' institutions – army, police, civil service, judiciary, etc. – and the 'democratic' ones – parliament, parties? How could the 'permanent' institutions be transformed, or even reformed?

If the 'State' – 'legal Italy' – was weak, the reason perhaps lay in 'society', in the complex, incoherent diversity of the 'real Italy'. In d'Azeglio's famous phrase, the *Risorgimento* had 'made Italy', but it had not 'made Italians'. Italian politics always had to be about reconciling, or containing, deeply ingrained social differences and conflicts – of class, of faith, of ideology, of ethnic or linguistic group, of regional culture and regional interest. Political institutions evolved a 'politics of accommodation', defusing overt conflict, reconciling incompatible views. Hence historians of modern Italy, even old-fashioned political historians, can hardly ignore social and economic issues. Southern Italy, for example, is the largest backward region in Western Europe. For over a century the 'Southern question' has affected every aspect of national politics – the nature of parties and parliamentary majorities, the degree of tariff protection, the pursuit of imperial glory, the recruitment of public officials. After 1871 Southern landowners were placated by being allowed a fairly free hand in local government and by Corn Laws (a high tariff on wheat); the peasants had little option but to emigrate. By 1971 landowners were no longer so important, but the wheat tariff was still there, thanks to the Common Market; and emigration was still an essential safety-valve. The main difference was that in 1971 more people had the vote. So there were more people to accommodate, and the costs of doing so had gone up. There were huge State-financed industrial plants over much of the South; education and welfare services prevented too much trouble from the plebs, and provided jobs for surplus graduates. By 1990 this whole arrangement was being bitterly criticized in the North.

As this example illustrates, the main themes of Italian politics have remained remarkably constant since Unification. Governments and administrators may talk of the need to 'make Italians', may even set out to do so, but in practice they have to balance, or rather 'absorb', the contending forces in Italian society. The Catholics, initially hostile to the new Liberal State, were partly 'absorbed' into the system by 1913 (Gentiloni Pact), and officially 'reconciled' to it in 1929 (Lateran Pacts). By 1948 they had become the rulers of Italy, although their title to rule was no more widely accepted than was that of their predecessors. The Socialists, 'subversive' by definition in the 1890s, were being wooed and placated by governments ten years later; they were finally 'absorbed' into the normal political game between 1948 and 1963.

2

In the 1970s the process was repeated for the Communists, and in 1994 for the Northern League. Normally this system works well enough; but occasionally it all goes wrong. Government attempts to 'absorb' Socialist trade unions and peasant leagues sparked off a sharp conservative reaction in 1920–21, a major factor in the rise of the Fascist movement – which governments then tried, unsuccessfully, to 'absorb' in its turn. Often the *leaders* of disaffected groups are perfectly willing to be 'absorbed', but the troops remain recalcitrant.

Even so, the pattern is fairly clear. The political history of Italy over the past 120 years has been that of the creation of organized lobbies for disaffected groups (the Church, the South, the industrial workers, the peasant land-owners, etc.), and the 'absorption' of these lobbies into the official political machinery. It is a history that disturbs many people, particularly recently. Radical historians like Salvemini have often denounced the whole business as corruption, and so it is: groups are bought off. Democratic theorists point out that the system is inherently élitist: the masses do not 'participate' in politics, they follow their upper-class leaders. This stricture, too, is valid. Italy has never had a Labour Party; it has had a Socialist Party and a Communist Party, both of them founded and controlled by middle-class intellectuals. The Catholic political movements were even more tightly controlled, not just by lay intellectuals but by the hierarchy. To use political-science jargon, Italy has had a system of 'corporate' politics. Each 'corporation' controls and represents large groups in society; each contends for money and influence. 'Corporate' politics inevitably means 'corporate' economics: a protected, State-dominated economy, more concerned with short-term social peace than with productive growth or consumer interests, and always liable to go bankrupt. And patronage is a wasting asset: there is never enough to go round.

'Corporatism' became much discredited in the late 1980s, but it had many redeeming features. Each important group won favours; as each was 'absorbed', so each became 'reconciled', and so the State became more 'legitimate' in the eyes of more people. Italy in, say, 1980 was not a peaceful and harmonious society, but she was a good deal more peaceful and harmonious since the Second World War than she had ever been before. There were fairly successful 'historic compromises' between Church and State, between Catholics and Communists, between North and South, between 'State' and 'society'. Perhaps ideology helped. After 1945 most political movements were linked by the overriding 'official' doctrines of anti-Fascism. These doctrines were, almost certainly, more widely accepted than the ideologies of Fascism or Liberalism had ever been. So the Italian political system had some legitimacy after all.

Yet not everyone was admitted to the feast. Non-union labour remained unprotected and often greatly exploited. Politically, too, several major groups remained outside. The neo-Fascists were excluded by definition after 1945, although they were the fourth largest party in the country. There were and are also, more significant still, several groups who choose not to join in – Radicals, anarchists, 'Leftists', Greens, regionalists, etc. These outsider groups have always been important. They consist of disaffected intellectuals and recalcitrant moralists, and they dominate much of the press. They are anticlerical, anti-militarist, and anti-Establishment. They are too influential to be ignored, and too high-minded to be bought off. They provide a constant challenge to 'legitimacy', today as over the past 120 years: a constant undermining of 'hegemony'.

1.2 HISTORIOGRAPHY

History-writing in Italy can only be understood in this 'corporate' context. Italian historians are rarely shy, retiring scholars, drenched in archival dust. They are far more likely to be busy professional politicians: one of them was Prime Minister in 1981–82. The history they write is essentially 'committed' history, designed to cheer on their own team. Catholic historians write dutifully about the Church; Marxist historians write about trade unions and workers' parties; Liberal historians write in praise of Liberal Italy. All of them concentrate on certain periods or issues – the formation of the key institutions in the new kingdom, the origins of Fascism, the nature of the Fascist regime, above all anti-Fascism and the Resistance. Sometimes the result is splendid: one thinks of Gabriele De Rosa's study of the Catholic political organizations, or Paolo Spriano's five-volume *Storia del Partito Comunista Italiano*, the only serious, well-documented history of any Communist Party anywhere.

Political commitment ensures that people do not shrink from writing contemporary history, as they so often do in Britain. But it also ensures that much Italian history-writing is hagiographical, or denunciatory, or 'Whig', and that unwelcome facts will be ignored. In the early 1970s there were, it seems, fifteen Institutes for the Study of the History of Anti-Fascism; there was none for the study of Fascism itself.[2] Historians have helped to perpetuate politically useful myths, for example by trying to show that during the Second World War the Resistance movement was a wholly Communist affair, or that it was a 'revolution betrayed', or (in the 1970s) that it was a precursor of some 'government of national unity'. Or, more simply, that it was a clash between Good and Evil. In short, too many Italian historians write in operatic terms. Life is a melodrama, full of villains and vendettas. Right must always triumph over Wrong, the Resistance over Fascism, Labour over Capital, the Church over Sin. Not for them the prosaic, contextual studies of the 'detached' outside observer, let alone new-fangled foreign ideas of history as structure. In Italy, the various schools contend – or rather, would contend, if serious debates among historians of different persuasions ever became frequent.

Of the main schools, the 'Liberals' are perhaps still dominant in academic circles, if not elsewhere. The major influence here has always been Benedetto Croce and his 'ethico-political' approach. Most post-war historians and their readers have been reared on Croce's *Storia d'Italia dal 1871 al 1915*, a commemorative hymn to Liberal Italy. Croce laid much stress on men and ideas, little on the economy, even less on social structures. Yet, strangely, the 'Liberals' have often been most impressive when writing economic history. In the 1950s Rosario Romeo opened up a real debate on economic growth in nineteenth-century Italy, a debate that forced even the Marxists to take economics seriously. Even when writing on non-economic topics 'Liberal' historians have paid due attention to economic and social themes: the outstanding example is Federico Chabod's *Storia della Politica Estera Italiana dal 1870 al 1896*, a magnificent work both of scholarship and art. In recent years 'Liberal' historians have, like others, succumbed to technology. Photocopying machines were installed in archives. Political history, in which the 'Liberals' specialized, was transformed overnight. 'History' became a mindless collection of 'facts', and historical works became indigestible chunks of documents. It was the very antithesis of Croce's teaching. Only a few biographies escaped this awful fate.

The 'Radicals' form another leading school, looking back to Salvemini and Gobetti as their intellectual precursors. Their best-known exponent today is an Englishman, Denis Mack Smith. These historians are a lively group, perhaps because recent Italian history provides such a lot to be radical about. Firmly anti-Fascist, anti-Catholic and anti-Communist, the Radicals are also anti-Liberal, in the sense that they stress the weaknesses of the Liberal governments, their lack of popular support and their ready acceptance of Southern corruption. The Fascist regime is, of course, a favourite Radical target, with the post-war Christian Democrat regime challenging it now for top billing. Italian history has always gone wrong; the historian's task is to analyse why. The Radicals are delightfully pessimistic. They may not write 'total' history, comprehending all sides, but most of them write engagingly, and they reach a huge audience.

Some of the other schools can be dismissed more briefly. There is a Nationalist or even neo-Fascist school, but it is not taken seriously either by the public or by the profession. Yet I suppose Gioacchino Volpe must be accounted a member, and his three-volume *Italia Moderna* has been rightly praised for its acute insight into the Liberals' defects.[3] The 'Leftists' – i.e. various types of Marxists to the Left of the former Communist Party – are no longer fashionable, even among the young. And the Catholics are, as one might expect, numerous but normally undistinguished by originality of thought: most of them write worthy studies of worthy men. However, the history of religiosity is attracting more young writers, and here perhaps is the nearest approach among Italian historians to the history of popular culture.

Probably the most influential school of historians in Italy after 1945 was that of the 'mainstream Marxists', i.e. the official Communist writers – Ragionieri, Procacci, Rosario Villari – grouped around their journal, *Studi Storici*. The dominant influence on this school was obviously Gramsci, whose reflections on Italian history and culture were published after 1945 and aroused enormous interest. Gramsci's stress on 'hegemony' and consensus, on the role of intellectuals in diffusing values, on the political importance of the peasantry, was evident throughout the work of his Communist followers. Here were intelligent historians at last, willing to think about their work, and anxious to debate with their rivals. Yet they had their limits. For Marxists, they were strangely uninterested in class divisions – a subject eventually tackled by an economist (Sylos Labini) rather than a historian; and 'working-class history' all too often meant the history of the working-class leaders. Abstract entities, like proletariats and petty bourgeoisies, filled their pages; real workers and peasants rarely appeared, much less details of factory work, labouring skills, or farming implements.

In short, the Marxists were 'ethico-political' too. Perhaps for that reason, in the 1970s the *Studi Storici* group seemed to be overtaken by changes in intellectual fashion. To their Left were the young Marxist hardliners, insisting on a real 'class-based', 'materialist' approach; to the Right, or rather to the North-West, lay attractive French models, stressing 'total' social history and the cult of '*mentalités*'. The Marxists could not hope to beat the *Annales* school, so they joined them. In 1972 the Turin publisher Giulio Einaudi produced the first volume of an encyclopedic *Storia d'Italia*, fathered by Gramsci out of *Annales*. It was a huge success both commercially and ideologically, confirming the Marxists' reputation for being open-minded and up-to-date. Yet, like all collective works, it lacked coherence; and as social history it was distinctly peculiar. It must be the only multi-volume social history ever written with barely a mention of the family, or of health, or even of the spread of welfare provision. And the central issue of how Italian society has been transformed in the past century was virtually ignored, at least initially.[4]

But it is unfair to single out the *Storia d'Italia* for such criticism. These defects were common to all the political schools. Until the 1980s none of them paid much attention to the social sciences, even essential ones like demography and anthropology. Very few Italian historians wrote military or colonial history – a big gap in our knowledge of the past century. The history of foreign countries was cheerfully neglected, and their languages were usually unknown. True, the *Storia d'Italia* was derived from French historical ideas, but there was no Italian *Annales*, nor even a *Past and Present*. This did at least avoid the wildest excesses of the New History – Italian computers did not write books, and Italian biographies were free of psychobabble – but it also avoided many vital issues. Social history was much neglected, at least for the contemporary period.

Eppur si muove . . . The 'official Marxists' were not the only historians influenced by *Annales* and by Anglo-Saxon innovations. In 1966 Alberto Caracciolo and Pasquale Villani founded the *Quaderni Storici delle Marche*, renamed simply *Quaderni Storici* in 1969. This journal has been the outstanding success of recent years. It has pioneered the 'anthropological' study of past societies, stressing the history of everyday life: food and health, leisure and work, sex and marriage, birth and death, rituals and magic. Unfortunately even writers in *Quaderni Storici* have rarely applied this approach to the past century, perhaps for good reasons. 'Long-period' history presupposes that things do not change too much too quickly; and 'microhistory' presupposes that local communities are not only small, but remain relatively isolated from the outside world. Neither of these propositions is true during the past 120 years, even for the most remote mountain village. Even so, *Quaderni Storici* and its imitators – especially *Passato e Presente*, *Meridiana*, and (for contemporary issues) *Polis* – meet the prime criterion of any historical writing. They tell us interesting things about the past.

By now it will be clear where my own sympathies lie. I have little time for narrative political history, and none for vulgar-Marxist views of economic change. I have the greatest respect for Gramsci, but I do not discern much sign of 'hegemony' in recent Italian history; like most Italian intellectuals, Gramsci exaggerated the importance of people like himself. This book will lay a fashionable stress on social history, in particular on the complex relationship between 'society' and 'State'. Occasionally I have used my own research, but essentially this is a work of synthesis, and one cannot synthesize work that has not been done. There are, alas, painful gaps in our knowledge, or at least in my knowledge. For these I apologize in advance.

1.3 SOURCES

History-writing, at least of the traditional kind, depends largely on the existence of reliable public records – government statistics, censuses, court records, tax documents, diplomatic papers, etc. – housed in accessible archives and libraries. There is no doubt about the abundance of such records for the period after 1870, nor about their accessibility. The *Archivio Centrale dello Stato* (central State Archives) in Rome houses most ministerial and Cabinet papers, and many personal ones. In particular, it holds the detailed Prefects' reports from the provinces, as well as the central security police files on political movements of every kind. They are an excellent quarry; perhaps too excellent. The police had informers everywhere; they tapped telephones, and scrutinized the mail. They thus amassed a huge amount of useless knowledge, eagerly awaiting its later historical justification. Research students naturally rejoice to find such a marvellous store of first-hand inside information. And so the policeman's view of history tends to predominate in Italian historical works. It is a racy, well-informed but usually short-term view; and, like the diplomatic reports so solemnly cited by historians of foreign policy, it is often cribbed straight from that morning's newspapers.

My impression, after reading much recent Italian political history, is that other archival sources are used less than they should be. The municipal archives in Tuscany, for example, are still almost unexplored; even the provincial ones, which include the local police records (*questura*), have been relatively neglected, although they are essential to any study of relations between Rome and the periphery. Local history has tended until recently to be a small-scale reflection of national history. The endless books on 'The Rise of Fascism in . . .' or 'The Origins of the Resistance at . . .' are usually worthy, but provide few surprises. Other 'local' archives – parish, episcopal, fiscal, judicial, industrial – are used mainly by students writing dissertations rather than by professional historians, despite one or two notable pioneering efforts (e.g. Ragionieri on Sesto Fiorentino). As for hospital, asylum or military call-up records, younger historians have now begun to investigate them, and regional history has become markedly more fashionable in recent years. Even so, most historians remain 'centralists', perhaps because they are too lazy to move out of Rome, or because of the fear that haunted all Italian intellectuals until recently, that they might be thought 'provincial'. Or perhaps it is because academic careers in Italy are made or broken in a handful of major cities. Still, the local archives exist, and the fashion now is towards using them. They are beginning to have a real impact on Italian historiography.

The obvious gaps in the records reflect political concerns. Crown papers are not accessible, so writing on the role of the monarchy is pure speculation. Vital episodes, like Italy's entry into the First World War or the fall of Mussolini in 1943, remain thereby obscure. Vatican documents are rarely available for any date after 1903. Few of the semi-public agencies in Italy – 'economic' bodies like ENI, local charities, cultural institutions, the State broadcasting corporation RAI – have opened their books, perhaps wisely. The result is that there are virtually no serious studies of them, although they link State, society and the economy in a host of vital ways. Of the political parties, only the former Communists are organized enough to have a respectable party archive. Labour history has to be written, for the most part, without trade union or Chamber of Labour papers, which were destroyed by the Fascists or disappeared mysteriously in the Second World War. So did many other military and civil documents of the post-1922 period, finding their way to St Antony's College, Oxford, or to the National Institute in Washington; just as well, since they were far more readily available to scholars there in the 1960s than they would have been in Italy.

Apart from archives, there is the usual range of printed sources, including of course parliamentary papers. Most Italian politicians write their memoirs; some are less mendacious than others. Much better are several indiscreet insiders' diaries: Domenico Farini, *Diario di Fine Secolo* (he was President of the Senate in the 1890s), Ferdinando Martini's diary during the First World War, and, of course, Foreign Minister Ciano's diary between 1937 and 1943. The interest, as always, lies not in what is revealed but in the atmosphere conveyed. Italian historians also rely heavily on newspapers and journals. Many local journals, however, survived only at the National Library in Florence, and the 1966 floods thus erased a major source of local and institutional history. As for printed books, it often seems that more people write them than read them. Perhaps that is not so surprising, given the chaotic state of many research libraries.

Less orthodox sources, like oral history, are just beginning to make an impact in Italy. A stroll round any Italian town, or through any part of the countryside, will reveal much about town-planning, about social and family structure, about farming methods – but only to those with eyes to see. In addition, many fine photographic and film records survive, as do the files of fashion magazines and journals like *L'Illustrazione Italiana*. It is far easier to see what Italy was like than to comprehend it; photography is not a source so much as a challenge.

Finally, there are official statistics. A census has been held every ten years, except in 1891 when the money ran out and in 1941 when the Second World War intervened; this latter gap is partly filled by the extra 'Fascist' census held in 1936. The census data are unusually unreliable, a fact deplored by successive census officials in their reports. Few people in the nineteenth century knew their own age; some were unwilling to reveal the existence of sons liable to military service. Local officials neither knew nor cared about how to classify people by profession. On the other hand, they cared greatly that the population of their municipality should not fall below a certain threshold, otherwise the number of seats on the council would be reduced and their own jobs would be at risk. In 1921 there were so many 'grave irregularities, due not to negligence or ignorance on the part of respondents but to negligence or deliberate intent by municipal administrations and their officials, especially in Apulia, Calabria and Sicily' that eventually the top officials in Rome knocked off over 750,000 people from the figures.[5] They also admitted that previous censuses had been equally unreliable. Similar heroic adjustments have been made by contemporary historians, notably Ornello Vitali. Vitali thinks that the data can be used, after much reworking, but his view is by no means universally shared.[6] In any case, it is extremely difficult to compare data from one census with that of another. Towns and even whole provinces were moved around between regions. Monterchi, for example, was transferred from Tuscany to Umbria in 1927, and back again in 1939; the province of Rieti hovered uncertainly between Umbria and Latium. Jobs were classified differently at each census, quite apart from any local variations; illiteracy, too, could be defined in different ways. Women and children were counted as 'active in agriculture', or not, on quite arbitrary grounds, and were probably always underestimated. Sometimes changes in the real world messed up the comparison: when bakers ceased to sell bread as well as make it, the census found a sudden decline in retail trading. 'Industrial' censuses used quite different definitions from 'population' censuses: in 1911, for example, the former showed 14.1 per cent of the active population in industry, whereas the latter, carried out by the same officials on the same people on the same day, gave 30.2 per cent.[7] These defects are important. Major historical debates have raged around utterly spurious data. Discussion of Italy's industrial 'take-off', for example, is not helped by the fact that the 1881 census, unlike those of 1871 or 1901, appears to move about 6 per cent of the Southern agricultural population into industry. And Italian historians, unlike many of their European colleagues, use the aggregate data worked out by census officials, rather than the original census sheets. I, too, have used census data occasionally in this book, on the grounds that poor information is better than none at all. Even so, I stress that quantitative history in Italy is, at best, an aspiration; usually it is a distortion. But perhaps that is true of all history.

REFERENCES

1. In P. Arcari, *La Coscienza Nazionale in Italia*, Milan 1911, p. liv.
2. G. Bocca, *La Repubblica di Mussolini*, Bari 1977, p. 341.
3. L. Valiani, in *L'Historiographie de l'Italie Contemporaine*, Geneva 1968, p. 35.
4. Cf. P. Villani, in P. Macry (ed.), *Società e Cultura dell' Italia Unita*, Naples 1978, p. 73.
5. Censimento Generale della Popolazione 1921, *Relazione Generale*, p. 11, quoted in U. Giusti, *Caratteristiche Ambientali Italiane*, Rome 1940, p. 243.
6. O. Vitali, *Aspetti dello Sviluppo Economico Italiano (1881–1961)*, Rome 1970, esp. pp. 164, 209–78.
7. V. Zamagni, in G. Toniolo (ed.), *Lo Sviluppo Economico Italiano 1861–1940*, Bari 1973, pp. 221–23.

PART ONE

1871–87

CHAPTER TWO

Italietta – a backward society?

In 1871 Italy had a predominantly agricultural economy – or rather, a number of agricultural economies, with very different characteristics. Most Italians – almost 60 per cent of the active population – worked on the land.[1] This fact would suggest, perhaps, a static traditional society, whose structure and values had been inherited from many previous generations. That was not the case. Italy was rural, but her agriculture was being rapidly transformed – in some areas by technical improvements, in others by the sale of vast Church estates, in yet others by foreign competition or export opportunities. The new unified State, with its tax exactions and its public works programmes, its abolition of tariffs within and its reduction of tariffs around the country, its stress on progress and improvement, was already having an effect in 1871. Above all, there was the gradual growth of industry and of a more complex trading economy, overwhelming 'traditional' values and practices and providing new opportunities for peasants willing to migrate. This chapter will attempt to trace some of these developments, and show how the Italian economy was brought into close and often brutal contact with the modern world.

2.1 AGRICULTURE

We know a reasonable amount about late nineteenth-century agriculture. The subject was constantly debated by knowledgeable men, for Italy's 'political classes' were nearly all landowners. In the 1880s a Parliamentary Commission of Inquiry under Senator Stefano Jacini investigated the subject, and produced fifteen volumes of detailed information. The *Final Report*, written by Jacini himself, remains a classic statement of the liberal, free-trading view. Jacini reminded his readers of a few basic essentials: nearly two-thirds of Italy's surface area was mountainous or hilly, and either could not be cultivated at all or was only just usable; even many of the plains were malarial, or had poor soil; grain was grown over far too large an area, in totally unsuitable conditions. The myth of Italy as 'the garden of Europe' was a myth, no more.

Moreover, regional variations were great, not merely in richness of soil or in suitability for various crops, but in land-tenure systems, capitalization, agricultural wages, and methods of cultivation. As Jacini proclaimed:

It may well be said that Italian agriculture, more than any other in Europe, shows all the varieties of rural economy as practised from Edinburgh to Smyrna, from Stockholm to Cadiz; from the medieval *latifundium,* using the most primitive type of extensive cultivation, to one using the most advanced intensive forms of cultivation; from small-scale farming of a single specialised crop to small-scale producers of everything; from an income of 5 lire per hectare of cultivated land to one of 2,000 lire per hectare; from the peasant-owner or long leaseholder to the casual day-labourer; from relative prosperity for agricultural workers of all classes, including the casual labourers, to the most squalid poverty among all workers, including owners and sharecroppers.[2]

In the Alpine and hill areas of the North, small peasant landowners were predominant. This was especially true in Piedmont – over a quarter of the 1.3 million Italian peasant-owners in 1881 were in Piedmont – but they were also numerous in Lombardy, Veneto and Liguria. These peasants usually owned small plots of infertile land, often held in scattered strips. They eked out a scanty living by seasonal migration to nearby cities or abroad, and by 'domestic' industry. Share-cropping tenancies were also found in these hill areas – they were prevalent, for example, in Treviso and Vicenza provinces – and sometimes on the Northern plains. The landowner provided the land and (usually) a house, on a yearly contract, in return for half the crop and various other dues. The variations on this theme were endless: sometimes seeds and cattle were provided as well as land; sometimes the crop was divided up in different proportions; sometimes the peasant received payment for improvements he might carry out; sometimes he enjoyed longer, or more secure, tenure; sometimes he paid rent, in cash or in kind. Often the peasant remained permanently in the landowner's debt – for example, for seeds – and had to pay usurious 'interest' in kind or cash, as did many of the small landowners themselves. The hill and mountain areas were devoted to subsistence farming, and rarely guaranteed even that. They had few large farms and little intensive or specialist farming, although vineyards and mulberry trees (for silkworms) formed a partial exception here and there.

The picture was very different on the fertile plains of Northern Italy. In the rice-growing areas of Vercelli, for example, farms often reached 100 hectares, and required between twelve and twenty-five families to work them. Capital investment was high, and agricultural labourers working for wages only were numerous – 112,000 in Novara province in 1871, according to the census. The farms were run by professional farmers who enjoyed fairly long tenancies of nine to twelve years, and who were paid for any improvements they introduced. Large farms, wage-labourers, modern methods of irrigation, and exporting of specialized products like rice and cheese: all these went together on the North Italian plains. The area formed a 'capitalist', market-oriented enclave in strong contrast to the neighbouring mountain areas. But agriculture had its problems even in Lombardy. One was its excessive reliance on foreign markets, which presupposed friendly relations with other countries, especially France. It also meant trying to maintain an unrealistically low exchange-rate, and trying to cope with new foreign competition, e.g. from America. For all their 'modernity', the irrigated farms of Southern Lombardy seemed in the 1880s no more likely to prosper than did the subsistence agriculture of the Alpine regions.

Central Italy was the classic home of the *mezzadria* (share-cropping) system. As late as 1901 over half of all those engaged in agriculture in Tuscany were share-croppers. Although half the crop was the normal rent, there were the usual variations according to local customs and soils. The aristocratic land-owners of Tuscany looked on share-cropping as an ideal system, guaranteeing social stability as well as the intensive cultivation needed by vines and other specialized crops. So it did, although it required an 'extended' peasant family, living in one house on a twelve-hectare farm, its members subject to their own patriarchal head and obliged to offer eggs, chickens and occasional labour to the landlord, as well as half the crop. As the rest of Italian society changed, was this system likely to survive? Share-cropping had other flaws. Capital could not be provided by the tenant, for he had none; and it was unlikely to be provided by the landowner, for he would get only half the return. More-over, the system rested on labour-intensive cultivation of specialized crops, like wine and olive oil. This was a fragile base, liable to be undermined by changes in taste or in international markets. Not all the peasants of Central Italy were share-croppers, of course. The 1881 census found 110,000 landless day-labourers in Tuscany, many lucky to find 180 days work in the year. And there were plenty of small owner-occupied plots near the villages, even though Jacini's picture of Umbria as a region of small peasant-owners was mistaken.

Latium, especially the *Campagna* to the South of Rome, was *latifundium* country. In 1871 the land was still owned by Roman aristocrats or by ecclesiastical corporations; the *Agro Romano*, all 200,000 hectares of it, was divided into 360 'farms' owned by 204 proprietors. The land was leased out to the so-called *mercanti di campagna*, prosperous middlemen who hired seasonal labour to do the work. The plains were malarial, and most of the land was used for pasture, except on the very outskirts of Rome. Indeed, in the 1870s only about 10 per cent of the *Agro Romano* was cultivated.

Further South, the picture was even bleaker. The summer heat and aridity precluded many crops; and malaria prevented cultivation in the low-lying zones of the Adriatic coast or the river valleys. The rural population lived in hill-towns, and scratched a living from the hillsides. Inland, especially in Sicily, stretched the vast empty *latifundia*, increasingly bare hills given over to pasture or to under-capitalized grain-farming. Land still normally belonged to absentee landowners, with a chain of sub-letting of various types. However, there were also many tiny peasant-owned plots – virtually allotments – near the towns, and in Sardinia small ownership and subdivision were so prevalent that the Commission of Inquiry found some owners with between 200 and 400 microscopic pieces of scattered land, making any improvements impossible. Even so, many peasants did not own or even rent any land at all.

The 1881 census found over 1 million day-labourers in the Southern provinces, chronically underemployed and very liable to become seasonal emigrants. And many others owned or rented land that was inadequate to support them and their families, so they too were forced to work as hired day-labourers, or to emigrate, for much of the year.

Of course, this picture needs some qualification. There were some prosperous exceptions – around the Bay of Naples, for example, or the Golden Horn near Palermo. The most productive agriculture in the South was along the Tyrrhenian coast, which was relatively malaria-free and where fruit and olive-trees flourished. And other tenure systems were sometimes found. Land had great prestige in the eyes of the Southern middle and professional classes, and in some areas their medium or small landholdings formed a significant proportion of the total – although they too acted as absentee landowners rather than as entrepreneurs. Share-cropping was also common in some regions, e.g. Sicily, Campania and Abruzzi-Molise, although it was almost unknown in others; where it did occur the peasant rarely kept half the produce.

The defects of Southern agriculture were much discussed. Clearly the South suffered from great natural disadvantages of soil and climate. During the nineteenth century Man the Despoiler made things worse. Forests were cut down for railway sleepers or industrial purposes, or simply to provide more land for cultivation. The results were disastrous: soil erosion in the hills, alluvial deposits on once fertile land in the valleys, landslides, less rainfall. The Agrarian Commission of Inquiry estimated that 10,000 hectares in Basilicata were permanently under stagnant water because of deforestation, and malaria became a far greater scourge. The main systems of land-tenure in the South – subsistence peasant-ownership, exploitative share-cropping, absentee landlordism, *latifundia* – were calculated to discourage capital investment and improvements. Too many Southern landowners thought in terms of a quick profit – sell off the woodland; squeeze the last bit out of the land or out of the peasant. In any case, the South was perhaps too far from European, or even from North Italian markets, for most investment to be worth the risk. Certainly the areas of advanced agriculture were few, and had little political power; they could not act as a counterweight to the influence of landlords elsewhere.

These patterns of landownership were undergoing great changes around 1870. The new entail laws required at least half a deceased man's estate to be distributed equally among his children; in the long run that was bound to lead to the break-up of large landed property. Moreover, younger sons were now insisting on their right to marry, and even daughters seemed reluctant to be placed in convents. Above all, feudal rights and customs – rights to grazing on common fields, to pasturage after the harvest, to woodgathering, etc. – had already been abolished; and much common or feudal land – on which these rights had been exercised – had already been split up into individually owned plots. In the South of Italy alone 265,000 hectares had been sold off by 1865, and a further 50,000 hectares were sold between 1866 and 1881.[3] These figures are probably underestimates, and in any case they do not include the public land illegally usurped, or the land later 'conceded' to usurpers (almost 400,000 hectares, according to Sereni), or the land rented out to private individuals, often at minimal rents. Thus land-tenure was not merely part of the 'economic background' to politics; it was a major political issue. Indeed, in the South, the 'demesne question' – i.e. who was to get the common land and the former feudal land of each municipality (*comune*) – was *the* vital issue.

Demesne land was managed and sold off by the local councils, under the nominal jurisdiction of the Prefect. Control of local government was therefore very important. The local government franchise was, of course, restricted; so municipal councils were normally run by a handful of men – usually landowners, sometimes merchants or lawyers – who had no intention of allowing the peasantry to acquire substantial amounts of good land. The results were sometimes worthy of a Gogol. At Ferruzzano, in Reggio Calabria province, a Commission of Inquiry found that 'there were 83 usurpers of one wood that was part of the demesne; they included 2 of the mayor's brothers, 17 of his cousins, 2 of his brothers-in-law, 2 of his nephews, 1 factor who worked for the mayor's brother, 6 municipal councillors, 2 councillors' wives, 1 councillor's brother, and one member of the provincial forest committee'.[4] Note that the land here was woodland: deforestation and the abolition of feudal rights went together. But the demesne lands were very extensive, and not confined to woodland.

Not surprisingly, the peasants of Southern Italy, including the small landowners and tenants, were in a constant state of ferment and revolt in the nineteenth century. Not only were they failing to benefit from anti-feudal legislation, but they were actually losing their immemorial rights. Even when the allocation system worked fairly, the effect was to grant small plots of land (often less than two hectares) to the poor of one generation, at the expense of the 'traditional rights' that the future poor might have expected. This may well have stimulated emigration from the South later on. And the new peasant owners acquired only the land. They had no water, animals, machinery, fertilizers, marketing knowledge, credit, capital, or political power. They did not last long, faced by the increased land taxes of the new unified Italy, and by the fall in food prices after the late 1870s. In 1879 Giustino Fortunato estimated that in the province of Teramo only 2,777 of the 7,260 plots originally allocated were still owned by the same peasant family that had purchased them; three-quarters of the plots granted at Barletta were by that time owned by large landowners. At Eboli, Prince Francesco Doria, son of the former owner, acquired eighty-four plots in 1877, thus regaining some of the lands his family had been forced to give up. The Jacini inquiry reported that nearly 62,000 demesne plots had been 're-expropriated' back to the demesne between 1873 and 1881 for non-payment of taxes; half of them could not be sold off again.

Moreover, history repeated itself. Another 500,000 hectares were sold off between 1867 and 1876, with the expropriation of the ecclesiastical estates. This time the land was sold off by a central State agency, in plots averaging

4.3 hectares. About half of it was in the South, and most of the rest in Central Italy. In Sicily another 190,000 hectares were put out on perpetual heritable leases. The price and area of the plots varied greatly from region to region – in Liguria they were less than 0.2 hectares, in the Marches over 13 hectares – and so did the social consequences of the transfer. Many Northern peasants, particularly in the Alpine areas of Piedmont and Liguria, did acquire land, although in very small quantities; and the same was true in Apulia, the region where the largest area of Church lands (over 96,000 hectares) changed hands. Elsewhere it was a different story. The agency itself seems to have acted reasonably impartially, but the sales took place at public auctions, and it took a bold peasant to bid against a powerful local notable. Purchasers also risked excommunication for buying Church land. Bertozzi estimated that in Sicily the maximum number of beneficiaries was 10,790, of whom only 15 per cent were labourers without any other land. And Sidney Sonnino found in Sicily that 'ecclesiastical property fell almost exclusively and with very rare exceptions into the hands of prosperous landowners, for the most part large landowners already'.[5] In any case, peasants who bought Church lands faced the same problems as those who had bought the demesne. Many were soon forced to sell out, because it was impossible in bad years to meet repayments of loans and pay the land taxes. In Sicily, the price of land fell from 2,075 lire per hectare in 1877 to 1,205 lire in 1882, and many lots remained unsold.

Still, there were some real and important changes in these years. A great deal of land had changed hands (over 2 million hectares in all). A new class of 'rural bourgeoisie' had arisen in many areas, i.e. non-noble owners linked to local government, including some former leaseholders or renters whose 'usurpations' of common land had been legitimized *post factum*. In the *Agro Romano*, 75,000 hectares passed from ecclesiastical ownership straight into the hands of these men, who had often been the tenants previously; attempts to sell the land in small plots failed, partly because of the lack of housing. In the former Papal States of Central Italy, the local landowners not only acquired extensive Church lands, but were also freed from clerical interference. But the main consequence was political rather than economic. A great opportunity for land reform had been lost, and a legacy of bitterness and hatred had been created. The land was available, the legislation was passed, the demand was enormous; yet small ownership did not become widespread – and one of the main reasons was the political power of the local élites. The peasants who lost their grazing rights and saw the common land sold off to the wealthy, or who – even worse – bought it themselves and then were forced to resell to meet tax payments, could have no love for the new political and social order. The 'Southern question' was not created in these years, but it was made more intractable; so much so that by the 1880s Southern Italy was being regularly compared to Ireland. It seems fair to conclude, with the 1910 Commission of Inquiry into the South, that 'the young Italian State did not succeed in creating a democracy of small landowners, of men who might have undermined the foundations of the old feudal system that had survived in fact if not in law. The new State became the slave of a new powerful group, the voting middle classes, just as the old State had been the slave of the feudal aristocracy . . . [it tolerated] usurpers who had the vote and used it to steal the land, with the more or less tacit complicity of the Prefects in that scandalous despoliation of the poor by the rich.'[6]

It has often been argued that the sales of demesne and Church lands absorbed whatever capital was available for agriculture, diverting it from land improvements or rural industries. Landownership conferred respectability and power, and it was obviously tempting for a local merchant to spend his money on buying up land cheaply. Morpurgo wrote that in the Veneto 'businessmen, industrialists, merchants and wealthy professional men embrace landed property, just as people who have had many adventurous love-affairs end up looking for marriage and a quiet life. They will earn a great deal less; they will have less excitement (to continue the comparison), but they will avoid tempests.'[7] Thus men 'disinvested' industrial capital into agriculture, for non-economic reasons. On the other hand, it may be that 'bourgeois' land acquisition led ultimately to more efficient farming than had ever occurred on the old estates.

These arguments are speculative, for we just do not have reliable enough figures for agricultural investment, or even for agricultural production. Rosario Romeo and Alexander Gerschenkron, using official figures, have argued for a substantial rise in agricultural production until about 1880. This seems dubious. Eckaus points out that value-added in agriculture may have risen at 1.96 per cent p.a. at current prices between 1861–65 and 1881, but most of this was accounted for by price rises. More recent calculations are by Orlando, who gives a rise in value-added of 0.1 per cent p.a. between 1872 and 1886, and by Toniolo: 0.9 per cent p.a. between 1862 and 1878. Romani found little evidence of a rise in grain productivity in Lombardy until the 1890s, but the number of dairy cows went up from 346,000 in 1869 to 463,000 in 1881.[8]

Whether production stagnated or rose in the 1870s, it is certain that Italian agriculture was dominated by cereals, and that productivity was low. Wheat was grown extensively, often in poor soil unfertilized by chemical or beast, and in many provinces (e.g. Sondrio and Cuneo) farmers reckoned on a return of 0.5 tonne per hectare. The national average was only about 0.8 tonne in the late 1870s, about one-third as much as in Britain. This meant that in an average year Italy produced around 3.8 million tonnes of wheat, not enough for home consumption; so she needed to import 150,000 tonnes, mostly from Russia and Turkey. In fact, wheat was an uneconomic crop in many regions, given the low productivity. Jacini thought that one-third of the land under grain should be put to other uses. No doubt he was right, but it could not be done in a country with over 1 million small landowners, and where at least 40 per cent of the cereals produced were eaten by the producers' families.

Apart from cereals (the importance of maize is discussed below), the largest area – almost 2 million hectares in the early 1870s – was devoted to vineyards. This was a much better proposition, on suitable soil, and in the 1870s both hectareage and production expanded rapidly, especially in the

Northern and Central regions and in Apulia. By 1883 there were 3.2 million hectares of vines. Jacini approved of vineyards. They required intensive cultivation, they were often suitable for small peasant landowners in hilly areas, and they produced a specialized export-oriented crop. The same was true of olive plantations (895,000 hectares), and of some fruit and vegetables. Yet these were also vulnerable crops, with vulnerable markets. Italian wine was not sought in France for its quality, but to mix with other wines to make up the quantity; and olive oil became less important as the century went on.

After 1880 Italy became immersed in the world-wide fall of agricultural prices. Official figures show the price of wheat falling from an average 331 lire per tonne in 1878–80 to 245 lire in 1883, and to 228 lire in 1885. Not only was there the competition of cheap American grain and Asian rice, but the lira's return to gold convertibility in 1883 lowered import prices still further. In 1886–87 a million tonnes of wheat were imported. The worst-hit farmers were the larger and middling landowners, and tenants paying rents in cash – i.e. precisely those most capable of investment. Small owners, growing grain for their own consumption, or share-croppers paying rent in kind, were of course less affected by price changes. Lombardy perhaps suffered more than any other region, because of its products (rice, grain, silk) and because of its foreign markets. Thus by the mid-1880s the most 'modern' sectors of Italian agriculture were apparently on the verge of collapse. Production was falling; investment seemed useless; markets were threatened, or already lost; landowners were trying desperately to pass on their losses to the peasantry, by cutting wages. The result was a persistent and ultimately successful demand for tariffs, i.e. for Corn Laws to safeguard the economic position of the landowners at the expense of everyone else.

Food was by far the largest item in the rural dwellers' budget, and observers were constantly surprised at how little, and how badly, the peasants ate. Meat was a rare luxury, eaten only on feast days or family celebrations. Foods which we think of today as typically Italian – tomato purée, for example – were virtually unknown, or far too expensive for most people. Even wine was beyond the means of many peasants, who had to content themselves with 'vinello' – mostly water, but passed through the must; and this was a serious matter, given the nature of the water supply. Worst of all, the Northern Italian peasantry relied mainly on bread or 'polenta' made from maize, often of low quality. It filled their stomachs, but it left them with malnutrition and niacin deficiency, resulting in pellagra. The disease was very widespread in Veneto and Lombardy. Further South, it was much less common, for bread was normally made from wheat; this was one of the few instances where Southerners were actually better off than their Northern counterparts. Chestnut bread was also found in many regions of Central Italy, and in Piedmont.

This diet, basically of bread, was supplemented virtually everywhere by such cheap additions as beans, onions, salt, lard, oil and potatoes. Other vegetables, and even most fruit, were a luxury. Many peasants managed to keep a pig, but eggs and chickens were not generally eaten by the rural poor, and share-cropping contracts often stipulated that such produce be paid to the landowner. In winter, when agricultural work was scarce, the peasants ate as little as possible, and even then went into debt. In the late nineteenth century the Italian peasantry was only just avoiding starvation, and many peasants were seriously undernourished. In 1881 11.8 per cent of conscripts to the Italian army were rejected as not tall enough, and a further 26.5 per cent were rejected on grounds of health or deformity.

As for housing, Jacini and his colleagues regularly found peasants living in mud huts, with roofs of straw, and no flooring; these conditions were common even in the Veneto and the lower Po valley. Most rural houses were built by the peasants themselves, on one floor or, at best, on two: humans above, animals below. In the South, conditions were even worse. Peasants refused to live near their land, and instead huddled into overcrowded towns. One room, without light, was shared by humans and animals, and this was true of the more prosperous peasants; the poor ones had no animals with which to share their houses. The best housing was often provided by landlords in share-cropping or fixed-renting areas; the worst in *latifundia,* especially in the *Agro Romano,* where shepherds from the Abruzzi or the Marches spent months at a time. Jacini argued that building decent houses in the countryside was vital. No intensive agriculture of the kind he advocated could be carried on without them, and the peasants could not build them or pay for them themselves – 'the worst hovels are the ones that are owned by the small landowners'.[9]

With such housing, hygienic provision was bound to be rudimentary. Water was rarely on tap, and was often polluted; toilets were rare even in many Northern regions. Refuse and manure were normally dumped near the houses, and sewage was often on the 'gardy-loo' system: local by-laws carefully regulated the hours when it could be thrown out on to the streets. Pigs were a vital part of the ecological cycle, for they ate the sewage and rubbish on the village streets. Nor were streets cleaned, except by rainwater; and 6,404 municipalities (out of about 8,000) had no gutters at all.

This idyllic picture of rural bliss would not be complete without mention of the cemeteries, or rather of their absence in the South. Pani Rossi's famous book on Basilicata described how at Muro bodies were thrown over a cliff, and how at Ripacandida they were put into a walled enclosure to be eaten by crows. Even those fortunate enough to be buried were rarely placed deep enough, so dogs nosed them up again and played with human bones in the street. 'In most places the dead are thrown on top of each other in church crypts, where their slow decomposition infects the inhabitants with lethal diseases.'[10] However, these conditions were not typical of the whole country. A much more reassuring picture was painted by the Commission of Inquiry into Hygienic Conditions in 1885; although even then 682 municipalities still had only mass graves.

It is not surprising that epidemic diseases were common. Cholera alone killed over 50,000 people between 1884 and 1886, 7,000 of them in the city of Naples. Typhoid deaths were 27,000 in 1887. Scarlet fever, smallpox, diphtheria and TB were all endemic; TB alone accounted for 63,000 deaths between 1887 and 1889. In 1885 nearly one-third of the municipalities had no doctor, and nearly one-half had no chemist. Peasants had recourse to local wise women or to traditional herbal remedies. Hospitals, of course, were urban institutions.

But the greatest scourge of the Italian countryside was malaria. It is impossible to overestimate the effects of this disease. At least 15,000 deaths occurred each year; 2 million people suffered its effects each summer. In many Southern regions malaria was reckoned to cause 20–30 per cent of all deaths. There is a lot of evidence that it increased in the late nineteenth century, perhaps because of public works schemes – especially cutting down trees for railway sleepers, or digging drainage ditches alongside railway lines. Italy was the most malarial country in Europe, and the South was the most malarial part of Italy. Malarial mosquitoes infested the coastal plains and the river valleys. Huge tracts of low-lying land – potentially the most fertile – could not be cultivated throughout the summer; housing had to be restricted to hill-towns, far from the fields, making intensive cultivation impossible in many areas. In some places railway lines could not be built. Even Rome was, or was thought to be, uninhabitable in summer because of malaria. Moreover, at this time nobody knew the cause, except that the 'exhalations' from the swamps had something to do with it. There were, therefore, many attempts to drain swampland in the nineteenth century, but it was not until the free distribution of quinine became general in the South – in the first decade of the twentieth century – that the disease declined.

2.2   THE INDUSTRIAL ECONOMY

I turn now to the other Italians, in the towns. Yet there was no neat distinction between a rural peasantry on the one hand, and an urban working and middle class engaged in industry and trade on the other. Most peasants in the South lived in hill-top towns, if only to avoid malaria or brigands: the most 'urban' province in Italy was Agrigento. But these 'towns' were simply dormitories for the nearby *latifundia*. Conversely, much 'industry' was domestic, and carried on by peasants' wives in the countryside. Moreover, there was regular seasonal migration between agricultural and industrial jobs, and many peasants found casual employment in the building trades during the construction boom of the 1880s. Even the 'fixed' urban worker was most probably an artisan, sometimes with his own plot of land nearby, and almost certainly with strong family links to the countryside. People were too versatile, or perhaps too unskilled, to stay in one job for long, or to rely on one job for their family income. They picked up a living as best they could, both in the towns and in the countryside; and they were lucky to make ends meet anywhere.

Thus only a very approximate picture emerges from the official job descriptions of the census, or even from those of acute social observers. There were probably around 2.2 million male 'industrial workers' (including artisans and employers) in 1881, and about 1.9 million females doing 'industrial' work. At least a quarter of the male workers were in the building trades, and most of the rest were engaged in clothing, in woodworking and furniture, and in the food industries. Most urban Italian men, therefore, were labourers or artisans – tailors, carpenters, masons and the like. Other town-dwellers were engaged in domestic service (around 350,000), or in small trading. The census figures, unreliable as they are, give us some idea of this vivid Mayhewesque scene. In 1871, for example, we find no less than 64,715 porters and packers, 3,199 water-carriers, 6,710 vegetable and ice-sellers, and 34,384 pork-butchers and sausage-vendors. Here, too, is a rich source of confusion, for there was really no distinction in many trades between 'industrial' worker, artisan, small shopkeeper, and street vendor. A single individual could easily be all of these, as the example of bread-making shows.

As for 'factories', they were small and few in 1871, and the workers in them were mainly women and children. Ellena's survey in 1876 found 15,202 'workshops' (*opifici*), employing 382,131 people, of whom only 27 per cent were adult men. Most were in Piedmont, Lombardy or Liguria; and three-quarters were engaged in silk, cotton or wool manufacture. Admittedly this survey omitted some industries altogether, including the mines, the engineering and metal industries, ceramics and glassmaking. Even so, the overwhelming impression is of a female 'factory' labour force. There was as yet no legislation to protect female or child labour.

The most important 'workshop' industries were silk and textile manufactures. Italy was the world's second largest producer of raw silk, second only to China; and silk was easily the country's largest export, bringing in about 300 million lire p.a., one-third of the value of all exports. By the 1870s all the stages of silk manufacturing were being carried out in Italy. Reeling employed 110,000 of the 'workshop' employees, 80,000 of them women; and throwing employed 75,000 more in the mid-1870s. However, less than 15,000 were employed in weaving, most of them in or near Como, and there were only 445 power-looms.

Several aspects of this silk manufacture need special emphasis. It was closely linked to agriculture. Not only did it process an 'agricultural' raw material, but it relied on 'agricultural' labour (peasants' wives and children). It also provided a big stimulus to agricultural investment. All stages of the process, even the mulberry trees, were overwhelmingly concentrated in Northern Italy, especially in Lombardy. The market within Italy was very small, and the whole silk industry depended on foreign sales, especially to France and Switzerland. Hence silk manufacturers had every interest in maintaining free trade with their European neighbours. And it was a chancy business. Silk-worm disease, for example, could wreck it at any time; and disease was wide-spread after 1875, reducing silkworm production by over 40 per cent. Moreover, long-distance transport became much cheaper in the 1870s, enabling Chinese and other Asian silk to undercut the Italian product in European markets. The price of a kilogram of silkworms fell from 6.75 lire in 1872 to 3.78 lire in 1881.

Thus the silk industry, for all its commercial nature and 'modernizing' influence, was in decline. It may well be, as many historians have argued, that silk was the first 'leading sector' for Italian economic development in the nineteenth century; but by 1880 it was leading straight into depression.

Cotton production, on the other hand, was expanding. Ellena in 1876 found cotton the second largest industry in Italy, in terms of production and numbers employed. He estimated there were 54,000 workers, 12,500 power-looms and 14,300 hand-looms in 'workshops',[11] plus a further 42,000 hand-looms in domestic households. Thus the hand-loom phase of production predominated, even in the most advanced sectors of Italian industry. However, cotton manufacturers were mechanizing rapidly and expanding their 'factories', and imports of raw cotton rose throughout the 1880s. Like silk, cotton manufacture was concentrated in Northern Italy, especially Liguria and Piedmont, but unlike silk the cotton market was essentially domestic and non-luxury. Hence cotton manufacturers soon turned against free trade in finished products, and agitated strongly for tariff protection.

The other main textile industry, wool, was also largely in Northern Italy, two-thirds of the looms being in Piedmont and the Veneto. Wool employed less than half as many people as cotton, but it needed tariff protection too. Italy's best-known industrialist – and best-known protectionist – Alessandro Rossi, was active in this sector, and founded the *Lanificio Rossi* at Schio in 1872. Both for cotton and for wool the major transformation of these years was the disappearance of thousands of household 'artisans' – hand-loom weavers and spinners – and their gradual replacement by factory hands, working powered looms and backed up by more complex commercial and financial organizations.

As for the other industries – food-processing, metallurgy, mechanical engineering and chemicals – the general picture is one of a slow increase in production before 1880, and of changes in technology and in organization of work, leading again to the decline of artisan trades. This was especially true in iron and steelmaking. The Bessemer converter and the Martin Siemens furnace were introduced, and the old charcoal-smelting plants were gradually closed down. New foundries arose in Lombardy, and Liguria was also well placed for this industry since Elban iron-ore could be shipped there easily. Even so, the industry could not cope with demand. Railways and ships were being built, and the cotton industries were anxious to mechanize. Italy's own production was still less than her imports. Indeed, the need to import iron, steel and coal, at high cost, was a great handicap for all Italian industries before 1880, as they struggled to compete in European markets or to preserve their own markets at home.

This portrait of Italian industry in the 1870s has emphasized its links with agriculture, the fact that 'industry' was still mainly artisanal or household, that it was concentrated in the Northern regions, and that it was dependent on foreign trade. Italian historians have recently been much concerned with two other interesting aspects. Firstly, how did Italy come to have a 'dual economy'? Was the South already so backward industrially in 1871 (or 1860) that it could never hope to compete with the North? Or was it rather Italian Unification itself that forced the South into backwardness? In other words, were the differences in the industrial development of the Northern and Southern regions innate, or were they acquired? Secondly, why was there a 'spurt' of economic growth in the early and mid-1880s, and why did this 'spurt' fail to develop into some kind of industrial revolution or 'take-off'?

The economic handicaps of the South in 1871 were overwhelming. The South relied on exports of agricultural produce or raw materials – citrus fruit, sulphur – and was remote from European markets. The agriculture was more primitive, the industrial workers were almost exclusively artisans, and the ruling class was mainly interested in securing unearned income from the peasantry or the State. The South lacked capital, entrepreneurial skills, foreign contacts, and skilled labour. The South also lacked regular water supplies for energy – it is no accident that so many of Italy's first factories were situated in Alpine valleys. The North may have been industrially backward too, but at least there were entrepreneurs like Rossi and Pirelli, Falck and Breda; and practically three-quarters of Ellena's 'factory' workers in 1876 were in Lombardy or Piedmont. Moreover, the North had commercial contacts with other countries, and was thus in touch with new ideas and values. Indeed, the Northern regions developed almost as 'sub-regions' of other European States: Piedmont had close links with French commerce and finance, as did Lombardy with those of Switzerland and Germany. Perhaps Italy did not yet have a 'dual economy' in 1871, but dualism was already implicit.

Even so, the impact of Unification was disastrous for Southern industry. Internal free trade within Italy, and the low Piedmontese tariffs on imports from abroad, meant that protective tariffs in the South (of up to 80 per cent by value) vanished almost overnight. The Southern silk industry, for example, could not compete with the Lombard products once the Bourbon tariff was removed. As Northern industry became gradually more mechanized, the crisis of the Southern artisans became more acute. Despite all one's reservations about the Italian censuses, it is still impressive to find that in Calabria, say, 323,612 people were classified as 'industrial workers' in 1881, whereas the comparable figure in 1901 was 204,643. In the late nineteenth century many regions of the South were 'de-industrialized', in the face of new competition and new opportunities for migration. Northern industrial products replaced Southern ones, even in the Southern market.

Unification also meant uniform tax rates throughout Italy, at far higher rates than had been known in the South before 1860. Many of the taxes, especially the grist-tax on milling (*macinato*), bore most heavily on consumers, including those with low incomes. As the peasants became impoverished by taxes, they were less able to buy industrial or semi-industrial products, and the difficulties of artisans increased. Moreover, most of the tax revenues were spent in the North or in Rome. There were more schools in the North; most military installations were there, to defend the frontiers; the military and naval academies were at Modena, Turin and Livorno; most shipyards were in Liguria. Land reclamation areas are another example. Between 1862 and 1897,

267 million lire were spent on them in the North, 188 million in the Central regions, 3 million in the South. And most of the railways were in the North. Many Southern historians have concluded that Italian Unification led to a net transfer of wealth from South to North (and to Rome), through the tax system. But this was not the case: most taxes were *paid* in the North too. However, one should also consider the purchase of demesne and Church lands by Southerners. The State used this money to finance public works further North. At any rate, the North was politically dominant, and decided on such matters as taxation, tariffs and trade; the South was unable to compete either nationally or internationally.

The second question that has been much debated concerns Italy's growth 'spurt' in the 1880s. Gerschenkron's index of 'weighted industrial output' shows a rise from 54 in 1881 to 73 in 1887 (1900 = 100).[12] The most rapid development was in metal-making (where the index rose from 22 to 66, and to 119 in 1889), in engineering (from 62 to 118), and in the nascent chemical industry (from 9 to 22). Iron and steel were the key sectors. Iron output climbed from 95,000 tonnes in 1881 to 173,000 tonnes in 1887. The rise in steel was even more dramatic: 3,600 tonnes in 1881, 73,000 tonnes in 1887, 158,000 tonnes in 1889. Italy acquired an important heavy industry, which could reasonably be expected to supply many other engineering sectors, from agricultural and textile machinery to shipbuilding and railway construction. This was an astonishing achievement for a country with virtually no coal and very little iron-ore. How was it done, and did the expected benefits materialize? Above all, why did this 'growth spurt' not lead into 'self-sustained growth', but instead into what Gino Luzzatto called the 'darkest years of the Italian economy', between 1887 and 1895?

Here again historians have concentrated on the role of the State and on public works. Rosario Romeo has argued that the higher rents received by landowners in the 1870s, and the increased taxation levied on agriculture, were used to build the vital 'infrastructures' (railways above all, but also roads, ports, ships, steelworks, etc.) that enabled Italy later to become an industrial country. On this argument, the foundations for 'primitive capital accumulation' and for later growth were laid between 1860 and 1880; the 'squeezing' of agriculture was an essential prerequisite for the 'spurt' and for the later 'take-off'. Hence Italian industrialization depended on a strong centralized State, levying high taxes and spending freely on communications and heavy industry; and it also depended on political power remaining in the hands of a class of 'investors', i.e. big landowners and rentiers, so that agricultural 'surplus' could be channelled into non-agricultural investments. If Italy had not been united, or if she had been united as a nation of small peasant-owners, industrial growth would not have occurred, or would have occurred more slowly.

These views have not been generally accepted. Agriculture probably was 'squeezed' in the 1860s and 1870s; but was the resulting 'surplus' significant enough to finance industrial or infrastructural investments? More important, was it so used or did most of the capital, even for railways, come from abroad? And

25

was infrastructure necessary anyway? Gerschenkron has argued cogently that 'infrastructure' often accompanies industrialization, rather than precedes it; it is misleading to talk of the 'prerequisites' for industrial growth. Public works may well have been irrelevant or even harmful, by diverting resources away from productive investment. Perhaps agriculture's main contribution to industrial growth was not capital at all, but a plentiful supply of cheap labour and raw materials.

Other historians have emphasized quite different factors as lying behind the economic growth of the 1880s. The agricultural crisis, for example, discouraged further investment in land and perhaps diverted resources towards industry. It certainly lowered food prices, thus keeping wages low and enabling Italian industry to be more competitive. Coal, too, became cheaper in the 1880s, and Italy's imports of coal leaped from 1.3 million tonnes in 1877–78 to over 4 million tonnes p.a. by the later 1880s, without imposing an excessive strain on the balance of payments. The return to gold convertibility between 1881 and 1883 acted as a disguised revaluation of the lira, and thus helped to reduce import prices of raw materials like coal and iron. Moreover, the new tariff of 1878 gave considerable protection to textiles (especially cotton) and to some other light industries, including glass and paper, as well as to iron.

Perhaps the most interesting argument has come from Stefano Fenoaltea. In his view, the boom of the early 1880s was essentially cyclical. Italian industry needed to renew its plant and machinery, and so steelmaking and engineering expanded; by the late 1880s this re-equipment was over, and so a depression began, which only ended in the late 1890s when the new machinery of the 1880s itself had to be renewed.[13]

The arguments will no doubt continue. It seems indisputable that the role of the State was vital, especially for investment in steelmaking, shipping and railways. Why was the State so keen on iron and steel production? The answer, strangely enough, is that Italy in the 1880s was dominated by a 'military–industrial complex', or more accurately a 'naval–industrial complex'. In 1886 the Terni Iron and Steel Works was founded, on the instigation of a naval commission; it was designed largely to provide for the needs of the navy. Admiral Benedetto Brin was the driving force behind the venture. He realized that cheaper coal meant that Italy could afford an efficient navy, with more steam-driven warships. However, this would also require a flourishing iron and steel industry, a skilled labour force, a civilian shipbuilding industry in which naval engineering skills could be perfected, and large well-capitalized shipping lines which could afford the new larger ships. Thus naval requirements were a vital spur for all these developments, and the 1880s were in fact the great age of the Italian navy. The *Dandolo* (1876) and the *Duilio* (1878) were among the largest and most efficient warships of the day. Admiral Brin, as Navy Minister, was in a fine position to ensure the construction of ships designed by himself. The Italian navy soon became the second largest in the world. Warships were aimed at making Italy an important Mediterranean Power, rather than at developing the steel industry; but arguably the latter was their most significant result.

And, of course, there were the railways. Like warships, railways were of great military importance, or were thought to be after the Franco-Prussian War. Unfortunately, in 1871 most of Italy's railway networks were owned and run by foreigners. In the next few years, therefore, the State stepped in. It spent enormous sums on railways (140 million lire a year in the 1870s, 130 million in the 1880s), either by assisting with their construction or by subsidizing them once built. When the companies were in difficulties, the State bailed them out. In 1873 it took over the *Romana* company; in 1875 the *Meridionale*; in 1876 *Alta Italia*. These were the three largest railway networks in the country. Management was normally left in the companies' hands, although this issue was very controversial politically, and indeed it was on this question that the famous 'Parliamentary Revolution' of 1876 (see §3.7) occurred. Even so, the State fixed the fares, insisted on a minimum number of trains, and issued the timetables; the *Romana* company was under direct State management until 1880–82, and *Alta Italia* until 1885. After 1885 management was entrusted to three main companies, *Adriatica* (the former *Meridionale*), *Mediterranea* and *Sicilia*, but even then 6,400 kilometres of their 8,900 kilometres of line remained in State ownership.

What were the results of this massive State spending? Italy acquired – and retained – a modern communications network. There were 6,400 kilometres of railway line in 1870, 9,300 in 1880, 13,600 in 1890. The number of passengers rose from 25.5 million in 1872 to 50.9 million in 1890; goods traffic increased from 678 million 'kilometre-tonnes' in 1872 to 1,120 million in 1880, and to 1,854 million in 1890 – most of it agricultural products, moving from South to North. Italy also acquired a cheaper and more efficient postal service, cheaper transport of soldiers and prisoners, some extra tax receipts (e.g. on tickets), and presumably a higher rate of return from other businesses. In a divided and mountainous country, with very poor roads, and with a ruling class anxious for national unification in every sense, railways must have seemed a godsend. However, they did not often cross mountainous terrain. The main lines went down the two coastlines of Italy, along the Adriatic and the Tyrrhenian seas. The inland peasant communities remained cut off from their neighbouring hill-towns; or rather, were brought into easier contact only with distant cities.

As for the 'spin-off' from railway-building, there was very little before 1876 – Cafagna writes that 'the demand for rails, engines, carriages and trucks, and iron for bridges continued to be supplied, with few insignificant exceptions, from abroad'.[14] This was because the companies running the railways were foreign, and also because the Italian iron and steel industry was tiny and could not meet demand; the same was true of the engineering industry. The *Alta Italia* lines bought 641 locomotives before 1878; only 39 of them were made in Italy. By the 1880s, however, things were changing. The State insisted that Italian engineering firms should provide some of the supplies. The need

27

for railway carriages was met within Italy, and the two major firms of Tosi (founded in 1882) and Breda (1886) became specialists in locomotive production. The railway boom did have a 'developmental effect' in Italy, but it was very late – only in the second major period of railway construction, in the 1880s. The most important effects on the Italian economy were probably the demand for sleepers, causing deforestation over vast areas; and the demand for labour, attracting peasants down from the hills.

Arguably the most important of the State's economic activities was Italy's commitment to virtual free trade in the early years after Unification, and her increasing disillusionment with this policy. Early on, free trade seemed to most Liberals a natural, rational and progressive institution, like parliament or the army; yet it had the great disadvantage of not giving protection. That did not matter much when there was little industry, and those worst affected were Southern artisans. It began to matter a great deal more when high-cost steel-works and their connected industries were founded with State money, and when the agricultural crisis dramatically lowered the incomes of politically powerful landowners. In 1878 a new tariff had been introduced (see above), and by the mid-1880s the pressure was building up again for more protection. In 1887 this was given, with ruinous results in the short term (see §5.1). Much of Italy's curious economic history in this period – her slow growth before 1880, the rapid industrial 'spurt' between 1880 and 1887, and the sudden deep depression thereafter – was directly caused by the State's general economic policies, especially on trading arrangements and tariffs.

To summarize, Italy before 1887 was a country with little capital, few skilled workers and few energy resources. Her economy was very dependent on international factors like the price of coal or of grain. Furthermore, there were as yet no major *new* industries, in which she might compete on a more equal footing with established industrial nations. For such an economy the State's role in modernization was crucial. State intervention can, in favourable circumstances, mean the building of useful infrastructures and rapid growth; but it can also mean the creation of parasitic industries and indeed parasitic classes, anxious to prevent change. Much of Italy's industrial growth was 'artificial', and purchased at great cost; it involved many distortions, including a 'naval–industrial complex' and neglect of the South. Even so, perhaps the really surprising thing is that it occurred at all.

2.3   THE ECONOMIC AND SOCIAL ÉLITE

So far I have discussed essentially economic questions – the problems of agriculture and of the nascent industries. But these issues cannot be treated in isolation. Steelworks and railways were not built solely, or even mainly, for economic reasons; and the 'economy' affected every aspect of social life, as is clear from the peasants' living conditions. Above all, the rulers of Italy were not essentially concerned with economic growth or prosperity. In 1881, according to Sylos Labini's estimates, there were about 200,000 'independent' landowners, rentiers and entrepreneurs, and about another 100,000 'professional' men – doctors, lawyers, engineers and the like. Often there was no real distinction between these two groups. Landowners and rentiers did not usually inherit until they were in their forties; until then, it was proper to follow a gentlemanly profession, like the law or the army. And the sale of demesne and Church lands had reinforced 'bourgeois' landownership. But sometimes the distinction was real enough, particularly after 1876 when the 'professional' classes enjoyed more political power, and when income from land began to decline. In any case, the two groups together formed the élite, who dominated Italian society, and about whom we know far too little. These 'independent' classes were, of course, outnumbered by their less prosperous 'petty-bourgeois' fellows: smaller landowners, shopkeepers and the 'dependent' middle classes, e.g. clerical workers. There were 100,000 Italians holding respectable white-collar jobs in the private sector, and there were also 250,000 in non-manual public employment, including around 75,000 teachers. A government post was the next best thing to unearned income, and the number of clerical employees on the railways never failed to surprise foreign observers.

Only in Northern Italy were there significant numbers of commercially minded businessmen, mostly engaged in activities linked to agriculture, or in banking and insurance. Even in these sectors professional managers often had to be imported from successful growth economies like Britain. Genuine industrial entrepreneurs were extremely rare, and even they sometimes flourished only because of State orders. This is, arguably, the chief reason why economic growth was so slow, and why the 'spurt' of the 1880s petered out. Italy lacked an entrepreneurial middle class, nor could the deficiency be supplied from below. Her skilled artisans were being squeezed by international competition, and in any case lacked the finance, contacts and literacy essential for founding successful businesses. On the other hand, she was over-endowed with a host of officials and clerks, squabbling among themselves for the spoils of office; and the holders of economic power were still mainly a landowning 'gentry' class, living off the peasants. Over most of Italy the upper and middle classes were not 'modern', not educated or travelled or enlightened. Many of them disliked and feared industry. They prized unearned income above earned, relied on rents or governments for their prosperity, and clung firmly to 'traditional' values. They even preferred to settle their quarrels by duel, to great public acclaim. In short, they were not 'middle class' at all, but aristocrats *manqués*.

And the real aristocrats were still numerous. Sicily alone could boast of 208 princes, 123 dukes, 244 marquises, and 104 counts; and the mainland South (the old Kingdom of Naples) did even better, with 172 princes, 318 dukes, 366 marquises and 81 counts. There were 321 patrician families in Rome, 28 of them with the title of prince. The other regions, especially Tuscany and Piedmont, were also well stocked with noble blood. Throughout Italy there were 7,387 noble families, plus 318 '*signori*' in Piedmont and 46 hereditary '*cavalieri*' in Lombardy and Veneto.

What role did all these aristocrats play in society? The Prefect of Naples, when asked this question by Carpi, gave an uncompromising answer: 'The ancient and modern nobility is powerless, uneducated, generally poor and with little influence, counts for nothing in politics, is honest in character, incapable of any initiative whatsoever, not at all diligent, and consists of a large number of needy families, a few moderately well-off ones, and a rare wealthy one.'[15] This seems fair comment for Naples, but the Italian aristocracy was by no means a spent force elsewhere, especially in the countryside. The princes and noblemen may not have enjoyed the social prestige or political power of their Russian, Prussian or English counterparts, but they still owned vast tracts of land, especially in Sicily and the *Agro Romano* near Rome: ten families owned 17 per cent of all Latium. The acquisition of Church lands enabled some of them to *extend* their landholdings in the 1860s and 1870s; this was true even of the Papal aristocrats in Rome, including those closest to the Vatican.

Moreover, as cities grew larger, there were plenty of opportunities for aristocratic landowners to benefit from property ownership. This was particularly the case in Rome, where the building boom was most intense. Via Veneto, for example, was built on the site of the former Villa Boncompagni Ludovisi, which Henry James had thought the finest park in Europe. Aristocrats were welcome on the boards of the banks that financed these operations. Then there were forests to be sold off for railway sleepers, and rich heiresses to be married. In hard times, too, there were certain Court posts, in diplomacy or the army, where outdoor relief was available for the upper classes: at least one-third of the diplomats in the foreign service were noblemen. Even politically some aristocrats survived. By 1879 the Papal aristocracy controlled local government in Rome again, and in 1882 Prince Leopoldo Torlonia became acting mayor. In short, aristocratic landowners retained much of their wealth, and formed an important, if often underestimated, part of the social élite.

2.4 MAKING ITALIANS

The Liberal élite that ruled Italy may have been divided on many issues, but on one thing it was agreed: the need to create a unified nation. Its inspiration was d'Azeglio's famous saying: 'We have made Italy; now we must make Italians.' This was a formidable task. 'Italy' in 1871 consisted of a number of very different regional societies, with different economies and ways of life, different cultures, different histories and different religious practices. Even 'regional' is too broad a term: there were plenty of economic and cultural differences within, say, Sicily, and the rivalry between the Tuscan towns was proverbial. Most of the Southern 'regions' were, in fact, invented in 1864 by the Statistical Office, to group its data more conveniently: they had no cohesion, and arguably the mainland South consisted of several differing rural economies, all dominated by their capital city of Naples. Furthermore, 'nation-building' was hampered by economic backwardness, by clerical hostility, and by the fact that most Italians could neither read nor write.

In one sense, of course, d'Azeglio's phrase was nonsense. There were plenty of Italians already – 26.8 million of them, according to the 1871 census – and the birth-rate was high. In 1871 there were 160.5 live births per 1,000 women of child-bearing age, and in 1881 there were 160.9. The birth-rate in the South was higher than elsewhere, but not all that much. One-third of the population was aged below 15, and the proportion would have been much greater had it not been for the high level of infant and child mortality: 22.7 per cent of the children born alive in 1871 died in their first year, and almost 50 per cent died before reaching their fifth birthday. But infantile mortality declined later in the century: 'only' 17.6 per cent of the children born between 1891 and 1900 died in their first year.

The general death-rate, also high in 1871 at 30 per 1,000 inhabitants, was down to 24.2 by the last decade of the nineteenth century, although the decline was much slower in the South. In other words, deaths decreased sooner and faster than births, an obvious recipe for population growth. By 1881 there were 28.5 million inhabitants, and by 1901 32.5 million. The picture is one of the early stages of the 'demographic transition', from a high birth–high death 'equilibrium' to a new equilibrium based on low birth- and low death-rates – a new equilibrium that was not achieved anywhere in Italy until this century.

Considering the rural nature of the economy, Italy's people were remarkably urban even in 1871. The census of that year found nearly 18 per cent of them living in municipalities (*comuni*) with more than 50,000 inhabitants; 31 per cent of them lived in *comuni* which contained a 'centre' of at least 6,000 people. Northern and Central Italy were covered by small and medium towns, each with its own proud history and traditions. As time passed, most of the Northern towns grew, some becoming important centres of industry. In the South, on the other hand, the end of brigandage gradually made the countryside safer, and the proportion of people living in 'scattered houses' increased quite markedly (from 10.7 to 16.6 per cent in Campania, and from 11.3 to 17.3 per cent in Calabria, between 1871 and 1901). In short, the North became more urbanized, the South more 'rural'. Both processes showed economic progress. Certainly many Southern peasants welcomed the chance of saving their daily two or three hours' travelling between house and fields, and possibly also the need to keep a mule.

The largest city in Italy was in the South. In 1871 the city of Naples was reckoned to have 415,000 people, almost twice as many as Rome, and more than twice the figure for Milan or Turin. But the city had problems. It had lost its Court, and therefore most of its *raison d'être* as an administrative, legal and diplomatic centre. It was grossly overcrowded, with housing and hygienic arrangements among the worst in Europe. And its hinterland, i.e. the rest of the mainland South, on which it had lived for centuries, had suddenly been brought into direct contact with the rest of Italy. It is not surprising that late nineteenth-century Naples grew far more slowly than Rome or most of the Northern cities, or even than some of the Southern ones (e.g. Catania). It could not hope to absorb the Southern population surplus, and this fact had important demographic and economic consequences, particularly affecting emigration (see §8.1).

Emigration was not a new phenomenon even in 1871. Probably around 120,000 Italians emigrated in that year. The 1871 census tried to count Italians living abroad and came up with the figure of 400,000, but some countries refused to supply information. There were two kinds of emigration. Mostly it was temporary, consisting of male peasants moving from Northern hill or mountain areas into France, Switzerland or Austria–Hungary for a season's work on building sites or the like. This was a well-established practice in parts of Piedmont, Veneto and Lombardy, and included some skilled workers (stonemasons, carpenters, etc.). The other main type of emigration was more permanent, and consisted essentially of Ligurian and other Northern emigrants settling in Brazil or the Argentine. Over half the Italians on the American continent in 1871 were Ligurians: clearly the spirit of Columbus was not yet dead. Both these kinds of emigration were still Northern. The great age of mass movements of Southern peasants had yet to come.

The broad picture of emigration after 1876 is as follows. Emigration to Europe rose slowly from about 80,000 p.a. in the late 1870s to just over 100,000 a year in the early 1890s. It became very characteristic of the Veneto, which provided practically half the European migrants by 1886–88, and nearly two-thirds ten years later. Piedmont, Lombardy and Liguria provided diminishing numbers of seasonal or temporary migrants, as economic growth began to be concentrated there. Transatlantic emigration rose much more dramatically, from about 20,000 a year before 1879 to 130,000 in 1887, and to nearly 205,000 in 1888. By 1891 it was officially estimated that over 1.4 million Italians were living in the Americas. Most of them were still Northerners, but by the late 1880s certain areas of the South – Abruzzi, Molise, Basilicata, the province of Salerno – had begun to provide significant numbers. Coletti estimated that in 1886–88 around 57,000 people a year left the South for America, slightly more per head of population than came from the North or Central Italy.

Why did they go? The short answer, and a true one, is 'poverty'. Looking at conditions in rural Veneto or Calabria, or even in Piedmont and Lombardy, the surprising thing is not that so many went away, but that so many stayed behind. Overpopulation, unemployment, land hunger, high taxation, conscription – all these could be avoided, but only by emigrating. The poor hill areas provided the most emigrants, for they were the zones of peasant land-ownership, where there was constant pressure on limited resources and where the chances of significant agricultural 'improvements' were small. However, other reasons besides poverty were also important. Many rural Italians, especially the day-labourers, had long been accustomed to seasonal migration into other regions of Italy; they were more mobile, and less attached to the land, than peasants are often supposed, by townsmen, to be. This tradition could easily turn into a preference for another country, if conditions and rewards were better 'over there'. As early as July 1871 the Prefect of Macerata had told one investigator that the peasants in his province had long been accustomed to find seasonal work in the Roman *Campagna*, but it gave them malaria, so now they sensibly preferred to go to America.[16] And, of course, the 'pull' was as important as the 'push'. There had to be somewhere for the emigrants to go, and some means of getting there. The crock of gold across the Atlantic, and the invention and spread of the steamship, 'explain' the emigration figures just as much as do rural conditions within Italy herself.

Above all, there were the agents acting on behalf of steamship companies or foreign employers, and getting their cut of 20 lire per head. They were the vital middlemen at local level – the lawyers, the teachers and mayors who advertised the voyage, arranged the passports, booked the passages, lent the money for the fares (at usurious rates) and sold the peasants' houses (for a commission). Those Italians who regarded emigration as an unmitigated disaster blamed it all on these venal speculators, trafficking in human flesh. The argument was convincing: how else could an illiterate peasant have got to America? The small-town 'political class' had a vested interest in emigration, which was an important unofficial source of income. This interest conflicted with that of the big landowners, who worried in case mass emigration put up wages; where the big landowners controlled local government, there was noticeably less emigration. But attempts to limit emigration were rarely successful in the long run. By the 1890s the middle class in most of the South was busy enrolling peasants, hiring ships and choosing destinations; sometimes it even managed to export its social dominance across the Atlantic, to reappear in America as 'bossism'.

It is an obvious fact, but usually overlooked until very recently, that half the Italian population were women. Surprisingly little is known about the position of women in nineteenth-century Italy. Certainly they were less educated even than men, as the illiteracy figures show. Novelists like Giovanni Verga and 'folklorists' like Giuseppe Pitré depicted a rigid patriarchal society, preoccupied by honour and sexual fidelity. This may have been true in parts of Sicily, but was not necessarily so elsewhere, even in the South. Our main source of contemporary information is Carpi, who in the early 1870s asked the Prefects about the 'woman of the people'. The Prefect of Foggia informed him that the women of the plain were cleaner than those in the hills, and less likely to be beaten. The Prefect of Bari reported that 'an ass, an ox, a sheep, are almost always worth more than a wife to the peasant, and the wife obeys her husband like a slave'; although he admitted that the slavery began only on marriage, and that girls were brought up on an equal footing with boys. In Sardinia, on the other hand, 'the woman is loved and respected, and is considered an integral part of the family, in which ties of kinship are greatly esteemed'. In Milan, the women were very religious (this was true almost everywhere) and of good sexual morality. But the Prefect of Agrigento was less favourably impressed: 'superstitious, gossipy, quarrelsome and turbulent, the women pay little attention to their personal cleanliness and none whatsoever to that of their houses'.[17]

In general, it seems that 'the family' was an unchallengeable institution. It was also the economic unit. In share-cropping areas family size was much larger for this reason: many hands were needed on the land. Indeed, in many areas women were expected to play their full part in agricultural work, even as hired labour (e.g. the rice-growers in Piedmont); and where this was not so, the women carried on domestic industry like weaving. The 1881 census reported that 5.7 million women (out of 11 million aged 10 or over) were 'active', a very high proportion by European standards. Ellena's survey of industry in 1876, which excluded domestic industry, found 230,000 female industrial workers out of a total of 382,000. Thus women and girls formed around 60 per cent of the industrial *factory* workforce.

The main job available to middle-class girls was schoolteaching, especially at primary level. The majority of the 45,000 elementary schoolteachers in the early 1870s were women; by 1901, there were 97,000 such teachers, two-thirds of them women. Many of them had an extremely difficult time. They had to teach unruly pupils, much given to truancy, with no support from parents or clergy, and often much obstruction from local officials. The fate of attractive single schoolmistresses in Southern towns was a constant theme of high-minded concern and low-minded gossip.

Very few other jobs were open to women, except telegraph-operator, domestic servant and, of course, prostitute. The indefatigable Carpi reported that there were 9,098 prostitutes in Italy at the end of 1875, but this figure refers only to the officially registered prostitutes operating in licensed 'houses of tolerance', and subjected to compulsory medical inspections. There must have been far more working freelance. William Acton, visiting Naples in the 1850s, saw thousands in special suburbs near the English cemetery. We know, in fact, very little about this subject, nor about the incidence of syphilis (which became a notifiable disease only in 1925). Apart from the usual obstacles to research in this field, the dominant school of positivist sociologists had little respect for women in general and regarded prostitutes, in particular, as innately primitive, like Red Indians or Negroes. They had 'strong jaws and cheek-bones, sessile [sic] ears, hypertrophy of the middle incisors, atrophy of the lateral teeth, and dullness of the sense of touch'.[18] One wonders how they secured customers. About the only credible finding to emerge from the contemporary research is that nineteenth-century Italian prostitutes, who took ample food and little exercise, soon ran to fat.

2.5   EDUCATION AND LITERACY

One obvious obstacle to realizing d'Azeglio's dream of 'making Italians' was the fact that most people could barely speak the Italian language, or understand what anybody from another region was saying. There were several minority linguistic groups scattered throughout the country – 80,000 French-speakers in the Valle d'Aosta, 96,000 Albanian and 30,000 Greek-speakers in the South, perhaps 30,000 Slav-speakers in Friuli and Molise – but these amounted to only about 1 per cent of the population, and were not the real problem. Far more important was the fact that most of the other 99 per cent spoke regional dialects and nothing else. This was true even among the upper classes: King Victor Emmanuel II himself nearly always spoke in Piedmontese, even to his Cabinet ministers. His famous remark on arriving at Rome, which the history books record as '*ci siamo e ci resteremo*' ('here we are and here we shall stay'), was actually '*finalment i suma*' ('we're here at last') – said after a long and tiring journey! In most of Italy Italian, like Latin, was a dead language, used occasionally for literary purposes by the intellectual élite. Only in Rome, which had long been a centre of immigration for Italians from other regions, and in parts of Tuscany, where the Italian language had been created from the Florentine dialect, was 'Italian' spoken by the man in the street. Tullio De Mauro has estimated that outside Tuscany and Rome perhaps 0.6 per cent of the Italian population knew Italian; even including them, the proportion goes up only to 2.5 per cent, i.e. 400,000 Tuscans, 70,000 Romans, and 160,000 others, out of a total population of 26.8 million.[19] There is no more impressive index of how 'regional' Italy was in 1871, of how few economic, social or political links had been created throughout the centuries. Many aspects of late nineteenth-century Italian history – the slowness to eradicate illiteracy, the low circulation of newspapers and journals, the amazing willingness of Italians to emigrate to foreign countries with strange tongues and stranger manners – become more comprehensible if one remembers that Italians did not normally speak the same language, and could not communicate with each other.

As long as 'Italian' remained only a written language, to be illiterate was to be ignorant of Italian. Conversely, since school readers and textbooks were written in Italian, and since the medium of instruction in schools was supposed to be Italian, to be ignorant of Italian was to be, and remain, illiterate. The illiteracy figures are, indeed, impressive. According to the 1871 census, 68.8 per cent of the Italian population aged six and over were illiterate (61.9 per cent of the men, 75.7 per cent of the women). As usual, this national figure disguised considerable regional variations (see Table 1). Among Southern peasants illiteracy must have been well-nigh total. However, it was by no means confined to the countryside: even in the provincial capitals over half the population was illiterate. Moreover, the official figures were certainly an underestimate, since if you could write your name legibly and read a short passage you were regarded as 'literate'. Still, other sources of information about illiteracy give roughly similar results. For example, 56.7 per cent of the youths born in 1851, and conscripted into the army in 1871, could neither read nor write; a further 4.7 per cent could only read. In 1871 67.2 per cent of people getting married did not sign the parish register (57.7 per cent of the men, 76.7 per cent of the women). This may perhaps be compared with a civilized country like Scotland, where the figure was 14.8 per cent; even in England and Wales, only 23.1 per cent failed to sign.

What incentives were there to become, or to ensure that your children became, literate? Very few, in the 1870s and 1880s. There was no popular press; and since little was written in dialect, there was no point in most

Table 1   Illiteracy by region: 1871, 1881, 1901 and 1911

	Illiterates per 100 inhabitants aged six and over (male and female)			
	1871	*1881*	*1901*	*1911*
Piedmont	42.3	32.3	17.7	11.0
Lombardy	45.2	37.0	21.6	13.4
Veneto	64.7	54.1	35.4	25.2
Liguria	56.3	44.5	26.5	17.0
Emilia-Romagna	71.9	63.5	46.3	32.7
Tuscany	68.1	61.9	48.2	37.4
Umbria	80.2	73.7	60.3	48.6
Marches	79.0	74.1	62.5	50.7
Latium	67.7	58.2	43.8	33.2
Abruzzi-Molise	84.8	80.6	69.8	57.6
Campania	80.0	75.2	65.1	53.7
Apulia	84.6	80.1	69.5	59.4
Basilicata	88.0	85.2	75.4	65.3
Calabria	87.0	85.0	78.7	69.6
Sicily	85.3	81.2	70.9	58.0
Sardinia	86.1	79.8	68.3	58.0
Italy	68.8	61.9	48.7	37.9

The figures are those of the censuses, as given in the census reports, in the various issues of the *Annuario Statistico Italiano*, and in *Annali di Statistica*, s. viii, no. 17 (Rome 1965), 300. Females were always more illiterate than males: the excess ranged from over 20 per cent in Veneto and Abruzzi-Molise in 1871 and 1881 to only 1.2 per cent in Lombardy in 1911.

Italians learning to read. Only conscripts had a real motive for learning to read and write, for otherwise they might not be discharged from the army after serving their time. According to the army's own figures, only 7 per cent of the 1871 conscripts were still illiterate when discharged three years later. If so, the regimental schools were the most successful educational institutions in Italy. However, in the early 1880s the army stopped enforcing longer service on illiterates, and its success rate dropped sharply: 22 per cent of the 1884 conscripts were discharged illiterate. And in 1892 the regimental schools were abolished. However, army service was still important indirectly. It brought thousands of young men each year into contact with the Italian language, and thus helped to lay the foundation for later literacy.

The persistence of illiteracy is less surprising if we look at the state of Italian education, especially in the primary schools. Only in Piedmont and Lombardy was there any tradition of lay education, and over most of the country there was not much tradition of education at all. Official figures showed 33,556 public (i.e. municipal) elementary schools existing in 1871–72, with 34,309 teachers and 1,545,790 registered pupils. There were also 8,157 private schools (mostly clerical), with 9,114 teachers and 177,157 pupils. As usual, these figures hide more than they reveal. Over 13,000 of the public elementary schools were in Piedmont and Lombardy; Apulia, Basilicata and Calabria had 2,228 between them. Many of the 'schools' had no actual building, the pupils being taught in the teacher's house or elsewhere. Over 6,000 of the teachers in the public schools, and 4,700 in private schools, were unqualified, according to Carpi. Finally, the 'pupils' were those who registered at the beginning of the year, not those who actually attended school regularly.

All aspects of public primary education were run by the local municipalities (*comuni*), which were obliged by the Casati Law of 1859 to provide school buildings, appoint and pay teachers, etc. Many local councils, especially in the South, failed to show much enthusiasm for this task, and in any case had very little money available. As time went on, the central government made loans and subsidies available to help the local authorities, but in niggardly proportions, and most of it went to the wrong regions. The result was not only inadequate buildings. Teachers were poorly paid; and although the pay scales were laid down centrally, small rural *comuni* would come to an 'agreement' with teachers to pay them less, sometimes giving them another job, e.g. as municipal secretary, to compensate.

Primary education was not legally compulsory until 1877, and even then children only had to attend two years' schooling. In 1888 this was raised to three years, but was still regarded by most educationists as inadequate to prevent illiteracy. But the legal compulsion was a fiction. In the South truancy was often well above 80 per cent. Nobody seriously tried to enforce attendance, and in any case children left school, quite legally, by the age of 8 or 9. Local councils were indifferent, the teachers were demoralized, the parents were unco-operative, and the local clergy were actively hostile. Furthermore, the education dispensed was often excessively formal, and quite irrelevant to most children's needs.

The most debated educational issue was not so much illiteracy as religious instruction. This was supposedly compulsory in elementary schools, although non-Catholic parents could opt out. It usually meant the catechism, taught outside school hours for one hour a week by a layman (since priests lacked teaching certificates); and whether even this was given in practice depended on the policy of the municipal council. Religious teaching was often a dead letter, at least in towns run by anticlerical politicians. The whole issue provided a great incentive for Catholics to fight local elections, stimulating the rise of 'clerico–moderate' alliances at local level (see §5.6). Even many Liberals, like Pasquale Villari, were uneasy at the thought that the new generation of Italians might grow up without any moral instruction at all. To reassure an anxious public, the Minister of Education issued a famous circular in 1886 recommending moderate religious instruction as the source of property rights: 'We must not forget that the primary school aims at rearing a population as instructed as possible, but principally honest, hardworking, useful to the family and devoted to the Country and to the King.'[20]

It is a mistake, therefore, to regard the elementary schools primarily as institutions devoted to combating illiteracy. Their real aims were rather different. From the point of view of the Liberal ruling class after 1870, the problem was to 'make Italians', and Italians who would be patriotic and free from clerical domination.

So a single State school system was gradually created. Furthermore, it was relatively free from class divisions and petty snobberies. Most elementary schools, at least in the Northern cities, had a reasonable social mix. The middle and upper classes were often reluctant to send their children to Church schools (although the really rich preferred to employ private tutors, until the children were old enough to go to the State *liceo*). De Amicis's famous book of school stories, *Heart* – a sort of Italian version of *Tom Brown's Schooldays*, set in a primary school in Turin in the 1880s – shows this clearly. It also shows how schools purveyed a constant, relentless diet of patriotism. Religion is barely mentioned throughout the book, and Church festivals are ignored. The pupils write essays on such subjects as 'Why do you love Italy?' The monthly stories are nearly always about heroic deeds done by boys on battlefields, preferably during the *Risorgimento*; the school bully is expelled, not for smoking or swearing, but for laughing during the commemoration of King Victor Emmanuel II; and the teacher, introducing a new boy from Calabria, warns that 'if one of you were to offend this comrade because he was not born in our province, he would render himself unworthy to raise his eyes from the earth when the tricoloured banner passes'.[21] This was nation-building, with a vengeance.

However, primary education enticed so few children into regular attendance that arguably it made little difference what was taught there. The secondary schools were rather more important, since some of them trained the country's future leaders. There were two main kinds of State secondary school. The *ginnasio* provided a five-year academic education, mainly in classics, which could lead on to a further three years at the *liceo* and thence to university. These schools, especially the *licei*, were the cradle of the new governing class, the lay, State-run equivalent of public schools in England. Although formally open to all, in practice poorer parents rarely sent their children to them, since they were not free (the fee at the *liceo* was 295 lire p.a.) and, above all, since they gave no worthwhile qualification in themselves: there was no point in starting at them unless you could afford to go on to university eight years later. The other major type of secondary school was the 'technical school'. This was much more popular with less affluent parents, for the technical schools' course was shorter (three years), the instruction was more useful in itself, and the pupil could go on to the four-year 'technical institutes' and thence to specialist qualifications in agronomy or commerce, or to university courses in mathematics or engineering. The 'technical schools' were perhaps still too bookish. Half the timetable was devoted to Italian and French, and the rest taught mathematics and science rather than crafts. Essentially they trained an engineering and accounting élite. Finally, there was a third type of secondary school, the *scuola normale*, training future primary teachers. Many girls were sent to these three-year schools simply to receive a general secondary education.

To receive any kind of secondary education was to be privileged. In

1870–71, according to Barbagli, the State *ginnasi* and *licei* had 12,000 pupils between them; by 1881–82 there were 20,000, and by 1891–92 34,700. The technical schools and institutes had 13,000 pupils in 1881–82, and 29,000 ten years later; the *scuole normali*, at the same dates, had 6,000 and 14,200. Private schools, which were normally run by Church organizations, were much more important in secondary than in primary education. Girls' secondary education, in particular, was still largely carried on in the convents. In the South the seminaries provided much of the secondary education available for boys, taking many pupils who did not intend to enter the priesthood. Barbagli, again, estimates that in 1881–82 there were over 27,000 pupils receiving private *ginnasio* or *liceo* schooling, usually in convents or seminaries.[22] Government inspectors were often not allowed into these schools, and in general it was extremely difficult for the State to 'control' them. The Ministry of Education, and most progressive Liberals, regarded them as centres of clerical subversion.

Even so, in nineteenth-century Italy the important distinction within secondary education was not really between State schools and private ones; it was between the 'classical' schools (*ginnasi* and *licei*) and the 'technical' ones. The development of the State technical schools, and of secondary education generally, formed a striking contrast to the situation in the primary schools, and also to that in other countries. In Italy, both kinds of secondary education could lead on to university, and so the technical schools had far more prestige than those of, say, Britain. Many educationists, indeed, complained that the technical schools were too successful, and that there would be no jobs for all the newly qualified engineers and accountants. The economic breakthrough achieved after 1896 must have owed something to the men trained in the technical schools, and to the new educational opportunities that had been provided for at least some of the lower middle classes. And technical, scientific education was certainly the terrain on which the traditional clerical dominance of secondary education could best be challenged. Even so, only a tiny minority of children (less than 10 per cent) attended any kind of secondary school.

At the top of the educational ladder stood the universities. For a country with a backward economy and a high rate of illiteracy, these were embarrassingly numerous. There were, in fact, seventeen State universities, plus four other private or province-run ones, as well as various other institutions of comparable status (e.g. the *Istituto Studi Superiori* at Florence, founded in 1872, or the *Accademia Scientifica e Letteraria* in Milan). All of them, except Naples, were far too small. Bologna, for example, which boasted of being the oldest university in Europe, had 577 students in 1872–73, and that was relatively large: Macerata had 47 in 1877, and Sassari 74. At Urbino, there were more staff than students in the Faculty of Science. However, nothing is more difficult than to purge the professoriat. All attempts – and many were made – to close down the smaller universities were beaten back by outraged local interests. Altogether, perhaps 13,000 students were attending the universities at any one time in the 1870s and early 1880s. Just under 40 per cent of them studied law, and just under one-third read medicine. Most universities had at least these two faculties, and some also had Faculties of Letters and Philosophy and Faculties of Science and Mathematics, as well as offering courses in pharmacy and veterinary medicine. The Theology Faculties were abolished in 1872. Students of mathematics and physics tended to stay at university only for a couple of years, and completed their applied studies (in engineering, for example) at specialist institutions like the *Istituto Tecnico Superiore* in Milan.

It is difficult to estimate what impact all these universities had on Italian society. Certainly doctors were badly needed in 1871, although the training was fairly primitive even by normal medical standards; but whatever happened to all those law graduates? Moreover, student numbers increased rapidly after the early 1880s, almost doubling by the end of the century. In 1881–82 the universities and similar institutions produced 2,625 graduates; in 1895–96 there were 4,560. The plethora of universities clearly diverted resources away from other needs. The education budget in 1873 made provision for the universities to cost 6.2 million lire, compared with 4.5 million lire for the secondary and 2.7 million lire for the primary schools. In other words, Italian education was incredibly top-heavy. It produced both too many illiterates and too many graduates. Few were called, but many were chosen.

This education system obviously had a great influence on the press and popular literature. Newspapers in the 1870s and 1880s were local and provincial, not national. They were often subsidized by the government (via advertising and subscriptions from public bodies, 'loans' from friendly banks, etc.); and they were read only by the élite. Circulations were small: *Il Secolo* of Milan boasted of 30,000 in 1871, and that was easily the highest in Italy. The prestigious *La Perseveranza*, regarded as the mouthpiece of the Lombard conservatives or even of the Establishment *tout court*, sold between 8,000 and 10,000 copies, as did the other main Liberal paper, *L'Opinione*. All the main papers in Rome were financed by politicians. Crispi's *La Riforma* was reckoned to cost him 100,000 lire a year in the mid-1880s. Why did he think it worth while to spend so much to influence so few? Partly because the 'political class', and the electorate itself, was so small; but mainly because, in the absence of organized parties, the press provided virtually the only forum for the discussion of public issues. Only through his newspaper could he gain the support of deputies. Thus the press, despite its small circulation, was influential in faction politics. Similarly, the local papers, with even smaller circulations, filled the need for local political organization. There were literally hundreds of daily 'newspapers' in the provinces. They consisted mainly of local gossip and political comment, and were often written by one man. National and international news, when included at all, was lifted out of the French press that had been sent by post from Paris. But there was not much news. Italian papers emerged from the 'literary' rhetorical traditions of Italian political debate. They were written for leisurely gentlemen in cafés, not for merchants or diplomats who needed reliable information.

As time went on, a 'seditious' press appeared. In 1881 Angelo Sommaruga began publishing his *Cronaca Bizantina*, full of anti-government gossip. Despite frequent libel actions and duels, it survived for four years. The first really successful weekly in Italy, *Le Forche Caudine*, was also run by Sommaruga. It reached a circulation of 150,000, before being closed down by libel proceedings in September 1885. It was a harbinger of things to come, but it was unique. Most of the 1,600 registered weeklies in 1887–88 were serious political, economic or educational organs, catering for a very restricted educated readership. What strikes a British observer is the absence of the 'pullulating variety' (Geoffrey Best's term) of periodicals to be found in Victorian Britain. But then, who could read them, and in what language?

2.6   LEISURE

In this respect, at least, the press accurately reflected realities. If there was no rich variety of periodicals catering for a range of leisure interests, it was partly because most people simply did not have the time or resources for leisure pursuits. Rural leisure focused on the traditional Church feast days, and on the processions and sacred dramas that were enacted on them. These passion plays, or lives of patron saints, were the most important public events of the year, and were firmly under clerical control. About the only non-religious recreation available was the wine shop, and even wine was expensive. Fishing and shooting were also common, but for most people had a utilitarian rather than a recreational purpose. In the towns, the wine shops were not alone, although they were, of course, very popular. Some games, for example *pallone* and *bocce*, were widely played on Sundays, and there were always the brothels. Milan and some other big cities even had cheap dance-halls open on Sunday afternoons. Above all, there was much free, or almost free, entertainment to be had on the streets, as anyone who has walked round, say, Naples, will appreciate. Ballad singers told their epic tales of human passion and brigandage, using themes and musical forms that had changed little since medieval times. Street musicians were popular with all classes: the famous 'Barbapedanna', who went round the restaurants of Milan, was even invited to sing before the queen. There were also the special local festivals for which Italian cities were and are renowned – the *Palio* in Siena, the *Calcio Fiorentino*; and there were fairs and circuses, often held in the town's main square. The Italian circus was not, perhaps, what it had been in the days of the Grimaldi, most of its star performers having been enticed abroad by higher rewards, but there were plenty of very popular one-family shows going the rounds. And there was a host of smaller-scale performers: weight-lifters, bearded ladies, sword-swallowers, quack-medicine sellers, conjurors and hermaphrodites, who turned up at markets or performed regularly in the cities, and who shaded imperceptibly into the criminal sub-world.

In short, popular leisure activities were still traditional in kind. This point becomes clearer if we look at what was *not* available – seaside holiday resorts, for example. At a time when the English factory hands were already flocking to Blackpool or Llandudno, Rimini was still a small provincial town, renowned for its anarchists rather than its beaches; and Ostia was a malarial swamp. Most sports were not available either, except to eccentric aristocrats or English immigrants. The one important innovation of these years was the State lottery. Extraordinary excitement centred round this institution, which was the subject of much popular mythology and superstition. All right-thinking Liberals deplored it for that reason. Successive Ministers of Finance deplored it too, yet none of them abolished it, for it brought in 7 per cent of their revenues between 1862 and 1896. Psychologists and functionalists have seen the lottery as an essential safety-valve, providing many Italians with their only chance of escape from an intolerable situation; sociologists of religion regard the cults surrounding the lottery as important evidence for popular religiosity; cynics say that it was the only official institution of late nineteenth-century Italy that actually offered the common people something. All agree that it was more than just a leisure activity.

Perhaps there is a more general lesson to be drawn. Since Gramsci's day, Left-wing historians in Italy have worried about the apparent absence of working-class or peasant sub-cultures and institutions, about the lower orders' distressing willingness to ape their betters and accept 'bourgeois hegemony'. As Asor Rosa has written, 'the people, in short, have neither ideologies nor viewpoints, except what is suggested to them by the bourgeois classes'.[23] In fact, a popular culture existed all right, but the forms it often took – gambling, drunkenness and superstition – did not commend themselves to the high-minded then and do not do so now.

The picture is rather different for the urban middle and upper classes. The theatre was well patronized, perhaps because it was one of the few places where well-bred ladies could be seen in public – although, when gas-lighting replaced candles, they could no longer be seen so clearly during the actual performance. And, of course, this was still the golden age of Italian opera. Verdi's *Aida* was first sung in Cairo in 1871; *Otello* had its triumphant *première* at La Scala in 1887, and *Falstaff* in 1893.

But perhaps the most characteristic middle-class leisure institution was the café. Sometimes Bohemian, more often unnecessarily respectable, the café (or its Southern equivalent, the *circolo*) provided practically the only informal meeting occasions for middle-class men, just as the wine shops did for peasants and artisans. It was in the cafés that newspapers were read (and sometimes written), that politics were discussed, and 'public opinion' was formed. The cafés were more than just centres of conspicuous leisure. They were places where middle-class values were created and diffused, and where the new ruling groups of united Italy sustained that self-confidence, that reassuring sense of being right among like-minded friends, that is so necessary for the comfortable exercise of power over others. They were, in short, the places where 'Italians' were 'made'.

REFERENCES

1. O. Vitali, *Aspetti dello Sviluppo Economico Italiano*, Rome 1970, pp. 152 and 294; and my calculations from *Censimento Generale della Popolazione 1871*, iii, pp. xviii–xix.
2. S. Jacini, *Relazione Finale sui Risultati dell'Inchiesta Agraria*, vol. xv of the *Atti della Giunta per la Inchiesta Agraria e sulle Condizioni della Classe Agraria*, Rome 1884, pp. 5–6.
3. E. Carnevale, 'I Demani e gli Usi Civici in Sicilia', in *Inchiesta Parlamentare sulle Condizioni dei Contadini nelle Provincie Meridionali e in Sicilia*, vi, tomo 1, Rome 1910, p. 267.
4. C. Cingari, *Il Mezzogiorno e Giustino Fortunato*, Florence 1954, pp. 92–93.
5. S. Sonnino, in L. Franchetti and S. Sonnino, *La Sicilia nel 1876*, Florence 1877, ii, p. 286.
6. G. Lorenzoni, 'La Sicilia', in *Inchiesta Parlamentare sulle Condizioni dei Contadini . . . cit.*, vi, tomo 1, p. 222.
7. E. Morpurgo, in *Atti della Giunta per la Inchiesta Agraria* (Jacini), cit., iv, fasc. 2, p. 367.
8. R. Eckaus, 'The North-South differential in Italian economic development', *Journal of Economic History*, xxi (1961), 306–7; G. Orlando in G. Fuà (ed.), *Lo Sviluppo Economico in Italia*, Milan 1969, iii, p. 20; P. Ercolani, *ibid.*, p. 401; R. Romeo, *Risorgimento e Capitalismo*, Bari 1958, pp. 111–12, 120–21; *idem, Breve Storia della Grande Industria in Italia*, Bologna 1961, pp. 29–30, 46–47; G. Toniolo, in *Lo Sviluppo Economico Italiano 1861–1940*, Bari 1973, p. 7; M. Romani, *Un Secolo di Vita Agricola in Lombardia*, Milan 1963, pp. 34–35, 37–38, 107.
9. S. Jacini, *Relazione Finale . . .*, p. 163.
10. E. Pani Rossi, *La Basilicata*, Verona 1868, p. 253.
11. V. Ellena, 'La statistica di alcune industrie italiane', in *Annali di Statistica*, s. ii, vol. 13, Rome 1880, p. 60.
12. A. Gerschenkron, *Economic Backwardness in Historical Perspective*, Harvard University Press 1962, p. 75.
13. S. Fenoaltea, in A. Caracciolo (ed.), *La Formazione dell'Italia Industriale*, Bari 1969, p. 109.
14. L. Cafagna, 'Italy 1830–1914', in C. Cipolla (ed.), *The Fontana Economic History of Europe*, vol. iv, pt. 1, London 1973, 287.
15. L. Carpi, *L'Italia Vivente*, Milan 1878, p. 162.
16. L. Carpi, *Delle Colonie e dell' Emigrazione d'Italiani all'Estero*, Milan 1874, pp. 31–48.
17. *ibid.*, pp. 161–78.
18. C. Lombroso, *The Female Offender*, London 1895, p. 98.
19. T. De Mauro, *Storia Linguistica dell'Italia Unita*, Bari 1963, p. 43.
20. Coppino circular of 7 Feb. 1886, quoted by D. Bertoni Jovine, *Storia della Scuola Popolare in Italia*, Turin 1954, p. 389.
21. E. De Amicis, *Heart* (English edn of *Cuore*, London 1894), p. 8. This book was a great success in Italy, and was soon translated into most other European languages. A Welsh edition appeared as recently as 1959.
22. M. Barbagli, *Disoccupazione Intellettuale e Sistema Scolastico in Italia*, Bologna 1974, pp. 106–7.
23. A. Asor Rosa, *Scrittori e Popolo*, Rome 1965, p. 64.

CHAPTER THREE

The Liberal State

This chapter is about the Italian political system in the late nineteenth century. Domenico Farini, President of the Senate, wrote in his diary during the grim days of insurgency and rioting in 1898:

Italy was united by the army (i.e. the material strength of the Italian people, her volunteers and soldiers) and by the plebiscites; and she can only be kept intact by the army and by parliament. From parliament must come the means needed to govern her, and to strengthen, where necessary, the activities of the government.[1]

The two bases of the regime, therefore, were coercion and consent. Similarly, the State's institutions may be separated, for purposes of analysis, into two branches – that of 'High Politics', revolving around the Crown and the army, much concerned with foreign affairs, internal order and sound administration; and that of 'Low Politics', revolving around parliament and local government, a grey, ignoble business of granting favours and buying support, of job-seeking and compromise. The two interacted, of course, and each 'side' needed the other's support; yet there was always some tension between them, and by the 1890s a latent hostility had flowered into an overt 'debate on the State', on how to reconcile the conflicting claims of the two branches.

A. HIGH POLITICS

3.1 THE CROWN AND ITS PREROGATIVES

The constitution of the new State remained the *Statuto*, granted by King Charles Albert in 1848. This document is remarkable mainly for the considerable powers that were formally retained by the monarchy. Article V proclaimed:

The executive power belongs to the King alone. He is the supreme head of State; he commands all the land and naval forces; he declares war, he makes treaties of peace, alliance, commerce, etc., informing parliament of them as soon as the interests and security of the State permit.

These were no empty phrases. In the late 1860s Victor Emmanuel had used the Civil List to finance a virtual 'Court party', and had chosen his ministers from among these men. However, lack of money soon put a stop to 'personal rule', and the Lanza government that took office in December 1869 insisted on a purge of the royal household. Thereafter governments were led by men who commanded the confidence of the Chamber of Deputies, for only the Chamber could vote taxes. Even so, there was nothing to stop the king appointing some reliable Piedmontese general as Prime Minister in time of emergency, and in fact General Pelloux was so appointed in 1898.

Moreover, the fact that governments were short-lived, and that there were no established parties, also increased the king's influence. When governments fell, the king had the task of consulting the most prominent deputies, and of appointing a Prime Minister-designate. Whenever there was no obvious candidate as next Prime Minister, the royal choice could count for a great deal; and so could Court intrigues. The same was sometimes true of the choice of individual ministers, especially the Ministers of Foreign Affairs, of War and of the Navy. The 'royal prerogative' remained considerable in these spheres, and ministers had to be acceptable to the Crown. In December 1893, in what appears to have been normal practice, the Prime Minister-designate suggested three names of potential Foreign Ministers to King Humbert. The king objected to all of them, and persuaded the leading candidate, General Baratieri, to withdraw. Sometimes, of course, the king's influence was useful, as when he persuaded di Robilant to accept the Foreign Ministry in 1885 after the Prime Minister had twice failed to do so. In any case, Foreign Ministers came and went, and did not bind their successors; they were usually cautious fellows, forever worried about diplomatic niceties. When there was a big decision to be taken, the king and his soldier-advisers were usually involved, together with the Foreign Minister and the Prime Minister. The other ministers, even most Prime Ministers, had little interest in foreign affairs. Depretis once remarked that diplomats were the most boring people on earth, except of course for academics. The politicians always had to accept a given foreign policy, however distasteful, for the alternative was to undermine the Throne, and hence the unity of Italy. This was a classic, recurring pattern. In 1899, when Italy threatened to use force against China, parliamentary opposition was muted. Senator Rattazzi wrote to Giolitti to say that however much one might deplore the foolish behaviour of the Foreign Minister, one could not vote against him without striking somebody much higher.[2] A similar situation had occurred in 1870, and recurred with even graver consequences in 1914–15 (see §9.1).

3.2 FOREIGN POLICY

In the circumstances it is surprising only that Italy's diplomacy was as professional and successful as it was. The main reason is that neither King Victor Emmanuel II nor his successor Humbert could be bothered too much about it, once they realized there was no money for a good war. Hence foreign policy was left to the diplomats – Visconti Venosta (Foreign Minister until 1876), Tornielli the director of the political division of the foreign office, the Secretary-General Artom, and a number of aristocratic ambassadors, usually Piedmontese or Savoyard. Their view of the world was perhaps too cautious to qualify as 'High Politics'. Italy had enough problems at home; she should therefore seek peace, and not draw attention to herself. In the years after 1870, their main worry was the Papacy. Would the Catholic Powers intervene to restore Rome to the Pope? Was the Pope intriguing with Catholic Powers against united Italy? It was essential to reassure Catholic Europe. Rome had been occupied, explained Visconti Venosta, in order to prevent rioting and disorder, perhaps even a Mazzinian Republic. Now that the city was the capital of a united Kingdom of Italy, order was assured. The Pope was safe in the Vatican, and the Church's position was guaranteed by the generous concessions of the 1871 law (see §4.5). These arguments were naturally well received. In any case, the Papacy's main protector, France, had just been defeated by the Prussians and was in no position to intervene.

The other major problem for Italian diplomats was in fact France, at least once French power began to revive in the late 1870s. Italians resented French pretentions to be the tutor of Italy; they also, paradoxically, suspected that the French wished to break up united Italy. France was, after all, a republic, and might favour republicanism elsewhere. There were quarrels, or potential quarrels, over Nice and Savoy, over colonial possessions, over trading agreements and tariffs, and indeed over control of the Western Mediterranean. The French occupation of Tunis in 1881, in particular, was a bitter blow to Italian prestige. There had been at least 9,000 Italian settlers there, compared with 200 Frenchmen. Moreover, the port of Bizerta might prove a useful French base in the Mediterranean.

Italy therefore sought friends elsewhere. In May 1882 she signed the Triple Alliance with Germany and Austria–Hungary. Italy promised to help Germany in the event of a French attack, or if Germany or Austria–Hungary were attacked by two Great Powers (clearly France and Russia were meant). In return, the Germans and Austrians promised to defend Italy against any French attack. Bismarck's Germany was a powerful ally. It was Protestant, and thus provided an excellent guarantee against French or clerical claims; it was military, industrialized and progressive. The alliance with Austria had less to be said for it, but it encouraged international conservatism and provided some 'guarantees' against revolutionary threats at home. The Triple Alliance was mainly a conservative, defensive alliance, which ensured that Italy was not isolated. It remained the basis of her foreign policy for over thirty years, and was still in force in 1914.

This unheroic foreign policy made sense, but undeniably it lacked glamour. There was a general feeling of disillusionment in post-1870 Italy. Rome had been won, but ingloriously; the *Risorgimento* had succeeded, but after too many lost battles; Italy had a large army, but other Europeans did not take it seriously. Furthermore, Italy came back 'empty-handed' from the Congress of Berlin in 1878. Could she ever become a really unified nation without a successful war? Sometimes the call took an 'irredentist', i.e. anti-Austrian, form; sometimes it was 'Mediterranean', i.e. anti-French; sometimes it was for colonial expansion.

We can see here two constant themes of Italian history. Firstly, Italians could never agree as to where their national interests really lay. Should Italy look southwards towards North Africa, especially Tripolitania, and aim at making the Mediterranean once more *mare nostrum*? Or should she look northwards towards the European power-game, and towards becoming one of the major industrialized States of North-West Europe? The debate has continued to this day, and of course it partly reflects the differing interests and expectations of different regions. When Northern (Piedmontese) politicians dominated Italy, her foreign policy was usually 'Eurocentric' (e.g. from 1861 to 1881); when Southerners held office, there was more emphasis on the 'Mediterranean' (e.g. 1881–85, 1887–1900). Secondly, many young Italians – and some older ones, like Crispi – saw Italy's conservative foreign policy as a 'jackal tradition'. High Politics, they proclaimed, should be high and noble, not cautious and base. They demanded, therefore, that there should be a more active interventionist policy, and that there should be greater democratic control of, or rather impetus to, foreign policy-making.

The first real response to these demands occurred in colonial policy. The acquisition of African colonies was fashionable, forceful and activist. Moreover, it avoided direct conflict with another Great Power, while being none the less directed largely against France and providing proof of a search for greatness among the nations. It appealed to important industrial interests, especially those connected with shipbuilding and the navy; and it appealed to the Court, to Catholics anxious to establish missions, and to Southern landowners worried about the increasing land-hunger of their peasantry. Colonies were a potential 'safety-valve' for Southern peasants: they would find a secure plot of land and a modest prosperity, and social unrest at home would be defused. Italian colonialism was not founded on any need to secure raw material supplies, and even less on any need to export excess capital or excess industrial production; it was the agricultural crisis of the mid-1880s and the need to export social problems that underlay it, together with a frustrated desire for self-assertion.

The earliest colonial settlement was by the Rubattino shipping company at the port of Assab on the Red Sea coast in 1869, but Italian colonialism really only began in February 1885, with an expansion along the coast to Massawa (see §5.4). This was the first real shift away from the austere, fastidious Piedmontese diplomatic policy towards some attempt to meet 'Southern' or 'popular' demands; and it occurred when a Neapolitan, Mancini, was Foreign Minister. Mancini presented the case for colonialism in 'Mediterranean' terms.

The Red Sea, he told a bewildered Chamber of Deputies, was the key to the Mediterranean. He presumably meant that taking Massawa might be a useful counter against French interests in North Africa. The only valid point in that kind of argument was that colonial disputes might easily upset the balance of power in Europe, and if they did then ships and armies might be needed nearer home. That was certainly the view of the Piedmontese Count Carlo di Robilant, who succeeded Mancini as Foreign Minister in June 1885. Yet even di Robilant was drawn into the Mediterranean. He signed the First Mediterranean Agreement with Britain in 1887, and insisted on clauses concerning Tripoli being included when the Triple Alliance was renewed the same year. Germany agreed then to help Italy if the French threatened Tripoli or Morocco – i.e. if the French took Morocco, Italy could have Tripoli. Even Piedmontese aristocrats had to take account of popular emotion, however much they might insist that Italy's real North-West frontier was in the Alps, or that Italy's real interests lay in Europe.

3.3 THE ARMY

The other major sphere of royal prerogative, and of High Politics, was the army. Successive kings were often tempted to take their formal command of the Armed Forces literally; whereas most Prime Ministers and other government members had little interest in such matters. Military policy (armaments, recruitment, etc.) was normally decided by the military themselves, in consultation with the monarch; until 1907 the War Minister was always a general, and the Navy Minister invariably an admiral. In the early years the army was run directly by the War Minister and by his Secretary-General. After 1882 strategy and army administration became the responsibility of the Chief of Staff, leaving the Minister of War as 'the spokesman within the government for the needs of the army',[3] a spokesman, moreover, who could always point to expert technical advice. Of course, the Crown did not always get its own way. General Ricotti was disliked by both Victor Emmanuel II and by Humbert, yet was Minister of War off and on for nearly ten years – although admittedly Humbert got rid of him in 1896.

Parliament's part in military affairs was normally restricted to voting the money, although there were some parliamentary inquiries into the more notable scandals. Military expenditure was high. Giorgio Rochat has calculated that nearly 25 per cent of all State expenditure between 1862 and 1913 was on the army and navy. But a further 42.5 per cent of expenditure was on interest and capital repayments of State bonds, and another 10.5 per cent went on the expenses of tax collection; so the Navy and War Ministries spent more than all the other ministries combined (23.7 per cent of the total, compared with 22.8 per cent on education, public works, the economy, administration of justice, and ordinary administration).[4] Moreover, much capital expenditure on public works – railways, ports, the Terni steelworks, shipbuilding – had an avowedly military purpose. These facts are especially important in considering popular disaffection. Italy seemed overburdened with taxes, and these taxes were used to support armed forces over which parliamentary control was minimal.

Why did Italy spend so much on her army and navy? There were sound reasons, including the soundest of all, a desire to keep up with the neighbours. Italy was surrounded by other Powers that spent a great deal more on their defence than she did. Italy could not, in fact, afford to be a Great Power, and in military terms never became one. But her kings felt themselves bound to maintain the military traditions of the House of Savoy. Victor Emmanuel II, his successor Humbert, and indeed Victor Emmanuel III, had all been given a strict military upbringing, enjoyed military training and campaigning, and regarded themselves as personally responsible for Italy's having a large and well-equipped army. The ideology of respectable Italians in the late nineteenth century included strong patriotism and a belief in the virtues of discipline and austerity. Few seriously doubted that European wars would recur, or that Italy would become involved in them when they did. Even if there were no wars, Italy needed the army. It was a force for Progress. It not only defended the frontiers of the new State, but instilled patriotism into the recruits, brought them into contact with men from other regions, often taught them to read and write, and even showed them how to wash and how to use a knife and fork. As elsewhere, the army was the School of the Nation. Writers like De Amicis glorified military life, and told recruits 'the regiment will seem to you like a big family: and all the honours that are paid to it will seem as if paid to you, and you will love your old Colonel like another father'.[5] Soldiers could count on better food and accommodation than many of them had known in civilian life. In this atmosphere, the army was bound to be influential.

Moreover, the army did have an important defence role. It was not, in fact, to defend the country against foreign Powers – the Italian army engaged in no military campaigns between 1870 and 1911 except in Africa (between 1885 and 1896) and in China (where an expedition was sent in 1900). The real defensive role was at home, defending the State against its internal enemies. The army's formative years were the dreadful period of brigandage in the 1860s, when troops 'restored order' in the South by ruthless repression (see §4.1). The army also had to cope with riots, illegal assemblies, strikes and demonstrations – the whole range of rural revolt and urban protest. 'States of siege' were proclaimed ten times between 1861 and 1922, whenever there was serious rioting, and sometimes when there was not – e.g. during the threatened general strike of 1904. A 'state of siege' meant military rule and martial law – military tribunals replacing the ordinary courts.

Military organization reflected this function. If the army were to be used against popular disturbances, it had to be a disciplined professional army, loyal to the Crown and run by conservative generals. There could be no question of a citizens' militia, or of the 'nation in arms'. Hence Italian regiments (apart from the 'Alpine' ones in the Northern mountains) consisted of recruits from two different regions, stationed in a third; and even so they were never stationed for more than four years in one place. This was to discourage contacts between the local populace and the barracks, so that the regiment might not be inhibited from its duty of repression. This system had many disadvantages. It was expensive; it made it very difficult to mobilize quickly in the event of war; and it meant that troops could not be concentrated in Northern Italy, where they would be most needed to fight invaders. Yet all these objections counted for nothing. As Farini told the king, 'local regiments are very dangerous for the country; he who advocates them is his country's enemy. I guarantee that if they were adopted the Romagna regiments would carry out a *pronunciamiento* every six months.'[6] The major debate on army organization was not about these issues, but about whether the army should have four divisions more or less. King Humbert consistently supported General Pelloux, who argued for more men, against General Ricotti, who favoured a streamlined army with better armaments. The king and Pelloux won, of course. They argued that in the event of a European war, it would be necessary to station large numbers of troops within Italy to maintain order; in any case it was too dangerous to dismiss officers.

The army in peacetime consisted of about 215,000 serving soldiers, with over 2 million in reserve. Most of these were conscripts. In the mid-1870s around 65,000 men were called up each year, at the age of 20, to serve a nominal three years in the infantry. This was less than a quarter of the age-group. Eldest sons were usually left alone, and in some years half the potential recruits were turned down for health reasons. Many NCOs were also conscripts in all but name. Those who signed on for five-year periods received higher pay and status than they would otherwise have enjoyed, and they might also save a brother from military service. In addition to the recruits, there was also, of course, a corps of about 15,000 regular officers. In the early years of united Italy, over two-thirds of the officers were from the Piedmontese army. That was essential if traditional disciplinary procedures and loyalty to the House of Savoy were to be maintained, and if anything that smacked of a Garibaldian popular militia were to be avoided. This Northern dominance of the officer class remained true until at least the end of the century. In 1897 Rodolfo Livi found that the ratio of officers to recruits was exactly twice as high in Piedmont as in Italy as a whole, although Liguria, Tuscany and especially Latium were also conspicuous recruiting areas.[7] Officers came from the large cities like Turin, Milan, Rome, even Naples – middle-class and aristocratic centres, with a tradition of State service and a need to place sons in gentlemanly employment.

The Italian army was, therefore, a powerful institution in the State. Loyal to the Crown and to its Piedmontese traditions, it perceived its task as the maintenance of law and order, as the repression of subversion, and as nation-building. It was a bastion of High Politics, set aloof from lesser concerns and lesser institutions. The army had its own food suppliers, its own medical and sanitary services, its own arsenals; but it did not have military chaplains. Like the diplomatic service, the army was criticized by nineteenth-century democrats as too professional and too cautious; and it was also attacked for being too costly, too repressive, and too much of a 'separate corps' – an enclave of parasitism, a refuge for the sons of the upper classes. This criticism was a little unfair. The army had important tasks, it was imbued with a stern sense of duty, and its ethos stretched down into society – the introduction of compulsory physical training in schools was a direct result of military pressure for healthier recruits. Para-military values were, in fact, very widespread. Duelling was still common: in 1898 the Radical deputy Felice Cavallotti was killed in his thirty-third duel, and the king's nephew had fought one the previous year against a French prince who had dared to criticize the Italian army. Moreover, the Armed Forces provided the necessary stimulus to all kinds of industrial development, from railways to shipbuilding, from steelmaking to Alpine clothing. The army was not so 'separate' and austere as all that. And it was, via the House of Savoy, well integrated into the general political system. It may not have been efficient, but it was loyal. There were no *coups*, no *pronunciamientos*, in Italy.

The real problem for the Italian army was that its 'nation-building' task could only be done if it were prestigious, yet its 'repressive' role exposed it to popular hatred. Moreover, the army's prestige was tied closely to that of the Crown. When the army lost its colonial war in Ethiopia (see §5.4), King Humbert's position was dangerously undermined. When General Bava Beccaris's troops shot down the Milan rioters in 1898 (see §5.5), the Crown became even more discredited. Italy was not yet a peaceful enough country to survive without periods of military law and military repression, yet each military intervention lowered the prestige of the Crown and made national unity even more precarious.

3.4 THE POLICE AND JUDICIARY

Most of the army was called on only occasionally to protect public order. But the 25,000 *carabinieri*, officially the 'First Arm' of the Italian army, were a regular military police force, and had many of the responsibilities of normal national police. Usually there was one division of *carabinieri* in each province, and in the rural areas they were the only policemen present in any strength. Essentially soldiers, or perhaps military policemen, they were subject to military discipline, had received a military training, and were organized by the Ministry of War. They seem to have been an effective and respected force. One astute and well-travelled American observer described them, just before the First World War, as 'a remarkable Corps, in many respects the finest police force in Europe'.[8] There was, indeed, something of a cult of the *carabiniere* among patriotic writers. He was portrayed as an honest, incorruptible hero, steadfastly doing his duty of maintaining public order and decency in a hostile and crime-infested Italy.

In the towns the *carabinieri* were not alone. Minor functions – traffic control, market regulations, begging and prostitution – were dealt with by municipal police. Some rural *comuni* also employed similar people, called 'rural guards'. There were about 18,000 of these local policemen altogether, but their activities depended very much on who controlled local government. More important was the national corps of 'public security guards', responsible to the quaestors and to the Prefects. The 'public security guards' were a civilian (but armed) police force, with 4,500 men throughout Italy in the 1880s. There was often sharp rivalry between them and the *carabinieri*; conflicts of competence between them could and did occur, especially in criminal investigations. Most of the complaints about policing concerned these 'public security guards'. There were not enough of them; they were virtually restricted to the towns; they were ill-paid and ill-equipped; they were recruited from poor shepherds in Calabria or the Abruzzi – often those rejected by the *carabinieri* or the army; and they were subject to inadequate outside, or even internal, control. At the apex of the Italian civilian police was a small élite of public security officials, normally university graduates and lawyers, known as quaestors and commissars. They were in charge of the 'guards', and in turn were made responsible to the Prefects and to the Ministry of the Interior. In practice they were left pretty much on their own, unless some disaster happened and a scapegoat was needed. These public security officials gradually became one of the most important, and least known, branches of the State. Civilian policing became more normal as the cities expanded, although the *carabinieri* jealously retained their rural police and military intelligence functions.

The various police forces were not, strictly speaking, supposed to investigate ordinary crime except at the request of, and under the control of, an investigating magistrate. The police's task was to maintain public order and security: 'prevention, not repression' of crime, to use a curious slogan of the period. Police work was seen as a branch of administration. The standard legal textbook proclaimed that the police 'protects the order and security of the State . . . it operates, therefore, not only according to the criteria of legality, but also those of utility . . ., propriety, convenience'.[9] If the police were to 'prevent' crime, they had to amass information on the citizenry; and yet the public security branch was a centralized force without local links. It was here that the system of licensing came into its own. No one could run a restaurant, café, wine shop, hotel, billiard hall, pawn shop or public baths without an annual police licence; nor could one act as porter, shoe cleaner, cab driver, boatman, guide, street singer, stallholder, acrobat or dentist without one. Licences could easily be revoked if information was not forthcoming. Thus the police came to rely on quasi-official 'informing classes'. That meant that they could acquire their information without ever developing close links with the local people, without ever becoming a 'community police' or needing to make concessions to 'popular morality'. The centralized public security police remained a largely 'separate corps', policing an often hostile and unruly urban society.

'Prevention' also meant that the police enjoyed other discretionary powers, including the right to arrest people on suspicion, to ban meetings, and to seize offending newspapers. They waged an unceasing struggle against the 'dangerous classes of society' – beggars, vagabonds, the unemployed, those just released from prison, or those 'renowned as habitually guilty' of various crimes, even when they had been acquitted of them.[10] The courts (i.e. usually the local magistrate) could 'caution' such people, i.e. urge them to settle down, take a job, and not go to the brothels too often. The police themselves could 'repatriate' – i.e. send back to his home municipality – anyone who 'arouses reasonable suspicion by his behaviour and who, at the request of public security officials, cannot or will not give an account of himself by some trustworthy means'.[11] Above all, there was the system of 'enforced domicile'. Those who failed to take jobs, or were *suspected* of criminal activity, or who – in many cases – had just been released from prison, were sent off to live on remote islands or in mountainous regions, well away from their betters. An 'enforced domicile' order was issued by a provincial commission, on the basis of police reports; there was no trial or investigation. Throughout the late 1870s and 1880s there were usually about 3,000 people affected, and in the 1890s well over 5,000.

These police powers were, at best, illiberal. 'Cautions' could be given out on suspicion or for personal reasons, or even to browbeat political opponents at election time; this was said to be extremely common in Naples. Once cautioned, a man could not easily find a lodging or a job, and so he would be condemned as an 'idle vagabond' and sent off to the islands or to prison – all without committing any crime. As for 'enforced domicile', it was a 'finishing school for vice and crime';[12] the exiles, inadequately supervised and fed, and with no work to do, simply terrorized the local inhabitants. 'Preventive detention' was also widely practised. Half of the 180,000 or so people arrested every year had to be released later, for lack of evidence against them. In short, the police guards controlled the fate of many poor citizens; and they sometimes abused their powers. In Turin, the local police force was itself a criminal band in 1880.

Perhaps the real problem lay in the unrealistic way the police perceived their task and, for that matter, perceived Italian society. The *carabinieri*'s first major task, in the 1860s, was to suppress brigandage in the South and grist-tax rioting in the North. Thereafter there was always a suspicion of the ordinary citizen and his doings, a suspicion that was confirmed by the frequent subsequent rioting and by the large numbers of 'subversives' (see Ch. 4). Moreover, the 'positivist' social doctrine of the day taught that criminality and 'subversion' were innate in certain people. Criminologists like Lombroso pioneered the study of 'criminal types', and filled their pages with measurements of the cranium and configurations of the ear. Such physical details could be used to reveal the authorship of crime, as in the detective novels of the day. Science had spoken. 'The whole criminal world', wrote one former policeman, 'is formed of individuals antisocial from birth, and neither the persuasive methods of education and morality, nor the repressive and preventive methods of social order, are adequate to curb their impulse towards evil.'[13] There was obviously no point in worrying about the civil liberties of such sub-human monsters. Even so, not everyone agreed with this analysis, and the powers of the police remained a contentious political issue.

Police powers might have been used less arbitrarily if Italy had possessed a strong-minded and independent judiciary. She did not. The judges were State officials. Normally they had no background as solicitors or advocates, and no chance of returning to lucrative private practice if dismissed. They were appointed, often in their mid-twenties, as *'pretori'* in some small town. As *pretori*, they had no security of tenure, and their career prospects depended entirely on promotion to be a judge in the Tribunals or Appeal Courts. These promotions were, to say the least, strongly influenced by the Minister of Justice. He, in turn, relied on local dignitaries – the mayor, the Prefect, the deputy – whose 'recommendation' was essential.

Once promoted to a Tribunal, a judge might be dismissed at any time during the first three years, and even after that could always be transferred. Transfer was a powerful weapon in the government's hands. It meant banishing independent-minded judges from Rome, say, to some remote backwater. A new government occasionally did this wholesale: 122 judges were transferred in six months in 1878–79, including the Procurator-General of the highest Court (of Cassation) at Rome and a former Minister of Justice. Political vendettas on this scale were unusual, but political reliability was always high on the list of judicial virtues. The Justice Ministry spent much time conferring with deputies about the judges; and, of course, many deputies were advocates. They rarely lost their cases. For serious offences judges could be 'tried' by other judges, who were themselves liable to transfer or disciplining. In short, the judges did not form an independent branch of the State. They could not protect themselves, let alone anyone else, against political abuses.

If this was true for the 'judicial' judges, it was even more true of the 'investigating magistrates' and 'procurators', who were also judges but were charged with carrying out enquiries into alleged crimes and with prosecuting offenders. These men were under the direct control of the Minister of Justice, and could be dismissed at any time. Hence it was unlikely that an investigating magistrate would enquire closely into politically delicate matters. Furthermore, these investigating and prosecuting magistrates were frequently promoted to the highest strictly 'judicial' posts, and this further undermined any judicial independence. The career of investigating magistrate or 'procurator' was not separate from that of the 'judging' judges; often it was superior to it, or a step in the path of advancement along it. In effect, the 'investigating magistrates' informed on and controlled their 'judicial' colleagues.

Thus government pressure was not applied merely at important trials. It was a routine matter, of which every judge was fully aware. And so it was normally unnecessary. In any case, judges were respectable men, with high social status. They naturally kept on good terms with the local gentry and the other local officials. Like them, they were horrified by riots and demonstrations, by attacks on property or by strikes. They shared most of the values of officialdom; they were officials themselves.

Judges did not, of course, determine the outcome of the more serious cases alone. The Courts of Assize had 'popular juries'. They consisted of a chairman (who was an Appeal Court judge), two judges, and fourteen 'laymen', i.e. electors. Verdicts were reached by majority from the sixteen votes: the two judges presumably had a big influence on the decision. Even so, this system produced some unfavourable verdicts, and in 1874 it was changed. Thereafter the 'lay' jurors were drawn not from the electoral rolls, but from certain even narrower categories of people with a rate-paying or professional qualification. After 1874, perhaps 30,000 people in the whole country – i.e. 60 per constituency, on average – were eligible for jury service, most of them by virtue of being landowners. Furthermore, the jurors were carefully selected for each case by a special committee of Tribunal President and municipal councillors. These juries tell us much about the realities of decision-making in Liberal Italy. Like the Armed Forces, the courts were centralized 'State' institutions, designed to maintain public order and run by a conservative and disciplined élite. There was no question of local initiatives, nor of concessions to popular morality.

3.5 THE CIVIL SERVICE

The same was true throughout the machinery of State. Italy's rulers believed firmly that they alone were qualified to determine the general interest, and that it was their duty to protect and enforce it. The best instrument for doing so was a powerful civil service, staffed by enlightened and politically reliable men. So they set up a centralized civil service, and entrusted it with vital tasks – education, railway-building, public works. In its upper reaches this civil service was highly politicized. Men moved easily from political to bureaucratic careers, and back again.

Italy was run by a Liberal Piedmontese Establishment: ministers, deputies, civil servants, judges and academics were the same people. Giovanni Giolitti's career illustrates the point well. He started as a Treasury official, then spent five years as secretary of the Court of Accounts scrutinizing government bills for their financial implications, and only then became a deputy. 'That long period of work checking all the decrees was an extremely effective administrative training for me. It gave me a knowledge of the whole machinery of State which proved very useful later on, when I had to run the machinery myself.'[14]

Throughout the nineteenth century the upper ranks of the civil service remained mostly Piedmontese, or at least Northern. Of 198 employees at the central offices of the Ministry of the Interior in 1875, 73 had been born in Piedmont or Liguria, 38 in Lombardy and the Veneto.[15] At the end of the century the picture was much the same. In 1899 Nitti found that almost 65 per cent of the Prefects, finance inspectors and generals came from the North, as did over half the higher civil servants in general.[16] At its best, this system worked admirably. The Piedmontese were high-minded and patriotic, devoted to Science, Liberalism and Progress. However, at its worst the system simply meant government jobs for the old Piedmontese 'martyrs of liberty' – the *patrioti* who were the plague of Italian administration in the early years of the new State. And always it meant a certain *omertà*, or secretiveness, that is typical of restricted social groups, and was perhaps accentuated by the fact that most of Italy's élite were Freemasons.

The civil service was still fairly small. In 1883 there were probably around 30,000 administrative and clerical civil servants (i.e. excluding cleaners and ushers as well as judges, teachers, policemen, etc.). Only about 3,100 of these men were in Rome. This was fewer than the various Italian States had employed before Unification, and it does not suggest the existence of a parasite class of State employees – although the picture was perhaps rather different at local government level. After 1883 the number of civil servants increased, mainly because of the spread of postal services and schooling.

We know far too little about the social origins and decision-making powers of nineteenth-century civil servants, especially those outside the top ranks. They had no legal, or even conventional, guarantees on tenure, dismissals, pension, etc., and no recourse to the courts. Conditions varied greatly from ministry to ministry, and each ministry recruited its own staff. Basic pay was usually low, and most civil servants depended on various bonuses or responsibility allowances to make ends meet. So ministers and senior ranks had great power over the junior civil servants.

These factors perhaps help to explain the features of the Italian civil service that aroused most criticism: the lack of co-ordination among the ministries, the incapacity for initiative at lower levels, the habit of referring everything to Rome, the insistence on checking and double-checking, the excessive legalism and slowness of the machinery. Here were the real weaknesses of the Piedmontese system. The top élite may have been mobile and interventionist, but most even of the administrative civil service was simply 'an army of ill-paid law graduates', seeing its task as applying general legal rules to particular cases. This made State intervention in the economy or in education cumbersome and ineffective. The Piedmontese relied on personal contacts, on the old-boy network and on Masonic links; but they failed to train a successor Establishment, a modern functional bureaucracy with some technical abilities that could inherit the top posts in later years.

However, there was some virtue in 'legalism'. The Piedmontese administration seems to have been generally regarded as 'honest'; certainly it regarded itself as an island of honesty and uprightness in a sea of corruption. Even so, abuses did occur, and it was difficult to put them right. The ordinary courts had no power to redress abuses, although they could declare ordinances and administrative acts null and void when they were plainly illegal, or when they infringed a citizen's civil rights. In practice, however, the courts rarely intervened. The civil servants could do pretty much what they liked, the main check being the doctrine of ministerial responsibility – i.e. a minister was responsible to parliament for what went on in his ministry. This sanction, too, was quite ineffective. Consequently the cry throughout the 1880s was for 'justice in administration': for a system of administrative justice on the French model, empowered to quash arbitrary acts and offer redress even when no law had been visibly broken. Eventually, in 1889, Crispi responded to this demand (see §5.1).

Criticism also focused on two other aspects of public administration, 'centralization' and 'political interference'. Centralization meant that too many decisions were taken inside the various ministries in Rome, and hence there was much delay and inefficiency. The obvious remedy was to let the local offices of the various ministries have more responsibility. That was never seriously attempted. The hierarchical traditions of the Piedmontese bureaucracy, and the overriding need for central 'controls' in troubled times, were powerful arguments against any shift of power from Rome. It is worth noting, too, that just as each ministry in Rome went its own way, so too did its local offices: the Italian provincial Prefect, unlike his French counterpart, never aspired to co-ordinate the various ministries' field services. Another possible answer to the problems of centralization was devolution, for example by setting up regional councils with extensive administrative powers. Minghetti had proposed this in 1864, but his arguments had been rejected then for the same reason they were rejected later: centralized government seemed essential, if national unity were to be maintained. Some of the 'subversives' – particularly if Republican or Catholic – favoured regionalism, but their motives were suspect to all good Piedmontese.

'Political interference' was an even more serious issue. Local 'notables' (powerful landowners, etc.) or deputies would sometimes request favours from ministers and civil servants, on pain of voting against the government in parliament or at the next election. If civil servants acceded to these requests, impartial administration became impossible; if they did not, parliamentary government might become impossible. It was an insoluble dilemma. The Piedmontese bureaucracy, high-minded and devoted though it was, could not always resist political pressure. The claims of 'Low Politics' could and did undermine the sacrosanct sphere of 'High Politics'; reality was breaking in.

B. LOW POLITICS

The great weakness of the system described so far was precisely its high-mindedness, its unwillingness to make concessions to lesser mortals down below. Men needed material benefits – jobs, favours, recommendations; they were offered patriotism and impartiality instead. This was an unimpressive and hypocritical mixture to those born outside Piedmont. The resulting tensions were most evident in two political 'arenas', local government and parliament. The centralizing patriotic Establishment tried to impose its authority on both, but with limited success.

3.6 LOCAL GOVERNMENT

Just as the ruling élites thought that regional government was too dangerous, so they thought that provincial and municipal government should be strictly limited in scope and subject to rigorous central 'control'. There were sixty-nine 'provinces' in the country, mainly with boundaries inherited from the pre-Unification States. Each had an elected provincial council and an executive. However, the most important political figure in the province was the Prefect, a centrally appointed official responsible for maintaining public order and informing Rome about political developments. Essentially the provinces were convenient areas for supervising the municipalities, and for structuring some of the State's administrative offices in the country. Provincial councils had few real powers of their own, except for maintaining roads and mental hospitals.

The most important level of local government was the municipality (*comune*). In 1871 there were 8,382 municipalities in Italy. Their boundaries, like those of the provinces, had been inherited, sometimes from centuries previously; they varied in size from tiny Alpine villages to big cities like Rome or Naples. A uniform legislation applied to all of them, and they were all supposed to carry out the same functions. The municipalities, too, had their own elected councils and executives. They also had mayors (*sindaci*), appointed by the government from among council members. Government appointment of mayors (which lasted until 1896 in most *comuni*) was an obvious means of maintaining central control, but it was not the only one. The leading local official, the *comune* secretary (Town Clerk), was a civil servant, responsible directly to Rome. Moreover, decisions of municipal councils were 'controlled', and could be vetoed, by the provincial executive. Municipal councils could even be dissolved for 'irregularities', and replaced by a government commissioner; this was frequently done. Above all, the Prefect in each province had the job of ensuring that local government was being carried on in line with the government's wishes. In practice, he recommended the names of possible mayors, he dissolved the councils, and he 'helped' the provincial executive to 'control' municipal decisions.

Yet all this was not enough. The weakest part of the whole centralized edifice of government was its supposed foundation, the *comune*. Over many areas central control of local government was virtually non-existent. Why? The main reason was that mayors were local men. The Prefects could hardly appoint reliable Piedmontese to all those posts, nor could they constantly be appointing commissioners throughout the country. In practice, they relied on local 'notables' to run local government, and interfered as little as possible. The system had the added advantage that the dominant local faction would then support government candidates at the next general election. Local government had to be left 'free', if deputies were to be reliable and if parliamentary government were to function at all. In late nineteenth-century Italy local 'notables' enjoyed greater practical autonomy, especially in regard to taxation, education and welfare, than almost anywhere else in Europe – or than in twentieth-century Italy.

The *comuni* were important. They were responsible for primary education, hygiene, local policing and public works, demesne land, and the supervision of many charities, welfare services and hospitals. These were all vital issues, affecting the lives and pockets of every citizen. Moreover, the *comuni* appointed their own staff, and thus controlled much local job-allocation and patronage. Above all, the municipal councils levied their own taxes, or their own surcharges on other taxes. They could decide what should be taxed, they could alter the tax rates, and they could give exemptions. When Sonnino examined the tax registers in Sicily he found that heavy taxes were levied on mules and donkeys (which the peasants owned), and negligible ones on cattle (which belonged to the bigger landowners).[17] In particular, the local councils could levy duties on food. These duties raised 79 million lire in 1873. They kept food prices high, and acted as a real barrier to internal trade. Furthermore, they were collected by locally appointed excisemen who could be guaranteed not to tax the produce of political supporters. For all these reasons passions often ran high during local elections. Controlling the *comune*, or being friendly with those who controlled it, was essential for many purposes. Indeed, local government was a constantly shifting battleground among the leading families and their supporters.

Despite their tax-raising powers, the *comuni* were chronically short of money. Perhaps this was deliberate government policy, to control them the better. Certainly one reason was that the Right-wing governments of the early 1870s off-loaded expensive tasks on to the municipalities, in an effort to balance the State budget. This policy backfired badly. The desperate financial plight of the larger *comuni* – especially Florence, which had spent a great deal in the late 1860s on equipping herself to become the capital of Italy, and which owed nearly 105 million lire in 1873 – led to a revolt by the Tuscan deputies and the eventual fall of the Right (see below, §3.7).

The condition of local government, particularly in the South, soon became a familiar theme of political debate. Franchetti deplored the 'absolute omnipotence of the wealthy class' in Sicily: 'the municipality is handed over to the total domination of the town council and the mayor'.[18] The municipal council was virtually a self-perpetuating oligarchy, since it also drew up the electoral rolls. Names of opponents could be left off 'in error', and the Court of Appeal would right matters only after the election. Mayors issued personal documents, passports, trading permits, etc.; they 'recommended' to the local magistrate names of people who needed a 'caution'; and they even had powers of arrest, in the absence of the police. Furthermore, many local welfare agencies were now run by the municipalities, with predictable results. The *monti frumentari* (grain and seed stores which traditionally had lent seed to the peasants at the beginning of the season, at low interest rates) became a usurious monopoly in the councillors' hands. Some rural banks lent only to councillors, often enabling them to buy up municipal land.

Many Northern writers on the South claimed that the corruption in local government was due to a different moral code being observed. Sicilians, wrote the Tuscan aristocrat Franchetti, simply could not understand why a friendly official should refuse a favour: 'all relationships are founded on the concept of individual interests and on obligations between individuals, to the exclusion of any social or public interest whatsoever'.[19] In such a society, *clientele* – personal relationships of obligation between 'client' individuals or families and their powerful protectors and patrons – were inevitable. But personal links were not everything. Franchetti, Pasquale Villari, and Sidney Sonnino all described Southern rural societies which were sharply divided into two main classes, the oppressors and the oppressed, the landowners and the peasants. Their comparison was with Ireland. No doubt they simplified matters. There were markedly different types of rural economy in the South (see §2.1). The local *comune* might be run by a handful of big *latifundia* landowners, or by squabbling local lawyers and shopkeepers, or by Mafia bosses. But it was never run by the peasants, or for them. What, then, prevented the peasants from revolting? Nothing, except the *carabinieri*. Peasant revolts had occurred in the 1860s, and had been brutally repressed. Sonnino – a Tuscan *conservative*! – thought that without Italian Unification, the Sicilian peasants would have been better off, because they would have had a revolution. As it was, they could act neither legally nor illegally – 'we have legalized existing oppression, and we guarantee impunity to the oppressor'.[20]

If the provincial Prefect intervened to prevent gross injustice in municipal affairs, howls of protest would reach the deputies in Rome, questions would be asked in the Chamber, and there would be demands·for the offending official to be removed forthwith. The Prefect's only support would come from an opposing local faction; and, at best, he would then be forced to rely. on and protect this new governing clique, just as iniquitous as the old one. Most Prefects were politically agile enough to avoid *that* outcome. Most of them had been, or would become, deputies or Senators themselves. All of them were 'political administrators', necessarily sympathetic to the government in office. One of their major tasks was to ensure that the right deputies were returned at the next general election. So they did nothing that might lose the government votes. In fact, their electioneering was usually fairly easy. There was a substantial payroll vote in the provinces – teachers, policemen, postal officials, pensioners, etc. – and the mayors and public security officials could be relied on to do their duty when it came to issuing gun-licences and so forth. Since the number of voters was smaller in the South, the system flourished most there. The Prefect was safe, so long as he did not alienate the local élites.

In short, the Prefect was the lynch-pin of the whole political system, the link between national and local government. He acted as the 'spokesman for his province' in Rome, and he supported the local élites in their dealings with the central civil service. His task was not so much to 'control' local government as to conciliate it, even to guarantee it against its victims. Often the power to appoint mayors was not an instrument of 'control', rather a means of winning reliable local supporters. In November 1884, for example, the Prefect of Caltanissetta gave the Interior Ministry a list of names of potential mayors: his main aim, he assured Depretis, had been to choose 'a citizen who is a competent administrator, loyal to the King and devoted to the present government; my intention is to secure people who will be effective in making government candidates prevail at parliamentary elections.'[21] Thus local government depended, ultimately, on national politics; but often the tail wagged the dog.

3.7 PARLIAMENT

What was true of local government was also true of parliament. Most nineteenth-century writers agreed that the Chamber of Deputies – the lower House of the Italian parliament – was essentially the home of 'influence' in domestic matters, the arena where political favours were traded. Deputies were elected in order to advocate their constituents' interests to the central administration in Rome. If a deputy failed to put pressure on a minister, he risked losing votes back home; if a minister refused a deputy's request, the government risked losing the deputy's vote in parliament. But in a world of scarce resources requests sometimes had to be refused. So deputies' allegiances were temporary, and governments were unstable.

The art of government, therefore, consisted between elections in conciliating deputies by granting them favours whenever possible ('buying deputies'); and at elections in using government favours to secure the right deputies ('buying votes'). The Prime Minister's job was largely that of 'parliamentary management', of creating and holding together a shifting coalition of support by persuasion and patronage. Some Prime Ministers – notably Agostino Depretis, who held the post for all but two years between 1876 and 1887 – were very effective at this activity, but their manoeuvres tended to bemuse the public and discredit the system. Governments were short-lived (by 1892 there had been 28 governments in the 32 years of the united kingdom's history) and were not bound by any convenient doctrine of collective Cabinet responsibility. They fell either when some faction or powerful individual had withdrawn support, or when the Prime Minister needed to rid himself of a minister so as to give the job to someone else. During the ensuing 'ministerial crisis' the king would consult the leading parliamentarians, and then appoint a 'Prime Minister-designate'; the latter would put together a new government, usually looking remarkably like the old one. Occasionally the Chamber would reject the king's nominee, as happened to Sella in 1880, but normally the deputies respected the Crown's choice – for a time. In practice, a few dozen men held the various ministries, almost in rotation. When parliament became really unmanageable, the king might be persuaded to dissolve it. At that point the Prefects and the Interior Ministry came into their own. Italian Prime Ministers nearly always held the Interior Ministry as well: parliament had to be managed, but so did elections.

All this helps to explain the complexity, but also the essential stability, of parliamentary politics. The one major political change in this period was the fall of the 'Right' government in 1876, although arguably that, too, was a classic example of this kind of politics. In the 1874 elections the Right-wing *'ministeriali'* had won 275 seats, as compared with their opponents' 233. A majority of 42 is fairly healthy in British terms; but in Italy it meant that only 22 deputies needed to change votes, and the 'Right' government was lost. Soon the Tuscan deputies became dissatisfied, mainly over the government's failure to rescue Florence from her financial problems. In March 1876 the government finally fell over a bill to nationalize the railways, and the 'Left' came to power. There had, of course, been no election. One was called shortly afterwards, and was managed carefully by the Left's Interior Minister: the new government's supporters won 414 seats out of 508. That was *too* large a majority. There were not enough jobs or favours to go round, and the squabbles among the various 'Left' factions became intense. Hence the 1880s was the classic period of *trasformismo*, i.e. of governments led by Depretis 'transforming' opponents into supporters, of factions being 'absorbed' into the government arena, and of the collapse of the old distinctions between 'Right' and 'Left'.

In assessing the deputies, one may perhaps distinguish, very roughly, between Northern and Southern ones, between 'Right' and 'Left', and between the periods before and after 1876. The archetypal 'Right-wing' deputy was a Northern landowner, aristocratic both by birth and temperament. He was devoted to the House of Savoy and to the 'general interests' of the country; and he regarded himself, sometimes justifiably, as one of the architects of Italian Unification. He was a member of the Liberal Establishment, and might well have served in the civil service or army. Often he was admirably competent and disinterested. The long series of probing parliamentary inquiries – into agriculture, industry, strikes, tariff reform, railway administration, the merchant navy, the Southern problem, the banks – were usually inspired by such men. Most of the criticism of parliament came from them too. These fastidious deputies of the 'Right' regarded the necessity for requesting favours with distaste. Sometimes they refused to soil their hands with such matters. So the atmosphere of kinship and personal friendships, of links with local notables and local authorities, did not always imply subservience to constituency interests. There were many deputies who were big enough names, or had important enough connections, or owned enough property, to be able to take an independent line. Luigi Pelloux, for example, was 'chosen' to sit for Livorno in 1881 by the former deputy, his brother-in-law Admiral Brin. He did not want the job, but 'the Prime Minister insisted so much that I had to resign myself to it, on condition however that I did not hold a single election meeting, that I did not put myself forward as a candidate, and that I did not even declare my willingness to serve if elected'.[22] At Cuneo, a year later, Giovanni Giolitti was more eager to become a deputy. He actually condescended to visit the place, and talked to the mayor for an hour. All went well at the election, because his cousin was mayor of nearby Dronero, and at Peveragno, in another part of the constituency, the mayor had been born in the Giolitti family house: he received a unanimous vote there.

The archetypal 'Left-wing' deputy, on the other hand, was rather closer to

Gaetano Salvemini's description of the Southern deputies of his day: 'unscrupulous manipulators and common fixers, with no personal convictions and no dignity'.[23] He was middle class rather than aristocratic, Southern rather than Northern, lawyer rather than landowner. He was less devoted to the Crown, less likely to have fought in the *Risorgimento*, and more concerned with his constituency. He probably regarded the State as a milch-cow, and he was more anticlerical. After 1876 such deputies became more numerous. By 1892 40 per cent of the deputies were lawyers; by 1913 it was 49 per cent.

These stereotypes are no doubt crude, but they have some validity. The nature of the Chamber did change after 1876: half the deputies elected in that year were new. Still, 'Right' and 'Left' were vague and confusing labels. The 'Right' stood for social progress, i.e. free trade, a strong army, and balanced budgets. The 'Left' also stood for progress: lay education, a wider franchise, and public works. The essential difference was over taxes and government spending. The parsimonious 'Right', with Sella and Minghetti at the Treasury, pursued far more austere and unpopular policies than did the Left's Magliani, with his 'cheerful finance' and his deficit spending. This was understandable. The 'Right' represented, after all, the rentiers of Northern Italy, who wanted sound money; the 'Left' represented the Southern bourgeoisie, who wanted public works and public jobs. Yet it was the 'Right' that favoured nationalization of the railways, State intervention in the economy, and social welfare schemes; it was the 'Left' that expanded the navy and engaged in colonial wars. Neither group had any coherent doctrine or organization, and each was split into factions clustered around some leading personality with influence. Every government contained men from different factions.

The issues of political debate were few, became fewer, and those few more prosaic. By 1883 the 'Left' had carried out its major promises – compulsory primary education, abolition of the grist-tax, and reform of the suffrage. There was really very little left to argue about, at least within the conventions of 'normal' constitutional politics and of 'normal' foreign and religious policy. As usually happens when there are no serious disagreements, men fussed instead about the economy. Parliament investigated agriculture, debated public works schemes and tariffs, and reorganized the railways. The leading politicians were men who knew, or claimed to know, about such matters. It was all rather dull, but it was a type of politics admirably suited to the small-town, backward Italy of the day. It was 'Low Politics': yet, even then, the navy was expanded and colonial wars began. While politicians squabbled over jobs and spoils, the real decisions were taken outside parliament.

The characteristics of the Chamber of Deputies naturally reflected those of the electoral system and of the electorate. Before 1882 deputies were elected in single-member constituencies on the 'ballottage' system, i.e. a run-off ballot was held when the leading candidate failed to secure 50 per cent of the votes at the first ballot. The voters had to be male, over 25, and literate. They also had to pay forty lire a year in direct State or provincial taxes, although there were some exceptions in favour of those living off government securities, or with professional qualifications. The electorate at parliamentary elections consisted of just over 500,000 men in 1870, rising to 622,000 by 1880, i.e. about 2.2 per cent of the total population (or 8 per cent of adult men). Less than 60 per cent of them bothered to vote; turnout in the South was consistently higher than in the North. Catholics were forbidden by the Pope to vote for the usurping parliament; and the Republicans also advocated abstention on principle. The effect of a limited electorate and a low turnout was that in 1874, for example, the median successful candidate received only 426 votes (the median constituency had over 50,000 population). Every vote counted, which was one reason why deputies were so solicitous of their electors' interests. The restricted suffrage also ensured that, in Sidney Sonnino's words, 'the vast majority of the people, more than 90 per cent of them, feel estranged from our institutions; they see themselves as subjects of the State, constrained to serve it with blood and money, but they do not feel that they form an organic, living part of it, nor do they take any interest in its existence and development'.[24]

One of the main planks in the Left's platform in the 1870s was their proposal to widen the suffrage. In 1882 the voting age was lowered to 21, and the tax-paying requirement came down to 19.80 lire annually. Those who had successfully completed two years' elementary schooling were exempt even from this, as were certain categories of tenants. The literacy requirement was maintained. Thenceforth over 2 million people had the vote – although that was still less than 7 per cent of the population. The educational qualification meant that the electorate was larger in the North and in the towns, where there were schools, than in the South or rural areas. In 1882 8.2 per cent of the Northerners had the vote, compared with 5.5 per cent of Southerners; to put it another way, 53 per cent of the electorate was Northern, 16 per cent lived in Central Italy, and 31 per cent in the South. A big political divide had suddenly opened up, and it grew wider as time went on: by 1895 the North had 56 per cent of the electorate, the South only 26 per cent. Some historians have written of two forms of parliamentary representation coexisting after 1882 – a reactionary, minority system in the South, a wider and more 'progressive' type in the North.

It was one thing to reform the franchise, and quite another to redistribute the seats. The South may have had many fewer voters than the North after 1882, but her deputies remained as numerous as ever – 144 from the mainland South, plus 59 from Sicily and Sardinia, out of the total 508. In 1882 the successful Northern deputies received an average of 5,651 votes each; in the South the figure was 3,991, despite the higher turnout. This outcome suited the Left very well. Their own position was maintained, that of their Northern Right-wing rivals undermined. Furthermore, they could claim to have pushed through a modern progressive reform. The wider suffrage helped to preserve the Left's power. It was the intelligent Right and landowners who had wanted a much wider suffrage again, so as to increase the political weight of the rural areas; the Left deliberately restricted rural representation, so as to combat the Right and/or the clerical threat. The Southern 'political class' dug itself into power, and survived with remarkably few changes until the 1950s.

The Chamber of Deputies was not, of course, the only House of the Italian parliament. However, the Senate was less significant. Senators were 'life-peers' appointed by the king, on the recommendation of the Prime Minister. A seat in the Senate was a political reward – it was a frequent consolation prize for unsuccessful pro-government candidates for the Chamber. On the other hand, a certain regional balance had to be maintained, and a certain gentlemanly tone had to be preserved. Giolitti caused great scandal in 1892 by nominating unworthy Senators. The Senate also served as a club for elderly gentlemen from various respectable élites – military, diplomatic, academic or landowning. It had little influence on domestic 'Low Politics', despite its constitutional right of veto; if it tried to oppose government policy, as it did in 1890 over Crispi's law on charities, it could always be overwhelmed by a huge influx of new Senators. The Senate's voice was influential, however, in foreign and military affairs, and on constitutional issues. On these 'High Political' matters it acted as an effective conservative counterweight to any dangerous proposals from the lower House.

The parliamentary system described here had some obvious weaknesses. By the late 1870s a host of commentators were complaining that elections were fixed, that deputies were corrupt, that the civil service was subjected to constant 'interference', and that the executive was too weak. Gloomy prognoses abounded. In 1884 Ruggiero Bonghi proclaimed of parliament, 'this is a man who will die'.[25] In the same year an eminent constitutional lawyer, Orlando, sighed for a *Deus ex machina*, a man of such unarguable superiority, of such untamable valour, as to grasp the helm of State with an iron hand'.[26] What could be done to improve the system?

One possible answer, much favoured by thoughtful statesmen out of office, was to decentralize the civil service. If there were no centralized government machine in Rome to secure favours from, the deputies would revert to honest debate and to zeal for the common good. Parliament would never work properly unless there were flourishing and independent local governments. This was a plausible view. Yet it was impractical. Nineteenth-century Italians were too Liberal to do without parliament; but they were also too Jacobin to abandon centralization, or to trust the Catholics and Radicals in the 'real country'.

Another possibility was to extend the suffrage even further. Deputies might have been less willing to press their constituents' case if more people had had the vote, or if they themselves had not sometimes owed their election to one or two local landowners or notables. Yet the suffrage could not be extended to illiterate Catholic peasants with any safety; nor could the Southern gentry be suddenly deprived of their local dominance, if their support for the new State were to continue. This remedy might prove worse than the disease, and destroy all the achievements of the *Risorgimento*.

The third remedy often proposed was sometimes associated with a wider suffrage. Deputies were too free to switch allegiances, and were too dependent on the local notables. Both traits could be avoided if only there were disciplined national parties, organized throughout the country, with Whips in parliament to keep dissident deputies in line. This was, again, a plausible argument, but quite unrealistic. There were no serious issues dividing the small political élite, and no real clash of interests or ideologies around which parties could coalesce. Strong Left-wing parties arose only later, as labour became more organized. Furthermore, the Vatican's rooted opposition to the whole idea of Italian unity ruled out religion as the basis of any effective conservative force. Mass parties emerged only in the 1890s, and transformed the political system only after universal male suffrage was brought in in 1912; and even then they proved no remedy against 'interference' in administration.

So, despite all the criticism, the Italian parliament continued on its unregenerate way. Perhaps the real problem was that Italians were not 'citizens' but subjects, and were treated as such by the State. Deputies could mitigate this in the short term, but could not alter it. Yet gradually things did change. Parliament may have been ineffective as a legislature, it may have failed to provide stable government, it may have been responsible for bending administrative decisions; but it provided a forum for discussion, and above all it helped to 'absorb' some of the disaffected groups into the political system. The Southern deputies in 1880 were, as Giustino Fortunato remarked, 'expressing the profound discontent caused by the Right's work of unification'.[27] Through parliament, these men were given favours and allowed to become ministers, or at least friends of ministers. That was an important part of Italian nation-building, however corrupt it may have appeared, or been. As Namier remarked, no one bribes where he can bully. Arguably it was better that governments should 'buy off' the Southern élites, rather than simply ignore them, or repress them. This was parliament's real function in the new united Italy: to make Piedmontese rule acceptable elsewhere.

I began this chapter by quoting Farini's view of parliament's task: to 'legitimize' government action. Yet in order to 'legitimize', parliament had to act 'illegitimately', and thus fall into disrepute. Northern Liberals always had to worry that the price of winning wider acceptance might be too high. The *people* (as opposed to the Southern bourgeois) might also demand concessions; and if the people accepted parliament it would only be through mass Socialist or Catholic parties, which would be a real threat to the whole system. So Liberal statesmen might easily be tempted, or panicked, into authoritarianism. Men might have to bully where they could not bribe.

3.8 CONCLUSION

This chapter has shown how influential the traditional organs of 'High Politics' were, and how small was Italy's ruling élite. Yet the State institutions never really dominated the rest of society. 'State' and 'society' interacted constantly, each trying to influence the other. The 'State' used its Prefects, police, courts, tax-gatherers and conscription-sergeants to intervene in 'society'; 'society' responded via elections, deputies' recommendations and so forth, to say nothing of riots and demonstrations. Political influence at the centre often rested on local power, especially after 1876. Furthermore, there was no centre from which the rest of Italy *could* be dominated. Rome herself – the very capital of the new State, the embodiment of civic dignity and ancient virtue – was in dispute, her people unreliable and *clericaleggiante*. Rome was no dynamic Jacobin centre of commerce or intellect, from which men could be ruled with a stern hand; she was a peaceful haven, where sheep grazed in the Villa Borghese gardens, and where agricultural labourers were hired by the day in piazza Montanara. Eternal Rome remained indolent, indifferent and sceptical: a city of bureaucrats, where men took the broad, long-term view, and gossiped among themselves. Gradually the *genius loci* imposed itself upon the austere Piedmontese incomers. They were trying to 'absorb' their rivals; but Rome absorbed them.

After 1876 the old élite of the Right became ever more pessimistic. They were out of office; and, as landowners, they suffered from the agricultural crisis of the 1880s. They were frightened of industry, Socialism, cities, emigration and the Vatican. They lamented the fate of the lay State, still beset by its many enemies and now in unworthy hands. As for the Left, we know remarkably little of these professional middlemen and politicians, or indeed of the 'Southern political class' in general. What, for example, were its relations with the big landowners? And why was it not more powerful than it was, in national politics? Why did the Left accept Depretis as Prime Minister for so many years – a Piedmontese, trusted by most Northerners? Why were the Southern notables apparently content with a subordinate role – local power, plus the occasional perk from Rome? My answer is necessarily speculative. The Southerners needed united Italy more than united Italy needed them; and they could never be quite sure of Northern support. The Left was nervous too, and with good reason.

REFERENCES

1. D. Farini, *Diario di Fine Secolo*, Rome 1961, p. 1302 (entry for 5 June 1898).
2. Rattazzi to Giolitti 10 Apr. 1899, in G. Giolitti, *Quarant' Anni di Politica Italiana*, i, Milan 1962, 360.
3. F. Minniti, 'Esercito e Politica da Porta Pia alla Triplice Alleanza', in *SC* iii (1972), 465–502 and iv (1973), 27–55, at iv, 37.
4. G. Rochat, 'L'Esercito italiano nell' estate 1914', in *NRS* xlv (1961), 295–348, at p. 297; A. Pedone, 'Il bilancio dello Stato', in G. Fuà (ed.), *Lo Sviluppo Economico in Italia*, ii, Milan 1969, pp. 203–40, at p. 217.
5. E. De Amicis, *La Vita Militare*, Milan 1880, p. 129.
6. D. Farini, *Diario . . .*, 1 Feb. 1891, pp. 4–5.
7. R. Livi, 'Saggio di geografia del militarismo in Italia', *La Riforma Sociale*, vii (1897), 550–52.

8. R. B. Fosdick, *European Police Systems*, London 1915, p. 93. The worst police in Europe, in his view, were in Glasgow.

9. O. Ranelletti, 'La polizia di sicurezza', in V. E. Orlando (ed.), *Primo Trattato Completo di Diritto Amministrativo Italiano*, iv, pt. 1, Milan 1904, p. 286.

10. Royal Decree 30 June 1889 n. 6144, art. 95.

11. *idem*, art. 85.

12. Jessie White Mario, 'Il Sistema Penitenziario e il domicilio coatto in Italia', *Nuova Antologia*, 1 July 1896, 16–35, at p. 27 (part Two of this article is particularly good, *Nuova Antologia*, 16 Sept., 313–35).

13. A. Bondi, *Memorie di un Questore*, Milan, n.d., p. 84.

14. G. Giolitti, *Memorie della Mia Vita*, Milan 1922, p. 26.

15. R. Fried, *The Italian Prefects*, Yale University Press 1963, p. 156; A. Caracciolo, *Stato e Società Civile*, Turin 1960, p. 125.

16. F. S. Nitti, *Nord e Sud*, Turin 1900, p. 184; *idem*, *La Riforma Sociale*, x (1900), 472–75.

17. L. Franchetti and S. Sonnino, *La Sicilia nel 1876*, ii, Florence 1877, p. 184.

18. *ibid.*, i, pp. 344–45.

19. *ibid.*, i, p. 61.

20. *ibid.*, ii, p. 462.

21. Prefect of Caltanissetta to Minister of the Interior, 5 Nov. 1884, quoted in G. Carocci, *Agostino Depretis e la Politica Interna Italiana dal 1876 al 1887*, Turin 1956, p. 476.

22. L. Pelloux, *Quelques Souvenirs de ma Vie*, Rome 1967, p. 125. For Giolitti's experiences, see his *Memorie . . .*, pp. 43–44.

23. Quoted in B. Caizzi, *Antologia della Questione Meridionale*, Milan 1950, pp. 364–5.

24. Sonnino's speech to Chamber of Deputies, 30 March 1881, in *Atti Parlamentari*, Cam. Dep., Sessione 1880–1, p. 4855.

25. R. Bonghi, 'Una questione grossa – la democrazia nel regime parlamentare', *Nuova Antologia*, 1 June 1884, 497.

26. R. De Mattei, *Il Problema della Democrazia dopo l'Unità*, Rome 1934, p. 48.

27. *L'Unità*, 6 Jan. 1912.

CHAPTER FOUR

The subversives

In the previous chapter I discussed the ruling élites of nineteenth-century Italy. I now turn again to those who were ruled – the vast majority. This chapter will concentrate on the political activities of those outside, or on the fringes of, the 'official' political system. Indeed, the workings of many of the institutions of Liberal Italy can only be understood in terms of the rulers' need to repress, control, or 'absorb', the 'parallel' institutions of the outsiders and protesters.

4.1 POPULAR DISAFFECTION AND ITS INSTITUTIONS

That was particularly true of brigandage, which had dominated much of the mainland South during the early 1860s. Brigands posed as the defenders of the peasants against the gentry and against the State. United Italy, to the peasants, meant conscription and higher taxes, especially on basic essentials like bread and salt. It also meant that such honourable traditions as blood-feuds and vendettas were liable to be regarded as crimes. Brigandage was also encouraged by the activities of the local gentry in taking over common and ecclesiastical land (see §2.1), and in operating the former Church charities to their own profit (see §3.6). So the brigand gangs of the 1860s lasted several years, despite thousands of troops, martial law, banishments and summary executions. In some regions the 'war against brigandage' was tantamount to civil war: the Government against the People. By 1871 the work of repression was done, and the 'military zones' in Southern Italy were restored to 'normal administration'. Even so, bands of brigands continued to operate for some years among the hills of Calabria, Abruzzi and Salerno province. The brigands were not particularly effective: they did little for the local peasantry, nor did they unite together to wage a co-ordinated guerrilla war. Yet their activities had major political consequences. They forced the Northern ruling class to abandon any idea of regional autonomy; they ensured that the army would be organized 'nationally'; and they contributed greatly to the North Italian belief that Southerners were a separate and inferior race. Above all, they were a shock to Liberal complacency. The educated, progressive, 'European' view of the world was clearly not shared by the bulk of the Southern population. A sense of unease, of fear, of dark subterranean hatreds waiting to be unleashed, was never absent from political debate thereafter.

When brigandage ended, crime remained – and there was at best a thin borderline between the two. Kidnapping, rustling and highway robbery were typical crimes of a 'para-brigand' type. According to Turiello, 'throughout entire regions you can only travel with an escort, and you cannot go into the countryside unarmed: sometimes, as in Sicily or the Romagna, this is true even in the towns.'[1] Arson, too, was a regular expression of popular protest in the *Agro Romano*, Sardinia, Liguria and the mainland South; and arson is the worst of all crimes against property – it destroys it, instead of merely redistributing it. The most widespread 'social crime' against property was the 'rural theft' of wood for fuel, of hay, vegetables, chestnuts, etc. These thefts were extremely common, especially among the landless labourers. Many peasants did not regard such thefts as crimes at all, unlike, say, petty thefts of cash. Why not? Presumably because they simply exercised the peasants' traditional entitlements, the '*usi civici*' of medieval times. If pigs had not been fed on stolen acorns, they would have starved; if people had not stolen wood, they would have had no fuel in winter. The thefts were invariably for the peasants' own family needs, not for trade or sale; that, again, was what the historic customs permitted. The 'rural theft' was vitally important to family budgets, and thousands of peasants were imprisoned each year for acts which they regarded as perfectly justified.

Needless to say, not *all* crimes, not even all crimes committed by Southern peasants, formed part of any social protest or had any political overtones. Italy in the nineteenth century was an armed and violent society, with around 3,000 known murders a year. Two-thirds of these murders were officially classified as 'Mediterranean' crimes: 35 per cent were caused by 'vendetta or hatred', 19 per cent by 'anger', 10 per cent by 'love', and 4 per cent by 'exalted sentiments of honour in particular family circumstances'.[2] They represented, not a protest against the modern world, but the old social code in action. Yet the old social code itself was now defined officially as criminal behaviour.

There were alternatives to crime and brigandage. Emigration, for example, meant young men taking to the emigrant ship instead of to the hills. Both emigration and brigandage (and conscription) may be regarded anthropologically, as a literal 'rite of passage' during which adolescents proved themselves as men. The increase in emigration correlated closely with a decline in criminal behaviour, another reason for regarding it as 'the great safety-valve'. Various popular religious movements of the late nineteenth century may also be regarded in this light. The Tuscan followers of Davide Lazzaretti were mown down by the *carabinieri* in 1878; they had been trying to establish the Reign of Justice upon Earth. Most peasants were too realistic to attempt this feat, but observers frequently noted millenarian aspirations among them, and other heretical cults flourished too, e.g. Pentecostalism.

It remains to consider two other classic institutions of social protest: the riot and the strike. Of these, the riot – the *moti in piazza* – was less frequent, but more spectacular. Riots were usually 'politically motivated': designed to let governments know what they could not get away with. In the rural areas, they were usually provoked by taxation. The grist-tax riots of 1868–69 are the classic example. They occurred in response to government proposals to introduce a tax on milling. This was tantamount to a tax on bread, the staple diet of the poor. Town halls were sacked, tax records burned, tax collectors' machinery broken up, and barricades raised. At least 257 people had been killed, and over 3,000 arrested, by the time troops and *carabinieri* restored law and order. The riots were spontaneous, and were accompanied by shouts of 'Long live the Pope' or 'We want the old laws'. They were also ineffective. When the troops had done their work the grist-tax remained (although it was abolished eventually, in 1883). Rural rioting continued sporadically throughout the nineteenth century, especially in Romagna and the South. In 1881 the mayor of Sanluri, in Sardinia, was killed, and the local tax collector forced to hand back some of the land tax; in 1879 the tax registers were burned at Calatabiano, in Sicily. And the Sicilian *Fasci* of 1893–94 (see §5.5) continued and amplified the tradition.

The city riot was rather different. It was most often caused by a temporary shortage of bread, or by price rises. The best-known examples were Palermo in 1866 and Milan in 1898. The city riot was more visible and more difficult to quell, and its repression had rather more serious economic implications once towns contained factories with expensive machinery. By 1900 it had become quite an effective political weapon, and could secure at least temporary concessions.

Strikes could also do this, with less risk – although troops were often used against strikers too. The first large-scale strikes in Italy occurred in the summer of 1872, in twenty-five different places. At Turin, a 'general strike' lasted nine days, and a similar movement in Milan lasted three days; at Verona the railwaymen stayed out for five days. It is tempting to think of the strike as a more 'modern' form of protest, especially as it occurred mainly in Northern Italy, among 'industrial' workers, and usually for 'economic' reasons; but its 'modernity' should not be exaggerated. Most early strikes were 'spontaneous', and had no trade union or other organization behind them. Moreover, the number of 'urban' strikes reached a peak in 1873, when there were 103, and thereafter declined as real wages rose; the 1873 figure was not reached again until 1889, when there were 126 strikes and 25,000 workers involved. Agricultural strikes reached a peak in 1885, when there were 62, with 8,857 strikers; this was the largest number of rural strikes before 1902. Most strikes were brief: 70 per cent of those in 1890, for example, lasted 24 hours or less. Over half the industrial strikes involved less than 100 workers; only 16 per cent of them were completely successful in their aims. Many of the successful ones aimed at a reduction in hours, or at resisting employers' proposals to increase them, rather than at increasing wages. Long hours were particularly resented because so many workers were women or children. Indeed, agitation on hours could normally expect public sympathy, even middle-class and Church support. To summarize, most strikes were local, Northern, short-lived, and unsuccessful. The industries most affected were textiles, mechanical engineering and the building trades.

Even so, there were signs that the strike could develop into a more serious affair. During the 1880s strikes became vitally important in the economy of the Po valley farms, especially in the Mantua and Rovigo areas. They were used by landless labourers at harvest time to push up hourly wage-rates, and to try to secure employment in winter. The peasants' strikes were naturally blamed on Socialist agitators, and it is true that there had been some Socialist penetration in the rural areas, at least in Mantua province, before the strikes. The main cause, however, was the impact of American grain on the Italian market after 1880. Food prices fell, and tenant farmers therefore reduced their labour costs, by paying lower wages and hiring fewer hands.

During the agitations, the peasants marched in processions, carrying not a Red Flag but a Tricolour, together with emblems of Virgil, Cincinnatus and Garibaldi. Altogether, there was not too much to worry about. Yet the government and many middle-class people became very nervous, and Carocci has written of a *grande peur* in 1884-85. The Prime Minister, Depretis, urged his Minister of Justice to dissolve the Mantuan mutual-aid society, so as to 'break up the ranks of the dangerous institution, and disarm the bold trouble-makers who are profiting from the peasants' ignorance'.[3] Soon 140 peasants were arrested, and 22 were later tried (only to be acquitted); the Italian Workers' Party (see §4.3) was dissolved. The Mantua agricultural strikes therefore collapsed in failure, but they were the first sign of an abiding characteristic of the Italian labour movement – the importance of the landless labourers in the Po valley, and of their organizations. Moreover, whether or not Socialist ideas had been important *before* the strikes, both the Italian Workers' Party and the Italian Revolutionary Socialist Party (see below, §4.3) held congresses in Mantua soon afterwards.

Strikes were not illegal, provided they had a 'reasonable cause'; but it was the judges who decided whether the cause was reasonable. This led to much confusion and uncertainty. In 1879 the Court of Cassation in Milan decided that the high cost of living was not a 'reasonable cause'; the fact that some workers had not gone on strike showed that the wages being paid must be adequate! Governments tended to see every minor agitation as politically motivated, and regularly issued orders to procurators urging them to make arrests. However, judges – and juries – proved surprisingly reluctant to convict on charges of striking without 'reasonable cause', and arrests were usually made only after violence or threats of violence – which were frequent enough in nineteenth-century Italy. In 1889 this *de facto* position was enshrined in a new law making strikes legal unless violence or intimidation occurred. This law, while obviously more 'liberal', in practice provided a rather more effective method of repressing strikes.

The riot and the strike were occasional episodes, not permanent institutions. Strikes could not become a major threat unless they were backed up by some relatively permanent workers' organization – a trade union, a trades council, a local 'league of resistance' – preferably one capable of organizing a strike fund. As in other countries, the printers led the way. The first national trade union, the *Associazione fra gli Operai Tipografici Italiani*, was founded at the end of 1872, and led a two-month strike in 1873–74. By 1878 it had 27 local branches, with over 2,000 members. The printers were probably the only 'trade union' in Italy before 1886, but the increasing frequency of strikes in the later 1880s, and the spread of Socialist political movements, led to many more permanent 'resistance' institutions in the early 1890s.

4.2 THE ANARCHISTS

Popular disaffection was, therefore, widespread in the 1870s and 1880s, but lacked expression in permanent organizations. Instead, anarchist ideas appealed to many Italians. Indeed, anarchist organizations (if the term is permitted) were regarded as the main threat by governments, which believed firmly that all unrest was 'fomented', 'instigated', by malevolent troublemakers. Actually this view had something to be said for it. The various anarchist groups, loosely associated in branches of the First International, incited the peasants to revolt, and played an important part in some strikes.

Anarchist ideas had come to Italy in the 1860s mainly through the Russian exile Bakunin, who stayed in Naples between 1865 and 1867. Naples was the first centre of Italian anarchism, and the first Italian 'section' of the International Working Men's Association was founded there in January 1869. It claimed 4,000 members in early 1870, mainly local artisans. Urban artisans – shoemakers, printers, carpenters and the like – in fact provided most of the anarchist membership throughout the nineteenth century, and many of them had every reason to oppose both capitalism and the new State. Bakunin himself placed much stress on the revolutionary potential of the Italian *peasants*, as shown by their constant rioting and brigandage; and his views seemed confirmed by the grist-tax riots of 1868–69. Bakunin was also delighted to find a revolutionary student class – 'ardent, energetic young people, without a career or outlets, who, despite their bourgeois origins, are not morally and intellectually exhausted as in the other countries'.[4] Numerous young intellectuals were attracted to anarchism, and provided the movement's leadership. Benoît Malon, who detested them, later calculated that half the leaders of the International in Italy had been to university.

Two important events helped anarchism, rather than rival doctrines, to spread. One was the Paris Commune in 1871, which seemed to show how revolution could occur spontaneously, and how the future society could run itself. The Commune was extremely popular among many urban artisans, and the anarchists' main rivals, the Republicans, lost much support when Mazzini failed to back it. The other development was the dispute within the International between the followers of Bakunin and those of Marx. Italians were forced to choose between them. Marx insisted on State ownership, central control, participation in elections, and an organized, disciplined political party. None of this had much appeal in Italy. Even Carlo Cafiero, who represented the 'Marxian' General Council of the International in Italy, broke with Marx and Engels in the summer of 1872, became one of the most prominent anarchists, and devoted his considerable fortune to the cause.

The Italians soon became the leaders of the 'anti-authoritarian' wing of the International. In August 1872 a national conference was held at Rimini. Even Garibaldi sent his 'moral adhesion'. The conference decided that the various Italian branches of the International should form an 'Italian Federation', with a permanent 'Commission of Correspondence' to transmit information, and a permanent 'Commission of Statistics' to do research on social and economic trends. It also decided to break with the 'Marxian' General Council in London, and to send representatives instead to the 'Bakuninist' International Congress held at St Imier the following month. The Rimini conference, in fact, formally founded an organized anarchist movement in Italy. Anarchism spread rapidly, partly thanks to the organizing abilities of Andrea Costa in the Romagna; and the anarchists were much encouraged by the Spanish Revolution of 1873. By the end of 1873 they were claiming 26,000 members, mainly in Central Italy. Anarchism in Italy – unlike Spain – was not a peasants' creed, and the South was not a stronghold, except in and around Naples and in parts of Sicily.

The first anarchist attempt to overthrow the established order occurred in 1874, at a time of food riots and some agricultural labourers' strikes. In August the anarchist Committee for Social Revolution called for an armed rising, and 150 anarchists marched from their base at Imola to seize Bologna. They reached Castel S. Pietro before the police stopped them; 50 were arrested, the rest fled. In Apulia, Errico Malatesta tried to arouse the peasantry at the same time, but could only persuade five people to turn out to help him. This was an inauspicious beginning. The anarchist risings failed, for the same reasons that brigandage or rioting failed – the strength of the police and army, the absence of weapons, the failure to co-ordinate local efforts.

After the Bologna rising most prominent anarchists spent the next two years in exile, or in prison. On their release, the International revived. In April 1877 Cafiero and Malatesta tried again, this time among the Southern peasantry. They chose the Matese area in Benevento province, sixty-five kilometres inland from Naples. Brigandage had been common there, and police repression had been fierce and recent. The peasants themselves were supposed to make the revolution; the anarchists' job was to spark them off, by preaching and performing revolutionary deeds. Their plans misfired. The police intercepted them, either by accident or design. The 'band' had to start its insurrection a month earlier than planned, in April instead of May, when many of the local shepherds had not returned from winter-grazing on the Apulian table-lands. That meant that local guides were lacking, that many of the insurrectionaries had not yet arrived, that they had no one with them who could understand or speak the peasants' dialect, and that the hills were still covered in snow. Despite these handicaps, twenty-six of them went to the isolated village of Letino, proclaimed the social republic, handed out a few old guns to the astonished peasants, and burned the land tax records. This performance was repeated at another village, until the troops arrived and captured the frostbitten insurgents. It is interesting to note that the local priests were fairly enthusiastic about these strange visitors, and one of them explained to the peasants that Socialism and the Gospel were really the same creed. The most outraged bourgeois in Letino is said to have been the local innkeeper, who had to feed the conspirators in return for an IOU for twenty-eight lire, payable after the revolution.

Was this episode as farcical as most people at the time, and most historians since, have assumed? Perhaps so; but were the anarchists' activities so very different from those of Garibaldi in 1860, or of Castro in Cuba in 1957–58? At any rate, the Matese affair discredited attempts at insurrection. Most of the anarchist leaders were again arrested or, like Andrea Costa, driven into exile – although the insurrectionaries themselves were acquitted in August 1878. Henceforth 'propaganda by the deed' tended to mean terrorism or assassination. In November 1878 an anarchist cook, Giovanni Passanante, tried to stab King Humbert at Naples. The attempt failed, partly because the Prime Minister, Cairoli, threw himself in the way. The next day a bomb was thrown at a patriotic procession in Florence, killing two people. Public outrage at these terrorist attacks had important results, including the fall of the Cairoli–Zanardelli government in December 1878 for being soft on anarchism. There was also much tougher action by the police.

The anti-anarchist drive of 1878–79 did not end Italian anarchism, but it drove many anarchists abroad (especially to France), disrupted the International's organization, and made 'legal' or 'Socialist' strategies more attractive to many workers. Even so, the anarchists were still numerous in Central Italy in the mid-1880s, and they had an important role in various agitations, especially by the landless labourers of the Polesine. They remained influential well into the twentieth century, agitating against legal reforms and against the 'parliamentary road' to Socialism. The pamphlets of Malatesta and of another brilliant writer, Francesco Saverio Merlino, circulated widely in Italy; *emigré* circles and *emigré* newspapers were often dominated by anarchist ideas. And it was Italian anarchists who carried out many of the political assassinations of the late nineteenth century – of the President of France in 1894, of the Prime Minister of Spain in 1897, of the Empress of Austria in 1898, and of King Humbert himself in 1900.

4.3 SOCIALISM AND LABOURISM

The anarchist decline after 1878 provided an opportunity for rival doctrines and rival organizations to spread. 'Legalitarian', 'evolutionist' Socialism had never died out, even though its supporters had been outnumbered by the anarchists during the quarrels between Marx and Bakunin. In Milan, Enrico

Bignami's *La Plebe* was influential, and in October 1876 another 'evolutionist', Osvaldo Gnocchi-Viani, founded the Upper Italian Federation of the International, to act as a rival to the anarchists and perhaps as an embryo of a Social Democrat Party on the German model. However, the Federation was dissolved in the police crackdown of 1877–78. It is mainly of interest as the forerunner of the later labour movement in Lombardy, and for its early attempts to organize the landless labourers in Mantua province.

The great problem for the early 'legalitarians' was that they were too respectable, too 'gradualist', to have much appeal when popular disaffection was high, and yet they were far too 'Socialist', too 'Marxist', in quieter times. After all, Italy had a number of 'respectable' workers' institutions already. Co-operatives, for example, existed for a variety of purposes, and many were founded in the 1880s to carry out public works schemes during winter unemployment. Dairy co-operatives were invented in Italy, and flourished in the mountainous areas of the Veneto, normally run by Catholic organizations. Small credit banks were especially important. The economist Luigi Luzzatti began founding these in the 1860s, and there were 171 of them by 1881. Rural credit banks also appeared during the 1880s, and they helped peasants with seed purchases, improvement works and crop insurance. And, of course, there were a host of normal consumer co-operatives on Rochdale lines. These institutions often owed much to upper-class organizers and patrons: the king himself lent 10,000 lire to the Ravenna labourers' co-operative. They are evidence for the non-revolutionary, sometimes even conservative, outlook of the Italian lower classes.

Above all, there were the mutual-aid societies, which provided a rudimentary social insurance – old-age pensions, sick pay, funeral costs – for urban artisans. They were essentially charitable institutions, and were particularly important at a time when traditional (ecclesiastical) charities had been disrupted, and when the State had not yet introduced its own social security. In 1873 official figures gave 1,447 societies; by 1885 there were 4,896, with 804,000 members. However, they were not workers' organizations in any strict sense. Their members included the master-craftsmen as well as the employees, and nearly 10 per cent of their members were reckoned to be 'honorary', i.e. non-workers – professional people, clergy, charitable gentlewomen and the like, who often (as in other countries) dominated and ran the whole society. Moreover, most mutual-aid societies were committed to particular political views – conservative, clerical or Republican – and there was little chance of their agreeing on any concerted action.

One of the major aims, therefore, of early Italian Socialist organizers was to create their own 'autonomous' mutual-aid societies, free from 'bourgeois hegemony', and preferably limited to a single trade. Single-trade societies had the potential to develop into some kind of local trade union. Moreover, 'legalitarian' organizers tended to extend the work of existing mutual-aid societies whenever possible, from charity to agitation. In education, for example, free lectures and distribution of books could easily lead to calls for better schools and free textbooks; and it was a short step from organizing unemployment relief to protesting against arbitrary dismissals. These efforts at transforming the nature of mutual-aid societies, and especially at founding new ones, had most success in Lombardy. The Lombard legalitarians – the 'Sons of Labour' – were committed to economic struggles, to organizing strikes and 'resistance'; they regarded political activity as a bourgeois delusion. Even so, they campaigned in Milan at the 1882 general election, and in 1885 the various Lombard institutions became branches of a new 'party', the Italian Workers' Party (*Partito Operaio Italiano, POI*). The party was open only to 'manual workers of both sexes, either in the fields or in the workshops, who are wage-earners and directly dependent on their bosses, entrepreneurs or capitalists'.[5] In fact, many of the party's urban members seem to have been artisans rather than wage-earners.

The POI was the first real 'class' organization of respectable North Italian artisans and peasants, protesting against capitalism as such (it regarded factory work, for example, as inherently degrading), and fighting strongly against the traditional dominance of working-class organizations by middle-class Radicals and political meddlers. It insisted on the independence of the working class, on the need for trade unions and on the right to strike. Yet it accepted most of the Radical platform on political issues – universal suffrage, tax reforms, freedom of the press, etc. – and indeed it rejected some 'Socialist' demands. The Workers' Party was opposed, for example, to State monopolies, or to any State mediation in disputes between capitalists and workers. It is also noteworthy how successful the party was among the peasantry. The Milanese workers helped to found 'leagues of resistance' and preached emancipation by the peasants themselves; they found a ready response in the Po valley. In 1886 a frightened government dissolved the POI, but it revived between 1887 and 1890, and became one of the main components of the Italian Socialist Party in the 1890s (see §5.7). Indeed, the Lombard labour movement retained its 'Workers' Party mentality' (*operaismo*) for many years. Some of the subsequent strength both of syndicalism and reformism in Milan, and of peasant unions in the Po valley, is attributable to the early propaganda efforts of men like Gnocchi-Viani.

Yet perhaps the main reason why, when organized agitation revived, it revived as 'Socialist' rather than as 'anarchist' lies not in the activities of the Lombard Workers' Party, but in the spectacular conversion to Socialism of the anarchist leader in the Romagna, Andrea Costa. Costa had fled abroad after 1877, and had been imprisoned in France. On his release, he wrote a famous letter 'To My Friends in Romagna'. Costa did not renounce his revolutionary views, but he admitted that insurrections like that of the Matese were imprudent. For the next two years Costa continued his agitation in the Romagna, winning over more support from the anarchists.

In August 1881, at Rimini – nine years after the famous anarchist congress there – Costa founded the Revolutionary Socialist Party of Romagna (PSRR). Its programme is worth looking at in some detail, because very similar proposals recurred later in the history of the Italian Left. It looked forward to a revolution, in which the working class (of town and country) would seize political power. But that would not occur immediately – 'the revolution generally achieves only what has already entered the consciousness of the majority, and if it is not to be exploited by the present ruling classes it must be preceded by successful spreading of social-revolutionary ideas'.[6] Hence the need for a political party, to spread the doctrines and to 'prepare' and lead the insurrection; the most effective thing this party could do in the short run would be to agitate peacefully for social, political, economic and educational reforms. Reforms were welcome, because they would increase 'Socialist consciousness'. Thus peaceful agitation was a means to revolutionary insurrection. After the revolution, there would be a temporary dictatorship of the working classes; but eventually a state of anarchy would be attained, with collective ownership first of the means of production, and later of the products of collective labour. These ideas were obviously aimed at a largely anarchist audience, but they were also clearly influenced by Marxist thinking, some ten years before the 'Communist Manifesto' was first published in Italian (by two Milanese anarchists, as a historical curiosity!).

In practice the PSRR – which in 1884 became the PSRI, the *Italian Revolutionary Socialist Party* – tended to emphasize the first steps along the road to revolution. It advocated universal suffrage, economic reforms, trade union rights, abolition of the standing army, i.e. many of the ordinary demands of Radicals and democrats. Soon Costa began to urge that Socialist candidates should stand for parliament, and in 1882 he himself became a deputy for Ravenna. Yet the word 'Revolutionary' in the PSRR's title was not entirely propaganda, and indeed the party's programme was criticized by the POI as being far too 'revolutionary'. In any case, there was no chance of the party's minimal, reformist aims being implemented by parliament at that time. Costa continued to support extra-parliamentary agitations and strikes, as well as using parliament as a platform for his Socialist convictions.

4.4 THE REPUBLICANS, RADICALS AND GARIBALDINI

This chapter has so far been mainly concerned with the 'opponents of Mazzini'. The anarchists, the POI and the Socialists all aimed to provide alternatives to the kind of mutual-aid and co-operative societies advocated and set up by the great Republican. Mazzini's failure to support either the grist-tax riots in 1869 or the Paris Commune in 1871 strengthened his rivals. Yet Republicanism did not die out, even though Mazzini himself died in 1872. The Republicans had a martyr, Pietro Barsanti, who had been executed in 1870 – despite a petition signed by 40,000 people – for his part in a raid on Pavia barracks. Throughout the 1870s policemen worried about what the Republican 'Barsanti Circles' might be up to, and certainly propaganda for a 'Constituent Assembly' was maintained. Above all, the Republicans controlled many of the workers' mutual-aid societies. In November 1871, 150 societies met in Rome and reconfirmed the 'Pact of Brotherhood' signed in 1864 – a characteristic Mazzinian programme, including agricultural credit, co-operatives, free lay education for all, extension of the suffrage, and the emancipation of women; it also called for some State social reforms, including pensions and accident insurance. But the Rome Congress envisaged the workers' societies essentially as organs of *self*-emancipation. Little was to be expected from the State or from parliament as long as the monarchy survived. At the next congress, in 1874, over 200 societies were represented, and they discussed tax reforms, unemployment assistance and the founding of consumer co-operatives – which already existed in areas of Republican strength like Romagna, the Marches, Tuscany and Liguria.

Most Republican activity was concentrated on these workers' societies, and five more national congresses were held up to 1889. The aim was to 'educate' the working man to be sober, industrious, and monogamous. Members of the societies were forbidden to carry guns, to get drunk, or to gamble – especially on the 'royal lottery'. The Mazzinians never accepted collectivist ideas, nor the class struggle, nor even the strike; and perhaps their hope of representing working-class interests while rejecting these developments was bound to fail. Yet, even so, they retained much influence among the independent artisans, and Molinelli has remarked: 'even today, anybody who spends some time in provincial Republican circles, even working-class ones, will be astonished at the unpopularity of terms like "class", "class struggle", "nationalization" etc'.[7] The Republican leaders were often honest, austere professional men – doctors and the like – who had suffered exile for their beliefs and were much respected locally.

The rivalry between anarchists and Republicans did not prevent the police from suspecting an alliance, or from arresting most of the Republican leaders in August 1874 on suspicion of plotting to join the abortive rising organized by the anarchists at Bologna (see §4.2). One of the main reasons for government concern was that the Republicans were often involved in 'irredentist' campaigns. 'Irredentism' meant, at the least, the 'national liberation' of Italians living in the Habsburg lands to the North or North-East of the Italian frontiers (Trent and Trieste); irredentists also sometimes laid claim to the Swiss canton of Ticino, to Nice and Savoy, and to Corsica. In 1877 a leading Republican, Matteo Imbriani, founded *L'Italia Irredenta*, an association to further these aims, and it soon had over 500 branches. In 1878 the irredentists tried to provoke war over Trent, and the Italian monarchy was bitterly criticized in 1882 when Italy allied with Germany and Austria–Hungary in the Triple Alliance. Irredentist passions grew even stronger in December 1882, when the Austrians hanged Guglielmo Oberdank, a Trieste student, for planning to assassinate the Emperor Francis Joseph. However, nationalist Republicanism had a fatal weakness. The House of Savoy was the main guarantee of the maintenance of national unity, and nearly everyone knew it.

By the 1880s Republicanism was in crisis. The old 'intransigents' clung to their anti-monarchism, to anti-parliamentarism and to their nostalgia for Mazzinian insurrections, but they seemed increasingly old-fashioned and became, indeed, increasingly respectable. The Republican leader, Aurelio

Saffi, was Professor of Public Law at Bologna University; as 'scholar, publicist and statesman' he was given an Honorary LL. D. at the tercentenary celebrations of Edinburgh University in 1884, and spoke feelingly of 'the harmony, the union, the intimate union, between religion, patriotism and science' that was so evident in Edinburgh.[8] Clearly governments did not have to worry much about *him*. A few students also played briefly at Mazzinianism, before taking government posts on graduation. But the movement was clearly in decline, and backsliding soon began. Leading Republicans began to come to terms with the monarchy, stood for parliament, took the oath of loyalty required of deputies, and even sometimes supported the 'Left' governments after 1876. Cairoli's government in 1878 enticed many prominent Republicans, including Carducci, away from the lost cause. These *transigenti* soon became known as Radicals, rather than as Republicans; in parliament they formed the *Estrema* (Extreme Left), urging on the 'Left' governments towards more extensive social reforms.

In accepting the monarchy, the Radicals were only following in the footsteps of the greatest democrat of all, Garibaldi; and Garibaldi himself played an important part in the affairs of the Radicals and democrats during the 1870s. In 1872 he issued an appeal to all Italian democrats to defer the 'political question' (i.e. the Republic). He also organized a Congress of Unity, to be held at the Colosseum, with a programme of universal suffrage, free compulsory lay education, tax reforms, land reclamation, female emancipation, a people's militia, and abolition of the clerical privileges enshrined in the Law of Guarantees. Although the government prohibited this congress, a truncated assembly was held in the Teatro Argentina, and the programme was approved. It was indeed a radical programme. But it was not too remote from political realities – after all, by 1877 there was a law for free compulsory lay education, and an extension of the suffrage was promised by the Left. Hence Garibaldi could accept the regime, after 1876, and become a deputy. It was all part of the lengthy process of inserting the 'democratic forces' into the machinery of State – the Radicals' historic role.

By April 1879 Garibaldi had become disillusioned with the 'Left' governments, mainly because of their failure to reform the suffrage or to abolish the grist-tax. In that month he founded a League of Democracy – the first real attempt to found a single party of the Extreme Left, including the Republicans. The League had the usual Radical programme, including administrative devolution and abolition of the parliamentary oath, but it also advocated support for irredentism and for the 'nation in arms'. Some Republicans, including Saffi and Campanella, joined the League initially, but were soon forced to resign by their supporters. Thus the League did not succeed in reconciling the 'pure' Republicans with the more conciliatory Radicals.

Still, the distinctions between Radicals, Republicans, and other 'democrats', were always vague. The main areas of Radical strength were in Lombardy and Liguria, with other pockets in Emilia-Romagna and at Rome. There were some links with Freemasonry, and many more with journalism. Their newspaper *Il Secolo* had the highest circulation in the country. In the South, which conspicuously lacked a modern-minded middle class, Radicalism was always weak, although some of the leading Radical individuals were Southerners – Giovanni Bovio, Mario Rapisardi, Matteo Imbriani. Radicalism in Italy (unlike France) remained an urban phenomenon. Indeed, many Radicals were worried about universal suffrage, as it would mean superstitious peasants getting the vote; whatever they might have said in public, in practice the 1882 compromise solution suited them very well. In short, the Radicals were enlightened bourgeois. Like most liberal intellectuals, they somehow regarded themselves as representing the interests of artisans and workers. In Milan, Antonio Maffi ran the 'Working Men's Consulate', and several of the later Socialist leaders, including Leonida Bissolati and Filippo Turati, started their careers as Radicals.

Throughout the 1880s the Radicals campaigned on such diverse issues as foreign policy (against the hated Triple Alliance), colonial policy (against any 'African adventures'), anticlericalism, civil rights and social legislation. After 1887 these issues became even more acutely debated, and the Radicals were poised to become a major force in the country and in parliament. Yet they also faced a real threat. The 1882 reform of the suffrage might have enabled them to represent, for decades to come, the newly enfranchised artisans and workers of Northern Italy. It did not do so, because of the rise of the Workers' Party, which firmly resisted 'bourgeois paternalism' and put forward its own candidates. The 1886 general election saw bitter quarrels between Radicals and 'Workers' in Milan. The Radical leader Cavallotti, angered by what he regarded as betrayal by the POI, even accused the Workers' Party of acting as the instrument of the government. This row between the POl and the Radicals lost the Radicals a good deal of working-class sympathy. The workers, in the largest industrial city of Northern Italy, had evaded the Radicals' grasp – and the surrounding peasantry, too, was far more influenced by the POI than by the Radicals.

4.5 THE CHURCH AND HER INFLUENCE

The most serious 'subversive' organization in the new united Italy was the Church. Informed public opinion and successive governments – especially those of the Left, after 1876 – were hostile to the Church, and her role in society was a constant theme of angry political debate. A lay education system was set up, deliberately designed to combat clerical influence on the young. Civil marriage was instituted, and couples who married in church were forced to go through a second marriage ceremony in front of the mayor, in order to have their marriages legally recognized. 'Legal separation', even of spouses married in church, could be granted by the civil courts, and the judges could issue decrees concerning maintenance and custody of children. Various attempts were made in parliament – even by Ministers of Justice, like Villa in 1881 – to introduce a divorce law, giving separated couples the right to remarry. Education and matrimony were just illustrations of a more general theme. The State claimed to represent a 'lay morality', of liberalism, rationality and progress, that was novel in a country where morality had always derived from the Church's teachings.

The Church naturally resisted the new doctrines, both explicitly – as in Pius IX's 'Syllabus of Errors' in 1864, especially Error no. 80 – and by making every effort to maintain her presence in civil society. This effort was made easier by the fact that some Right-wing politicians supported her – or rather, sought her support. If religion were the foundation of morality, they reasoned, how could a stable State survive without it? Religion might not be true but it was necessary, to educate people to their duty; and doubly so in a country where the mass of people were Catholic, illiterate, and excluded from political life. Moreover, there were always the susceptibilities of foreign Catholic States to be considered. And so caution prevailed, and the worst excesses of anticlericalism were avoided. There was no actual persecution of priests, legislation on sensitive subjects like divorce was unsuccessful, and the catechism was taught in State primary schools. Despite the occasional rhetoric of both sides, there were never two 'irreconcilable Italys' – just an uneasy cohabitation, punctuated by many petty quarrels.

If we examine the State's legislation on strictly ecclesiastical issues, we find the same picture. On the one hand, pilgrimages were prohibited, and military service was introduced for priests. The ecclesiastical estates were expropriated, and their lands sold off at auctions. Male religious orders with a 'communal life' were disbanded, their goods confiscated, and their members 'dispersed' – i.e. forbidden to live communally. These provisions were extended to Rome in 1873, which meant that the headquarters of the various religious orders were closed, and that the goods of the Congregation for the Propaganda of the Faith – which financed foreign missions – were seized. The mendicant and contemplative orders were particularly badly affected by these measures. Over 4,000 religious houses were suppressed in all. To this day official buildings in Italy – schools, hospitals, prisons – are often housed in former monasteries or convents.

On the other hand, most charitable foundations (teaching, hospitals, etc.) were not affected, nor were institutions concerned with the 'cure of souls'. Moreover, the 'right of free association' remained as valid for monks as for other citizens. This all left plenty of legal loopholes. The Jesuits, for example, characteristically managed to save their priceless library in Rome by claiming it was the private collection of their General, Beckx. A monastery might become a national monument, and the monks would be left in it as 'custodians' – the Benedictines did this at Monte Cassino; it might become a cathedral, and the monks would then turn into officials of the chapter – as at St Paul's Without-the-Walls; it might become registered as a charitable organization; it might become the private house of an individual monk, who left it in his will to another – the Rosminians and Salesians survived by using this device; or, most commonly of all, it might become a private landholding company. The Trappists, for example, took over 485 hectares of the *Agro*

Romano in 1879, and cultivated them silently and successfully for over fifty years with the help of convict labour (they are now part of the EUR district of Rome). As time went on, there was a gradual return to the old monastic houses; available figures for membership of religious orders show a marked rise after 1880. The female orders were unaffected by the new laws, except that when any community's numbers declined to six, the remaining members were to be rehoused in larger communities. That implied – but did not state explicitly – that they should not recruit new members, but the implication was widely evaded: novices were presented as servants. In any case, teaching and charitable orders *were* allowed to recruit, much to the annoyance of anticlericals and officials. Nursing remained in the hands of nuns, as did nursery teaching. By 1900 there were over 40,000 nuns in the country, 12,000 more than in 1880.

The main result of all this legislation was that the more old-fashioned kind of religious life – the contemplative closed community, the mendicant order – was discouraged or suppressed. Instead, energies were diverted into activity within Italian society. The teaching orders, for example, had to secure professional qualifications, i.e. pass State examinations; so Church schools acquired for the first time a qualified body of teachers. The revival of Italian Catholicism in the late nineteenth and early twentieth centuries owed much to the anticlerical laws of the 1860s and 1870s.

This picture of fractious cohabitation between Church and State is also valid for the vexed issue of ecclesiastical appointments and benefices. Liberal politicians agreed that in principle the Church, as an autonomous 'separate' institution, should be free to order her affairs as she wished. In practice, things were not so easy. Could the State tolerate the appointment of a turbulent priest or intransigent bishop, who might denounce government policy from the pulpit and even stir up peasant revolt? And could the Pope really be allowed unfettered dominance over the clergy, who after all were Italian citizens? Moreover, parish priests and bishops normally enjoyed considerable 'temporal benefices' – at the least a place of residence, often extensive lands. Should the State have no control over how this property was used? On these issues politicians were greatly, even bitterly, divided. On the whole, the moderate Right (Lanza, Minghetti, Visconti Venosta) was 'separatist', but the Left was reluctant to give up traditional royal prerogatives and State control.

The legislation on this topic passed in 1871 was therefore a compromise. The Law of Guarantees laid down that, although the Church was normally free to make her own appointments, the income (benefices and ecclesiastical goods) associated with episcopal sees or parishes could not be enjoyed without a royal decree of *exequatur* or *placet*. This was more important than it sounds, for it was difficult for a bishop to carry out his duties without access to the bishop's palace. Refusing the royal *exequatur* for episcopal benefices meant a *de facto* veto on episcopal appointments; and, of course, it was an easy way of increasing the State's revenues. Moreover, the Law of Guarantees also laid down that in those regions (e.g. Sicily) where some bishops had traditionally been royal nominees, the king would maintain his rights –

although in practice the State made concessions on this point. There were other concessions too. Bishops no longer had to take an oath of allegiance to the Crown. Above all, bishops or priests could not be controlled once they had been appointed. Could the *exequatur* be revoked? For some years nobody was quite sure, but in 1885 the Council of State said it could not. These disputes between Church and State, and among politicians, generated a good deal of warmth. The Law of Guarantees remained one of the most controversial pieces of legislation in Italy. Even so, the new Italian State was probably less interventionist, less 'jurisdictionalist', than the various previous States in Italy had been, or than other Catholic Powers still were.

The key issue affecting Church–State relations was, of course, the 'Roman question'. Pius IX and his successors took the view that the former Papal States had been annexed by brute force, and that some territorial sovereignty – some 'temporal power' – was necessary in order to guarantee the Pope's independence. The Pope must be subject to no man. But no Italian government was willing to abandon Rome to the Papacy. On this issue, too, the Law of Guarantees represented an attempt at compromise. It recognized a kind of Papal sovereignty. The Pope was accorded all the rights of a sovereign, including even diplomatic representatives being accredited to him; he was proclaimed immune from arrest or trial; his person was declared sacred and inviolable, on the same footing as the king's; and separate postal and telegraph offices were guaranteed. The Pope retained the Vatican and Lateran palaces in Rome, and his villa at Castelgandolfo. Yet these enclaves, immune from taxation and interference as they were, were part of the Italian State. The Pope's 'sovereignty' was personal, not territorial. Finally, the Pope was offered compensation for the loss of his territories, in the form of an annual payment of 3,225,000 lire.

That was quite unacceptable to Pius IX, who had no intention of becoming 'chaplain to the House of Savoy'. In any case, what was guaranteed by the Law of Guarantees? It was simply an Italian law like any other, liable to repeal or amendment at any time; it did not even have the status of an international treaty. The Pope could not be beholden for all time to the goodwill of Italian parliaments. He therefore rejected the law and the compensation. He proclaimed himself a 'prisoner in the Vatican', and the Italian government a usurper. So on this issue the attempt at compromise failed. Or did it? The argument that 'temporal power' was essential for Papal independence became less and less convincing as time went on, especially as the modern State began to take over far wider responsibilities than previously. As Binchy has remarked, the Papacy was lucky to lose its lands, for its renowned incompetence as a secular government would otherwise have discredited its spiritual claims. Instead, the influence and reputation of the Papacy greatly increased after 1870, and 'it was surely no mere coincidence that the masterly Encyclicals on the relations between the Church and the modern State should have come from the pen of the first Pope for centuries who had no State to govern'.[9]

At all events, the Roman question embittered Church–State relations for many years after 1870. In March 1871 the Penitentiary Tribunal was asked whether it was 'expedient' for Catholics to take part in parliamentary elections. The reply became famous: *non expedit*. This formula was repeated in 1874, with specific reference to the general election of that year. It was not, perhaps, a total prohibition, but in April 1881 Leo XIII removed all doubts. *Non expedit*, he declared, meant a 'true and proper prohibition', and in 1886 a decree of the Holy Office laid down again that *non expedit prohibitionem importat*. Catholics were thus formally forbidden either to vote or to stand as candidates at parliamentary elections – although both were allowed, even encouraged, at local and provincial elections. What effect this may have had on voting is difficult to estimate, but the *non expedit* certainly prevented the rise of any 'national conservative' party with mass Catholic support, such as was dreamed of by some Roman aristocrats and conservative gentry. And abstentionism had some advantages. It was a proud slogan for all Catholics outraged by the Liberal State's treatment of the Papacy; it focused attention on the Roman question, and maintained it as a live political issue. It became, too, a refusal of political clientelism and corruption, of parliamentary jobbery and intrigue. Above all, it had the advantage that the Church could claim to represent the 'real country', the *paese reale*, without ever having to submit this claim to be tested in the field.

I have written of 'the Church', yet in 1871 there was no Italian Church. There were several regional Churches, with different organizations, different traditions of piety and observance, and different attitudes to the laity and to the civil authorities. In Tuscany (except Lucca province) there was a tradition of State control. 'Liberal Catholicism' survived longer there than elsewhere, 'intransigent' Catholic organizations were weak, Catholics were important in local government, and pressure for 'reconciliation' with the State was always strong. In the South there had never been a strong parish structure. Bishops had little authority over priests, and in their tiny dioceses were little more than parish priests themselves. Most clerics were monks or friars. The 'cure of souls' had often been entrusted to 'sanctuary-clergy' attached to some local monastery or chapter. They were local men, usually members of a religious order; they lived in the family home, supported other members of their family and were invariably immersed in family rivalries and parish-pump politics. When the new Italian State dissolved ecclesiastical corporations and confiscated their property, it destroyed the Church's whole foundations. The Southern Church thereafter was absent from political or even much social life, for a generation or more. She simply did not have enough resources at local level, and in any case the clergy were often suspected of sympathy with the Bourbons. The Church languished, cut off from her revenues, cut off from the sources of patronage, and harassed by the men who had taken over her lands and who now controlled local government. As for her influence, Bakunin's remarks are famous: 'Your peasants are superstitious, but not at all religious. They love the Church because she is very dramatic and interrupts, with her theatrical and musical ceremonies, the monotony of country life. The Church is for them a ray of light in a life of hardship, backbreaking toil, grief and poverty.'[10] These remarks were confirmed by many other clerical and lay observers in the nineteenth century, and some of them went further than Bakunin. The German Protestant scholar Thomas Trede thought that in the South Catholicism had long since been defeated by Graeco-Roman paganism, which he found still flourishing in many local cults – pilgrimages, miraculous images, exorcism, the *jettatura* (evil eye) and so forth.

In Northern Italy there was apparently more religious observance among the peasant landowners of the hill and Alpine zones than on the cities of the plain. In the Veneto, the parish structure was strong, and the clergy retained their traditional social prestige and political power. The loss of Church lands merely prevented the Church from running as many charitable organizations as before, and thus made life for the peasants even more insecure. The priests became the natural spokesmen for the peasants' discontent against the new order. There were no anarchists or Socialists in the Veneto, no labour leagues or strikes, not even any riots; instead, a resentful 'clerico-populism' settled over the static and traditional countryside. The peasants sought their salvation elsewhere on earth, and in Heaven. Even so, the clergy were not satisfied. A recent study of manuals of devotion used in this period reports a constant uphill struggle to transform 'popular', 'social' observance into something more akin to 'true piety'; religious sentiment often seemed indistinguishable from superstition.[11]

Whether or not the Church represented the 'real country', she was determined to do so in future. Just as 'legal Italy' had become united under the House of Savoy, so did the Church endeavour to become a united organization under the Papacy. The year 1870 may have seen the loss of the temporal power, but it also saw the proclamation of the doctrine of Papal Infallibility; and the First Vatican Council (December 1869 to July 1870) was the first occasion for centuries when bishops from different regions of Italy had met together to discuss common problems. After 1870, there was a new generation of bishops: 135 out of the 298 dioceses in Italy were filled between May 1871 and May 1875. The new men were predominantly 'intransigent' Papalists. Many of them came from prosperous families – after all, they had to live for some time without temporalities – or from the religious orders; they were pious, zealous and determined. Their task was to reform the seminaries, to train and supervise a new generation of priests, and to purge the existing clergy. By the 1890s the Church was a far more centralized and far more effective organization throughout most of the country.

Nor were the laity forgotten. Catholic laymen had long been organized, for pious or charitable purposes, in local 'confraternities' – Congregations of Mary, 'third orders', Christian Mothers, etc. Italian Unification led to changes. The laity were to be the front-line troops in the Catholic *reconquista* of civil society. National laymen's organizations were founded, on an 'intransigent' Papalist basis, with far more central control. They, like earlier bodies, had charitable or religious aims – looking after roadside Madonnas, buying out priests from military service – but their real work was in education. They were to teach the young, run journals and libraries, provide leisure facilities, influence the local schools and so forth. The most influential lay organization, the *Opera dei Congressi e dei Comitati Cattolici*, was founded in 1874. It had a structure of lay committees based on the parish or diocese, quasi-annual congresses, and a national standing committee whose president was appointed by the Pope. It was much stronger in Northern Italy, especially in Veneto and Lombardy, than elsewhere: in 1883–84 there were 993 parish committees in the North, 263 in Central Italy, and only 57 in the South, including Sicily and Sardinia. As time went on, the *Opera dei Congressi's* activity tended to move away from education towards more directly political and economic ends – co-operatives, rural credit banks, organizing petitions against divorce bills; this was particularly marked in the 1890s. But it was always consistent in one thing – it was 'intransigent' on the Roman question. It always defended the Papacy, and it always sought to organize the laity according to the Syllabus of Errors. Its leaders' attitudes were admirably illustrated by *L'Unità Cattolica's* famous headline on the death of King Victor Emmanuel II: 'The King is Dead; the Pope is well'.

How important was the *Opera dei Congressi*? It was certainly not very numerous in the 1870s and 1880s – even in Northern Italy, only about one parish in ten had a committee, and many of them were inactive. However, it showed the Church's determination to preserve, or create, a Catholic 'sub-culture' outside the Liberal State. It was the lay counterpart of the new generation of bishops and clergy. As in the Church herself, the new centralized organization enabled Catholic leaders from different regions of Italy to meet more often, and thus helped to create a more 'national' Catholic movement, opposed to the nation-State.

Above all, the lay 'intransigents' and their organization prevented religion from becoming an *instrumentum regni*. Organized Catholicism had come into being to fight against the established Liberal order. The *Opera dei Congressi's* constant worry was that Right-wing politicians might seek to use the movement to create a conservative party with mass support. The danger was a real one. Many Catholic laymen still hoped for a 'reconciliation' between Church and State. 'Reconciliation' seemed especially desirable to conservatives worried about anarchism and social unrest; and it is no coincidence that it was most discussed at periods of political tension – 1878–79 and 1886–87. In 1879 a group of Catholic laymen did, in fact, hold a meeting to discuss the founding of a 'National Conservative Party', able to fight parliamentary elections. Most of them were Roman aristocrats, who had the most immediate interest in settling the Roman question, but Tuscany was also a centre of conservative 'conciliatorism'. The initiative soon faded out, as Leo XIII reaffirmed Papal intransigence on the Roman question, but the whole argument revived again in the summer of 1887. After the tragedy of Dogali (see §5.4), Leo XIII spoke of his wish to end the 'lamentable quarrel' between Church and State. The Abbot of Monte Cassino, Fr Luigi Tosti, published a pamphlet entitled *La Conciliazione*, urging moves towards a settlement; he had apparently discussed it beforehand both with the Minister of the Interior, Crispi, and with Vatican officials. It naturally raised a great storm of criticism from the Catholic 'intransigents' and from the anticlericals and Radicals; both

Crispi and the Pope decided that the time for 'reconciliation' had not yet come. The failure of 1887 ushered in a period of much sharper conflict between Church and State.

4.6 CONCLUSION: STRATEGIES AND COUNTER-STRATEGIES

This chapter has outlined some of the forms that popular and clerical disaffection took between 1871 and 1887. Clearly major changes occurred in this period – the rise and decline of anarchism, the decline of intransigent Republicanism, the shift of some mutual-aid societies towards 'resistance', i.e. strikes, and the increasing importance of the Workers' Party in Lombardy. Moreover, in 1882 the vote was given to most literate urban workers (see §3.7), and this led to the election of the first 'Socialist' deputies, including Costa. Here were the beginnings of a modern labour movement, with its own institutions and practices.

Even so, the labour movement was still very weak in 1887. Only the printers had a national trade union. The mutual-aid societies were the most important labour organizations. Traditional forms of popular protest – riot, brigandage – had by no means died out, especially in Southern Italy. Above all, Italy was not yet an industrialized country. Building workers and railwaymen were the largest groups outside agriculture, and most of these had recently been peasants or still had family links with the land. The early labour institutions were being founded by craftsmen and artisans – printers, bakers, tailors, shoemakers – not by industrial workers; and those industrial workers who were found in them were often semi-rural, like the Como silk-workers. The really distinctive feature of the most 'advanced', Northern, labour movement in Italy, the POI, was its success among the landless labourers of the Po valley, especially in Mantua province in 1884–85. This rural base remained a characteristic feature of Italian Socialism in years to come. It is dubious, therefore, whether this period should be seen – as many Left-wing Italian historians have argued – as one in which 'spontaneous' popular disaffection gradually became more disciplined and more organized into a 'modern' labour movement. Popular disaffection continued to worry governments, and usually on grounds of public order.

How did the ruling classes deal with protest and opposition? A variety of methods were employed, with considerable success. Military force was certainly one answer. It was used against brigandage, against anarchist bands, and often against strikes. Preventive detention, forced exile, house arrest and the like were less drastic variations of 'repression'. Nor was it only the State machinery that used force. The late nineteenth century was also the golden age of the Sicilian Mafia, the period when non-legal violence became a recognized method of defending landowners and new property rights against the peasantry. What was unusual about Sicily was that the *dominant* class was engaged in overt crime. But disaffection did not always have to be repressed; it could also be diverted. The 'great safety-valve', emigration, was often opened by members of local political élites – although most governments tried to curb emigration, and the number of emigrants was far fewer in this early period than after 1887. Similarly, rural poverty could be blamed on foreigners, and used to justify protectionist policies – this was very evident by the mid-1880s. Above all, disaffection was 'absorbed'. Workers' self-help organizations were encouraged by enlightened gentlemen; the 'industrial spurt' of the 1880s, with a rapid expansion of building activity in the main cities and the abolition of the grist-tax in 1883, relieved the worst of the pressure on many urban Italians; and the advent of the Left to power in 1876 helped to pacify many Southern opinion-makers.

Indeed, perhaps the most important factor is that the Left governments after 1876 were not *too* alien from popular feeling on vital issues. Men like Cairoli and Crispi still regarded themselves as democrats, and angrily rejected charges of betraying their early Garibaldian ideals. Garibaldi himself was prepared to come to terms with the political regime after 1876. The 'political classes' and the Radical or Socialist 'disaffected' had much in common, after all – a belief in progress, in science, and in evolution. They adhered to vaguely positivist views, and often to Freemasonry. It is noteworthy how 'official', how 'bourgeois', anticlericalism was in the late nineteenth century. In Bologna, for example – the home of Republicanism, of Saffi and Carducci – anticlericalism focused on the local cremation society, which was run by upper-class Liberals and army officers. Cremation, they claimed, was patriotic, scientific, liberal, hygienic, egalitarian, respectful, progressive and cheap.[12] Irredentism, too, may have been officially discouraged – especially as it touched on the royal prerogative in foreign policy – but certainly many Establishment politicians sympathized quietly with expansionist aims.

In short, the 'outsiders and protesters' were not so far outside as all that. They shared many of the values of the insiders. Yet the story of the Radical Party is instructive. The Radicals helped to 'absorb' some popular disaffection, but they failed to carry the Milan working class or Lombard peasantry with them, and by 1887 governments had reason to worry about whether the younger generations of Northern Italy would be as easy to handle as previous ones. Moreover, just when strikes and Socialism became more of a threat, the first attempts at 'reconciliation' with the Church ended in failure. Social Catholicism, with a mass basis, was becoming far more active in the Northern countryside, and this was a real threat to Liberal 'hegemony'. The political classes had been fairly successful in containing disaffection in the 1870s and 1880s; the task was much more difficult in the 1890s.

REFERENCES

1. P. Turiello, *Governo e Governati in Italia*, i, Bologna 1882, p. 52.
2. L. Bodio, *Di Alcuni Dati Misuratori del Movimento Economico in Italia*, Rome 1891, p. 37.

3. Letter of 24 Feb. 1885, quoted by G. Neppi Modona, *Sciopero, Potere Politico e Magistratura 1870–1922*, Bari 1969, pp. 24–25.

4. Bakunin to Francesco Mora, 5 April 1872, quoted in E. De Laveleye, *Le Socialisme Contemporain*, Paris 1881, pp. 349–50.

5. G Manacorda, *Il Socialismo nella Storia d'Italia*, Bari 1966, p. 163.

6. G. Manacorda, *Il Movimento Operaio Italiano attraverso i suoi Congressi*, Rome 1953, repr. 1971, p. 366 (the programme is on pp. 362–71).

7. R. Molinelli, *Una Città delle Marche dopo il 1860*, Urbino 1971, p. 59.

8. *Records of the Tercentenary Festival of the University of Edinburgh*, Edinburgh 1885, pp. 162–63.

9. D. Binchy, *Church and State in Fascist Italy*, London 1941, p. 13.

10. Bakunin quoted in G. Manacorda, *Il Socialismo nella Storia d'Italia*, pp. 119–20.

11. M. Bendiscioli in Autori Vari, *Chiesa e Religiosità in Italia dopo l'Unità*, ii, Milan 1973, p. 175.

12. Speech of Gen. Costetti at the cremation of Col. Arturo Brin, in Società di Cremazione di Bologna, *Inaugurazione dello Stendardo e Commemorazione del Colonnello Arturo Brin*, Bologna 1896.

PART TWO

1887–1914

CHAPTER FIVE

The first crisis of the Liberal State, 1887–1900

In the summer of 1887 Agostino Depretis died. He had been Prime Minister for most of the preceding eleven years, and to many Italians his death symbolized the end of an era – the grey era of *trasformismo*, of parliamentary intrigues and corruption, and of timidity in foreign affairs. It was time for a change, time for a proper concentration on High Politics. Certainly Francesco Crispi, the incoming Prime Minister, thought so. He remained Prime Minister until February 1891, and held the office again from December 1893 to March 1896. Crispi was a hero of the *Risorgimento*, a man of great patriotism, vigour and determination. He saw himself as the Italian Bismarck. He intended to abolish corruption, strengthen the executive, reinforce the army, defend Italy's interests abroad and promote social reforms; and no one was going to stop him. He was a great believer in liberty; but in liberty under the law. Convinced of his own rectitude and contemptuous of social, economic or even political complexities, Crispi (and some of his successors in the 1890s) attempted to run Italy as if she were a vast volunteer army, mobilized for glory and progress. The attempt failed. He (and they) succeeded mainly in disrupting the economy, endangering the whole Liberal regime, and provoking far more widespread and effective movements of political opposition.

5.1 CRISPI THE REFORMER

Like most zealous reformers, Crispi found it easier to tamper with the machinery of State than to achieve his other goals. A new Ministry of Posts and Telegraphs was set up, and the Ministry of Finance was formally separated from the Treasury. The top civil service post within each ministry, the 'general secretary', was abolished; henceforth no civil servant was responsible for all the ministry's work, and the head of each 'directorate' reported direct to the minister. To compensate, 'under-secretaries' were set up to help the minister, i.e. each minister would have a deputy (or Senator) to help him with his administrative and parliamentary work. The aim was to give the 'politicians' greater control over the 'bureaucrats'. The main consequence was to double the number of government jobs, thus making the Prime Minister's task of maintaining a parliamentary majority rather easier. It also made it easier for Crispi and his successors to hold various ministries as well as the premiership. In particular, the Prime Minister was nearly always the Minister of the Interior; and to be the Interior Under-secretary soon became a very important government post.

Crispi's other major reform was to reorganize the Council of State, a body of lawyers that advised the government on legal and constitutional issues. In 1889 it was given a 'fourth section', with a monopoly of administrative justice. It heard appeals against official decisions, and decided whether the official had violated the law or exceeded his powers. Italy had acquired a group of ombudsmen, with high prestige and some teeth. The reform was supposed to keep both parliament and the ordinary courts out of public administration, and to give the citizen some guarantees against administrative abuses. On the whole the new system worked reasonably well, although civil servants themselves remained without any guarantees against arbitrary acts by their superiors. Abuses were even more frequent in local government, and in 1890 a similar system of administrative law was introduced for the municipalities and provinces. This was a less successful innovation. Justice was dispensed by a new body, the 'provincial administrative *giunta*' (GPA); but the GPA was dominated in practice by the Prefect, who was far from being a neutral figure.

Crispi also introduced two other important changes in local government. In 1889 the suffrage at local elections was extended. Henceforth all literate males over twenty-one might vote, provided they paid five lire p.a. in local taxes; the local electorate therefore rose from about 1½ million to nearly 3½ million. The other innovation was to permit the larger councils, in municipalities with over 10,000 inhabitants, to elect their own mayors. In 1896 the concession was extended to all municipalities. This was a real revolution in government. The two measures together did much to strengthen Catholic and Socialist positions at local level, and – in the long run – to undermine the Liberal regime.

5.2 THE 'TARIFF WAR'

The economic problems of these years also undermined the Liberal regime. I have shown in Chapter 2 that there was rapid economic growth in the 1880s, but that some industries – notably steelmaking and shipbuilding – flourished only through State subsidy and a State-guaranteed market, and that some other sectors, including cereals and textiles, faced an increasing threat from foreign competition. It is true that they were protected to some degree by the tariff of 1878, which had imposed levies varying from 10 per cent to 40 per cent on textiles; but these terms were often reduced by commercial treaties with particular countries, especially the treaty with France signed in November 1881 – and France accounted for about two-fifths of Italy's foreign trade. Textile and light industrial interests were particularly vociferous in demanding more protection. These demands became even louder after 1883, when gold convertibility was restored and the lira was thus 'revalued'. Above all, the worsening agricultural crisis of the 1880s discredited free trade. Most regions were affected by the increasing imports of cheap American grain, and farmers also had to worry about Asian competition in rice or silk and about exporting cattle or dairy produce at a time of collapsing world prices. Southern landowners, who were threatened with increased land taxes under a new land register introduced in 1886, were anxious for some compensation. Early in 1885 the Agrarian Defence League was founded at Turin, and parliament began receiving petitions.

And so an important political lobby was formed. It was essentially a North Italian alliance of textile manufacturers and Po valley landowners, but it was a more complex and subtle alliance than that bare description would suggest. Many Northern workers'· organizations and mutual-aid societies were protectionist too, for jobs were at stake. For Catholics, free trade and competition were Liberal heresies, whereas protection might help to retain the peasants in Italy and preserve traditional values. Moreover, the strikes and labour unrest of the mid-1880s had persuaded many politicians that free trade was too risky. Perhaps public order could only be maintained by protecting agriculture and key industries; and certainly desirable social reforms like the abolition of child labour could only be enforced if there were some economic prosperity. Thus protectionism promised the most tempting of all prizes – an answer to the 'social question'; and indeed the protectionist campaign was led by the most enlightened employer of the day, Senator Alessandro Rossi. Protectionism also offered, of course, the prospect of a national steel industry, a national shipping industry, and a strong navy. Social reforms, public works, military spending, national prestige, anti-French sentiment and 'corporate interests' all fused together.

The tariff campaign transformed the Italian political scene. It has often been described as a stage in the creation of a *national* ruling class. More subtle historians have argued that it created a 'permanent' alliance of interests and values – a 'historic bloc', to use Gramsci's term – that dominated Italy until after the Second World War. There is much to be said for this view, although the 'alliance' was not a simple one between Northern industrialists and Southern grain-growing landowners. Southern landowners played a very minor part in the protectionist campaign, and derived surprisingly little benefit from its success (see below). If there was an 'alliance', it was a very one-sided one. The 'Agrarian Party' was Northern, and it was Northern agriculture that was faced with collapse in the mid-1880s. Moreover, many leading protectionists had wanted protection for industrial goods only. Even Crispi himself opposed raising the duty on wheat, partly because he was a lifelong enemy of the Sicilian absentee landowners, but mainly because he had no desire to impose a policy of dear food. The tariff's consequences increased the South's sense of betrayal, and provoked open revolt in some areas – especially the grain-growing areas of Sicily!

In July 1887 parliament approved the new 'general tariff'. It applied a 15 per cent levy on imported luxury foods like sugar and coffee; this levy was allegedly for revenue purposes only, but in practice it gave effective protection – and a great stimulus – to home sugar-beet growers, refiners and alcohol distillers. In addition, the duty on imported wheat had been raised (on 21 April) from the existing 14 lire per tonne to 30 lire; it was raised again to 50 lire on 10 February 1888, and to 75 lire in 1894. These were real Corn Laws, and caused great immediate hardship to the poor. Above all, the tariff also introduced a much higher, and much more complicated, duty on nearly all imported manufactures, especially steel and textiles. Whole industries, like steelmaking or shipbuilding, were to depend on protection for decades to come. The 1887 tariff and the duties on wheat remained in force until after the First World War, and had a major impact on Italy's economic development during the crucial phase of industrial 'take-off'.

The new tariff was a 'general' one, i.e. it applied only to imports from countries which had no detailed commercial treaty with Italy. Hence the protectionists had only won half the battle. They still had to prevent concessions being made in new treaties, particularly in any new treaty with France. In December 1886 the Italian government had 'denounced' the existing French treaty, and so that treaty was due to expire in January 1888. The two governments, therefore, had to negotiate new terms, but their efforts to do so were lukewarm. Crispi had always been wary of the French, and in any case was convinced that France would suffer far more than Italy from failure to reach agreement; and he could not afford to 'sign away the tariff', for fear of losing political support. Moreover, he was anxious for Italy to assume a more important role within the Triple Alliance. In October 1887 he visited his mentor Bismarck; and in December Italy signed a commercial treaty with Austria–Hungary, granting many concessions. The French, for their part, insisted that any renegotiation could only be on the basis of the 1881 treaty (which they had assumed would expire in 1892), not on the basis of the new Italian general tariff. Negotiations proved fruitless. On 27 February 1888 the French imposed a special discriminatory tariff on many Italian goods, and applied their maximum general tariff on all the rest; two days later Italy replied in kind. The 'tariff war' had begun. It continued at full strength for two years, until the Italians abolished their *discriminatory* (anti-French) tariffs in January 1890; the French followed suit, but only two years later. Only in 1898 was agreement finally reached, and even then silk was excluded.

The short-term effects of the 1887 tariff – and especially of the subsequent 'tariff war' – were dramatic. Trade between the two countries was halved. Italian exports to France fell from an average of 444 million lire in 1881–87 to an average of 165 million lire in 1888–90; the French share of Italian exports fell from 41 per cent to 18 per cent. Imports from France went down from 307 million to 164 million lire. Only about one-third of the lost export market could be made up elsewhere. Silk and wine were particularly affected, although rice, dairy produce and cattle exports all suffered. Italian wine exports, averaging nearly 2¼ million hectolitres p.a. in the mid-1880s, were below 1 million hectolitres in 1890. Prices also fell, from 33.5 lire per hectolitre in 1881–87 to 25 lire per hectolitre, so by 1890 wine-growers' receipts from exports were running at below one-third of those three years previously. Many of the wine-producers had turned to vines fairly recently, and many of them were in the South, especially in Apulia. They never recovered from the blow, especially since phylloxera was at last spreading among the Italian vineyards. In 1886 Italy had produced 38.2 million hectolitres; the average in 1888–90 was 28.0 million hectolitres. Much the same story applied to olive oil exports, and to fruit and vegetables; and these products were characteristic of the most modern, intensive, agricultural areas in the South. Whole regions of Italy were ruined, all for the sake of Italian prestige.

Even grain-growers did not benefit by as much as they perhaps anticipated. The average wheat price rose between 1887 and 1891, from 221.4 lire per tonne to 252.9 lire, but it then fell for the next three years: by 1894 it was 192.2 lire per tonne, 13 per cent less than before the 1887 tariff. This was perhaps just as well, for the last thing Italy needed was encouragement to produce even more grain. Thus although the wheat tariff was high – the highest in Europe by 1894 – and although things might have been even worse for some farmers without its protection, it did not resolve the agricultural crisis. Emigration increased dramatically after 1887, even from the grain-growing areas.

The immediate effects of the 1887 tariff and the 'tariff war' on industry are more difficult to assess. The tariff had been introduced to meet a serious cyclical crisis of overproduction, and it is difficult to disentangle the effects of the tariff from those of the cycle. Steel production rose for a time, from 73,000 tonnes in 1887 to 158,000 tonnes in 1889, but this was partly because the Terni steel plant was still coming into full operation; after 1890 production fell rapidly as demand collapsed. As for the engineering industry, it has become a commonplace among economic historians to deplore its fate after 1887. Enjoying little protection itself, forced to buy costly home-produced steel which priced it out of foreign markets, and faced with lack of orders at home, the Italian machinery and engineering industries took years to recover. Gerschenkron's index for the period 1888 to 1896 gives an astonishing negative 'growth rate' of 7.4 per cent p.a. for engineering.[1] Only the cotton industry seems to have derived immediate advantages from the tariff. Imports of cotton textiles halved between 1885 and 1890, but raw cotton imports went up over 65 per cent. But the cotton industry had very limited export opportunities, and could hardly sustain industrial expansion on its own. All in all, the immediate effects of the tariff were pernicious. Its long-term effects are more debatable, and are discussed in Chapter 6.

5.3 THE BANKS

Among the immediate effects of the 'tariff war' was a hasty withdrawal of foreign investment from the country. This had particularly dramatic results in Rome. Rome in the 1880s had enjoyed, or suffered, a building boom. Speculative builders had put up flats for the hordes of civil servants that had to live in the city, and ten new suburban zones had been created. The whole operation was based on credit, especially on advances from Piedmontese and foreign banks. When the French suddenly wanted their money back, and when business confidence was in any case suddenly undermined by the 'tariff war', the bubble burst. The lira came under pressure on the foreign exchanges. Some of the smaller Piedmontese banks failed; small savers lost several hundred million lire; and 80,000 building workers in Rome – mainly immigrants – found themselves out of a job. In February 1889 some of them rioted, and Liberal Italy was faced with a major problem of public order in the capital city.

The various governments of these years naturally tried to mount a rescue operation. Crispi convinced himself that the banking and building crisis was all due to a plot by French financiers. He, therefore, asked Bismarck to put pressure on the leading German banks to support the lira by buying Italian government paper. The episode marks the virtual beginning of the important influence of German banks on Italian economic fortunes; and it also shows how Italian dreams of prestige, at a time of economic weakness, could lead only to subservience within the Italo-German alliance. The other government remedy was to persuade the six note-issuing banks to bail out the smaller banks and finance-houses that were in difficulties. As recompense, these issue banks were allowed to print extra bank notes, far in excess of their reserves or of the legal limits. This was simply creating money to avoid a recession, and soon there were 50 million lire of 'illegal' currency in circulation.

Even so, the smaller banks failed, and dragged down some of the larger ones with them. At the end of 1893 the two largest credit institutions in Italy, the *Banca Generale* and the *Società Generale di Credito Mobiliare*, closed their doors. These banks had financed industry, agriculture, commerce and railways as well as property, and their fall was an economic disaster. The country had no large credit institutions left, and many of the smaller ones had also disappeared. Prospects for industrial or commercial investment looked hopeless. Only the local savings banks remained, important no doubt for small-scale agricultural expansion, but hardly capable of meeting industrial needs. And, of course, there were the six issue banks – but even they had lost much money in rescue operations, and one of them, the *Banca Romana*, also collapsed in 1893.

The fall of the *Banca Romana* was probably not so serious economically as that of the *Banca Generale* and the *Credito Mobiliare*, but it had far greater repercussions politically. The *Banca Romana* had also been involved in property speculation in Rome, and by 1888 was in deep trouble. However, since it was an issue bank, the printing press was the obvious solution to its liquidity problems. Soon it was rumoured that 60 million 'illegal' *Banca Romana* notes were in circulation, including 9 million duplicates. In December 1889 the Crispi government ordered Senator Giacomo Alvisi and Gustavo Biagini, a Treasury official, to carry out inquiries. Both reports were damning. After a lengthy and well-documented catalogue of errors and omissions, Chapter 1 of the Alvisi report concluded roundly:

At the *Banca Romana* the accounting system is defective, the creation of bank notes is abnormal, their issuing is excessive and partly camouflaged, the arrangement of the general reserve fund is confused, the store of notes for circulation and withdrawal is inadequately protected, and further illegitimate and illegal issues must be expected.[2]

Naturally this report was shelved. It was far too embarrassing. To begin with, many of the bank's losses had been incurred from loans granted to tottering businesses favoured by governments or politicians. Nor did politicians want it known that the *Banca Romana*, like other banks, had made large 'loans' to leading politicians, often without expecting any interest; it was customary to finance election expenses in this way. So no action was taken, and the Bank's Governor, Bernardo Tanlongo, was even nominated to the Senate in November 1892.

Yet eventually the Radicals managed to get hold of Biagini's report, Napoleone Colajanni made impassioned speeches in parliament, the 'subversive' press had a field day, the *Banca Romana* collapsed, and Tanlongo was arrested. The new Prime Minister, Giolitti, claimed unconvincingly that he had never read the Biagini or Alvisi reports, but rumours flew around that he himself had had a 40,000 lire loan from the bank, that Crispi was also deeply involved, and that even the king and his family had benefited. Other committees of inquiry had to be set up. The Mordini committee, reporting in November 1893, confirmed the financial irregularities, including illegal circulation and duplicate notes. It also named twenty-two deputies as having received payments from the bank, blamed Giolitti for wilfully ignoring the bank's activities and for nominating Tanlongo to the Senate, and revealed that Giolitti himself had borrowed (but also repaid) at least 60,000 lire, and possibly 100,000 lire, from the bank. The Giolitti government promptly resigned. Crispi was also mildly censured, for failing to do anything about the original Alvisi report in 1889, when he had been Prime Minister. The Mordini committee was distinctly hostile to Giolitti but favourable to Crispi: it ignored other accusations against Crispi, for example that he had asked Tanlongo for 60,000 lire in December 1892, or that he had sold honours. Indeed, Crispi became Prime Minister again two weeks later.

Yet the *Banca Romana* scandal was not over yet. The judicial inquiries continued; and Giolitti, nursing his grievance, bided his time. In December 1894 he handed over a packet of documents to the President of the Chamber. The packet contained proof that Crispi had 'borrowed' 55,000 lire from the bank, and that Crispi's wife and other relatives had also 'borrowed' on the strength of his credit. Faced with these unpleasant revelations, Crispi chose to prorogue, and later dissolve, the Chamber. In the whole of 1895 parliament sat for less than three months. The accusations of corruption thus threatened to turn into a real political crisis.

The *Banca Romana* was Liberal Italy's major financial scandal. Even so, the Radicals' moral zeal was a little exaggerated. There is no evidence that Tanlongo's payments achieved any startling results. It was simply that politics was an expensive business. Banks and businessmen were expected to contribute towards the expenses of elections and of running (or bribing) newspapers, and they were expected to be discreet about it; in return they might receive the odd perk, like a seat in the Senate or a public-works contract, but they were not normally allowed to influence policy. However, the constant rumours and revelations, the constant reports of bribes and cover-ups, were important. They helped to discredit Italy's rulers and her institutions. Pareto wrote that 'a band of brigands is governing our unhappy country'.[3] Bank 'loans' may have been just part of the system; in that case the system was corrupt. The scandals were a gift to the Radicals and to the press. The *Banca Romana* had revealed very clearly just how low 'Low Politics' could be. The alternative, as ever, was High Politics; yet the royal house, too, had not been above suspicion.

5.4 AFRICA

But it was not only economic collapse and domestic scandals that undermined Liberal governments in the 1890s. Italy also found herself fighting, and losing, a hugely expensive colonial war, for no apparent reason. Italy had become involved in Africa largely by accident, under the Depretis governments (see §3.2). Initially her interest lay on the Red Sea, around the port of Massawa which she occupied in 1885. However, Massawa was useless unless the Abyssinian trade went through it; the Abyssinians were reluctant to use it, and even more reluctant to see the Italians in it. Skirmishes soon began. In January 1887 500 Italian troops were massacred by Abyssinians at Dogali, and that, of course, led to a great outcry at home. Italy blockaded Abyssinia, and parliament voted an extra 20 million lire to strengthen the Massawa garrison.

This was the situation Crispi inherited when he came to power. Fortunately his initial preoccupation with France prevented him doing much to aggravate matters early on, and in March 1888 the Abyssinian Emperor John IV agreed to give compensation for Dogali and to use Massawa as a trading-post. The following year John was killed by his Sudanese enemies, and the King of Shoa, Menelik, became Emperor. Menelik was a personal friend of Count Pietro Antonelli, who was in charge of colonial policy, and the Italians had been supporting him for some years against John; so in May 1889 he signed, in return for 5,000 rifles and a loan of 3 million lire, a treaty of friendship with Italy, the Treaty of Wichale (*Uccialli*). Article 17 of the treaty laid down, in the Italian version, that 'His Majesty the King of Kings of Ethiopia agrees to make use of (*consente di servirsi*) the Government of His Majesty the King of

Italy, for all business negotiations he might have with other Powers or Governments'.

So far so good. Italian honour had been saved, and an Italian 'protectorate' established over Abyssinia. Soon the Italians pushed further inland and along the coast, and in 1890 Crispi joined up Italy's Red Sea possessions (Massawa and Assab) to form 'Eritrea'; he also began the conquest of Somalia, which formally became an Italian colony in 1905. Menelik became very mistrustful of the Italians, and in September 1890 he wrote to King Humbert explaining that the words 'agrees to' in the treaty were a mistranslation: in Amharic the word was 'may'. There was no Italian protectorate after all.

What was to be done? Clearly Italy could not afford to become bogged down in a ruinous colonial war at a time of economic crisis. When Crispi fell from power early in 1891, his successor di Rudiní thought the best thing to do with Africa was to get out of it. He told the President of the Senate: 'that African business is impossible; we might spend 50 million a year on it . . . let someone else spend it, not me. I'll end up by bringing everybody home, come what may.'[4]

Farini agreed, yet he told di Rudiní that withdrawal was impossible. The blow to Italian prestige would be too great. He noted in his diary that 'the day that our helplessness was revealed in this way would cause serious damage to the monarchy'. Here is a recurring theme of modern Italian history. The Italian State seemed threatened by numerous enemies, both within and without – regional disruption, the Vatican, French ambitions in the Mediterranean, anarchists and Socialists. Patriotic men realized that the Crown was the country's major unifying force; and the Crown's prestige was closely linked to 'successes' in foreign and defence policy. Liberal politicians, therefore, had to play along with reckless foreign adventures. Di Rudiní did not, therefore, withdraw from Africa, but he did pull back to the Red Sea and its immediate hinterland.

In Crispi's second term of office (December 1893 to March 1896) the Abyssinian campaigns resumed. The French had started building a railway from Addis Ababa to Djibouti, which would give the Abyssinians a trading outlet on the Red Sea outside Italian influence. Something had to be done. In January 1895 General Baratieri occupied Tigré, and that summer came to Rome for his 'triumphal' welcome. In September he went back to fight off Menelik's counter-offensive, but suffered a series of humiliating defeats. Finally, on 1 March 1896, came the disastrous battle of Adowa, when 5,000 Italians were killed, and nearly 2,000 taken prisoner. It was the first time that an African army had defeated a European colonial power. It brought Crispi down in disgrace, and it was, of course, a disastrous blow to Italy's prestige. Once again, Crispi's successor as Prime Minister was di Rudiní; and once again di Rudiní pulled the army back to Eritrea. In October 1896 Italy and Abyssinia made peace. The Treaty of Addis Ababa recognized the Mareb River as the frontier between Abyssinia and Eritrea, and ended any claim to an Italian 'protectorate' over Abyssinia. It was not, however, the end of Italy's colonial ambitions. She retained her Eritrean and Somalian territories; and she nursed a sense of shame and a thirst for revenge, that were to become powerful influences on Italy's foreign (and domestic) policies in the early twentieth century.

5.5 RIOT AND INSURRECTION: THE SICILIAN *FASCI* AND THE RIOTS OF 1898

So far in this chapter I have discussed the 'tariff war' and its disastrous economic repercussions, the bank scandals, and the collapse of Italian prestige in Africa. Clearly 'legal Italy' was in deep trouble, and it is not surprising that the 'outsiders and protesters' were vocal, or that the problems of public order became far more acute in the 1890s. Riots became almost commonplace. The most important episodes came from opposite ends of the country, Sicily and Milan.

Sicily had been in endemic revolt against government – any government – for most of the nineteenth century. There was much hatred of the newly rich landowners or large tenants who had taken over ecclesiastical and common lands. Sicily had also been badly hit by the slump in the world price for grain and sulphur. The more prosperous coastal areas, where wine production had flourished, were trying desperately to cope with a major outbreak of phylloxera. The 'tariff war' with France was the last straw. It deprived Sicily of its major export market, virtually overnight. And these 'economic' grievances were only half the story. At least as important was the unusually appalling – and unusually well-documented – state of local government in Sicily. When, as often happened, the mayor was also the largest landowner, he controlled virtually all jobs, both private and public; he and his friends decided who paid local taxes, and how much; and they controlled the local police forces as well. Moreover, the Sicilian 'municipality' (*comune*) was the largest local government unit in Europe; the very nature of many Sicilian 'villages' – large dormitory-towns inhabited by 10,000, sometimes even by 40,000 peasants – made riots more likely to break out, and far more difficult to control. Local excise duties and municipal taxes were a hated burden; burning down the town hall and the tax records was the obvious solution.

So rioting was endemic. But the riots and disturbances of 1893–94 were rather different from their many predecessors. They were, at least in many areas, connected with the rise of the so-called 'Sicilian *Fasci*' (the word '*fasci*', literally 'bundles', was adopted from ancient Rome to denote a group or alliance, especially if aspiring to political power). The first *Fasci* had been founded in the towns by Radical or Socialist artisans and intellectuals. They were partly mutual-aid societies, partly 'leagues of resistance' of the kind familiar in Northern Italy (see §4.3). In 1893 the *Fasci* spread into the rural areas, and became virtual peasant leagues. Although there were all kinds of *Fasci* – some were run by anarchists, some by local gentry, some by *Mafiosi* – most were 'Socialist' in some sense, and their spread in Sicily in the early

1890s owed much to contacts with North Italian workers' organizations and with Northern ideas. The rural *Fasci* were, therefore, a curious phenomenon: both ancient and modern. They managed to combine peasant 'millenarian' aspirations with urban 'intellectual' leadership. The 'millenarian' aspects were the most picturesque, and impressed contemporary observers the most. The cross was carried in processions; children were 'baptized' by the local *Fasci* leaders; the movement set out to emancipate humanity, and preached complete equality among all men. But the leadership and organization were the keys to the *Fasci*'s effectiveness. Enlightened 'bourgeois intellectuals' – Giuseppe De Felice Giuffrida at Catania, Dr Nicola Barbato at Piana dei Greci, Rosario Garibaldi Bosco at Palermo, Giacomo Montalto at Trapani, Bernardino Verro at Corleone – inspired the peasants, mediated with Prefects and governments, and were elected on to local councils to 'change the laws'. They also led 'modern' strikes, made hard-headed immediate demands for higher wages and lower rents, and demanded the expropriation and division of the *latifundia*. Contemporary observers thought that the Sicilian *Fasci* were 'caused' by a generation of radical students at Palermo University. This was too simple, but certainly without the 'organizers' there would have been no *Fasci*, merely peasant riots. However, even *with* the organizers there were still peasant riots, which eventually provided the justification for government action.

These novel organizations, and the successful strikes over agricultural contracts, naturally alarmed the landowners and larger tenants. Towards the end of 1893, as violence and arson became more common, the gentry's alarm turned to panic. The Giolitti government showed little sympathy. Strikes were not illegal, and Giolitti was well aware of the state of local government on the island. He affected neutrality, at least initially. But this lofty attitude could not be maintained. The government infuriated the landowners by being unwilling to use force, and it annoyed the peasants by being unwilling to redistribute the *latifundia*. The king himself urged firm action against the 'subversives'. At this point the Giolitti government resigned, mainly over the *Banca Romana* affair (see §5.2 above); and Giolitti was replaced by a man who could restore law and order, Francesco Crispi.

Crispi's initial strategy seems to have been to conciliate the *Fasci* by promising reforms. He consulted Napoleone Colajanni, one of the leading Radicals in parliament, asked for his help in calming things down, and even offered him the job of Minister of Agriculture. But Crispi soon changed his mind. In his paranoid way, he thought that only a conspiracy could have brought about all this rioting. He imagined that the Vatican, or the French, might be trying to undermine Italian unity; and Italian unity was his lifelong passion. As he told parliament, 'he who loves, fears; and I love Italy greatly, and fear that she may collapse'.[5] Crispi's fears were not totally ludicrous. Italian unity was still felt to be a fragile achievement, and even some quite sensible people agreed that the French were probably responsible for the riots, or at least were financing the ringleaders. As for the Vatican, plenty of anticlerical Republicans were prepared to believe the worst – Jessie White Mario wrote in Crispi's paper *La Riforma* that the true instigators of the *Fasci* were clerical troublemakers. Although there was never any conspiracy, it is true that the anarchists in the *Fasci*, and even some of the Socialists like De Felice, hoped that revolution might break out. De Felice tried to contact sympathizers elsewhere in Italy, so as to create a network of quasi-*Fascist* organizations to help Sicily in the event of insurrection. And an anarchist insurrection did occur at the same time (January 1894), in the Lunigiana area of North-West Tuscany.

On 3 January 1894 the government dissolved the *Fasci* and all other workers' associations in Sicily, ordered the arrest of all the ringleaders, proclaimed a State of Emergency, and appointed Lieutenant-General Morra di Lavriano as Royal Commissioner to govern the island under military law. In the short run repression worked. Over 1,000 people were deported without trial to nearby islands. Many of them had nothing to do with the *Fasci*, or at least nothing to do with the riots. Military tribunals were set up and handed down lengthy sentences. De Felice was given 16 years for 'incitement to civil war'; Barbato was sentenced to 12 years, and Montalto to 10. The *Fasci* movement soon collapsed. The government also seized the opportunity to 'revise' the electoral rolls. At Catania 5,000 of the 9,000 electors were struck off. There were to be no more Socialist deputies or mayors if Crispi could help it.

Yet in the long run the repression was a mistake, even from Crispi's own point of view. The military tribunals gave the *Fasci* leaders a chance to make impassioned and well-reported speeches in their own defence; and, above all, they revolted the Liberal consciences of many Northern Italians. The tribunals were too obviously repressive, too reminiscent of Bourbon rule. Moreover, the repression was not confined to Sicily or the Lunigiana. In October 1894 the Socialist Party was dissolved, and its deputies arrested; and the electoral registers were 'amended' everywhere. All this meant that Crispi found his former 'Left-wing' support vanishing. In July 1894, in an attempt to recoup, he suddenly introduced a bill to take over the large estates (*latifundia*) and any uncultivated land; the land would be rented out on long leases in medium-sized holdings, and leaseholders would be given cheap credit and tax concessions. This project failed to convince the Radicals and democrats of Crispi's good intentions, but it infuriated the Sicilian landowners, who were now – after the suppression of the *Fasci* – feeling a good deal more secure, and were unwilling to make any needless concessions to their disloyal peasantry. They fought hard against the project, under the leadership of the Marquis di Rudiní; when Crispi fell from power after Adowa in March 1896, di Rudiní became Prime Minister. The Sicilian Establishment was safe. The peasants had no choice but to vote with their feet, and the years after 1894 saw a massive increase in emigration from the island.

The other major 'insurrectionary' episode of the 1890s was the food rioting that occurred in most regions of Italy in the spring of 1898. There was a simple, if perhaps mistaken, explanation for these riots. The wheat harvest in 1897 was the lowest since Unification – 2.4 million tonnes, compared with an average of 3.5 million tonnes in 1891–95. The dearth could not easily be made good, partly because the Spanish-American War in 1898 made it more costly to import American grain. The result was high prices: wheat at Milan rose from 225 lire a tonne in mid-1897 to 330 lire a tonne in April 1898. The government was urged to 'repeal the Corn Laws', i.e. abolish the duty on imported wheat; and there were also calls for local councils to abolish the municipal taxes on bread, and to open subsidized bakeries.

The succeeding events followed the classic pattern of political rioting. The government of di Rudiní reacted too little and too late, and so pleased nobody. In January 1898 it lowered the tariff on imported wheat from 75 lire a tonne to 50 lire a tonne. That was quite inadequate. Street demonstrations began in the South, spread up the peninsula and affected most regions by April or early May. During these demonstrations some 'incidents' occurred, i.e. some of the demonstrators were shot by nervous policemen. That, in turn, led to more violent demonstrations, shading into riots, and to new political demands for greater liberty as well as for cheaper food. The most serious rioting – a virtual insurrection – was at Milan in early May. It was sparked off by police attempts to arrest Socialist pamphleteers; and it was suppressed by the army. Official figures later gave 80 killed and 450 wounded, practically all of them 'insurgents'; these figures probably understated the facts by at least half.

The army had clearly over-reacted. So did the government. It arrested most of the well-known 'subversives' as ringleaders (which they were not), and imposed martial law in four provinces. Once again, journals and newspapers were suppressed; thousands of people were arrested; and military tribunals handed down lengthy sentences. The Socialist leader Turati was given 12 years, and the fiery 'intransigent' priest Davide Albertario was sentenced to 3 years. The 'subversive' parties and associations were dissolved, including most Socialist, Republican and Catholic bodies. Perhaps the most striking example of over-reaction was the king's public telegram a month later to General Bava Beccaris, who had been in charge of the troops in Milan. King Humbert awarded him the Cross of Savoy, 'to reward the great service which you rendered to our institutions and to civilization, and to attest to my affection and the gratitude of myself and the country'.

Once again, repression worked in the short run. Yet the events of 1898 had important political repercussions. They made popular national heroes out of a few relatively unknown 'subversives', not just in Milan but in many provincial towns throughout Italy. Furthermore, they discredited the 'agrarian' politicians who dominated the di Rudiní government and the State in general; and they strengthened the position of more 'progressive' Northern leaders. Above all, they exposed the Crown to hatred and contempt. King Humbert's telegram was a great boost to Republicanism, and of course the Crown was already being attacked for its links with colonial policy, militarism and the Triple Alliance. Thus the riots brought Liberal Italy sharply up against unwelcome reality. Popular disaffection seemed to be stronger than ever. Successive governments continued to wrestle with this problem, certainly for the next two years, arguably right until the Fascist regime was firmly installed in 1925–26.

5.6 THE CATHOLICS

But 'public order' in the 1890s was not just a matter of coping with popular unrest or spontaneous rioting. There were also the *organized* 'subversive' associations – clerical, Socialist, Radical or Republican; they were as troublesome as ever, and even more difficult to suppress. Potentially the most profound challenge to Liberal Italy still came from the Catholics, and successive Italian governments responded in kind. In June 1889 a monument to Giordano Bruno was formally unveiled in the Campo de'Fiori in Rome. The 20 September, the day in 1870 that Rome had fallen to the Italian troops, was declared a public holiday in 1895. An enormous monument to Victor Emmanuel II was built in Rome, on the site of a Franciscan friary and of Paul III's Tower. It soon became generally known as 'The Wedding-Cake'. Everyone agreed it was hideous, but 'Italy has to put up something big to show the Vatican'.[6]

Most seriously of all, in 1890 Crispi pushed through a major reform of charities. In the 1880s there were an estimated 22,000 charitable bodies in Italy, spending 96 million lire a year, of which 31 million lire were subsidies from local government. Welfare provision differed markedly between different regions. Most of the charities were run by 'congregations of charity', normally laymen appointed by each municipality and subject to a vague supervision by the provincial authorities. Crispi's new law strengthened this lay control, and specifically excluded all priests from membership of the 'congregations'. The more old-fashioned charities were suppressed altogether; and many others were 'merged' together – nearly 6,000 by 1908. Yet others were 'transformed', i.e. their funds diverted to quite different purposes from the founders' original intentions – this happened to 1,193 charities by 1903, mainly those which had provided retreats, hospices for pilgrims and dowries for novice nuns. It was all a major challenge to traditional welfare provision, affecting all alms-giving bodies and those caring for the orphans, the old and the sick. It was also a major challenge to the Church's remaining role in 'civil society'. Inevitably the Church fought back. The bishops made a public appeal to the people, deploring the effects of the new measures on the poor, deploring the overruling of founders' wishes, and above all deploring the inefficiency and corruption that would inevitably follow. But another law passed three days later expropriated the property of the various lay 'congregations' and 'confraternities' in Rome, and diverted the income to officially approved causes.

There was, of course, much to be said for reforming the charities. Most of them were small, inefficiently managed, and often a source of patronage in local government; and the Church had already lost control of many of them in 1862. Moreover, the intellectual fashion of the day was for 'indoor relief', in different kinds of welfare institutions – orphanages, mental hospitals, old people's homes – and these required large sums and some degree of provincial co-ordination. Even so, the Church's reaction was understandable. Crispi's laws on charities had some important repercussions. They made it even more vital for Catholics to gain or share control of local government, and the broader local suffrage made that easier in some areas. Several cities fell to them in 1893, and 'clerico-moderate' alliances between Catholics and conservatives became more common: one took over Milan in 1895. More generally, once the Church and the Catholic laity lost some of their traditional charities they began to engage in more active kinds of social work among the peasants and industrial workers.

This tendency was strengthened in 1891 by Leo XIII's famous encyclical on the social question, *Rerum Novarum. Rerum Novarum* not only condemned existing capitalist society, it ordered devout Catholics to transform it, and this seemed particularly apposite at a time of agricultural crisis, industrial depression, and high emigration. Employers should pay a 'just wage', enough to permit the worker to save and acquire property. The State might legitimately intervene to safeguard workers' rights and prevent blatant exploitation, but essentially reforms should come by mutual agreement, through a series of 'private' associations. Mutual-aid societies, co-operatives and mixed 'corporations' of workers and employers were the most favoured kinds of association, but workers' trade unions were also permissible provided they did not engage in the class struggle. All this 'Papal Socialism' seemed dangerous nonsense to Liberals, and it was perhaps partly intended to *épater les bourgeois.* But its real purpose was to stimulate the Catholics to greater efforts – and to combat the ever-present threat of Red Socialism. In 1890 the German SPD had become the largest party in the *Reichstag*, and in Italy a Socialist Party was being formed (see below). 'Social Catholicism' seemed an urgent necessity, and it was not restricted to Italy.

A further boost came from Giuseppe Toniolo's 'Union for Social Studies', founded in 1889. Toniolo was a sociologist at the University of Pisa; his ambition was to 'Christianize' the 'pagan–positivist–Marxist' social sciences. His writings were very influential, and he also founded a scholarly journal, the *Rivista Internazionale di Scienze Sociali,* to discuss the main issues. The Union's most important document was the 'Milan Programme' of 1894, entitled the 'Programme of Catholics faced with Socialism'. The 'Milan Programme' agreed with the Socialist view that State Socialism was the natural outcome of liberal capitalist society. But it did not welcome the prospect. Socialism would be a disaster, denying God, family life and the right to property; 'under a mask of emancipation it prepares an even more cruel and universal servitude'.[7] The remedy was 'corporations' – i.e. 'guilds' of employers and workers – profit-sharing in industry, small landownership, share-cropping or long leases in the countryside, co-operatives to organize commerce, and banking to be run as a public utility. The 'Programme' ended by looking forward to the 'Christian democracy of the twentieth century', in which all classes would work together in social harmony.

Toniolo was essentially a theorist; the practical work had to be done by others – in particular, by the lay organizations affiliated to the *Opera dei Congressi* (see §4.5). The '*Opera*' officially adopted the 'Milan Programme' in 1894, and the 1895 Congress proclaimed that Catholic provincial and municipal councillors should do all in their power to implement it. This was the great period of the '*Opera*'. In 1892–94 the movement was reorganized, and its 'permanent committee' was divided into sections to organize the various branches of activity – youth work, education, press, local election campaigns, rural banks, co-operatives, charities, etc. The second section, called 'Christian social economy', was perhaps the most effective, especially in the North Italian countryside. The 'rural banks' (*Casse Rurali*), in particular, soon gave the Northern peasants real protection against usury. By 1897 the '*Opera*' claimed 3,982 parish committees, 708 youth sections, 17 university circles, 688 workers' associations, 588 rural banks, 24 daily newspapers, 105 periodicals, and many other organizations and activities. The movement remained far stronger in Veneto, Lombardy and Piedmont than elsewhere, but even in the South there were some signs of life – in Sicily there were 207 parish committees and 9 periodicals. The '*Opera*' was a major national movement, or movements – prominent as a confederation of workers' societies in one area, as a league of rural banks in another, as an alliance for local elections elsewhere. It crusaded joyfully for the '*reconquista*' of Italian society, while still remaining firmly committed to Papal claims and to 'intransigence' on the Roman question. Perhaps its greatest achievement was in creating a 'Catholic sub-culture', distinct from the established order.

Yet the Catholic social movement had its weaknesses. It was weak in most of the South and some regions of Central Italy. It made little headway among industrial workers, or among landless labourers; and it was riven by factions. The most open split was between the 'old intransigents', who insisted on the Roman question and engaged in 'traditional' activity (charities, education, etc.), and the younger men who were more concerned with the social question, including trade unionism and new kinds of militancy. But there were plenty of other issues in dispute too. If the '*Opera*' admitted the State's right to intervene in the economy in order to prevent abuses and exploitation, then what was the sense in denying the legitimacy of the Italian State, or in abstaining at general elections? Similarly, if free trade produced all the evils denounced in the Papal encyclicals, it seemed odd to refuse votes to candidates pledged to protective tariffs. Hence by 1896 even Don Davide Albertario, the editor of the 'intransigent' *Osservatore Cattolico* in Milan, was urging that Catholics should vote at parliamentary elections, and hoping to become a deputy himself. As the '*Opera*' became more lay and more 'social', it seemed likely to evolve into some kind of a political party. Yet if it did that, would the clergy and hierarchy be able to retain control of it?

However, these splits were not yet too evident, and the rapid spread of the Catholic movement seemed a real political threat to the Liberal Establishment. In 1897 the government of di Rudiní decided to act. On 18 September the Prime Minister instructed Prefects throughout the country to crack down on Catholic associations and to ban meetings whenever there was a danger to public order. On 8 October he again urged the Prefects to act, for clerical associations had often expressed 'views contrary to the free institutions that govern us, and even in favour of the destruction of the Italian State. These guilty and insane statements cannot and must not be tolerated any longer.'[8]

The Prefects responded zealously. Hundreds of Catholic associations were dissolved, journals were banned, meetings prohibited. In December Zanardelli, perhaps the most anticlerical of the leading Liberal politicians, became Minister of Justice, and carried on the good work. All this was *before* the crisis year of 1898. When, in that year, bread riots spread up the peninsula, and when the fiftieth anniversary of the 1848 revolution in Rome was celebrated by anticlericals throughout Italy, passions were inflamed still further. The Milan riots were the last straw. On 9 May Don Albertario was arrested; on 27 May di Rudiní ordered the Prefects to dissolve all 'subversive' Catholic organizations, including economic and educational ones. All the Catholic dailies were suppressed, as were many weeklies; 2,500 parish committees, 600 youth sections and hundreds of rural banks were dissolved. The whole Catholic network of social, educational and economic bodies, so laboriously built up over the previous decades, was crushed.

Yet the clerical response was surprisingly muted. Paganuzzi, the President of the 'Opera', protested that Catholics were law-abiding citizens, not rebels or 'subversives'. Pope Leo XIII took the same line. His 'Letter to the Clergy and People of Italy' was far from being a cry of protest; indeed, it could reasonably be interpreted as a conciliatory gesture. The dissolution of Catholic associations, he claimed, was an 'undeserved and unjust measure . . . the community is being deprived of a powerful conservative force, since the organization itself and the spread of its ideas were a bulwark against the subversive theories of Socialism and anarchy'.[9]

In other words, the Vatican (and the 'old' leaders of the 'Opera') were coming round. They had had a whiff of grape-shot, and they realized that there was something to be said for 'bourgeois liberties' after all. They worried about the Catholics being left isolated, possibly facing an 'anticlerical alliance' of Liberals, Radicals and reformist Socialists. It was far more prudent for the Church to emphasize the social danger, and offer the more Right-wing Liberals some useful support in the struggle against Socialism.

Thus the persecution of 1897–98 had very important results for the Catholic movement, and for Italian politics generally. Traditional 'intransigence' was quietly dropped; and in return the new government of General Pelloux allowed most of the Catholic associations to be refounded. Italian governments thereafter could count on tacit Catholic support, and in the next few years the '*non expedit*' was gradually abandoned. So, too, was the *Opera dei Congressi* (see §7.3). Social activity continued, of course, but Catholic politics moved into an era of 'clerico-moderate' alliances at both national and local level; the Catholic threat had apparently been 'absorbed'.

5.7 THE ITALIAN SOCIALIST PARTY

There were various working-class movements in Italy before 1890 (see §4.3). They were all jealous of their independence, and they were all committed to different ideologies and aims. Government repression in the late 1880s greatly weakened all of them; but it also increased the tendency for working-class 'economic' organizations – co-operatives, 'leagues of resistance', mutual-aid societies – to press for political liberties and 'legal' reforms, so that their normal peaceful activities could safely continue. It also led some 'bourgeois intellectuals', like the young Milanese lawyer Filippo Turati, to have a greater interest in social problems and a greater sympathy for labour. This intellectual support was to prove a vital factor. Turati and his friends in Milan founded a journal, *Cuore e Critica* – later renamed *Critica Sociale* – which rapidly became required reading for progressive intellectuals. In the 1890s it was fashionable to be a Marxist of the 'evolutionist', positivist kind, to deplore the evils of early industrialization, to press for social reforms and demand the right to engage in 'legal' political activity.

Engaging in legal political activity meant, however, having a legal party to work in; and so Turati and his colleagues set themselves the task of forming an Italian 'Social Democratic Party' – a party that would be legal and reformist, would have mass working-class support, and yet would be quite distinct from the older middle-class Radical movements that the Italian Workers' Party (POI) so much detested. For Turati – as for Crispi – the model was Germany, where the SPD won 20 per cent of the vote at the 1890 *Reichstag* elections. An Italian party might do no less, by proclaiming Socialism with a German face.

And so Turati's group in Milan wooed the Northern workers. In July 1889 he founded the Milanese Socialist League, open to workers and intellectuals but not to anarchists. The League rapidly became influential in Milan, partly because two months earlier some of the Italian Workers' Party leaders had been arrested; the POI had been forced to move its headquarters to Alessandria, in Piedmont. This move left a gap in Milan, and Turati seized his opportunity. He was helped also by the split in the Republican ranks in 1889–90, when the 'collectivists' founded what was virtually a 'Republican-Socialist' movement within the workers' associations. Even so, Turati had an uphill struggle. Many POI members were hostile to interfering intellectuals, and suspicious of anything that smacked of 'political' activity. The POI still existed, after all. It was a loose federation of workers' 'economic' associations, and many Lombard workers wanted to keep it that way.

In August 1891 Turati convened an 'Italian Workers' Congress' in Milan. The delegates were mainly Lombard, but there were some from most regions of Northern and Central Italy, and from every persuasion – Socialist, POI, Radical, Republican, anarchist. The congress approved a motion calling for social reforms, e.g. the eight-hour day. It also set up a committee to organize, within a year, the founding congress of a new 'Party of the Workers'. After many vicissitudes and intrigues, this latter congress finally met in mid-August 1892, in Genoa. The city was chosen because it was celebrating the 400th anniversary of Columbus' discovery of America, and the Italian railways offered cheap fares to anyone wishing to attend. Over 200 delegates, representing 324 associations, came to the Genoa Congress; 80 of them were anarchists. Most were from Lombardy or the Po valley, but some came from the Sicilian *Fasci* and others from Tuscany, Apulia and, of course, Romagna. The 1892 Congress was not the first national 'labour' congress, nor was it even the first to approve a vaguely 'Socialist' programme – the Milan Congress had done that a year earlier – but none the less it is usually regarded as the foundation of the Italian Socialist Party, because it was in Genoa that the acrimonious split between 'Socialists' and 'anarchists' took place. By the second day, in fact, two congresses were being held. The 'majority' – 197 societies – approved a 'Socialist' programme drawn up by Turati. It called for an 'economic struggle' by organized workers, to win immediate advantages; and also a 'more general struggle', to win control of the 'public powers' in the State and local government. Meanwhile the anarchists and some of the POI delegates – representing 97 societies – had formed a rival, and short-lived, Party of the Workers. This party was also committed to 'economic' action, but was opposed to fighting elections and did not expect reforms from the bourgeois State. Some delegates were reluctant to join either group; Costa and his Romagna followers joined Turati's party only a year later. Neither party was ideologically homogeneous. Turati's party contained 'collectivist Republicans' and some Lombard POI men, as well as the Milanese positivist Marxists and a few ex-Radicals; the rival party was divided between intransigent POI members and anarchists of different persuasions. These differences persisted over thirty years: although the basic 'Genoa' division between 'Socialists' and 'anarcho-syndicalists' remained valid, each group was itself divided on ideology, strategy and tactics.

Ideology was the key issue. The Genoa Congress discussed programmes, not organization; the initiative remained with the intellectuals. The 'Turatian' 'Party of the Workers' – renamed the 'Italian Socialist Party' (PSI) in 1895 – was based essentially on the Genoa Programme, and it was the Programme which provided much of the moral fervour and idealism of early Italian Socialism. Indeed, the PSI soon became almost a 'religious' movement. The party's preachers and evangelizers spread the Gospel among the peasants of the Po valley; its intellectuals refined and disputed the articles of the Creed; and it even had a Pope, Filippo Turati, with all the qualities of a great pontiff – personal saintliness, dedication to his followers' welfare, and subtle political skills.

What the party lacked, as yet, was an organization. The 'Statute' remained that of the old POI. In other words, the party was a loose association, attempting to co-ordinate a couple of hundred local 'leagues of resistance', co-operatives and so forth. Individual membership was permitted, but the basic structure was that of a federation of disparate groups. These rules made it vulnerable. When Crispi dissolved many of the Socialist and labour organizations in 1894, in the wave of repression that followed the crushing of the Sicilian *Fasci*, the party was threatened with collapse. The Third Congress, held clandestinely at Parma in January 1895, therefore decided to restructure the party on the basis of individual membership. When the repression was relaxed, the new structure remained. Soon the PSI developed all the 'German' features of a modern party – individual membership cards, a network of local sections, internal electoral procedures, regular congresses. By 1897 it had over 27,000 members, and the party ran a daily newspaper, *Avanti!*; even the title was taken from the German model, *Vorwärts*. The national newspaper helped in the vital task of uniting the party, of overcoming local traditions, and of giving full publicity to the parliamentary struggles of the late 1890s.

Thus the Socialist Party after 1895 no longer depended necessarily on workers' or peasants' 'economic' organizations, on the co-operatives, mutual-aid societies and 'leagues of resistance'. Local party branches might easily come to be dominated by a leading local 'intellectual' – lawyer, teacher, journalist and the like – and Socialist activists might fight their political struggles more or less independently of the 'economic' bodies. In many areas the party became an electoral machine, run by a relatively small number of activists. It was a fairly successful machine. By 1900 the Socialist Party secured 216,000 votes in a general election, and returned 32 deputies, nearly all of them middle-class intellectuals. Meanwhile the 'economic' organizations fought their own battles, without reference to the party as a whole. Few working-class leaders (and even fewer peasants) found their way into Socialist *Party* politics. In any case, the PSI was founded before there was a fully established trade union movement, indeed before Italy's industrial revolution.

However, the distinction between party and economic organizations was never quite so absolute in practice as on paper. The co-operatives and peasant leagues were themselves often run by 'bourgeois intellectuals'. There was also the possibility that the 'economic organizations' might use the party and its deputies to secure concessions from central or local government. This development became part of the 'Giolittian system' of government after 1900 (see §7.1); it clearly implied a 'subordinate' role for the party, which would be 'integrated' into the machinery of the Liberal State. Even in the repressive 1890s, there were some occasions when Socialist co-operatives won public works contracts in Northern Italy or the Po valley. Arguably, too, the strength of the Socialist labourers' leagues and co-operatives in the Po valley blinded the party to conditions elsewhere in Italy, or to the need to win support among other agricultural classes. And there was very little Socialist activity among the small landowners, a class whom the Socialists regarded as doomed to disappear.

The main 'economic' innovations of the 1890s were the Chambers of Labour, another good example of how the 'economic' organizations influenced the party. The 'Chambers' were founded to co-ordinate the various workers' associations and leagues in each city or province, and to act as labour-exchanges. Their main concern was to protect employment and to place workers in jobs, although they also collected funds for workers on strike and watched over apprenticeships, arbitration procedures and the like. They were nearly all in Northern or Central Italy, they often received subsidies or free accommodation from the local municipality, and they often acted to prevent overt labour disputes. In short, they were usually conciliatory bodies, seeking better conditions for their members. They were *not* 'resistance' organizations, as the POI's leagues had been. Even so, they sometimes supported strikes, and so most of them were dissolved in di Rudiní's repression of 1897–98. The subsequent rioting in 1898 convinced many Liberals that the Chambers of Labour were useful bodies which helped to maintain labour discipline; it was dangerous to shut them down.

Thus the Socialist Party, founded at Genoa on an ideological basis and led by middle-class intellectuals committed to a programme of evolutionary Marxism, was flanked by 'reformist' economic organizations that might easily become integrated into bourgeois society. And there were forces pushing the party itself the same way. The PSI's early years were much influenced by successive periods of official persecution – Crispi's in 1894–95, di Rudiní's in 1897–98, Pelloux' in 1899–1900. At times of repression, the PSI naturally allied with the Radicals and democrats, even eventually with the 'Left wing' of the Liberals. Despite the occasional rhetoric, the PSI leaders in the 1890s were normally 'collaborationist' – and Engels himself, in his famous letter of 26 January 1894 to Anna Kuliscioff, approved the policy of allying with bourgeois Radicals for bourgeois reforms. The party gradually became more committed to the values of parliamentary democracy. Turati himself joined with the Radicals to found the 'League for the Defence of Liberty' against Crispi in November 1894; and the Socialists and Radicals formed an alliance for the local elections in Milan in February 1895 – a precursor of later national alliances. Although the party fought general elections as a separate party, its programme of basic economic and political reforms was mainly the standard Radical package – universal suffrage, abolition of censorship, legal and political emancipation of women, progressive income tax, the eight-hour day; and indeed Socialists were permitted to vote for a non-Socialist candidate at the second (run-off) ballot provided he supported civil liberties. The Socialist leader Filippo Turati was an ex-democrat, took a 'positivist', 'evolutionary' view of social and political progress, was ignorant of the South and its problems, and was very Milanese in his ideas and aspirations. So, too, was Felice Cavallotti, the leading Radical of the day, and the man who led the various 'moral' campaigns of these years. By 1898 the PSI was an important part of the parliamentary coalition against the government. The party's role was to lead the working and peasant masses into their rightful place in society, and to defend bourgeois liberties.

5.8 THE RADICALS AND REPUBLICANS

But the chief fighters for freedom were the Radicals. The 1890s was their golden age, and their trump card was 'morality'. The Radicals denounced the bank scandals, and made a great fuss about other people's sexual irregularities – especially the king's open relationships with his mistresses, or Crispi's alleged bigamy. Many of them were pro-French, and therefore hostile to the Triple Alliance; and virtually all of them were 'anti-Africa' and hostile to high military spending. As for economic policy, the Radicals were very close to the free-trade liberal school: protectionism in general, and the 1887 tariff in particular, were regarded as anathema. Tariffs pandered to selfish vested interests, at the expense of the general good. In general, the less the State intervened in economic matters the better; for the Crispian State was oppressive, and the only way to avoid corruption was to reduce its role.

In May 1890 Felice Cavallotti convened a great democratic congress at Rome, at which the famous 'Pact of Rome' was agreed. The 'Pact' rejected ideas of insurrection or of direct action, and argued that parliament should be made to work more effectively. Parliament should be convened whenever fifty deputies demanded it; deputies should be paid; various civil rights, such as free speech, a free press, and freedom of assembly, should be guaranteed; the judiciary should be independent; there should be administrative decentralization, and autonomy for local government; primary education should be free, compulsory and lay; military spending should be cut, and the army gradually transformed into a people's militia; social legislation should be passed, with guarantees on female and child labour, pensions, etc.; there should be no tariffs or other taxes on basic foods; above all, article 5 of the *Statuto*, which gave the king the right to declare war and to make treaties of peace, alliance and commerce, should be abolished. These issues remained the Radical programme for many years to come. Most of them concerned the working of the political institutions rather than, say, economic or social arrangements. The Radicals, indeed, demanded changes in the three key institutions of Liberal Italy – the Crown, the army, and the bureaucracy.

Much the same programme was also adopted by the Republicans. The Mazzinian 'Pact of Brotherhood' was dissolved in 1893, and a younger generation of Republicans refounded themselves as a party – the Italian Republican Party – in April 1895. The PRI was committed to fighting elections to the king's parliament, and elected twenty-eight deputies in 1900; and it, too, paid much attention to regionalism, local government, bureaucracy, the courts and the tax system. However, the Republicans were more 'intransigent' than the Radicals, and less willing to support governments during the occasional periods of Liberal reform. They also naturally tended to see the Crown as the bulwark of the hated political system, and fiercely attacked its power to determine foreign policy, to declare war, and to dissolve parliament. Like the Radicals, the Republicans were a minority group: only in the Romagna did they enjoy significant working-class or artisan support.

Throughout the 1890s the Radicals and Republicans kept up the pressure. Parliament was the main platform for their denunciations; and so the maintenance of parliamentary freedoms – questions to ministers, committees of inquiry, debates on motions of censure – was vital to them. They also relied heavily on journalism, especially on the *Secolo* in Milan, and they were formidable pamphleteers. Thus press freedom, too, mattered more to the Radicals than to any other political grouping. In 1895, with the bank scandals and Crispi's prorogation of parliament, the 'moral question' became the major domestic political issue of the day. Cavallotti published his most famous pamphlet, the 'Letter to the Honest Men of all Parties'. The 'Letter' denounced Crispi for selling honours and receiving bank 'loans'. The Radical campaign certainly contributed to a shift of opinion during 1895–96, although Crispi's fall was caused eventually by the Italian defeat at Adowa.

The Radicals were always a mere 'handful of officers without soldiers'.[10] They never won a real electoral victory. Even in 1900 there were only thirty-four Radical deputies returned, together with twenty-eight Republicans – although the Radicals and their allies had more success in local elections after the broader suffrage was introduced there in 1889. There were just not enough enlightened Northern bourgeois, or artisans, to provide mass backing for the Radicals' ideas. Yet during the 1890s the Establishment was genuinely frightened of them, as Farini's diary shows. The Radicals had a concrete and realistic programme which threatened some of the ordinary assumptions of conventional politics, including the need for a strong army and the Triple Alliance. They represented, if not an alternative government, at least a credible alternative mode of governing, one in which the role of the Crown would be greatly curtailed; and, of all the 'subversives', they were the ones closest to the parliamentary system, and most able to influence some of the Liberal politicians like Zanardelli. In a period when mass parties were just beginning, and when effective political debate was still restricted to relatively small groups of enlightened gentlemen, the Radicals were a real threat. Above all, the Radicals seemed to represent progress – modern, lay, bourgeois ideas, geared to the developing industrial needs of Northern Italy, rather than to the corrupt Court intrigues of Rome and the parasitic colonialism of the South. No wonder Crispi and di Rudiní worried about the loyalty of Milan; and no wonder the influence of the Radicals was greatest precisely when the 'crisis of the State' was most acute.

5.9 THE DEBATE ON THE STATE, 1896–1900

The lengthy political crisis of the 1890s naturally led to much debate among the beleaguered Liberals. Parliamentary government was not working well; but was there any alternative? Many conservatives thought that there was. In 1893 Ruggiero Bonghi called on the king to exert 'a high moral surveillance over the State' and over parliament; Pasquale Villari, too, appealed to the monarchy to unite the Italian people once again in the hour of danger, and called for an 'honest government above party'.[11] In 1895, as we have seen, Crispi had governed for many months without a factious and inquisitive parliament. In 1897 came the most famous contribution on the conservative side, Sidney Sonnino's article 'Let us return to the *Statuto*'. He repeated the familiar anti-parliamentary arguments – the deputies' corruption, their obsession with local interests, their 'interference' in administration, etc. – and he emphasized also that a parliamentary regime in Italy must necessarily mean unwelcome concessions to Catholics and Socialists. He concluded that the only remedy was a return to the strict letter of the *Statuto* (Constitution), in which the Crown would have a far more active role. 'Your Majesty . . . You alone are responsible for the executive power. You alone are responsible for the nomination or dismissal of Ministers, who must countersign and answer publicly for Your acts of government. The nation looks to You, and has trust in You.'[12]

Sonnino's article caused a great fuss. It looked like, and probably was, yet another attempt to prod King Humbert into action. That was silly, for the king was not particularly sympathetic to the 'conservative' cause, at least until 1898–99. When Farini had mentioned, in November 1893, that Humbert might choose a Prime Minister irrespective of parliament's wishes, the king had soon interrrupted him: 'I am deaf in that ear!..'[13] Sonnino's arguments simply showed up the weakness of the conservatives. They were unnecessarily frightened of the Republicans and Socialists; they were even frightened of the Vatican, or at least unwilling to come to terms with the clericals; and they were obsessed by High Politics and the need for sound administration. The patriotic appeal was all they had. No wonder they turned to the Crown. They failed to realize that parliament's essential role was (and is) to legitimize government action and make it more acceptable. By attempting to undermine parliament, the conservatives undermined the effective government that they claimed to favour.

The 'constitutionalists' counter-argument to Sonnino was that the 'subversive' parties were not as subversive as all that. They could easily be 'absorbed' into the parliamentary system, given time and a few concessions. But it was vital to keep parliament functioning, so that this process could occur, and so that legitimate interests could be represented and conciliated. 'Interference' in administration was a small price to pay if it avoided disorder and revolution. In any case, if the monarchy tried to rule as well as reign, it would bring about its own collapse and perhaps that of united Italy.

The conflict between the two views was particularly evident in 1899, during the great parliamentary row over the so-called 'political provisions'. The 'provisions' were a series of bills on public order – prohibiting strikes in the public services, bringing railwaymen and postal workers under military discipline in some circumstances, tightening up the laws on the press, public meetings, etc. They had originally been put to parliament by the di Rudiní government in June 1898, and were inherited by the new government that General Pelloux formed after the Milan riots. Pelloux was a Savoyard Liberal who initially did nothing about them; on the contrary, he lifted martial law and permitted a free press once more. But in the spring of 1899 he reshuffled his government. The new Cabinet was far more conservative, and the 'provisions' appeared once more. The Radicals and Socialists started a filibuster: points of order, endless speeches, constant calls for a count to check the quorum and so forth. Since there was no guillotine procedure or time-limit on debates, the filibuster was successful.

On 22 June the government's patience snapped. Since the 'provisions' could not be pushed through parliament, some of them – e.g. on the press, on public meetings and on associations – were issued as a royal decree, to take effect a month later whether parliament approved or not. This was unconstitutional, and prudent men were horrified. The President of the Senate lamented into his diary 'so now the *Statuto* is being trampled on, just as many conservatives have been demanding and wanting for so many years . . . long live the "Return to the *Statuto*" '.[14] Farini was right to be alarmed. The government was breaking all the rules of the game and exposing the Crown to danger. A week later the parliamentary session ended, after further scenes of uproar during which the voting urns were overthrown.

Clearly the government's days were numbered. Pelloux' parliamentary support began to vanish; Zanardelli and Giolitti went into open opposition. In February 1900 the Court of Cassation declared the decree-law invalid. Pelloux had to start all over again. He brought the 'provisions' back to the Chamber, and filibustering resumed. By this time the Establishment had convinced itself that parliament must have a guillotine procedure if it were ever to work 'properly'; Westminster, after all, had had one since 1881. Sonnino told di Rudiní that 'for me the important question now is that of procedure, the "provisions" are very secondary'.[15] So a guillotine motion was introduced, and there were further unseemly rows. Eventually the new procedure was approved, after the 'Extreme Left' (Socialists, Republicans and Radicals) and Zanardelli's group of 'constitutional Liberals' had walked out. The government then promptly withdrew the original bill on the 'provisions'; they did not seem necessary, once parliament had a guillotine procedure. But the Left stayed away from the Chamber. Pelloux decided to dissolve parliament and appeal to the country. The ensuing elections were a victory for the Left. The Socialists, Radicals and Republicans won 96 seats between them, 28 more than in 1897. The whole Left, including the 'Constitutional Liberals', won almost as many votes as the government's supporters, and far more in Northern Italy. A fortnight later Pelloux resigned.

Superficially, the results of the parliamentary dramas of 1899–1900 were negligible. The 'provisions' had not been approved; and after the elections parliamentary procedure was soon changed back to the old system. But the political results were extremely important. Sonnino and strong government were discredited. Zanardelli and Giolitti had allied with the Extreme Left, had won a famous victory, and soon came back to power pledged to more 'conciliatory' policies. The lesson of the 1899–1900 rows was that governments could not govern without being attentive to parliament. Indeed, it is noticeable how very 'parliamentary' the battles had been. Although the 'subversives' were leading the campaign, there were very few popular demonstrations, no petitions, and no disorders. Men had rioted for bread in 1898; they did not riot for liberty in 1899. Perhaps these issues were of interest only to the educated élite – an ominous lesson for the future. Or perhaps the lesson was rather different. The 'real country' could get rid of a repressive government just as easily through parliamentary agitations and elections, as she could by rioting. At any rate, that was the lesson that most of the 'subversives' were anxious to draw.

5.10 CONCLUSION

A month later King Humbert was assassinated at Monza by an anarchist, Gaetano Bresci. It was the culmination of a decade of riot and 'subversion'. Yet the 'subversives' were horrified. Church bells tolled throughout the land, and bishops invited mayors and Prefects to attend requiem masses: 'in those circumstances patriotic and religious sentiments were united in common agreement'.[16] The Socialist paper *Avanti!* appeared with black margins, and called the assassin a 'criminal madman'. Even the Republicans denounced the killing, perhaps forgetting their support for Orsini and Oberdank earlier in the century. The chorus was symbolic. By 1900 the main 'subversive' groups had been 'absorbed' into the system and 'constitutionalized' – not fully, of course, but to a far greater degree than had seemed possible ten years earlier. They had even become the defenders of liberty and the Constitution, against many 'conservative' groups.

REFERENCES

1. A. Gerschenkron, *Economic Backwardness in Historical Perspective*, Harvard University Press 1962, p. 76.
2. E. Vitale, *La Riforma degli Istituti di Emissione e gli Scandali Bancari in Italia*, Rome 1972, iii, p. 51.
3. Pareto's letter to Colajanni 25 Aug. 1893, in S.M. Ganci (ed.), *Democrazia e Socialismo in Italia: Carteggi di Napoleone Colajanni*, Milan 1959, p. 355.
4. di Rudini's words as noted on 19 March 1891 by D. Farini in his *Diario di Fine Secolo*, i, Rome 1961, 13.
5. S. Romano, *Crispi-Progetto per una Dittatura*, Milan 1973, p. 196.
6. D. Farini, *Diario . . .*, i (22 Dec. 1892), 157.
7. The 'Milan Programme' is given in G. De Rosa, *I Partiti Politici in Italia*, Bergamo 1972, pp. 164–70.
8. G. Spadolini, *L'Opposizione Cattolica da Porta Pia al '98*, Florence 1954, p. 442; G. De Rosa, *Storia del Movimento Cattolico in Italia*, i, Bari 1966, pp. 310–11.
9. De Rosa, *Storia del Movimento . . .*, p. 326; Spadolini, *L'Opposizione Cattolica . . .* p. 476.
10. R. Michels, *Il Proletariato e la Borghesia nel Movimento Socialista Italiano*, Turin 1908, p. 239.
11. R. Bonghi, 'L'Ufficio del Principe in uno Stato libero', in *Nuova Antologia*, 15 Jan. 1893, pp. 340–55; P. Villari, 'Dove andiamo?', in *Nuova Antologia*, 1 Nov. 1893, pp. 5–24.
12. Un Deputato (S. Sonnino), 'Torniamo allo Statuto', in *Nuova Antologia*, 1 Jan. 1897.

13. D. Farini, *Diario . . .*, i (27 Nov. 1893), 340.

14. *idem*, ii (23 June 1899), 1506.

15. Sonnino to di Rudiní, 23 March 1900, quoted in S. Sonnino, *Diario*, i (ed. B. Brown), Bari 1972, 435.

16. L. Vitali (ed.), *L'Episcopato Italiano in morte di S.M. Umberto I*, Milan 1900, p. vii.

CHAPTER SIX

The first 'economic miracle': industrialization and the economy, 1896–1914

The political troubles of the 1890s had, of course, been linked to Italy's real economic difficulties between 1887 and 1895 (see §5.2). In the early twentieth century the political scene was transformed; and this, in turn, was partly a reflection of the country's rapid and unexpected economic progress after 1896. In this chapter I will discuss the growth of the Italian economy between 1896 and the First World War, and how it was that Italy developed a particular kind of industrial economy.

6.1 INDUSTRY

There is no difficulty in showing that Italy experienced a spurt of economic growth after 1896. National income as a whole rose from over 61 billion lire in 1895 to over 92 billion lire in 1911–15, at constant 1938 prices; per head, from 1,888 lire in 1891–95 to 2,478 lire in 1911–15. Gerschenkron's figures for six key industries also indicate rapid growth between 1896 and 1908 (although not later). He gives *annual* growth figures of 12.4 per cent for iron and steel, 12.2 per cent for engineering, and 13.7 per cent for the chemical industry.[1] More recently a group of economic statisticians led by Giorgio Fuà have estimated that the value of manufacturing industrial production rose from 11.2 billion lire (at 1938 prices) in 1896 to 20.6 billion lire in 1908, and to 22.1 billion lire in 1913.[2] Moreover, there was a perceptible shift from 'traditional' textile or food-processing activities towards 'newer' engineering, metal-making and chemicals, which by 1911–15 accounted for over 30 per cent of all industrial production. This was also a shift towards heavy industry, producing capital goods. One should not exaggerate. Italy in 1914 was still '*Italietta*', an agricultural economy, and her most important industry was still cotton; it was the First World War that provided the real stimulus to the engineering industries. Even so, the industrial expansion of 1896–1908 was impressive, whether we call it an 'industrial revolution', a 'take-off', a 'big spurt', or just an intense phase of the 'normal' business cycle.

119

Why did this expansion occur? Historians have suggested many possible explanations, ranging from the long-term effects of the 1887 protective tariff to the role of the new 'German' banks, from the advent of unexpectedly sound government finance to cheap energy, from mass emigration to the rise of a new industry, car manufacture. Perhaps the fundamental divide is between 'Liberal' historians (e.g. Romeo, Gerschenkron, Fenoaltea) who emphasize market, technological or financial influences, and 'Statist' historians, more concerned with the State's role in subsidizing and protecting particular sectors. The arguments are inconclusive, for the available data are as inadequate as the available theories. Certainly Italian economic growth was part of an international business cycle. By 1896 the world 'agricultural crisis' was over. Prices had begun to rise again, markets were expanding, and investors everywhere were looking for opportunities. It seems safe to conclude, rather tamely, that economic expansion was the fortuitous result of many factors combining, and between them creating one of the most vital, and fragile, factors of all: confidence.

The development of hydro-electricity is one obvious explanation. Industrial growth elsewhere had been based on coal, but Italy had virtually none. Her industries had always had to import it at great cost: the price at the Italian factory gate was sometimes eight times what English factories paid. By the mid-1890s it was possible to 'transport' energy cheaply, and this meant that hydro-electric power from the Alpine valleys could be used throughout Northern Italy. Milan was the second city in the world to have electric street lighting. She also had electric trams by 1893; and industry followed suit. In 1898 Italy had 50,000 kilowatts of hydro-electric capacity, by 1911 she had nearly 500,000 kilowatts, by 1914 1 million kilowatts; 90 per cent of it was used by industry. Coal imports none the less continued to rise, from 4 million tonnes in 1896 to nearly 11 million tonnes in 1914, but the cost of imported fuel no longer made Italian engineering uncompetitive in world markets. Hydro-electricity was a great boost to confidence and to investment. A native energy source had been harnessed at last; and it would never run out.

The development of hydro-electric power naturally required capital – over 500 million lire by 1914. Here government intervention and private initiative were both important. The government thoughtfully nationalized the railways in 1905 and compensated the former shareholders; so they moved their money thankfully into electricity companies. The leading electric companies – Società Alta Italia, Edison, Negri, Officine Elettriche Genovesi – also received finance from several new 'mixed' banks, founded in Italy in the mid-1890s. The old Italian banking system had crashed in 1893–94 (see §5.3); the new 'mixed' banks replaced it. Most of them were foreign in origin, and perhaps in expertise. The most famous, the *Banca Commerciale Italiana*, was a 'German' bank founded in 1894 with German and Austrian finance, and the other new banks – the *Credito Italiano*, founded in 1895, the *Società Bancaria Italiana* (later *Banca di Sconto*) founded in 1905 – also relied heavily on German, Swiss or French capital and techniques. The other major 'new' bank, the *Banco di Roma*, was linked closely to the Vatican, and so it, too, had many international connections. The essence of the new 'mixed' banks' activity was channelling depositors' money into large-scale enterprises, i.e. turning savings into investment. It was all a great boost to the stock exchange, and the banks' underwriting meant that industry could usually raise money from the markets without trouble. The new banks also took the initiative in founding and helping to manage new industries, e.g. shipbuilding and chemicals. Indeed, Gerschenkron has argued that the industrial upsurge of 1896–1908 was mainly brought about by the banks: their role in remedying the weak national capital market, their nursing of infant industries, and their zest for technological and managerial innovation, were all vital. This was particularly true of the electric power industry. The *Banca Commerciale* created a special holding company, which controlled many of the leading firms, and the bank always insisted on a seat on the board.

Even so, the new banks' achievements should be kept in perspective. Most savings still went to local savings banks and co-operatives, and so were not available for this kind of investment. The small saver was not exposed to the risks of the new industrial projects, nor did he enjoy the benefits. Moreover, the 'new' banking techniques were not all that new. The old banks, especially the *Credito Mobiliare*, had also been active in financing industry. In any case, banks by themselves could do little, unless there were a high demand for capital, and few alternative sources. The real novelty was the fact that profitable investment in certain capital-intensive industries was now possible, thanks to world economic expansion, State protection and improved hydro-electric technology.

The banks were not free to invest as they liked, or wherever the profit lay. The *Banca Commerciale*, for example, was initially managed by three Jewish foreigners. Such men were vulnerable, and could not easily refuse loans to the politically and industrially powerful. Moreover, the bank had 'inherited' most of its customers from the old banks: Terni, for example, had to be supported, whatever the bankers thought of its prospects. And, being a 'foreign' bank, the *Commerciale*'s managers also had to conform to pressures from abroad – for diversification of risks, for high liquidity ratios, for financial orthodoxy and caution. They were pulled two ways. They had to make some 'political' loans, and they also had to look for investments that were acceptably orthodox. Hydro-electric schemes and electric companies were the ideal answer to their problems. No wonder they poured money into them. They were lucky that it turned out to have been well spent.

After the brief economic crisis of 1907, however, the *Banca Commerciale* became more deeply drawn into various dubious political ventures, especially the rescuing of heavy but lame industrial ducks. Its liquidity began to suffer. By this time, too, only a minority of the managers were 'Germans'; and the majority of shares were owned by Italians. So the pressures changed. The bank became more 'national' and more of a political milch-cow, closely linked to the Prime Minister Giolitti. It resolved its new set of conflicting pressures by financing naval and munitions deals: 'on the eve of the war, the *Commerciale* credit was largely geared to military contracts'.[3] The 'German' bank financed the growth of the Italian arms industry, which was used against Germany in 1916.

The banks had to operate, therefore, in harmony with the politicians. The State was paramount in financial matters. Much of Italy's economic success after 1896 is attributable to the State's action, or lack of action. The end of the Ethiopian War in itself relieved a huge strain on resources and morale. And Sonnino, Treasury Minister between 1894 and 1896, reordered public finances. He imposed new taxes – an extra 100 million lire p.a. – and cut public spending. He also imposed income tax on the interest paid by government stocks, but since the net return (4 per cent) on Italian bonds was still higher than on most other governments' stocks, people still bought them. The budget deficit was sharply reduced, from 174 million lire in 1893–94 to 36 million lire in 1896–97. By 1898–99 there was a surplus, and deficits did not appear again for another eleven years. Healthy State finances made it possible to spend more on public works; these in turn stimulated the market and encouraged investment. Sonnino also strengthened the powers of the Bank of Italy. This central bank, founded by Giolitti in 1893, acted closely with the Treasury and issued the bulk of the paper circulation, thus regulating the money supply as well as rediscounting bills and acting as lender of last resort to the other banks. The post of Governor of the Bank of Italy soon became the key economic job in the country.

In short, after 1894 the State contributed to a general confidence in money and in the banks' continuing solvency. Confidence in the lira also depended on the balance of payments. Here, too, Italy was fortunate. These were the years of massive emigration, especially to the Argentine and the USA, and the emigrants sent foreign money home, partly to support relatives and partly to buy land. It amounted to well over 300 million lire a year. Together with tourism and shipping revenue, emigrants' remittances enabled Italy to run a considerable trade deficit with impunity, and to import machinery and raw materials for her growing industries. By 1912–13 imports exceeded exports by 34 per cent, yet the balance of payments was still in surplus. There was no need for credit restrictions or cuts in public spending, no need for 'stop-go' policies to 'save the lira'. Italy may not have enjoyed export-led growth, but she did at least avoid import-led stagnation.

Much of the argument among historians about Italy's economic growth has revolved around the tariff of 1887. As I have shown (see §5.2), the short-term effects of the tariff were very unfortunate, both for Italy's agriculture and for most of her industries. Yet after 1896, with the tariff still in force, imports resumed at their old levels, and the economy expanded. Was it despite the tariff, or because of it, or did the tariff not make much difference either way? It seems that what really hit Italy after 1887 was the disruption of her trade with France; once that quarrel was settled, in 1898, there were no other major obstacles to business confidence. On the contrary, a series of commercial treaties with particular countries helped mitigate the tariff, guarantee outlets and boost trade. It also seems largely agreed that the tariff helped to protect certain industries, notably steelmaking, shipbuilding and cotton, from what might otherwise have been too severe competition. However, arguably these sectors absorbed resources which might have been more profitably used elsewhere. The engineering industry, for example, had to use dear Italian steel, and its chances of exporting were thereby reduced. Fenoaltea, indeed, has argued that if the engineering industry had retained its export outlets, it might have maintained its growth at the 20 per cent p.a. level of 1880–87, and been five times as large in 1913 as it in fact was.[4] But it is foolish to project early growth rates indefinitely, and there is no way of quantifying what the effects of cheaper steel might have been. There was, in fact, much dumping of German and French iron and steel in Italy, much to the annoyance of the native producers. Certainly the iron and steel tariff did not abort the engineering industry. Motor vehicles, railway equipment and textile machinery remained in steady demand. Gerschenkron, himself a leading advocate of the view that the steel tariff harmed Italian engineering, writes that 'as far as the period 1896–1908 is concerned it is engineering and metalmaking that are mainly, if not solely, responsible for the big industrial movement of those years'.[5]

Thus the steel industry was, and is, at the centre of the tariff controversy. Pig-iron production rose from 20,000 tonnes in 1900 to 430,000 tonnes in 1913; steel from 140,000 to 930,000 tonnes. But it was not enough. Despite all her efforts, Italy never built up a fully adequate heavy industrial base. Iron and steel imports remained high, despite the tariff; in 1913 221,000 tonnes of pig-iron were imported, and 362,000 tonnes of scrap. Italy still had to rely on foreign suppliers for basic industrial necessities, for iron and steel as well as for coal and (later) oil.

The steel industry was, therefore, not so important economically as all that; but it was very important politically. The industry soon came to be dominated by a handful of giant firms, organized in trusts. Terni (see §2.2) continued to supply nearly all the armour plate for the Italian navy, at vastly inflated prices. By the late 1890s it was evident that this plating was inadequate, and in 1904 the Navy Ministry finally decided to insist on Krupp processes. The ensuing parliamentary inquiries revealed much that was embarrassing about Terni's past relations with the navy, and about the firm's financial and political connections. Terni may have made poor steel at high cost, but its position was none the less unassailable. By 1914 it was the largest hydro-electric steel plant in the world. And it was backed by the *Banca Commerciale Italiana*, which also financed and co-ordinated the activities of nearly all its leading rivals.

By 1900 other large steel firms had been founded. In 1899 the *Società Elba* began mining iron-ore on Elba. The iron was to be used in Italy's first coke blast furnace, built at Portoferraio by the firm. Thus fuel would be saved, steel would be built, and Elban iron would no longer be exported to France or Belgium. It was an exciting prospect, holding out the promise of a native iron and steel industry. Furthermore, in 1897 another large firm had been founded, the *Società Altiforni e Fonderie* at Piombino, and in 1900 appeared the *Società Siderurgica* at Savona. It looked as if there might soon be some competition in the Italian steel industry after all, despite the tariff; so deals were struck.

Elba and the Savona plant came under the owners of Terni. In 1905 the group also helped to form a new company, *Ilva*, which built a huge steel plant at Bagnoli, near Naples, with government subsidies and a government-guaranteed supply of Elban ore. Despite these agreements and despite the tariff, the steel companies still had to face foreign competition in the home market. By 1911 they were faced with bankruptcy, and so the Bank of Italy organized a rescue operation. The five major firms set up a cartel under the general 'management' of *Ilva*. The cartel accounted for all Italian pig-iron, and over half her refined steel. Henceforth none of the five firms could modernize its plant without the agreement of the others; nor would any of them be forced to close down unprofitable operations. The industry continued to rely on State orders, boosted by the arms race and by the nationalization of the railways in 1905; and the State continued to pay needlessly high prices for its steel.

Much the same story is true of the sectors closely linked to steelmaking. The shipbuilders, too, were protected by the tariff; they, too, relied mainly on State contracts and subsidies; they, too, soon became dominated by a handful of large firms, which sought political and financial backing and formed cartels or mergers among themselves. In 1900 the navy placed an order for four battleships – one from each of the four biggest shipyards in the country. The largest shipping line, the *Navigazione Generale Italiana*, also relied heavily on State subsidies, and on its monopoly of the postal service to the African colonies. Shipping, shipbuilding and steel firms were interconnected. Shipbuilders like Orlando and Odero sat on the boards of the steelworks: Giuseppe Orlando was even president of Terni in 1912, and Attilio Odero was vice-president of *Ilva*. A handful of big industrial families prospered through their ability to corner public funds and private backers. Again, perhaps one should not exaggerate all this. Italy was not yet a 'corporatist', autarchic economy. Just as the steel industry could never prevent foreign dumping of cheap steel, so the big shipping companies could not control all their market either. There were plenty of small private shipping lines, mainly transporting cargo, and they usually bought cheap British or German boats: in 1914 only one-third of Italian tonnage had been made in Italy. But it is, none the less, significant that these heavy industrial sectors were, like the electricity companies, linked to the two main banks, the *Banca Commerciale* and the *Credito Italiano*. Shortage of capital implied both State-sponsored industrialization and a major role for financial institutions.

Italy's economic growth after 1896 meant essentially the rise of a healthy engineering sector. It flourished for two main reasons: a 'cyclical' demand for machinery, and the birth of a new industry, motor vehicles. By the late 1890s the textile machinery installed during the 'industrial boom' of the 1880s was obsolescent. It had to be replaced, particularly since the Italian cotton-spinning industry was flourishing behind the tariff.[6] Furthermore, the railway locomotives and rolling stock had been run down in anticipation of future nationalization, and they also had to be replaced when the railways were finally nationalized in 1905. Between 1905 and 1908, the State railways ordered over 1,000 locomotives, 3,000 passenger carriages and 25,000 freight trucks; preference was given to Italian producers. It was not exactly a 'railway boom', but it all helped, especially during the industrial recession of 1907. The spread of electric power helped engineering, too, for the railway machinery firms were asked to build trams: the public transport system of Italian cities even today largely dates from this period.

The major breakthrough was in motor vehicles. Here at last was a new sector, in which other countries had no established position, and where entrepreneurship, engineering skills and flair could win massive rewards. The car was new, and exciting. For years it remained a millionaire's toy; before 1912 the small car was almost unknown in Italy, unlike France or Britain. Those who could afford a car at all wanted a splendid one, to demonstrate their success ('*fare figura*'). Italy's car factories, like Scotland's grouse moors, depended on the existence of a rich sporting aristocracy with a passion for discomfort. The *Fabbrica Italiana Automobili Torino*, better known as Fiat, was founded at Turin in 1899 by a group of ex-cavalry officers, including not only Giovanni Agnelli himself but also Count Emanuele Cacherano di Bricherasio, Count Roberto Biscaretti di Ruffia, and Marquis Alfonso Ferrero di Ventimiglia; even the first factory was in a *chic* part of town, the Corso Dante. Its leading racing driver, Nazzaro, in 1907 won the *Targa Florio* and the *Grand Prix de France* at Dieppe. The Duke of Abruzzi also raced Fiat cars, losing a famous wager in 1901 but winning great public acclaim.

In short, a car craze swept through early twentieth-century Italy. By 1907 there were 71 car firms in the country, including 32 in Turin. They were surrounded by a host of ancillary industries – coachworks, tyre factories, headlight manufacturers, etc. Indeed, it was the existence of these other firms, especially coachworks and railway workshops, that had attracted the motor manufacturers in the first place, for here were the skilled engineers and craftsmen that the industry needed. Coachworks were particularly important, for Italy led the world in styling: Alessio, Farina and Ghia all flourished in these years. The 1907 recession led to the collapse of many small manufacturers, but even so six major firms survived in Turin alone. Within a decade the staid old capital of the House of Savoy had become dominated by the new industry, and in 1911 there were 6,500 car workers in the city.

Some far-sighted manufacturers, like Agnelli, could see that there were just not enough sporting aristocrats around to support a flourishing industry. In 1912 there were only 12,373 privately owned motor vehicles in Italy; the market was still mainly abroad. So Fiat also made lorries and buses, and the first Fiat aeroplane flew in 1907. But by 1912 the bus network was already as large as that of the railways, and the room for expansion was clearly limited. The future lay with mass production of cheap cars, and in 1912 Agnelli visited the Ford plants in the USA. When a fellow-industrialist asked him whether it might be possible to introduce American methods into Europe,

Monsieur Agnelli avoided answering. His eyes lighted up briefly but his face, which I was scrutinizing, remained impassive. He changed the conversation rapidly.[7]

Fiat did, in fact, adopt such methods, and expanded its production rapidly:

150 vehicles in 1903, 4,500 in 1914. In 1912 the first 'utility' car was begun, the Fiat 'zero': 19 horse power, top speed 72 km.p.h., price 8,000 lire – not cheap (for 8,000 lire you could buy a 35 horse power car in America), but a good deal cheaper than anything previously produced in Italy. In 1914 the Italian car industry was poised for mass production.

The picture drawn here of industrial expansion is not, of course, complete. In an atmosphere of optimism all sorts of new ventures will take root, and some will flourish – as did, for example, Camillo Olivetti's typewriter firm, founded in 1908 at Ivrea in Piedmont. Another example is the chemical industry, which before 1908 enjoyed the highest rate of growth of any sector; it benefited greatly from cheap power and from the increasing demand for agricultural fertilizers. Several traditional industries continued to flourish too; indeed, without the expansion and prosperity of the old industries there could not have been the growth of the new. Textile machinery is the best-known example, but note too that Giovanni Buitoni installed the new thermo-mechanical drying process in his very traditional industry, pasta-making. The cotton industry arguably derived more benefit from the 1887 tariff than any other sector – the duty on imported cotton goods was between 30 and 50 per cent – and it was also greatly helped by mechanization: the number of spinning-frames doubled between 1900 and 1914. The domestic market was secure, and by 1907 over 10,000 tonnes of spun yarn were being exported. However, the industry was badly hit by the 1907 recession, and in 1913 the leading producers formed a cartel, the *Istituto Cotoniero Italiano*, to maintain prices and limit production. Even so, the industry had made great progress over the previous twenty years, and in 1914 600 million lire were invested in it. Wool and silk also prospered, especially up to 1907. Silk exports were valued at 500 million lire in 1914, almost as much as the value of cotton and of all agricultural products combined.

The economic spurt after 1894 was largely confined to the North and to the Po valley. Piedmont, hitherto lagging behind in industrial development, became a major European centre of car manufacture. The Ligurian coast became the home of many of the steel and shipbuilding firms. The 1911 industrial census, which counted only people in 'workplaces', found 2.2 million 'industrial workers': almost half of them were in the three regions of Lombardy, Liguria and Piedmont, i.e. the famous 'industrial triangle' with Milan, Genoa and Turin at its apices. In Lombardy 26 per cent of 'active' persons were in industry; in Liguria the figure was 21 per cent and in Piedmont 17 per cent. Nowhere else had more than 14 per cent, and Basilicata had only 4 per cent.[8] To these figures should be added a further million or more artisans or employers, as should at least 300,000 'domestic' workers, spinning or weaving at home, as well as 500,000 'garment workers' – a loose category of tailors, cobblers, hatters, seamstresses, laundresses and so forth – and 500,000 in the building industries. The bulk of the strictly 'industrial workers' were in traditional industries: textiles, food-processing and the like. Over a quarter of them were women, mostly under twenty-one.

Women left industry on marriage, or at least on childbirth; thus labour turnover was high, just as skills were low. Much industrial work was still seasonal, something to turn to in the winter when there was no work in the fields. In textiles, 'the figure of the "worker-peasant" was almost the rule'.[9] Italy was still an agricultural country. The 1911 census found that almost 59 per cent of employed adults worked in agriculture; many of the others were part-time peasants. And most of the peasants who flocked into the Northern cities found jobs as building labourers or domestic servants, not industrial workers: Milan had no less than 33,000 domestic servants in 1901, and that was the official figure. In short, the Italian working class was small, heterogeneous, Northern and mostly unskilled. The skilled workers were to be found among the artisans, or among a few traditionally favoured groups in engineering, printing and the building trades. The 'factory system' was only just beginning to break down the social and economic gulf between the old skills and the new unskilled. These years saw not so much 'the making of the Italian working class', as the expansion of the Italian working cities.

6.2 AGRICULTURE

The story of Italian agriculture in this period has many parallels with that of industry. It, too, experienced tariff protection, the end of the long world slump in prices, markedly increased production, some exciting technical innovations, major improvements confined to certain areas of Northern and Central Italy, and the rise of a major State-subsidized 'industry' that depended greatly on maintaining its political influence.

In 1887 the tariff on imported wheat had been raised from 14 lire per tonne to 30 lire, and ultimately – in December 1894 – to 75 lire per tonne. Wheat was not the only foodstuff to be protected. The duty on rice was even higher, and dairy products were also sheltered from foreign competition. Even so, agricultural incomes fell in the early 1890s, and only picked up later in line with the general world price rises of foodstuffs, in turn connected to the food required by larger cities and an expanding population. The price of wheat within Italy, which had fallen from 221.4 lire per tonne in 1887 to a minimum of 192.2 lire in 1894, rose steadily thereafter: 257.0 lire in 1900, 260.8 lire in 1905, 285.3 lire in 1910, and 291.7 lire in 1913. These prices were over 50 per cent higher than in Britain.[10]

The tariff was not high enough to make marginal land profitable, but it was a marvellous bonus for the grain producers on good land, especially in the Po valley where modern machinery could be used and where land reclamation could be carried out. In such areas productivity rose rapidly. By 1913 the four Northern regions of Piedmont, Lombardy, Veneto and Emilia had doubled their wheat production, compared with forty years earlier; they produced 40 per cent of the country's wheat, compared with only 25 per cent in the early 1870s. By 1911–13 total Italian wheat production had reached over 4.6 million tonnes, 1 million tonnes more than fifteen years earlier. The improvement had occurred, as in the case of industry, before 1907. But it was confined to the 'agricultural quadrilateral' of the North and Emilia-Romagna. In 1909–13 seven provinces had yields of over 1.5 tonnes per hectare: all were in Lombardy, Veneto or Emilia-Romagna. And thirty-three provinces had yields below 1 tonne per hectare: all were south of Emilia, and several provinces in Sicily were below 0.6 tonne per hectare (the figure for the UK was 2.2 tonnes per hectare). In other words, these were the years of 'take-off' for Northern cereal agriculture, thanks to capital investment and State-guaranteed profits; but the South was left behind. In the mainland South the hectareage under wheat actually declined by almost 8 per cent during the thirty years after 1879–83, although it rose in Sicily. In Calabria, yields per hectare also fell in the twenty years before the war.

So far I have discussed only wheat, for it still covered over one-third of the country's cultivated surface. But the same story is true of many other crops. Maize yields in 1911–13 varied from 2.51 tonnes per hectare in Lombardy to 0.52 tonne per hectare in Sicily; nearly 70 per cent of the crop was grown in Piedmont, Lombardy, Veneto and Emilia-Romagna. Rice was grown only in these same regions. Silkworms and dairy produce were also concentrated there, and two-thirds of Italy's cows grazed there in 1908. Sugar-beet was almost restricted to Emilia-Romagna and the Veneto; 36 per cent of Italy's wine production came from the four Northern regions too. The other regions did, of course, specialize in some things, notably fruit, olive oil and sheep. They recovered some of their export markets after the disastrous early 1890s, and even opened up new ones: Germany, for example, took two-thirds of Italian fruit exports in the early twentieth century, and the USA was a big market for citrus fruit until the Californian orange-groves expanded production. But, even so, the 'agricultural revolution' remained a Northern phenomenon. Serpieri estimated that 1 hectare of agricultural land in the North produced 429 lire in 1914, compared with 280 lire in Central Italy, 237 lire in the mainland South, and 194 lire in Sicily and Sardinia.[11]

How were these increases in production in Northern Italy achieved? The 'demand side' accounted for part of the answer – tariff protection within Italy, a world market that was expanding again. But the 'supply side' had to meet these demands, and that meant more use of fertilizers and machinery. The fertilizers came from Italy's nascent chemical industry, or were imported from Germany: superphosphates applied in agriculture rose from about 0.3 million tonnes in 1900 to over 1 million tonnes in 1913, and the amount of nitrates also doubled. The farm machinery was supplied by Italy's nascent vehicle industry. To finance their purchases, farmers could borrow from the rural savings banks if need be; tenants paying fixed rents in cash obviously benefited when food prices rose, and so had some money available for investment. But there was another vital requirement, knowledge: how, and when, to use the new techniques? Here the 'itinerant chairs' (*cattedre ambulanti*) of agriculture played a vital role in spreading awareness of the new industrialized agriculture. There were 41 such 'agricultural experts' employed by local or provincial authorities in 1900, and 191 by 1909 – as well as 3 'Higher Schools of Agriculture', 2 university faculties and 77 other schools of agriculture or agronomy, plus specialist institutions for viticulture, veterinary medicine, etc., and numerous private schools. The 'itinerant chairs' began in the Po valley, and there were always more of these experts in lower Lombardy and Emilia than elsewhere. They had most influence on a few 'enlightened' landowners and large tenants, anxious for commercial success and untroubled by tradition or ecological scruples. But they also advised the many new co-operatives of small farmers, founded throughout Northern Italy under clerical, Socialist or Liberal auspices. In the South the experts were largely ignored, except by a few major landowners and by the Sicilian co-operatives organized by Sturzo. Areas of peasant landownership and of share-cropping were suspicious of innovation, and unsuited to benefit from it.

Another major cause of Northern agricultural expansion was land reclamation – irrigation, drainage of marshes and the like. Various laws from 1882 onwards encouraged landowners and local authorities to carry out this work, and made State grants available to cover up to 60 per cent of the cost. In the early twentieth century the concept of reclamation widened to include reafforestation, house and road-building, drinking water and schools – i.e. everything needed to encourage settlement in remote areas. By 1915 352,000 hectares had been 'improved' under these laws; only 2,300 of these hectares were in the South. Southern landowners just were not willing, or able, to invest in agriculture, even when the State 'topped up' their contributions and granted tax concessions. The major 'improvement' areas were around the mouth of the Po, especially in the Polesine and Ferrarese where the area of cultivated land had been doubled by 1910; but the Tuscan *Maremma* and the *Agro Romano* were also greatly 'improved'. The various 'reclamation' laws were much criticized, and there was plenty of opportunity for diverting public funds into private pockets; but the achievements, in certain zones, were real too.

Agriculture also benefited from the new food-processing techniques. Canning, for example, became a major industry only in the twentieth century, and greatly expanded the market for tomatoes and fruit. But the outstanding example is sugar-refining, which had some curious parallels with steelmaking. Sugar was considered a luxury, and as such heavy revenue duties were levied upon it: 740 lire per tonne on domestic sugar, and a 990 lire per tonne tariff on the imported product. Thus the effective protection was 250 lire, ample to ensure the growth of a native sugar-refining industry and the spread of sugar-beet cultivation. The first refinery was founded in 1891; by 1910 there were 41 of them, employing over 13,000 workers (mainly in Emilia and Liguria) and processing 1.6 million tonnes of beet. The *Banca Commerciale* financed many of these refineries, and advised on management. Sugar production rose from about 6,000 tonnes in 1898 to 305,000 tonnes in 1913 – more than twice the annual consumption. The industry soon formed a cartel, the *Unione Zucchieri*, to maintain prices within the country. It became an extremely successful pressure-group. Furthermore, the Emilian sugar barons became very prominent in Right-wing politics; their mouthpiece, the Bolognese paper *Il Resto del Carlino*, waged spirited campaigns in favour of economic nationalism. In August 1912 the Italian government renounced the international sugar agreement, and began dumping the surplus produce abroad while maintaining the tariff barrier at home. The high price of sugar probably inhibited the spread of secondary processes – biscuit-making, jams, confectionery and so forth – rather as costly steel is said to have handicapped the engineering industry.

All these changes naturally had an impact on the structure of the rural economy. I outlined Italy's different agricultural zones and land-tenure systems in Chapter 2 (§2.1), and much of what was true in the 1870s and 1880s was still true thirty years later, especially in the hill areas of peasant ownership and share-cropping. But on the North Italian plains the irrigation schemes and 'improvements' were pioneered by a new type of landowner, the limited company, and by tenant farmers with large farms and long leases. These people simply hired and dismissed agricultural labourers as they required them, and the older landowners followed suit. The old system of share-cropping or of renting small plots rapidly declined. The result was a much more efficient 'capitalist' agriculture, but also a mass of labourers who could find work only at the busiest times of the year: in short, an 'agricultural proletariat'. By 1900 landless labourers and their families formed between 55 and 60 per cent of the rural population in Ferrara province, and it was a similar picture in several other provinces of the Po valley. Furthermore, it was an agricultural proletariat with a grievance. Many of the labourers had been thrown off long-held land. Others had migrated to the area to work on the irrigation schemes, and were left jobless once they had been completed. The areas of advanced 'capitalist' farming in Emilia, lower Lombardy and Apulia soon became the centres of labourers' leagues and of protracted strikes and labour battles, whose outcome was to determine the political complexion of the whole country.

The other major rural changes were those connected with emigration, either to the towns or abroad. Again, I discuss this at length elsewhere (see §8.1) but I stress here that in some emigration zones so many peasants left the land that those who stayed behind secured substantial wage rises. This was especially true in Calabria and Basilicata. Daily wages in the South in 1907 were at least 50 per cent higher than in 1882. Later calculations show an average rise over all Italy from 1.61 lire a day in 1905 to 2.11 lire in 1913.[12] The landlords and rentiers of the South became seriously alarmed, as their profits were squeezed. They were sometimes forced to grant their tenants longer leases, on better terms. Moreover, returning emigrants brought back a zest for commercial success, and sometimes brought large capital sums. Thus in some areas, particularly of Sicily, new owners began to take over the land. However, this was untypical. In most of Italy it was the members of owner-cultivator families in hill areas who were emigrating, and the number of owner-cultivators in the country actually fell sharply between 1901 and 1911 (from around 2.5 million to 1.7 million). Moreover, the overall number of landless labourers increased from 3.0 million to 3.38 million.[13] Even so, the massive emigration affected the whole structure of the rural population, and the total number of people engaged in agriculture fell between 1901 and 1911 – a marked contrast to what happened before and after.

In short, Italian agriculture underwent great changes in this period, perhaps greater than at any other time in its history, at least until after the Second World War. New landowners, technical innovations, networks of co-operatives and credit banks, technical advisers, export markets, rising prices and wages, whole new agriculture-based industries, land reclamation – they all coincided and reinforced each other. Furthermore, they obviously helped Italy to feed her own population and to pay for necessary imports. But the benefits were concentrated in the 'agricultural quadrilateral' (Southern Piedmont, Lombardy, Southern Veneto and Emilia), that overlapped the 'industrial triangle'. Jacini had clearly been prescient when he wrote in 1885 that 'the experience of all places and all times has shown that purely agricultural countries are never rich countries, not even in agriculture; but where trade and industry flourish, private initiative will create rural wealth'.[14] In the South, change of a different kind was evident. Emigration was relieving the demographic pressure on resources, and thus raising real living standards. However, it was creating political strains back home, and it obviously rested on other countries' continued willingness to import large numbers of illiterate unskilled labourer. The 'Southern problem' was beginning to be seen as the most acute problem facing the changing Italian economy.

6.3   THE LIMITS TO GROWTH

Both the industrial and agricultural sections of this chapter have shown, I hope, that the South was left behind economically after 1896, and became mainly a pool of migrant labour. By 1911 income per head in the South was probably around half that in the Northern 'industrial triangle'. But the South's political importance remained as great as ever; and its economic grievances soon became a vital political issue. A chorus of lament arose from the Southern provinces, complaining of emigration and excessive taxation, and demanding government help – more public works, cheaper credit, relief from land taxes, and the costs of primary education to be taken over by Rome. Taxes were the greatest grievance. The provincial councillors of Avellino even wrote a booklet about them in 1903, claiming that direct taxes in their province were 5.32 lire per inhabitant, compared with only 5.01 in Turin and 4.18 in Bologna.[15] In July 1902 seventy mayors threatened to resign *en bloc*, if nothing were done. The Prefects often acted as spokesmen for these demands, warning that public order could not be maintained much longer unless some relief were given. This was a real threat, and all too credible.

And so Italian governments embarked on a series of measures designed to promote economic growth, or at least to buy off unrest, in the huge backward Southern regions. In September 1902 the Prime Minister, Zanardelli, astonished everybody by actually visiting the South. Clearly the government was in earnest, although it was unfortunate that Zanardelli died the next year, for many Northerners attributed his death to the hazards of Southern travel. One of the first major laws on the South was, in fact, for the benefit of Basilicata, where the Prime Ministerial feet had trod. It provided a package of measures, costing over 50 million lire, for reafforestation, irrigation, drinking water, road-building to isolated communities, etc. There were also various tax concessions, e.g. on land and cattle, and an agricultural credit fund was set up, to grant mortgages for land purchase and improvement. Similar laws followed for Calabria in 1906 and 1907, as did other subsidies: money for the Apulian aqueduct, for Sicilian railways and sulphur mines, relief for Messina and Calabria after the 1908 earthquake, and so forth. In 1906 the various tax concessions were extended to the whole of the South. A parliamentary commission was also set up, to investigate the conditions of the Southern peasantry. Like most parliamentary inquiries, it produced an admirably detailed survey of its subject, but few practical changes.

As for industry, here too government money was forthcoming. The Bagnoli steelworks owed its existence to government insistence that 200,000 tonnes of Elban iron-ore be reserved for it each year. In 1904 came a law for the industrial development of Naples. The harbour was enlarged, new roads were built, tax exemptions were given for new industrial projects, and State orders were guaranteed. The idea – a modern one – was to create an industrial growth area in the South. The results were disappointing. The industrial zone was never built, nor was cheap electricity provided by the municipal council, as promised. Some Northern capital and technical skill were induced to move to Naples, only to find the local labour force unskilled and fractious. In any case, the tax concessions encouraged capital-intensive projects rather than a range of local entrepreneurs and small businesses. There was little 'spin-off', and few signs of an emergent industrial bourgeoisie. Indeed, according to the census figures, fewer people had industrial jobs in the South in 1911 than had done in 1871.

Reforms also foundered on political realities. In 1906 Sidney Sonnino, who had written a famous survey of Sicily thirty years earlier, became Prime Minister with Radical support. He proposed major changes. Land taxes were reduced by one-third, except for the really big landowners; and tenants were to be entitled to borrow money from their landlords. Sonnino also proposed to set up provincial banks and to subsidize the schools. His general aim was to transform Southern Italy into a land of literate owner-cultivators or long leaseholders, engaged in intensive cultivation of specialized crops, and forming co-operatives to process and market them. These projects aroused great hostility from most ruling groups in the South, and the government fell after a mere 100 days. In any case, Sonnino's proposals were not economically feasible: in most of the South a family would have required at least thirty hectares for a comfortable living. There was just not enough land to go round, at least until after further massive emigration.

This was an objection not merely to Sonnino's project, but to the Basilicata and Calabria laws that were actually passed. In practice, they were glorified public works schemes. They had little economic impact, although they probably helped to reduce ill-health and mortality, and they certainly relieved landowners of some burdensome taxes. The legislation's failure was not surprising. The problems of the South were huge. Planned intervention of this kind was in its infancy, and required far greater resources than the hard-pressed Italian State possessed. Moreover, the earthquakes of 1905 and 1908 destroyed much of the engineering work begun by those dates; and the First World War prevented many more being started. Less than one-third of the projects initially approved for Basilicata had been implemented twenty years later. There was also much Northern resistance to the idea of granting 'privileges' to Southern agriculture and industry. The town council at Livorno protested solemnly against the law on Naples, and in 1906 the island of Elba demanded to be included in 'the South'.

More high-minded Northerners saw the legislation as an inevitable fount of corruption. The schemes were normally administered by 'special offices' in the Ministries of Agriculture and Public Works in Rome, and the Prefects were responsible for how the money was spent locally. Central control of resources was probably just as well, given the nature of local government in the South, but it meant constant pressure on the ministries by local interests. Here are the beginnings of constant themes in twentieth-century Italian politics: the distribution in the South of subsidies and patronage by central State development agencies, and the use of such agencies to win political support.

So Italy's economic growth was somewhat peculiar. In many leading sectors – steel, shipping, sugar – it was a handful of State-sponsored, tariff-protected, cartelized firms that succeeded; and they succeeded by virtue of their financial connections and their political weight. Saraceno has termed this the 'guaranteed model' of industrial development,[16] one in which both banks and industry came to depend on public subsidies and, indeed, ended up in the public sector. Meanwhile a few enterprising firms (e.g. Fiat) flourished in world markets without State protection, and a host of smaller firms provided the specialist craftsmanship and support services, often the innovatory ideas, that the large firms needed. An incipient 'dual economy' was growing up. On the one hand, there was the 'quasi-State' sector, with a protected home market, guaranteed finance and little interest in exporting, except possibly to the underdeveloped South-East of Europe; on the other was a 'market', export-oriented sector, often small-firm or even artisan in character, anxious to maintain trading links with North-West Europe. This distinction is, of course, a crude one, and some large firms spanned both sectors: Fiat itself was heavily involved in submarine engines and military trucks by 1914. Yet the distinction existed, and it was to be the basis of many political and economic conflicts in years to come.

The other important point to stress is that after 1907, and particularly between 1912 and 1914, the growth process slowed down. In some sectors, e.g. silk, there was an absolute decline in production. Even in chemicals,

133

Gerschenkron estimates an annual growth rate of only 1.8 per cent p.a. between 1908 and 1913, compared with 13.7 per cent p.a. in the previous twelve years. The 'big spurt' was petering out. This had important political consequences. The 'market sector' faced grave difficulties, and began organizing cartels – in chemicals, in paper, even in engineering; and the 'quasi-State' sector needed to exert more political pressure, to win greater subsidies and larger government contracts. The government was forced into deficit spending again: the budget deficit reappeared in 1909–10, and by 1912–13 was running at over 250 million lire. Relations between government and industrialists became both closer and more tense. Many influential people began to think that the easiest solution to Italy's economic difficulties was to spend more money on weapons. Defence spending did in fact rise (from 21 per cent of total public spending in 1897–1906 to 27 per cent in 1907–12), and there was a nationalist clamour for imperialist expansion abroad. Such were the benefits of Italy's economic take-off.

REFERENCES

1. A. Gerschenkron, *Economic Backwardness in Historical Perspective*, Harvard University Press 1962, p. 75. Cf. R. Romeo, *Breve Storia della Grande Industria in Italia*, Bologna 1961, pp. 67–68.
2. G. Fuà (ed.), *Lo Sviluppo Economico in Italia*, iii, Milan 1969, pp. 401–2.
3. R. Webster, *Industrial Imperialism in Italy 1908–15*, University of California Press 1975, p. 133.
4. S. Fenoaltea, in G. Toniolo (ed.), *Lo Sviluppo Economico Italiano 1861–1940*, Bari 1973, p. 178.
5. Gerschenkron, *Economic Backwardness . . .* p. 404.
6. Fenoaltea in Toniolo, *Lo Sviluppo Economico Italiano . . .*, pp. 135 ff. Cf. O. Vitali, in G. Fuà, *Lo Sviluppo Economico in Italia*, ii, p. 106 (he gives figures for new machinery installed in the cotton industry).
7. L. Bonnefon-Craponne, *L'Italie au Travail*, Paris 1916, p. 120.
8. V. Zamagni, *Industrializzazione e Squilibri Regionali in Italia*, Bologna 1978, p. 193 and pp. 226–27.
9. G. Procacci, *La Lotta di Classe in Italia agli Inizi del Secolo*, Rome 1970, p. 14.
10. E. Avanzi, *L'Influenza che il Protezionismo ha Spiegato sul Progresso Agrario in Italia*, Pisa 1917, p. 235; G. Porisini, 'Produzione e produttività del frumento in Italia durante l'età giolittiana', *QS* no. 14 (1970), 507–40, at 513–14.
11. His estimate is quoted in M. Bandini, *Cento Anni di Storia Agraria Italiana*, Rome 1957, p. 86.
12. P. M. Arcari, 'Le Variazioni dei Salari Agricoli in Italia, dalla Fondazione del Regno al 1933': *Annali di Statistica* serie vi, vol. xxxvi, Rome 1936, esp. pp. 214–15, 252–53, and 270–71.
13. Figures from O. Vitali, *Aspetti dello Sviluppo Economico Italiano*, Rome 1970, p. 294.
14. S. Jacini, *Relazione Finale sui Risultati dell'Inchiesta Agraria*, vol. xv of the *Atti della Giunta per la Inchiesta Agraria e sulle Condizioni della Classe Agraria*, Rome 1884, p. 113.

15. Deputazione provinciale di Avellino, *Voti al Governo del Re e al Parlamento Nazionale*, Avellino 1903, p. 13.

16. P. Saraceno, 'Le radici della crisi economica', *Il Mulino*, no. 243 (Jan.–Feb. 1976), 3–26.

CHAPTER SEVEN

Politics in the age of Giolitti, 1900–14

7.1 THE 'GIOLITTIAN SYSTEM'

In the years after 1900 a new political 'regime' emerged in Italy. The constitutional debates of 1898–1900 had largely been resolved by Pelloux' ineptitude and by the general election of June 1900 (see §5.9). The assassination of King Humbert a month later proved, if proof were needed, that authoritarian rule aroused much hostility. Italy entered a period of stable parliamentary government, without excitement or adventures; a period of social reforms and economic prosperity, during which popular discontent could be 'bought off', and the Catholic, Radical or Socialist 'subversives' could be integrated even further into the existing political system. She also acquired a safe, reliable, shrewd parliamentary leader, trusted by the Establishment and yet willing, when necessary, to concede influence to chosen outside groups. Giovanni Giolitti, aged 58 in 1900, Piedmontese, deputy since 1882, former civil servant at the Court of Accounts, former Treasury Minister, even former Prime Minister, familiar with the intricate workings of the bureaucracy, respected by the new young king, Victor Emmanuel III, and admired by the leading parliamentary Socialists, stepped forward to meet his destiny. In February 1901 he became Minister of the Interior; by November 1903 he was Prime Minister. The Giolittian Age had begun.

Giolitti had a bad press at the time, but most historians have judged his rule favourably, perhaps because they know what came later. In the 1920s Croce, for example, saw him as having been devoted to the Crown and to the public good, mindful of popular misery, and anxious to reconcile the masses to the parliamentary system. This picture seems valid. Giolitti sought to 'reconcile' the people to the regime, 'real Italy' to 'legal Italy'. What he did not do was seek to reconcile 'legal Italy' to 'real Italy'. He had no wish to see fundamental political change, and certainly did not intend to allow the Socialists, or the Radicals, or the Catholics, or the Nationalists, any autonomous role in Italian politics. These groups – or rather, their leaders – had to be bought off, perhaps eventually 'absorbed into the system'; but that was all. He was a clear-headed and rather cynical Liberal, not a democrat. And, in the long run, his policies did not work.

Giolitti's policy of concessions took various forms, including attempts to develop the Southern economy (see §6.3). Public works were also important, and by 1907 the government was spending 50 per cent more on them than in 1900. Above all, there was social legislation. This period saw the first effective State welfare measures. In 1902 a new law limited the working day for women to eleven hours, and forbade employment of children under the age of 12. In 1910 a Maternity Fund was set up, compulsory for female industrial workers: the State gave 10 lire at each birth, with another 30 lire coming from the employer's and worker's contributions. There were also laws making a rest-day compulsory each week (1907), prohibiting night work in bakeries (1908), and founding a State-subsidized sickness and old-age fund for the merchant navy (1913). Moreover, in 1898 accident insurance had become compulsory in industry, the employer paying the cost; and in the same year a non-compulsory national insurance fund for health and old age was set up for industrial workers. The Socialist Party welcomed this scheme and recommended its members to take out a policy; but the mutual-aid societies, which already provided pensions for their members, were naturally more cautious. Here was an important limit to Giolitti's policies. The State had already come up against established interests in the social welfare field in 1890, when Crispi had pushed through his law on charities against clerical opposition (see §5.6); in the early twentieth century reforming State-paternalists found they might have to reckon with parts of the 'lay' labour movement as well. It was not surprising that little more was done until after the First World War.

The most important concession to the Socialist-led trade unions of industrial workers and agricultural labourers in Northern and Central Italy was the government's new policy of intervening as little as possible in labour disputes. This policy was cautious and limited. Giolitti remained implacably hostile to strikes in the public sector (e.g. by railwaymen), and to 'political' or 'general' strikes. Even so, it was a major innovation. In 1901 there were many agricultural labourers' strikes in Emilia and lower Lombardy. The government did nothing, except sometimes to urge landowners to settle. And in 1906 Giolitti exhorted the Prefects and police chiefs:

in particular, I remind all State officials that in this period of profound social transformation government action must be inspired both by absolute neutrality in the struggles between capital and labour, and by affectionate concern for the legitimate aspirations of the working classes. And it must be the government's special task to persuade everybody that the struggles for progress can only be fruitful when they are peaceful, disciplined and non-violent.

Whoever represents the government, whether at the highest or the lowest level, has therefore the duty not only of rigorously applying the law, but also of fulfilling a real apostolate of social peace.[1]

The social apostolate was helped by 'arbitrators', an unpaid body of concili- ators chosen by unions and employers in each province to settle individual (not collective) disputes. By 1905 they had laid down a body of precedents and 'case law' that made a major contribution to social harmony. They insisted, for example, that 'good cause' was necessary before anyone could be sacked; taking part in a strike was not sufficient reason. Thus workers had some safeguard against sudden unemployment. The reformist Socialists were very enthusiastic about these conciliatory 'courts', and Turati even wrote a book about them. They were cheap, quick, knowledgeable, not too formal or bureaucratic, and likely to favour the workers: the ideal labour institution for Giolittian Italy.

Another institutional 'concession' was the Supreme Council of Labour, founded in 1902 as an advisory body to examine labour issues and to give its opinion on proposed legislation. It contained employers, civil servants, parliamentarians, various experts, and representatives of various reformist-Socialist bodies like the National League of Co-operatives and the Italian Federation of Mutual-Aid Societies. It even contained a few token workers – just seven out of the forty-four members, and those seven appointed by the Ministry of Agriculture and Industry. The Council was hardly ideal. It excluded the Catholics altogether, and did not even represent the Socialist trade unions as such. But it was effective on some issues. It could take the initiative in proposing legislation, and the laws on weekly rest-days and on the Maternity Fund, among others, were drafted and approved by the Council before going to parliament. The Council's real importance was political. It was the first visible attempt to 'absorb' part of the labour movement into the existing political structure, the first formal recognition that labour had to be allowed its own institutional role in the Italian State.

These 'concessions' often had most impact at local level. Trade unions were small and locally based, and so were strikes. The new government policy meant, in practice, that the central State remained 'neutral' in provincial disputes. That in itself was a nasty shock to local businessmen, but Giolitti went further. By the early twentieth century many municipal councils in Northern and Central Italy were bent on 'improvements' – building cheap houses and new schools, orphanages and old people's homes, or providing a safe water supply and free school meals. In Milan the council ran a tram service to the cemetery, and took hearses and mourners free of charge; in Turin there were even public baths. Giolitti's governments gave benevolent support to such policies, and subsidized some of them (e.g. building co-operatives). There were fewer Prefectoral vetoes, and sometimes Prefects and police chiefs actually tried to see that welfare legislation was properly applied. In 1903 parliament even passed a law permitting local councils to 'municipalize' – i.e. take over and run as a local monopoly – virtually all industrial or commercial activities 'of public interest' in their area. Most major cities started running their own trams, water and electricity boards, etc., amid much controversy; elsewhere, however, lack of finance prevented the law from having much impact. But many of the other aspects of 'municipal Socialism', especially council houses and school-building, were evident even in the smaller centres; and the Socialists ran some of Italy's big cities, including Milan, before 1914.

It would be wrong to exaggerate the extent of Giolitti's 'concessions' to local government. The full range of central controls remained intact, and was used. The transfer of primary education from municipality to central State (see §8.3) greatly reduced local government's powers. The government regularly dissolved local councils, and appointed 'Prefectoral commissioners' to run municipalities for months on end, until new elections could be held. Often the reason was genuine concern for sound administration; but not always. In December 1904, for example, the voters of Bassano elected a Catholic local council. A month later the council was dissolved and a commissioner appointed. The Prefect had urged that this measure was indispensable 'to allow the Liberal party a relatively long period of time to reorganize and regroup its forces' so as to combat 'those parties which are not those of order'.[2] This was a typical example, and it illustrates an important point. If the Giolitti governments tolerated 'municipal Socialism' in Northern Italy, that was a deliberate choice on their part; other local councils were not so fortunate.

Giolitti's Prefects were still expected to win elections for 'ministerial' candidates at general elections, in the time-honoured manner. One Prefect's *Memoirs* relate how, despite all his careful efforts, 'his' candidate lost in 1900, the first such blow to the Prefect's career;[3] another tells of how, when the wrong candidate was elected at Formia in 1904, he simply quashed the result and counted again.[4] Many historians have written of elections, especially in the South, as if they were entirely corrupt, and of Giolitti's parliamentary support as consisting of Southern placemen. It is true that most Southern deputies were pro-government (103 out of 137 in 1904), but none the less Giolitti's majority was Northern: there were always more 'ministerial' candidates elected in Northern and Central Italy than in the South. In fact, we know surprisingly little about Giolitti's electoral methods or his parliamentary support; the period awaits its Namier. Certainly there were plenty of accusations of corruption at elections. The government would ask for detailed reports; the Prefects and police chiefs would deny that any irregularity had occurred. Part of the problem was that the administration of elections was in the hands of local mayors and officials. Governments were not likely to dissolve a friendly town council, just before the elections, merely because of allegations that the mayor was not issuing voting cards to government opponents, or was blocking opposition candidates' meetings. Another factor was that the pro-government candidates expected government officials and pensioners to vote for them, and no doubt it was prudent to do so. But Giolitti himself appears to have acted in reasonably good faith. Certainly he always detested the Southern landowners, and refused to support them in their battles against the peasantry. Often it was the deputies who wanted to be known as 'ministerial', and who wanted the Prefect's support and prestige, rather than the Prefects or government who tried to 'corrupt' them.

The deputies were still much the same as in previous Italian parliaments. In 1900 and 1904 one-third of them had sat in five previous Chambers. In one sense they were local men, born in the province where their constituency lay, yet they usually came from the provincial capital. In short, they were urban men, 'representing' rural areas; an educated élite, trained in the classics, law and rhetoric. Nearly half of them were advocates, and teachers and journalists were also prominent. There were a few industrialists and bankers, but their number did not increase and the number of landowners fell steadily (from 114 in 1900 to 73 in 1913). The Socialist deputies, too, were almost invariably lawyers or teachers. This continuity is perhaps a little surprising. Italian society, the *paese reale*, was changing rapidly; the *paese legale* was not. The deputies' social composition did not change even in the 1913 elections, when almost universal male suffrage was introduced. The deputies' capacity for survival explains much about Giolitti's methods of government. He, like they, was a member of the 'educated ruling class'. His majority was conservative, but his government was 'open' to, and therefore often tacitly favoured by, the new 'organized social forces' in the country.

7.2 THE RADICALS AND SOCIALISTS

The Radicals were hardly an 'organized social force', but they provide the clearest example of how opposition groups were 'absorbed'. Giolitti was not the only Prime Minister to play this game, and in fact it was Zanardelli in 1901 who began the whole process by inviting two leading Radicals into his Cabinet. They refused, on the grounds that they could not support high levels of military spending, but thereafter the Radicals abstained benevolently in votes of confidence. In 1904 came another major advance. On Giolitti's suggestion, the Radical Marcora became President (Speaker) of the Chamber of Deputies – a key post, and a decisive step in any party's approach to government. In 1906 Ettore Sacchi and Edoardo Pantano joined Sonnino's brief government, attracted by his promise of reforms. In the next few years several Radicals (e.g. Nitti and Credaro) served in Giolitti's Cabinets, and they became a normal part of Giolitti's parliamentary majority.

Why was the Radicals' 'absorption' so easy? The main reason is that most of them had little reason to stand aside. The new king was no reactionary; Giolitti was no threat to parliamentary institutions or civil liberties; industrial progress and welfare legislation were welcome. A few Radicals remained in opposition, mainly 'free-traders' like De Viti De Marco who thought that government policy gave excessive benefits to the protected 'corporations' and trade unions of Northern Italy, and who were sceptical about 'collectivist' welfare schemes. But most Radicals had no such qualms. They were the party 'of political liberty and economic Socialism'; and their base was among the teachers and civil servants – the 'intellectual classes', enjoying the benefits of State employment and anxious for more. Perhaps for this reason, their share of the Southern vote rose from below 5 per cent in 1904 to 17.3 per cent in 1913, and their Southern deputies increased in number from 9 to 35. The Radicals remained Masonic and anticlerical, but Giolitti did not seem over-tender towards the Church, at least until 1913; and they were usually mildly pro-French, but that did not matter much until 1914. The Radicals became Giolitti's most faithful allies, and gave him many years of support.

The Socialists proved more resistant to Giolitti's blandishments, despite the various social reforms. Indeed, some conservatives thought that the Socialists were dominating governments, because the constitutional crisis of 1898–1900 had shown that Italy could not be ruled by force. It is more plausible to say that Giolitti 'absorbed' some of the Socialists, especially the union leaders and deputies, but could not buy off the Socialist Party in the country: he swallowed the head, but not the backbone.

Socialist trade unionism enjoyed rapid growth. Many new unions were founded in 1901–2, usually as 'federations' of existing local or craft-based unions. By 1902 nearly 250,000 industrial workers were 'organized' in the Socialist national federations. The best-known example was the Metal-Workers' Union, FIOM, founded in 1901; by 1902 it had 50,000 members, although for some years the different crafts continued to act with virtual independence. The 'federations' were overtly 'resistance' bodies, i.e. formed to resist capitalists. Their whole aim was to fight for higher wages, to conduct disputes with employers and to organize strikes. They were important in periods of labour militancy, channelling and directing what had often started off as 'spontaneous' disputes. The early years of the century were such a period, partly because of the new government policy of non-interference. In 1901 official figures showed over 1,000 strikes, involving 189,000 workers; and strikes became even more common later. The new unionism appealed mainly to skilled men – metal-workers, railwaymen, printers and the like. Where unskilled or female labour predominated, as in road-building or textiles, or in the South, there was little scope for any kind of organization. And, of course, many small traditional unions of local tradesmen or artisans survived. Sometimes the new 'national federation' was simply the old local association renamed, as with the hatters of Monza or the dockers of Genoa.

The unions were not always successful, especially after 1910 when slower economic growth meant that militancy was less likely to pay. FIOM had 30,000 members in 1907, but only 10,000 by 1911. The fact that the large trade unions were 'federations' of different trades made it difficult to find issues on which all their members could unite, except in agitating for general social reforms. When the Socialist unions, together with the Chambers of Labour, formed a 'General Confederation of Labour' (CGL) in 1906, this problem became even more acute. The CGL was an admirable institution for Giolitti, making it easier for him to co-opt union leaders on to all kinds of consultative committees, but it was ineffective as a 'resistance' organization. Moreover, there were often competing rival unions, organized by Catholics or syndicalists. And one of the largest and most militant unions was the Railwaymen's. Even Giolittian governments could not stay neutral in rail disputes, and in 1905 railway strikes were made illegal – though they still occurred on occasions thereafter.

The most important labour organizations in Italy were still the Chambers of Labour (see §5.7). They also expanded rapidly in the early years of the century: in 1900 there were fourteen, in 1902 seventy-six. They were usually run by skilled workers or artisans (tailors, cobblers, barbers); sometimes a local schoolteacher or a 'professional Socialist' lent a hand. They were always more popular than the 'federations', and had many more members. Above all, they were the centres of a Socialist popular culture and a Socialist morality. The workers who spent their evenings at the Chamber of Labour were upright, responsible men, firmly anticapitalist and anticlerical. They had little knowledge of Marxism, and were mainly concerned with religious and educational issues. The Chambers, or their offshoots, organized housing co-operatives, co-operative shops, and educational associations. They often produced their own magazines and ran their own recreational facilities. They preached against drunkenness, wife-beating and infanticide, and in favour of strict sexual fidelity and eventual suicide. In Sesto San Giovanni, for example, all this was going on long before the Socialist Party branch was founded in 1911; the Chamber of Labour had created a series of workers' institutions, active in political education and self-improvement. Rivalry with Catholic associations was intense: 'Socialism' and 'anticlericalism' were virtually synonymous. The Chambers were, in fact, challenging the Church's monopoly of ritual fervour. May Day processions provided a counter-attraction to traditional religious festivals. There were 'Socialist funerals' with bands, banners and processions, giving the humble worker a far more lavish send-off than he could hope to receive from the Church; and there were 'Socialist baptisms', during which the mother dedicated her infant 'to suffering humanity. You will struggle for the redemption of the class to which you belong by birth. You will be a courageous champion of Socialism, the light of the future.'[5] The Chambers of Labour were ideal institutions for diffusing these values in the rapidly industrializing towns of Northern Italy. They illustrate how the allegedly 'modern', Socialist labour movement was deeply impregnated with the older, Mazzinian ideals of local co-operatives and self-help, of laicism and mutual aid.

In some areas the Chambers of Labour took over other functions as well. In Emilia the peasant leagues and Chambers of Labour between them sometimes managed to control the labour market. Farmers could not hire labour except through the Chamber, and the Chamber determined the rates of pay. Moreover, after 1904 municipal councils could have public works and irrigation schemes carried out by co-operatives (cheaper projects, costing below 100,000 lire, had been allowed since 1889); and after 1906 agricultural co-operatives were allowed to buy up land at public auctions. Chambers of Labour, Socialist co-operatives and Socialist local councils became an intertwined group of public bodies, supported by and supporting the hordes of landless labourers. They dominated both local politics and the local economy.

This was the Italian labour movement's great peculiarity, its source of greatest strength and weakness. Strength, in that Italy was the only industrial country before 1914 where a substantial number of agricultural labourers were Socialists. The *Federterra* ('federation' of agricultural labourers) was one of the first major national unions to be founded, in 1901, and accounted for at least one-third of the CGL's members in this period; in 1913 it had 157,000 out of 327,000. By 1910 there were 1,500 'Socialist' agricultural co-operatives with 218,000 members, and 37,000 hectares were being farmed collectively. Emilia-Romagna was the party's fortress – it won five of the eight seats in Bologna province in the 1904 general election – and it was a fortress built on agriculture, not industry. Yet it was a fragile edifice. It rested on government benevolence, indeed on active government willingness to concede public works and subsidies. It also rested on success in the battle for jobs for landless labourers, and on the labourers' accepting the Socialist aim of land nationalization. And it rested, above all, on employer weakness.

The main targets of Giolitti's 'absorption' policy were the Socialist deputies. They were mainly moderate, humane positivists like Turati, similar in outlook to the Radicals. In 1904, twenty-two of the twenty-eight Socialist deputies had been to university, and nine were university teachers; only two had been manual workers. They needed middle-class votes to be elected, and they usually allied with Radicals or Republicans at election time, at least for the second ballot. Socialist firebrands like Lazzari or Mussolini, although very popular with the party in the country, did not win parliamentary seats. The Socialist vote was a large one, even in these years. The PSI won about 20 per cent of the votes on the first ballot in 1904 and 1909; in Emilia it won almost 40 per cent. Yet the vote was not too high. If more people had voted Socialist, the party could have put up 'revolutionary' candidates who did not need Radical support, and they might have been elected; that was one reason why the Socialist deputies were so lukewarm about universal suffrage. As it was, the Socialist deputies were safe. Usually they did not need to take much notice of the rest of the party. The 'reformist' deputies had, in any case, majority support at party congresses between 1900 and 1904, and again from 1908 to 1912. But they came under fire from the Left-wingers, for 'collaborationism' or worse. In 1912 the party congress condemned the 'feeble, skeletal report of the parliamentary deputies, and notes and deplores the lack of political activity by the group, which has helped to demoralize the masses'.[6] It was true that the Socialist deputies had taken few initiatives. They were supplicants relying on government favours, not revolutionaries trying to overthrow government.

But the Socialists could not be fully 'absorbed' into the Giolittian system for several reasons. One was that in early twentieth-century Italy strikes meant violence. Strikes were legal, as was picketing; but so, too, was the right of non-strikers to work. The police were sent in to protect 'blacklegs' from angry crowds. This was a recipe for disaster, since strikers were used to settling their personal conflicts robustly, and the police were ill-trained, inexperienced and armed. Between 1900 and 1904 over 200 people were killed or wounded in battles between strikers and police. The 'proletarian massacres' continued in the next few years. Every time the police fired, there was a public outcry. Giolitti, in his *Memoirs*, complained that 'the Socialist deputies, ignoring all the work done by the government in favour of freedom and the working people, made continuous protests in parliament and supported the claims of the extremists'.[7] But what else did he expect? All Socialists were genuinely outraged by the deaths, and the deputies did not relish losing control of the party to the 'intransigent' wing.

This pattern was seen most clearly in September 1904. A series of 'massacres' culminated in the shooting of a striking miner at Buggerú, in Sardinia. In many cities, including Milan, the Chambers of Labour called a 'general strike' in protest. It looked very like a national strike, the first ever in Italy, although in reality it was a number of unplanned and unco-ordinated local strikes taken on local initiative, evidence of popular hatred of police repression. The strike was far more complete in the Northern cities and the Socialist strongholds of the Po valley than elsewhere; the Socialist deputies, and the party directorate, provided little leadership or co-ordination. Giolitti ordered his Prefects to do as little as possible. In his view, the movement would soon collapse, and when it did the 'myth of the general strike' would be over. He was right about the strike collapsing, but wrong about the myth. Indeed, the whole affair boosted another powerful belief – in government weakness in the face of unlawful militancy. Once the danger was over, the respectable middle classes railed against the government; and so did the frustrated revolutionaries.

Later 'general strikes' reinforced this impression. Official repression was fierce enough to kill people and infuriate the Left, but not fierce enough to destroy the peasant leagues or reassure the Right. It also meant full 'Socialist funerals' for the victims, with all the panoply of the Socialist counter-culture being paraded in public. In these circumstances it was impossible for the Socialist deputies to compromise overtly with Giolitti. Parliamentary manoeuvres were one thing; public avowals of affection were quite another. In 1903 Giolitti invited Turati to join his government. Although Turati admired most of Giolitti's policies, it was an offer he had to refuse.

The PSI in the country was small – it never had 50,000 members before 1914 – but it was active, it was usually militantly Left-wing, and it was always in ferment. More than one-quarter of its local branches were dissolved each year. Party congresses were chaotic and disputatious affairs, seldom taking decisions but always providing drama and excitement. Inasmuch as anyone ran the party, it was the Directorate elected by the congress, but even the Directorate spent most of its time on propaganda – where it was less significant than the party's newspaper, *Avanti !* The party was dominated by middle-class 'professional Socialists', very different from the people they claimed to represent. The PSI won the peasant vote in Central Italy, but it had few peasant leaders. Socialist mayors, town councillors, peasant league organizers and co-operative managers nearly all came from the middle classes. The town council of Turin – a major industrial city – had 15 Socialist councillors in 1902: 3 doctors, 3 advocates, 6 teachers or professors, 1 accountant, 1 railway clerk and just 1 manual worker, and even he owned his own business.[8] Robert Michels called the PSI the 'party of university teachers', but he exaggerated. It was the leaders who were bourgeois intellectuals; most of the members (72 per cent in 1903) were manual workers.

It would be tedious to recount the details of the party's splits and faction disputes. The essence of them was always the same: would the 'reformists' (deputies and union leaders) retain control, or would they be defeated by the Left-wing 'intransigents'? Since there was nothing much to control anyway, the outcome hardly mattered. In 1904 the 'intransigents' won a majority at the party congress, but did little with it. In 1908 the 'reformists' won 'power' back. In 1912 passions had been aroused by the Libyan War (see below, §7.5), and the 'intransigents' triumphed once more.

Neither the 'reformists' nor the 'intransigents' agreed among themselves. Turati regarded the State, under Giolitti, as essentially a neutral guarantor of peaceful working-class advance. He prized liberty, and feared that legislative reforms might lead to Bismarckian authoritarianism. His fellow-reformist Bonomi regarded the State in a very different light. It was a set of institutions to be taken over, precisely in order to provide legislative reforms. Thus he, and Bissolati, were far more willing to ally with the Radicals, to join governments if possible, and to push for reforms; and they were also far more interested in foreign policy.

The 'intransigents' were even more divided, for example between the 'revolutionary syndicalists' and the 'revolutionary Socialists'. The syndicalists believed in direct action by the workers themselves, and in seizing power by a revolutionary general strike. The economy would then be run by workers' 'syndicates', or unions. In practice, the 'reformists' retained control of the main unions, and the syndicalists had to make do with some of the Chambers of Labour. Apart from occasional strikes in protest at police repression, they achieved very little. In 1908 they were expelled from the party, and various syndicalist movements flourished thereafter in rivalry to the PSI and to the CGL unions. The 'revolutionary Socialists' were orthodox Marxists, but with no trust in parliament or interest in reforms.

In short, Socialist politics was a complex business. At local level, party branches came and went, largely run by their secretaries; a Socialist sub-culture was slowly spread by skilled workers and artisans, via Chambers of Labour, co-operatives, etc. At national level, efforts centred on propaganda and journalism, and around the struggle for victory at the next party congress. The deputies went their own way, as much as they dared. And the unions, grouped together in the CGL, pursued their own interests independently of the party and of each other. All this explains why Giolitti's 'absorption' of the labour movement was at best partial and temporary. He could count on the tacit support of the Socialist institutions that mattered, i.e. the deputies, the industrial unions, and the labourers' leagues; but that support was bound to remain tacit. The Socialist Party in the country remained aloof. It firmly denounced the capitalist class, and indignantly rejected the corrupt political manoeuvres of the exploiting bourgeoisie.

7.3 THE CATHOLICS

Much the same is true of the other major ideological group outside 'the system', the Catholics. Giolitti was extremely cautious and reticent about the Church. His only striking pronouncement was in 1904, when he described Church and State as being 'two parallel lines, which should never meet'.[9] Even in his *Memoirs* he made no mention of the major disputes, nor did he name a single Pope. Giolitti did not want to alienate the anticlerical Radicals and Socialists. Probably he was suspicious of clerical scheming, and possibly he was quite indifferent to religious issues. Yet he needed the support of Catholics, if only as a counterweight to Socialism; and for a time he secured it. He was the first Liberal statesman to win the organized Catholic vote. In return, he was expected to make some 'concessions'. The two parallel lines were beginning to converge.

The long process of cautious *rapprochement* began as soon as Giolitti became Prime Minister. A divorce bill, which he had inherited from his predecessors, was quietly allowed to founder. In 1904, at the election called after the September general strike, the '*non expedit*' was relaxed for the first time. Catholics were permitted to vote in constituencies where otherwise a Socialist might be elected; and sometimes for other reasons. At Bergamo the Catholics' Liberal allies threatened to stop backing the Catholic-dominated *local* administration unless the Catholics supported the Liberals in the *parliamentary* election. This was a real threat, for Bergamo was one of the centres of social Catholicism: there was a whole network of co-operatives, rural banks and charities, ultimately dependent on a benevolent municipal council. So Pope Pius X himself told the Bergamese to 'do as your conscience dictates'.[10] In 1905 a Papal encyclical *Il Fermo Proposito* explained that the '*non expedit*' still applied in principle, but might be lifted in practice 'to help the maintenance of the social order'. In the 1909 elections the '*non expedit*' was suspended in about 150 constituencies, and voters' turnout rose markedly in the Catholic North (in Veneto, from 48.5 per cent in 1900 to 65.2 per cent in 1909; in Lombardy, from 52.9 per cent to 65.9 per cent). By this time debate concerned not whether Catholics might vote at general elections, but whether they might stand as candidates; forty-one of them did, and seventeen were elected. The Vatican paper, *L'Osservatore Romano*, invented a new formula: '*cattolici deputati*' were permissible, but '*deputati cattolici*' were not. In other words, Catholics might become deputies, but no deputies should claim to represent Catholic opinion, or be elected for their clerical affiliations.

The lay Catholic movements had come to be dominated, after 1898, by the 'clerico-moderates', respectable men of conservative views anxious for reconciliation with the State. There was no more talk of 'intransigence' or 'usurpation'. In 1912 the king narrowly escaped assassination; leading Catholic laymen promptly went to pay homage to him in the Quirinal Palace itself, the historic site of the Papal conclaves. Giolitti's officials constantly reported back how the clergy and laity had become reconciled to Liberal institutions, and how horrified the Catholics were by Socialism. For example, the bishop of

Verona's pastoral letter for Lent 1901, to be read by clergy in church, stressed that:

Socialism is the most abject slavery, it is flagrant injustice, it is the craziest folly, it is a social crime, it is the destruction of the family and of public welfare, it is the self-proclaimed and inevitable enemy of religion, and it leads to anarchy.[11]

The Prefects also noted, with some alarm, how influential the various Catholic movements were becoming. By 1911 the 'clerico-moderates' were part of local government majorities in many major cities – Turin, Bologna, Florence, Venice – and hundreds of smaller centres, especially in Lombardy and Veneto. In some areas they controlled most economic and social activity. In Vicenza, Giacomo Rumor owned a printing works, helped found the *Banca Cattolica Vicentina*, was president of the Vicenza Catholic Workers' Society, sat on both the municipal and provincial councils, and was president of the Chamber of Commerce. Such men were obviously part of the Establishment, whether the fact was publicly avowable or not.

Yet the network of Catholic co-operatives, rural banks and welfare agencies never received official recognition by the State, nor even much support from the Church. The Vatican worried that if lay Catholics were too successful in political or social affairs, they might be less willing to accept Papal directives, and above all might begin to regard the Roman question as irrelevant. In July 1904 Count Grosoli, president of the *Opera dei Congressi*, annoyed the new Pope, Pius X, intensely by claiming that the Catholics were 'anxious that the work of the living should not be impeded by dead issues'.[12] Pius dissolved the *Opera dei Congressi* two weeks after Grosoli's blunder. In 1905 the lay Catholic movements were reorganized into three separate 'unions': the *Unione Popolare* to organize pious activities and propaganda, the *Unione Economico–Sociale*, and the *Unione Elettorale* to mobilize the vote. The Catholic youth movement, *Gioventù Cattolica Italiana*, was also reorganized and given the same status as the other 'unions'; and in 1908 the *Unione Donne Cattoliche* was founded for women. Each was independent of the others, and each was brought under the immediate control of the bishops. This change was important. It reasserted clerical control. It meant that the rising generation of younger Catholics, inspired by Leo XIII's *Rerum Novarum* and firmly committed to encouraging social change, was left without national lay leadership or central organization. Yet Pius X was probably right in thinking that the *Opera dei Congressi* had had its day. It was too much of a hybrid, with its economic, political, charitable and religious activities all overlapping; and it had risked involving the whole Church in political, even trade union, affairs. If Catholics were going to 'take over' society, they would need various institutions and differing perspectives. In the long run Pius X's decision probably helped the growth of autonomous political Catholicism, and of more independent Catholic social movements. It was, perhaps, the first step in reconciling the Church to pluralism.

Catholic lay activities were now under the bishops, so it made a good deal of difference who the bishops were. They were, increasingly, of peasant origin, educated solely in seminary schools, men of little culture and less independence. They did what Rome required them to do, and lived in fear of 'apostolic visitations'. There were, of course, some exceptions: at Bergamo Bishop Radini Tedeschi, supported by his young secretary Fr Angelo Roncalli, backed local strikes from the pulpit. But the general picture was one of hesitation and perplexity. The great advances that Catholic social and economic institutions had made in the 1890s were not continued in the 1900s. The *Unione Popolare*, for example, had only 78,000 members by the end of 1910 (the equivalent Catholic organization in Germany, the *Volksverein*, had 652,000). It had become largely a debating club for Catholic intellectuals, and made little attempt to convert the masses or to provide a focus for social life. The *Unione Economico–Sociale* shows a similar picture. In some regions, notably Lombardy and Veneto, the Catholic organizations continued to flourish. In 1910 there were 105,000 members of Catholic trade unions, working mainly in textiles, agriculture and the railways. The agricultural co-operatives had over 50,000 members, and the rural banks had 94,000 accounts. But in the South the economic movement never recovered from the blows it had received in 1898, and in many other areas the Catholics were isolated and defensive. In the Northern cities a historic opportunity was missed, in this crucial decade of rapid industrialization. The Socialists often stepped in where Catholic organizers feared to tread, and in 1911 only about one-fifth of the 'organized' workers were in Catholic unions.

One reason for this relative decline was that the young Catholic enthusiasts for social, economic and political action were liable to be accused of 'modernism'. 'Modernism' was an ill-defined term, originating outside Italy. It referred to a 'historicist' or, worse, 'immanentist' approach to theological issues, and to rigorous historical and philological study of the Gospels; and it usually included demands for reform of clerical abuses and of Church organization, and for acceptance of the lay democratic State. In Italy the movement was essentially political, i.e. social-reforming 'Christian Democrat', opposed to conservative 'clerico-moderatism'. Pius X firmly condemned the theological doctrines in 1907, and for a few years there was a virtual witch-hunt against 'modernists'. As with all witch-hunts, the original motives were soon forgotten, and anyone suspected of excessive political or social zeal came under a cloud. Romolo Murri, an energetic priest from the Romagna who had become the leader of the younger 'Christian Democrats', was 'defrocked' and excommunicated in 1909 (he became a Radical deputy, and sat on the Extreme Left benches of the Chamber, still in clerical dress). Many other Catholics lost heart, or bided their time. Thus 'modernism' apparently collapsed, although many 'modernist' doctrines proved very influential later. The whole 'Christian Democrat' movement became tainted with heresy.

It was rescued, eventually, by another political priest, Fr Luigi Sturzo, the acting mayor of Caltagirone in Sicily. Sturzo was also suspect for a time, and in 1907 an apostolic visitor arrived to check up on his orthodoxy. Fortunately, all was well; and in any case Sturzo was willing to keep silent on religious issues. His interest was in local government, which was perfectly acceptable.

He argued that the Socialists would hold sway over the people, if the Catholics did not act quickly. He wanted regional autonomy for Sicily and elsewhere, and he hoped for an eventual 'lay' Catholic political party, based on flourishing local organizations and committed to democracy and social reforms. He was horrified in 1904, when Catholics started voting for Liberal candidates. This was the 'politics of eunuchs'; Catholics were 'prostituting their vote' for minimal returns. Sturzo was much concerned about the Southern question, and part of his opposition to 'clerico-moderatism' stemmed from the fact that it was essentially Northern, enmeshed in the 'Giolittian system' of industrial protection. There was little he and his friends could do, outside local government; but at least they prevented political Catholicism being solely identified with 'clerico-moderatism', and built up the first real network of Catholic organizations in Southern Italy. His group was not, of course, alone. The 1904 election convinced many laymen, including Filippo Meda, the influential editor of the *Osservatore Cattolico*, that a 'non-confessional' polical party for Catholics was inevitable, once the 'modernist' crisis had died down. When it became clear, after 1913, that a Catholic party would be reasonably successful and tolerable to the new Pope, this view was strengthened. Sturzo was best placed to lead the way; and Giolitti was unlikely to 'absorb' *him*.

In the 1901 census, only 36,000 Italians (0.1 per cent) declared they had 'no religion'; in 1911, 874,000 (2.5 per cent) did so. Was this a real decline in belief, or was it simply that people were more willing to proclaim their lack of faith? Alas, we have no idea. We also have little idea why religious observance fell in some places and not others, or whether industrialization and urbanization had anything to do with it. However, we know that proclaimed religious belief fell most in Central Italy – by no means the most industrial or most urbanized part of the country – and held up remarkably well in industrializing Piedmont and Lombardy. The success or failure of trade unions and peasant leagues, and who organized them, had a great deal to do with the outcome. Even more important was the attitude of the local clergy. Father Burgalassi quotes the diary of a parish priest in Basati, a marble-quarrying area in Lucca province: in 1900 all the villagers in his parish took Easter communion, in 1910 'only a few men' did so. What had happened was that a Socialist union organizer had come along and founded a 'league'. It had secured pay rises and lower hours, but the priest had warned his parishioners not to join, and a Capucin friar had told them that trade unionists were not allowed to take communion. So religious practice fell very sharply, mainly because of the lack of imagination of the local priest – and there were many such priests in Italy.[13]

Catholic education and propaganda were hampered by the fact that priests were not well-educated men. Their libraries rarely contained the Bible or even the Gospels, let alone anything else. Bishops made their usual efforts to improve seminary training, but it was a slow business. Literary Catholics, recognizing the problem, wrote uplifting novels for the people. Even Sturzo wrote several plays, although characteristically on secular themes like *The Southern Prefect* or *Winning the Freedom to Vote*. These works were not much of a challenge to the Socialist or Nationalist rhetoric of a De Amicis or a D'Annunzio, but at least the Catholics tried. Perhaps the clergy's major problem was that they had always acted as 'mediators' between the people and the outside world. This high status was undermined once other people could read and write too, and it was also challenged by lay politicians and trade unionists, including lay Catholics. Naturally the priests sometimes resented it, and their authority was diminished whether they resented it or not.

Even so, one should not exaggerate. Italy in 1911 was not a 'secular' country. Catholic social action may have flagged, but the women's union and the Catholic youth movements both expanded, indeed flourished as never before. The Church may have lost out on funerals and trade unionism, but she found alternative – perhaps more successful – ways of proselytizing, e.g. sports clubs. The 'Catholic sub-culture' could compete on equal terms with the Socialists in most of Northern Italy, and certainly it could outbid the Liberals when it came to winning the popular vote.

Thus Giolitti's compromise with the Catholics was always uneasy, and always unstable. To speak of 'two parallel lines' was simply to fudge the issue. Church and State could hardly avoid influencing each other, if only because the Church's influence on education and welfare was immense. In practice, Giolitti used the Catholics to bolster his majority, but he could not, or would not, give them much in return. He was unwilling to yield a centimetre of Italian soil, and so could not settle the 'Roman question'. He relied heavily on the conservative 'clerico-moderates', and on the fact that the 'Christian Democrats' were out of favour in the Vatican. And he was hostile to anything resembling a 'Catholic party'. He thus missed a possible chance of founding a more stable and more democratic regime which would satisfy the Catholic laity. He tried to 'absorb' the Catholics quietly, without anybody noticing; but he was bound to be found out in the end.

7.4 THE NATIONALISTS

However difficult Giolitti's relations with the Catholics, it was the Nationalists who posed the biggest threat of all to 'Giolittianism'. Italian nationalism, as an organized movement, barely existed at the beginning of the Giolittian period, or even in 1908; yet by 1914 it was a major force, influencing many sectors of the Establishment, powerful enough to resist being 'absorbed', indeed powerful enough to transform the whole political system in the next few years. How, and why, were the Nationalists so successful? Why was Giolitti unable to cope with them?

Part of the answer is that the Nationalists caught a public mood – a sense of national inferiority, a feeling that Italy was being left behind in the race to industrialize, a concern that Italy, alone among the European Powers, was not acquiring colonies, a sense of shame that so many Italians had to emigrate, that Italy was overshadowed by Austria and Germany in the Triple Alliance, above all that Italy had been defeated – by Abyssinians! – at Adowa in 1896. Writers and intellectuals returned to these themes again and again (see §8.4). Twentieth-century Italian nationalism, like its predecessors, started off as a literary movement, as an attempt at cultural renewal. But it was never just literary. It always claimed to command men's obedience, and to tell people what they must do to be saved. Italy was a 'proletarian nation', entitled to struggle against her oppressors; she could be redeemed, but only through sacrifice and conflict. The Nationalists' prophet, Corradini, proclaimed the need for a new kind of religious fervour – 'a religious feeling, gentlemen, which when it becomes widespread in Italy will at last make the trains run on time'.[14]

Nationalism, in short, was a revivalist movement, stressing past guilt and future redemption. It competed directly and consciously with Socialism. Virtually all the Nationalists' pamphlets stressed the similarities, and differences, between them and the Socialists, and often used very similar language. But the Nationalists' chief target was Giolitti. Giolitti's cunning parliamentary manoeuvres, his tacit deals with interest-groups, above all his caution in foreign policy, aroused the Nationalists' fury. They were impossible men to 'buy off' or to 'absorb' into the 'Giolittian system', for they were not interested in economic or social 'concessions'. They were visionaries, and they thought history was on their side.

And so it was, at least for a time. Nationalist propaganda also stressed various concrete themes, each highly relevant to sensible, practical men. Their anti-union agitation went down well among many middle-class Italians, who had long thought that Giolitti was making too many concessions to the Socialists. Giolitti did little to reassure them. During one labourers' strike, for example, Count Arrivabene sent an urgent telegram to the Minister of Agriculture: 'I want you to know that to prevent the loss of crops I, Count Arrivabene, am forced to labour in the fields day and night with other members of my family and friends.' Giolitti's reply was hardly diplomatic: 'I am happy, *Signor Conte*, that you have taken work which can only improve your health, and which will help you to understand how hard and bitter is the life of your peasants. Distinguished compliments.'[15] Episodes like that convinced conservatives that Giolitti was handing over the State to their enemies. The recurrent strikes reinforced this view. In 1906, during a general strike at Bologna, a strike-breaking vigilante group of 'volunteers for order' was formed, encouraged by the *Corriere della Sera* and other Liberal papers. Clearly the Nationalists' message was reaching receptive ears.

Admittedly the Nationalists did not produce any original ideas for some time. They simply urged that public sector strikes should be banned, and that police powers should be strengthened. But gradually new themes crept in. By 1911 Corradini was arguing that the State should settle labour disputes, by creating a 'national consensus' on wages. Even more important, he embraced 'productivism'. The State should organize the economy and allocate resources, in order to maximize production. Naturally that could only be done if Italian industry were protected from foreign competition. 'Productivism' and protectionism became important aspects of Nationalist thinking. They would boost production, maintain profits, and help to conciliate labour. They were not temporary expedients but necessary, desirable features of a modern industrial State. All this pleased many industrialists, especially in industries reliant on State orders or tariffs. It also pleased many politicians. 'Productivism' was a widely accepted idea among Radicals as well as Nationalists – Nitti, for example, wrote in 1907 that the whole aim of the Radical Party was 'the greatest elevation of the national soul, together with the greatest development of production'.[16] The two concepts were becoming fatally linked.

The Nationalists' leading thinker on political and economic issues was Alfredo Rocco, himself an ex-Radical. In 1914 Rocco persuaded the Nationalist Congress to adopt a far-reaching policy of constitutional reform, setting up a new kind of State that would replace the discredited Liberal parliamentary system. Rocco provided, at last, an answer to the 'trade union question'. The unions, he proclaimed, should be welcomed, not fought. They were national, centralizing bodies that disciplined labour; all that was needed was that they themselves should be brought under firm central control. There should be a compulsory closed shop for all workers; employers, too, should be organized into recognized legal associations, preferably into the same ('mixed') unions as the workers. Disputes could then easily be settled, if necessary by compulsory arbitration; and the economy could be planned nationally on 'productivist' lines. The congress resolved that 'mixed' unions were 'the most effective way of moving from a system of free competition to one of national producers' solidarity',[17] and of transforming the unions into organs of national co-operation rather than class conflict. All this sounded a bit too good to be true to most conservatives and Liberals, but gradually Rocco's 'extremism' made headway. The Nationalists, unlike Giolitti, did at least have some ideas about how to avoid 'Socialist tyranny'.

But the main reason for the Nationalists' success lay abroad. Italian nationalism was conceived in disgust at the 'cowardice' and past failures of Italian foreign policy. It was essentially a demand for High Politics, indeed for a victorious war. It flourished after 1908, in the dangerous and unstable Europe of the Bosnian, Agadir and Moroccan crises, when colonial rivalry had become intense and when alliances had become more fluid. In 1909 and 1910 many Nationalist journals were founded: *Il Tricolore* at Turin, *La Grande Italia* at Milan, *La Nave* at Naples. In 1910 came the first Nationalist Congress, mainly propaganda for a more active foreign policy. The main Nationalist journal, *L'Idea Nazionale*, began publication the following year, on 1 March – the day the ancient Romans had assembled their armies, and also the date of the battle of Adowa. The Nationalists agitated for a stronger army and higher defence spending, and in the new international climate they were successful. Spending on the army had been more or less constant, at 250 million lire p.a., between 1900 and 1907; by 1909–10 it had risen to 340 million lire, and Right-wing politicians like Salandra argued that even this was hopelessly inadequate.

The Nationalists did not, of course, agree on everything, even in foreign policy. Most of them were primarily interested in colonial expansion, and so remained in favour of the Triple Alliance with Germany and Austria–Hungary. Yet the Triple Alliance was showing signs of strain by 1908 if not earlier, and Italy's interests clearly conflicted with Austria's in the Balkans. Furthermore, 'irredentism' (see §4.4) always had a powerful emotional appeal, especially among the radical and democratic young. A 'National Trent and Trieste Association' was founded in 1903, and by 1910 there were several para-military student groups, e.g. the 'Hunters of the Tiber' and the *sursum corda*, receiving military training from army officers. And some of the leading 'irredentists' – particularly Scipio Sighele and Alberto Caroncini – were early members of the Nationalist movement. They preached a Holy War against the traditional enemy Austria, to reclaim the 'Italian' territory of Trent and Trieste; and they saw Italy as essentially a great *European* Power. They made little immediate headway, and in fact were virtually expelled from the Nationalist Association in 1912, in the heady pro-colonial aftermath of the Libyan War. But they were Nationalists too, and their hour was to come two years later.

7.5 THE LIBYAN WAR

In September 1911 the Italian army invaded Libya. This was an uncharacteristic decision, but Giolitti and his Foreign Minister, San Giuliano, had their reasons. In 1902 Italy had signed an agreement with France, whereby Italy supported French expansion in Morocco, and France agreed to back Italian influence in Libya. When the Agadir crisis blew up in July 1911, it was clear that the French were consolidating their rule in Morocco. It was time for the Italians to act. Giolitti had to assert Italy's claims in Tripolitania, before the French stepped in there too. Libya was not much use in itself – Giolitti did not fool himself that the desert could easily be made to bloom – but it had a few ports, and Italy could not allow them to fall into potentially hostile hands.

The Great Power chess-game was not the only consideration in Giolitti's mind. The *Banco di Roma* had founded a branch in Tripoli in 1907, and had built up major banking, shipping and agricultural investments throughout North Africa. Furthermore, it had powerful friends. Its president was Ernesto Pacelli, uncle of the future Pope Pius XII; its vice-president was Romolo Tittoni, brother of Tommaso who had often been Foreign Minister between 1903 and 1909. The bank financed some of the Catholic press, e.g. the *Corriere d'Italia*, which campaigned for war. Indeed, San Giuliano complained that 'every little incident in Tripoli and between Italians and Turks is deliberately magnified by the press for various motives, including money and the intrigues of the *Banco di Roma*, which has an interest in securing a quick Italian occupation of Tripolitania'.[18]

The *Banco di Roma*'s involvement meant that Catholic opinion – or, at least, 'clerico-moderate' opinion – would support invasion. Public opinion in general was militant, and would not tolerate the government 'standing idly by' while the French took over Tripoli. The Nationalists led the chorus, but many others joined in, including even some Socialists like Bissolati and Bonomi. Some of the press campaign was no doubt orchestrated by the government: pro-Giolittian papers like *La Stampa* and *La Tribuna* were prominent in depicting Libya as a Promised Land. But the government could hardly have resisted for long, even if it had wanted to. It was faced, in fact, with an extraordinary spectacle of nationalist enthusiasm, particularly extraordinary to those who remembered how unpopular Crispi's Abyssinian War had been less than twenty years previously. In Giovanni Pascoli's famous words 'the great proletarian [nation] has stirred'. Ironically, only the proletarian parties, on the extreme Left, stayed aloof. The bulk of the Socialists and syndicalists, most Republicans and some Radicals were hostile to the war; and they were immediately accused of lack of patriotism.

Thus the decision to invade Libya was not just a hasty diplomatic move, forced on the government by the Second Moroccan Crisis. It was also consciously taken for reasons of internal policy, to placate the Nationalists and the 'clerico-moderates'. Public opinion – i.e. the restricted world of politically-minded gentlemen – played its part; so did economic interests; and so did Giolitti's constant, cautious efforts to 'absorb' and conciliate his opponents.

The war itself was a military success, at least by Italy's previous standards. Italy declared war on Turkey on 29 September 1911. Her navy and marines seized most of Tripolitania's ports and coastal towns within three weeks. Then the difficulties began. The Italians had somehow expected the local Arabs to welcome them as liberators from the Turk, but this unaccountably failed to happen. Soon there were 70,000 Italian troops in Libya, fighting not only the Turks but the Arabs as well. After some months, Giolitti realized that the only real hope of victory lay in putting military and diplomatic pressure on Turkey elsewhere. In May 1912, therefore, Italy occupied thirteen Turkish-held islands in the Aegean, including Rhodes; and in October Italy had a stroke of luck. Montenegro, Serbia, Bulgaria and Greece started the Balkan War, and the Turks were really in trouble. On 8 October they formally surrendered Libya (i.e. Tripolitania and Cyrenaica) to Italy. The Arabs, however, continued their guerrilla resistance for many years, especially in Cyrenaica. The Italians were forced to keep 50,000 troops in the country on garrison duty, and even so their writ only ran in Tripoli and the larger towns. The year of official war had cost nearly 3,500 Italian dead, and 1,300 million lire. Still, Italy had a North African colony at last, and the shame of Adowa had been assuaged.

The war had a major impact on domestic politics. Initially Giolitti's hand was strengthened. He could take the credit for a victorious war and a successful peace. Yet that mood was short-lived. In the longer term the Libyan War broke up the 'Giolittian system'. It was, for example, an immense triumph for the Nationalists. Giolitti had hoped that invading Libya would placate them, but in fact it simply made them more popular and enabled them to forge alliances with the 'clerico-moderates'. The Nationalists had softened up public opinion for the war: Corradini's novel *La Guerra Lontana* and his propaganda book *L'Ora di Tripoli* were both published in 1911, as was Castellini's *Tunis e Tripoli*. The Nationalists claimed (wrongly) the credit for having forced a reluctant government into war. And the Nationalists provided many of the war correspondents in Libya, and made the most of their opportunities for bellicose propaganda. They complained bitterly that the Italian army had not been ready to fight. The soldiers had been betrayed by the politicians; Italy had been stabbed in the back by her own leaders. This was good propaganda, for by late 1912 Italians were counting the cost of the war and wondering why its benefits were so meagre. The Nationalists had the answer: Giolitti was to blame. Soon they became a real Right-wing political party, and in 1913 five of them were elected to parliament. They were still a small group, but they had infiltrated the Liberal Establishment, and they were undermining Giolittianism.

Moreover, the Catholics were slipping out of Giolitti's grasp. Most of the Catholic press had welcomed the Libyan venture, and many priests had preached a crusade against the heathen Turk. Pius X tried to discourage this, but in vain. The war provided Catholics with a fine opportunity to demonstrate their patriotism, and many of them seized it eagerly. They, too, were now part of the national unity. Indeed, they were now part of the Nationalists' unity, or at least some of the 'clerico-moderates' were. Both Catholics and Nationalists campaigned hard against Freemasonry, for Masons were obviously bound to be pro-Turk; both favoured colonial expansion and praised Italy's 'civilizing mission' abroad; both hated the French Revolution and its detestable democratic principles. Catholic support was vital for the Nationalists. Their five deputies owed their election to it, and in 1914 a Catholic–Nationalist conservative alliance won control of Rome's local government.

Yet talk of a Catholic–Nationalist 'wedding' was exaggerated. It was more like a heady but strictly temporary affair. Certainly it never received the blessing of the Church. The Vatican newspaper dismissed the Nationalists as 'supporters of the most tyrannical and odious Caesarism'; and, reporting the Nationalist Congress of 1912, it wondered 'why a small group of people have recently founded a new Italian Nationalist party, warmongering and arrogant, with helmet and sword ready to cut down their neighbours in the name of a parody of Italian imperialism'.[19] Perhaps the Vatican did not want the Nationalists spoiling the game, just when the Catholics were entering the political arena under *Giolitti's* auspices. Certainly many lay Catholics were anxious to keep their independence, and to show that it was possible to be patriotic without being Nationalist.

The real domestic losers of the Libyan War were the Socialists. In March 1911 Giolitti had offered them a post in his new government, but they had refused him again. Still, the offer showed Giolitti's good intentions, and Bissolati for one rejected it most reluctantly. It looked as if the PSI was on the threshold of power. The war changed all that. It isolated the party's deputies, and strengthened the 'revolutionary' wing. The PSI opposed the war on principle, but its attempts to mount anti-war demonstrations established the party's reputation as a treacherous fifth column undermining national security. Giolitti could no longer look to the Socialist deputies if he needed support, and they in turn felt betrayed by him.

Moreover, the war split the party. Some of its main reformist leaders, including Bissolati, Bonomi and Cabrini, were expelled for supporting the war, or rather for congratulating the king on escaping assassination. They soon formed the 'Italian Reformist Socialist Party', with little support except in the South and Liguria. Although Turati and most other reformists remained inside the old party, the 'reformist' wing never recovered from this blow. The 'revolution-aries' captured the leadership in 1912, and appointed a fiery twenty-nine-year-old Socialist from Romagna, Benito Mussolini, to be editor of the party newspaper *Avanti!* Mussolini, like other Socialist editors before and after him, used the job to become virtual party leader. He was a brilliant journalist, and under his leadership *Avanti!* campaigned fiercely against the corrupt placemen and militarists who murdered ordinary workers both in Libya and at home. So did the syndicalists, 100,000 strong by December 1913, militant and anti-militarist, and always ready to denounce any 'betrayals' by Socialist leaders. Henceforth there would be much less chance of Socialists being 'absorbed' into the bourgeois political system, and many fewer compromises between Giolitti and the moderate Socialist leadership. Giolitti had betrayed his main allies, and his system would have to take the consequences.

7.6 THE SUFFRAGE OF 1912

Thus the Libyan War demolished the old familiar bases of Italian politics. The most important change of all was also partly a consequence of the war. For some years there had been a desultory debate about widening the suffrage, and in March 1911 Giolitti had made it part of his new government programme. In 1912, as Italy's conscript soldiers faced death in the Libyan desert, it was impossible to deny them the vote any longer. A new law brought in almost universal male suffrage: all literate men aged 21 and over would have the vote, as previously, but so would those who had completed military service, and all men aged 30 whether literate or not. The electorate, which had been below 3 million in 1909, rose overnight to nearly 8.5 million; the age of mass politics had arrived. Many argued that the change was premature. The existing voters would be swamped by 5 million illiterates; and indeed one estimate is that in 1913 70 per cent of Italy's voters could neither read nor write.[20]

This reform was not the result of any irresistible popular agitation. It was introduced from above, by Giolitti and the 'constitutional' Liberals. They argued that it would be a symbol of national unity during a war, that it would strengthen the conservative rural areas against the 'subversive' towns, and that it would make the working classes more responsible and less given to extremism. In fact, most of the 'subversives' were literate Northerners who had the vote already; and the really troublesome illiterate ones were aged below 30, and still would not get it. Most observers assumed it would make little difference, for governments would still 'manage' elections, and the same people would still be elected. Others, more perceptively, saw that it would weaken the traditional hold of the provincial towns over their surrounding countryside.

The first elections under the new system were held in 1913, and at first sight did indeed show little significant change. Admittedly the Socialist vote rose from 19.0 per cent in 1909 to 22.8 per cent, and the PSI deputies increased from 41 to 79; yet only in Apulia and Latium were there signs of a dramatic Socialist breakthrough (in Apulia the Socialist vote rose from 3 per cent to 17.3 per cent). The 'constitutional' parties retained 56.7 per cent of the vote. More than two-thirds of the deputies had sat in the Chamber before, a higher proportion than in 1909.

Yet Giolitti's new majority was not quite so comfortable as usual. The Liberal and 'constitutional' seats fell from 382 to 318, out of the total 511. Above all, it rested heavily on organized Catholicism. There were 65 Catholic candidates, and 29 were elected. Furthermore, Count Gentiloni, president of the Catholic Electoral Union, had thought it was pointless to give Catholic votes to Liberal candidates without secure guarantees that they would support Catholic interests if elected. So the Electoral Union had asked parliamentary candidates to sign their agreement to 'seven Points' (on religious education in schools, no divorce law, etc.) in return for the Catholic vote. Many did so, and were duly elected. Gentiloni boasted after the election that 228 deputies owed their seats to Catholic support, although the figure was hotly disputed (especially by the ones who were Masons or known freethinkers). Giolitti always denied he had had anything to do with this 'Gentiloni Pact', and indeed denied it had ever existed. But the informal arrangements were real enough in many constituencies. The 'Pact' showed that the Catholics could reasonably press for more 'concessions'. Their political organization was, in many places, much stronger than that of the Liberals; they were better equipped for the new age of mass politics, now that the rural areas had the vote. The Catholics, and only the Catholics, could provide the mass anti-Socialist turnout. Henceforth the Liberal regime rested on Catholic support.

7.7 THE END OF THE 'GIOLITTIAN SYSTEM'

There were many other reasons for the collapse of Giolittianism, besides the Libyan War and the introduction of semi-universal male suffrage. Giolitti was a good political juggler, but even he could not keep all the balls in the air at once. If he made concessions to the Socialists, he annoyed the Catholics. If he allied with the Catholics, he lost the Radicals. If he invaded Libya, he betrayed the Socialists. It was, for example, all very well to set up a Supreme Council of Labour to consult with and help 'absorb' the Socialist labour movement, but what about the Catholic labour institutions, or the syndicalists? Political systems that rest on 'absorption' and 'concessions' are always faced with this 'me-too' problem; it is still a major issue in Italy today. It was particularly acute in the later Giolittian years, because economic growth had slowed down; there was simply not enough money available to keep everybody happy.

Another problem was that Giolitti was soft on Socialism, but after the Libyan War Socialism was unfashionable. In any case, moderate leaders like Turati had lost control of the PSI, and the revolutionary syndicalists were winning support away from the moderate Socialist unions. Any hope of 'absorbing' the party and the unions into the system had to be abandoned after 1912. All 'Comrade Giolitti' had done, and continued to do, was to alienate other powerful groups, particularly among the industrialists and landowners. In 1911–14 Giolitti continued to make influential enemies. In 1911 he brought in a bill to nationalize life insurance: profits made by the new State monopoly would pay for sickness and old-age pensions for the poor. This proposal smacked of Socialism. It was furiously opposed by financial institutions at home and abroad (60 per cent of existing policies had been issued by foreign companies), and by the Catholics (whose banks and insurance companies had a major interest). The bill was eventually passed in 1912, after being amended so that existing companies might continue operating for ten more years, but it had antagonized many powerful people.

In 1913 Giolitti repeated this error. During a major dispute in the Turin car industry, the Prefect of Turin informed the local employers that, if they locked out their workers, the police would not protect their factories. Moreover, the Giolittian newspaper La Tribuna published a sharp attack on Bonnefon Craponne, the president of the Industrial League. The industrialists protested against 'the inexplicable declarations of the political authorities and their illegal attitude',[21] but they had to give in. Three weeks later the dispute ended, with real concessions to the Socialist-led Engineering Union, FIOM. Bonnefon Craponne resigned his post. The industrialists did not forget or forgive their defeat, and they drew the appropriate conclusions. If the government was going to become the arbiter of labour disputes, it was important to have the government on their side. Giolitti was on the other side – and would any democratic government act otherwise? Craponne's successor, Dante Ferraris, was soon financing L'Idea Nazionale.

Thus by 1914 a complex bloc of opposition to Giolitti had built up. What brought him down eventually was Gentiloni's public claims about how indispensable the Catholics had been to the new government's majority. This made it impossible for Giolitti to keep his other allies happy. The Radicals withdrew their support, and their deputies hastily left the government. Giolitti immediately resigned. Now it was the Catholics' turn to feel betrayed: had not Giolitti passed up a marvellous opportunity to work with them and grant 'concessions', free from Radical anticlerical pressure? Thus Giolitti's 'system' ran into the sands, amid much bitterness and recrimination.

Giolitti's downfall highlighted the major defect of his system: the weakness, indeed the virtual absence, of an organized Liberal – constitutional party. This was, of course, an old theme of political debate. But it became far more acute in 1911–13. Giolitti was a Liberal, trying to reconcile new political and social organizations with traditional dynastic and bureaucratic authority, and attempting to remain the arbiter in a contending pluralist world. He wooed the Socialists and the unions, or made deals with the Catholics, in order to gain legitimacy for the State and its institutions. He never attempted to form a mass party of the moderate Right, for this would have needed full Catholic support, and might easily have meant Catholic dominance. In any case, it was not necessary. The provinces remained reliable; the Prefects and local 'notables' could still get out the restricted vote. His was an old-fashioned style of politics, restricted to an élite and concerned with the ancient issues of clericalism and consensus, progress and patronage.

But mass suffrage changed everything. It meant mass parties. And there were no possible bases for a mass Right-wing party except patriotism or religion. Giolitti's rival, Antonio Salandra, realized this clearly:

we, unlike our Catholic colleagues, cannot offer Paradise in heaven; nor, unlike our Socialist colleagues, can we offer Paradise on earth ... nevertheless a flame of idealism inspires us too, for the flame, the very essence of Italian Liberalism, is patriotism, is love of one's country.[22]

After 1913 most governments in Italy were either nationalist, or Catholic, or both; or, to be more exact, they wore nationalist or Catholic labels. The old Giolittian game of parliamentary manoeuvres and 'concessions' to organized groups might well continue, but only under new auspices. The Church's influence was accepted, and there was more overt patriotism, more sabre-rattling, certainly more public profession of interest in the High Politics of international diplomacy. And all this was happening on the eve of August 1914.

REFERENCES

1. Giolitti to Prefects 1 June 1906, in G. Giolitti, *Quarant'Anni di Politica Italiana*, ii, Milan 1962, p. 423.
2. Prefect of Vicenza to Minister of the Interior 8 Jan. 1905, in *ACS*, Min. Int., Dir. Gen. Ammin. Civile, 'Comuni', b. 196. These files contain a great deal of unexplored material on central–local relations.
3. A. Nasalli Rocca, *Memorie di un Prefetto*, Rome 1946, p. 131.
4. F. Cordova, 'Alcuni ricordi inediti di un prefetto dell'età liberale', *SC*, v (1974), 334–39.
5. M. Sylvers, 'L'anticlericalismo nel socialismo italiano', in *Movimento Operaio e Socialista,* xvi (1970), 187.
6. Mussolini motion, quoted in L. Cortesi, *Il Socialismo Italiano tra Riforme e Rivoluzione*, Bari 1969, p. 545.

7. G. Giolitti, *Memorie della mia Vita*, Milan 1922, repr. 1967, p. 144.

8. R. Michels, *Il Proletariato e la Borghesia nel Movimento Socialista Italiano*, Turin 1908, p. 104.

9. G. De Rosa, *Storia del Movimento Cattolico in Italia*, i, Bari 1966, p. 433.

10. G. Suardi, 'Quando e come i cattolici poterono partecipare alle elezioni politiche', in *Nuova Antologia*, 1 Nov. 1927, 121.

11. Published in Verona 1901; now in *ACS*, Min. Int., Dir. Gen. Aff.Culto, b. 136.

12. Quoted in G. De Rosa, *Storia del Movimento Cattolico . . .* , i, p. 423.

13. S. Burgalassi, *Italiani in Chiesa*, Brescia 1967, pp. 16–17.

14. E. Corradini, *Il Nazionalismo Italiano*, Milan 1914, p. 44.

15. N. Valeri, *Giovanni Giolitti*, Turin 1972, p. 8; C. Sforza, *Contemporary Italy*, New York 1944, p. 163.

16. F. S. Nitti, *Il Partito Radicale e la Nuova Democrazia Industriale*, Turin 1907, p. 115.

17. Resolution of the 1914 Congress, quoted in F. Gaeta, *Il Nazionalismo Italiano*, Naples 1965, p. 120.

18. Memorandum to Giolitti 28 July 1911, in *Quarant'Anni di Politica . . .* , iii, p. 55.

19. *L'Osservatore Romano*, 25 Sept. 1913 and 23 Dec. 1912; quoted in L. Ganapini, *Il Nazionalismo Cattolico*, Bari 1970, pp. 196–97.

20. A. S. Hershey, 'The recent Italian elections', *American Political Science Review*, viii (1914), pp. 50–56.

21. Resolution of the Industrial League, 27 May 1913; quoted in M. Abrate, *La Lotta Sindacale nella Industrializzazione in Italia*, Milan 1967, p. 116.

22. Speech to Chamber of Deputies 17 Dec. 1913, quoted in B. Vigezzi, 'Il suffragio universale e la "crisi" del liberalismo in Italia', in *NRS*, xlviii (1964), 534.

CHAPTER EIGHT

An Italian people?

The first half of this book has emphasized the varied nature of Italy and of the Italians: their regional diversity, the fragility of their national institutions and so forth. It has also shown how both the political system and the economy were transformed in the early twentieth century. How far, then, had Italian society been transformed too? By 1914, after all, the ruling élite had been trying for over fifty years to 'make Italians' in their own image. Had they succeeded? Or had the Italians somehow 'made themselves' despite, rather than because of, the efforts of their rulers?

8.1 POPULATION AND MIGRATION

In one crude sense they were doing so less than before. The birth-rate had begun to decline in the towns, and even in the rural areas of two or three Northern and Central regions. In 1911 live births per 1,000 women of child-bearing age were 147.5 over all Italy, but only 107.0 in Piedmont, 106.4 in Liguria, and 132.1 in Tuscany. The South had much higher figures – Basilicata 174.1, Apulia 172.2. Even so, it was too early yet to talk of a North–South divide, or of 'demographic dualism'. Rural Veneto and Lombardy, with their Catholic traditions, retained high birth-rates too (over all Veneto it was 173.4), and in the share-cropping areas of Central Italy family size tended to be much higher than elsewhere. The sharpest decline in births took place in the cities – Turin showed only 74 births per 1,000 child-bearing women in 1900–1, and both Bologna and Florence had only 79. The death-rate was also declining, and here the North–South distinction was actually diminishing. It was still fairly high at the turn of the century, with deaths per 1,000 inhabitants varying from 19.6 in Liguria to 27.4 in Basilicata (the national average was 22.4). By 1909–13 the national average had come down to 20.0, with a smaller regional range (Apulia 22.8, Piedmont 17.5).

This improvement had several causes. Much of the money spent on the

161

South went on aqueducts, irrigation and water supply, and the disastrous cholera epidemics of the 1880s were less frequent. Furthermore, the two secular scourges of rural Italy, malaria and pellagra, were both being conquered. Over 1 million people had suffered bouts of malaria in 1898; but in the next decade the disease was greatly curtailed everywhere except Sardinia, and deaths from malaria in 1905–9 were less than a quarter of those twenty years earlier. Sir Ronald Ross had discovered the cause; people began to put wire netting on their windows; and after 1900 quinine was distributed at government expense throughout the affected provinces. A vast propaganda campaign began, to persuade people to take their free quinine, and to assure them that it would work better than wine. This was a real social revolution. It opened up vast dreary regions of low-lying land in Southern and Central Italy to possible cultivation and improvement. People began living in the countryside again for the first time in centuries: in Basilicata the rural population almost doubled between 1871 and 1911. As for pellagra, the breakthrough also came in the early twentieth century, as the rural inhabitants of Northern Italy came to supplement their maize-based diet with richer foods. The disease was disappearing by 1914, and was virtually wiped out soon after the First World War.

The population data indicate clearly that the classic 'demographic breakthrough' to fewer births and fewer deaths was well under way in the towns. The lower birth-rate is partly explicable in terms of late marriages. The median overall age of marriage in 1906–10 was 28.6 for men, and 24.5 for women. Many urban dwellers, like soldiers, prisoners or priests, were not encouraged to marry at all, and many others – particularly the 'intellectual classes' whose careers began late – could not marry early. The median age for teachers was 32. In 1911, one-third of the people aged 31–35 in Turin were unmarried. Housing was scarce in the towns, and marriage – or rather, childbirth – meant less income in an age when female labour was in great demand in industry and domestic service. Thus people married late; but the vital question about marriage is not so much when, as who? The answer was that they usually married people like themselves. Industrial workers, in particular, tended to do so, perhaps because they often lived in working-class ghettoes near factories. A survey of Milan in 1909 found that 1,519 male industrial workers out of 1,838 had married female industrial workers, or their daughters. Rome, however, was different. It was the only 'melting pot' in Italy, with little industry. There, only farmers and the intellectual professions were likely to choose spouses from among their own kind.

As an institution, marriage survived the demographic transition without serious challenge. The nuclear family ruled supreme, at least outside the share-cropping areas. Illegitimate children were surprisingly rare, and not likely to survive – in Milan, in 1905, over one-third of them died in their first year, more than twice the mortality of legitimate offspring. Orphans were similarly at risk. Indeed, the foundling hospitals were a national disgrace. In Rome nearly half the babies in them died in their first year. A society in which family ties were so important, in which the family was the economic unit, could not be expected to waste resources or sympathy on defenceless outsiders. The urban family was helped by a network of day nurseries, usually run by nuns, and by the farming-out of city babies to be wet-nursed in the nearby countryside: in Milan, again, one-third of the babies born in 1900 were living outside the city on census day in February 1901. Wet-nursing also gave rural families friends and contacts in the city – very useful later on if the peasants moved to the city and needed a job or a house. And it was the shortage of urban wet-nurses that partly explains the slaughter in the orphanages.

The family was also helped by a flourishing literature of an improving kind, preaching the virtues of family life and explaining the delicacies of woman's role. A host of illustrated magazines and booklets explained that the woman's task was to please her husband, and to make herself and her home so attractive that he would no longer go off to the wine shop. Italian women, proclaimed 'Donna Clara', had never learned to choose the right wallpaper or, more generally, to 'embellish the nest and win their husband for family life' – as in England.[1] Big department stores grew up to cater for these curious new aspirations. Shopping became a respectable, even enjoyable, female activity, instead of a tedious chore for the servants. So, too, did cooking. The first really successful cookery book for the middle-class housewife appeared in 1891, Pellegrino Artusi's *Science in the Kitchen and the Art of Eating Well* (note the 'progressive' title). Modern plumbing and the new electric light helped too, by making homes more pleasant.

All this was very important. Rapid economic and social change was helping to emancipate women and give them education and employment. The family might easily have been threatened. Yet the effect was quite different. Lombroso found that in working-class areas of Turin family cohesion was strengthened, if anything, by women finding industrial jobs, for grandmothers and aunts became essential as child-minders. The family was the worker's best protection against sickness and old age; it was often the only source of comfort and satisfaction in an extremely harsh life. And middle-class women found new outlets and satisfactions within the family framework. The 'Italian Lady' was, indeed, invented as an ideal in the years before 1914; she flourished, graceful, tender and self-sacrificing, for the next fifty years.

Yet even the Italian Lady was known to complain at times. Women were excluded from certain professions, e.g. advocate; even a professor of law at Rome University, Teresa Labriola, was turned down by the Bar in 1913. Another obvious grievance was the lack of a vote. Committees for Female Suffrage existed in all the major cities, even Naples, by 1906. Although most women's organizations concerned themselves with charitable works – organizing hostels for young working girls, founding schools for illiterates, providing school meals – they also debated political and social issues, and founded national organizations to do so. In 1898 various Radical feminists formed an association 'For Woman'; in 1903 came the more respectable National Council of Italian Women, presided over by Countess Gabriella Spalletti Rasponi; the Union of Women, a section of Catholic Action, was founded in 1908; in 1910 there was a (Catholic) women's trade union. In 1911 Radical women shocked the bourgeois by holding a congress in Castel

Sant'Angelo. All this ferment even produced Italy's first feminist novel, *A Woman* by Sibilla Aleramo (actually by Rina Faccio, cousin of one of Italy's best-known feminists 70 years later). Radical, Socialist and Catholic feminists agreed about opening up the professions and about the vote, about the need for maternity leave and more factory inspectors, about closing the brothels and introducing legal investigation of paternity; but they were split on most other family and educational issues.

The strength and nature of marriage as an institution was seen clearly in the courts, and in the fate of the various proposals for a divorce law. Wives were not permitted to administer their own property or even have a bank account without their husband's permission. Another good example is adultery, which in law could be committed only by a woman. In 1903 the Supreme Court of Cassation ruled, in a famous judgment, that a woman could commit adultery with a man 'even if he lacked, through amputation, his male organ'.[2] The courts also regularly annulled marriages where the husband had discovered, too late, that his bride was not a virgin. But divorce was a different matter. It was supported by Radicals, Socialists, and even by a few Liberals like Zanardelli, but by few others. The civil code proclaimed firmly that 'marriage is only dissolved by the death of one of the spouses'. Most 'lay' conservatives thought a divorce law would undermine social stability. It would also needlessly antagonize the Church, just when her support was needed against the rising tide of Socialism. When bills were introduced into parliament, clerical bodies in the country organized huge petitions. There were 637,000 signatures against Villa's bill in 1881, 700,000 in 1893, and 3.5 million against Zanardelli in 1902. The Italians may have married late, but they married for ever.

Late marriage does not explain all the decline in births. For working-class couples, there was an average gap of four years nine months between marriage and the birth of the first child; even the 'educated classes' took two and a half years. Clearly there was some voluntary birth-control going on, but how? One enterprising demographer sent a questionnaire round to doctors and gynaecologists, but they did not know, or if they did they would not say. Sheath contraceptives were easily available in the cities, their use justified by the need to ward off venereal disease, so this was presumably part of the answer. Some priests and confessors still followed the old canon law in permitting abortion within 40 days, while condemning contraception as wicked.[3]

The urban population was growing faster than ever before. In 1881 23.6 per cent of the Italian people had lived in municipalities with over 20,000 inhabitants; by 1911 31.3 per cent did. Urban growth – i.e. the number of people living in such *comuni* – was about 3 per cent p.a. between 1901 and 1911, which remained a record rate of increase until after the Second World War. Both Milan and Rome doubled in population between 1871 and 1911, and each had over 500,000 inhabitants by 1911. Naples, with 678,000 inhabitants in 1911, was still larger than either.

Immigration accounted for most of the increase, probably about three-quarters overall. In 1901, less than half the population of Rome or Milan had been born there. Usually the incomers were relatively local; there was, as yet, negligible movement from the South to the Northern cities. In the Northern 'industrial triangle' of Piedmont, Liguria and Lombardy, only about 12 per cent of the inhabitants in 1911 had been born in a different *province*. A crude conclusion emerges. The Northern cities absorbed much of the surplus population of the surrounding rural areas. The Southern ones did not, and so rural Southerners went to American cities instead. Admittedly some Southern towns expanded rapidly too – Catania and Taranto became successful industrial centres and busy ports in this period – but in most cases the growth was 'artificial', restricted to provincial capitals that 'specialized' in administration.

The great problem in the expanding cities was housing. Middle-class urban dwellers lived in flats with running water, central heating and indoor toilets; some even had lifts and telephones. The residential blocks were built by major development companies, linked to and often founded by the commercial banks. Working-class housing was more primitive. There were one or two 'model villages' built by enlightened industrialists, e.g. Crespi on the Adda, near Milan, but a cheap subsidized housing programme was only just beginning. In 1903 building co-operatives were given tax concessions, and savings banks were similarly encouraged to move into housing finance, but the incentives proved inadequate. As the cities grew, lack of housing became a desperate social problem, bringing many other evils in its train. The building industry, and local government, clearly could not cope. In Milan, where net immigration was running at about 14,000 a year, only 15,436 rooms were officially declared furnished and habitable in 1913; in 1911 over half the city's population lived in a one- or two-room dwelling. Nowhere else was quite so crowded, except Messina where the 1908 earthquake had destroyed the city; but in Naples the figure for those living in a one- or two-room dwelling was 43.2 per cent, and in Turin 42.4 per cent.

Nevertheless, people were anxious to move to the towns. They offered better jobs, better education, even better hygiene and living conditions. Most of the new immigrants settled on the city outskirts, not in the centre. For the most part they were unskilled peasants, and their work was in the most menial and lowest-paid sectors – domestic service for girls, building or food-processing for men. A few employers, like Pirelli, deliberately took on unskilled immigrants, so as to pay low wages and be free of union trouble, but this was unusual. More often it was the 'natives' who had the industrial jobs, the immigrants who took what was left. In Milan only 11 per cent of servants in 1901 had been born there; 53 per cent of the city's printers had. We cannot conclude, therefore, that it was a period of great *social* (as opposed to geographical) mobility, although there was surprising social flexibility in Rome. Chessa found, using 1908 data, that 22 per cent of the sons of manual workers there had white-collar jobs, and 27 per cent of white-collar workers' sons had manual ones.

These were the years of massive Southern emigration to '*La Merica*'. Between 1898 and 1914 there were never less than 150,000 emigrants crossing the Atlantic each year, and in the peak years five times as many. Over 70 per cent of them were Southerners, and 25 per cent came from Sicily. Emigration to Europe also increased, mainly temporary and by North Italians, but it was the sudden Southern exodus to the New World which attracted the most attention, and which had the most impact. Many of these transatlantic emigrants – roughly 40 per cent betweeen 1897 and 1906, and over 66 per cent later – returned to Italy after making, or failing to make, their fortunes; many of them later went back to America again. Indeed, a kind of seasonal migration developed across the Atlantic: Southern peasants set off in November to work in the Argentine or the USA and returned in the spring for agricultural jobs. In short, migration was a complex business. Different groups of Italians went in different directions, and most of them came back – nine-tenths of those who went to Europe did so. Even so, over 1½ million Italians must have left their native country for good between 1901 and 1911. And the ones who came back brought new ideas and new values. Few artisans or industrial workers left Italy, for they could easily find jobs at home. Most emigrants were young, male, unskilled and rural. As the peasants and labourers moved out, whole regions took on a peculiar demographic colour. In Calabria, for example, there were only two men for every three women in the 25–45 age-group. And Calabria was not extraordinary: Abruzzi, Molise, and Basilicata saw an even higher proportion of their people leave, and Veneto was little different.

The causes of emigration were both obvious and complex. Poverty, unemployment, high taxes, above all the disastrous effects of Crispi's 'tariff war' on the Southern rural areas in the 1890s – all these contributed to the process. So, obviously, did the need of American cities for labour, and the need of local shipping company agents for their commission (see §2.4). Once started, the process was self-perpetuating and self-expanding. A few pioneers crossed the Atlantic, then sent word back home, and soon their relatives and neighbours joined them. Emigration may be seen as an 'individualistic' alternative to labour militancy: it was highest in the hill areas of Abruzzi-Molise and Basilicata, but it was low on the neighbouring Apulian plateau, where 'capitalist farming' prevailed, where the labourers' unions managed to win many concessions, and where there was little chance of buying land on your return. The same contrast could be seen in the North, between the hills of Veneto and the plain of Emilia.

Most Italians welcomed this exodus. It was, they thought, an acceptable remedy for grievous problems. It would reduce the pressure of population on resources, raise wages for those labourers who remained, provide thousands of people with capital for investment in agriculture or housing, and give a great incentive to become literate and 'modern' in outlook. Nitti, in a famous phrase, described emigration as 'a powerful safety-valve against class hatreds'[4] – a good argument in the troubled 1890s. Sonnino thought that to prevent emigration would be to attack the poor. However, the State should certainly prevent exploitation by shipping agents or other countries. In fact, in 1901 a General Commission for Emigration was set up. It provided advice to emigrants, and supervised conditions on the ships. Much was also done by private or clerical charities, particularly the *Opera Assistenza agli Operai Italiani* founded by Bishop Bonomelli of Cremona.

Such views were realistic and compassionate, but also somewhat Olympian and detached. Emigrants were often victims of abject poverty and vicious local greed, virtually driven out by brutal landowners and an indifferent country. De Amicis, in *On Blue Water*, described their sufferings with masterly sentimentality, and aroused much indignation on their behalf. Emigration came to be seen as shameful, and as a refutation of any claim to be 'making Italians'. Catholics deplored its effects on family life, and indeed on religious belief – thousands of the emigrants to America came back as Protestants, often as Pentecostalists. Nationalists worried that Italy was losing too many of her potential soldiers: Southern overpopulation should be remedied by colonies in Africa, not emigration to America. Thus after 1907 the debate on emigration gradually changed. It ceased to be a gentlemanly discussion of economic and social change, and became instead a clamour for imperialism.

8.2 THE USES OF LEISURE

With greater prosperity, Italians now had more leisure. Some had it in abundance. There were around 200,000 men with private incomes – rentiers, absentee landowners and the like. These were the 'idle rich'; or rather, the jobless upper classes. Many of them were, in fact, extremely poor, and clamoured for government posts. Others worked hard at their pleasures. The social élite, and even some others, took to manly sports. Gymnastics, shooting and fencing were all popular – the last two not merely for recreation, since duelling was still fairly common among the upper classes. Mountaineering was also much favoured by the affluent. The Italian Alpine Club's Milan branch had 2,338 members by 1914. The Alpine Club published maps and guidebooks, built huts, diversified into winter sports (skiing was also becoming fashionable) and, above all, organized school trips. Why? Because if Italy were ever to enter a European war, her soldiers would have to fight it out in the Alps. G. C. Abba, one of Garibaldi's 'Thousand', published a school textbook on the subject in 1901. Mountains, being nearer to God, make people virtuous. Climbing them makes boys manly, and 'so, almost without noticing, they are trained as citizens and as soldiers . . . the youth who wears the Alpine Club's badge will, if the country calls on him in future, make an excellent Alpine soldier in war'.[5]

Thus sport could and did have an overt patriotic purpose. However, gymnastics and other martial exercises had little mass appeal. Cycling was the first sport to become generally popular in Italy. The *Touring Club Italiano*, now Italy's equivalent of the Automobile Association, was founded in 1894 for cyclists. By 1900 it had 20,000 members. One of the *Gazzetta dello Sport*'s first activities was to organize cycle races round Lombardy, and later round Italy. Even cycling had originally been an aristocratic pursuit – it depended on people being affluent enough to buy bicycles and having leisure enough to ride them. And even cycling could be politicized. Soon 'Red cyclists' were setting out every Sunday from the Lombard and Emilian towns, to convert the local peasantry to Socialism.

Another new sport that soon became popular was association football. It, too, was originally a diversion for the gentry, and foreign gentry at that. The first clubs were founded by Englishmen and bore English names: 'Milan' and 'Genoa', not 'Milano' or 'Genova'. Indeed, they were usually founded as much for cricket as for football – 'Genoa' was originally the 'Genoa Cricket and Athletic Club', founded in 1892, and 'Milan' started life in 1899 as the 'Milan Cricket and Football Club'. Even Palermo had a cricket club in 1897. However, cricket unaccountably failed to catch on in Italy (unlike Corfu), whereas the sporting upper classes adopted soccer eagerly. In 1898 came the first championship, won by 'Genoa' whose team contained only five foreigners. In 1910 Italy played her first international, beating France 6–2; the match was played in Milan, and attracted 6,000 spectators. Football was still the sport of gentlemen, but it, too, could be politicized or, rather, sanctified: many of the first teams were founded as Catholic sports clubs.

Then there was the greatest new mass entertainment of them all, the cinema. 'Moving pictures' arrived in Italy early in 1897, being shown at circuses and fairs. The first cinemas were built a few years later, and by 1910 most provincial capitals had at least one. An Italian film industry arose, specializing in documentaries. Vitrotti made a famous film about *The Cavalry School at Pinerolo*, and there were several about the Libyan War. Another favourite *genre* was the grand historical epic, often celebrating the achievements of the *Risorgimento*: the first film made by the leading Alberini and Santoni company was *The Taking of Rome* (in 1870). 'Moving pictures' provided a marvellous opportunity to combine entertainment with patriotic uplift. The glories of ancient Rome soon became remarkably familiar to Italian cinemagoers. So, too, did battles and violent armed conflict. The political uses of leisure were all too evident in the cinema: where else could Italians be shown their past so vividly, or be taught their true destiny?

Finally, the cafés and wine shops still flourished. Wine had become cheaper over the years, and consumption had risen from 80 litres per head per year in 1870–80 to 125 litres in 1911–14. That is, of course, a national average. Drinking was more common in the towns, or at least more measurable there. In 1906 the people of Milan drank 213 litres of wine each. A study of manual workers in the Testaccio area of Rome in 1911 found that virtually all of them drank two litres of wine a day, and 40 per cent drank three litres or more; they spent, on average, two hours a day in the wine shops. In Turin there were nearly 2,500 wine shops in 1907, one for every 150 inhabitants; this figure does not include clubs, or the 500-odd restaurants and *trattorie* where wine was also obtainable. All this was a real sign of prosperity, unthinkable a generation earlier. The most bibulous region of Italy was now the Veneto. Many peasants emigrated during the summer for seasonal work, returned in the autumn with enough money and nothing to do, and spent the winter in an alcoholic haze. In 1913 a prudent law provided that habitual drunkards should be struck off the electoral register. This was a necessary measure for the new era of universal male suffrage.

8.3 EDUCATION AND LITERACY

Arguably the most important changes to occur before 1914 were in the schools. Illiteracy was still high, but it was falling. The census of 1901 was the last to find that most Italian women were illiterate. By 1909 nearly three-quarters of Italian bridegrooms were able to sign the marriage register, as could nearly two-thirds of the brides. Regional differences were still very noticeable, as Table 1 in Chapter 2.5 shows, but Southerners now had a real incentive to learn to read and write: emigrants to America needed to send money and news home. Within Italy, the new townsmen found that they needed to speak 'Italian' rather than dialect, and Italian was a language that might be written and read. Furthermore, illiterates in towns were more noticeable by the élite, who felt that something should be done.

One obvious thing that could be done was to pass laws. In 1904 the larger municipalities, those with 4,000 or more inhabitants, were told to start up fifth and sixth-year classes in their primary schools. These classes would be compulsory for pupils not going on to a secondary school. The new law had some effect in the towns, but in rural areas the primary schools still offered only three years' schooling, and most children still left school at the age of 9. In any case, truancy was the norm rather than the exception, especially in the South. Local councillors were not keen on enforcing attendance, because the council had to pay the costs of schooling, and councillors needed the parents' votes. The only weapon that the occasional zealous mayor had over recalcitrant parents was, literally, a weapon: after 1904 firearm permits were not supposed to be issued to illiterates. But zealous mayors were few, and recalcitrant parents were many. Disputes over education were far more likely to be between mayors and teachers, over non-payment of salary.

In 1907–8 a close friend of Giolitti, Camillo Corradini, carried out a survey of Italian education. He drew public attention to the illiteracy and truancy, to the diverse provision in different regions, to the lack of schooling in the countryside, and to the local pressures against improvement. The result was a major reform, the Daneo–Credaro Law of 1911, which took primary education away from the municipalities. Control of the schools and teachers in each province was entrusted to a Provincial Schools' Council; half its members were elected, the other half appointed by the government. It all meant greater central control of primary education than previously, although one should not exaggerate: in the whole of Italy there were only ten inspectors of primary schools. Most local dignitaries made little protest: they may no longer have had responsibility for the schools, but neither did they have to pay for them any more. But the new law greatly annoyed the Catholics, especially in areas like the Veneto where they ran local government. Catholic hostility towards Giolitti was much increased, an important factor in the years ahead. Indeed, the law had been designed, at least partly, to counter Catholic influence, and to rescue the 'lay' school, the school of progress and patriotism, from 'Catholic' teachers and local councils.

Another way of tackling educational problems was to build schools. Before 1911 the lay State financed school-building on the Biblical principle: to him that hath shall be given. Municipalities that were rich enough to pay for buildings received State subsidies or loans to cover part of the costs; the others received virtually nothing. So the poorest and most backward regions stayed backward. Basilicata received 568,000 lire for school-building over the whole period 1861–1911, out of total national spending of 100 million lire; Cosenza province, in Calabria, got nothing at all. After 1911 it became compulsory for municipalities to build decent schools, and money was allocated for this purpose to each province – 240 million lire over the next ten years. But fate intervened. The First World War started before building had seriously begun, and by 1920 the lira was worth one-quarter of its previous value. In Reggio Calabria province not a single new school had been built by then; many of the schools were still the same temporary huts put up after the 1908 earthquake.

The structure of secondary education was left substantially unchanged. However, the number of pupils in technical schools and technical institutes (see §2.5) doubled between 1901 and 1912, from 55,180 to 123,909, as did the number of future primary teachers in the 'scuole normali' (from 20,000 to 50,000). This expansion was in sharp contrast to the more traditional *ginnasi* and *licei*, where pupil numbers remained little altered at around 65,000 (including private schools). There was also more emphasis on mathematics and physics in the technical institutes, and in 1910 a '*liceo moderno*' was introduced – a new senior secondary school, teaching more science than the other *licei*, and a modern language instead of Greek. In practice, much 'secondary' education was also provided by the 'popular universities', extension courses started by various university faculties and workers' organizations from 1901 onwards. By 1906 there were fifty-one of them, nearly all in the North. There were also libraries run by the Italian Union of Popular Education, as well as by the larger Chambers of Labour and other Socialist or Republican bodies.

These changes were very significant. Secondary education, at least in Northern Italy, was shifting away from a 'classical' to a practical, scientific, engineering emphasis, and more pupils were choosing this kind of training. It all meant that innovations could spread more easily. Artisans and craftsmen could develop new skills, and were literate and numerate enough to run small businesses successfully.

Only the universities continued relatively undisturbed, bastions of the old 'positivist' culture. True, they had to cope with a few more students – they had 27,388 in 1901–2, and 30,612 ten years later – and they were expected to put on extension courses, but otherwise little was changed. Even the growth in student numbers was much less than it had been in the late 1880s or 1890s.

Nearly one-third of the students still read law. The Italian universities produced each year a steady 1,700 law graduates, 700 doctors and 230 scientists and mathematicians. It was not an impressive achievement for an industrializing society, and it was much less impressive than what was happening in secondary education. Inevitably, the State stepped in. Some of the professors had to suffer the indignity of no longer running their own entrance examinations, and in subjects like accountancy and medicine even the final qualifying examinations came under ministerial supervision in 1906–7. Here was the State insisting on a core curriculum and on minimum national standards. Moreover, key professional groups were being brought into the State's orbit. There was the usual anguished debate about 'academic freedom' and ministerial tyranny. Even so, this was not a serious reform of the universities, much though they needed one. Most subjects were not affected, and on the whole universities continued to operate with the same splendid incompetence as before. Examinations, for example, covered only the work done in class, so if students could disrupt the lectures, they would not have to sit the exams. Every spring, as the examination season approached, the students would riot and the universities would be closed.

The *licei* and the universities were often accused of being breeding-grounds for parasites. Clearly 1,700 new lawyers each year were not all going to find jobs, even if they took to public administration or journalism. In Naples the Radical economist Francesco Nitti realized that he was surrounded by an 'intellectual proletariat' – hordes of unemployable lawyers and doctors, unable to find clients and desperately seeking government posts. He thought they were the really 'dangerous classes' in Italian society, and perhaps he was right, for Southern intellectuals were soon found leading the Socialist, Communist, syndicalist and Nationalist movements. Doctors and engineers could always emigrate, and Barbagli estimates that between 1901 and 1914 over half of Italy's annual production of graduates went abroad – a real brain-drain.[6] As for the others, governments tried to create jobs for them somehow. Established posts in the State administration, even excluding the post office and the railways, rose steadily. In 1882 there had been 98,354, in 1907 there were 139,216, in 1914 there were 165,996; and the top jobs increased faster than the rest (there were 103 'heads of division' in 1882, but 314 in 1914).[7] Before 1914 Italy had twice as many officials running its Colonial Ministry as Britain had. Even so, the problem of graduate unemployment remained overwhelming, and so did its political implications.

Thus education in Italy was clearly split. An industrial bourgeoisie was growing up, with engineering and accounting skills; yet the country was also overproducing lawyers and classicists, who demanded more jobs in teaching and administration. Since few of the technical schools and institutes were in the South, this was tantamount to a North–South split. And it was worsened by the fact that the top bureaucracy was still firmly in Northern hands. But the pressure for jobs came mainly from the South, and in the long term the traditional Northern control of the State machinery was bound to be challenged.

8.4 THE PRESS

The growth of the press was a natural outcome of greater literacy. Newspapers had always been an influential forum for debate in Liberal Italy (see §2.5), but from around 1900 onwards they became a real 'fourth estate', an important channel of political persuasion and mobilization. In Milan, Luigi Albertini took over the *Corriere della Sera* in July 1900. By 1913 its circulation had tripled to 350,000, and it had become almost the official 'opposition'. Its constant high-minded 'free-trading' criticism of government policies did much to undermine the Giolittian 'system' in Northern Italy. In the South the same job was done by Alberto Bergamini's *Giornale d'Italia*, founded in 1901 at Rome. Giolitti kept some support, of course: *La Stampa* in Turin, *Il Mattino* at Naples, and – especially – *La Tribuna* at Rome, were normally faithful to him, at least until 1910, and the Interior Ministry handed out regular monthly bribes to journalists on a wide range of papers. Even so, it was the two leading opposition papers that set the tone for the whole press.

The newspaper industry was changing fast. The big national papers had the advertising, and flourished; the smaller provincial papers did not, and declined. Telephone lines existed by 1903 between Rome and Milan, even Rome and Paris; news from France could appear in Italy on the same day it appeared in Paris. The big papers introduced foreign news pages, and sent out 'special correspondents' to cover major events. They also introduced linotype machines to set up the print, and began to cater for a wider audience. They started weekly magazines, devoted to sport or women's interests: the *Gazzetta dello Sport* had been founded in 1896, and the first mass circulation weekly, with 1.5 million copies, was the *Domenica del Corriere*, produced in Milan from 1899 onwards by the *Corriere della Sera* presses. Sports pages appeared in the dailies themselves. So, too, did the 'cultural page' (*terza pagina*), introduced in the *Giornale d'Italia* in 1902 and soon a characteristic feature of the serious press. It carried book and theatre reviews, short stories, extracts from novels, and articles by the leading writers and critics of the day. The 'cultural page' enabled newspapers to influence taste and opinion on a wide range of non-political issues; and it enabled a rather more uniform taste to be formed. When Croce wrote for the *Giornale d'Italia*, his words reached all the Southern intellectuals. It was a huge advance towards 'making Italians', or at least towards influencing the educated Italians.

Businessmen noted the power of the press and began buying into it, especially after 1908 when the economic climate was harsher. By 1910 even the Giolittian *La Tribuna* was owned by the *Ilva* steel trust, by Genoese shipbuilders and sugar-refiners, and by the *Banca Commerciale*. Many 'Liberal' papers became mouthpieces for big industry or the big banks, and the Catholic *Corriere d'Italia* was closely linked to the *Banco di Roma*. This development left public opinion wide open to manipulation by vested interests, as was evident before and during the Libyan War (see §7.5). However, there were enough rival papers to prevent excessive uniformity, and certainly the *Corriere della Sera* was independent enough: it campaigned for free trade, even though it was owned by cotton manufacturers, who were among the chief beneficiaries of protection.

The press was still the main arena of political and ideological discussion in Italy. There were great national newspapers, but as yet no great national parties. The leading journalists and editors were politicians, for all practical purposes, and indeed success in journalism was becoming almost a necessary prerequisite for a political career. Sturzo, Meda, Serrati, Gramsci, Nenni, above all Mussolini: they all built their political careers on journalism. Even much lesser figures could have enormous influence: a handful of Nationalist journalists in 1911–12 softened up public opinion for the Libyan War. But the great journalists and roving correspondents of the Giolittian Age rarely had a good word to say for Giolittian politics. The press had become a great 'national' institution; and in so doing had acquired its classic function, that of 'delegitimizing' the national government.

8.5 THE REVOLT OF THE INTELLECTUALS

This was not true only of the press. Giolitti's cautious and cynical policies were despised by most writers and intellectuals, either of the Right or the Left. His social reforms seemed dull, demeaning, even contemptible to them; his foreign policy was said to abandon Italy's vital interests; his parliamentary manoeuvres were regarded as corrupt. Fashionable intellectuals insisted that the Italians were not yet properly 'made', and never would be unless they abandoned the 'Giolittian system' and embraced new ideas, new literary movements, and new politics.

The new ideas can be briefly, if crudely, summarized as a 'revolt against positivism' – 'positivism' meaning here not so much a philosophy as a set of views about human behaviour and society: materialist, determinist, behaviourist and evolutionary. Benedetto Croce, the leading intellectual in Italy, was in the forefront of the 'anti-positivist' campaign, and constantly asserted aesthetic and 'spiritual' values. His extremely influential journal, *La Critica*, carried fierce reviews of works by 'positivist' writers, and helped to discredit 'official' (university-based) culture; and Croce's friendship with the publisher Giovanni Laterza enabled him to issue hundreds of suitable books or translations of literature, philosophy and history, and virtually control what literate people read. But Croce, the 'lay Pope', was too austere, and his idealist philosophy too obscure, to satisfy the more ardent spirits. In practice, positivism was challenged not so much by idealism as by irrational, mystical doctrines in philosophy, and by nationalism in politics. The writers who mattered were not great thinkers or poets, but journalists and publicists like Prezzolini, Papini, Corradini, Marinetti: young, excitable men who wrote essays in cultural reviews, with a frenetic message of urgent change. For a few brief years such intellectuals really counted for something in Italy. They gave Italians a new image of themselves: active, passionate and warlike.

The most spectacular of these intellectual groups were undoubtedly the Futurists. Filippo Marinetti and his fellows insisted on originality at all costs. The whole Italian 'past', with its piety and its pathetic liberal institutions, was a detestable burden on the living: it should be jettisoned forthwith. It was time for Italy to stop being a museum and become a factory, better still an arsenal. Venice should be encouraged to sink, and Florence should be burned down. The Futurists admired the modern, industrial world of the great Northern cities. They gloried in speed, violence, power, danger, youth, and virility. Machines, not works of art, were the greatest creations of mankind. Antonio Sant'Elia thought houses should be built of concrete and steel, like giant machines, although he was, typically, more interested in designing power stations than dwellings. Futurist composers wrote noise, not music, and Luigi Russolo built mechanical noise-machines, each producing its own sound – crackling, buzzing, exploding, etc. But it was not just fast machinery that fascinated the Futurists. Revolution and war were even more exciting. Painters depicted rioting crowds (e.g. Carrà's 'Funeral of the Anarchist Galli', and Boccioni's 'Riot in the *Galleria*'), and war was welcomed, in a famous phrase, as 'the only cure for the world'.

All this was designed to shock the bourgeois, but Marinetti and his fellows were not just clowns. Some of them, for example Boccioni, had real talent. Above all, the Futurists were among the first real prophets of the industrial age. They recognized modern technology was transforming men's sensibilities and their whole view of the world. Art must not ignore these changes; on the contrary, it should contribute to them and express them. Futurism was propaganda for the modern world, and Marinetti was a genius at publicity. The Futurists constantly put on spectacular stunts, demonstrating their rousing message throughout Europe. In February 1909 Marinetti succeeded in having the first 'Futurist Manifesto' printed on the front page of continental Europe's most influential daily, *Le Figaro*. Other manifestos followed in quick succession, to keep up the momentum and generate more excitement. For the next few years Marinetti remained the darling of the media. Perhaps his greatest innovation was the 'Futurist Evening', a mixture of music-hall, political demonstration, and happening. He used the theatre to spread the Futurist Gospel, to entertain, to provoke his enemies, and if possible to start a riot. Often he succeeded. It was all fairly good-humoured, and great fun; and it worked. The Futurists were the first *avant-garde* artistic movement to reach a mass audience. Their message was original and liberating; and much of it was political. The first 'Futurist Evening' was held in Trieste, and aimed at rousing the local Italian population against Austrian rule. The second Futurist Manifesto, in 1911, proclaimed that 'the slogan ITALY should dominate the slogan LIBERTY'.

The Futurists were not the only important group of bellicose intellectuals, nor were they the first to become prominent. In 1903 Giuseppe Prezzolini, Giovanni Papini and others had founded *Leonardo* in Florence, a cultural review that was also firmly political and Nationalist. It soon folded, but its successor *Il Regno* (1903–4) was even more overtly political. In its first issue,

Corradini explained that it aimed to be 'a voice against the present cowardice'.[8] *Il Regno*'s nationalism was rather conservative. The journal had little time for irredentism, or for anything that might upset stability in Europe; it favoured Mediterranean and colonial expansion. Moreover, 'the present cowardice' also meant the bourgeoisie's cowardice when faced by a militant proletariat, or rather by other bourgeois claiming to represent the proletariat. The message was that the middle classes should fight back hard, and not be hampered by sentimentality. *Il Regno* thus attracted support from many non-Nationalists, and acted as a 'respectable' focus for opposition to Giolitti's compromises with the Socialists.

The longest-lived and most influential of the Florentine journals was *La Voce*, which appeared from December 1908 to November 1914. *La Voce*, dominated initially by Prezzolini, was not a Nationalist journal, nor did it have any sympathy with Futurism. Like *Il Regno*, it attracted contributors of different persuasions: the Southern democrat Gaetano Salvemini was a regular contributor until 1911, as were Romolo Murri and Giovanni Amendola. It was written clearly, in simple language, and its contributors educated a large public in European ways of thought. But although the sober writers of *La Voce* were not Nationalists, they were all anti-Giolittian, anti-parliament, anti-egalitarian and anti-emigration. They all agreed that the bourgeoisie had become too soft, and they all hoped that the industrial revolution might lead to a regeneration of national politics. They all agreed, too, that Italian foreign policy after 1896 had been a series of further humiliations. Most of them welcomed the Libyan War in 1911. On occasion, they could be heard lamenting that too little blood had been shed during the *Risorgimento*, and 'even that little had not been all Italian'.[9]

Not all these 'new' writers were young. The spiritual fathers of all this ferment were Alfredo Oriani, born in 1852, and Gabriele D'Annunzio, born in 1863. Oriani was a dull fellow and a duller writer, but his tedious reflections on history and politics (especially *La Rivolta Ideale*, published in 1908) somehow became the Old Testament of the Nationalist intellectuals. It is strange how youthful revolts always seem to need aged pedantic father-figures in the background. D'Annunzio was a very different personality, and far from dull. He poured forth a stream of extravagant, narcissistic, sadistic, erotic plays, novels, poems and vituperation. His favourite themes were incest and vendetta, virile conflict and death. *La Nave*, a bloodthirsty play about medieval Venice, glorified Italy's past naval role in the Mediterranean; its famous call, 'Arm the prow and sail towards the world', became a slogan for all true patriots. Many men, and women, took his macho posturing surprisingly seriously. His well-publicized love-affairs helped maintain his flamboyant image as aesthete, superman and hero. In fact, D'Annunzio had simply adopted the ancient infallible recipe for literary success: sex and violence. But he did it *con brio*. He made militarism not merely glamorous, but erotic.

Yet politically D'Annunzio was a modern. He saw that industrial Italy had come to stay, and welcomed it. The problem was how to reconcile technology and individualism, the machine age and humanity. It was not a trivial problem, indeed it exercised the best minds of his generation. D'Annunzio's solutions – mass mobilization, romantic nationalism, and eroticism – were no doubt morally deplorable, but they were politically and psychologically feasible. Circuses, not bread, were required. Like the Futurists, D'Annunzio saw this clearly, and provided them.

The 'new' writers in Italy were very different from each other. Some of the most influential, like Georges Sorel, were not even Italians. Others, like Gaetano Mosca or Vilfredo Pareto, were not writers in the 'literary' sense, but sociologists or political theorists who evolved theories about how States were always ruled by élites. Some were anxious for war as the only redeemer of the world, others stressed the problems of *anomie* in the industrial age. D'Annunzio exalted the superman – in *La Gloria* he wrote presciently about a leader with burning eyes and strutting chin, standing on a balcony and urging a huge crowd in the piazza below to rebuild the Roman Empire. Yet they all had something in common too. They all despised parliamentary democracy, and they all detested positivism and Socialism, which were, indeed, connected. The 'reformist' Socialists had always claimed that their ideas were 'scientific' and evolutionary; Turati's *La Critica Sociale* appeared fortnightly throughout this period, with scarcely a concession to the new fashions. And the 'new' writers were all part of a general European mood of self-questioning, of interest in primitive societies and anthropology, of mistrust of the claims of 'civilization'. Pareto insisted that men were irrational creatures of passion, that progress was a myth, that Marxism was simply a smokescreen behind which ambitious intellectuals sought power for themselves, not the masses. Sorel insisted that strikes and group terrorism were acts of ritual purification and heroism, vitally necessary in impersonal industrial societies if men were to retain their self-esteem and their solidarity with others. The message to the bourgeoisie was that Socialism was a false, pernicious doctrine, and could legitimately be fought. Bourgeois rule was perfectly justified, provided it rested on bourgeois heroism.

Perhaps the real importance of these writers is that they transformed the whole debate about 'making Italians'. In the nineteenth century most disputants had assumed that 'real Italy' was rather a conservative place – rural, Catholic and reactionary. Now it was suddenly being portrayed as dynamic, urban and modern. The 'legal Italy' of the Liberals had lost its monopolistic claim to represent progress, indeed was beginning to look old-fashioned in the new industrial age. By 1912 Prezzolini and the others had set up a kind of established counter-culture: their views dominated the serious periodicals, had become almost the common sense of the age. Liberal politicians found themselves hard-pressed to justify their habitual routines. The collapse of Giolittian Italy was at least partly due to this intellectual climate. Adventures like the Libyan War were extremely popular in fashionable circles. It was difficult, in practice, to distinguish a cultural *'aggiornamento'* from a national *Risorgimento*, or a national *Risorgimento* from a successful war; or a successful war from a new political regime.

8.6 CONCLUSION

Can we conclude that 'Italians' had been 'made' into a nation-State by 1914? Urbanization and growing literacy were certainly having some effect: 'Italian' had become a *lingua franca* in the army and the towns, and perhaps 6 or 7 million people spoke it. Most people, too, had gone through some patriotic propaganda at school. A national economy existed, linked by roads and railways. Many institutions – trade unions, Catholic Action, newspapers – had become larger, more centralized, more 'national'; and some 'national' institutions, e.g. the *carabinieri*, had become fairly popular. Above all, the State had existed, for good or ill, for fifty years. People had grown used to it. Even the Church appeared 'reconciled'; even most of the 'subversives' had become respectable parliamentarians.

But one should not exaggerate. Nation-States are, in fact, very rare beasts indeed, and certainly pre-1914 Italy was not one. There was no unified 'lay' consensus, no Liberal 'hegemony', no agreement on basic ideological, educational or social aims. Most people still spoke only dialect; nearly 40 per cent of the adults were still illiterate. A popular press barely existed. Marconi had invented the wireless in 1896, but as yet there was no broadcasting, no central control of the people's information. The social and economic gap between North and South was all too evident; so, too, was the chasm between town and country. The urban petty bourgeoisie may have flirted with nationalism, but few rural dwellers were impressed, and many of them relied on income from family members abroad. And one of the great engines of uniformity in other countries, the social welfare system, did not work that way in Italy. State welfare antagonized not only conservatives, but also the existing welfare bodies, usually clerical but sometimes Republican or Socialist. It was noticeable how many of the Giolittian social and economic provisions benefited particular groups of workers, like seamen or bakers, or particular industries like steel. Italy was becoming a 'corporate State', a country of institutionalized, legally guaranteed privilege. Above all, she was still run by much the same people: a small élite, with little title to rule except its belligerent patriotism and its historical myths.

REFERENCES

1. 'Donna Clara', *L'Arte di Arredare la Casa*, Turin 1906.
2. Judgment of the Cassation Court in Rome 8 May 1903; quoted in R. Canosa, *Il Giudice e la Donna*, Milan 1978, p. 90.
3. G. Mortara, *La Popolazione delle Grandi Città Italiane*, Turin 1908, p. 146.
4. Quoted by R. Foerster in *The Italian Emigration of our Times*, Cambridge, Mass. 1919, p. 476.
5. G. C. Abba, *Le Alpi Nostre e il Monferrato*, Bergamo 1901, p. 24.

6. M. Barbagli, *Disoccupazione Intellettuale e Sistema Scolastico in Italia*, Bologna 1974, pp. 55–58 and 63–64.
7. R. Faucci, *Finanza, Amministrazione e Pensiero Economico*, Turin 1975, p. 136.
8. *Il Regno*, 29 Nov. 1903.
9. G. Amendola, in *La Voce* 28 Dec. 1911, in A. Romano (ed.), *La Cultura Italiana del '900 attraverso le Riviste*, iii, Turin 1960, p. 400.

PART THREE

1914–43

CHAPTER NINE

Italy and the Great War

9.1 THE SALANDRA GOVERNMENT AND 'RED WEEK'

The government that Antonio Salandra formed in March 1914 was not expected to last long. Most deputies still thought of Giolitti as the 'natural' Prime Minister; many of them had owed their election to him only four months previously. Salandra was a useful stop-gap, perhaps able to 'absorb' the Nationalist challenge, certainly able to hold the ring until Giolitti could win back his Radical friends and his tacit union support. Yet Salandra had other ambitions, or had other ambitions thrust upon him. His was a more conservative government than Italy had seen for many years, and it was pledged to 'national policy'.

Moreover, the new government was soon pushed even further Right. Early in June there was yet another 'proletarian massacre', when three anti-militarist demonstrators were killed at Ancona. The syndicalists, Republicans and anarchists protested furiously; the Directorate of the Socialist Party proclaimed a general strike. Even the CGL agreed to support it. The strike soon escalated into the most widespread movement of popular protest since 1898. There were riots and demonstrations in most major cities, and some small towns in Romagna and the Marches were taken over by insurgents. Railway stations were seized, telephone wires cut, tax-registers burned, and trees of liberty planted. Armed peasants near Ravenna even captured a general. 'Red Week', as the movement was later called, was quite spontaneous, although central organizations had called the original general strike, and although national revolutionary figures like Mussolini joined in with encouraging rhetoric. After two days the CGL called the strike off, but it took thousands of troops to restore law and order. 'Red Week' was a very old-fashioned revolt, but it had important consequences. The 'revolutionaries' were bitter at their defeat, blamed the reformist CGL leadership for betraying them, and were more hostile to the bourgeois State than ever. And middle-class property-owners had had a nasty fright. The 'Red Threat' had become a reality. Vigilante groups were formed again at Bologna and elsewhere; there were street battles between 'revolutionaries' and Nationalists. Giolitti's policy of 'absorbing' working-class leaders was thoroughly discredited. It seemed time for a more robust approach to domestic problems – a real factor during the next few weeks, as Europe slid haphazardly into war.

9.2 THE INTERVENTION CRISIS

On 28 June, only a fortnight after 'Red Week', the Austrian Archduke Francis Ferdinand was assassinated at Sarajevo. Austria–Hungary determined to punish Serbia. As a member of the Triple Alliance, Italy was pledged to stay neutral if an ally declared war on another country; she was not committed to joining in. There were, in fact, many reasons for caution. War on the Austrian side might mean bigger and rougher Red Weeks throughout Italy; the Austrians were seen by many Italians as the aggressors; the Italian army was still trying to subdue Libya; and Britain was on the other side. It was one of the few firm principles of Italian foreign policy to remain on good terms with Britain, which supplied most of Italy's coal and which had a powerful navy able to threaten Italy's immense coastline.

Moreover, the Foreign Minister San Giuliano had always been perhaps excessively interested in the Balkans: it is striking how high a proportion of the published Italian diplomatic documents, even in July 1914, are about Albania. He was firmly opposed to Austrian expansion there, and he was determined to secure compensation if Austria–Hungary did occupy any more Balkan territory. Indeed, article 7 of the Triple Alliance formally stipulated that such compensation would be given, and it also committed Austria–Hungary not to occupy Balkan lands without previous Italian agreement.[1] Yet Austria declared war on Serbia at the end of July without consulting Italy. This gave San Giuliano a marvellous extra excuse for declaring Italy's neutrality. The Triple Alliance remained formally in force, and Italy continued to negotiate fitfully with Austria about possible compensation, under article 7; but Italy's allies naturally felt betrayed. Some Italians felt dishonoured too, but most were thankful to have stayed out of the war, and industrialists looked forward to supplying the munitions needs of both sides.

Yet neutrality did not solve Italy's problems. If the 'Central Powers' (Austria–Hungary and Germany) won the war, they might seek to avenge Italy's 'betrayal'. If the 'Entente' – Britain, France and Russia – won, it would have no reason to grant Italy any of the Austrian territory she coveted (Trent and Trieste); moreover, Russia would then be a major threat in the Adriatic and Balkans. San Giuliano considered these alternatives coolly. Italy would probably have to join in, if she wanted to join the 'victory banquet'. But whose would be the victory? By 9 September, after the battle of the Marne, it looked as if the *Entente* would probably win; and most of the land Italy wanted was in Austrian hands. So the *Entente* looked a better bet; but Austria–Hungary might be persuaded to grant hefty concessions without Italy needing to fight at all. As the war would probably be a short one – over by the late summer of 1915, at the latest – Italy had better act fairly quickly; but she could hardly act before spring, especially as the army was not ready to fight. San Giuliano decided to negotiate with both sides. If Austria–Hungary were willing to grant adequate 'compensation', well and good; if not, perhaps the *Entente* would make a better offer.

San Giuliano died in October, but the negotiations were continued by his successor, Sonnino. The slogan was '*sacro egoismo*' (sacred egoism), an unfortunate but revealing phrase used by Salandra in a speech to Foreign Ministry officials in October. But it was not just selfishness, and certainly not just cool calculation. Salandra was obviously emotionally committed. On 17 September he told Martini: 'I cannot hesitate: if I thought I had had the opportunity to restore Trent and Trieste to Italy and that I had let it slip, I would not have a moment's peace for the rest of my life.'[2] Moreover, he was convinced that 'the monarchy and our institutions would not survive the conclusion of a European peace from which Italy did not emerge politically and territorially strengthened'.[3] But the Austrians were unwilling to give much territory away, even with German prompting. By January 1915 Sonnino thought the most he could hope for was the Trentino and a boundary revision along the west bank of the Isonzo. The Austrians did eventually concede these regions and agreed also to give Trieste an Italian university, a free port, and the title of 'imperial free city', but they did so only at the last minute – 10 May 1915 – and by then it was too late. Early in March 1915 Sonnino had turned to London. The *Entente*'s bid was much higher – not merely Trentino and the Isonzo, but also Trieste, the South Tyrol, Istria and nearly half of Dalmatia. On 26 April Italy and the *Entente* signed the Treaty of London, which pledged these lands to Italy in return for her entry into the war within a month. On 4 May 1915 Italy denounced the Triple Alliance, and three weeks later she was at war with Austria–Hungary. If all went well, Italy could expect to 'complete her unification', and to dominate the Adriatic. It was a triumph for '*sacro egoismo*'.

Italy's entry into the war was essentially the work of two men only, Salandra and Sonnino. The army's general staff was not informed about what was going on: in August 1914 Italy declared her neutrality just as the generals were preparing mobilization, and in April 1915 Italy signed the Treaty of London just when the generals were beginning to think the war might be a long one after all. The king also played a restricted role, at least until the last few weeks. Indeed, the two politicians had to plot to involve him somehow, in order to guarantee no last-minute reversals of policy; and so, after the Treaty of London had been signed, they persuaded him to send official telegrams to the other *Entente* Heads of State. As for parliament, it was kept completely in the dark about the various negotiations and about the Treaty of London: mere deputies were not fit to discuss High Politics.

Yet the 'intervention crisis' of 1914–15 was not just a matter of diplomatic manoeuvring. Public opinion counted for a great deal. The government's main problem, especially after it had signed the Treaty of London, was how to win enough support for a war. Even some of the Cabinet ministers were neutralists. It is true that by April 1915 some very respectable people were pro-war, including most of the Radicals and prominent Masons, reformist Socialist leaders like Bissolati, and the editor of the *Corriere della Sera*, Luigi Albertini. So, too, were many non-respectable people – the Futurists, for example, and D'Annunzio. The Nationalists and irredentists were naturally in favour; some of them formed armed bands to raid Austria, hoping to provoke reprisals which would lead to war. University students needed little encouragement. They usually rioted in the spring anyway, and the war agitation provided a wonderful excuse. Many Republicans, including the young Pietro Nenni, were fervent in the cause; some syndicalists, like Corridoni and De Ambris, looked to war to trigger off revolution.

But the most spectacular convert was the revolutionary Socialist, Benito Mussolini. As editor of the Socialist daily, *Avanti!*, he took a public stand against outright neutralism as early as 18 October 1914. By the end of the month he had resigned from the paper. On 15 November he produced the first issue of a rival daily, the *Popolo d'Italia*, pledged to war and revolution; on 29 November he was expelled from the Socialist Party. The new paper was financed initially through Filippo Naldi, editor of the Bolognese daily *Il Resto del Carlino*, who used funds provided by big industrial firms and possibly by the government. From early 1915 onwards the French press office in Rome provided much of the cash, although the British and Russians also contributed.[4] Mussolini took very few Socialists with him, and his closest contacts in the next few months were with Republicans and syndicalists, but his conversion proved immensely important. Henceforth the 'interventionists' had a superb journalist, a very effective speaker and a shrewd political brain on their side.

However, most Italians were still opposed to the war. The Socialist Party, despite Mussolini's defection, was the only one in Western Europe not to abandon its internationalist principles. As a result it remained what the Libyan War had made it – the unpatriotic party. Most Catholics were also anxious to keep Italy out, as was Pope Benedict XV; but Luigi Sturzo was an 'interventionist', and many patriotic speeches were made at the executive meeting of Catholic Action in March 1915. In April 1915 the Prefects were asked to report on public opinion in their provinces. They replied that people feared war, and that hardly anybody cared much about Trent or Trieste. In Teramo province people 'perceive war simply as a disaster, like drought, famine or plague'.[5] Businessmen, apart from a few steelmakers and ship-builders, were as anxious as everyone else. They feared for their raw material supplies and their markets, and worried that war might lead to excessive State regulation of industry. Yet, despite all the apparent neutralism, there was no very strong anti-war feeling. War was coming to be seen as inevitable, always a dangerous sign.

The decision to join the war was part of the domestic political battle. The various politicians manoeuvred among themselves as well as among the belligerent Powers. Salandra wanted a successful war to establish his position as national leader; Giolitti, in opposition, had no intention of letting him have it. On 4 December 1914 Giolitti spoke in parliament in favour of neutrality. A few weeks later he wrote a famous letter, published in *La Tribuna* on 2 February, claiming that Italy could make 'considerable' gains (*parecchio*) without needing to fight. His aim, presumably, was to bring the Austrians to make concessions, so as to avoid war. His advice was counter-productive. The Austrians concluded that Italy was unlikely to enter the war, and so dug their heels in; and Salandra became determined to win more than just *parecchio*, and so more likely to fight. Giolitti had miscalculated. In any case, his hands were tied. He could not use his parliamentary majority to bring the government down, for any new government would obviously be more 'neutralist', and as such less able to wring concessions from Vienna. So he pledged his support to Salandra, and hoped that Salandra was still negotiating seriously with the Austrians.

Only in early May 1915 did Giolitti realize what was going on. On 9 May he returned to Rome, furious that the government had denounced the Triple Alliance and gone back on its word. He told Malagodi that 'the people who are in government deserve to be shot'.[6] As a sign of support 300-odd deputies – a majority of the Chamber – left their cards at his hotel. He painted a gloomy picture of what war might mean – mutinies in the army, Austrian troops occupying Milan, revolution, the end of the monarchy and of Liberal institutions. Yet, as previously, Giolitti could not form a government himself. All he could do was try to persuade the existing government to accept the latest Austrian offer, that of 10 May; but it was a hopeless task. Salandra was not going back on his signed pledges to the *Entente*, just so as to 'live for a short time under Giolitti's protectorate'.[7] On 13 May Salandra called Giolitti's bluff by submitting his resignation. The king asked Giolitti to form a new government. By this time Giolitti almost certainly knew about the Treaty of London: it would be fatal for Italy to betray *both* sides. And, of course, the king felt committed by his telegrams, and might abdicate if the Treaty of London were not honoured. So Giolitti refused. After all, he was a good Piedmontese monarchist at heart. He was not going to risk overthrowing his king, merely to avoid a world war. Three other leading politicians refused as well. Meanwhile D'Annunzio and others made inflammatory speeches to excited crowds in Rome, Mussolini gathered a crowd of 30,000 in Milan, and telegrams of support for Salandra flooded in. On 16 May the king recalled Salandra. Giolitti left Rome the next day, and on 20 May parliament voted the government exceptional powers and finance.

Thus Giolitti's parliamentary moves against the war were conspicuously unsuccessful. That was not surprising. Italy joined the European war for normal diplomatic reasons, and in the normal manner. Giolitti knew the rules of the game. Kings, Prime Ministers and Foreign Ministers, not parliament, made policy; international treaties were, at best, ratified by parliament later. He himself had not bothered about parliamentary approval before invading Libya in 1911; Salandra and Sonnino had acted quite constitutionally in 1915. As Salandra later wrote, Italy was pledged to war, the king had committed himself, 'parliament should merely have drawn the consequences'.[8] Instead, her leading statesman, with a parliamentary majority behind him, had made himself the symbol of neutralism. Henceforth the war could be presented as a crusade against '*Giolittismo*' and against parliament, as well as against Austria–Hungary.

In short, Giolitti had helped to create the myth of 'interventionism': the belief that a tiny handful of far-sighted statesmen, spurred on by a few bellicose intellectuals and some noisy street demonstrations, had swept Italy into war despite all the efforts of parliament and Establishment to stop them. I emphasize again that this *was* a myth. Italy's entry into the war was actually a 'normal' diplomatic decision, taken by conservative-minded men worried about preserving Liberal institutions and public order. It owed little to the 'interventionists', however vocal. In any case, not all the 'interventionists' were ranting nationalist demagogues: many of them, like Gaetano Salvemini or Giovanni Amendola, were noble and far-sighted men. Yet myths are powerful and tenacious, and this one was disastrous. It helped to make many 'interventionists' more willing to suppress parliamentary criticism, more nervous about unpatriotic plots, more determined to win extra territory. Above all, it greatly exaggerated the importance of men like D'Annunzio and Mussolini, and enabled them to claim the 'credit' for the war. Years later, in March 1919, Mussolini summoned the inaugural meeting of the *Fasci di Combattimento* in these terms:

we are the only people in Italy who have the right to talk of revolution . . . we have already made a revolution. In May 1915. We started off that May, which was exquisitely and divinely revolutionary, because it overturned a shameful situation at home and decided . . . the outcome of the World War.[9]

That was the real legacy of the intervention crisis.

9.3 THE GREAT WAR: FIGHTING AND CAMPAIGNS

In May 1915 Salandra expected a brief, offensive campaign, leading to quick territorial gains. His hopes were soon disappointed. When the government fell, a year later, nothing of any significance had been won. The 'interventionists' were disappointed too. They had anticipated not merely a glorious victory, but a glorious, manly war. Trench warfare, or rather escarpment warfare in the Alpine foothills, turned out to be very different from the romantic Garibaldine crusade of interventionist rhetoric. It was a squalid, prosaic slogging-match, unheroic and apparently interminable, marked only by the capture of Gorizia in August 1916. The stalemate was finally broken in October 1917, but not by any Italian triumph. The Austrians pushed through the Italian line above Caporetto, and the Italians had to retreat down to the Piave. The second phase of the war was, therefore, mostly on Italian soil. The Italians fought a defensive campaign until almost the last minute, under a new commander and a new government. As the Austro-Hungarian Empire collapsed, Italy emerged victorious from her ordeal. But the cost had been enormous – at least 600,000 lives lost, whole provinces devastated, and the traditional political system in ruins.

The commander of the Italian army, from July 1914 until the disaster at Caporetto, was General Luigi Cadorna, son of the man who had taken Rome in September 1870. Cadorna was a typical soldier of the old traditional Piedmontese type – authoritarian and unimaginative, contemptuous of civilians, and devoted to the House of Savoy. He insisted on a free hand. It was his war, to fight as he chose. The war was run, therefore, from his headquarters at Udine, not from Rome. The politicians were remote from the combat, and in August 1916 Cadorna forbade them entering the war zone; he even refused to meet the minister charged with maintaining relations between government and army command. In other words, Italy had no civilian war leader like Lloyd George or Clemenceau. She had Cadorna instead. There was no national mobilization, no rousing of the national energies in a great cause. The government's main role, in fact, was to take the blame when things went wrong, and Cadorna naturally encouraged this tendency. In June 1917 he wrote three times to the Prime Minister, complaining that the government's tolerance of 'subversive' (anti-war) propaganda made it impossible to maintain discipline. He blamed the army's low morale on the Minister of the Interior, Orlando, and tried to have him replaced, but the plan failed. Cadorna's letters were not discussed in Cabinet, and Orlando remained in office. After Caporetto he had his revenge, becoming Prime Minister and sacking Cadorna.

Cadorna was an austere man, and he took an austere view of his officers. By October 1917 he had dismissed 217 generals and 255 colonels from their posts. The constant reshuffles did little for the army's efficiency. Most of the junior officers were, of course, not professional soldiers at all. Italy had just over 15,000 serving officers in 1914, but in the next four years 160,000 young men were commissioned in the army: more than 16,000 of them were killed. In the infantry over half the new officers were Southerners: Northerners tended to serve in the more 'technical' or mobile units, further away from the front line. And they were conscripts. 'Interventionist' volunteers and pro-war enthusiasts were regarded with great suspicion, as being unstable, 'subversive' or Republican; they were normally excluded from officer-training centres. Certainly there was no question of 'Garibaldi brigades', nor of 'volunteer corps', nor of special units of irredentist *Trentini* – all concepts that were anathema to the hard-bitten professionals. In the field, the old Northern military caste was transformed into a 'Southern', conscripted officer corps. At headquarters, however, little changed. Cadorna did not understand his officers, nor they him.

The soldiers, too, were conscripts. Nearly 5 million men were called up into the army; more than half of them were peasants or agricultural workers. Again, Southerners were over-represented in the front-line infantry regiments, for trained Northern workers were needed in the artillery or engineering corps – or else were drafted into armaments factories well away from danger. Ideals of 'nationality' were rare among Southern peasants. 'Trent and Trieste' meant nothing to them, and they were staggered that anyone should think the rocky wastes of the Carso or Bainsizza were worth fighting for. So this was no 'nation in arms', enthusiastic and zealous for glory, or inspired by the ideals of the *Risorgimento*; on the contrary, it was a sullen, often illiterate, ill-equipped army, torn away from its homes and fields to fight on foreign soil for incomprehensible reasons. Furthermore, the soldiers were well aware that back home there were plenty of 'shirkers' (*imboscati*) – Northern industrial workers, sons of notables or politicians, etc. – all free from danger, all believed to be earning huge wages, and all full of contempt for the army and for the war.

So the troops' morale was low, and it became lower still. Pay was exceptionally low – half a lira a day for a fighting infantryman, with similar paltry sums for his family. The troops' rations, too, were none too generous. In the first winter a front-line infantryman received 750 grams of bread daily, 300 grams of pasta or rice, and 375 grams of meat. However, in December 1916 the bread ration was reduced to 600 grams, the meat to 250 grams and the vegetables more than halved; it was only four months later, after much agitation in parliament, that the bread ration was raised again, and then only to 700 grams. During the winter of 1916–17, therefore, the army had a real grievance, and was probably genuinely undernourished. One post-war calculation is that the daily ration, excluding wine, was less than 3,000 calories that winter, compared with 3,846 calories previously and 3,200 later in 1917.[10] Reducing the rations was an astonishing blunder for professional soldiers to make, especially in an Alpine campaign at the onset of winter. The surprise is not that morale was low in 1917, but that it was not far lower.

The troops' welfare was also neglected in other ways. There were no war newspapers, and no entertainment. Soldiers were forbidden to enter cinemas or bars even when on leave, if they were still in 'war zones'; and there was just one leave per year, of 15 days. Alcohol was made freely available before offensives, and improvised brothels were hastily set up; but otherwise morale was maintained by propaganda lectures about Italy's rightful claims to Trent and Trieste. Even these had to be given by regular officers: when Mussolini offered to give some, the Minister of War forbade it, although he allowed D'Annunzio every facility (not that D'Annunzio was satisfied – he complained to Albertini of having to clean his own shoes). But one vital change did occur. From 1878 to 1911 the army had had no chaplains; even in the Libyan War it had admitted only about 20, to attend the wounded in field hospitals. But in 1915 a 'field bishop', Mgr Bartolomasi, was appointed, and 2,400 priests served as army chaplains during the war, in addition to the 22,000 priests called up as ordinary soldiers. The chaplains, and perhaps especially the soldier-priests, helped illiterate soldiers write home, and generally provided what comfort and assistance they could. One of them, Fr Giovanni Minozzi, founded the 'Soldiers' Homes', usually small barracks-like buildings for about twenty to thirty people, with a few books, a piano, perhaps even a film-projector. By October 1917 there were about 250 of them. They were the most important new initiative taken up to that time to make life slightly more bearable for the troops. They were organized by a priest, and were treated with total neglect, sometimes even suspicion, by the military authorities.

Cadorna relied on more robust methods. He constantly harried his commanders to take a tough line with transgressors. Indeed, there was more than a touch of hysteria about discipline. Between May 1915 and the post-war amnesty of September 1919 nearly 290,000 soldiers – nearly 6 per cent of the total – were tried by courts martial for wartime crimes, usually desertion. The courts themselves were surprisingly lenient: 120,000 men were acquitted, and nearly all the rest were released at the amnesty. Even so, over 4,000 death sentences were passed, and 750 were carried out. The high number of trials and desertions – 55,000 between the spring of 1917 and that of 1918 – are a clear indication of low morale among the troops and of nervousness among the young officers. They also indicate that the army command simply failed to adapt to the new conditions. It insisted on blind obedience, and could not grasp that a mass war needed a different style of leadership altogether.

Summary punishments in the field are another sign of this. Monticone reckons that at least 100 soldiers were shot by their officers before November 1917, and possibly several hundred.[11] Sometimes, after some collective crime like mutiny or disobedience, there was a 'decimation': individual victims were chosen by lot from among a whole company or regiment, and shot in front of the others. Cadorna issued circulars making it 'an absolute inescapable obligation' for all commanding officers to do this whenever individual responsibility could not be ascertained; the circulars were read out to the troops. They were not well received. If 'decimation' was meant to maintain morale, it not surprisingly had the opposite effect; and Cadorna had to sack some commanding officers for 'cowardice', i.e. refusing to 'decimate'.

Not that Cadorna approved of the practice, but he could see no alternative, given the low morale of the troops. For this he blamed everyone except himself. He claimed that the Socialists were busy undermining morale; the government tolerated this 'defeatism', and allowed hundreds of thousands of 'shirkers' to avoid the war. By the summer of 1917 the Russians were to blame, for giving up and making the war more difficult to win. After August 1917 the Pope was added to the list of villains, for condemning the war as a 'useless slaughter' (see §9.6). Yet Cadorna's real problem, especially in 1917, was that he had not won any significant territory except Gorizia, and did not look likely to. After all, Italy had attacked Austria, and was out to make real gains; and they had to be real, for a considerable amount (*parecchio*) could have been obtained without fighting. As the months went on, and as useless offensive succeeded useless offensive, morale was bound to suffer. So was Cadorna's reputation.

Even so, no one expected disaster. Yet on 24 October 1917 disaster struck, if not exactly out of a clear sky, then out of a sky no greyer than usual. The Austrians, with German support, suddenly broke through the Italian lines above Caporetto in Venezia Giulia. They did so by shelling the Italian artillery, by infiltrating fresh troops at night, by concentrating on two short sectors, by sweeping through the valleys and ignoring the heights, by using gas and by attacking in the fog. These tactics won an initial victory, and enabled them to cut off the Italian rear. But then the Italians turned defeat into rout. Their defences behind the lines were weak, and they failed to bring up reserves quickly; sometimes they even failed to move their troops back from exposed positions. Most of the Second Army was left confused and without orders for two days. The other corps managed to retreat, for the most part, but whenever there was Austrian harassment Italian discipline was likely to crack.

And so hundreds of thousands of Italian soldiers streamed down from the hills, some without weapons, some looting and pillaging, some shouting for joy that the war was over at last, some shooting their friends and comrades in a Dionysian frenzy, most simply exhausted and relieved. It was an extraordinary spectacle, and it haunted official Italy for a generation. Yet it was far less chaotic and violent than it might have been: officers were unmolested, and both Cadorna and the king were treated respectfully. Eye-witnesses reported hearing shouts of 'Viva la pace! Viva il Papa! Viva Giolitti!' ('Long live peace! Long live the Pope! Long live Giolitti!') rather than anything more menacing.[12] At least 200,000 soldiers lost contact with their regiments, and ended up behind the River Piave. Fortunately the river was in its autumn flood, the Austrians could not cross it, and the rout was halted. Most of the Veneto had been lost, together with vast quantities of arms; 300,000 men had been taken prisoner.

Cadorna attributed the Austrian breakthrough to 'the violence of the attack, and the inadequate resistance of certain units, some of which surrendered ignobly while others took to flight in a cowardly manner'.[13] This was itself ignoble, and in any case confused cause and effect. Caporetto was a normal military engagement, which the Austrians won for good tactical reasons; the surrenders and desertions, the acts of cowardice and hysteria, came later. Even so, Cadorna was half-right. Low morale did not cause the military defeat, but it must have contributed to the military collapse afterwards. In any case, after Caporetto Cadorna had to go. The new Orlando government kicked him upstairs to be head of a newly created 'Supreme Inter-Allied Council'; thereafter the army was commanded by General Armando Diaz.

Caporetto changed not only the commander, but the war. Italy was no longer fighting for Trent and Trieste – they seemed impossible dreams early in 1918 – but to defend her sacred soil against the invaders. She had to regroup her army, survive the winter somehow, and prepare to hold off renewed Austrian attacks in the spring. Most Italians realized this, and as the Piave line was held both civilian and military morale gradually rose. Moreover, General Diaz paid far more attention to the soldiers than had Cadorna. Trench newspapers began in 1918, and some were soon very popular. Propaganda units (*Uffici 'P'*) were attached to each regiment. Above all, the troops' rations were raised. They were also given ten more days' leave each year and free life insurance – although whether this last concession improved morale must be questionable. Two divisions of special shock-troops, '*Arditi*', were set up. These volunteer commandos soon became the legendary heroes of the Italian army, at a time when it badly needed some; and the adventures of fighter-pilots and of naval anti-submarine units received similar publicity. In December 1917 the government founded a servicemen's association, the *Opera Nazionale Combattenti*, to look after the welfare of troops and their families; and there were frequent promises of 'land to the peasants' once the war was won. Strict discipline continued, of course, but there were no more 'decimations'.

In short, the army became more 'national'; and so did the war. By First World War standards, Diaz was a cautious general who refused to risk his men's lives unnecessarily: 143,000 Italian soldiers were killed or wounded in 1918, compared with 520,000 the previous year. Even at the end of September 1918, when it was obvious to the politicians that Austria–Hungary was collapsing, General Diaz was still reluctant to attack. By this time the government desperately needed a token victory, both for appearance's sake and to strengthen Italy's hand at the peace negotiations; and so Italy 'intervened' in the war again. On 24 October, the anniversary of Caporetto, General Giardino began an offensive near Monte Grappa, and two days later the Italians began crossing the Piave. This time it was the Austrians who retreated in disorder, or surrendered without a fight. On 30 October the Italian army could proclaim a victory at last, as it entered Vittorio Veneto twenty kilometres from the Piave. On 3 November it took Trent, and the navy landed troops at Trieste. The next day the war with Austria was over. In ten days the Italians had won what had eluded them for 3½ years.

9.4 THE WAR AT HOME: THE ECONOMIC IMPACT

The Great War had dramatic effects on the Italian economy. It was a 'war of exhaustion', which would be won by the side with the most men, arms and resources. Yet Italian steel production in 1913 was less than 1 million tonnes, compared with 2.6 million tonnes in Austria and 17.6 million tonnes in Germany. Cadorna claimed that he had only two machine-guns per battalion in May 1915; the Austrians had twelve.[14] Certainly the army was very short of essential artillery, even of bullets, until at least the spring of 1917. Yet somehow the deficit was made up. Italy ended the war with over 7,000 cannons in the field, more than the British had; on Armistice Day she had nearly 20,000 machine-guns, compared with 613 in May 1915. She had also created an aircraft industry, producing over 6,500 planes in 1918. Fiat, in Turin, had become the leading producer of trucks and lorries in Europe, making almost 25,000 vehicles in 1918 (compared with 4,500 in 1914). Here was a real 'economic miracle' of high-speed armaments and vehicle production. It was attained despite continuing shortages of raw materials, especially steel and coal. Steel production rose, but only to 1.2 million tonnes in 1918; coal imports fell, from 4.6 million tonnes in 1913–14 to 1.0 million tonnes in 1917–18, although the shortfall was partly made up by extra hydro-electric power.

How was the miracle achieved? The answer is by 'production at any cost'. The State was the sole consumer for all these industrial goods, and the State did not bother much about prices or costs. A special Under-secretariat (later Ministry) of Arms and Munitions was set up under General Alfredo Dallolio. Dallolio was an energetic and effective organizer, and his priorities were clear: 'the time factor must have precedence over any other consideration'.[15] The ministry made payments in advance, arranged cheap loans and rapid depreciation allowances for favoured firms, and granted generous contracts. Much of the detailed negotiation was done by central and regional 'committees of industrial mobilization', on which the leading industrialists sat; below them there were local cartels, distributing the available raw materials and the contracts. There were plenty of opportunities here for abuse, and in May 1918 Dallolio was forced to resign after a particularly flagrant series of scandals; but it was an ideal system for achieving rapid growth. For a few giddy years Italian industrialists could do no wrong. There were no risks, and both the banks and the State smiled upon them. There was not even much bureaucratic interference: for the most part they ran the 'industrial mobilization' system themselves. To cap it all, they were patriots, nobly sacrificing their energies for the national good.

But the costs were real none the less, and had to be paid later. One calculation is that the State spent about 41 billion lire, at pre-war prices, on military supplies, pensions, food subsidies, etc.[16] The State budget went heavily into deficit: from 2.9 billion lire in 1914–15 to 23.3 billion lire in 1918–19. Governments could only pay for the war by borrowing, and so the National Debt rose five-fold, from 15.7 billion lire in June 1914 to 84.9 billion lire in June 1919, including war debts of over 15 billion lire to Britain and 8.5 billion lire to the USA. When governments can borrow no more, they print. There were almost six times as many bank notes in circulation in June 1919 as five years previously. Inflation was the inevitable result, or cause. The wholesale price index rose from 100 in 1913 to 412.9 in 1918, and even this probably understated the real position.

There were other disadvantages to the 'industrial mobilization' system and to the 'war economy'. Only a few regions enjoyed a war boom. Most of the arms firms were in the 'industrial triangle' of Piedmont, Liguria and Lombardy. The war worsened the already grave regional imbalance, especially as Southern savings in government stock were used to finance Northern industrial investment. Only a few sectors of industry were affected: steel, engineering, vehicles, cement, hydro-electric power, chemicals, rubber, woollen textiles. And only a few firms – Ilva, Breda, Ansaldo, Fiat, Montecatini, Pirelli – really benefited from wartime conditions. Only they had their men on the right committees to ensure raw material supplies and profitable contracts; only they were large enough to produce the goods in the right quantities and at the right time. They made huge profits, and ploughed much of them back into new investment: sometimes they swallowed up their pre-war competitors. Fiat's capital grew from 25 million to 125 million lire; it employed 30,000 workers by 1919, compared with 6,000 before the war. Ansaldo bought up the Cogne iron mines, installed hydro-electric plant, and acquired two shipping lines. Ilva, essentially a steel trust pre-war, acquired shipyards and engineering plants as well as the Lloyd Transatlantico shipping line. Such firms were widely detested as war profiteers; they may have grown bigger, but they became far more vulnerable politically.

They had also become vulnerable economically, if the war ever stopped. By 1918 the leading firms were fighting desperately to take over the banks, so as to deny credit to their competitors and secure it for themselves. The Perrone brothers, who ran Ansaldo, bought up the *Banca di Sconto* and tried to take over the *Banca Commerciale* as well. Max Bondi, who ran Ilva and was linked to the *Banca Commerciale*, tried to take over the Bastogi finance-house; Giovanni Agnelli, who ran Fiat, attempted to buy up the *Credito Italiano*. Eventually the Treasury Minister imposed a truce, but hostilities resumed after the war.

'Industrial mobilization' naturally implied a big increase in industrial jobs. By November 1918 1,976 firms, with 905,000 workers, were organized by the 'industrial mobilization' system. Over one-third of the workers, i.e. 331,000 people, were men of military age, most exempted from military service but 151,000 of them actually in the army and seconded to the munitions factories. Thus many skilled engineering workers spent the war at home in their usual jobs – a fact of great political significance. For the rest, peasants flocked into the main munitions centres from the surrounding countryside; and women easily found unskilled jobs in transport or engineering – over 20 per cent of the armaments workers were women by 1918. It all meant that the industrial centres grew rapidly. Milan had just under 600,000 inhabitants in 1911, according to the census; by 1921 there were 718,000. Turin increased from 427,000 to 518,000, and became a 'proletarian city': about one-third of its population had industrial jobs, and in 1918 the city contained twice as many industrial workers as in 1913. There was serious overcrowding, especially as house-building stopped during the war.

The 'industrial mobilization' system also rested on strict control of labour. All the workers in arms factories were placed under military discipline. Armed soldiers patrolled the factories. No one could change jobs without the local regional committee's permission, which was rarely given. Indiscipline was tried by military officers and punished by terms in military prisons – or by dispatch to the front. Strikes, of course, were prohibited. Most industrial workers detested this military supervision and discipline. They saw themselves as slaving away in intolerable conditions and working excessive hours – a seventy-five hour week was normal at Fiat by 1916. Moreover, they also had to cope with transport delays and food shortages. Admittedly by 1917 bread and pasta were rationed and sold at controlled prices, but most other foods were not. Meat and sugar consumption fell sharply in the towns. Industrial workers were less sheltered than peasants from the effects of inflation, and most urban families had to cut down even on basic essentials. Although their pay rose regularly, the cost of living rose even faster: during the war real wages probably fell by 25 per cent, on average, although the position obviously varied from industry to industry.

There was, therefore, much discontent among the Northern workers. Most of them had opposed the war from the outset. They knew their employers were making huge profits, and they knew that many shopkeepers were selling only on the black market. By May 1917 the chief of police recognized that the workers of Turin were 'in a state of compressed effer- vescence'.[17] Their unrest could probably be contained by firm discipline and regular pay rises, but only if food supplies were readily available. He was very prescient. In August bread shortages in Turin caused major rioting. Barricades were built, and troops had to be rushed in. About fifty people were killed before order was restored. The riots showed how morale in the cities had fallen to dangerously low levels, and they shocked politicians and generals alike. Yet they were an isolated episode, and they soon died down when bread arrived. Economic grievances and class antagonism remained acute in the Northern cities in 1918, but more care was taken over food supplies and propaganda at home as well as in the army, and there was no more rioting.

The workers' grievances were real to them, but to no one else. Most soldiers thought that the urban workers were extremely lucky: they had nice safe jobs well away from danger, they lived at home with their wives and families while their fellow-Italians were being slaughtered in the trenches, and their wages were fabulously high. Indeed, they received an average 6.04 lire per day in 1918 (piece-rate workers at Fiat earned 14.48 lire), while combat troops were still getting only half a lira. Furthermore, the troops' rations were far more meagre than normal consumption at home. Many of the peasants in the army naturally resented the urban workers' privileges, and they resented them even more after the Turin riots. In fact, only about 36 per cent of the armaments workers were men of military age; but the idea that all industrial workers were contemptible *imboscati*, 'shirkers', became deeply rooted among the 'interventionists', and among the soldiers.

The Great War also had sudden and dramatic effects in the countryside. Over 2½ million peasants and labourers were taken into the army, leaving only the older men, women and adolescents to till the fields. In some areas women had always done farm work while the men went off to foreign building sites, so the position was not much different from usual apart from the lack of emigrants' remittances, but in other regions – e.g. Latium, Apulia, Sardinia – a woman's place was in the home, and families suffered accordingly. The share-croppers of Central Italy probably coped best with the new conditions, for share-cropping had always been an activity for large families. Among the small peasant landowners of Northern Italy, the loss of the bread-winner could be a disaster. On balance, the real incomes of peasant families probably went down, but not much. Italy had long suffered from rural overpopulation; war, like emigration, was one way of relieving it. A vast reserve army of labour – women, the old, the young – went into action. So food production was not seriously affected. During the war it amounted to almost 95 per cent of pre-war production, although admittedly many more animals were slaughtered than usual, and fertilizer thus reduced.

But the value of this produce did change. Indeed, the great inflation transformed the Italian countryside. Inflation reduced debts, and many peasants had been chronically in debt – for seeds, for animals, for the cost of a boat ticket abroad. The village usurers suffered for once; the peasants paid off their debts, and even began to save. Deposits in the rural savings banks almost trebled. Fruit and vegetable growers did best, for these prices were not government-controlled. But anyone who rented land for money was likely to benefit, especially since rents were frozen during the war. Many peasants found themselves making money, in some cases using money, for the first time in their lives. Hundreds of thousands of them began to think that buying their own land might not be an impossible dream. Here was a 'revolution of rising expectations', a shift from hunger to land hunger. The corollary was that existing landowners lost out badly, especially the absentees. They no longer had a stranglehold over their tenants through debt, and the rents they received became trivial. By 1918 many of them were in despair. They had to sell – or fight back.

Governments naturally had to adapt to these changes. They encouraged the impression that after the war there would be ample 'land for the peasants'. This slogan was repeated again and again in the official propaganda of 1917–18. There were several bills in parliament, referring mainly to the Southern *latifundia*, and even one or two decrees in favour of agricultural co-operatives on uncultivated land. These schemes all fed the peasants' land hunger, and worried the landowners. In 1918 some lands in Latium and Emilia were 'occupied' unofficially by peasants. It was easy to predict that when the vast peasant army went back home there would be a tremendous agitation for land throughout Italy (see §10.3).

9.5 WARTIME POLITICS

In May 1915 Salandra's supporters had expected the war to transform domestic politics. After a rapid victory, a new 'conservative-liberal' regime would emerge, very different from the hated Giolittian system. The 'democratic interventionists' – Radicals like Nitti, respectable Republicans like Barzilai, reformist Socialists like Bissolati – also looked to victory, but they expected it to induce a more 'open' type of government, with mass participation and enthusiasm, and more stress on social progress, education and industry. Giolitti's men, still a majority in the Chamber, licked their wounds and bided their time. They did not expect victory at all; and they feared they would have to pick up the pieces after a disappointing armistice. Wartime politics was essentially the story of the intrigues of these three groups. It was complicated by the fact that there was no pro-war majority in parliament. 'The Chamber never wanted war, and never pretended to want it', remarked Martini bitterly in March 1917;[18] and he was right. Governments were therefore weak and unstable. The politicians behaved with their characteristic blend of calculating shrewdness and short-sighted naivety. They failed to grasp how much the fighting soldiers despised them; and they underestimated, or ignored altogether, changes within Italy's other three main political groups, the Catholics, Socialists and Nationalists.

Giolitti had been the war's first political victim, before it even started. He remained horrified by it, and horrified that Italy should have entered it; and he remained virtually helpless. He could not act against the Crown. He and his followers could bring governments down, but they could not form a new one. Nor could they influence policy. In 1917 the Giolittians favoured negotiations and a compromise peace: '*parecchio*' all over again. But Sonnino was obdurate, and after Caporetto the victorious Austrians were not anxious to negotiate. At home, the Giolittians had to take much of the blame for low morale. Camillo Corradini, Under-secretary at the Ministry of the Interior, was sacrificed after the Turin riots; and had not the retreating Italian soldiers of Caporetto shouted '*Viva Giolitti*'? So Giolitti remained isolated, the personification of 'neutralism' and corruption. He feebly urged more parliamentary control over the conduct of the war. Over 100 Giolittian deputies formed a 'Parliamentary Union' to this end, but this move only aroused further suspicions of defeatism.

Giolitti's great enemy Salandra was also an early political casualty of war. His government proved unable to control Cadorna, unable to achieve the promised victories, unable to rally the country and unable to win friends in parliament. In June 1916, after an Austrian counter-attack in the Trentino, Giolitti had his revenge. Salandra's government fell – the first government to fall in a belligerent country – and he never held high office again. His successor was Paolo Boselli, seventy-eight years old and not noted for energy even when in his prime. He formed a 'National Coalition', including several 'democratic interventionists' – a Republican, two Radicals, two reformist Socialists – and even a Catholic, Meda. With Salandra gone, Sonnino was the leading 'conservative-liberal' in the Cabinet; as Foreign Minister, he embodied Italy's determination to achieve her war aims. But Boselli's government was just as unsuccessful as Salandra's; and on 25 October 1917, the day after the Austrian breakthrough above Caporetto, it fell.

The Sicilian lawyer Orlando then formed Italy's third and last wartime government. He retained Sonnino as Foreign Minister, but the Radical economist Nitti became Treasury Minister, and soon dominated most of his colleagues. In general, the 'democratic interventionists' were more influential than before, and far more so than the Salandrian conservatives who had begun the war. In December 1917 all the various pro-war groups, from democrats like Bissolati to Nationalists like Federzoni, formed a 'Parliamentary Group (*Fascio*) of National Defence'; by April it had 156 members. The *Fascio* was a response to Caporetto and to 'defeatism', and it was a very significant development. It showed that the 'democratic interventionists' could ally politically with the Right-wing Liberals and Nationalists in the patriotic cause – and against Giolitti. Indeed, it was formed specifically to oppose Giolitti's 'Parliamentary Union'. Moreover, the *Fascio* was intolerant. He who was not with it, was against it. It called for a tougher line against 'subversives', and for tighter press censorship. Thus the 'democratic interventionists' certainly became more influential, but at a cost. They acquired some strange bedfellows, and their 'interventionist' credentials were often more evident than their democratic ones. This was even more true outside parliament. Local '*Fasci* of National Defence' and 'Resistance Committees' sprang up; Republicans, Radicals, Masons and Nationalists worked together in the common cause – combating the neutralists. These local bodies, patriotic and paranoid, became centres in which landowners, eminent citizens, labour agitators and youthful careerists met to exchange ideas and to deplore government inertia. Many lasting friendships began there, and some of them were the nuclei of later Fascist organizations.

The 'democratic interventionists' had another major problem. At the end of 1917 the Bolsheviks published the Treaty of London, showing that Italy was fighting not only for Trent and Trieste but also for, *inter alia*, Northern Dalmatia and the South Tyrol. These areas were not inhabited by 'Italians'. Bissolati and his colleagues were horrified to learn, after nearly three years of war, that Italy was fighting for the wrong things. So were many Liberals, including Albertini of the *Corriere della Sera*. The Giolittians and the Socialists stepped up their attacks on the war. In January 1918 President Wilson of the USA issued his 'Fourteen Points', proclaiming that Allied war aims included the right of 'autonomous development' for oppressed nationalities. Point Nine laid down that 'a readjustment of the frontiers of Italy should be effected along clearly recognizable lines of nationality'. Here was the democratic interventionists' opportunity. They climbed hastily on to Wilson's platform. In April they organized a 'Congress of Oppressed Nationalities' (oppressed by Austria–Hungary, that is) in Rome. Delegates came from Poland, Czechoslovakia, Yugoslavia and Rumania; the congress proclaimed their rights to national independence. Sonnino refused to attend. He thought all this talk of 'nationalities' was dangerous nonsense, and he certainly did not want a strong Yugoslavia on Italy's doorstep. He wanted the Treaty of London, and continued to defend it. Orlando, as Prime Minister, equivocated. He allowed a 'Czech legion' to be formed from Czech prisoners-of-war, to fight against Austria, and he encouraged talk of 'nationalities' as a good propaganda weapon against the enemy troops. In 1918 it often seemed as if Italy were fighting a war of national liberation. But he kept Sonnino on as Foreign Minister, despite the press clamour. On Armistice Day in November 1918 Italy's war aims were still undefined. The 'democratic interventionists' had not imposed their views, and still needed to rely on President Wilson.

9.6 THE OUTSIDERS' POLITICS

Ambiguity also prevailed within the 'outsider' political movements – the Catholics, Socialists and Nationalists. Catholic attitudes to the war ranged from nationalism to pacifism, with pro-war feeling more common in the South. Most bishops thought the war was a divine punishment, to be borne as patiently as possible, i.e. they thought the same as most soldiers. The faithful were urged to do their duty, but there was not much enthusiasm. Some priests, including Fr Semeria, chaplain at Cadorna's headquarters, had real crises of conscience as the appalling slaughter went on. But usually the line of 'moderate patriotism', of rendering unto Caesar, prevailed. The Prefect of Verona boasted that the local clergy always adopted the propaganda lines he suggested to them.[19] Organized religion became an indispensable prop to a weak State fighting an unpopular war. In the field, open-air mass became a regular feature of army life; between 80 and 95 per cent of the soldiers in many regiments took Easter communion in 1916. Mussolini wrote in his diary that the chaplain's cry of 'Italy before all and above all' was the first real patriotic speech he had heard in sixteen months in the army.[20] At home, parish priests organized aid for soldiers' families; and Nitti thought they might persuade the peasants to produce more food.

This helpful attitude brought the various Catholic movements many benefits. Baron Monti, an old school friend of the Pope, was made director of the *Fondo per il Culto*, in charge of government subsidies to the Church. The cousin of the Vatican Secretary of State was made a Senator. And in 1916 Filippo Meda became Finance Minister in Boselli's government. He was not the first Catholic to be a government minister in united Italy, but he was the first to become a minister because of his Catholicism. In May 1918 another Catholic deputy, Cesare Nava, became Under-secretary of Arms and Munitions on Dallolio's resignation. The State needed these men in government, just as it needed the bishops' help on the home front and chaplains and soldier-priests in the field. Thus the war boosted the long process of 'reconciling' united Italy and organized Catholicism.

And yet the Vatican itself did not join in, apart from organizing a great deal of relief work – exchanges of sick or wounded prisoners, repatriation of displaced civilians, etc. Benedict XV refused to declare that the war was 'just', and in May 1915 he called it an 'appalling butchery'. In August 1917 he issued a famous Note, urging disarmament, arbitration and an international conference to settle the outstanding issues. The initiative failed. The main impact of the Note came from one phrase in it, where the Pope declared that the war was a 'useless slaughter'. This caused a great fuss, and probably did have a devastating effect on Italian morale. The top brass at Cadorna's headquarters said the Pope should be hanged. He certainly took some of the blame for the rioting at Turin three weeks later, and for the defeat at Caporetto in October. In any case Sonnino, as Foreign Minister, resented secret Papal diplomacy, and was determined to keep the Vatican out of any peace negotiations. All the 'democratic interventionists' thought the Pope was far too sympathetic to Catholic Austria. The Italian Establishment's Masonic traditions died hard: the Catholics were still too suspect, too 'defeatist', to be welcomed fully into the political fold.

So 'reconciliation' had its limits. Indeed, the war also boosted a contrary process – of building up independent Catholic institutions. For example, the war gave the peasants new wealth; much of it flowed into the Catholic rural banks. Charity was needed in wartime as never before; it was Catholic organizations that relieved distress. In March 1915 the Pope had reorganized Catholic Action yet again, putting its various component bodies under a single national executive run by Count Giuseppe Dalla Torre as president and by Fr Luigi Sturzo as secretary. The executive stimulated a host of local and diocesan initiatives – helping peasant landowners, founding rural banks and Catholic newspapers, promoting co-operatives, agitating for land for the peasants and votes for women. In March 1918 it even managed to found a national trade union confederation, to rival the Socialists' CGL. By 1918 the provincial Prefects of Northern Italy had become quite alarmed.[21] Catholic Action was clearly taking on a more direct political role.

Thus the Catholics took part in the war effort, but they kept their distance. They took a longer view. When the war was unpopular, they appeared as 'neutralists', seeking to mitigate disaster; when men rallied to the flag, the Catholics rallied too. Catholic ambiguity, like Giolitti's, was inevitable: the Socialists could not be left as the sole defenders of the neutralist cause. But, like Giolitti's, it caused much resentment.

There was, on the face of it, less ambiguity about the Socialists' attitude to the war. They were opposed to it. Militarism was widely detested; and skilled industrial workers, natural Socialist supporters, had no contact with the troops or their experiences. The PSI was the only political party openly committed to peace; it acted as spokesman for popular discontent. Yet the Socialist Party could not be too unpatriotic. It clearly could not support the Austrians, nor could it sabotage the war effort. The party secretary, Lazzari, therefore coined a formula to define the party's attitude: 'neither adherence nor sabotage'.

So here was more ambiguity. And, as the war went on, many Socialists inevitably became involved. Socialist local councils organized rationing and welfare payments; Socialist co-operatives helped to keep down the cost of living and to prevent profiteering; Socialist trade unionists sat on regional 'committees of industrial mobilization', and helped to settle labour disputes. These committees granted wage rises, safeguarded working conditions and helped workers gain exemption from military service. No wonder Socialist trade unionists and ordinary workers welcomed them. Yet they were undoubtedly part of the war effort: their job, essentially, was to make more weapons. Socialist deputies, too, sat on commissions and influenced social and economic legislation; that, too, helped the workers, but it also helped the war. In any case, some Socialist deputies were sympathetic to the war. After Caporetto they became quite open about it, and Turati himself proclaimed that the country was in peril and all should rally to the cause.

Thus many Socialist leaders and institutions did little to oppose the war, and much to support it. However, there were exceptions. The party's formal leadership, the Directorate, remained in the hands of the party's 'revolutionary', 'intransigent', 'maximalist' wing; and the Directorate appointed the editor of the party's newspaper, *Avanti!*. So Socialist propaganda, under *Avanti!*'s new editor Serrati, remained firmly anti-war. The paper was much censored, but in October 1915 it managed to publish the resolutions of the international anti-war conference at Zimmerwald. When the Turin rioting broke out in August 1917, the Socialists took the blame, or credit. Serrati was arrested as an instigator, along with the party's secretary, vice-secretary and various other leading Left-wingers. Naturally, the Socialists were also blamed for Caporetto. In fact, Socialist anti-war propaganda was fairly ineffective. Only the Bolsheviks' success in Russia gave the Socialists much of an argument, and even then President Wilson soon provided other attractive ideals to counter Lenin's. By 1918 the maximalists were very frustrated. Their leaders were in gaol, they were detested by all true patriots, and they had become spokesmen for the 'shirkers' rather than for the workers.

Above all, they distrusted the Socialist deputies and trade union leaders for being soft on militarism, and for being too close to the renegade Bissolati and other expelled ex-Socialists. In September 1918 the party held a brief congress in Rome, and condemned the deputies' conduct. There were many other rows later. The Socialist movement was irremediably split, essentially on the war issue. On the one hand, the 'maximalist' Directorate, the constituency parties and *Avanti!* regarded opposition to the war as the test of revolutionary virtue; on the other, 'reformist' trade unionists, local government leaders and most deputies 'collaborated' as a patriotic necessity.

The Nationalists, of course, had no doubts about the virtues of war, although they too were divided about war aims. They took part in the 'Congress of Oppressed Nationalities' in 1918, but few of them were willing to give up any claim to Dalmatia. Indeed, they agitated strongly for *more* territory, especially in Asia Minor and Africa. They were also prominent in the national and local '*Fasci* of National Defence'. The Nationalists fought the defeatists and the neutralists, sometimes literally. Their favourite target, apart from the Socialists and Giolitti, was Orlando, for being too feeble as Minister of the Interior in 1916–17. Orlando told Malagodi in September 1917 that the Nationalists wanted to 'become masters of the Interior Ministry, so as to govern Italy with partisan aims and methods, organizing demonstrations with the help of the police and striking terror into their opponents'.[22] That was true. A powerful weapon was being forged. The war gave the Nationalists deeper local roots and greater local support, and it made them even more paranoid.

Indeed, it confirmed many of the Nationalists' deepest suspicions about parliamentary government. Federzoni argued that the Italian State was failing to run the war properly, and might fail to win the benefits of victory. The old parasites of parliament and bureaucracy must be swept away. 'Industrial mobilization' must continue in peacetime. The slogans of 'productivism' (see §7.4) reappeared. Italy should be run by the 'producers', especially the technical experts; and she should be run on military lines. The State, in peace as in war, should control prices and incomes, should regulate foreign trade, should distribute raw materials, should ration consumption and should discipline labour. The Nationalists promised radical, progressive change: an efficient economy, full employment, social welfare and social harmony. It was not too unrealistic a programme, for much of it had apparently happened already, in the war; and it was very attractive to arms' manufacturers and to many young officers and patriots. Above all, it provided a marvellous excuse for excluding large unwelcome groups – Socialists, Catholics or Giolittians – from political influence. Such an argument was badly needed in 1918, for it was clear that the Socialists and Catholics would dominate post-war parliamentary politics. 'Productivism' offered a way out of this nightmare. It provided allies, even among the 'democratic interventionists'; and it provided good grounds for setting up a new kind of State, welcome to all who had supported the war. The Nationalists had won their major battles before the war; would they win again after it?

9.7 CONCLUSION

The Nationalists had expected the Great War to 'make Italians', to cement the disparate people together into a united community. In some ways it did so. Shared hardships, bread-rationing, urbanization, the army's use of the Italian language rather than dialect, all helped to unify the country. Yet the contrary was far more true. The Italians were also deeply divided by the war. The opposition to it included not only the Giolittian majority in parliament, but the two major organized forces in the country, the Catholics and Socialists. The disputes of 1914–15 refused to die down, even long after the war was over. To the victorious 'interventionists' 'Italy' henceforth meant wartime Italy: noble, self-sacrificing and disciplined, the 'Italy of Vittorio Veneto'. 'Italy' also meant wartime Italy to the defeated neutralists and to many ordinary peasants and workers, but it was seen by them as repressive and reactionary. To both, patriotism meant war. The Italians had been divided before, but by November 1918 they were more divided than ever – 'combatants' against 'shirkers', peasants against workers, patriots against defeatists. No conceivable form of government could suit them all.

The war left other major legacies. They included a thirst for justice ('land for the peasants') and a transformed industrial economy. The very bases of the Liberal State were being questioned. The government was dominated by Nitti, who welcomed State intervention in economic and social affairs and encouraged demands for a 'broader democracy'. The war also produced tens of thousands of new officers, drunk with patriotism and greedy to command. They had won the war, and did not intend to let anyone forget it. The Great War, like the Resistance of 1943–45, provided a whole generation with patriotic credentials and a claim to reward. But perhaps the greatest legacy of the war was psychological, or medical. It left men utterly exhausted. The overwhelming impression given by the letters and diaries of this period is of strain, of not being able to cope any more. Perhaps that was why almost as many Italians died from influenza in 1918–19 as were killed in the whole war. This was the people that had to deal with Italy's post-war crisis.

REFERENCES

1. For the text of article 7 of the Triple Alliance, see Z.A.B. Zeman, *A Diplomatic History of the First World War*, London 1971, p. 3; A. F. Pribram, *The Secret Treaties of Austria–Hungary*, Harvard University Press 1920, vol. i, 248–51.

2. F. Martini, *Diario 1914–18*, Milan 1966, p. 106.

3. Salandra to Bertolini, as noted in Bertolini's diary 29 October 1914 (P. Bertolini, 'Diario agosto 1914–maggio 1915', *Nuova Antologia*, 1 February 1923).

4. On the financing of the *Popolo d'Italia*, see W. A. Renzi, 'Mussolini's sources of financial support, 1914–15', *History*, lvi (1971), 189–206; F. Naldi's articles in *Il Paese* 12–14 Jan. 1960; R. De Felice, 'Primi Elementi sul finanziamento del Fascismo dalle origini al 1924', in *Rivista Storica del Socialismo*, 22 (May–Aug. 1964), 223–51; and R. De Felice, *Mussolini il Rivoluzionario*, Turin 1965, pp. 275 ff.

5. B. Vigezzi, *Da Giolitti a Salandra*, Florence 1969, p. 382.

6. O. Malagodi, *Conversazioni di Guerra 1914–19*, i, Milan 1960, p. 56.

7. A. Salandra, *L'Intervento*, Milan 1930, p. 270.

8. *idem*, p. 267.

9. '23 marzo', *Popolo d'Italia*, 18 March 1919.

10. G. Zingali, *Il Rifornimento dei Viveri dell'Esercito italiano durante la Guerra*, Yale University Press and Bari 1926, p. 548.

11. A. Monticone, *Gli Italiani in Uniforme*, Bari 1972, pp. 218–23.

12. See, for example, Amendola's account in O. Malagodi, *Conversazioni . . .*, i, p. 184.

13. Cadorna's bulletin is quoted in F. Martini's *Diario* cit., 28 Oct. 1917, on p. 1023; cf. also p. 1036.

14. O. Malagodi, *Conversazioni . . .*, i, p. 78.

15. Circular of Dallolio to inspectors of artillery construction, quoted in L. Einaudi, *La Condotta Economica e gli Effetti Sociali della Guerra Italiana*, Yale University Press and Bari 1933, p. 61.

16. F. Repaci, *La Finanza Pubblica Italiana nel Secolo 1861–1960*, Bologna 1961, pp. 244–45.

17. O. Malagodi, *Conversazioni . . .*, i, p. 124. Cf. also R. De Felice, 'Ordine Pubblico e orientamenti delle masse popolari italiane nella prima metà del 1917', *Rivista Storica del Socialismo*, 20 (Sept.–Dec. 1963), 467–504.

18. F. Martini, *Diario . . .*, p. 873 (entry for 2 March 1917).

19. Prefect of Verona to Ministry of the Interior 10 June 1918, in *ACS*, Min. Int., Dir. Gen. P. S., 'Conflagrazione Europea', b. 32B, f. 'Verona'.

20. On 31 Dec. 1916; quoted by A. Prandi, in G. Rossini (ed.), *Benedetto XV, i Cattolici e la Prima Guerra Mondiale*, Rome 1963, p. 169.

21. See, for example, reports by Prefects of Piacenza (25 Jan.), Genoa (30 Jan.), Rovigo (15 June) and Florence (27 June), in *ACS*, Min. Int., Dir. Gen. P. S., AA. GG. e RR., 1918, b. 49, 'Partito clericale'.
22. O. Malagodi, *Conversazioni* . . ., i, p. 167.

CHAPTER TEN

The strange death of Liberal Italy, 1919–25

In November 1918 the war ended at last. Italy had won. She had gained Trent and Trieste; her historic rival, Austria–Hungary, was destroyed; her monarchy and her Liberal institutions were respected and intact. Yet less than four years later the Fascist leader Mussolini was Prime Minister; a few years again, and the old Liberal institutions were no more. Liberal Italy collapsed suddenly and unexpectedly in her hour of triumph. Why?

10.1 HIGH POLITICS: PATRIOTISM INSULTED AND PATRIOTISM AVENGED

One major reason is that her statesmen lost at diplomacy, just when the game mattered most. Italy had won the war but she bungled the peace, and bungled it spectacularly and publicly. Orlando and Sonnino went to the Versailles peace conference in 1919, demanding the full terms of the 1915 Treaty of London, i.e. Trent, Trieste, the South Tyrol to the Brenner, Istria and Northern Dalmatia. Most of these demands were granted, even though they ran counter to the 'principle of nationality' dear to the American President, Woodrow Wilson. But Wilson drew the line at Dalmatia, and the atmosphere was not improved when the Italians also asked for Fiume (Rijeka), the former Hungarian port on the Croatian coast. Fiume had not been mentioned in 1915, and rarely mentioned later; and it was not much use – Italy now had a much bigger Adriatic port at Trieste. But its citizens were mainly Italians (if the suburbs were not counted), and they wanted to be included in the Kingdom.

The Fiume question revealed again the differences among Italian politicians about Italian war aims. Did Italy want the Treaty – a good old-fashioned document of secret *Realpolitik* giving her control of the Adriatic – or did she want to embrace the new 'democratic' ideals and claim Fiume on national grounds? The answer, it seemed, was that she could not make up her mind.

In fact, Sonnino did not really want Fiume. He only asked for it to strengthen his hand when it came to arguing about Dalmatia: in his view Dalmatia, with its splendid naval bases, was the key to the Adriatic. The Navy Minister agreed with him. The high-minded 'democratic interventionists' like Bissolati, however, held fast to the 'principle of nationality'. Fiume was 'Italian'; Dalmatia was not, and so should be given up. The army commander, General Diaz, agreed with *them* – he feared that Italy might acquire an 'Ireland', with the army having to fight constant guerrilla campaigns against recalcitrant Dalmatian Italophobes.[1] So the government wavered. At Versailles, it publicly demanded both Fiume and the Treaty; on the Adriatic, it intrigued with Croat and Montenegrin separatists, and tried to subvert the new state of Yugoslavia.

The result was a disastrous rebuff. President Wilson refused to 'concede' either Fiume or Dalmatia to Italy, and published his arguments in a leading Paris newspaper. Sonnino and Orlando, affronted, went back home and were greeted as popular heroes. Conversely, Wilson became the arch-villain – a great change from the virtual adulation he had received in Italy a few months previously. The collapse of 'Wilsonism' had very important consequences for Italian politics: it destroyed the credibility of the 'democratic interventionists', as well as of the Allies.[2] Two months later the Orlando government fell, with the Adriatic question still unresolved. Italy had acquired Trent and Trieste, and the Italian army occupied Istria and Northern Dalmatia *de facto*, but her Allies had failed her over Fiume – and also over the ex-German colonial territories in Africa, which the British and French carefully kept out of Italian hands. It seemed, in D'Annunzio's phrase, a 'mutilated victory'. 'Interventionists', Nationalists, and even many ordinary Italians, greatly resented the sanctimoniousness of the Americans, the selfishness of the British and French, and the feebleness of their own government – especially when, in June 1919, Francesco Saverio Nitti became Prime Minister.

Nitti was an economist. Like most devotees of the Dismal Science, he overrated both its importance and its dismalness. Italy lacked coal and money; only the Allies could provide them; therefore the Allies must not be affronted. He and his Foreign Minister Tittoni played down Italy's claims; and the 'interventionists' clamour grew. D'Annunzio called Nitti '*Cagoia*' (abject coward). The nickname stuck. Nitti issued an amnesty to the wartime deserters, which affronted all right-minded patriots. He also cut down military spending, and this infuriated all the Right, especially the many new army officers. Soon the loyalty of some army units was dubious. Throughout the country a host of 'interventionist' groups railed against the 'renouncing' government.

In September D'Annunzio agreed to lead a military *coup* organized by prominent Nationalists, top army officers and one or two industrialists. He marched into Fiume with 2,000 'legionaries', mainly deserters or mutineers from the army. The '*Comandante*' remained there for fifteen months, hurling defiance at '*Cagoia*' and at Nitti's successor Giolitti. Fiume became a symbol of patriotic fervour and youthful vitality. Futurists, ex-servicemen, Nationalists, syndicalists, anarchists and adventurers flocked there from all over Italy. They swaggered round in cloaks and daggers (literally), bullied the local citizens, and enjoyed themselves immensely. The regime was a permanent *festa*, full of processions and ceremonies, of dancing and slogans. D'Annunzio's idea of democratic decision-making was rather like Mussolini's later: long rhetorical speeches from balconies to the eager crowds below, punctuated by massive acclamations. D'Annunzio also invented many of the other trappings of the later Fascist regime, including the militia, the 'Roman salute', the compulsory castor-oil 'purgation' for dissidents, and even the meaningless warcry 'Eia, eia, alalà'. However, D'Annunzio's Fiume was not just comic opera, nor merely a 'May 1968' of the Right. The *'Comandante'* issued proclamations *urbi et orbi*. He founded a 'Fiume League', a kind of Anti-League of Nations for oppressed peoples; and, within Fiume itself, he promulgated a revolutionary Constitution, largely written by his syndicalist friend Alceste De Ambris. It proclaimed that Fiume was a 'Producers' State'. Everybody was to be a member of one of ten 'guilds', or 'corporations', which would run the economy; the upper house of parliament would be elected by these corporations.

Initially there was not much that Italian governments could do. Nitti could not expel D'Annunzio by force, for the 'invasion' was very popular in Italy. The army in Venezia Giulia had clearly helped D'Annunzio to prepare it; certainly it would refuse to move against him. So Nitti ignored D'Annunzio as best he could, although D'Annunzio was not an easy man to ignore. Giolitti, who succeeded Nitti as Prime Minister in mid-1920, was more effective. He began negotiating directly with the Yugoslavs, and in November 1920 the two countries reached agreement. The Treaty of Rapallo declared that Fiume was to be independent. Italy kept Trieste and Istria. In Dalmatia, Zara and four islands were to go to Italy, but the rest was to be Yugoslav. This treaty was generally welcomed in Italy, perhaps because by late 1920 most people had got bored by D'Annunzio. Even in Fiume itself many of D'Annunzio's followers thought it acceptable, for it kept Fiume out of Yugoslav hands. On Christmas Day 1920 Giolitti took the final step, and sent the navy in. D'Annunzio surrendered almost immediately. The *'Comandante''s* regime was no more.

Yet Fiume was an important episode, or rather an important symbol. D'Annunzio had held the city, in defiance of Italian governments and international opinion, for over a year. He had proved that the Italian State was weak, and that the Armed Forces might prove disloyal. He had also pioneered a new style of 'mass politics', adopted by later demagogues in Italy and elsewhere. And although the manner of his fall – the 'Christmas of Blood' when Italian warships shelled the city – damaged his prestige as hero and war leader, it also tainted Giolitti yet again as anti-patriotic and fratricidal. D'Annunzio had helped to convince many Italians that they had been robbed; and he had shown that daring and activism might win back what had been lost. The plight of Fiume and Dalmatia provided slogans for all kinds of super-militant patriotic groups; it kept the spirit of 'interventionism' alive throughout the post-war years.

10.2 ECONOMIC PROBLEMS

Another major reason why the Liberal regime collapsed was its failure to cope with the transition to a peacetime economy. The problems were, indeed, intractable. The Nationalists, and some wartime 'technocrats', argued that there should be no transition at all. Some industrialists, especially those in heavy industry, electricity and shipbuilding, agreed; it was their only chance of survival in the post-war world. They could never sell all their guns, aeroplanes and ships on the open market; nor could they easily sell them to peaceful governments anxious to cut public spending. So the Perrone brothers of Ansaldo financed all sorts of Right-wing nationalist movements and newspapers, and Oscar Sinigaglia helped to organize the Fiume expedition. Such industrialists advocated what was, in effect, an alternative model of economic development: ships, steel, and hydro-electricity were to be vital in peacetime international competition, as well as in war.

But their arguments failed. Neither the Nitti nor the Giolitti government was willing to listen. The wartime controls were removed, and Italy went back to a semi-market economy and free-ish international trade. The results were dramatic. In 1920 the Perrone brothers tried desperately to buy up the *Banca Commerciale*, hoping thus to secure credit; Max Bondi of Ilva tried to diversify, by taking over the Edison electricity company. The various manoeuvres failed too. At the end of 1921 Ansaldo went bankrupt, and brought down the *Banca di Sconto* with it. Ilva, its great munitions rival, had failed a few months earlier, as had Lloyd Mediterraneo. True patriots naturally blamed the government for these bankruptcies: national idealism and dynamic initiative had once again been trampled underfoot by short-sighted, time-serving politicians.

In the meantime Italy suffered all the ills of hasty adjustment. As millions of men left the army, unemployment reached a peak of 2 million in November 1919; as industrialists 'reconverted' their plant to peacetime production, share prices halved. Above all, there was inflation. The wholesale price index (1913 = 100) rose from 412.9 in 1918 to 590.7 in 1920. The lira fell from 30 to the pound sterling in March 1919 to 50 in December of that year, and to 100 in December 1920. This post-war inflation was almost as bad as in the war itself. It wiped out the middle-class's savings, crippled the huge rentier class, and drastically reduced the wages and pensions of State employees. And civil servants had suffered enough already – senior administrative salaries in 1918 were less than half what they had been in 1914, in real terms.[3] A few firms, like Fiat, kept working normally during 1919–20, mainly because of the continuing need for army vehicles and ambulances; but by early 1921 the recession was international, and it badly hurt Fiat just when it was able to produce more vehicles from the new Lingotto factory.

These dark economic prospects were worsened by intense labour militancy. For 3½ years severe factory discipline had been enforced on recalcitrant workers. Suddenly a new era dawned. Socialist and anarchist leaders came out of prison or exile. Socialist trade unionists began organizing again: although – or perhaps because – most of them were 'reformists', they needed to prove their virility. Some valuable reforms were won, including the eight-hour day, State-financed labour-exchanges, and old age, health and unemployment insurance. Much of the militancy was defensive, for inflation hit workers' income as much as anyone else's. But much was not defensive at all. Many workers were convinced that revolution was imminent, 'as in Russia', and at least some of the agitations were designed to 'prepare' or help carry out the revolutionary task. Strikes, lockouts, riots, factory occupations and gang warfare became commonplace. Over 1 million people went on strike in 1919, and more again in 1920. Membership of the Socialist unions in the General Confederation of Labour rose from 250,000 in 1918 to 2 million by late 1920; the recently founded Catholic confederation claimed 1.2 million, mainly in textiles and agriculture; and the anarcho-syndicalists of the Italian Syndical Union claimed 300,000 members in September 1919, with much support in the steelworks and shipyards of Liguria. Industrialists nervously bought off trouble whenever they could, and governments seemed helpless.

More traditional modes of social protest were not forgotten either. Food riots broke out spontaneously in Central and Northern Italy in June 1919, provoked mainly by a sudden sharp increase in prices. The rioting was 'revolutionary' in the old-fashioned style: granaries were plundered, shops were looted, trees of liberty were planted, little local republics were set up. But the authorities reacted very differently from usual. Nitti had just become Prime Minister, and he was not going to start off by shooting women and peasants. So mayors and Prefects were ordered to set up food committees, often with the aid of the local (Socialist) Chambers of Labour; these committees requisitioned stores and issued price decrees, halving the price of many foods at a stroke. The rioting died away. But the shopkeepers were furious. How could they trade, if they were forced to sell at half-price, and if looters went unpunished?

And so a fateful pattern was set. When riots or strikes broke out, governments sought to compromise, to settle, to 'absorb' or buy off popular discontent. The policy worked, in the short run; but it fatally antagonized the middle classes. They complained it was not just the workers they had to contend with, but also the government; and the issues at stake were exacerbated by the 'patriotic question' – the new 'strikers' were the old 'shirkers'. Not all strikes were successful, of course. In July 1919 there was a twenty-four-hour 'international' strike of solidarity with the Russian Revolution, which aroused little enthusiasm; and in April 1920 a ten-day 'general strike' in Piedmont also failed to achieve its aims, this time of defending the new workers' councils in the factories. But unsuccessful strikes annoyed respectable opinion too, and public sector stoppages were particularly resented. The railwaymen came out in January 1920, as did postal and telegraph workers; they came out again in April and September; and in July even the troops went 'on strike', in protest against possible posting to Albania.

The most famous example of labour militancy was the 'occupation of the factories' in September 1920. It started as part of a normal wage dispute in the engineering industry. The unions feared an employers' lockout, and occupying the factories seemed the logical way to prevent one. In addition, the anarchists and syndicalists had long advocated 'direct action' of this kind as a prelude to revolution. So over 400,000 workers took over their factories or shipyards, expelled the managers, ran up the Red (or Black) Flag, and carried on working – sometimes at making barbed wire or guns for self-defence. They stayed there for nearly four weeks, living off 'Communist kitchens' in the factories, or off 'wages' taken from factory safes. It looked remarkably like a revolution, and it was a terrible shock to the *benpensanti.* Yet the Giolitti government affected to ignore it, at least initially. In Giolitti's view, the workers would do less harm inside the factories than outside, and in any case the army could not expel them without a bloodbath. The movement would collapse when raw materials ran out and when orders were cancelled, and he wanted the extremist ringleaders to take all the blame for failure. Even so, after ten days or so the government began to be alarmed, especially when news of weapons manufacture leaked out. So it started putting pressure on the employers to settle, using both stick and carrot – the stick being a threat of credit restrictions, the carrot a more protective tariff. By this time wages were no longer the issue. Something more 'revolutionary' was needed, if honour were to be satisfied and the workers persuaded to withdraw. The solution was 'trade union control of industries', a resounding phrase that sounded important and could be applied to all industries. Giolitti set up a commission to draft a bill making it compulsory; and the occupation ended, amid much recrimination.

But, once again, the price was too high, or seemed so. Many industrialists were furious at the government's 'interference' in the dispute, and had no intention of allowing the unions any say in management. They need not have worried. The commission failed to agree on a draft, and although Giolitti put a bill to parliament in February 1921, nothing came of it. Even so, the occupation had disastrous consequences. In itself, it was a dramatic threat to the bourgeois order; and the government response to it seemed no better. Arguably Giolitti had little choice – he had to persuade the workers out of the factories somehow, and 'control' was as good a way as any. But that was not how it looked to industrialists. Moreover, employers had to worry about other aspects of government policy. Giolitti had appointed a former syndicalist, Arturo Labriola, as Minister of Labour; there was a government bill to introduce a public register of shareholdings, which would make tax evasion much more difficult (this bill greatly alarmed the Vatican); the Minister of Finance was introducing a wealth tax, and talking about taxing war profits at 100 per cent. There were plans to give the trade unions even greater control over the labour-exchanges, so that employers could no longer hire whom they pleased. Where would it all end? Was the government in league with the unions?

In late 1920 an economic recession hit Italy, and deepened the industrialists' gloom. Some of them became more willing to finance strikebreakers and Right-wing extremists, although many others (e.g. Agnelli of Fiat) still relied on the Socialist unions as the best guarantors of industrial discipline. Things also looked bad for the militants. The 'occupation of the factories' had failed to bring about revolution, and had destroyed the syndicalists' great myth, the idea that seizing factories would bring down the bourgeois regime. There were far fewer strikes in 1921. But they had left a legacy of bitterness and fear, and there were many accounts to be settled.

10.3 AGRICULTURE

Much the same was true in the countryside, only more so. The soldiers left the army in 1919, and went home expecting 'land to the peasants'. Often they acquired it easily enough, buying from frightened or impoverished landowners; sometimes they took it by force, although in practice very little force was needed. Peasants would march symbolically on to barren or uncultivated land, would raise their flags and set to work. These 'land occupations' were nothing new: they had occurred sporadically throughout the nineteenth century. And they were not 'revolutionary'. They were usually reassertions of traditional claims, in the new post-war climate where promises were more likely to be kept. Sometimes they were spontaneous, but many were organized by local priests or by the ex-servicemen's associations, which could also help with such matters as seed purchases, insurance and marketing. Most of the occupations were in Latium and the South, where most of the uncultivated land was. Taking sales and occupations together, nearly 1 million hectares came into peasant ownership. By 1921 there were probably about 3½ million peasant-owners, twice the number of 1911; in the South, between 30 and 40 per cent of rural heads of families owned some land by then. Many Southern '*latifundia*' disappeared altogether. The turmoil of 1919–20, so alarming and revolutionary in appearance, in reality established a new, deeply conservative social structure in much of rural Italy.

Land occupations and purchases also occurred in Central and Northern Italy, but the general pattern there was rather different. Where small tenant farming predominated, as in some of the Northern hill areas, the agitations were over rents, food prices or co-operative enterprises; priests and Catholic union organizers were prominent. In much of the Veneto the landlords had fled during the Austrian occupation of 1917–18, whereas the clergy had stayed behind to share the people's sufferings. No wonder that, in the words of the Prefect of Vicenza, 'the rural population, under the influence of the Catholic party, are greatly agitated and regard their bosses with real hostility; the landowners are regularly described – even from the pulpit – as covetous speculators'.[4] In Tuscany and Umbria, where the share-cropping system was widespread, the peasants already 'occupied' the land physically; what they wanted was full ownership, or at least guaranteed tenure, a greater say in deciding land use, and a larger proportion of the produce. In areas like Emilia where there were large tenant-farmers hiring wage-labourers as required, the Socialist Labourers' Union *Federterra* demanded higher wages, a closed shop, above all the '*imponibile di mano d'opera*' – i.e. enforced overmanning, one worker per six hectares in Ferrara province throughout the winter. The ultimate Socialist aim was 'collectivization', which would follow 'after the Revolution'. The unions failed to achieve nationalization, but they often secured their other demands by well-organized strikes, particularly effective at harvest-time. In the 'red' provinces of Ferrara and Bologna no labourer could get a job except through the Socialist unions' labour-exchange; no employer could hire non-union labour. The Socialist Chambers of Labour could 'dictate conditions of work, wage-rates, even, if they so desired, the choice of crop'.[5] Any attempt to beat the system was countered by rick-burnings, physical violence, boycottings and even expulsion from the province.

Altogether, these were years of social upheaval in rural Italy. If there was a common factor in the different regions, it was that the larger landlords and tenants were threatened. And if there was a factor common to agriculture and industry, it was that governments sometimes seemed to be acting directly against the employers' interests. In September 1919 a government decree instructed Prefects to 'recognize' occupations of uncultivated land: peasant co-operatives (usually of ex-servicemen) could keep it for four years. The new law naturally encouraged further occupations, or at least landowners naturally supposed that it did. In October the unions' 'labour-exchanges' were officially recognized, and granted State subsidies. In the summer of 1920 a prominent member of the Catholic Popular Party (see below, §10.4), a party which relied heavily on the peasant vote, became Minister of Agriculture. Micheli behaved true to form. In October 1920 he issued a decree giving permanent, as opposed to four years, guaranteed tenure to illegal land occupiers. In January 1921 he introduced a bill guaranteeing all agricultural jobs until the end of 1922. Landowners everywhere bitterly resented these new decrees; and those in the North feared that land occupations might spread to their areas.

Landowners had other reasons for worry in late 1920. At the local elections of October–November nearly a quarter of the municipal councils, including most of the rural *comuni* in Central Italy, were won by the Socialists; the Catholic *Popolari* did almost as well. That meant that only union leaders and their friends would get local government jobs and subsidies, public works would be entrusted only to peasant leagues and to Socialist or Catholic co-operatives, and party propaganda would be subsidized from the rates – which would rise sharply. Furthermore, militant peasant unionism, both Socialist and Catholic, showed no signs of diminishing, and after the poor wheat harvests of 1919 and 1920 (4.6 million tonnes and 3.8 million tonnes respectively, less even than the wartime average of 4.56 million tonnes), many landowners were genuinely short of funds. The Giolitti government, with its *Popolari* ministers, seemed bent on destroying the position of landowners throughout the country. Who would act to save them?

10.4 POLITICAL BREAKDOWN

All these problems were serious, but not insuperable. Liberal Italy might have weathered the storm, given time and a stable political framework. But post-war Italy did not have a stable political framework. It had been precarious enough in 1913, but by 1919 it was weaker still. The old ruling class had been bitterly divided by the war: 'interventionists' against neutralists, Salandrians against Giolittians. The 'democratic interventionists' – Republicans, reformist Socialists, pro-war syndicalists – were also divided among themselves, and in any case were discredited by President Wilson at Versailles. The Nationalists, proud of their victorious war, trumpeted that a stronger State and a warlike economy were necessary. Indeed, in early 1919 there was much agitation, especially by the 'democratic interventionists', for a 'Constituent Assembly', to draft a new Constitution and push through thorough-going political and social reforms.

The two major groups of 'outsiders' were also more troublesome than ever. The Catholics, building on their wartime efforts, founded their own political party. The Popular Party (*Partito Popolare Italiano*, PPI) was an uneasy fusion of Right, Centre and Left-wing Catholics, supported mainly by the small peasant proprietors and tenants of Northern and North-Central Italy, and anxious to win over the Southern peasantry too. It naturally backed the peasants' land and rent agitations, and indeed often organized them. The PPI was formally 'non-confessional', and its policy programme carefully omitted any mention of the Roman question or of ecclesiastical legislation. Thus it did not aim to represent the Church's interests. It was a lay political party founded for lay purposes; yet it was led by a priest, Luigi Sturzo, and virtually all its supporters were practising Catholics, hostile to Liberalism, laicism and landlordism. The Catholics had now returned *en masse* to Italian politics. Unsympathetic Liberals suspected the PPI of being too 'clerical'; but the Vatican suspected it of not being clerical enough.

The founding of the PPI meant that the Liberals could no longer win Catholic support tacitly and cheaply, e.g. by promising not to bring in divorce, as in 1913. The days of 'Gentiloni Pacts' were over. The Catholics had emerged from the war as *combattenti*, with radical claims that had to be met. However, there was no guarantee that the PPI would keep any bargain it made; it was too disparate, and it was not under the Church's control. It refused, for example, to join an anti-Socialist coalition at the 1920 local elections in Milan, with the result that Milan came under Socialist control, much to the annoyance of its archbishop. No government in this period managed to win lasting backing from the PPI. Yet the Liberal regime had come to depend upon such backing.

The Socialists were, apparently, even more threatening. The PSI ended the war committed to immediate revolution and to the dictatorship of the proletariat. For two years the party Directorate and its newspaper, *Avanti!*, continued to preach revolution. The 'reformists' – trade union leaders, old

211

parliamentary hands, co-operative organizers, local councillors – counted for little; and the unions had to give regular proof of militancy, if only to ward off the strong syndicalist challenge. However, the Socialists' revolutionary slogans were purely verbal. They had no idea how to lead a revolution, and by the late summer of 1919 they were totally absorbed in election campaigning. Only in Turin, where the young Sardinian journalist Antonio Gramsci led a campaign for 'factory councils' in industry, was there any appreciation of the real issues involved. Even so, slogans are important in politics. The PSI's revolutionary posturing meant that it was not 'available' to friendly politicians like Giolitti; it could not be tacitly 'absorbed' into the system by public works schemes or union concessions, as in pre-war days. The PSI joined the Third International, and sent a high-ranking delegation to Moscow in July 1920 for its second congress. Serrati, editor of *Avanti!,* was elected on to the Comintern's executive committee. The PSI's public Bolshevism, its support for strikes and factory occupations, frightened the respectable middle classes away from a Liberal regime that seemed incapable of dealing with overt subversion.

The Liberal regime admittedly made things unnecessarily difficult for itself. Orlando's government introduced universal male suffrage in December 1918, to reward the soldiers. The following August Nitti brought in proportional representation as well, partly to please the Catholics, partly to strengthen the reformist Socialists, partly to stifle calls for a Constituent Assembly, partly because many moderate Italians hoped, as usual, that it would provide a safeguard against an extremist takeover. Henceforth there would be fifty-four huge constituencies, and the 508 deputies would be elected on a party-list system. The new electoral law was a real constitutional upheaval, although few realized it at the time. Nitti himself was confident in September 1919 that not more than sixty Socialists would be elected, half of them moderate men 'willing to take part in government'; in mid-November, more realistically, he thought that 'at the Chamber we will have to overcome an initial period of confusion, which will last perhaps a month or two'.[6] Giovanni Amendola was more perceptive: 'the list system means the abdication of the Liberal Party . . . into the hands of a Red–Clerical alliance'.[7] He was right about the end of the Liberal regime, but not about its successors.

In November 1919 the first elections were held under the new rules. The results were a disaster for the government, and indeed for the political system. The Radicals won 67 seats, and the reformist Socialists 21, much as expected; but the Giolittians won only 91, and the Right-wing Liberals only 23. The new Chamber was dominated by the two organized mass parties, the Socialists with 32.4 per cent of the vote and 156 seats, and the *Popolari* with 20.5 per cent and 100 seats. 'Government' parties (including the Radicals) won over half the votes only in the South; everywhere North of Rome, and even in Latium itself, the 'subversives' triumphed. The North–South split was unmistakable. One hundred and forty six of the 156 Socialist deputies came from Northern or Central Italy; so did 76 of the 100 *Popolari.* But 162 of the 239 'government' deputies were elected in the South. Could the backward

South really rule the industrial North? In any case, Liberal governments could only survive if they secured support either from Northern Catholics or from Northern Socialists. Such support would be difficult to win in the time-honoured manner. Most deputies were now dependent on party machines, and could not be bought or 'transformed' as easily as before.

The Nitti government fell in June 1920. The new Prime Minister was Giolitti himself, a sure sign of how the Establishment was trying to forget its old quarrels. Giolitti approached his tasks in the old complacent spirit. He assured Malagodi that there was 'no need to take the threats of Serrati, Bombacci and Co. too seriously. They are people who calm down immediately when they become deputies . . . in general the Socialists are not to be feared. Their very organization gives them a sense of responsibility and makes them used to discipline.'[8] Giolitti also wooed the PPI, brought it into government, and gave it some key posts, including the Treasury and Agriculture. But Giolitti and Sturzo were uneasy bedfellows. Giolitti, as a Piedmontese Liberal, could not abide meddling priests; Sturzo, as a Southern democrat, disliked corrupt fixers of elections. Moreover, Giolitti's concessions to Socialist trade unions (see above, §10.3) greatly annoyed Catholic unionists, as well as alienating the Liberals' essential middle-class supporters – and the Church. So Giolitti's liaison with the PPI was always fragile, and both sides constantly looked around for other partners. The local elections of autumn 1920, with their sweeping Socialist and *Popolari* gains, simply confirmed that the old regime was no more.

In May 1921 Giolitti played his last card. Hoping that the Socialists were by this time discredited, he called new elections. And hoping as ever to 'absorb' troublemakers, he offered Mussolini's Fascists a place on the government parties' lists. The gamble failed. Certainly the government parties' vote went up, from 36.9 per cent in 1919 to 47.8 per cent; but the Socialists lost fewer votes than expected, and the PPI vote remained stable. There were now 123 Socialist deputies, 15 Communists and 107 *Popolari* – still virtually half the Chamber. What was worse, the 'government' parties had become far too disparate. They included not only 64 Radicals and 24 reformist Socialists, but also 35 Fascists. No stable government could be formed from such a Chamber, and Giolitti resigned forthwith. He was succeeded by a series of short-lived coalitions under weak premiers, living from hand to mouth as public order collapsed. Salandra, Orlando, Nitti, Giolitti – all had been tried, and all found wanting. There was no other Saviour in sight, or rather none among the Liberals.

10.5 THE RISE OF FASCISM

This complex crisis clearly offered immense scope for paranoid patriots. Continuing the hysterical traditions of 1917–18, they founded various movements – the '*Fasci* of Resistance', the 'Italian *Fasci* of National Defence', the 'Association of Italian Volunteers' and so forth; the term '*Fascio*' (which literally meant 'bundle', and came to mean 'group') was deliberately reminiscent of the '*Fasci* of National Defence' (see §9.5), as well as of the revolutionary Sicilian *Fasci* (§5.5). The most prominent 'interventionist' group was that of D'Annunzio's legionaries, whose sights were set on Rome as well as on Fiume. After Fiume had fallen, D'Annunzio's supporters founded a 'National Federation of Fiume Legionaries', both patriotic and syndicalist. Former members of the '*Arditi*' (shock-troops) also founded a semi-political movement after the war; it soon had 10,000 members – men who had been chosen in war specially for their murderous qualities, and who enjoyed a good fight. The Futurists were also still active, and indeed Marinetti was the acknowledged leader of the *Arditi*. He, too, founded '*Fasci*' throughout Italy, the '*Fasci Futuristi*', loosely co-ordinated by a 'Futurist Political Party' with a programme based on 'total and intransigent anticlericalism'.

These 'interventionist' movements had much in common. They attacked the same targets: parliament, government, Nitti, Giolitti, Socialists, Catholics, bureaucrats and war-profiteers. They were urban, and strongest in Northern and North-Central Italy; they were para-military in organization and style; and they relied heavily on patriotic myths and bellicose sentiments. They appealed to students, both those who had fought in the war and those who had, unhappily, been too young. And they all recruited ex-officers. At least 130,000 officers were discharged from the army in 1919; over 20,000 of them took crash courses at university, either before or after formal demobilization. So the distinction between officers and students was never a clear one. All the 'interventionists' were active, all were glorious, all needed honour and excitement. They were available for political adventurers like D'Annunzio or Marinetti.

The most formidable Right-wing demagogue in Italy was Benito Mussolini, thirty-five years old in early 1919 and with very varied experiences behind him. Born in anarchist Romagna, the son of a blacksmith and a schoolmistress, he soon became that classic figure of Italian society, the embittered and penniless intellectual. He read voraciously, especially in literature and philosophy; he kept himself by a series of short-lived jobs – schoolteaching, building worker; and he joined a revolutionary political movement, the PSI. He served his time in Switzerland, as all good revolutionaries should; he wrote an anticlerical novel. Mussolini was intelligent, yet impatient of complexities; he was energetic, yet anxious for instant panaceas; he was inconsistent, yet always convinced of his own righteousness.

In short, he was a born journalist. Journalism was how he – and many others – made his way to the top; and he remained a journalist at heart all his life. From the local Socialist paper at Forlì, *Lotta di Classe*, he became editor of the official Socialist daily *Avanti!* in 1912, at the age of 29. This was a post of great political influence, and he was hugely popular and successful in the job. Two years later, however, he broke with the PSI over the intervention issue. He had made sure he had funds enough to found another paper, the *Popolo d'Italia* (see §9.2), but even so his action was not that of a calculating careerist. On the contrary, Mussolini was a violent and impulsive man, and he enjoyed living dangerously. War seemed desirable and exciting to a man of his temperament – and it made good copy. Naturally he went off to fight, and was honourably wounded; and naturally he came back to battle against 'the internal enemy' in the columns of his newspaper. He never forgot those glorious war years. He had campaigned for the war, wrecked his Socialist career for the war, and fought in the war: the war was the great ennobling experience of his life, indeed the great ennobling revolution of the twentieth century.

When peace came Mussolini, too, founded a political movement, the *Fasci di Combattimento*, whose inaugural meeting was held in a building on piazza San Sepolcro, Milan, on 23 March 1919. The *Fasci* were often indistinguishable from the *Arditi*. Captain Ferruccio Vecchi of the *Arditi* was chairman of the Fascists' inaugural meeting. The *Fasci di Combattimento* had the usual radical programme – a Constituent Assembly, abolition of the Senate, land for the peasants, seizure of Church property and major tax changes. But there was not much of a market for all this, and what there was had been cornered by the Socialists. The movement remained strident but ineffective in 1919–20, restricted to a few major centres of ultra-patriotism: Milan, Bologna, Trieste. It had only 870 members in December 1919. In November Fascists, Futurists and *Arditi* stood together in the parliamentary elections in Milan: they won a derisory 4,657 votes, out of 270,000.

It was the *Popolo d'Italia*, not the *Fasci*, that kept Mussolini in the limelight; it was in the newspaper, not in 'interventionist' politics, where his word was law and no rivals like D'Annunzio could challenge him. Mussolini remained an editor, first and foremost, long after he had become the '*Duce*' (leader) of Fascism. He successfully turned the paper into the spokesman for all the discontented extreme 'interventionists'. But the newspaper continually needed money, money which could only be provided by industrialists – sugar barons, steel magnates or shipbuilders. For nearly two years Mussolini struggled to keep his newspaper alive, and to find a political opening.

It came, eventually, from setting up armed 'squads', real para-military organizations run by Fascist ex-officers. Trieste, where national passions ran deep, was soon dominated by these groups, well-armed and enjoying army help. In late 1920 the Fascist para-military movement – '*squadrismo*' – really took off, rather to Mussolini's surprise. Many factors helped it. The Treaty of Rapallo was good propaganda for nationalists; and so was the fall of Fiume. Above all, the Giolitti government seemed soft on militancy. The 'occupation of the factories' frightened many people; the local election results in October–November frightened even more. It was time to stand and fight.

The really important breakthrough came not in the North, nor in the cities, nor even in centres of nationalist excitement like Trieste. It owed little to Mussolini or to his newspaper. It came in the 'red' provinces of Central Italy, in Emilia and Tuscany, where landlords and leaseholders reacted against the victorious Socialist labour leagues, against the new local councils and against government agricultural policy. Fascist squads were the ideal instrument for breaking up Socialist or *Popolare* dominance in the countryside. A lorry-load of ex-officers or students would descend on some village at night, beat up the local unionists, 'purge' them of their iniquities by making them drink castor-oil, burn down the local party offices, and depart. The police would stand by, when not actively joining in; the Prefect would wring his hands, but stay well clear. Landowners naturally encouraged these exploits: destroying the labour leagues was well worth the cost of the odd lorry.

Yet '*squadrismo*' was not just class conflict, nor was it just thuggery. Many ordinary peasants were sick of the petty Socialist dictatorships too, and joined the squads willingly enough. Once the labour leagues' 'closed shops' had been broken, these men could expect jobs, leases or even smallholdings. Above all, the squads were convinced of their own righteousness. They were restoring law and order, they were rescuing their country from tyranny, and they were avenging their fallen wartime comrades. That was why so many respectable Liberals wished them well, initially. Luigi Albertini wrote that the Socialists deserved all they got; Giovanni Amendola agreed, and expressed his 'complete support both with my head and my heart'.[9] Mario Missiroli described Fascism as 'the emergence of a besieged army'.[10] And it was victorious. The 'red' provinces of the Po valley and of Tuscany were transformed, sometimes in only a few weeks, from being the home of the most powerful peasant unions in Europe to being the main strongholds of the Fascist squads.

All this transformed the Fascist movement too. The initial stereotype of Fascism, the 'revolutionary' 'interventionist' 'Fascism of the first hour' in Milan and the big cities, the Fascism of Mussolini, syndicalists, ex-officers and students, was replaced by another stereotype: *squadrismo*, reactionary and rural. But stereotypes are deceptive, and perhaps there was not that much difference between the earlier and later Fascist movements, except that the later one had found its vocation. Both were, in fact, urban – the squads started out from provincial towns, usually provincial capitals – and both initially contained much the same people, i.e. ex-officers and students. At Bologna, for example, the squads could only begin serious operations when the university term began in the autumn of 1920. Even so, '*squadrismo*' made Fascism a mass movement, and gave it a much wider base, or series of bases, in Central Italy. Small leaseholders and owners, farm managers and artisans, share-croppers in Emilia, those who had bought or hoped to buy land, joined the squads and joined the *Fasci*. The squad leaders – the '*ras*', as they were soon called – like Farinacci in Cremona, Balbo in Ferrara, Arpinati in Bologna, soon became the great *condottieri* of Northern and Central Italy.

Mussolini, in Milan, could not control these men, and the local *ras* remained one of his biggest headaches for years to come. But his position outside *squadrismo*, above the *mêlée*, also gave him a marvellous opportunity for manoeuvre. On the one hand, he was the *Duce* of Fascism. He and his paper acted on the squads' behalf, as national organizer, financier and propagandist. He was the man who could unleash the squads, and he threatened to do so unless given concessions. But he also played a very different role, that of moderate statesman, far-sighted and patriotic. He was the man who could tame the squads, if only he were given the authority to do so. Whenever the squads were particularly violent, Mussolini murmured soothing words about national reconciliation and restoring law and order. Mussolini needed squad violence. It had given him an effective political movement to lead. He needed to support it; but he also needed to deplore it.

For most of 1921 Mussolini played the squad-tamer, reassuring his city followers that Fascism had not sold out to the rural bourgeoisie, and reassuring the Establishment that he was respectable at heart. He proclaimed that land should be leased out to the peasants. Mussolini also reaffirmed his republicanism, to console his more radical supporters. Even so, the Fascist movement was clearly becoming more conservative. By July 1921 Mussolini had become the peace-maker. He proposed a 'pact of pacification' between the Fascists and the Socialist unions, and one was actually signed on 2 August. It was a great risk to take, and he soon paid the price. The *Fasci* of Emilia rejected the pact angrily, and some prominent leaders – including Roberto Farinacci of Cremona – resigned from the Fascist central committee. Dino Grandi of Bologna and Italo Balbo, boss of Ferrara, even went to Gardone and asked D'Annunzio to take over the Fascist leadership. The Fascist movement very nearly split, and for a few months Mussolini's authority was precarious. Yet the squad leaders distrusted each other at least as much as they distrusted Mussolini; and there was no alternative leader except D'Annunzio, who refused to act.

So Mussolini kept his hold on the movement, after many harsh words and a brief tactical resignation. He had to give up the 'pact of pacification': *squadrismo* continued to flourish, spreading out from Central Italy into fresh provinces in the North. But he managed, in October 1921, to put Fascism on a proper footing as a formal political party, the National Fascist Party (*Partito Nazionale Fascista*, PNF). The new party founded local branches, welcomed 'respectable' recruits, collected regular dues; it was obviously designed to be a centralized body under Mussolini's control, a counterweight to the local squads and their insolent commanders. With over 200,000 members by the end of 1921, and over 300,000 by May 1922, the party gave Mussolini a real political base other than his newspaper. It greatly improved his hand in negotiations with other politicians. The PNF rapidly became the party of the middle classes, filling the vacuum left by the collapse of Liberalism.

Organized mass unions proved useful too. Here the militant syndicalist legacy of early Fascism was vital. The *squadristi* and the syndicalists joined forces, like the stick and the carrot. *Squadristi* destroyed the Socialist peasant leagues; syndicalists followed on their heels and herded the former members into Fascist bodies. Sometimes the 'closed shop' system was simply taken over, the Socialist league being replaced by a Fascist 'syndicate' and by a Fascist labour-exchange. More generally, Fascist volunteers not only broke strikes among railway and postal workers, they also founded alternative unions. Syndicalism was organization, strength, political power; it was also 'the conscience of the revolution'. The union, or syndicate, linked the old radical aspirations to the new reactionary reality; or rather, it showed that Fascism was not merely reaction. And it worked, or seemed to. It was literally true, in 1920–21, that the Fascists made the trains run on time, indeed run at all: a remarkably high proportion of the early provincial leaders, including Farinacci himself, were station-masters or other railway officials. In January 1922 the various local unions formed a National Confederation of Syndical Corporations, with Edmondo Rossoni as secretary. By June it claimed nearly 500,000 members, mainly peasants. In many regions landowners negotiated only with the syndicates, and were threatened if they tried to do otherwise. The Catholic and Socialist peasant unions melted away. The Fascists were 'bringing the workers into the system', while making sure they did not dominate it. And who else could do that?

By late 1921 'Fascism' already meant several quite distinct phenomena. To many, it meant strike-breaking – seen either as a vicious attack on workers' rights, or as a heroic, patriotic duty. To others, it meant the 'national' unions, a new way of disciplining and mobilizing labour. To a few, it was still a revolutionary, republican movement, 'Fascism of the first hour'. But this last kind of Fascism was obsolescent, and indeed was rapidly turning 'anti-Fascist': the *Arditi* Association went over to D'Annunzio in June 1921, and publicly declared its opposition to Fascism. To most people, and to most Fascists, 'Fascism' now meant *squadrismo* – a number of different para-military groups, fiercely independent, sometimes in league with large landowners, sometimes more 'syndicalist', but always recruiting from the urban middle class or from leaseholders and small owners, always run by local bosses, always intransigent and, increasingly, a menace to public order as well as to Socialists. To the more sophisticated, 'Fascism' also meant local groups, but more complex and varied ones than the term '*squadrismo*' implied: republican in the Romagna, irredentist in Trentino, syndicalist in Emilia. Alternatively, 'Fascism' meant 'Mussolinism': a cult of personality, full of bellicose rhetoric and nationalist sentiment; necessary to hold the disparate groups together, but essentially theatrical.

These different kinds of Fascism explain why historians disagree even about such basic questions as who the Fascists were. Were they 'bourgeois' or 'petty bourgeois', 'rising' or 'falling', members of 'new' or 'old' élites, or of none? Traditional views have stressed the 'humanist petty bourgeoisie' – teachers, civil servants, lawyers, rentiers – hit by inflation, desperate for jobs, and resentful of working-class prosperity. Many of these men were ex-officers and some were landowners, needing to control labour and avoid taxes. The problem with this argument is that it simply describes the traditional middle classes of pre-Fascist times – particularly in the South, where Fascism was weakest. Renzo De Felice has argued, so far with little evidence, that many Fascists were members of the 'rising middle class', who had recently acquired land or small businesses.[11] They were, in short, 'petty bourgeois', but aggressive and successful rather than defensive. Our only real evidence comes from a survey of about half the Fascist Party members in the autumn of 1921, which revealed an unusual number of landowners, shopkeepers, clerical workers and, above all, students – Petersen has calculated that 12–13 per cent of Italian students must have been PNF members at this time.[12] Fascism was a typical militant student movement, except that these students knew how to fight, and their parents approved of their activities.

The only indisputable conclusion is that Fascism was a number of complex local movements, linked by patriotic sentiment, by hatred of Socialism and by the myth of the *Duce*. However, Liberal politicians had no doubt what Fascism meant. It meant, by late 1921, the thirty-five Fascist deputies and the PNF leaders, who represented substantial middle-class interests, and who were willing to collaborate with other respectable parties in parliament. Such people might also be willing to give up Fascism's para-military aspects, as the attempted 'pact of pacification' had shown. Was it not wise, therefore, to strengthen the Fascist Party and the deputies, perhaps even by bringing them into the government, so that they could assert their authority more effectively over their own followers?

In these circumstances Mussolini had only two real worries. Firstly, some tough-minded Liberal politician might yet 'restore law and order' against the Fascists rather than with them. This was unlikely, if only because there was no parliamentary majority for such a policy. In fact, after Giolitti's resignation in June 1921 there were three more Liberal governments, one led by the reformist Socialist Ivanoe Bonomi (June 1921 to February 1922), and two by Facta, a Giolittian (February to July, and July to October 1922). Both Bonomi and Facta were weak men, anxious only to compromise, and neither of them could ensure police or army loyalty in fighting Fascists.

In any case, there were no tough-minded Liberals around, except Salandra, Giolitti and (possibly) Orlando. Salandra showed little sign of activity or ambition, had little support in parliament, and was not noticeably anti-Fascist anyway. Giolitti was the man who had brought the Fascists into parliament; and he had alienated the *Popolari* – in February 1922 Sturzo 'vetoed' his return to power. Orlando, the 'President of Victory', was still reasonably prestigious despite Versailles, but he had not been a tough Minister of the Interior in 1916–17 and there was no reason to suppose he would be any tougher in peacetime. The same argument applies to tough-minded police action. The squads might have been suppressed by the police and *carabinieri*, if strong orders had been issued to the Prefects, and if these orders had been believed. Giolitti and Bonomi issued the orders, but the Prefects did not believe them – after all, in national politics both men were trying to conciliate the Fascists, not repress them, and the Fascist candidates were on government lists at the 1921 elections. Only exceptional Prefects like Mori at Bologna were willing to risk acting on their own; and he was soon transferred. So, too, were other 'neutral' (i.e. not actively pro-Fascist) Prefects, especially in Tuscany. It was the Prefect's job to keep in with the local élites; and the local élites sympathized with Fascism. Most policemen and judges, too, were well-disposed towards Fascist aims; the police had had to face all the demonstrations and riots of the Socialist years, and they welcomed their new allies.

The second possible threat to Mussolini was more serious. His followers might slip out of his control; even worse, they might desert him and go over to D'Annunzio. The crisis over the 'pact of pacification' had shown that this was a real possibility. D'Annunzio helped Mussolini out by being hostile to *squadrismo* – he called it 'agrarian slavery'[13] – and by posing as national peace-maker. There was not much point in the squad leaders going over to him; better the devil they knew. In any case, Mussolini had learned his lesson. After September 1921 he backed the squads, very loudly. Together they won some famous victories. They took over town after town in Northern Italy in the summer of 1922. The *Duce* was leading his troops again.

The opponents of Fascism helped Mussolini too. In January 1921 the Socialist party split, and thereafter Italy had a real Communist Party, sectarian and financed by 'Russian gold'. It was too small to be a threat, but its existence was excellent propaganda for the Fascists. Most of the Left-wing Socialists stayed in the PSI, and so the reformists were still outnumbered there and still unable to ally with 'bourgeois democrats' in defence of the Liberal regime. But the greatest boost of all to Mussolini came from outside the formal political parties. In the summer of 1921 anti-Fascist defence squads were formed, the *Arditi del Popolo*, mainly consisting of anarchists, syndicalists, Republicans and Socialists. This movement soon collapsed for want of money and arms, but it had frightened the bourgeoisie a little. And it left a legacy. An armed anti-Fascist struggle had been attempted, and had collapsed within a few weeks.

In July–August 1922 Mussolini's opponents helped him again. Some of the main trade union bodies – the anarcho-syndicalists of the Italian Syndical Union, the reformist Socialists in the CGL, the Railwaymen's Union, the Dockworkers – had formed an 'Alliance of Labour' in February, mainly to fight wage cuts and unemployment. The 'Alliance' had the benevolent backing of several political parties – PSI, Republicans, even the Communists and anarchists; but it was dominated by the reformist Socialists. On 31 July it called a twenty-four-hour general strike, hoping to ensure that the new government then being formed would be anti-Fascist and contain reformist Socialist deputies. This was a disastrous error. The strike was not widely supported: only 800 of Fiat's 10,000 car workers came out, and Fascist volunteers kept public services running. It discredited the CGL, and ensured that the reformist Socialists would *not* be in the next government; and it frightened respectable opinion yet again. The Fascists could pose, once more, as saviours of their country, their own thuggery forgiven if not forgotten.

After the 'Alliance of Labour' strike, the question was no longer whether the Fascists would come into government, but on what terms. The parliamentary manoeuvres of autumn 1922 were over this issue, as was the Fascists' violent pressure – their continuing murders, their seizure of provincial towns, the mass rally of 40,000 Fascists at Naples on 24 October, even the so-called 'March on Rome' on 27–28 October. Mussolini succeeded brilliantly, both in keeping up the morale of his supporters by militant action, and in confusing the politicians by offers of compromise. In early October, he was negotiating with Giolitti, among others, demanding four Cabinet posts in a new government. By mid-October Mussolini could insist on becoming Prime Minister himself, unless the politicians used force against the massed Fascists. The Facta government, still formally in office, was obviously reluctant to do so. But early on 28 October, after much hesitation, it finally asked the king to sign a decree establishing martial law ('*stato d'assedio*').

The king, after initially agreeing, refused. Why? No one can be sure, but his military advisers seem to have told him that the army might not be willing to fire on Fascists. Marshal Diaz is reported to have said, in a splendid phrase, 'Your Majesty, the army will do its duty; however, it would be well not to put it to the test'.[14] The king may also have worried about his cousin, the Duke of Aosta, who was near the Fascist headquarters in Perugia and might have been hoping for the Crown. More probably he thought resistance was not worth it. Why risk a bloodthirsty civil war, when the only question was how many Fascist ministers were to be included in the next coalition government? And the Fascists had already taken over most of the country – the 'March on Rome' of 28 October was actually a successful 'March on the provincial capitals'. So the king refused to authorize martial law, and instead made one last effort to persuade Salandra to form a government. Salandra, realistically, refused. Two days later Mussolini arrived on the overnight sleeper from Milan, summoned by the king to form the new government.

Thus Mussolini did not really seize power. He did not, by 28 October, need to use force. He won by threatening to use it, and by having the squads ready to obey. Formally, he became Prime Minister constitutionally, appointed by the king; the 'March on Rome' happened afterwards, when hordes of Blackshirts were allowed to roam around the capital exulting and rampaging in the rain. Mussolini won by being 'brought into the system' by a king and a governing élite that could see no other way of containing organized violence. Although it is right to stress the longer-term causes of his victory – the 'mutilated victory' of Versailles, agrarian class conflicts, ex-officers seeking social promotion, proportional representation and so forth – there was nothing inevitable about it. If there had been a 'respectable' conservative able to exploit anti-union sentiment in 1920–21, if Giolitti had not made Fascism respectable in May 1921, if the *Popolari* had not been so opposed to a new Giolitti government in February 1922, if the reformist Socialists had not called a general strike in August 1922, if Facta had resigned earlier in October, if Giolitti had been in Rome instead of Piedmont later in the month, or if the king had not been worried about his cousin, all might have been different. And the idea of 'absorbing' the Fascists into the Establishment, of allowing them a few posts in someone else's government, may have been ignoble but was not foolish. It might have worked – Mussolini himself recognized on 17 October that 'they would like to imprison me; joining a government would be the liquidation of Fascism'.[15] 'Absorbing' troublemakers is normally sound Italian politics; on this occasion it misfired, but the politicians cannot be blamed too harshly for trying it.

10.6 MUSSOLINI AS PRIME MINISTER (OCTOBER 1922 TO APRIL 1924)

On 28 October 1922 a new era of Italian history began – literally so, for the Fascist regime dated its documents thereafter from the March on Rome. But few people realized it at the time. Mussolini formed a coalition Cabinet – a 'National Government', as he called it – including himself and three Fascists in the key posts, but also including two *Popolari*, four Liberals of various types, a Nationalist (Federzoni), and three prestigious names – Marshal Diaz at the War Ministry, Admiral Thaon di Revel at the Admiralty, and the philosopher Giovanni Gentile at Education. The talk was all of 'normalization' and restoring law and order. Mussolini even invited the CGL leader Baldesi to join his government, although opposition from the Fascist syndicates and from the Nationalists ensured that the offer was not taken up. Most observers welcomed this work of reconciliation. Gaetano Salvemini, who was to spend twenty years in exile fighting the Fascist regime, wrote in April 1923 that 'a return to Giolitti would be a moral disaster for the whole country. Mussolini was able to carry out his coup last October because everybody was disgusted by the Chamber.'[16] Similarly, a month after the March on Rome Anna Kuliscioff, a lifelong Socialist, wrote that she was looking forward to pacification and to the 'absorption' of the Fascists: 'the victory of a subversive bloc now would foment Fascist violence and would encourage them to maintain their armed squads'.[17] And few people supposed the new government would last long.

The main losers from the March on Rome were, in fact, the Fascist *squadristi*, numbering perhaps 100,000 by this time. Mussolini's government was far too parliamentary for their tastes. Its economic policy was depressingly orthodox, it was allied to the hated PPI (until April 1923), and Mussolini continued to intrigue with the even more hated CGL. In Rome, the career bureaucracy was still entrenched. Even at local level Prefects tried to keep some semblance of control. Had the revolution been betrayed? Where were the jobs for the boys?

Mussolini the squad-tamer had to answer these complaints somehow. His answer was brilliant. In January 1923 the Fascist Militia (MVSN) was formed, 'to defend the Fascist revolution'. The Militia was recruited from party members, usually ex-*squadristi*; it was paid out of public funds; and it was answerable directly to the *Duce*. Here was a marvellous way of ending undisciplined *squadrismo*. The Militia was designed to keep the rank and file squad members under control, and to make the *ras* impotent; it gave Mussolini a private army too. Of course, this was not achieved overnight. The Militia remained for several years a loose federation of local squads, run by local bosses, but at least it showed that the government was trying to control the hard men. Apart from that, the Militia had few functions. It guarded public buildings, and it allowed Fascists to parade around in uniforms; but its main purpose was to exist. It provided the *squadristi* with rewards, both in cash and in glamour. It was an outward and visible sign that the Fascist Revolution had succeeded – and that it was over.

Most important of all, the Fascist movement risked being taken over by the Establishment. The PNF had 300,000 members in October 1922; it had 783,000 by the end of 1923. A vast crowd of careerists and place-seekers threatened to swamp the old believers. And in February 1923 the Nationalist Association joined the PNF *en bloc*. This 'fusion' of two movements, which at local level often detested each other, transformed Fascism yet again. Luigi Salvatorelli called it, perhaps prematurely, 'the undeniable victory of the Nationalist spirit over the Fascist one'.[18] The Nationalists were monarchist, anti-Masonic and conservative. They had far more in common with the old landowning élites and with the Roman bureaucracy than the Fascists did, and they soon dominated the Southern branches of the party. They provided able leaders; and they provided novel yet respectable ideas. 'Fusion' gave the Fascist Militia another 80,000 members, who had formerly been in the Nationalist para-military organization, the '*Sempre Pronti!*' That, too, helped to weaken Fascist *squadrismo*. Moreover, some of the old Fascists were expelled from the party, including even the boss of Naples, Padovani. De Vecchi of Turin was sent to Somalia. Mussolini seemed to be favouring 'revisionist' Fascists like Giuseppe Bottai, who argued that *squadrismo* had become anachronistic. To sugar the pill, the *Duce* set up a new Fascist body, the 'Grand Council'. Like the Militia, it did little – most political decisions were still taken by the government coalition – but it created a formal Fascist 'Cabinet', parallel to the constitutional one, and it gave the top Fascist bosses the opportunity to look important while the party beneath them was slowly transformed. The PNF was becoming respectable. It could be used already as a weapon against the *ras*; it might become the mass party of the bourgeoisie.

Mussolini's major political achievement in 1923 was also geared to this aim. In April the PPI Congress was very divided on the party remaining in the Fascist-led government, and ten days later Mussolini brusquely dismissed the *Popolari* ministers. Clearly the government's parliamentary majority was now at risk, so Mussolini immediately proposed a new electoral system. This was a shrewd move. Proportional representation was generally regarded as disastrous, except by Socialists and *Popolari*. Most Liberals wanted to return to single-member constituencies. The Fascists proposed a 'corrected' pro-portional system, in which the party grouping with the largest number of votes, provided it amounted to at least 25 per cent of the valid votes cast, would receive two-thirds of the parliamentary seats. This would ensure, in theory, a stable government majority. In practice it would mean that Mussolini could form a 'national bloc' of pro-government groups, and that the Liberals would be forced to climb on to his bandwagon. On the other hand, they would be elected; and so most of them supported the measure, however half-heartedly. The losers would be the Radicals and the more 'Left-wing' Liberals (Nitti, Amendola, etc.), who had lost most of their influence already; and – above all – the PPI. Mussolini would no longer need its support. The PPI was confused and hopelessly split by this time, and the Vatican, clearly impressed by Mussolini's concessions on education, Freemasonry and the like (see §12.4), applied some delicate pressure. Most PPI deputies abstained in the vote on the electoral bill, and Sturzo resigned from the post of party secretary, 'by the Holy See's wish'.[19] The bill passed its second reading by 235 to 139; Giolitti, Salandra and Orlando all voted in favour. Mussolini's position seemed secure.

Soon came the elections, to consolidate it still further. In April 1924 the *'listone'* of approved candidates – Fascists, former Nationalists, Right-wing Liberals including Salandra, Orlando and De Nicola, Agrarians, even a few *Popolari* – won 66.3 per cent of the valid votes, and was thus entitled to two-thirds of the seats anyway. Of the bloc's 374 victorious candidates, about 60 per cent were 'Fascists'. The government's success was particularly marked in the mainland South (81.5 per cent of the vote) and in Central Italy; in the North the bloc received less than the opposition. Yet the 'opposition' covered a huge range: the Giolittians (strictly speaking, not an 'opposition' at all, but 'parallel' to the government bloc), Amendola's 'constitutional list', Bonomi's Democrats, the *Popolari* (9.1 per cent of the vote), the Republicans, Matteotti's reformist Socialists (5.9 per cent), the PSI (down to 4.9 per cent), and the Communists (3.8 per cent). These parties had little in common, and they squabbled ceaselessly. Mussolini had, it seemed, succeeded in his aims. He had brought Fascism under control, and had made it respectable and parliamentary. He had destroyed and discredited the main opposition parties, especially the Socialists and Catholics. He had won over the Nationalists and Right-wing Liberals to his cause, and allowed them influence and office. He was the hero of a grateful Establishment, and could look forward to a long dull reign.

10.7 THE MATTEOTTI CRISIS

But it was not to be. On 30 May Giacomo Matteotti, who had replaced Filippo Turati as leader of the reformist Socialists, spoke in parliament. He denounced the recent elections as a fraud and a sham. What he said was true: the 1924 elections had indeed been much worse than usual, and many opposition candidates had been beaten up or tortured. His speech was a conscious act of defiance, designed to discredit Mussolini's claims to respectability and 'normalization'. He may also have been trying to prevent the CGL leaders from coming to terms with the *Duce*. At any rate, he infuriated Mussolini, who was alleged to have told his personal gang of thugs (the so-called 'Cheka', set up in January) 'if you were not cowards, nobody would have the courage to make a speech like that'.[20] On 10 June Matteotti disappeared. Everyone assumed, rightly, that he had been murdered by Fascists. The main opposition parties walked out of parliament in protest, and the Liberal press denounced both government and Fascist movement as assassins. The 'Matteotti crisis' had begun; Mussolini's 'Watergate'.

The immediate issue, as in Watergate, was one of complicity. Was Mussolini, or the Fascist government, or the Fascist movement, 'responsible' for Matteotti's death? Matteotti had been seized by Mussolini's hit-squad, led by Amerigo Dumini; Dumini was also assistant to Cesare Rossi at Mussolini's press office. Clearly the operation had been planned by men close to the centre of power – i.e. not by Fascist 'extremists', but by 'normalizers'. Was Mussolini's remark tantamount to an order to kill Matteotti? Did Mussolini have any later part in the plot, or in a cover-up? The long-term issue was political. If the Fascist thugs were rampant, if the Fascist government could not guarantee law and order after all, or if it was itself a criminal band of murderers, then it would obviously have to go. But how? It had just won a solid parliamentary majority, and its supporters were entrenched in office throughout the land.

As in the Watergate crisis, the government's chief enemy was the press. Amendola's *Il Mondo* and Albertini's *Corriere della Sera* thundered against the government, and their circulation rose alarmingly. Mussolini also had to worry about his Cabinet – four ministers offered their resignations, and some of the others were doubtful – and about the Liberal elder statesmen like Giolitti, Orlando and Salandra. These men remained in parliament. They might well influence the king, and the king might, constitutionally, dismiss the government. Even so, things could have been a lot worse for the *Duce*. There were a few popular protests and strikes after 10 June, but nothing serious: even for Matteotti's funeral there was only a ten-minute stoppage, in which the Fascist syndicates themselves joined. The general public seemed reluctant to blame the government. D'Annunzio remained silent, perhaps because he was about to sell his manuscripts to Mussolini for over 5 million lire. In the Chamber, the opposition parties had conveniently walked out – 'gone to the Aventine hill', to use the old Roman expression – so there was no chance of the government being overthrown by a parliamentary vote. This was a vital advantage, as Giolitti complained: 'Mussolini has all the luck: the opposition was always very troublesome to me, but with him it just walks out and leaves the field free.'[21] And the Senate voted on 26 June in favour of justice and pacification, by 225 to 21. Above all, the king stayed inactive. He failed to see how he could dismiss the government as long as it enjoyed a parliamentary majority, and the Senate's vote was a clear indication of Establishment views.

So Mussolini hung on to power. He refused to admit any complicity in the murder, he sacrificed some of his more unpopular henchmen, and he carried on 'normalizing'. A career Prefect, Crispo Moncada, became chief of police, and the Nationalists were given the key security jobs. Federzoni became Minister of the Interior, and Rocco Minister of Justice. Several other Right-wing Liberals and monarchists were brought into the government; one of the king's former adjutants, General Clerici, became Under-secretary of War. Above all, the Fascist Militia was reorganized. In August it was 'brought into the Armed Forces', i.e. Militia members would henceforth be subject to military discipline, the officers would be ex-army regulars, and everybody would take an oath of loyalty to the king.

As time went on, the opposition's impotence became clearer. The Vatican implicitly supported the government, and ordered Sturzo into exile. The opposition parties continued to squabble. The 'Centre-Left' parties had a secret committee to co-ordinate the anti-Fascist struggle, but it had no arms, and it was also supposed to fight against the Communists if need be, as the Communists well knew. The Communists, in turn, saw the situation as 'going to the Right. This is very favourable to us. It helps even now to sow lack of confidence in the opposition parties among the proletariat and peasants and even some strata of the bourgeoisie.'[22] There was clearly no chance of any concerted opposition action against Mussolini.

Yet, once again, Mussolini's attempts at 'normalization' failed. They were all a bit too obvious. The *squadristi* were furious at the various conciliatory moves, and they greatly resented the press campaign against them. Why were such newspapers still allowed in Fascist Italy? In their view, it was the opposition parties that had acted illegally, even treasonably, by walking out of parliament. In September the Fascist deputy Casalini was murdered in Rome, and the *squadristi* became more furious still. Why should they suffer the opposition's moralizing over Matteotti, while their own men were being slaughtered with impunity? Thus the Matteotti crisis entered its second phase, that of squad reaction. The leading *ras* had learned to distrust Mussolini. They feared that they, too, might be called to account for their past crimes, as Matteotti's murderers had been. They also worried about the Militia. De Bono had resigned as commander in June, because of his involvement in the Matteotti murder; his successor Balbo had to resign in November, implicated in various other crimes. This time the new commander was an army general, Gandolfo, who promptly sacked all the regional commanders and replaced them by ex-army officers.

When parliament reopened on 12 November it soon became clear that, despite the opposition parties' absence, the government was in danger. The respectable conservatives, elected on the '*listone*' six months previously, were unhappy. Giolitti was anti-government, and his supporters voted against the Foreign Ministry budget. Orlando abstained on the Interior Ministry budget, and Salandra made a critical speech. Various industrialists and generals spoke up in the Senate, and on 5 December the Senate vote on the Interior budget showed fifty-four anti-government votes and thirty-five abstentions. This was a real blow to Mussolini, especially as the Minister of the Royal Household abstained. Orlando, in the Chamber, urged the king to take the situation in hand. On 20 December forty-four Fascist deputies, mainly from the South, met in the house of the ex-Nationalist para-military leader Paolucci, and agreed to support 'normalization'. Mussolini tried to oblige. On 20 December he delighted the Liberals by producing a bill for returning to single-member constituencies, a gesture which also implied new elections fairly soon to resolve the crisis.

But 'normalization' still eluded him, if indeed he was still pursuing it. The day after Christmas Salandra resigned as president of the budget committee. The next day Cesare Rossi's 'memorandum' on the Matteotti affair (and other Fascist crimes) was published in the opposition press, and fully implicated Mussolini. On 30 December the Cabinet met, and the two Liberal ministers,

Casati and Sarrocchi, urged it to resign. Meanwhile, back in the provinces the *ras* had decided to act. Now that Balbo had gone, how long would any of them keep their jobs in the Militia? They wanted their Militia to stay Fascist, and no more talk of pacification. Thirty-three of them visited Mussolini on 31 December, and demanded a 'real' Fascist regime at last; in Florence, the Fascists rioted. So Mussolini had little choice. He could not remain as 'constitutional' Prime Minister; 'normalization' had apparently failed. But he could still play the *squadrista* card. He was still, just about, the man who could tame the squads; or rather, by this time, the man who could unleash them. It was his last card, but it was a trump – provided he played it quickly before the squads got out of control.

And so Mussolini decided to stay on, as the unashamed *Duce* of Fascism. On 3 January 1925 he spoke to the Chamber of Deputies. The Fascist government, he claimed, had always sought peace and 'normality'. It was absurd to imagine that he had ordered Matteotti's murder. He had always acted legally – even in the previous six months the budgets had been regularly approved, the Militia had taken an oath to the king, and an electoral reform had been proposed. Alas, none of this statesmanship had made the slightest impression on the opposition. It had 'seceded' from parliament – itself an anti-constitutional and revolutionary act – and had continued its scurrilous and libellous press campaign. Mussolini was therefore reluctantly forced to take sterner measures. 'I now accept, I alone, full political and moral and historical responsibility for what has happened . . . if Fascism has been a criminal association, then I am the chief of this criminal association.'[23] Henceforth Italy would have a strong government, one that would not tolerate slanders or sedition; and with such a strong government, there would be no need to unleash the squads.

It was a masterpiece of ambiguity. Many people at the time, and many historians since, have taken his speech to mean that he accepted responsibility for Matteotti's murder; but that is not what he said. Indeed, he specifically denied any involvement in the murder. What he claimed responsibility for was Fascism. That greatly reassured the *ras*, who imagined that the government would now be more responsive to their wishes. But most of the old ruling class was also reassured. The squads were not, after all, to be unleashed, and it was the normal State machinery – Prefects, police, etc. – which would restore law and order. Mussolini had accused the opposition of unconstitutional behaviour, a reminder that the king and the Chamber were still backing him; respectable conservatives had every excuse for doing the same. Above all, Mussolini had seized the political initiative. He could now make serious moves against the opposition parties and their newspapers. He had survived his Watergate.

His victory, once again, owed much to the militant squads and to their power in the provinces; and, once again, it owed much to the king's unwillingness to use the army against the Fascists. Yet, once again, it was not inevitable. If the opposition parties had been present in the Chamber, especially in November–December, or if the Rossi memorandum had not been published when it was (on 27 December, a foolish time because nothing could be done about it over the holiday period), or if General Gandolfo had not dismissed the Militia commanders, or if the Militia 'consuls' had not conveniently put pressure on in late December, or if the elder statesmen – especially Salandra – had shown more initiative, then Mussolini might have fallen. On 30 December Casati and Sarrocchi had expected the Ministers of War and Navy to support their call for Cabinet resignation; but they did not. The king had decided, and Mussolini was safe. Italian politicians learned another lesson, which they have never forgotten: in a crisis, it makes a great deal of difference who is Head of State.

REFERENCES

1. O. Malagodi, *Conversazioni di Guerra*, ii, Milan 1960, p. 503; his conversation with Diaz, 29 Jan. 1919.
2. P. Melograni, *Storia Politica della Grande Guerra*, Bari 1969, p. 560.
3. P. Frascani, *Politica Economica e Finanza Pubblica in Italia nel Primo Dopoguerra*, Naples 1975, p. 80; P. Ercolani, 'Documentazione Statistica di Base', in G. Fuà (ed.), *Lo Sviluppo Economico in Italia*, iii, Milan 1969, p. 455.
4. Prefect of Vicenza to Ministry of Interior 5 May 1919, in *ACS* Min. Int., Dir. Gen. P. S., AA. GG. e RR., 1919, b. 57.
5. P. Corner, *Fascism in Ferrara*, Oxford 1975, p. 90.
6. Nitti's views of 13 Nov. 1919, reported by Antonio Albertini to his brother Luigi, in L. Albertini, *Epistolario*, iii, Milan 1968, p. 1325.
7. Giovanni Amendola to Luigi Albertini 31 March 1919, *ibid.*, iii, p. 1192.
8. Giolitti's comments on 15 June 1919, in Malagodi, *Conversazioni*, ii, p. 707.
9. Letter to Albertini 26 Nov. 1920, in L. Albertini, *Epistolario*, iii, pp. 1438–39.
10. M. Missiroli, in his *Fascismo e la Crisi Italiana* (1921), quoted in R. De Felice, *Fascismo e Partiti Politici Italiani 1921–23*, Bologna 1966, p. 328.
11. R. De Felice, *Intervista sul Fascismo*, Bari 1975, pp. 30–33. Cf. A. Lyttelton, *The Seizure of Power*, London 1973, pp. 67–68.
12. J. Petersen, 'Elettorato e base sociale del Fascismo negli anni venti', in *SS*, xvi (1975), 660. There were 19,763 students, 13 per cent of the PNF membership. Cf. A. Tasca, *Nascita e Avvento del Fascismo*, Florence 1950, p. 247.
13. R. De Felice, *D'Annunzio Politico*, Bari 1978, p. 171.
14. A. Repaci, *La Marcia su Roma*, ii, Milan 1963, p. 386.
15. Reported by Col. Vigevano to Min. of War 17 October 1922; quoted in N. Valeri, *Da Giolitti a Mussolini*, Florence 1958, p. 188.
16. Quoted in A. Aquarone, *Alla Ricerca dell'Italia Liberale*, Naples 1972, p. 334.
17. Letter of 24 Nov. 1922, in *Carteggio Filippo Turati – Anna Kuliscioff*, v, Turin 1953, p. 600.
18. *La Stampa* 28 February 1923; also in his *Nazionalfascismo*, 1923, reissued Turin 1977, p. 70.
19. Sturzo to Card. Bourne 15 June 1925, quoted in P. Alatri, 'Luigi Sturzo nel centenario della nascita', in *SS*, xiii (1972), 211.
20. A. Landuyt, *Le Sinistre e l'Aventino*, Milan 1973, p. 95. Cf. R. De Felice, *Mussolini il Fascista*, i, Turin 1966, pp. 622–24.

21. M. Soleri, *Memorie*, Turin 1949, p. 183.
22. Togliatti report to e.c. of Comintern 7 Oct. 1924, in P. Togliatti, *Opere*, i, Rome 1967, pp. 824–38, at p. 828.
23. *Atti Parlamentari*, Cam. Dep., Legisl. xxvii, Sessione 1924–25, Discussioni 3 gennaio 1925, iii, 2028–32; excerpts in O. Barié, *Le Origini dell' Italia Contemporanea*, Bologna 1966, pp. 164–67.

CHAPTER ELEVEN

The Fascist State: the new authoritarianism

Mussolini's speech of 3 January 1925 was not merely the end of the Matteotti crisis. It was also a foretaste of things to come. He had made three main promises, or threats. He had promised that press freedom would be curbed and that the opposition parties would be disciplined; he had promised a 'strong State'; and he had promised that the Fascist squads would not be unleashed. So the outlines of a new 'regime' were already discernible. It would be illiberal and authoritarian, but it would not be fully 'Fascist' – although naturally some face-saving concessions would be given to the Fascist enthusiasts. It would strengthen the institutions of High Politics; and it would do its best to abolish the trivial concerns of Low Politics.

11.1 THE DEFEAT OF THE OPPOSITION

Mussolini's first aim, to curb the opposition, was achieved with remarkably little fuss or protest. The two Liberal ministers, Casati and Sarrocchi, resigned after the 3 January speech, as did Salandra from his post as head of the Italian delegation to the League of Nations. But the two Service ministers, General Di Giorgio and Admiral Thaon di Revel, continued in office, symbols of royal favour, and that reassured the conservatives. The Minister of the Interior, Federzoni, ordered wholesale police raids on party offices, and over 100 people were arrested; but the main target was not the 'official' opposition parties, but the Radical–Republican '*Italia Libera*', a small, recently founded, specifically anti-Fascist network of local clandestine groups. That was reassuring too. '*Italia Libera*' was dispensable, especially as dissolving it could be portrayed as necessary to restrain the Fascists. So the main opposition parties continued to exist, and to hope for royal intervention or for new elections. They did nothing very much in 1925, except to issue a futile appeal to the king and to squabble among themselves.

Soon they lost their main weapon, the press. Mussolini, ever the professional journalist, had decided to run the newspapers himself. The government tightened up press censorship immediately after 3 January, and unflattering papers were regularly seized. In 1925 the leading Liberal journals were brought under government control. There was no need for a set battle, for newspaper proprietors, like other industrialists, knew they could not afford to quarrel with the government. They simply replaced offending editors: Luigi Albertini was dismissed as editor of the *Corriere della Sera*, and Senator Frassati lost his post at *La Stampa*. Some newspapers changed hands completely – in Naples, *Il Mattino* was bought up, in order to be rid of its owner-editors, the Scarfoglio brothers; but this was unusual. Normally the whole process was smooth and legal. If all else failed, there was always the closed shop. The Press Law of December 1925 laid down that only registered journalists could write for the papers; and the Fascists ran the register. Editors and journalists knew that they held their jobs on sufferance, and that Mussolini read the papers every day. Only the strictly party newspapers – the Communists' *L'Unità*, the Socialists' *Avanti!* and so forth – provided alternative viewpoints (until November 1926), and even they were rigorously censored and available only in the big cities.

Without king or the main newspapers, and cut off from the Chamber, the opposition parties were helpless. They were not so much attacked as allowed to fade away. Soon their deputies began trying to re-enter the Chamber, only to be repulsed – except, curiously enough, for the Communists, who had made a symbolic reappearance in parliament as early as November 1924. The Socialists had split into several squabbling groups, and their trade unions were still trying to come to terms with Mussolini; the *Popolari* struggled on, but by 1925 the Vatican had obviously abandoned them. The Nationalists had joined forces with Fascism, as did many Right-wing Liberals in 1925–26. A few courageous Radical or Republican groups, such as Giovanni Amendola's *Unione Democratica Nazionale*, survived but had little influence. Inasmuch as a focus of opposition remained, it was the Senate. Senators were appointed by the king, and could not be purged without a direct challenge to the Crown. So the Senate held up Mussolini's press law and other illiberal measures in 1925, and for many years individual Senators like Benedetto Croce could speak their minds and influence the young. But that was all. There was no other political outlet. Even the traditional ways of influencing governments, through local administration and/or Masonic lodges, were closed. Elected mayors were replaced by appointed '*podestà*'; local councils by consultative bodies; and the Masons, many of whom had been prominent anti-Fascists during the Matteotti crisis, were banned, like all other secret societies, in 1925.

When normal political activity is denied, men turn to abnormal means. Despair of the opposition ever doing anything led a respected reformist Socialist deputy and war hero, Zaniboni, to try to kill Mussolini in November 1925. There were three other attempts in 1926, and all brought the government more sympathy. After the last, allegedly by a sixteen-year-old Bolognese anarchist named Zamboni, the government seized its chance. Amid a clamour for law and order, it withdrew all passports, banned all opposition parties and their journals, declared that the mandate of opposition deputies had expired (so they lost their parliamentary immunity), and set up a 'special tribunal' to repress anti-Fascist activity. Few people minded much. The Prefects reported that the ban on opposition was 'greeted with relief' as being 'severe but just',[1] and in any case the parties had been dormant for at least a year already, as had the press and the Chamber. Thus the classic Liberal institutions of informed public opinion were brought down. 'Public opinion' henceforth would be what the government said it was: the newspapers, like the radio, would be under the 'Great Editor'.

11.2 THE STRONG STATE

Mussolini's second promise on 3 January had been to strengthen the traditional machinery of High Politics. This presented even fewer problems. The repression of 1925–26 was repression by the police and the courts, both subject to conservative ex-Nationalist Ministers: Federzoni at the Interior and Rocco at the Ministry of Justice. From November 1926 the police were allowed, once again, to banish suspected persons to remote provinces or Southern islands; this 'confino' was used quite extensively against minor anti-Fascists and rumour-mongers as well as against ordinary criminals. It had unexpected consequences. Northern intellectuals found themselves in the South for the first time, and were shocked by what they saw; the Fascist 'confino' contributed much to public awareness of the Southern problem after 1945. Otherwise the police continued in their customary manner, scrutinizing the usual 'subversives', organizing networks of informers, and investigating the sexual or financial peccadillos of the Fascists themselves. Sometimes other iniquities were found, like a Masonic past or a shocking plagiarism – Farinacci, for example, was discovered to have cribbed the thesis for his law degree at the University of Modena word for word from someone in Turin.[2]

Admittedly police activity was on a much larger scale than previously. Renzo De Felice says that in a typical week the political police alone would carry out 20,000 'visits', searches, arrests, seizures of literature, etc.[3] The secret funds were greatly increased, and 500 plain-clothes men (the 'applause squad') were assigned to surround Mussolini on public occasions. But policing remained in traditional hands. Mussolini's chief of police from 1926 to 1940, Arturo Bocchini, was a career Prefect, as was his successor Carmine Senise. Both men were intensely suspicious of the provincial Fascists, and both prevented the Fascist Militia's attempts to found an effective rival political police force. This was an important achievement, which greatly affected the whole nature of the Fascist regime. There was no SS in Italy, and very few political appointments to top police jobs. But, as so often in politics, reality was disguised by rhetoric. In December 1930 Mussolini suddenly announced that the 'OVRA' had made important arrests. Nobody knew what the initials stood for. Most Italians assumed there was a new secret police. In fact, the OVRA was mainly the traditional secret branch of the Ministry of the Interior, but using more informers than previously. In the absence of a free press, the secret policemen were the only people in Italy who knew what was going on – and Bocchini was the only man in Italy who dared tell Mussolini.

As for the courts, the only real innovation was the 'Special Tribunal for the Defence of the State', set up in November 1926 to try terrorists and other political criminals. The tribunal was run by Militia consuls presided over by military judges, and it applied military law. It could, but rarely did, inflict the death penalty – there were twenty-six executions up to the fall of the Fascist regime in 1943, including nine in the fourteen peacetime years. Usually it imposed prison sentences or '*confino*'. Its most famous victim was the Communist leader Antonio Gramsci, who was sentenced to twenty years' imprisonment. Once again, the result of Fascist policy was paradoxical. The ordinary courts had nothing to do with political offences. So, although they may not have protected the citizen or defended civil liberties, they did not become servile instruments of the Fascist regime. The legal system remained unchanged and 'unFascist' – although admittedly no more independent of the executive than before 1922. Judges simply joined the party, and kept their jobs. And Rocco's new penal code in 1931 was far from 'Fascist' in tone: most of its provisions emerged from pre-Fascist discussions, and remained in force for many years after 1945.

Another vital institution to be placated was the army, which in early 1925 was restive: not about the nascent Fascist regime, needless to say, but over the government's anti-Masonic campaign and in particular over the Minister of War's plans to cut down its size. In April 1925 Mussolini bowed to the inevitable. The Minister of War was dismissed, Mussolini took on the post himself, and new army regulations were pushed through the following year – basically the old structure, the 'garrison army', restored. Mussolini also became Navy Minister in May 1925, and Air Minister in August. This sounded impressive, but even the *Duce* could not do all the work himself. In practice the three Armed Forces were run henceforth by the under-secretaries, who were nearly always generals or admirals. There was not much 'Fascistization' – as late as December 1940 the Ministry of War was still trying to get army officers to join the party[4] – but equally there was not much planning or efficiency. Each branch continued to go its own way, despite Marshal Badoglio's fitful efforts, as chief of the general staff, to co-ordinate them. Badoglio was also Governor of Libya until 1934, which hardly improved matters. The army, navy and air force each prepared for a different war, or rather for no war at all. Generals and admirals proliferated; arms – especially tanks – were neglected. Mussolini's attitude to the services was shown best in 1933. He sacked Italo Balbo from the Air Ministry, and wrote to him saying that there were only 911 serviceable planes instead of the 3,125 that Balbo had claimed: 'I add immediately that I consider this number satisfactory'.[5] Mussolini did not care about efficiency, but he did care about Balbo becoming too popular or troublesome, and the fact that the air force was at less than one-third strength was a useful political weapon against him. In the long run the Fascist settlement proved disastrous; but it maintained the jobs of career officers, and it ensured their support for the regime. In one respect only did the Fascists undermine the army's role: troops were no longer needed to maintain order against strikers or rioters. This innovation, too, helped the officers enjoy a quiet life.

The 1925 law on 'secret associations' affected the civil service too, for Freemasons were supposed to be dismissed. Civil servants could also be dismissed if they were 'in conditions of incompatibility with the general political directives of the government'. Mussolini's much vaunted 'purge of the bureaucracy' went little further. He had come to power pledged to reduce the swollen wartime civil service, but most of the cuts were in 1922–24, when the number of ministries was reduced from fifteen to eleven and when 50,000 railwaymen were sacked. After 1925 civil servants kept their old jobs, and apart from Masonry kept their old practices. In January 1926 the government tried to prevent them issuing statutory instruments with the force of law, but inasmuch as the new rules made any difference at all, they probably strengthened the real powers of senior civil servants. So, too, did Mussolini's habit of accumulating ministries. He ran eight ministries himself by 1929, quite apart from the fact that as Head of Government he had assumed, in December 1925, many of the powers previously exercised by the whole Cabinet. Fascist government was centralized government, and one man was supposed to be responsible for virtually everything. Other ministers came and went at frequent intervals, and counted for little; there was minimal scrutiny by parliament or press. In such circumstances the bureaucracy flourished. In the 1930s it began expanding again, and by 1939 there were fifteen ministries once more. Most of the top administrative posts were held by career civil servants, not party men. Even in characteristically 'Fascist' ministries like the Ministry of Corporations all the senior staff in 1938 had been civil servants since 1916.[6] Naturally they joined the party, but they remained civil servants first and foremost. Many Fascists disliked this outcome. There was much party pressure for 'a new Fascist State', or at least for more jobs for the faithful, but only in 1939 did the Fascists begin appointing civil servants 'for political reasons'. Other institutions existed, after all, to keep the Fascists happy – the Militia, for example, or the *party* bureaucracy, or the syndicates and corporations.

In the early years there was pressure of a different kind, for a streamlined civil service, more able to administer efficiently the new industrial State. These suggestions were also ignored. When De'Stefani presented proposals on these lines in March 1929, Mussolini pointed out that 'we have to adopt a policy of the maximum number of jobs in the State bureaucracy, if we don't want an insurrection on our hands – an insurrection caused by the hunger, I repeat hunger, of intellectuals'.[7] In the 1930s, pressure for jobs became greater, and the State became far more involved in detailed economic intervention and welfare. The existing civil service avoided any major changes in its own structure by off-loading the new tasks on to public and semi-public agencies or 'quangos'. These new bodies provided not only the necessary regulations, but also jobs for needy Fascists. This was a happy outcome, for it kept the ministries themselves safe; and the State needed a permanent, non-political executive.

Even most of the Prefects, always the most 'political' branch of the civil service, were career civil servants. Only 29 of the 86 new Prefects appointed between 1922 and 1929 came from outside the Prefectoral Corps. This proportion was maintained in later years: 37 of the 117 Prefects in office in 1943 were political appointments. Their powers remained as wide as ever. In 1927 Mussolini stressed this point in a well-publicized circular:

I reaffirm solemnly that the Prefect is the highest State authority in each province. He is the direct representative of the central government. All citizens, and especially those who have the great privilege and honour to be Fascist party members, owe respect and obedience to *the highest political representative of the Fascist regime* [my italics].[8]

Mussolini needed the Prefects in the early years to suppress '*squadrismo*' and to control the provincial Fascist leaders, so he insisted that there could be no dual authority in the provinces. He also increased the number of Prefects (from 78 in 1923 to 100 in December 1926) and the number of provinces (from 69 to 91); two more provinces, Littoria and Asti, were created in 1934–35. The Prefect's job was to organize the police, to repress the 'subversives', to defend the regime, and to watch over the 'social and intellectual order' of the province. Most Prefects performed their task admirably. The Prefect, not the party secretary, was in charge of the province. Later on, once the *ras* had been tamed, party secretaries were given more latitude, especially in labour relations and in dispensing patronage. Even so, the Prefects remained dominant, and indeed they had an easier time in the Fascist period than ever before. There were no elections to worry about, nor was there significant labour militancy to curb. The Prefects enjoyed government confidence and support; they controlled and spied on the local Fascist party branches.

They also had far more control over local government, as part of the general programme of increased central authority. All local councils were dissolved in 1926, and mayors were dismissed. Thereafter the municipalities (*comuni*) were run by one man, the *podestà*, sometimes helped by a purely consultative appointed council. The *podestà* was appointed by the Prefect; he could be dismissed at any time by the Prefect; and he could be transferred to another *comune* by the Prefect. The Prefect's main task – a difficult one – was to find a reliable *podestà*. In the South, they usually chose elderly conservative gentlemen, especially landowners or ex-army officers; Fascist enthusiasts were not suitable, and local lawyers even less. In Tuscany, however, the *podestà* was often a local aristocrat: the Fascist 'reform' simply meant that the Tuscan nobility regained control of local government. In the North, too, local landowners predominated, but 'strangers' were often brought in when the favouritism and corruption became too blatant; again, retired colonels were ideal, having plenty of free time and needing no pay. Rome was given a Governor, usually an aristocrat – a Borghese, a Colonna, a Boncompagni Ludovisi – responsible directly to the Ministry of the Interior. Altogether, the *podestà* were typical of the new 'strong State'. Although party members, they were rarely 'Fascists'; their job, indeed, was to prevent control of local government by the real Fascists. They were the old ruling class, watched jealously, as of old, by the Prefect. But they were in office only because elections had been abolished. That was the real meaning of the 'Fascist State'.

11.3 THE DEFEAT OF THE FASCISTS?

Mussolini's third promise on 3 January 1925 had been not to unleash the squads. He would tame Fascist violence, while governing through the normal machinery of State. Many of the measures just described were in fact aimed largely at the Fascists themselves. It was, after all, the *Fascist* deputies who dominated the Chamber and who, therefore, suffered most as parliament was emasculated; and the local Fascists would have run local government, had it not been for the *podestà* and the Prefects. Mussolini had 'assumed full responsibility' for the Fascist movement; this was a threat to the Fascists as well as to others.

The Fascist National Party (PNF) in early 1925 was still a loose organization, in which various factions contended. The local bosses enjoyed considerable autonomy and power, as they had proved in December 1924. How could they be tamed, without provoking another rebellion? Mussolini's solution was imaginative. In February 1925 he appointed the most intransigent *ras* he could find, the '*Fascistissimo*' Roberto Farinacci of Cremona, to be party secretary. Farinacci was an ideal front man. Many provincial bosses regarded him as their spokesman. He had a reputation for ruthlessness and extremism, which he enhanced in 1925–26 by acting as flamboyant defence counsel in the trial of Matteotti's murderers, and by loudly proclaiming that he had a secret list of 8,000 Freemasons in government jobs. He frightened many conservatives, so that Mussolini by contrast appeared the soul of moderation. And he was a political innocent. He thought his job was to create an effective and disciplined Fascist party, which would impose its will on the old conservative ruling class; but his real functions were firstly to reassure the *ras*, and secondly to discredit them by his behaviour.

For much of 1925 Farinacci was allowed a fairly free hand. He imposed tough discipline, cracking down hard on dissenters, purging many members – including six deputies – and even expelling two of the leading Militia 'consuls', Galbiati and Tarabella. Yet he tolerated, even encouraged, squad violence in the provinces, especially when directed against Catholics and *Popolari*, and there were bitter rows between him and the Minister of the

Interior, Federzoni. In October, when Fascist squads killed eight Liberals and Masons in Florence 'in front of the tourists', Mussolini at last intervened. Yet again he ordered the squads to be dissolved; any squad members would henceforth be expelled from the party. The Florence *fascio* was ruthlessly purged. Six months later, once the Matteotti trial was safely over, and once the 'constitutional' laws were safely through parliament, Farinacci was dismissed and banished to Cremona without a job. He languished there for almost a decade, watched carefully by the police and writing occasional letters of frustrated recrimination to Mussolini. The news of his dismissal was greeted by considerable disturbances: the Fascist intransigents realized that the days when they could lord it over the old ruling class were over.

The new party secretary was Augusto Turati, dull but reliable. Under him the PNF was transformed into a tool of Mussolini's personal policies. In January 1926 the Grand Council had decided to allow in new members, and membership figures rose in a year from just under 600,000 to 938,000. Most of the recruits were prudent men who could see where the best hopes of advancement lay. This in itself changed the party's nature. The process continued in later years. No new members were admitted between 1927 and 1932 except from the youth organizations, but in 1933 another influx brought the party up to over 1,400,000 members – a 40 per cent increase in one year. It almost doubled again in the next few years, reaching 2,633,000 by 1939, not counting the women or youth organizations. As new men came in, so older and more intransigent Fascists left or were thrown out; 7,400 were expelled between April and September 1926, and the purge gathered momentum later. Probably 50,000–60,000 members had been expelled by March 1929, and a further 100,000–110,000 had left voluntarily. In 1927 7,000 people were expelled from the Rome *fascio* alone. A further major purge took place under Turati's successor, Giuriati, in 1931–32; possibly 120,000 members were then expelled. No doubt many ex-*squadristi* remained, disgruntled but still loyal to their *Duce*. Nevertheless, by 1928 the PNF was no longer a Fascist vanguard, merely a new and much-extended 'Freemasonry' based on patronage: the initials PNF were jokingly read as '*per necessità famigliari*', 'for family reasons'.

A high proportion of the members, even in October 1927, were clerks and white-collar workers in local government or minor public employment.[9] For these groups membership was semi-compulsory, and became fully compulsory in 1933. Party secretaries, even at provincial level, also came from the lower middle class, but real influence often remained in the hands of the same local notables who had flourished in the pre-Fascist era. At Verona, for example, the Fascist federation was not merely purged, but actually dissolved for some time, and when it was refounded there were no public jobs for anyone unless he joined the party; but the real bosses remained the *comune* councillors, 'coming from the old cliques, more clerical than the Pope, pupils of General Pelloux. They run things from outside, via the Prefect.'[10] In the South, where many *fasci* were founded for the first time in 1926, this tendency was even more marked. Job-seekers and local employees formed the mass membership; landowners, Freemasonic and formerly Liberal, provided the leadership. The jibe that the PNF consisted of 'the old ruling class in black shirts' was fully justified in many areas.

The changes in the PNF were not of membership alone. The Fascist provincial press was virtually suppressed; and in October 1926 the party itself was given a new Statute, or Constitution. The elective principle was abandoned. Henceforth all posts were filled by appointment from above. The Grand Council was termed the 'supreme organ of Fascism', and was empowered to appoint the national Directorate; federal secretaries, at province level, were to be appointed by the general secretary; secretaries of individual *fasci* would be appointed by the federal secretaries. Local and provincial congresses were abolished. So the ordinary party members, whether old or new, had no way of influencing policy-making. The party became a mere supporting organization. Its members paid dues, secured their meal-tickets and (sometimes) furthered their careers, but their political role was restricted to showing 'moral leadership' and mouthing the correct slogans on request.

Perhaps the process even went too far. The PNF was not just tamed, it was emasculated. The last party congress ever held was in 1925. From 1931 to 1939 the party secretary was Achille Starace, a notoriously stupid man who was the butt of many 'Irish' jokes. With him in charge, the problem was to find something for the party to do. The party failed to influence policy, failed to form a new élite, failed to inspire the young or reassure the old. At local level, true, its leaders sometimes enjoyed considerable patronage and influence – which they fully abused. They were not punished for their misdemeanours, for that would have meant admitting that Fascism had not restored hard work, patriotism and morality after all. So corruption soon became endemic. The Fascist party secretaries, linked to the national headquarters in Rome and dispensing favours in return for political support, were often tiresome local bullies, but at least they were little more.

What was true for the party was also true for the Militia. The Militia had been brought under greater army control in August 1924, much to the annoyance of the consuls (see §10.7). In September 1925 General Gonzaga, a career soldier, was made commander of the Militia. By late 1926 the fight against the consuls and against the ex-*squadristi* had been largely won. The Militia remained in being, disciplining restless Fascist youths and providing an employment outlet for retired army officers; but its members had less and less to do. They provided some pre-military training for young people, they tried to muscle in on the work of the police, and they organized parades on Sundays. That was all. With the rapid decline in organized opposition, the squads were indeed anachronistic. Mussolini's reliance on the *State* machinery of repression ensured that the voluntary Militia was left as the army's appendix – quite useless but occasionally troublesome.

In December 1928 the party's 'supreme organ', the Grand Council, was 'constitutionalized'. Henceforth it would consist almost exclusively of ministers or holders of top State jobs – Speaker of the Chamber of Deputies, etc. Above all, it would advise on constitutional issues, including the succession to the throne, the composition and functions of parliament, relations with the Vatican and so forth. It was also supposed to draw up a list of names of possible heads of government, to be submitted to the king in case of vacancy. In principle, this law struck at the heart of the old Constitution. It limited many of the Crown's prerogatives, including that of nominating future Prime Ministers, and it even threatened to prevent the normal succession to the throne (the heir-apparent, Prince Humbert, was widely believed to have anti-Fascist sympathies). In practice, its effect was limited. Mussolini was far too astute to draw up a list of his own successors. In any case, the Grand Council could not 'advise' unless it met, and Mussolini convened it irregularly at best and, in later years, rarely. The new law was probably passed to ensure that the king did not obstruct Mussolini's 'reconciliation' with the Holy See (see §12.4), a settlement which involved him giving up a small piece of territory in Rome. It was certainly a public humiliation for the Crown, but what it really symbolized was the 'fusion' of party and State.

11.4 SUMMARY

Between 3 January 1925 and December 1928 the Italian State had been transformed. It had not been 'Fascistized'. The intransigent provincial Fascists were a spent force by November 1926, with their leader Farinacci isolated at Cremona. Nevertheless, an authoritarian regime had been set up, with an authoritarian slogan – 'Everything within the State, Nothing outside the State, Nothing against the State'. It was based essentially on the old bureaucratic-military ruling class, and designed to protect that class from the new political and economic forces that had arisen during the Giolittian period and/or the First World War – organized industrial labour, militant agricultural labour, political Catholicism, and indeed Fascism itself. New organizations, like the Fascist Militia or the syndicates, were set up to absorb or control the 'new forces'; or, in the later years of the regime, to protect established economic interests. But the important institutions of the new State were the old traditional ones writ large – the army, the Prefects, the police and the courts. Most of the old institutions survived, despite all the talk of revolution. The Chamber of Deputies, although transformed in membership, was still needed to pass laws; the Senate remained untouched, as always a forum for respectable opinion. In 1932 there were 148 Senators who were not members of the PNF; even in 1942 there were still 34 left, and many others were 'Fascist' only in name. Above all, Italy was still a monarchy. When Mussolini died, it would be the king who would decide the future government, and everyone knew it. Admittedly some features of the old Liberal State, e.g. political parties and elected town councils, were abolished, but even this affected fewer members of the old ruling classes than might be imagined. The 'Great Electors' interests continued to be protected; local government remained largely in the same hands as before 1920.

Yet the new political system was not simply the old regime in more authoritarian form. The loss of certain traditional (or not so traditional) liberties – a free press, free speech, free association, etc. – was not trivial, and certainly hurt many members of Italy's former élite: the respectable Liberal anti-Fascists of the Aventine, and the Freemasons, were the great losers of 1925–26. The price may have been worth paying if it secured law and order, political stability and maintenance of privilege; but it was still a high price. Moreover, Mussolini was always setting up new institutions and adopting new policies – the battles for wheat and for births, the corporations and the labour tribunals, the youth movements and the *Dopolavoro*, the welfare schemes and the 'reform of customs' (see Ch. 12 and 13). Many existing State institutions were left largely unchanged, but that is not necessarily proof of continuity of policy. The Fascist government was always innovating, always invading new areas of society and indeed new areas of the world.

Another major weakness of the new system, from the point of view of its beneficiaries, was the excessive personal power of the *Duce* himself. What if he betrayed, or misjudged, their interests? In fact, Mussolini proved to be a rotten manager. He had a lively journalistic intelligence, but he was impulsive. He over-simplified and dramatized everything, and had no patience for prosaic long-term planning. He was also distressingly vulgar and vulnerable to flattery. Corruption and incompetence were tolerated, even encouraged. Intensely suspicious of rivals, he dismissed most of his more competent subordinates – Rossoni in 1928, Turati in 1930, Grandi, Rocco, and Bottai in 1932, Arpinati in 1933; even Balbo was banished to be Governor of Libya in 1934. These men were replaced by mediocrities or intriguers – in the 1930s Starace was head of the PNF, Buffarini Guidi was running the Ministry of the Interior, Ciano was Foreign Minister. Worst of all, he deliberately isolated himself. Mussolini had no confidants after his brother Arnaldo died in 1931; he had no friends, and no social life except with his mistresses. He could not even enjoy a decent meal, for after his ulcer in 1925 the doctors had forbidden virtually all food: the *Duce* lived off sugared milk and fruit. He worked long hours, but to little purpose. Much of his time was spent reading newspapers, or deciding trivial questions like when the Rome policemen should wear their summer uniforms. His initial, M, was needed on every document, and it was rarely refused. Senior civil servants and ministers pursued their own policies, often quite contradictory to those of their rivals, and each of them would produce an initialled paper from the *Duce* in order to overcome his colleagues' opposition. The Council of Ministers met only once a month, and even then did not co-ordinate policy. Perhaps Mussolini had grown bored; perhaps he was simply too contemptuous of arguments and of men to take any of them seriously; or perhaps it was a deliberate device to keep everyone dependent on him. At any rate, it was no way to run a country.

There was one consolation. Mussolini's was a 'Roman Dictatorship'; it would not survive him. The chief of police thought the regime would collapse immediately on Mussolini's death. Federzoni, Farinacci, and most anti-Fascists agreed on this, if on nothing else. The king and the army also realized that

240

the regime would not last: the king had appointed Mussolini to be Prime Minister in 1922, and what he had given he could take away. The Vatican prepared quietly for a future post-Fascist regime. Fascist or anti-Fascist, conservative or progressive, they all bided their time, and waited for the end.

REFERENCES

1. R. De Felice, 'La situazione dei partiti antifascisti alla vigilia della loro soppressione secondo la polizia fascista', in *Rivista Storica del Socialismo*, 25–26, a. viii (1965), 79–96.
2. *ACS*, Seg. Part. del Duce, Cart. Ris., b. 37, sottof. 2.
3. R. De Felice, *Mussolini il Duce*, i, Turin 1974, p. 83.
4. Circular of Minister of War 3 Dec. 1940, in *ACS*, Fondo Primo Aiutante S. M. il Re, sez. spec., f. 67.
5. Letter of 12 Nov. 1933, quoted by G. Rochat in G. Quazza (ed.), *Fascismo e Società Italiana*, Turin 1973, p. 108.
6. Taylor Cole, 'Italy's Fascist Bureaucracy', in *American Political Science Review*, xxxii (1938), 1143–57.
7. A. De' Stefani, *Una Riforma al Rogo*, Rome 1963, p. 12.
8. Circular of 5 Jan. 1927, in A. Aquarone, *L'Organizzazione dello Stato Totalitario*, Turin 1965, pp. 485–88.
9. S. Tranquilli, 'Elementi per uno studio del PNF', *Lo Stato Operaio*, i (1927), no. 8, 875–90.
10. *idem*, p. 882. Cf. A. Lyttelton, *The Seizure of Power*, London 1973, pp. 303–5.

CHAPTER TWELVE

The Fascist regime: the quest
for consensus

In the previous chapter I outlined the main features of the new 'Fascist State', stressing – perhaps overstressing – the undeniable continuity of many institutions. But, equally undeniably, the Fascists did not merely form a government. They claimed to have set up a 'regime'; and the regime was, or purported to be, 'totalitarian', affecting every aspect of ordinary people's lives. The Fascists also preached an ideology of national solidarity and individual self-sacrifice, and tried to train a new generation of true believers in patriotism and war. This chapter will examine how far their policies were successful.

12.1 IDEOLOGY AND INDOCTRINATION

There were many strands in Fascist thought. The syndicalists, revolutionary and anticapitalist, were anxious to build a new kind of 'producers' State' (see §12.2). The provincial radicals, populist and impatient, yearned to sweep away Church, king and parliament. There were spiritual revivalists, preaching national pride and a 'new Rome'; and there were ex-Nationalists, royalist and anti-democratic, drawing up blueprints for a strong State and a planned economy. The various groups disagreed with each other violently over such matters as corporatism, or the Church, or the powers of old élites; but uniting most of them was an urge to be in the *avant-garde* in all spheres, and an urge to rescue Italy from foreign domination. Fascists knew whom they were against: Bolsheviks, Freemasons, international bankers – anybody, in short, engaged in a secret conspiracy against the nation. These ideas were mainly a legacy from pre-war days, especially from the Nationalists and Futurists (see §8.5), and indeed from the war itself. The Fascists may not have had a coherent doctrine, but they had a powerful one. They had won the war, and vanquished the Bolsheviks after it; they had built a new State and a new economy, the envy of the world; they were the new élite, vigorous in mind and body. They would spread civilization and order throughout the

Mediterranean and North Africa, as their Roman forefathers had done. Admittedly there were also conservative, clerical, or 'rural' elements in Fascist doctrine, but even these were perfectly compatible with nationalism, Empire and 'Roman-ness' (*romanità*). Indeed, this cult of ancient Rome was perhaps the most striking feature of the regime. The word '*Duce*' itself came from *Dux*; the *Fasci* were, of course, the Roman lictors' symbols of office; the Militia and the youth organizations all had a pseudo-Roman hierarchy and titles – legions, cohorts, centurions and so forth.

Furthermore, this ideology was not just for Fascists. To achieve their noble purpose, the Fascists had to 'mobilize' every Italian to the cause. 'The thoughts and wishes of the *Duce* must become the thoughts and wishes of the masses', wrote Gentile.[1] Theirs was a mass regime, founded on war: 'real' Italy had vanquished 'legal' Italy, in 1922 as in 1915. The Fascists never forgot their origins. Mussolini 'considered the whole nation in a permanent state of war';[2] and so the morale and fighting spirit of the masses had to be constantly maintained.

They had numerous instruments to hand. The press, for example, was not merely censored, but primed. Government subsidies were increased, in return for fulsome praise of the regime. Despite his militarism, Mussolini always believed the pen was mightier than the sword. His press office sent out detailed instructions on what to print and how to print it – 'the *Duce*'s speech may be commented upon. We will send on the comment ourselves.' Hence the relentless Fascist rhetoric: the 'unsleeping' *Duce*, his 'masculine profile forged in bronze', marched 'audaciously' at the head of his invincible legions. Foreign words were Italianized – 'cocktail' became '*coda di gallo*' – and even the word '*Mezzogiorno*' was banned, as too redolent of the 'Southern question'. Reports of crime, or suicide, or traffic accidents, disappeared from the newspapers. Nothing was allowed to disturb the national harmony.

Yet the result was emasculation rather than indoctrination. Educated Italians continued to read their old familiar newspapers rather than Fascist ones – in 1933 the *Corriere della Sera* had a circulation of over 600,000, compared with the *Popolo d'Italia*'s 100,000. The government concentrated on other means of persuasion – youth movements, recreation schemes, syndicates (see below, §12.2) – rather than on mass propaganda. It also 'took over' one or two worthy bodies like the Dante Alighieri Society; and it founded both a National Fascist Institute of Culture and a Royal Italian Academy, on the French model, to mobilize or flatter the intellectuals. Few people took much notice. In 1935, however, things became more serious. The press office became an under-secretariat for press and propaganda, and in 1937 this in turn became a full-scale Ministry of Popular Culture, vulgarly known as Minculpop. It had many tasks. Press supervision continued, but by this time other mass media had become more important. The first radio stations were set up in 1924–25; there were over 300,000 registered sets by 1932, and over 1 million by 1938. Each set was listened to by numerous people – at least a family, often a café, and occasionally a whole piazza. And broadcasting was State-controlled. Hence news broadcasts and newsy chats, in particular Roberto Forges Davanzati's 'Chronicles of the Regime', provided a marvellous opportunity for official propaganda.

So, too, did the cinema, which became the most popular entertainment in Italy in the 1930s, and which brought spoken Italian to the ears of many citizens for the first time. The regime built an 'Experimental Centre of Cinematography', training 100 students a year, including Michelangelo Antonioni; and it took over *Cinecittà* – Italy's Hollywood – in 1938. After 1934 many Italian films were subsidized, although the industry remained essentially in private hands. Most films were escapist entertainment, depicting 'white telephones' and other such symbols of opulence. But there were also several films glorifying Fascism and the regime's achievements: Blasetti's *Vecchia Guardia* was a major success, as was *Luciano Serra, pilota*, which the *Duce*'s son Vittorio helped to make – the title was suggested by the *Duce* himself. Augusto Genina's *Siege of the Alcazar* has been praised by both Antonioni and by Mario Isnenghi.[3] Admittedly the most popular films were American, but the regime did its best to censor them and restrict imports. In any case, official newsreels had to be shown, by law, at every performance, so the customer could not escape propaganda. Altogether, 'it may well be argued', as Philip Cannistraro says, 'that Fascist Italy was the first State in Western Europe to recognize the potential value of the mass media for purposes of political control'[4] – although Nazi Germany soon outpaced Fascist Italy in this dismal enterprise.

The other mass entertainment in Fascist Italy, and one constantly featured in the cinema newsreels, was sport. These were the years of spectacular racing cars, of Nuvolari and the *Mille Miglia* race around the country. Balbo flew across the Atlantic, and a surprisingly large number of other Fascists were airmen – Ciano, Pavolini, Muti, the *Duce*'s sons Bruno and Vittorio; even Mussolini himself acquired a pilot's licence in 1939. Skiing became genuinely popular, and the regime encouraged it – future European wars would probably be fought in the Alps. Cycling, too, was a mass sport with patriotic overtones – the *Giro d'Italia* was a way of unifying the country, and the party secretary started the cyclists off. 'Mussolini's boys' won twelve gold medals at the Los Angeles Olympics, and Primo Carnera was world heavyweight champion from 1933 to 1935. Football became the second obsession of Italian men. Arpinati, for some years Under-secretary of the Interior, was a genuine fan. In 1926 he became president of the Football Federation, and built a huge stadium in his home town of Bologna. In 1934 came a real propaganda triumph. Italy not only staged the World Cup, but won it. The *Duce* himself attended the final, and handed out the medals to his victorious team. The Italians also won the Olympic Football Championship in 1936, and the World Cup again in 1938. These sporting achievements contributed much to the government's general popularity, and the Fascists knew it. The Football League championship continued to be played even during the Second World War. The regime helped sport; and sport helped the regime.

The most successful 'ideological' body of them all was undoubtedly the

Dopolavoro (literally, 'after work'). The Fascist squads in the early 1920s had closed down the old Socialist recreational and welfare centres; the Fascist syndicalists sometimes took them over. In 1925 the various local clubs were federated into a national network, the *Opera Nazionale Dopolavoro* (OND), and in 1927 the Fascist Party took over control. The movement soon expanded enormously, from 280,000 members in 1926 to 1¾ million in 1931, and to nearly 4 million by 1939. Most clubs were local, organized on a *comune* basis, but the OND also persuaded some 3,000 industrial firms to set up recreation schemes, and public employees naturally had their own facilities. So the OND was easily the largest Fascist organization for adults, and easily the most popular. The *Dopolavoro* clubs had bars, billiard halls, libraries, radios and sports grounds; they put on concerts and plays; they provided virtually free summer holidays for children; they organized charabanc trips, ballroom-dancing, mountain walks, and days at the seaside. They also handed out welfare relief in poor areas: both circuses and bread. No wonder they were popular. It was the first time in Italian history that mass leisure activities had existed, let alone been encouraged and subsidized by politicians. And it was not too solemn. The *Dopolavoro* was fun, not propaganda: it was recreation, not self-improvement. Some Fascists worried about this, and high-minded Italian bourgeois looked down on it all as irredeemably vulgar, but Mussolini knew better. He, like thousands of others, went to Riccione for his holidays.

This stress on sport and recreation typified the Fascist obsession with physical fitness and vigour, and more generally with the cult of youth. Fascist posters and films always depicted *young* heroes. '*Giovinezza*' – 'Youth' – was the party song. Young people are, of course, the prime target for every 'totalitarian' regime; the Fascists were no exception. In 1926 they founded the *Opera Nazionale Balilla* (called *Gioventù Italiana del Littorio*, GIL, after 1937), a youth organization with many branches. There were the '*Sons of the She-Wolf*' for six- to eight-year-olds; the '*Balilla*' itself for boys aged 8–11; the '*Balilla Musketeers*', for boys aged 11–13; the '*Little Italians*' for girls aged 8–14; the '*Avanguardisti*' for thirteen- to fifteen-year-olds; and so forth up to the age of 21. These various organizations were youth clubs with sports facilities, but they were also pre-military training bodies with indoctrination sessions, and their leaders were present and active in the schools as well as at Saturday afternoon rallies. It was difficult to avoid joining them, at least in Northern Italy and while at school. And they had little competition. The (Catholic) Boy Scouts were closed down in 1928, and although Catholic youth organizations did exist they were not allowed to engage in serious matters like sport. So, superficially, the Fascists were successful. They brought up a new Fascist generation, imbued from childhood with patriotic zeal and military fervour.

The education system itself was diverted to similar ends. In the primary schools, teachers were fairly young and easily replaceable. Fascist textbooks and readers could easily be imposed upon them. Forges Davanzati himself wrote a highly successful text, *Il Balilla Vittorio*, for fifth-grade pupils. In general, 'political education' seems to have worked at this level. By the time they left primary school most eleven-year-olds had learned something of the war, of the shameful post-war treatment of returned heroes, and of the Fascists' great campaign to rescue Italy from Bolshevism. In the secondary schools it was more difficult. The teachers were not anxious to lower academic standards, and the subjects studied – including philosophy, in the *licei* – discouraged total conformity. The headmaster was usually a Fascist, and the *Balilla* officials taught PT, but there was little opportunity for full-scale indoctrination. Pupils were not hostile to Fascist ideas, indeed they accepted them as normal; but they were not committed enthusiasts either. In the universities the same arguments applied even more strongly. The regime founded Faculties of Political Science, but these were naturally despised. It also forced university teachers to take an oath of loyalty – 'I swear to be faithful to the king, to his royal successors, and to the Fascist regime, and to observe loyally the *Statuto* and the other laws of the State, to exercise the office of teacher and to fulfil all my academic duties with the aim of training hardworking, upright citizens, devoted to the country and to the Fascist regime. I swear that I do not belong nor will belong to associations or parties whose activity is irreconcilable with the duties of my office.' Only 11 out of 1,200 professors refused to take the oath, and were dismissed.[5] That in itself was a good propaganda victory for Fascism, although it demonstrated nothing but the truism that nearly all university teachers are venal. Afterwards, the universities were left alone by the regime, and carried on much as before, until the anti-Semitic laws of 1938.

So, for the most part, did the world of High Culture. Croce continued to publish *La Critica*, although he had organized an anti-Fascist 'manifesto' in 1925. The major publishing houses like Laterza and Giulio Einaudi presented exciting new works: Ungaretti, Montale, Moravia, Pavese and Vittorini all wrote their best, or first, works in the Fascist period. Above all, the *Enciclopedia Italiana* included articles on anti-Fascist themes: Rodolfo Morandi, for example, wrote about Communism, Socialism and Historical Materialism. One of the eleven 'non-juror' university teachers even remained on its managing committee. In general, intellectuals were tolerated and flattered, indeed bought off, rather than persecuted. Many prominent writers and artists received government prizes: even the young Amintore Fanfani was given 2,000 lire for his work on economic history.[6] Others – e.g. Guttuso, Ungaretti, Quasimodo – were given university chairs. The *Duce* himself loved to show off his wide reading to impressionable foreign journalists. The regime was endorsed by Pirandello and Marconi at home, by Freud and George Bernard Shaw abroad. Mussolini asked no more. He ruled with a light rein, and subsidized the intellectuals.

Altogether, the Fascists probably succeeded in indoctrinating most children in primary school, but they did not create a really 'Fascist' élite via secondary or higher education, let alone create a 'Fascist' intelligentsia. That was very significant, for training a new Fascist élite was a vital task for the regime. The Fascists did their best, but it was not good enough. Their key institution was the *Gioventù Universitaria Fascista* (GUF), the Fascist student organization which had been quite active in the days of *squadrismo*. After 1926 most students joined it, if only for career purposes, and its social activities (film clubs, etc.) were reasonably popular. The main activity of GUF was to run the *Littoriali* – cultural and debating competitions in which teams from all over Italy competed. They were well attended, if only because they provided a rare opportunity to speak fairly freely on important issues; but they did not have the desired effect. If anything, they showed young people how stifling most normal political discussion was. They also provided a marvellous opportunity for anti-Fascist infiltrators.

Did all this Fascist effort at 'social control' actually work? The judicious historian gives a prosaic answer: yes and no. Yes, in the sense that until 1936 most people swallowed most of the propaganda most of the time, at a fairly superficial level. Italy was stable, the *Duce* was popular, open dissenters were rare. It made sense to go along with the regime, and patriotism is a natural feeling even in Italy. But there was little enthusiasm for Fascism – as opposed to patriotism or to Mussolinism – and the regime's claims to 'totalitarianism' were laughable. Religion, family sentiment, individual ambition and cunning, the parish pump, the art of *arrangiarsi* – all these traditional institutions and values survived and flourished. The Fascists totally failed to arouse warlike zeal among the general population, a failure which became very evident by the late 1930s. In short, there was acceptance but not devotion, consensus but not commitment, let alone 'hegemony'. Still, even the Fascist consensus was a great deal more than most Italian regimes had achieved. On balance the ideological efforts paid off. It took years for most people to see through Fascism.

12.2 FASCIST SYNDICATES AND CORPORATIONS

Arguably the Fascists' key achievement was to 'discipline' labour. The Fascist movement had taken off in 1920–21 as a reaction to trade union militancy. The Fascists had destroyed the existing unions and co-operatives. But that was not enough. To avoid renewed trouble in future the Fascists needed to 'represent the workers' interests' within their own organizations. So the Fascist unions – 'syndicates' is the Italian term – had to be reasonably successful in negotiations, if they were to attract some working-class support. For a time they were. The Fascist syndicalists built up their empires rapidly after 1921 (see §10.6). The Matteotti crisis in 1924 further strengthened them. Mussolini needed all the working-class support he could get, if only to put pressure on wavering businessmen; so he backed the syndicates. In 1925 there were several major strikes led by the Fascist unions, sometimes supported tacitly by the government. These strikes culminated in a major engineering dispute in Lombardy, involving over 100,000 workers. The strike was a success for the Fascist syndicalists, but it alarmed many conservatives. Mussolini had to redress the balance by a purge of the more militant syndicalists. Even so, in October 1925 the industrialists were forced to recognize the new facts of industrial and political power. The industrialists' confederation and the Fascist syndicates' confederation recognized each other's right to represent exclusively their respective side's interest, and pledged themselves not to negotiate with any other body. It was a triumph for the Fascist syndicalists: they had cornered the labour market. Henceforth their rivals could only fade away, impotent and unheeded.

And yet the Fascist syndicalists' battle was only half won. They had been fighting on several fronts. They had triumphed over the Socialist and Catholic unions, and had over 2 million working-class members by 1927; they even succeeded, for a time, against the industrialists; but they failed to impose their ideas about labour relations upon the government. Many syndicalists had been arguing for years that the syndicates should become the basic institutions of the State. They had been impressed, too, by De Ambris's and D'Annunzio's schemes at Fiume (see §10.1), where 'corporations' of both employers and employed had been supposed to run the economy in a spirit of national harmony. In short, the Fascist syndicalists were not just trade unionists, competing with rivals and fighting for higher wages in a capitalist system. They were prophets of a new economic order, in which the class struggle would be abolished, private enterprise would be strictly regulated, and the national interest would prevail. And in this new order they themselves would play an essential part.

The more conservative Fascist sympathizers naturally dreaded this prospect. Trade unions might be necessary in any industrial State, but they certainly should not be allowed to run the economy. Mussolini could not afford to alienate these men, who included the leading industrialists, nor could he afford to alienate the syndicalists. The result was a prolonged balancing act, ending in a compromise. In April 1926 a major new law was passed, which owed much to the Minister of Justice, Alfredo Rocco. Rocco was no syndicalist. His whole aim was to *discipline* labour: as he told the Chamber, 'the State cannot allow, the Fascist State least of all, any other States within the State. The regulation of trade unions must be a means of disciplining them, not a means of creating powerful, uncontrollable bodies that can dominate the State.'[7] The law confirmed the syndicates' monopoly of negotiations, as agreed six months previously, and provided for compulsory arbitration of collective disputes by special labour tribunals. This pleased Rossoni and the syndicalists. But strikes, go-slows and lockouts were strictly forbidden, and strike leaders were promised prison sentences. Moreover, the syndicates were to represent workers only. They were not to be 'mixed' guilds of employers and employed, embracing whole industrial sectors; and hence they would not be able to decide economic policy. In particular, they would not decide government policy. Syndicates were specifically prohibited in the key ministries (article 11). Specially severe prison sentences were provided for strikes or go-slows that 'aimed at coercing the will or influencing the decisions of a department or organ of State, province or municipality, or a government official' (article 21). As for the major firms, they would need to negotiate with the Fascist syndicates, but they would not be dragged into any corporatist planning network, and the absence of strikes was naturally pleasing to employers.

The 1926 law did not work out quite as planned. In practice, the labour tribunals had little work to do: they dealt with only forty-one cases in the next ten years, and settled only sixteen of them by judicial decree. Most disputes continued to be settled by negotiations between syndicate and employer; the more serious ones were settled by officials of the Ministry of Corporations. 'Individual' disputes were also settled in this way, or by the ordinary local courts. National collective agreements were also less important than might appear. Minimum wages were set, until 1934, by the provincial 'unions' rather than at national level. Moreover, the syndicates had no representatives in the factories. The pre-Fascist internal commissions (elected shop stewards' committees) were abolished in 1925, and although Fascist *fiduciari* often existed in the major factories, they were legally recognized only in 1939. Hence it was difficult to ensure that any collective agreements that the syndicates made were actually enforced. Strikes and demonstrations continued to occur, often over precisely this issue, although only on a local scale and without any press publicity. Yet, on balance, the legislation did its job. There was remarkably little labour unrest in the Fascist period. The syndicates and the local courts seem to have been reasonably successful in dealing with individual grievances, and in the 1930s low wages could always be blamed on the Depression. Perhaps the technology of the time – the introduction of conveyor belts, the 'Bedaux system', time and motion studies – made authoritarianism in the factories virtually inevitable. Skilled men would have lost their jobs, and craft unions would have been undermined, in any case. In that perspective the Fascist unions do not appear so unsuccessful, and they clearly attracted some working-class support, especially after 1930.

The 1926 law did not settle the union question for ever. 'Corporatist' ideas of national economic harmony were still very much alive, and Mussolini still needed a threat against independent-minded employers and against independent-minded syndicalists. His balancing act, therefore, continued. Later in the same year he set up a new ministry – the Ministry of Corporations. 'Corporations' implied 'mixed' unions of workers and employers, and national economic planning; and the new Under-secretary, Giuseppe Bottai, was exactly the kind of empire-building intellectual that industrialists most feared. He soon helped to push through a 'Charter of Labour', proclaiming grandiose guarantees on social issues and labour relations. Yet, in practice, the Ministry's main achievements were to mediate in labour disputes, and to reduce the syndicalists' influence. In 1928 Rossoni was dismissed, and the Confederation of Fascist Syndicates was split up into six component parts: thenceforth there were six workers' confederations of syndicates (one each for industry, agriculture, commerce, etc.) with six corresponding employers' confederations and one genuine 'mixed corporation' – of artists and professional men. This was a major blow to syndicalism: 'corporatist' ideology had been used to undermine 'syndicalist' reality.

This process continued in the next few years. In 1930 a National Council of Corporations was founded, to act as a joint consultative body on the economy. It met and deliberated regularly, to little effect. Only in 1934 were real 'mixed' corporations actually set up. There were twenty-two of them, containing representatives of employers and workers and also of the PNF. They were empowered to fix wage-rates, settle disputes, distribute labour, regulate apprenticeships, advise on economic issues, and generally 'encourage improvements in production'. But it was just propaganda. The workers' syndicates and the employers' associations continued to exist 'below' the level of the corporations; the corporations themselves did little, except to provide jobs for bureaucrats. Pius XI himself complained that 'new syndical and corporative organizations tend to have an excessively bureaucratic and political character',[8] and his views were echoed by many leading Fascists, including Turati, Arpinati and Farinacci. When the Fascists did begin regulating the economy on a major scale after 1933, they used quite different machinery, and the corporations were not even consulted.

But although the corporations were only propaganda, they were very good propaganda. They were propaganda, indeed, that many Fascists – including Mussolini himself – fervently believed in. They were original, at least to people who knew nothing of Fiume, and they tackled the right issues. They promised both 'workers' self-management' and 'managerial authority', both dynamic innovation and protection of established interests, both free enterprise and State monopoly. They seemed to offer 'a third way', between capitalism and Bolshevism, which looked attractive in the Depression. They justified Mussolini's whole regime. The class conflict had apparently been overcome: the national interest prevailed, the trains ran on time. Gaetano Salvemini remarked in 1935 that 'Italy has become the Mecca of political scientists, economists and sociologists, who flock there to see with their own eyes the organization and working of the Fascist Corporative State', and who 'flood the world with articles, essays, pamphlets, and books, which already form a good-sized library'.[9] Until imperialism replaced it, 'corporatism' was one of the major elements in Fascist ideology.

But while the corporations may have been just propaganda, the syndicates were real. The impact of trade union activity is always debatable, and the figures for the Fascist period are particularly controversial, but it seems probable that real wages in industry declined a little between 1924 and 1926, i.e. while the Socialist and Catholic unions were being destroyed; then rose and fell again over the next four years; and thereafter were maintained until 1934. Thus the Fascist syndicates, together with government policy, cushioned the worst effects of the Depression. Private consumption per head went down by only 2.5 per cent in the real Depression years of the early 1930s. However, in November 1934 the forty-hour week was introduced in response to syndicalist demands for work-sharing to combat unemployment. This policy reduced the monthly wages of those already in jobs, by about 10 per cent. That was a major blow to the established working class, and it was directly attributable to government and union policy; but the decline was partly recovered by 1939, and of course reduced hours were also a real benefit. In any case, the policy did mitigate unemployment: the official figures went down from 1.2 million in December 1933 to 960,000 a year later and to 700,000 in 1936, although the true rate was probably at least 75 per cent higher at all times.

These figures are, as always, inconclusive: effective wage-rates depend on many other factors besides trade union strength or government policy. But they do at least show that the absence of strikes and of free trade unions did not lead to vicious exploitation of industrial workers. I have deliberately quoted figures for *real* wages. Perhaps the real impact of Fascist syndicalism was to make it easier for cuts of about 25 per cent in money wages to be imposed between 1928 and 1934, as the cost of living fell. More militant unions might have successfully resisted these cuts, and thus increased unemployment.

The syndicates had, of course, other ways of courting popularity. Indeed, as Vannutelli has argued, 'the very lack of power to work directly for salary increases encouraged the labour movement to pursue other compensatory goals'.[10] Grievances were often freely discussed at local syndicate meetings. The unions also helped to find jobs, and often controlled the local labour-exchanges. During the Depression at Turin, they arranged for 1 per cent of workers' pay to go to subsidizing the unemployed, and 'persuaded' the employers to contribute as well. The syndicates claimed the credit for, and sometimes distributed, some of the regime's best-known welfare measures. Family allowances were started on a large scale in 1934, to compensate workers with families for the forty-hour week; they were paid in all sectors by 1937. Christmas bonuses and holiday pay also began in the late 1930s; accident and sickness insurance was included in most pay settlements. Above all, there were subsidized leisure activities, the 'Dopolavoro' (see §12.1); and there was job protection. All this was not exactly a Welfare State, rather a medley of different provisions and different 'semi-State' welfare bodies; but it was novel, and it helped defuse working-class unrest. Union membership rose rapidly. In Milan, the industrial unions had 176,000 members in 1933, but 560,000 by 1940. In that sense the syndicates 'mobilized' the workers. The Communist underground organizer Curiel thought syndicates comprised 'the only organization in which the working class has managed, intermittently, to express its wishes'.[11]

12.3 ANTI-FASCISM

For all these reasons anti-Fascism was weak. It remained weak until 1938, indeed until 1943. The mass political parties of 1919–20 retained, at best, a few clandestine bridgeheads in areas of traditional strength. The Socialist Party was very feeble, since both Communists and reformists had split off to form separate parties in 1921–22. Relations between these three parties were usually uneasy, although the reformists and 'maximalists' (Socialists) managed to fuse their two parties together again in 1930. This move only increased hostility between Socialists and Communists; the Communists spent much of the period between 1929 and 1934 denouncing the 'Social-Fascism' of their rivals. None of these parties could operate freely in Italy, although some ex-*popolari* were still active in Catholic Action (see below, §12.4). Anti-Fascist politics meant, for the most part, writing articles in the anti-Fascist press or agitating among Italian emigrants in Paris or Switzerland, with occasional efforts at smuggling pamphlets into Italy. Only the Communists had any idea of underground organization. They managed to print a surprisingly wide range of journals in Italy, but even the Communists were few in numbers – between 2,500 and 7,000 – and sectarian in strategy, until the late 1930s. The other parties showed little sign of life, and had no organization within the country. The Republican Party was influential among the exiles, for it could claim that it had been right all along: the anti-Fascists had relied on the king in 1924, and he had let them down. He would have to go. So republicanism became an article of faith among most anti-Fascists – but the party stayed tiny.

However, anti-Fascism was not just the parties. Equally important, indeed far more important before 1936, were various small dissident groups of intellectuals, journalists and students, usually Radical or Republican in sympathy, who would found an association or journal, produce a few clandestine issues, and then be forced into years of exile. A rather different 'group' was *Giustizia e Libertà* (GL) founded in 1929 by Carlo and Nello Rosselli, Ernesto Rossi and others. *Giustizia e Libertà* aimed to unite Republicans, Socialists and democrats in an activist 'super-party', and it went in for spectacular gestures like dropping anti-Fascist pamphlets from aeroplanes. It had considerable appeal for young intellectuals, and soon it had an underground organization in Italy – by 1933 it may have had as many adherents as the Communist Party. There were also a few respected intellectual figures like Croce in Italy, Sforza and Salvemini in exile, keeping alive the spirit of independence and inquiry. But that was all. Without institutions or organizations, the Italian anti-Fascists were like the Russian dissidents forty years later – sometimes infiltrated, usually persecuted, and always harmless.

There were two major exceptions. Italy's newly acquired lands in the North-East, 'Venezia Tridentina' and 'Venezia Giulia', both contained substantial ethnic minorities – 228,000 'Germans' in the South Tyrol, 327,000 Slovenes and 98,000 Croats in Venezia Giulia – who were determined to preserve their languages and customs. The Fascists were far too nationalistic to permit any such thing. They insisted upon the use of Italian in the primary schools, although hardly any of the local children could understand it, and although this meant sacking the local teachers. They also suppressed private teaching. Italian also had to be spoken in public offices, courts, etc., so local officials lost their jobs too; and German and Slav surnames were Italianized. Even the inscriptions on the tombstones were changed. This was a real *Kulturkampf,* and it was not restricted to cultural symbols. Jobs were at stake, in teaching and in administration, and Italians from other regions were encouraged to settle in North-East Italy. After 1934 a new industrial zone was set up in Bolzano, partly to speed on this 'Italianization'. By 1939 there were about 80,000 'Italians' in the South Tyrol, far more than in 1921.

But the policy did not work. The local priests led the cultural resistance, continuing to preach and catechize in German or Slovene, and organizing clandestine private schools. Church–State relations were much worse in these regions than elsewhere in Italy, and in 1936 Bishop Fogar of Trieste was even forced out of office. In the South Tyrol, the 'Germans' were isolated rather than assimilated. Deprived of schools and urban jobs, they remained defensive and despondent in their rural ghettos. In Venezia Giulia sterner forms of resistance appeared. Italian teachers were driven out of schools, bombs went off regularly in public buildings, and local terrorists assassinated police and militiamen. There were five Slavs out of the nine people condemned to death by the Fascist Special Tribunal before 1940. In these regions anti-Fascism became deeply ingrained, and became synonymous with anti-Italianism.

The feebleness of organized anti-Fascism in 'mainland Italy' is, at first sight, surprising. It certainly surprises and dismays many Italians today. Communist membership was a few thousand at most; *Giustizia e Libertà* never had more, and the Socialists had far fewer. Money was always short – if the Communists and 'GL' were the most influential groups, it was mainly because of the Comintern's subsidies and the Rossellis' private fortune. No foreign States except France and Russia had an interest in harbouring anti-Fascist exiles, and the French and Russian interests were strictly limited. Obtaining arms was virtually impossible. Moreover, people remembered that the anti-Fascist parties had lost badly, not only in 1922 but also in 1924–25. They were split, and they offered no credible political alternative. The various assassination attempts on Mussolini in 1926 had associated them with terrorism, and this naturally reduced public sympathy. Part of the explanation for the anti-Fascists' weakness lies in effective policing: Bocchini's informers were everywhere, and *confino* or worse awaited dissidents. But perhaps the real reason for anti-Fascism's failure was that the Fascist regime seemed tolerable and was even popular, at least until 1937–38. It was careful not to alienate vested interests: even the workers had some safeguards, and journalists were flattered and bribed. Active resistance seemed pointless.

Yet 'latent', submerged forms of anti-Fascism, or at least of non-Fascism, were extremely widespread. Catholicism provided an alternative ideology and focus for loyalty; so did Liberalism. Far more people went to Catholic Action meetings, or read Croce's work, than were ever reached by *Giustizia e Libertà* or by the clandestine Communist press. The self-proclaimed anti-Fascists were much less important for many years than they – and some historians – have believed; but the quiet, dissembling trimmers, in schools and offices throughout Italy, kept their jobs and prevented the Fascists from creating a new ruling class. That was a real achievement, though it was not done by the official anti-Fascists.

12.4 THE CHURCH

The Catholic Church was the greatest obstacle to any 'totalitarian' regime in Italy. All the others – parliament, press, opposition parties, unions – could be smashed or emasculated; but not the Church. Nor could she simply be ignored, for she had immense influence in education and welfare, and she proclaimed values quite incompatible with those of Fascism. Mussolini, therefore, needed all his political skills. He had to reassure the hierarchy of the Church by material concessions, he had to obscure the ideological differences, and he had to win tacit or explicit endorsement for his regime. But he also had to limit the Church's hold on society whenever possible, especially once the endorsement had been won. Of these various aims, winning endorsement was the most important, because success there would be a propaganda triumph. The Church's major interest, on the other hand, lay in protecting, or if possible increasing, her influence in society. If that could be done, it was certainly worth an endorsement. The Church of Pius XI was still a defensive body, inward-looking and suspicious. She felt she had been rejected by progressive Europe for over a century, and that she was beset by powerful enemies. She needed to carry out her tasks, without hindrance or persecution. So it made sense to render unto Caesar that which was Caesar's anyway, and to take from him whatever she could obtain.

Thus the atheist and anticlerical Mussolini, pre-war author of *Claudia Particella, The Cardinal's Mistress*, gradually became the prodigal son. In its first few years in office Mussolini's government increased clerical salaries, granted 3 million lire for damaged churches, restored the Crucifix in schoolrooms, law courts, and Colosseum, rescued the (Catholic) *Banco di Roma*, and closed down fifty-three brothels. It also set up national examinations, thus enabling Church schools to enter pupils for them on an equal footing with State schools, and recognized degrees given by the new Catholic University of the Sacred Heart in Milan. It banned Freemasonry, and closed down anticlerical journals; it dropped the Liberal proposals to tax ecclesiastical property and to introduce a public register of shareholdings; and it destroyed the Socialist menace. Moreover, Mussolini flattered the Church. In his maiden speech to parliament he praised her as representing 'the Latin and imperial tradition of Rome'. He had his first three children baptized, at quite advanced ages; and in 1925 he even married Donna Rachele in church, ten years after the civil ceremony. True, Fascist squads wrecked Catholic co-operatives and unions throughout Italy, and the Popular Party was dissolved along with the others, but that was different. Those were lay bodies, with secular tasks; they were dispensable. Mussolini did not attack the Church as such. On the contrary, he wooed her.

By 1926 the Vatican Secretary of State, Cardinal Gasparri, was confident that Mussolini was going to stay in power. A major long-term deal could be done. On 11 February 1929 Mussolini and Gasparri signed the 'Lateran Pacts' – a treaty, a financial convention and a Concordat. The treaty set up a separate sovereign State of 'Vatican City', with forty-four hectares of land and full diplomatic rights. The financial convention gave the Pope 750 million lire, plus a further 1,000 million in Italian State bonds, as compensation for the loss of his pre-1870 territories. And the Concordat granted various privileges to the Church. Religious education was brought into secondary as well as primary schools, seminarists were exempted from military service, and church marriages were deemed legally valid – they no longer had to be followed by a civil ceremony. The Concordat also guaranteed the future position of Catholic Action organizations 'in so far as they carry out their activities independently of all political parties, and immediately subordinate to the Church hierarchy, for the diffusion and realization of Catholic principles'. This was perhaps the most important provision of all, at least to the Pope. It ensured that the Church could continue to run her own organization for the laity.

The pacts were a triumph for the *Duce*. The cost was negligible, the benefits huge. Mussolini had 'solved the Roman question', which had baffled even Cavour and Crispi; he could count on world-wide prestige and a chorus of admiration. He was 'the man sent by providence', as Pius XI called him.[12] His regime was sanctified and blessed by Mother Church. At home, nobody could touch him now; abroad, he could assume the agreeable mantle of Defender of the Faith. The Church, too, could rejoice. She had achieved sovereign territory at last, financial security, above all recognition and immunity for her work. In short, she had the right to peaceful coexistence – no mean achievement in an avowedly totalitarian state.

But like later forms of peaceful coexistence, this one went through various phases. There was real '*détente*' for a few months in 1928–29, and again in 1935–36; but there was virtual 'cold war' in the summer of 1931 and in 1938–39. The early rows were over the Catholic youth movement. There had been disputes in 1927–28 over the Catholic Boy Scouts, which had been dissolved before the Lateran Pacts. In 1931 a major storm blew up. Catholic Action was accused of organizing sport, of being led by ex-*popolari*, and of trying to form 'occupational groups' – trade unions by another name. There were police raids and squad violence, and the State formally closed down Catholic Action's youth organizations. Pius XI retaliated with an encyclical '*Non abbiamo bisogno*', in which he recommended anybody who had to take an oath of loyalty to the Fascist regime to do so with 'mental reservations'. After some months the quarrel was patched up, but the Fascists insisted on confining Catholic Action to strictly religious activities. Former members of the PPI were henceforth ineligible as leaders. Catholic youth associations were not allowed to organize athletics or sport, which was to be a Fascist monopoly; but they were permitted to engage in 'recreational and educational activities having religious purposes'. This seems to have been sufficient. They flourished during the 1930s, and membership rose from just under 250,000 in 1930 to 388,000 in 1939. The Catholic youth movements were always a rival to the *Balilla* and to the GIL, and by their very existence they mocked any claim that the *Duce* was rearing a new Fascist generation.

The Catholic student movement, FUCI, deserves a special mention. It had been founded in 1896, and had always been an important branch of Catholic

Action. In the Fascist regime it was especially significant, for it was the only authorized non-Fascist organization for students. In 1932 it even managed to set up a 'graduate movement' for ex-students. It was led by a devoted enthusiast, Igino Righetti, and from 1925 until 1933 its chaplain was none other than Mgr Giovanni Battista Montini, the future Pope Paul VI. FUCI had long-term aims: to prevent any Fascist monopoly of student life, and to train a Catholic lay élite. This élite would defend the Church's interests in the uncertain future, and most thinking Catholics, indeed most thinking Italians, knew Fascism would not last. After Mussolini would come the deluge, in the form of a revived Liberalism or, even worse, Communism. The Catholics had to build, not in order to take over the country – few dared hope for that; but to hang on to what they had won. They wrought better than they knew. Many of Italy's Christian Democrat leaders after 1945 came up through FUCI. Both Aldo Moro and Giulio Andreotti were presidents of it, and its members included Emilio Colombo, Mario Scelba, Benigno Zaccagnini and Francesco Cossiga, as well as many future administrators, judges and businessmen. A new Catholic ruling class was being formed, under Fascist eyes. No wonder the Fascist police had informers in all Catholic Action branches, or that the chief of police urged that Catholic Action members should be excluded from jobs in government service.[13]

Thus although the Church undoubtedly contributed to the Fascist consensus between 1926 and 1938, she was also a rival, and a rival who was building up her strength. Northern and Central Italy seem to have had a mild religious revival in the 1930s. Church marriages became even more common; the median age at baptism declined from fourteen to ten days, in conformity with Church teaching. The various branches of Catholic Action had over 1 million members. A new Freemasonry had arisen to replace the old, and it had some claim to be the real 'internal opposition'. Church-run secondary schools had 31,000 pupils in 1927; by 1940 they had 104,000. However, Catholic Action was still feeble in the South – in Gallipoli 'usually it's one poor boy who is trying to organize Catholic Action, and his parish priest who is trying to stop him'.[14] And the Church herself had rivals. Worried Catholic attempts to curb the Pentecostalists and prevent the distribution of Protestant Bibles were at least as prominent in the religious history of these years as any revival of Catholic piety; on the only occasion Mussolini met Pius XI, that was the issue the two men discussed. Still, the number of clergy undeniably increased during the Fascist period, from 68,264 in 1921 to 70,652 ten years later; admittedly most of the new men were monks or friars, but some regions (for example Piedmont) saw an increase in secular priests too, and the monks were less cloistered than previously. And the nunneries were transformed. Not only were there far more nuns (129,000 in 1936, compared with 71,000 in 1921 and 45,000 in 1911) but many more were working in schools or hospitals, and over half were in the North. The increase was no doubt a consequence of the First World War, for many girls could no longer hope for marriage; but it helped the Church's '*reconquista*' of Italian society.

12.5 THE BREAKDOWN OF FASCIST CONSENSUS

The Fascist regime remained fairly popular until about 1936, but the late 1930s saw a marked change. 'Youth' was a difficult cult to keep up. By the mid-1930s the youthful heroes of 1915–18, and even the youthful *squadristi* of 1921–22, were youthful no longer. They were sweating middle-aged Fascist *gerarchi*, performing their physical jerks in public and ranting on about *Giovinezza*. They were simply ridiculous, to none more so than to the genuinely young. Their parade-ground antics symbolized the paradox of Fascist ideology. The Fascists claimed to be 'revolutionary', to be sweeping away the traditional strait-jacket of the Liberal past; yet in practice they had compromised with the older institutions, and even in propaganda they regularly appealed to traditional values like 'the family' or 'rural life'. In De Felice's phrase, they had founded a 'movement', but had set up a 'regime'.[15] Fascist ideas had emerged from the years of turmoil, from the First World War and revolutionary unrest; yet they were preached during the ossified years of Depression and stagnation. Many Fascists were radical demagogues at heart, and the Fascist ethos was deeply anti-Establishment; yet for years they had been part of the Establishment, and it showed. Many of them had somehow acquired aristocratic titles – *Count* Dino Grandi, *Count* Ciano *di Cortellazzo*, *Count* De Vecchi *di Val Cismon*. It was a classic case of rhetoric being out of joint with reality. The young intellectuals grew ever more cynical, especially in the 1930s when they could not find jobs; and, in the factories, disaffection became more noticeable.

In the end the rhetoric won, as it often does. Just as apocalyptic sects proclaim their beliefs with redoubled fervour the day after the world has failed to end, so the Fascist government stepped up its ideological campaign in 1938. It introduced the so-called 'reform of customs'. Italians were suddenly forbidden to shake hands – they had to use the 'Roman salute' instead. They were given detailed instructions on how to give it: it was all right to keep your hat on, but not to do it sitting down. They were also forbidden to call each other '*Lei*', the normal polite form of address; they had to use '*Voi*' instead. Civil servants were told to wear uniform. The army and Militia were forced to adopt the '*passo romano*', or goose-step – another risible sight to most Italians and deeply offensive to the king, who at the age of 69 could not manage it. These ludicrous measures antagonized virtually everybody, but it was difficult to ignore them.

The most odious aspect of this renewed ideological zeal in 1938–39 was the government's anti-Jewish campaign. It began, quite suddenly, in 1937. Until then individual Fascists like Farinacci and Preziosi may have been anti-Semitic, but the movement as a whole had not been racialist, except of course towards Libyans and Ethiopians. Mussolini had had a Jewish mistress for years, and in 1932 he appointed a Jewish Minister of Finance. In any case, there were only about 45,000 Italian Jews in the country, plus about 10,000 who had been born abroad, mainly refugees from the Nazis; the Jews were about 0.1 per cent of the population, not enough to be a plausible threat or to generate much popular resentment. Yet by 1938 Minculpop was distributing a 'Manifesto of Racial Scholars', and a press campaign was well under way. In November came legislation. Foreign Jews were to be deported. Italian Jews were forbidden to marry 'Aryans', to hold public office (including teaching and civil service jobs), to join the PNF, to own more than fifty hectares of land, to run any business with over 100 employees, or to have 'Aryan' servants. Some exceptions were allowed for war service or devotion to Fascism in the past, but even so the laws had an enormous impact: 6,000 Italian Jews left the country in the next three years. Many business firms closed down; Jewish children were expelled from State schools; one in twelve university teachers, including the Principal of Rome University, lost their jobs; the brilliant physicist Enrico Fermi left Italy in protest. Thus the academic and business élites were outraged; and so was the Church. The laws were denounced from many pulpits as immoral, and the Pope spoke out frequently against racialism. The Vatican also regarded the laws as a clear breach of the 1929 Concordat, since they prohibited 'mixed' marriages between Catholics and Jews, even baptized Jews.

The Fascist laws coincided with the first major pogroms in Germany – *Kristallnacht* was on 9 November 1938 – and so they were naturally regarded as simple subservience to Germany. In fact, there is no evidence of any Nazi pressure for the laws. Why, then, were they passed? Fascist propaganda against the Jews concentrated on their alleged lack of martial spirit. On 5 November 1938, for example, the main anti-Semitic journal *La Difesa della Razza* contained four articles on this theme: 'Un Popolo senza Eroi', by G. Cogni; 'Gli Ebrei e la Guerra', by E. Canevari; 'Giudeo e soldato: un' antitesi', by G. Lucidi; and 'Gli Eterni Imboscati', by E. Gasteiner. Most of its other issues were surprisingly full of militarist rhetoric, all jackboots and expansionism. Perhaps this is the key. The only semi-rational explanation for the government's measures is that the Fascists, like Pharaoh in Egypt (Exodus 1 : 9 ff.), feared that the Jews might not be loyal in time of war. Better to exclude them from the army and government service first.

If this was Mussolini's calculation, it misfired badly. The laws were much resented in the country, and were a source of shame to many Fascists. They discredited the 'activist', 'revolutionary' aspects of Fascist ideology, by showing where they led; and they alienated the conservative élites of Church, business and Court, on whom Fascist consensus had mainly relied. Moreover, the laws made it clear that Mussolini's foreign policy was dangerous. The Germans were feared and distrusted even by many Fascists. Fascist rhetoric was tolerable at Militia parades; but suddenly the game had become serious. The ultra-nationalism, the zeal for domination and Empire, the general belligerence of Fascism were dragging Italy into unnecessary wars, fought in order to prove the Fascists' virility rather than for any real national interest. Thus it was not just the young and idealistic who began to reject Fascism in the late 1930s; the old and cautious did so too.

In short, the anti-Semitic campaign and the 'reform of customs' were disastrous political errors, although not inexplicable ones. All parties, in all countries, profess lunatic and antiquated ideas, and on occasion act accordingly. The Fascists simply provide an outstanding example of how destructive an ideology can be. They always had to be doing something new and dangerous. Their rhetoric prevented them from retaining the stable, authoritarian, 'Francoist' policy so ardently desired by the Establishment, and so laboriously constructed in 1922–29. The 'movement' had subverted the 'regime'.

The anti-Fascist parties naturally benefited from the changed climate. The Socialists and Communists had signed a 'pact of unity of action' in 1934, and this alliance lasted until the Nazi–Soviet pact five years later. Moreover, Italian intervention in the Spanish Civil War (see §14.1) had a major impact on anti-Fascism. The mass Left-wing parties joined with others to raise a 'Garibaldi battalion' from among the emigrés, to fight in Spain for the Republic. These units included Nenni and Longo, and were commanded by the Republican Pacciardi. In March 1937 they helped to defeat Italian troops fighting on Franco's side at the battle of Guadalajara. News of the victory soon percolated back to Italy. So the anti-Fascist parties still existed, and could defeat the Fascist Militia; Fascism was vulnerable after all. Rosselli's famous slogan 'today in Spain, tomorrow in Italy', began to appear on walls. Guadalajara was a huge boost to Left-wing and anti-Fascist morale. The anti-Fascists used the wireless from Madrid or Barcelona to spread their message, far more successfully than hitherto. Indeed, the Communist Party's rise to influence in Italian politics dates from Togliatti and Longo's time in Spain. But the Socialists, Republicans and GL benefited too. The comradeship forged in battle was sometimes stronger than the inevitable rivalry, and had a major impact on post-war Italy: Togliatti, Longo and Nenni dominated the Communist and Socialist parties until the mid-1960s, and Pacciardi was Minister of Defence in the Italian Republic. The Left-wing parties were learning to work together. And they were no longer the inevitable losers: prudent men might soon have to consider changing sides. Rosselli's slogan turned out to be true: the Spanish Civil War *was* a rehearsal of things to come in Italy.

12.6 SUMMARY

Italian Fascism has provoked intense arguments among historians and sociologists. There are three main schools of thought. The 'Radicals' see Fascism simply as a tougher version of Liberal Italy. Some of them regard it as the inevitable consequence of the *Risorgimento*'s limited achievements, as a 'revelation, not revolution'. This perspective seems to me valid for the 'High Political' institutions of the regime (see §11.2). There was much continuity between Liberal and Fascist Italy here, although 'continuity' does not mean continuing on from the troubled years of 1918–22, nor does it preclude strengthening. But in other fields, and even in other political institutions, 'continuity' was less evident. The Fascist National Party, as a mass organization of the middle classes, was new; so was the Militia. Giuseppe Prezzolini may have exaggerated when he said that Fascism was 'the only really original political idea ever invented by the Italians' since the medieval communes and *Signorie*,[16] but his view is more realistic than that of Nicola Tranfaglia or other contemporary Radicals.

A second, and larger, group of historians recognizes that Fascist Italy was different from Liberal or Republican Italy, indeed regards Fascism as essentially revolutionary, but sees it as a European or even world-wide phenomenon which just happened to occur in Italy first. Such writers normally stress the similarities between Fascist Italy and other Fascist regimes, especially Nazi Germany. They stress also the long-term structural changes in European societies, selecting suitable themes according to academic interests or political preference: the fall – or rise – of an independent peasantry; the fall – or rise – of the lower middle classes; the rise – or betrayal – of the 'masses', and of 'mass parties'; the limited nature of 'bourgeois' revolutions in previous centuries; the concentration of industrial or financial capital; the absence or sudden loss of Empires; the 'moral crisis of the West'. These historians are right to stress the lower middle-class composition of early Fascism, and to emphasize that nationalist and activist ideas were extremely influential in many countries. It also seems to me correct to argue that the Fascists aimed at and partially created a 'mass society'. But Italy was very much *sui generis*. There is no Grand Structural Explanation that accounts for the Fascist regime. As for the Nazis, most Fascists had little in common with each other, let alone with them.

Finally, there are the dullards, who rigorously reject any schematic interpretations, and often any attempt at thought. If the king had not changed his mind on the morning of 28 October 1922, they claim, there might never have been a Fascist regime at all. This group is, alas, right. All crises can have multiple outcomes. Fascism was not inevitable, nor was it bound to succeed – indeed, in the early years it went through repeated crises that threatened its very existence. It emerged from the First World War, from Versailles and Fiume, and from the peculiar clashes of the new post-war politics; in 1924–26 it became a 'regime', through a further complex series of manoeuvres and misunderstandings. The only way to understand why Italy became Fascist is to study its detailed history.

Furthermore, Fascism meant different things at different times. De Felice has stressed the distinction between 'Fascism-movement' (revolutionary, intransigent, and syndicalist) and 'Fascism-regime' (conservative, compromising, and corrupt). But this distinction is itself too simple. 'Fascism-movement' included syndicalists like Rossoni, provincial squad-leaders like Farinacci, and would-be cultural revolutionaries like Malaparte. And 'Fascism-regime' – the conservative regime of 1926–34, of consensus and conciliation, of Mussolini in top hat and frock coat, the regime of Alfredo Rocco and the constitutional changes of 1925–26 – was also the regime of intense corporatist propaganda and disputes over Catholic Action; it was not as conservative as all that.

Moreover, by 1938 this conservative regime had somehow turned stridently nationalist. It had become the regime of Empire and racialism, with Mussolini as the victorious *Duce* never out of military uniform.

So here is another continuity problem. Was the real Fascist revolution in 1936–38? Or was 1936–38 the beginning of the regime's breakdown, the extremism being due to panic and hysteria as the failure of Fascism became daily more apparent? Perhaps both views are true – it was a 'real' Fascist revolution at long last, arousing intense antagonism as the implications of it all eventually struck home. But, once again, there was nothing inevitable about it. The regime might, just might, have evolved in other directions, as Franco's Spain did after 1939; it was not Fascist militarism alone that prevented this happy outcome. And even in this late Fascist period Mussolini was less warlike than he pretended. He kept Italy out of war in 1939, and only joined in when the outcome looked certain.

Nevertheless, my own view is that Fascism, like Communism, was essentially the child of war. Its origins lay in pre-1915 humiliations and agitations. Its appeal was to the officers of the war generation, to the 'real Italy' of the trenches and of Vittorio Veneto, to men who had won the first major victories of Italian arms. Together these men had overcome not only the Austrians, but also the hated neutralist Establishment, the cowardly Giolittian parliament, the treacherous Socialists and the peace-mongering Church; and in the post-war ferment, braving insults and violence, they had conquered them all again. They never forgot. The regime's slogans and symbols were always military – 'believe, obey, fight'. Mussolini's working office after 1929 was in Palazzo Venezia, which had until 1915 been the Austrian Embassy. Wartime memories accounted for many Fascist policies. 'Intervention' in the economy was geared mainly to national glory. So was 'industrial mobilization'. Factories had recreation centres, like the soldiers had had in the war; the *Balilla* had chaplains, as regiments had had in the war; newspapers were censored, as they had been in the war.

'War alone', proclaimed Mussolini's official 'Doctrine of Fascism' in 1932, 'brings up to their highest tension all human energies, and puts the stamp of nobility upon the peoples who have the courage to meet it'.[17] When there was no war to fight, the Fascists found surrogates; when there was, they joined in. Mussolini was always the *Duce*, the military leader, the man on horseback. His regime was neither conservative, nor revolutionary; it was bellicose.

REFERENCES

1.   G. Gentile, *Origini e Dottrina del Fascismo*, Rome 1929, p. 48.
2.   Speech to Chamber of Deputies 11 Dec. 1925, quoted in R. De Felice, *Mussolini il Fascista*, ii, Turin 1968, 269.
3.   M. Antonioni, 'La Sorpresa Veneziana', *Cinema*, 25 Sept. 1940 (quoted in F. Savio, *Ma L'Amore No*, Milan 1975, p. 30); M. Isnenghi, '30–40: l'ipotesi della continuità', in *QS*, no. 34 (1977), 103–7.

4. P. V. Cannistraro, 'Mussolini's cultural revolution – Fascist or Nationalist?', *Journal of Contemporary History*, vii (1972), 137.

5. The oath is given in A. Aquarone, *L'Organizzazione dello Stato Totalitario*, Turin 1965, p. 179.

6. F. Tempesti, *Arte dell'Italia Fascista*, Milan 1976, pp. 211–12.

7. Speech of 10 Dec. 1925, in A. Aquarone, *L'Organizzazione...*, p. 130.

8. '*Quadragesimo Anno*' (1931); quotation from Part Two, section 5, on p. 43 of English edn, London n.d.

9. G. Salvemini, *Under the Axe of Fascism*, London 1936, p. 10. This claim was not exaggerated. A. Gradilone's *Bibliografia Sindacale Corporativa*, published in 1942, contained over 1,000 pages.

10. C. Vannutelli, 'The living standard of Italian workers, 1929–39', in R. Sarti (ed.), *The Ax Within*, New York and London 1974, p. 147.

11. E. Curiel, 'Masse Operaie e sindacato fascista', in *Scritti 1935–45*, i, Rome 1973, p. 236.

12. Pius XI to visitors from Sacro Cuore University, Milan, 13 Feb. 1929 ('e forse ci voleva anche un uomo come quello che la Provvidenza Ci ha fatto incontrare').

13. M. C. Giuntella, 'L'Organizzazione universitaria fascista e Ia federazione universitaria cattolica in una relazione del segretario del G.U.F. di Viterbo', in *Rivista di Storia della Chiesa in Italia,* xxvi (1972), 130–36.

14. Police report of 13 Sept. 1938, quoted in P. Borzomati, *I 'Giovani Cattolici' nel Mezzogiorno d'Italia dall' Unità al 1948*, Rome 1970, p. 157.

15. R. De Felice, *Intervista sul Fascismo*, Bari 1975, pp. 27ff.

16. Interview with R. Gervaso, in *Corriere della Sera*, 22 Oct. 1978.

17. 'The political and social doctrine of Fascism', in A. Lyttelton (ed.), *Italian Fascisms*, London 1973, p. 47.

CHAPTER THIRTEEN

The economy and society under the Fascists

Mussolini's economic and social policies, like his other policies, were geared to political propaganda rather than to real achievement. This chapter will examine government monetary, industrial and agricultural policies, and discuss whether they had any effect upon reality; and will also look at some of the Fascists' 'social' policies, e.g. urbanization, demography and education, in the same light. The general message will be that inasmuch as the Fascists had a long-term aim at all, it was to 'mobilize' resources for some great national purpose, usually war; but it did not work, or worked only very partially.

13.1 ECONOMIC POLICY

In his first years in office Mussolini tried, as always, to balance 'Fascist' demands – syndicalism, etc. – with the need to win over the Establishment. He appointed an orthodox financier, De'Stefani, as Treasury Minister; and he made many concessions to business interests. The telephones were handed back to private companies; private life insurance was also reintroduced; Giolitti's proposal for a register of shareholders was dropped; taxes on 'excess' war profits were reduced or abandoned. The huge shipping and steel firm of Ansaldo, owned by the Perrone brothers, was reconstructed with government cash, and the (Catholic) *Banco di Roma* was rescued. Furthermore, these were boom years. The index of manufacturing production rose from 54 in 1921 to 83 in 1925 (1938 = 100); not until the late 1950s were similar rates of growth achieved in Italy. Many businessmen were delighted by the new government's policies. But others remained sceptical. They disliked the Fascist unions, detested the Fascist squads, and distrusted the Fascist leader. In October 1922 many of the leading Milanese industrialists had tried to prevent power being handed over to an 'erratic and impressionable despot' like Mussolini,[1] and during the Matteotti crisis many Liberal industrialists not only failed to support the government, but spoke actively against it. Ettore Conti even made a speech in the Senate in December 1924 thanking Mussolini for his past services!

In 1925–26, as the political climate became harsher, so too did economic policy. De'Stefani was replaced by Count Volpi di Misurata, the Fascist syndicates were allowed to lead a major engineering strike and acquired sole negotiating rights, and the Ministry of Corporations was founded. The industrialists were being taught a lesson. A serious balance of payments crisis provided a further occasion. Mussolini proclaimed that the regime would not tolerate an undervalued lira (at the time almost 150 to the pound sterling). Henceforth the exchange-rate would be '*quota novanta*', i.e. 90 lire to the pound – a figure selected, if not quite at random, at least mainly for prestige reasons. Many businessmen complained that 90 was far too low, but to no avail. Mussolini had decided to show them who was boss. Inflation would be curbed, the host of small savers and rentiers in Italy would be satisfied, foreign bankers would lend money, the lira would be stable and the regime would be safe.

The revaluation to '*quota novanta*' was a real economic turning-point, especially as it was accompanied by other deflationary measures – high interest rates, a lower money supply, a credit squeeze, wage cuts, etc. The economic boom of 1922–26 had been export-led, indeed exports had doubled in those four years: more than half Italy's cars were exported. The new exchange-rate priced Italian products out of world markets; cars, light engineering, and textile producers suffered most. Conversely, importers ought to have prospered, since '*quota novanta*' lowered the Italian price of foreign goods. In fact, this did not help consumers much, because of higher tariffs and lower wages – there was a 10 per cent cut in all wages in autumn 1927. But the new exchange-rate did benefit steel, armaments and shipbuilding interests, which had traditionally required huge quantities of raw materials – especially coal and iron – from abroad. Even so, the shipyards languished for lack of orders, and had to be heavily subsidized. Steel and chemicals were the only industries which flourished. By 1929 Italy had become self-sufficient in chemicals; and steel production was up to 2,122,000 tonnes, compared with 982,000 tonnes in 1922. So the Fascist economic pattern was becoming set. Italy was turning away from her export markets, and boosting instead the industries which stood to gain most from Empire and rearmament.

In the Depression years of 1929–33 this policy was continued. The government again lowered money wages in November 1930, by around 12 per cent, and encouraged price-fixing and cartel agreements. Mergers became common, and producers were even forced into compulsory 'consortia', i.e. employers' closed shops. Anticipating Keynes, the Fascist government boosted total demand and employment by public works and welfare benefits: the money spent on road-building doubled in four years. Even so, the general policy remained deflationary. Money supply declined from 19 billion lire in 1929 to 16 billion lire in 1932, and to 15.3 billion lire in 1934; the cost of living dropped by 16 per cent between 1927 and 1932.

The main thrust of government policy was directed towards the banks. The major banks – the *Credito Italiano*, the *Banca Commerciale* and the *Banco di Roma* – had lent large sums to industry and commerce on the security of shares in the debtor firms; as the firms became insolvent, however, they ceased repayments. The banks were left holding worthless pieces of paper, and threatened to collapse in their turn. So did the Bank of Italy, which had been trying to support them. Something had to be done. Governments had rescued banks on previous occasions, and the Fascists themselves had rescued the *Banco di Roma* in 1923. So they simply continued this policy. A larger and wealthier rescue institution, the *Istituto Mobiliare Italiano* (IMI), was founded in 1931 to provide industrial credit, and in 1933 another agency, the Institute for Industrial Reconstruction (IRI), was founded. These agencies bought up the useless industrial shares from the banks, paying real (taxpayers') money for them. They also took over long-term loans to industry. The banks were saved; or rather, they were swallowed. IRI ended up owning the banks' shares itself, in return for lending them the money to continue operations. But the banks did not continue as before. They were debarred in future from long-term or even medium-term commercial lending. The 'mixed bank', which had dominated Italian business since the 1890s, was no more. Henceforth investment capital would come either from the stock exchange – and this was not probable in the 1930s – or from the new State-owned financial institutions. It would not come from the banks.

This was a real revolution in Italian finance. The State took over much new industrial investment, and did so to public acclaim. Millions of small savers were protected, and confidence was restored. Italy weathered the storm of 1929–33 rather better than some other industrial countries. Gross national product fell 5.4 per cent between the 1929 peak and the 1931–33 trough, and industrial production fell by 22.7 per cent; the figures for Western Europe as a whole were 7.1 per cent and 23.2 per cent.[2] This relative success was a boost for Fascist propaganda. Liberal economics seemed to be discredited by events world-wide; government intervention seemed to work in Italy.

The IRI was a particularly important innovation. It was founded to hold the industrial and commercial shares that the State had acquired, and then to sell them off again, recouping as much as possible of the initial outlay. It started as a company hospital, where patients were given financial and technical injections and nursed back to health; but it soon became a business school, where new management techniques were taught and applied. By 1939 IRI and its subsidiaries controlled Ilva, Terni and Dalmine (steelworks), L'Italia, Lloyd Triestino, Adriatica, and Tirrenia (shipping lines), Ansaldo and Cantieri Riuniti (shipbuilding). It also dominated the electricity and machine-tool industries as well as the telephone system. After 1936 'the Italian State owned a proportionally larger part of industry than any other State in Europe except the Soviet Union'.[3] Normally, however, these firms were not wholly State-owned, and IRI sold off part of its stock at regular intervals to private investors.

Fascist propaganda presented IRI as part of the corporate State. In fact, IRI was kept well away from the corporations. It was not run by a Fascist but by

Alberto Beneduce, a former Minister of Labour in the Bonomi government of 1921–22. Yet it soon became responsible for a new kind of 'mixed' and 'semi-State' enterprise. Surprisingly competitive and efficient, run on private lines, sometimes co-operating with major private firms (e.g. with Fiat in aircraft), sometimes selling off unwanted assets, always 'mobilizing' national resources and managing them 'progressively', it was the key economic legacy of the Fascist period.

The Depression was followed by further storms. In 1935 Italy invaded Ethiopia (see §14.1), and the League of Nations imposed economic sanctions upon her. These sanctions were limited – they did not include oil – and they had little direct impact on consumers; but they naturally boosted the government's drive for self-sufficiency. 'Autarchy' became the slogan. Imports would be replaced by *ersatz* goods. Lanital (made from cheese) replaced wool; rayon replaced cotton. Exports henceforth would go to the Empire – Africa alone took over 25 per cent of Italian exports after 1936, a huge shift of Italian resources overseas. A further 25 per cent went to Germany.

Thus in the late 1930s Italian economic policy can be summed up as Autarchy, Rearmament and Empire, and the greatest of these was Empire. Long after sanctions had been abandoned in 1936, foreign trade remained curtailed by trading licences and import quotas. The cartels, the price-fixing and the 'consortia' also remained in being. It was a policy geared to heavy industrial interests – steelmakers, shipbuilders, chemical manufacturers and the like; and in some ways it succeeded. By 1938 industrial production was back at 1929 levels. But the disadvantages were obvious. It was immensely expensive. The budget deficits were alarming – 12,750 million lire in 1938–39 – and the currency reserves were running out. Nobody liked paying the many extra taxes and capital levies of 1936–39, especially the 'forced loan' of 5 per cent of the value of housing. There was no future in being Germany's client State, whoever won the forthcoming war; and many bankers and businessmen were Jewish. People began shifting their capital abroad, always an easy feat in a country with a Swiss border. By 1939 economic policy was evidently leading to disaster. Whatever successes it had achieved in the past seemed about to be destroyed.

But what successes had it achieved in the past? Surviving the Depression relatively painlessly was one; and the banking system, although now State-owned, was less vulnerable than before. There were no more liquidity crises to disrupt Italian business, and the old chronic shortage of risk capital had been, if not overcome, at least mitigated. Some of the public works projects, especially roads and hydro-electricity, provided huge benefits: virtually all Italy's electricity came from water power, and it amounted to 14.8 billion kilowatt-hours by 1937. IRI built up the 'infrastructure': the iron and steel plant may have been used for arms in the 1930s, but it became useful for many other purposes in the 1950s. So, too, did the State-owned oil corporation, AGIP, which was already negotiating directly with Middle Eastern oil suppliers, and had already discovered natural gas in the Po valley. Some new industries became firmly established, e.g. chemicals (Montecatini), artificial fibres (Snia Viscosa), paper and electricity supply. Light engineering, although often neglected by government policy, none the less continued to expand: there were over 800,000 mechanical workers in the late 1930s, almost twice as many as ten years earlier. Italy by 1939 was more industrialized than she had been in 1922, and rather more prosperous. Gross domestic product had increased by 1.2 per cent per year on average, more than double the growth of population; manufacturing production had gone up by 3.9 per cent p.a. A new generation of managers had emerged, trained in State enterprise and political manoeuvres as well as in strictly business methods.

However, the costs had been high. The Fascists cannot be blamed for 'mobilizing' and organizing their industrial base – most twentieth-century States have done that, usually for military reasons; nor can they be blamed for the manner of their intervention, which was the fashionable doctrine of the day; but they can certainly be blamed for doing it for quite such foolish purposes. In the late 1930s military spending (including the Empire and Spain) was running at about 15 billion lire per year, over one-third of all public spending.[4] Even much of the civilian expenditure was imperial; roads in African deserts were no use to Italy. Ethiopia absorbed scarce resources and capital, and provided virtually no benefits. Furthermore, the welfare side of the Fascist 'warfare–welfare' State was also alarmingly expensive, despite the undoubted political benefits. Welfare spending rose from 1.5 billion lire in 1930 to 6.7 billion lire by 1940, i.e. from 6.9 per cent to 20.6 per cent of all State and local tax receipts. Italy, with less than half the gross national product per head of Britain, could barely afford either imperialism or a Welfare State; certainly she could not afford both.

Even more important were the 'opportunity costs', the shift of resources away from profitable exporting (textiles) towards autarchy and Empire. Among the big firms, some natural exporters diversified into more politically rewarding channels. Olivetti, for example, started making machine-guns as well as typewriters. Fiat prudently kept up its aircraft manufacture and its iron and steel interests, although it continued to make cars for export – after all, car factories could easily be converted to make military vehicles if necessary. Even so, it made and exported fewer cars in the late 1930s than it had in the mid-1920s. Other exporting industries, especially cotton and silk, declined very rapidly in the Fascist period. In general, the 'consortia', cartels, mergers, trading licences and controls on investment, all protected existing firms but discouraged innovators. By 1940 Italy had five private firms that were virtually monopolies in their sectors – Fiat, Pirelli, Montecatini, Snia Viscosa and Edison – as well as the largely State-owned steel plants and shipyards.

Another major economic cost was excessive State interference and parasitism. IRI may have been a success, but for every one skilled manager in the public or semi-public enterprises there were ten political hangers-on in the corporations. Quangos flourished as never before. The Fascists proclaimed the State's duty to intervene in the economy, and expanded the public sector; but they also created a vast network, or rather many competing networks, of 'jobs for the boys' and corruption. That was inevitable when no business could be started or expanded without a licence from the ministries or from the corporations. These bureaucratic organizations provided jobs for otherwise unemployable members of the middle classes, and possibly helped in this way to boost demand, but they were immensely expensive, produced nothing but paper and delays, and were incapable of any serious planning. The National Council of Corporations, supposedly the 'general staff' of the economy, was not even consulted when IRI was set up; and IRI was run by a non-Fascist along 'private' lines. The Fascists had turned away from Liberal 'market' policies, but they could control neither their State enterprises nor their private cartels.

And there was much else that they could not control. Italian economists, contemplating the rather similar economic bureaucracy of the mid-1970s, have recently turned their attention to the flourishing 'black economy' (see §17.1) – the millions of 'clandestine' workers, paying no taxes and belonging to no union, who provide the personal services and even the manufactured goods that keep the Italian economy afloat. All this happened in the 1930s too. 'Official' figures and 'official' policy are only half the story, and often the wrong half. Autarchy was never complete; there were always the tourists, at least. Some measures of affluence obstinately continued to go up. In 1929 a survey of eating habits found, for the first time in Italian history, that in the North the upper classes were consuming fewer calories per day than the poorer ones – a sure sign of prosperity.[5] Army recruits grew taller each year, another good index of better hygiene and diet: the median height rose from 164.4 centimetres in 1928 to 166.2 centimetres in 1938. Cars provide a further illustration. In 1922 there had been 47,164 registered cars on Italian roads; by the end of 1938 there were 345,000. How and why all this happened is by no means clear, although Fiat made car ownership easier by mass-producing excellent cheap models like the *Topolino*. Many Italians must have prospered in the grim years of Depression and autarchy by adaptability and imagination, without any official blessing.

13.2 AGRICULTURE

The Fascists took over a country where there were 3½ million landowners, many of them 'new' peasant-owners anxious to keep newly acquired land. Furthermore, it was the peasants who had fought the war, and who would fight any future war. So the Fascists backed the peasantry, or rather they backed the new landed peasantry. In some Liberal or Catholic areas Fascist syndicates even took over big estates after 1922, selling them or leasing them out to landless peasants. 'Land to the peasants' was a constant propaganda cry throughout the regime, justifying reclamation schemes in Italy and imperial dreams in Africa. Mussòlini proclaimed the need to 'ruralize Italy'[6], and told the Prefects to give particular attention to agriculture, 'in precedence over all other forms of economic activity ... the regime is predominantly rural, and intends to remain so'.[7] This was not just rhetoric. In many regions the small farmers were the backbone of the Fascist regime. Mussolini's rural conservatism had a solid basis in fact.

Yet, as ever, Mussolini was not content to be a mere conservative. He had grandiose ambitions for the land, ambitions which were military in nature. The government would 'free the Italian people from the slavery of foreign bread', so that the people would not starve in time of war. In 1925, after a poor harvest had made it necessary to import 2.3 million tonnes of wheat, he proclaimed a 'Battle for Wheat'. A high tariff was put on imported grain, thus raising food prices and discouraging consumption. By 1933 the tariff was 750 lire per tonne, and the Italian farmer was benefiting accordingly. Landowners grew wheat even on unsuitable soil, using all the advances of modern science – selected seeds, chemical fertilizers, farm machinery and so forth, most of them subsidized by new government grants. Annual wheat-growing competitions began, to stimulate 'wheat consciousness' and rural Stakhanovism. Storage deposits were built up, and after 1936 farmers had to sell their wheat to compulsory marketing agencies. The Fascists made an intense effort to spread knowledge of new farming techniques, and even the priests were expected to play their part. The archbishop of Reggio Calabria, for example, instructed his clergy to be model farmers and to spread technical skills – 'be therefore true apostles also in this respect; and you will have the blessing of your parishioners, of the national government and, above all, of God'.[8] More land, mainly on Southern hills, came under wheat; and more wheat was grown per hectare – startlingly more in Northern and Central Italy, where there was a 50 per cent rise on pre-war days. Yields by 1931–35 (2.18 tonnes per hectare in the North, 1.07 tonnes in the South) were still low by French or British standards, but much of the land was unsuitable for wheat anyway.

The 'Battle for Wheat' undeniably produced more wheat. The average harvest rose from 5.39 million tonnes in 1921–25 to 7.27 million tonnes ten years later, and imports fell off markedly. But the costs were high. They were paid by consumers, in lower consumption, high tariffs and needlessly high prices: one estimate is that each family had to pay about 400 lire per year extra.[9] Some costs were also paid by farmers, in the form of 'opportunity costs' and soil exhaustion. The campaign probably did little harm in Northern Italy, where it essentially meant a switch from maize to wheat, and hence less pellagra; but most of the extra arable land was further South, where the climate was too hot and dry for efficient wheat-growing. More land for wheat meant less for pasture, olive trees, citrus fruit, and vineyards. The South lost 20 per cent of its cattle and 18 per cent of its sheep between 1918 and 1930, as pasture was ploughed up; and that in turn meant less manure. Italy had fewer cows in 1930 than she had had in 1908, and the decline was evident even in Lombardy, the centre of Italy's dairy industry. Centuries-old orchards were destroyed, and fruit and wine exports fell off markedly. Spain was allowed to corner the European market in citrus fruit, and for some years Italy even became a net importer of olive oil. So Mussolini's wheat policy made little economic sense. But then it was not an economic policy. It was politics and propaganda, like everything else he did: not bread, but circuses. It made Italy self-sufficient in basic foods, it cut the balance of payments deficit, and it protected essential rural interests, especially those of larger arable farmers.

The same was true of Fascism's other major agricultural policy, the famous land reclamation and improvement schemes. Such schemes were not new in united Italy – over 500,000 hectares of marsh land had been drained before 1911 – but the Fascists decided to do it on a larger scale. In 1928 the so-called 'Mussolini Law' promised to throw huge sums of public money into reclamation. The work was supposed to be comprehensive ('integral'), including irrigation, road-building, housing and aqueducts. It was also to be compulsory – landowners who did not carry it out would be expropriated. In practice, the new Fascist reclamation was mainly the old Liberal drainage, writ large. It worked in the Tuscan *Maremma* and in the Roman *Campagna*, i.e. where drainage was the answer; it failed, or was not attempted, in the Southern hills, where there was a need for irrigation, reafforestation and the settling of peasant cultivators. The outstanding success was in the Pontine Marshes, which by 1935 had been turned into an area of small farms, cultivated by ex-soldiers from the Po valley. The Pontine Marshes were only fifty-six kilometres from Rome, a convenient distance for foreign journalists and visiting agricultural experts; and, just in case they missed the point, Mussolini created a new province there, Littoria.

But the Pontine Marshes were not typical. In 1934 the government claimed that reclamation had been 'completed' or was 'under way' on 4¾ million hectares, i.e. one-sixth of the total area of the country; in reality half this land had scarcely been touched, and most of the other half had been drained or irrigated decades previously. Perhaps 5 per cent of the claimed total (i.e. 250,000 hectares) was actually improved significantly by the Fascist regime, at a cost of nearly 8 billion lire. Furthermore, the scheme was badly administered. Landowners who formed 'consortia' were put in charge of their own reclamation, and received government subsidies. Soon there were 357 'consortia', and some 4 billion lire were handed over to private landowners over a ten-year period. The scheme's compulsory purchase powers were hardly ever used. Fewer than 10,000 landless peasant families were settled on land in the 1930s, a trivial proportion of the total. Land reclamation probably had more impact on public health – reducing malaria by almost half – and on unemployment than on agriculture. It was a huge job-creation scheme during the Depression, and accounted for one-third of all public works jobs.

The Fascists were pursuing different and quite incompatible goals. They wanted to encourage and settle small peasant landowners, yet they also wanted more wheat – and wheat can best be grown on reasonably large farms. And the Fascists relied on the landowners not only for wheat, but for political support. So when they attempted a major experiment in State-directed planning, they put the private landowners and tenant farmers in charge of it. Moreover, the post-1926 deflation made mortgages more onerous. Much land had been bought on credit, but as food prices fell, the new owners could not keep up the repayments. The failure of many rural Catholic banks after 1926 also cut off a major source of credit. Both these factors hindered new or would-be peasant landowners. So despite all the rhetoric, peasant landownership expanded immensely just before and just after the Fascist regime, but not during it, at least not after 1926. It probably declined. Almost half the new land holdings in upper Lombardy had been sold off by 1935, and Vitali has estimated that the number of peasant landowners in Italy went down from 3.4 million in 1921 to just under 3 million in 1931.[10]

The problem of reconciling the need for larger farms with the need to attract peasants to the land was solved, if at all, by various half-way houses – more leases, more fixed tenancies, more share-cropping and so forth. These were the normal outcomes on privately owned 'improved' land. Consequently there were fewer landless labourers by the mid-1930s than there had been fifteen years earlier – 1.3 million fewer, according to Vitali.[11] But the new tenants, and indeed many of the new owners, were hardly better off than the old labourers. Their holdings were too small, their best products – fruit, vegetables, wine – were without official favour or subsidy, and they were too numerous. Their changed status was not a sign of 'rising social mobility'; on the contrary, it simply tied them to the soil.

And this was perhaps the whole point. Mussolini had proclaimed his intention of 'ruralizing Italy'; but Italy had become less rural than ever before, and at least 500,000 men left the land in the Fascist period. There were still 8 million people working there, as in 1871; but now there were more people busy elsewhere. It is probable that in the 1930s, for the first time in Italian history, less than half the active population was engaged in agriculture – although many of the new 'industrial' or 'service' jobs were in food-processing or food-retailing, and some were linked to the new agricultural policies, e.g. jobs in tractor or fertilizer manufacture. Still, several mountain zones were becoming virtually depopulated. The government was trying to put the clock back. This policy was bound to fail, although the Fascist efforts may have slowed the rural exodus down, and in the Depression many urban workers went back more or less voluntarily to their tiny family farms.

13.3 SOCIAL CHANGE AND THE POPULATION

Perhaps the most significant economic change in the Fascist period was in the civil service and public agencies. The number of public employees doubled during the 1930s from 500,000 to 1 million, quite apart from the extra jobs in the Fascist Party, Militia or syndicates. Fascism offered the middle classes security – not just against trade unions, socialism or inflation, but also against unemployment. There were more jobs for them, more prestige, and more power; and the salary–wage gap – the middle class's differential – widened for the first time since figures began. The Italian middle classes (unlike the German) held on to their money and their privileges after the early 1920s.

Indeed, the Fascist educational changes (see below, §13.4) reinforced their position. Most of the new public sector jobs were in teaching; a degree was becoming almost as essential a meal-ticket as the party card. Yet only 3 per cent of university students in 1931–32 came from working-class families, compared with 5 per cent in 1911.

Still, most middle-class people had humbler aspirations and activities. They were small shopkeepers, rather than bureaucrats. Many of them were small landowners or self-employed artisans selling their own produce, economically not all that distinct from their 'working-class' counterparts. The number of shops was striking – there were about 550,000 at the end of the 1920s, quite apart from the pedlars and stallholders. Italy lacked chain stores, major department stores or retail co-operatives; but she was, nevertheless, a nation of shopkeepers. So the growth of the middle class was deceptive. It did not necessarily imply more social mobility, or better educational opportunities, or less rigid social patterns. It meant stability, not change. Similarly, although 'service industries' – welfare, administration, commerce, domestic help, etc. – undoubtedly expanded, this was not necessarily a sign of a more advanced modern economy.

The economic changes also widened the gap between North and South. The industries which grew fastest in the Fascist period were mechanical engineering, steelmaking, chemicals and hydro-electricity supply. They were all in the North, indeed mainly in the famous 'industrial triangle' of North-West Italy. By 1937 almost half Italy's industrial workers and almost two-thirds of her engineering workers were in Lombardy, Liguria and Piedmont. In the South, only Campania and Apulia had any real industry, centred around steel and shipbuilding at Naples and Taranto. In the other Southern regions 'industrial workers' were artisans or, at best, engaged in food-processing or in the building trades. Electricity prices in the South were two or three times those in the North; and Southern savings had been wiped out by the great post-war inflation. Moreover, the 'Battle for Wheat' did the South much harm, and land reclamation schemes did little good. Thus the North grew more prosperous, admittedly slowly, but the South stagnated.

In any case, Fascism was a Northern movement, born in Milan, Trieste and the Po valley. It neglected the South, although Mussolini made enough concessions to landowners and lawyers to prevent any overt opposition. The main Fascist achievement in the South was Prefect Mori's famous 'Battle against the Mafia' in the late 1920s. Mori was effective if brutal. Most leading *Mafiosi* were imprisoned, driven underground, or forced to emigrate to the USA. This was a real success. Murders in Palermo province dropped dramatically – from 278 in 1924 to 25 in 1928; so did kidnapping and rustling. The big landowners could safely set foot on their estates once more. But neither Mori nor the government tackled other issues: Sicily received far less funds for drainage and irrigation than did the Roman *Campagna* or the Tuscan *Maremma*.

Indeed, the 'Southern question' became far more serious after 1921, when the Americans cut down the number of immigrants they were willing to admit. The USA had taken 233,000 Italian immigrants a year on average between 1901 and 1910, most of them Southerners; in the 1920s they took 42,000 p.a., and in the 1930s 11,500. Emigration to Europe fell off too, especially during and after the Depression. The Fascist government also did its best to keep its people in, by making the regulations more bureaucratic. So here was a dramatic and sudden change in Italian society. Total emigration fell from over 600,000 p.a. before the war, to below 50,000 (gross) in the late 1930s. The 'great safety-valve' had suddenly been closed. Economically, the period from the late 1920s to the late 1940s was perhaps the worst in recent Southern history: by 1950 income per head was about 60 per cent that of 1924.

Yet emigration, like time, is an ever-rolling stream, that bears all its sons away; when one stream is dammed, the current flows elsewhere. Fewer people went abroad. Instead, they moved from the country to the town, from South to North, from East to West, from hills to plains. Italy ceased to be a country of emigrants, and became a mobile society. After 1928, over 1 million Italians moved from one municipality to another each year; indeed, more people moved in the 1930s than in the 1950s. And why not? The countryside was still overpopulated, especially in the South; not everyone could have land, and labourers' wages were inadequate even when work was available. So the peasants came into the towns. Southern immigration into the Northern cities, which became a familiar pattern after 1950, began on a large scale in the 1930s. By 1931 over half the population lived in municipalities of over 10,000 people. Rome expanded from under 700,000 inhabitants in 1921 to 1.4 million in 1940; indeed, Rome grew more rapidly than any other city in Western Europe in the inter-war years, and Milan was not far behind.

The cities not only grew but were transformed. In Milan, the artisans and workers were pushed out from the centre. Their houses were replaced by office blocks, and they themselves by clerks and businessmen. Milan became a commercial city, dependent on commuters – a strange new breed who vanished at night along suburban railways. Turin was different. It remained a predominantly industrial city, with its cars, light engineering, printing-presses and typewriters, but it became bigger, and it became more 'Southern'. The city took in 31,000 immigrants a year in the 1930s, particularly from Apulia and the Veneto. In Milan, too, most of the homeless were Southern immigrants, especially Apulians. The old dream of 'making Italians' was coming true in unexpected ways.

As for Rome, imperialism united with archaeology in a frenzy of 'romanità': the city was to be the visible seat of a new Roman Empire. Thousands of houses were pulled down, and much of the medieval and Renaissance city was contemptuously destroyed. Perhaps only the coming of the Second World War saved the rest. The city centre began to appear much as it had in the Dark Ages, a desert dotted with ancient ruins; but there were new monuments too. A new Triumphal Way, *Via dell'Impero* (now *Via dei Fori Imperiali*), replaced the houses between the Capitol and Colosseum. It covered over much of the old Roman Forum area, which had just been laboriously excavated; but no matter, for it symbolized the new Empire built on the structures of the old. A vast area south of Rome was set aside for a 'Universal Exhibition', to be held in 1942 on the twentieth anniversary of the March on Rome. The exhibition was never held, but the buildings were started, and after the war 'EUR' (*Esposizione Universale Romana*) was turned into a luxury suburb, much celebrated in Antonioni's films. Five thousand people in the Borgo district were made homeless as the government constructed yet another symbol of triumph, the *Via della Conciliazione* leading to the Vatican.

So just as peasants flooded into Rome, many ordinary houses were destroyed. Where, then, did the immigrants – and many native residents – go? The lucky ones went to huge new working-class estates on the 'periphery' – Primavalle, San Basilio, Pietralata and the rest – hideous wastelands bereft of many basic services, but prudently sited near military barracks. The unlucky ones went to makeshift shanty-towns. Neither group had much chance of an industrial job, apart perhaps from demolition and building work. In that sense the city was not transformed. Rome remained the administrative centre for Church and State, a place for tourism and idle pleasures. Rome preserved her *romanità*, in short. But all around arose the desolate new suburbs, with their isolated but menacing sub-proletarian inhabitants. The Fascists boasted of their new Imperial Rome, the Rome of Julius Caesar and of Mussolini; but it was the Rome of Pasolini that they built.

It was not altogether their fault. The government tried, Canute-like, to stop the tide of urban immigration. After all, urban unemployment was a good deal more visible and dangerous than rural underemployment. In 1928 the Prefects were given powers to send unemployed migrants back to their place of origin; in 1931 a 'Commissariat for Internal Migration and Colonization' was set up, which could send people back to their own province if they moved without its permission. In 1938 people could only be registered as unemployed (and thus hope to find an official job) in the municipality (*comune*) where they were registered as being resident. A nice refinement followed. In July 1939 it was laid down that you could not transfer your officially registered residence to a municipality with over 25,000 inhabitants, unless you already had an official job there; but, of course, because of the 1938 law you could not get a job there unless you were already registered. Yet all these laws were ineffective. Prefects did not use their powers, except to send back troublesome individuals, as they had done for decades on public order grounds. The 1931 Commissariat spent most of its time settling peasants on 'improved' land, i.e. moving rural people from North to South against the current, rather than dealing with urbanization in the other direction. The 1939 law was overwhelmed by the war. There was a great deal of propaganda, both about rural virtue and urban vice, but little real action, and none capable of reversing the profound long-term changes in Italian society.

This was also true of other aspects of Fascist population policy. Mussolini did not merely want more people in the countryside; he also wanted more people. The 41 million Italians of 1931 were not enough. Indeed, one of the main reasons for trying to 'ruralize' Italy was the fact that rural people were more fertile. Once again, government policy was a mixture of propaganda (for example, Mussolini's Ascension Day speech in May 1927) and prohibition (for example, of birth-control information or equipment); but there were also incentives. Family allowances, introduced in the 1930s, became an important part of a wage-earner's income (see §12.2), and there were also tax reliefs – although you had to have ten children before you were finally exempted from income tax. Some of the new measures were imaginative. 'Marriage loans' cost 89 million lire in 1939: part of the loan was cancelled every time the happy couple produced another child. 'Marriage grants' to newly-weds cost a further 55 million lire, and 'birth grants' to the newly-fecund came to 86 million lire; there were special prizes for the super-prolific. Jobs and promotions in the civil service were reserved for the fertile married; after 1938 university professors had to be married. Over 1 million Italian bachelors paid a 'celibate's levy' (it raised 230 million lire in 1939); only priests, soldiers, and the infirm were exempt, and after 1937 even the servicemen had to pay for their privilege. The tax was extraordinarily high – by 1936 a thirty-year-old bachelor had to pay *double* his normal income tax, plus 155 lire p.a.

Yet, once again, it did not work. Italians contrived, somehow, not to have too many children. Despite the bachelor tax, there was no rush to the altar, at least until 1937. Non-marriage remained socially acceptable – 8.3 per cent of Italian men aged over 50 were bachelors in 1936 – and fairly late marriage remained the norm (the median age in 1936–40 was 28.3 for men, 24.9 for women, almost a year higher than in the early 1920s). The birth-rate declined steadily at least until 1936, and went below replacement level in some Northern and Central regions. By 1936 there were 102.7 births for every 1,000 women of child-bearing age; in 1911 there had been 147.5. Admittedly more of the children now survived – infant mortality in 1938 ranged from 6.41 per cent in Liguria to 14.9 per cent in Basilicata, with a national average of 10.4 per cent – but even so Mussolini's demographic policy had clearly failed. However, the various provisions were not totally futile. They may have prevented the birth-rate falling even lower, and the Fascist National Agency for the Protection of Motherhood and Infancy, by putting a stop to the iniquitous old orphanages, helped to lower infant mortality. Even so, by 1937 a note of hysteria was evident in government pronouncements, as the figures kept coming out wrong. Many of the provisions in favour of large families were increased or tightened up. Thereafter the birth-rate did rise slightly for two or three years, at least according to some measures.

Population policy – *la politica della razza* – was closely linked to other major policies – ruralization, land improvement, and the 'Battle for Wheat' – and also to more general issues, such as religious observance, autarchy and *italianità*. Ultimately they were all geared to Empire and to war. Mussolini wanted '60 million Italians' by 1950, enough to populate an Empire or to fight a major European war of attrition; without births 'there will be no Empire, we will become a colony'.[12] Apart from hindering emigration, he failed in every respect. As Melograni remarks, Italy (or rather, Northern Italy) 'became an industrial country precisely during the years of Fascist ruralization'.[13] Northern

Italy also became a society of small urban families during the years of pronatalist propaganda. Furthermore, because of the First World War Italy remained a predominantly female country during all the years of masculine posturing and aggression (there were 957 males to every 1,000 females in 1931). In 1950, as it turned out, there were only 47.5 million Italians – and no Empire.

Pronatalist policies naturally had most impact upon women. The Fascist attitude to women was, frankly, male chauvinist. Women were to be 'exemplary wives and mothers', 'guardians of the hearth', subject to 'the legitimate authority of the husband'. 'War is to man what motherhood is to woman' proclaimed the *Duce*.[14] Certainly females were not to have jobs, if the government could help it – and the government could sometimes help it. The State railways, for example, sacked all women taken on after May 1915, unless they were war widows; and women were discouraged in private industry as well, except for 'female work' (e.g. as telephone-operators, secretaries, etc.). The decline of textiles, which had traditionally employed a female labour force, was also a major blow to women's chances of a job. Admittedly there was more work available in shops and domestic service – the servant problem was perhaps the only social question that the Fascists ever solved – but essentially a woman's place was in the home, preferably pregnant.

As jobs became scarcer, more women stayed on at school or even began to go to university. In the long run the Fascist regime probably helped, rather than hindered, female emancipation. It mobilized women into public organizations – 500,000 'Rural Housewives' by 1939, another 500,000 'Fascist Women' in the party. It helped with summer holidays and advice on child-rearing, it encouraged female sport in general and women athletes like Ondina Valle in particular, and it kept girls out of dead-end jobs. In 1925 it even gave women the vote at local elections, a huge concession marred only by the fact that there were no more local elections. Above all, it greatly expanded the educational opportunities for women. By 1935–36 17.4 per cent of university students were female, compared with less than 4 per cent before 1914. Women were not allowed to apply for the most competitive jobs in senior secondary schools, but that simply meant that Latin, Italian, History and Philosophy were taught by men, whereas Mathematics, Physics and Chemistry continued to be taught by women. This was an apt comment on Fascist male chauvinism.

13.4 EDUCATION

So, too, was the shift in Italian education from technical to non-technical subjects. The Fascists inherited a 'three-stream' system of secondary education: the *ginnasio* and *liceo* for the social élite, the technical schools and technical institutes for the commercial middle classes, and the *scuole normali* for girls wanting to become primary teachers. The second of these streams had expanded rapidly since 1900, and by 1922–23 had over 140,000 pupils, twice as many as the traditional *ginnasi* and *licei*. The Fascists soon changed all that. In 1923 Giovanni Gentile, as Minister of Education, reorganized secondary education. Henceforth children would spend five years, not four, in primary schools. Most of those staying on at school would then enter a '*scuola comple-mentare*' where they would receive a general academic education lasting three years. These new schools replaced the old technical schools, which were abolished. The new 'complementary schools' did not give access to the technical institutes, nor indeed to anything else. They were simply junior secondary schools, and one Senator suggested that above their doors should be inscribed 'Abandon all hope ye who enter here'.[15] Children who wanted a technical education had to avoid them, and go direct to technical institutes at the age of eleven. The technical institutes were, therefore, given junior classes, but even so only about half as many children attended these courses as had gone to the old technical schools. And what the technical institutes were given at one end of the age-group they lost at the other. Their physics and maths departments were hived off, as were the 'modern' departments of the *licei*, into new four-year 'scientific *licei*' for the fifteen to eighteen-year-olds. Only the 'scientific *licei*' gave access to university science and engineering, although pupils from the technical institutes could still enter the university economics and business studies faculties. The other secondary schools, i.e. the *ginnasi* and *licei*, and the *scuole normali*, remained basically unchanged, except that special girls' *licei* were set up, and the *scuole normali* were renamed '*istituti magistrali*' and given an extra year's classes. The new system was far more complicated than the old. Another stream had been added, the '*scuola comple-mentare*', which provided secondary education of a kind for more people; but access to, and the status of, the technical institutes were greatly reduced, as was admission to the university science faculties. Gentile reorganized the curriculum as well as the schools. More stress was put on Italian literature and history; and Latin, previously restricted to the *ginnasio–liceo* stream, was introduced to the technical institutes and the *istituti magistrali*, as well as to the 'scientific' and girls' *licei*. Philosophy – especially ethics and epistemology – was to be taught not only in the *licei* but in the *istituti magistrali* and even in the 'scientific *licei*'. Indeed, it was supposed to become the key subject, unifying the pupil's studies and encouraging individual thought.

The effects of these changes were considerable. Many people acquired a rhetorical style of abstract 'thought' that unfitted them for more vulgar concerns. Indeed, the schools prepared people only for more education. After 1928 university students became more numerous – their number doubled in the 1930s – but most of them were training to become lawyers, civil servants, teachers, or professional intellectuals. Italy produced fewer engineers, scientists and doctors in the late 1930s than in the early 1920s. Admittedly economics and business studies became one of the most popular faculties, with 13,000 students in the late 1930s, and these people may have contributed to the post-war 'economic miracle'; but for the most part Italy's schools and universities were becoming 'parking lots', where youths passed their days acquiring the pieces of paper essential for a bureaucratic career.

In short, Italian education assumed some of its contemporary character-istics. Most children, even most girls, went to primary schools by this time. Illiteracy slowly declined – although in the South 21 per cent of brides could not sign the marriage register in 1936. Secondary schooling was becoming more common (there were over 500,000 secondary pupils in 1938–39) but it was formal, often pedantically so, and was more impractical than in pre-Fascist times. And Gentile's other major innovation, State examinations at the end of secondary education, provided a great boost to private, i.e. 'Church', schools. This was a lasting achievement, and it ensured that many more pupils came under clerical influence (see §12.4). Some of his other innovations were less durable. Parents were so unwilling to send their children to the 'complementary schools' that in 1930 these schools were replaced by 'schools of preparation for work', from which pupils could pass to technical institutes or to teacher-training colleges. And in 1939 Giuseppe Bottai, as Minister of Education, recast the schools system yet again. Manual labour was brought into the last two years of primary school, the 'schools of preparation' were renamed 'artisan schools', the technical schools were partially restored as 'professional schools', and the other streams of eleven- to fourteen-year-olds – previously at *ginnasio*, technical institute or *istituto magistrale* – henceforth attended a single three-year lower secondary school with a common curriculum including the vital Latin. This new junior secondary school fed into the normal streams – *ginnasio–liceo, liceo scientifico*, technical institute and *istituto magistrale* – at age 14. The junior secondary school remained until 1962 the sole channel to any kind of higher education; below it, the 'artisan' and 'professional' schools trained the peasants and artisans of the post-war world.

13.5 CONCLUSION

Previous chapters have argued that Fascism was essentially a *military* regime. So, too, Fascist economic and social policy was essentially military, indeed militarist. Fascist agriculture was a strategic resource designed to feed an army; Fascist demographic policy was supposed to breed one. The industrial sector became a vast 'military–industrial complex', geared to armaments and Empire. The regime can, therefore, be assessed in military terms. Did all the effort at mobilization and *italianità* really help to 'make Italians', or to make weapons? Was Italy an efficient military machine in 1939? The answer is clearly no, she was not. By 1939 the regime had become more unpopular than ever before. Land reclamation had been virtually abandoned, pronatalism had evidently failed, and the economy as a whole faced bankruptcy. Worst of all, both the army and navy still lacked modern weapons. Admittedly other countries, including France and Britain, were in like state, but they had not been trumpeting their military values for the previous seventeen years. Fascist Italy failed by her own criteria and, in failing, transformed the Italian economy and society once again.

REFERENCES

1. Luigi Albertini's phrase, in letter to D'Atri 28 Oct. 1922 (in L. Albertini, *Epistolario 1911–26*, iii, Milan 1968, p. 1594).
2. P. Ciocca and G. Toniolo, *L'Economia Italiana durante il Fascismo*, Bologna 1976, p. 36.
3. R. Romeo, *Breve Storia della Grande Industria in Italia*, Bologna 1961, p. 173.
4. Giorgio Fuà's figures, quoted in Ciocca and Toniolo, *L'Economia Italiana...*, p. 189; F. Repaci, *La Finanza Pubblica nel Secolo 1861–1960*, Bologna 1961, pp. 168–70, gives over 21 billion lire, i.e. over 50 per cent.
5. A. Niceforo and G. Galeotti, 'Primi risultati dell'inchiesta alimentare condotta in varie provincie d'Italia', in *Quaderni della Nutrizione* (1934); quoted in S. Somogyi, '100 Anni di Bilanci Familiari Italiani', in *Annali dell'Istituto Giangiacomo Feltrinelli*, ii (1959), 176–79.
6. Letter to Giuriati, March 1927, quoted in P. Melograni, *Gli Industriali e Mussolini*, Milan 1972, p. 198.
7. Circular to the Prefects 15 Feb. 1930, in *ACS*, Seg. Part. del Duce, Cart. Ris., b. 28, f. 28.
8. Archbishop of Reggio Calabria, pastoral letter to clergy 8 June 1930, quoted in M. Mariotti, *Forme di Collaborazione tra Vescovi e Laici in Calabria negli ultimi cento anni*, Padua 1969, pp. 279–80. A national wheat-growing competition for priests was held every year after 1930.
9. C. T. Schmidt, *The Plough and the Sword*, New York 1938, p. 68.
10. O. Vitali, *La Popolazione Attiva in Agricoltura attraverso i Censimenti Italiani*, Rome 1968, Table 1.
11. *ibid*.
12. *Discorso dell'Ascensione*, Rome 1927, p. 23.
13. P. Melograni, *Gli Industriali...*, p. 261.
14. Speech to Parliament 26 May 1934, in *Scritti e Discorsi*, ix, Milan 1935, p. 98.
15. Senator Tamassia, quoted in M. Barbagli, *Disoccupazione Intellettuale e Sistema Scolastico in Italia*, Bologna 1974, p. 218.

CHAPTER FOURTEEN

Fascist diplomacy and Fascist war

14.1 FOREIGN POLICY

Foreign and military policy were the key activities of the Fascist State. It was predictable that the Fascists, nursing the grievances of Versailles, would be expansionist, and fairly brutal in their methods. But Mussolini was also erratic. He was no diplomat, and seemed incapable of taking a long-term view. Far from being the cold, tough-minded realist of Fascist mythology, Mussolini was a shrewd, insecure journalist, ever liable to be carried away by his own bellicose mythology, and ever seeking further military glory on the cheap. He relied on intuitions, not appraisals; he mouthed slogans instead of analysing situations; he was obsessed with his own prestige rather than his country's interests – or rather, he identified the two. As his rise to power in the 1920s had shown, Mussolini knew how to manoeuvre, how to play people off against each other, how to threaten and bluff, how to make propaganda, how to exploit temporary advantages; but he knew little of other countries, and he ignored the underlying strategic realities. For him, foreign policy could not be a cautious matter of making compromises and gaining limited advantages. It was an exhilarating game, played for high stakes. It was also a marvellous way of rousing and transforming the recalcitrant Italian masses. As he told his Foreign Minister in 1937, 'When Spain is finished, I will think of something else. The character of the Italian people must be moulded by fighting.'[1] And so it proved.

Furthermore, foreign policy was in his hands, at least after 1926 when Contarini, the head of the Foreign Office, resigned. His Foreign Ministers had some influence, but did not take the key decisions; his diplomats and ambassadors were usually ignored. The king's occasional efforts to suggest moderation simply goaded Mussolini into resentful wrath. Churchill's famous remark in 1940, about Italy having entered the war because of 'one man, and one man alone', was true of many earlier decisions as well.

Mussolini's early ventures were at least limited in scope. In August 1923 an Italian general, heading an Allied commission to draw the frontier line between Greece and Albania, was assassinated. Mussolini promptly bombed and occupied the Greek island of Corfu, on the grounds that the Greek government was responsible for the murder. Eventually the Greeks apologized and paid an indemnity; the Italians withdrew. But the Corfu episode, however revealing of Mussolini's aims and methods, was untypical. Mussolini needed to reassure foreigners, and he had few weapons with which to do anything else. In any case, Italy had little real quarrel with the Versailles settlement in Europe, and could not raise frontier disputes without risking the loss of German-speaking South Tyrol. So Italy acted respectably, and played her part at the League of Nations. In 1924 Yugoslavia was at last persuaded to recognize Fiume as being part of Italy. In October 1925 Mussolini turned up in person at Locarno, in Switzerland, to initial the treaty settling the French–German border. Britain and Italy settled their frontier questions in Somalia and Libya. All this did not stop Mussolini meddling in the Balkans, but that was a relatively harmless Italian tradition, annoying only to the French who were doing the same thing.

Another traditional area of meddling was Africa. In the 1920s much effort and expense were still going into 'pacifying' the Sanusi tribesmen in Libya; by 1932, this done, Mussolini began to look further afield. An obvious target was Ethiopia, where Liberal Italy had suffered her disastrous defeat in 1896, and where the prestige pickings therefore looked good. The Italian army could probably defeat the Ethiopians fairly quickly, given enough transport, and Eritrea would provide the necessary bases. The only real problem was diplomatic. The British and French would hardly approve of a rival European Empire arising in East Africa, next to the Sudan and threatening Djibouti. But by January 1933 the British and French had another preoccupation – Hitler. They might be persuaded to turn a blind eye in Africa, in return for promises of support in Europe. So Mussolini set the diplomatic and military machine in motion. While the generals planned their Ethiopian campaigns, the diplomats squared the French, and tried to square the British. In January 1935 the French Foreign Minister, Pierre Laval, signed a series of Franco-Italian agreements in Rome; in April the Italians, French and British met at Stresa, reaffirmed the Locarno treaty and agreed to contain Germany; in June the Italian and French generals signed a military convention, agreeing to act together if Hitler were to threaten Austria. All seemed to be going well. But Britain let the *Duce* down. People in Britain worried less about Hitler than the French did, and they were more attached to the idea of settling international disputes through the League of Nations. Few people felt much sympathy for the bullying *Duce*, or saw any particular reason to buy him off. In August 1935 Britain moved the Home Fleet into the Mediterranean, as a vague threat against Mussolini's war plans. This bluff failed. The fleet had very little ammunition, as Mussolini probably knew, and by this time Mussolini's preparations were too far gone: he could not stop without excessive loss of prestige.

On 3 October 1935 Italian troops invaded Ethiopia. Mussolini had acted alone, against the advice of the king and most of the generals, and had defied the British. Soon Italy had to face the League of Nations' economic sanctions –

a ban on taking Italian exports and on supplying her with strategic imports, although oil was not included. Economic sanctions failed, as usual. Indeed, they provided a marvellous occasion for propaganda: Italy was self-sufficient, and could defy the world. Meanwhile Italy poured troops and equipment into East Africa – 400,000 men by December 1935, another 250,000 early in 1936. This was no minor colonial skirmish. The whole nation was mobilized for the cause; 250,000 married women, including the queen, donated their wedding rings to boost the gold reserves (they put steel rings on instead, although steel was more use in wartime than gold). By May 1936 Marshal Badoglio's troops had defeated the Ethiopians, partly by using mustard gas. Adowa was avenged at last. From the balcony of Palazzo Venezia in Rome Mussolini proclaimed the founding of the new Italian Empire, with Victor Emmanuel III as Emperor.

It was his finest hour. Mussolini had triumphed *contra mundum*. The Empire was popular, and so was the *Duce*. Italians flocked to Ethiopia, to escape provincial boredom and to make their fortunes. But in every other respect the conquest of Ethiopia was a disaster. The economic cost was huge, and became huger: in the next few years it bled Italy dry (see §13.1). Militarily, the easy victory led to complacency: the navy and the air force seemed to be the strongest in the Mediterranean. Meanwhile there was disquiet in Whitehall, for the same reason. The 'Mediterranean crisis' of August 1935 ensured a rapid improvement of British naval and air strength, which paid off handsomely in 1940. Diplomatically, Italy was left isolated in a hostile world. The agreement with France was shattered. The British, Italy's traditional allies, never forgave Mussolini.

Mussolini, overconfident, drew the wrong lessons. Italy did not need false friends like the British or French. She could go it alone. The democracies might complain at the League of Nations, they might even try to wreck the Italian economy, but they would not fight. And they were scared of Hitler, as was proved by their failure to act when Hitler marched into the demilitarized zone of the Rhineland in March 1936. If Italy flirted with Germany, the British and French would be even more scared. They would turn more blind eyes, make more ineffectual gestures, at anything the Italians might do in Africa, in the Balkans, in the Middle East – who knows, perhaps even in Tunisia. They would swallow anything, to keep the *Duce* out of a real German alliance. His calculations were short-sighted. Despite the new Empire, Italy was not a Great Power. Nor was she even the 'determining weight' in the European balance of power, as Mussolini thought. He overestimated Italy's bargaining position; and he underestimated Hitler.

By October 1936 Mussolini was talking about a 'Rome–Berlin Axis', and was beginning to fight alongside the Germans, in Spain. Italy had no particular interest in the Spanish Civil War, but the French (now led by Blum's Popular Front government) were backing the Republicans, so Mussolini supported the Nationalists. If General Franco won, France would have lost a Mediterranean ally, and Italy would have gained one. There might also be other benefits – possibly the concession of naval bases in the Balearic islands.

Ideology no doubt played some part. Franco was hardly likely to set up a Fascist regime in Spain, but many people in France and Britain thought he would, and at least he was safely anti-Communist and anti-Socialist. Certainly Fascist Italy did not want too many close neighbours under Left-wing control.

So in 1936–37 Mussolini poured 'volunteers' and aircraft into Spain. The troops achieved little, except to lose face for Fascism at the battle of Guadalajara (see §12.5), but the 1,400 pilots, the 400 fighter planes and the 200 bombers destroyed Republican supply lines, and bombed British and French shipping in Spanish ports – eleven British ships were sunk or seriously damaged in the early summer of 1938. That wrecked any prospect of reconciliation between Britain and Italy. Altogether, Italian intervention in the Spanish Civil War was another diplomatic disaster. It drew Italy into Hitler's embrace, it provided Mussolini with yet more evidence that the democracies were unwilling to fight even when attacked, and it further alienated influential people in France and Britain. It also distracted Italy from realizing the implications of what was happening in Central Europe and indeed on her own frontier. In March 1938 Hitler annexed Austria, and became an obvious threat to Italian security.

Another threat was the existence of over 200,000 discontented 'Germans' (i.e. German-speakers) in Italy's South Tyrol region. Hitler realized this clearly. He always proclaimed that the South Tyrol 'Germans', unlike their counterparts in the Sudetenland or in Poland, were of no concern to him. The Great German Reich stopped at the Brenner, and Hitler said so publicly in Rome two months after annexing Austria. Even so, South Tyrolese unrest remained worrying. In 1939 the *Duce*, therefore, offered the inhabitants of the South Tyrol the 'option' of voluntary 'repatriation' to Germany–Austria. He was almost certainly trying to get rid of a few troublemakers rather than an entire population, but in fact three-quarters of the German-speakers, i.e. about 185,000 people, 'opted' to leave. Many of them, no doubt, did so without having any real intention of going – the plebiscite could be seen as an excuse for the Germans to annex the region, or simply as a demonstration of ethnic solidarity. Still, it looked for a time as if the South Tyrol might be cleared of its German population (that was not how it worked out: see §14.5).

Mussolini was still playing along with Hitler, in order to wring concessions from France and Britain, and to extend the new Empire. It was a dangerous game, but to some extent it paid off. In September 1938 he won prestige by posing as peace-maker between Germany and the West over Czechoslovakia, as the man who had restrained Hitler and single-handedly avoided a world war. In March 1939 Hitler marched into Prague anyway. A few weeks later Mussolini annexed Albania, although it was already virtually an Italian protectorate. In May 1939 Italy increased her stake on Germany. She signed the 'Pact of Steel' with Hitler, committing herself for the first time to a military alliance. This was a very foolish move. Mussolini and his youthful Foreign Minister Galeazzo Ciano (the *Duce*'s son-in-law) clearly underestimated Hitler's designs on Poland. Indeed, they thought that Hitler had promised not to start a war anywhere before 1943, so there were no staff talks or military build-up after the Pact. Mussolini's heart was still set on winning gains in the Mediterranean and Africa – Corsica, Djibouti, Tunisia, perhaps Malta or even Egypt. His policy in 1938–39 was essentially still that of manoeuvring for advantage among the contending Powers, meanwhile hoping that a European war would be avoided. But the Pact of Steel reduced his room for manoeuvre, and threatened to trap him in Germany's war.

In August 1939 Ciano visited Hitler and Ribbentrop at Salzburg, and was told there the horrifying news. Germany intended to make war on Poland. He returned to Rome 'completely disgusted with the Germans, with their leader, with their way of doing things. They have betrayed us and lied to us. Now they are dragging us into an adventure which we do not want and which may compromise the regime and the country as a whole.'[2] Clearly Italy had to abandon the Germans very rapidly, but that presented problems. The *Duce* worried about his honour, and about Italy's too – he had talked at length in 1937 about 'the necessity for redeeming Italy's reputation as a faithless nation'.[3] And, of course, he wanted any spoils that might become available. Still, Ciano worked on him, as did others. Ciano and the army High Command had the bright idea of sending Hitler a huge list of urgently needed munitions, without which Italy could not possibly join the fight. That did the trick. On 3 September, when war began, Italy remained 'non-belligerent', a felicitous term coined by the *Duce* himself to avoid using the hated word 'neutral', with its overtones of 1914–15. The Italian people were greatly relieved. The Nazi alliance had been unpopular even with many Fascists, and the prospect of suffering British air and naval bombardment in order to help aggrandize Hitler was hardly appealing.

So Italy stayed out of the war, or rather out of the 'phoney war' of 1939–40. Mussolini made vague offers of mediation: once Poland had been partitioned, he thought there was no point in continuing the war. In January 1940 he told Hitler he could never defeat the British and French ('the United States would never permit the total defeat of the democracies'); he should attack Russia instead.[4] But Italy's extravagant claims on France were not dropped: the *Duce* would not mediate for nothing. This manoeuvring could be maintained indefinitely as long as neither side looked like winning, and perhaps if the war had turned out to be a tedious, lengthy slogging-match like 1914–18 (as most people assumed it would) then Mussolini might have had some chance of success. But Hitler had other ideas. In the spring of 1940 the war suddenly became real. The Germans invaded first Denmark and Norway, then Belgium and Holland. By mid-May they were on the verge of defeating France. Meanwhile the British had cut off German coal shipments to Italy. What would the *Duce* do, in these new circumstances?

The answer was that the *Duce* would join in. It must have seemed to him as if he had little choice. Since September 1939 he had been chafing at the bit, desperate to play the warlord, yet mindful of the fearful risks. His military and economic advisers kept telling him that Italy was in no position to fight. Suddenly, in May 1940, it looked as if there were no risks, or few to speak of, and no time to lose. Perhaps, too, Italy might be able to restrain the victorious

Führer. Furthermore, if she did not join in, Hitler might wreak vengeance: for had not Italy betrayed the German alliance, in 1939 as in 1914? Hitler, having absorbed Austria, might well want Austria's traditional Southern regions of Trentino and the South Tyrol, and Austria's traditional Southern port of Trieste. Fear mingled with greed in Mussolini's frenetic mind. Important, too, were his sense of honour, his urge to transform his sheeplike people into wolves, and above all his need to be *doing* something. Mussolini was a bellicose nationalist. He could not sit around in Rome, while the map of Europe was redrawn. His whole past, his whole propaganda, his whole regime had glorified war. Now there was one, and he had to join it.

On 28 May 1940 Mussolini finally decided to join the war, and did so on 10 June. This time there were no enthusiastic crowds shouting for war, as in May 1915; but there was none shouting for peace either. The king, Ciano, and the leading generals were all worried by the prospects, but they were helpless once Germany seemed victorious. Mussolini made a famous speech from the balcony of Palazzo Venezia, setting out Italy's 'Mediterranean' war aims: 'a people of 45 million souls is not truly free unless it has free access to the oceans'.[5] An African Empire, based upon control of the Mediterranean, had been the one constant theme in his policy; it was not surprising that it had led to conflict with Britain and France.

14.2   THE WAR: CAMPAIGNS

Mussolini in 1940, like Salandra in 1915, looked forward to a short, sharp war. A quick campaign in the Alps, a share in the booty, and another triumph for the regime: that was what he expected. And that was what he got, for the first two weeks. On 21 June Italian troops advanced into the French Alps, meeting little opposition except from severe weather: most of the casualties were from frostbite. On 22 June Marshal Pétain's new French government signed an armistice with Germany, and so the Alpine campaign soon ended. But there was little booty. Hitler saw no reason to humiliate the French further, and the *Duce* was strangely unwilling to press his case. Instead, he went home and ordered partial demobilization. It had not been a glorious war, but at least it had been short.

Yet the war was not over. It was still to be fought, not in the Alps but in East and North Africa, in Greece and the Balkans, even in Russia. These zones were remote. They needed long supply lines and specialized equipment. Mussolini had not anticipated anything like that. Nor had his generals, who had as usual assumed the next war would be like the last – a series of Alpine campaigns on Italy's Northern borders. Italy was ill-equipped even for that; she was certainly incapable of fighting lengthy campaigns on two continents. So the rest of the war was a succession of military disasters.

On 28 October 1940 – anniversary of the March on Rome – the Italians suddenly attacked Greece, believing there would be little resistance. In fact, the Greeks defeated the main Italian forces, and indeed captured a quarter of Albania. Even worse, the Italians lost three cruisers and two destroyers at the decisive naval battle of Cape Matapan in March 1941. Hitler had to move in and rescue his ally, and in the spring of 1941 it was the Germans, not the Italians, who took over Greece. The whole Greek campaign was a huge blow to Italian prestige and morale. It had one important political consequence. Marshal Badoglio was made the scapegoat, and was replaced as Chief of Staff by General Cavallero. So the elderly Marshal retired to his club life in Rome, where he was ideally placed to contact Court circles later on.

Africa was next. In the spring of 1941 the Italians lost Eritrea, Somalia and Ethiopia. The Duke of Aosta's army, with 250,000 men, surrendered to the British. The East African Empire was no more. And in December 1940 General Graziani's troops had been chased back into the Libyan desert beyond Benghazi; 130,000 Italian prisoners had been taken, together with 380 tanks. Once again the Germans had to step in, in the shape of Rommel's Afrika Korps. Thereafter the Desert War was fought hard and bitterly on both sides. The Allies lost Tobruk, but in October 1942 Montgomery won at El Alamein, and by May 1943 the entire Axis army in North Africa had surrendered. Libya, controlled by the Italians since 1912, was lost. By then Italy was suffering yet another disaster. In 1941 Mussolini had insisted on sending an Italian expeditionary force to help Hitler attack the Soviet Union – he seems to have thought, as in 1940, that the Germans would win quickly and that they must not win alone. By 1942 there were 227,000 Italian troops on the Eastern front: ill-equipped, and dominated by an overbearing ally.

Low morale contributed much to these defeats, and so did poor intelligence – e.g. about British weakness in North Africa, or about Greek equipment and morale. There were also major errors of strategy. Greece and Russia were campaigns that the Fascists did not need to fight, whereas no sustained attack was made on Malta, vital to Italy's whole Mediterranean and North African position. Nor did the Italians launch major attacks on the British bases at Gibraltar and Alexandria, even though the war was ostensibly being fought so that Italy might cease to be a 'prisoner in the Mediterranean'. It is difficult not to connect these strategic errors with the fact that there were no unified lines of command. Mussolini was Minister of War, Minister of the Navy, Minister of the Air Force and 'supreme commander'; but neither he nor the Chief of the General Staff had more than a skeleton organization. When Cavallero tried to build one up after mid-1941, the navy and air force took little notice of it. The lack of co-ordination, particularly that between navy and air force, had disastrous results. At Punta Stilo, in July 1940, the air force bombed its own ships; at Matapan, the following March, air support arrived too late. Worst of all, the navy had hardly any aircraft-carriers, for the admirals had refused to believe that aerial bombing of ships could be effective, and the *Duce* himself had proclaimed that 'the whole of Italy is an aircraft-carrier'. Without them, Italy could not hope to attack enemy bases, or to control the Mediterranean. The real reason why nobody built aircraft-carriers was that they cut across service demarcation lines, and the same was true of parachutists, marines, and anti-aircraft defence. This last was conspicuous by its absence, which left the Italian cities open to bombing raids, and greatly lowered civilian morale.

The years of neglect had left their mark in other ways. The army had too many senior officers: there were 600 generals in 1939. The military academies were years out of date. The British military mission in Greece was astonished by how poor Italian tactics were, and reported that the Italian field officers were clearly ill-trained and had no idea of what to do, other than advancing to cries of '*A Noi!*'[6] There were, it seems, no plans drawn up for war in the Mediterranean. Military doctrine relied on numbers, i.e. the famous '8 million bayonets', which did not exist and would have made no difference if they had. It also relied heavily on morale, or rather propaganda. In fact, the soldiers' morale was never high. Many of Italy's defeats, e.g. Greece and East Africa, were in the first year of war. By the spring of 1941 the army was used to losing. Rations were low, below 3,000 calories a day, and clothing was far worse than in the First World War, for the Germans had little wool or cotton to spare. Most infantrymen were peasants, as in 1915–18. They were fighting, and dying, far from home for a cause which very few of them understood. They fought, for the most part, with discipline and courage. Nearly 300,000 Italian troops lost their lives in the Second World War. But it was, all too obviously, to no purpose.

But perhaps the essential Italian weakness was in equipment. Minniti has estimated that Italy could not arm more than thirty to thirty-five divisions properly, but she put seventy-five to eighty in the field,[7] then left them to fight modern mechanized warfare without enough tanks or other vehicles. In 1939 the army had only 1,500 tanks, nearly all of them light (three-tonne). By the end of 1940 there were 100 tanks (of all types) a month being produced, and production reached a maximum of 185 in June 1942, but this was still totally inadequate. In any case, many weapons never reached the right combat zones. Italy's best artillery and anti-tank guns were sent to Russia rather than to Libya, where they might have made a big difference in 1942. Furthermore, supplies for Africa had to cross the Mediterranean, patrolled by British submarines and bombers. Losses were not considered excessive until the second half of 1942, but by then they were disastrous, and even in late 1941 General Cavallero estimated that one-third of the tanks and one-quarter of the artillery were being lost in transit.[8] As for vehicles, the army had acquired about 25,000 wheeled vehicles in the four years before the war; another 83,000 were produced in the three years of 'full war' (June 1940 to July 1943), but these were still too few. All too often the Italian infantry in the Second World War moved just as Caesar's legions had done, on foot.

Thus the army remained an infantry army, geared to the First World War and often using the same rifles and cannons. The navy was in rather better shape. In 1939 it had 115 submarines and 155 surface ships, most of them new; but it had hardly any aircraft-carriers and only a tiny air arm, and these proved real weaknesses in distant naval battles. It also lacked radar equipment, and above all it lacked oil – there was only five months supply in

1939, and stocks soon declined. The air force had similar fuel problems, and was worse equipped in other ways. It had at most 1,369 serviceable planes in 1939, including 191 fighters and 647 bombers – of 19 different types! The factories produced almost 300 planes a month in 1940 and 1941, but only 215 by December 1942. In the air quality mattered more than quantity. Italian fighters were too slow: the Macchi 200 had a maximum speed of 500 km.p.h., the Fiat CR 42 of 435 km.p.h., both of them less than a Spitfire's 580 km.p.h. And there were no long-range bombers, able to attack British naval bases in Egypt and Gibraltar. The three services naturally ordered their own arms, without any co-ordination or reference to each other – the Ministry of War Production acquired 'co-ordinating powers' only in February 1943, and only then when arms common to all three were being ordered. The supply problem was the key to Italy's disastrous war. It made many of her defeats inevitable; and it made Italy dependent on Germany, for whatever fuel and weapons the Germans were willing to spare.

14.3   THE WAR ECONOMY

It is easy to list these supply problems; and to explain them. There simply was not enough fuel or raw materials with which munitions could be made. Italy managed to import about 1½ million tonnes of oil a year during the war, mainly from Rumania, but that was less than half her normal *peacetime* requirements. The Italians had controlled Libya for thirty years without noticing any oil; they had to take oil there by sea from Europe, and were down to a month's supply by the end of 1941. Italy's native hydro-electric power could not easily be increased when needed most. So the Italian war effort depended essentially on German coal. The Germans could only send just under 1 million tonnes a month. That was why Italy's arms production was low in the Second World War compared with that of other countries, or even with her own rapid expansion in 1915–18. Steel production actually fell in the war, from 2.3 million tonnes in 1938 to 1.9 million tonnes in 1942 and 1.7 million tonnes in 1943. These were risible figures for a would-be Great Power (Germany produced 23 million tonnes pre-war, Russia 25 million tonnes, Britain 14 million tonnes). Arms production was unimpressive, especially in the first two years: Fiat and Spa together produced 2,550 vehicles a month in 1941, but they had made 4,883 a month in 1938. Many factories lacked coal, oil, iron and steel, aluminium and rubber; there was little even the most enterprising industrialist could do. Only by the spring of 1942 were reasonable levels of arms production reached, but even then the Italians were still often making antiquated weapons like the Macchi 11 tank. In any case, the period of maximum production was brief – spring to autumn 1942. After that, the major industrial cities were systematically bombed. Some large firms – Lancia, Alfa Romeo – were badly disrupted; many smaller firms and skilled workers hastily left for the countryside, and the specialized accessories they had made could not easily be reassembled. To quote the best economic history of these years, 'none of the economic benefits of war were reaped in Italy; its disasters were reaped in full'.[9]

The structure of the Italian economy, therefore, changed remarkably little between 1940 and 1943. It had long been used to State intervention and military procurements. Industrial workers were subjected to quasi-military discipline in 'auxiliary' factories, as in the First World War; but in one respect their bargaining position improved. After October 1939 the Fascist syndicates were allowed to have representatives ('*fiduciari*') in the main engineering factories, to settle individual grievances and smoothe over potential unrest. Wages held up reasonably well until 1943, factory canteens provided extra food off-rations, and family allowances were much increased. But the working week also went up, from forty to at least forty-eight hours, and industrial workers were peculiarly exposed to air raids.

Indeed, Northern Italy was one of the few places where mass aerial bombing proved effective in the Second World War. It disrupted production, it shattered morale, and it forced thousands of people to flee from the cities. In Turin, 25,000 dwellings had been wrecked by the end of 1942; and 500,000 people had left Milan. The bombing also helped provoke the first real labour trouble for eighteen years. In Turin, over 100,000 industrial workers downed tools, usually for short periods, during the week after 5 March 1943; these 'internal strikes' soon spread throughout Piedmont and into Lombardy, Veneto and Emilia. The protests were triggered by the government's decision that only heads of families, who could prove they had in fact moved house, were to receive an 'evacuation allowance' of an extra month's wages. But the stoppages were also clearly political – anti-government, anti-war, anti-Fascist. In some factories, especially in Turin, Communist organizers helped stiffen the protest, and the Fascist syndicate bosses were helpless. Eventually the government and employers promised to pay up, and work was resumed. The strikes were the first mass protest demonstration in Axis Europe; they revealed how weak the Fascist regime had become by March 1943.

It was not, of course, the bombing raids alone which lowered morale. People had to cope with all the inevitable wartime shortages. There was very little heating fuel in the Northern cities in 1942–43, and shoes were virtually unobtainable. Soap became a luxury, as did coffee. Petrol had soon disappeared, and in 1942 private cars were requisitioned. Italian cities became quiet, or at least less polluted, and for a few brief years the tram and the bicycle recovered their old pre-eminence. Real wages may have been maintained, but that is an economist's calculation based on *official* prices, which had supposedly been more or less frozen in 1940. Most basic foods, including bread after October 1941, were rationed. The system seems to have held up until 1943; but the rations were extremely low. An adult civilian was allowed about 1,000 calories a day, even in winter: in 1942–43 the ration was 150 grams of bread a day, 400 grams of meat a month, 500 grams of sugar a month and so forth. This was quite inadequate, especially as the bread was 30 per cent maize. The whole 'corporate' structure of control and intervention provided only a quite inadequate diet. So the black market flourished. By June 1943 bread was being sold in Rome at eight times the official price, eggs at fifteen times; and the city's cats had long since disappeared.

The food shortages were not all that surprising. As in the First World War, half the soldiers had come from the fields; and animal feeds or artificial fertilizers were unobtainable by 1942. So food production fell (the wheat harvest was 6.51 million tonnes in 1943, compared with 8.18 million tonnes in 1938), but that only partly explains the long queues and poor diets of urban workers. Farmers could easily avoid selling their produce at fixed prices to the official agencies. Instead, they could eat it themselves, give or sell it to their relatives, or sell it on the black market. Mussolini himself told his ministers that only a quarter of Sicilian grain went to the State warehouses, most of the rest being smuggled into the towns in carts and sold under the counter.[10] As in 1915–18, many peasant families became relatively prosperous. They began buying land, and inflation soon reduced their mortgages. Sensing their chances, they simply ignored the regime: it was in the countryside, not the towns, that the Fascist system first collapsed.

14.4 PROPAGANDA AND THE PARTY

Yet it was the towns that mattered most politically; and morale in the towns was never high. Police informers in Milan had reported as early as July 1940 that many people were listening to Radio London, and after the fiasco in Greece a few months later 'lack of confidence is very widespread and discontent is growing'.[11] The chief of military intelligence spoke privately, in December 1940, of 'a state of mind similar to that which overcame the French on the eve of their catastrophe. It is the same moral bankruptcy; most people, as in France, want the war to end, at whatever cost.'[12] People spoke out freely, without shame or fear, blaming Ciano, the Germans, or even the *Duce* himself; 'defeatism' was far more widespread than in 1915–18. As food became scarce, as prices rose steeply and as bombing became more frequent, civilian morale naturally grew worse, and by Christmas 1942 it had visibly collapsed – visibly, for slogans began to appear on walls: '*Il Fascismo è Fame*', '*Morte al Duce*', '*Viene Baffone*' ('Fascism is Hunger', 'Death to the *Duce*', 'Moustachio, i.e. Stalin, is Coming').

Moreover, it was not just the man in the street who complained. Fascist party officials stressed that the upper classes, young people and intellectuals were the most hostile to the war. Few private organizations sprang up to help soldiers' families or the war-wounded. The number of university students suddenly doubled, presumably because they were exempt from military service. And Mussolini went out of his way to annoy influential people. In October 1941 he ordered all Sicilian-born government employees working in Sicily to leave the island, an evident sign of his suspicion about their loyalty. There were plenty of Sicilians in government service throughout the country, and it was idiotic to alienate them in this way; the Minister of Public Works called it, in his diary, 'an act of sabotage'.[13] In 1942 Mussolini stepped up his campaign. He brought in a compulsory register of share-ownership, one of the main issues that had frightened the wealthy and the Vatican away from Liberalism in 1920–21 (see §10.2). He even proposed to abolish officers' messes in the army. Mussolini's old contempt for the complacent bourgeoisie had clearly surfaced again, although the rhetoric was partly a response to events – he told newspaper editors in April 1942 that 'we always said we despised the comfortable life, and now the uncomfortable life has arrived'.[14]

That was not, perhaps, a very effective way of cheering people up; but what else could he say? Despite the State radio, the controlled press and the *Duce*'s undoubted gifts as pro-war journalist, government propaganda was feeble and ineffective after 1940. It compared unfavourably even with that of 1917–18. In the First World War Italy had been fighting for Trent and Trieste: incomprehensible ideals, no doubt, to the peasant-infantry, but ones which fired the enthusiasm of many officers and volunteers. In 1940–43 Italy was fighting for – what? For Corsica, Nice, Tunisia, Greece? Or for Hitler? Mussolini recognized the problem. It was put to him that he should use the clergy more for propaganda, but he dismissed the idea: 'How would the clergy explain to the people that we are fighting for Timor and Java?'[15] In these circumstances propaganda just could not succeed. If it bore any resemblance to reality it was liable to be 'defeatist'. The most popular radio commentator, Mario Appelius, was sacked in February 1943 for some incautious revelations. In practice, Fascist radio propaganda was simply abuse of the 'Anglo-Saxons'. That was fair enough in its way, but not too convincing to the millions of Italians who had relatives in the USA.

In any case, the Fascist propaganda machine had rivals. Colonel Stevens of Radio London became a national figure. The BBC's version of events, although no doubt doctored too, was a good deal more credible than RAI's. The Vatican also had a radio; a British Foreign Office official minuted in July 1941 that it 'has been of the greatest service to our propaganda'.[16] Furthermore, it had a newspaper, the *Osservatore Romano*, whose circulation shot up to 200,000, and which on occasion even dared to publish Churchill's speeches, as well as many other items of unwelcome news. The regime could not even produce any popular new songs: such efforts as the *Ode to the Duce* or the *Song of the Submarines* somehow failed to catch on.

Propaganda at home was primarily a matter for the Fascist Party. But the party had not been effective for years. After 1940 all servicemen were allowed to join it, so there were formally 4¾ million members by 1942, but the party lacked organization and credible leadership at every level, particularly at the top. There were constant personal squabbles. In December 1941 the party secretary challenged a government minister to a duel, and had to be replaced. The new secretary was Aldo Vidussoni. It was a symbolic appointment. Vidussoni was twenty-eight years old, and thus represented Youth; he had been wounded in the Spanish Civil War, and so incarnated Valour. But unfortunately he was naive, indeed *fesso*: he had no judgement of men, no skills as an organizer, no gifts as an orator. He inspired derision, not devotion, from the public; and the Fascist old guard detested him as an upstart. The faction-fighting continued more bitterly than ever. Other 'outside' factions, for example the Petacci 'clan' (the family and friends of Mussolini's favourite mistress Claretta Petacci), joined in the *mêlée*. In short, the party not only failed to boost morale, but positively lowered it. Its one success was to divert public criticism away from Mussolini himself, but by late 1942 even that was beyond it.

Thus the party disintegrated from within. 'The party is absent and impotent', lamented Farinacci after the strikes of March 1943,[17] and he was right. The Grand Council had not met since December 1939; the *Duce* had not spoken from his balcony in Palazzo Venezia since June 1940. Admittedly in the spring of 1943 Vidussoni was replaced by a tough-minded ex-*squadrista*, Carlo Scorza, and a new chief of police took over, but by then the whole Fascist regime was crumbling. Reality had caught up with it. The facades of bellicose activism, of controlling the economy, of Youth and Patriotism, all were collapsing in the harsh glare of war.

14.5 ON THE FRINGE

Like earlier Roman Empires, the Fascist one crumbled first at the periphery. The Sicilians nursed their grievances, and founded secret 'autonomous associations' to struggle against the 'Continentals'. In the South Tyrol, most of the inhabitants were '*Optanten*' who had voted to leave (see §14. 1), and who were regarded from 1940 onwards as German citizens subject to German law. So the Nazis set up a Delegation for Repatriation, with its own adminis-tration, its own courts, and its own schools. The whole economy came under German control, and in many rural areas Italian schools were shut down. The 'option' itself was not seriously enforced. By June 1942 only 72,000 South Tyrolese had actually 'gone back' to the *Reich* – most of them only as far as the North Tyrol. Often they did not like what they found – 500 of them were in Dachau concentration camp by April 1940 – and many returned clandestinely to their old homeland. In any case, there were still over 110,000 '*Optanten*' in the South Tyrol, living as German citizens without having to give up their farms. This was the ideal solution from their point of view, and one which they were not anxious to change. There were also 60,000 German-speakers who had chosen to stay, or not bothered to vote: these '*Dableiber*' were victimized as anti-Nazis. The South Tyrol had, in effect, slipped out of Italian hands.

Venezia Giulia was similarly threatened. The Germans, moving down the Balkans to help their Italian allies in Greece, took over Yugoslavia in April 1941. The country was carved up. Croatia became a petty kingdom, and the Italian Duke of Spoleto was made king, much to his horror (he wisely never went there). The Italians occupied, and administered directly, much of

Slovenia and parts of the Croatian and Dalmatian coast. These new areas, bordering on Venezia Giulia and with much the same ethnic composition and history, posed huge problems. The Fascists could not hold them by force; nor could they reconcile the local Slavs to Italian rule, except perhaps by making far more concessions (on schools, use of Slav languages, administrative autonomy, etc.) than they had ever tolerated in Venezia Giulia itself after 1919. By late 1941 the Italians had a Slav revolt on their hands – the first armed Resistance movement in Axis Europe. Terrorist attacks became frequent. Guerrilla bands of the Liberation Front, a nationalist movement mainly led by Communists, controlled much of the countryside. The Fascists tried everything they knew. They took and executed hostages, burned villages, tortured captives; to no avail. By the summer of 1943 the Slovene and Croat Resistance movements were, in effect, alternative governments, and their organizations had spread far into Venezia Giulia itself. The various Slav regions under Italian rule looked like sharing the same fate: the Fascists were losing them all.

14.6 UNDERGROUND STIRRINGS

Fascism was crumbling; what of the anti-Fascists? They were debating and squabbling as usual, either in exile or on the remote Southern islands where the Fascist tribunals had confined them. In 1940 the USA had replaced France as the main centre of intellectual exile, although some individuals like Silvio Trentin remained active in Toulouse, and indeed a 'Committee of Action for the Union of the Italian People' was set up there in 1941 by Communists, Socialists and 'GLists'. But there was no action, no union, and no impact on the Italian people. In America, the formidable Carlo Sforza – aristocratic, anticlerical, ex-Foreign Minister, in exile since 1927, contemptuous of Fascism and of much else, including the king – pressed a rather different case on the State Department: a 'democratic' case, with few unpleasant Socialist overtones and certainly nothing dangerous like full Communist participation in a Popular Front. In August 1942 Sforza helped to organize a Pan-American Anti-Fascist Congress in Montevideo. The congress demanded a 'social and democratic Republic', a new Constitution, and European federalism; worthy aims, if anyone in Italy wanted them. These exiles were out of touch: 1942–43 was a bad time to be a *republican* anti-Fascist, for the king was by far the most likely person to rid the country of Mussolini. There was no point, either, in disdaining the Church and the Communist Party, since they were the only non-Fascist bodies with an organization in Italy.

Yet the exiles were not the whole of anti-Fascism. Indeed, 1942–43 saw the revival of 'indigenous' anti-Fascist politics, after some seventeen years of quiescence. Seventeen years, after all, are not as long as all that: many people could remember pre-Fascist politics, and there were plenty of 'survivors' around, still young enough to be competent. The old intellectual radicalism of

Amendola's *Unione Nazionale* and of the Rossellis' *Giustizia e Libertà* resurfaced in 1942. After much debate, the movement was broadened to include Republicans, Radicals and Left Liberals, and renamed the 'Party of Action' in January 1943. It was, as always, run by professors – De Ruggiero, Salvatorelli, Fenoaltea, Calamandrei – but now the professors had something to do: publishing clandestine journals like *Italia Libera*, proposing reforms that might actually be implemented, drafting Constitutions that might actually be adopted. The Communists also found it easier to spread their propaganda and organize their cells. *L'Unità* began to appear again in mid-1942 as a clandestine monthly, and Umberto Massola's network in Piedmont and Lombardy, although tiny, helped to foment the stoppages of March 1943. Socialists were fewer, but they too still existed and new groups like Lelio Basso's *Movimento di Unità Proletaria* were being formed within Italy. Most surprising of all, a Catholic – but formally 'non-confessional' and secular – party existed again by mid-1942. The new Christian Democrat (DC) party was headed by the old Popular Party leaders, men like De Gasperi, Gronchi, Spataro and Scelba. It was indebted for recruits to the million-strong branches of Catholic Action and to numerous local 'discussion groups'. The Catholics, too, had their clandestine papers, especially *Il Popolo*; they, too, had their plans for the future, including political and trade union liberties and regional devolution; they, too, realized that the hour was rapidly drawing nigh. What was more, they had the Vatican and the Church behind them. That implied international links and information, a ready-made organizational network, and unrivalled opportunities for propaganda.

So four major anti-Fascist groupings – Actionists, Communists, Socialists and Catholics – were showing signs of life. There were also many Liberals or Liberal sympathizers, issuing the occasional manifesto or dropping a word in an important ear. Then there was Ivanoe Bonomi, last Prime Minister but one, still busy twenty years later and claiming to be the heir of Giolitti and of the 'Historic Left'. Bonomi was respected at Court, and had friends among Roman bureaucrats and Southern landowners. He was a key link man in any political intrigue, particularly as he thoughtfully founded his own 'political party', the largely spurious Democratic Party of Labour, in order to guarantee his place at the negotiating table.

Did all this matter? No, in the sense that it was all very limited. None of the opposition parties, not even the Communists, had an effective organization: at the main Fiat works in Turin, there were 80 Communist Party members in March 1943, out of 21,000 workers. The police usually knew what the anti-Fascists were up to, and there were over 1,400 political arrests between March and June 1943. May Day 1943 was greeted by posters and circulars, but by nothing more militant, despite the successful strikes of a few weeks before. But yes, anti-Fascist activity did matter in the sense that these politicians were actually present in Italy and might influence events: Bonomi talked to everyone, the Communists provoked strikes. These people, whatever their faults, were more sensible than most of the exiles. Some of them, like Bonomi and Casati, had served in previous governments; others, like De Gasperi and

Romita, had been prominent in party politics. They had learned to live with each other. In April 1943 Bonomi persuaded all the main anti-Fascist groups, except the anti-monarchist Republicans and Actionists, to join a 'United Freedom Front'. They would all work together against Fascism, and set up a democratic political system thereafter.

Here was something new, and important, in Italian politics: Catholics, Communists and Socialists agreeing to collaborate. And it was not just words. The agreement stuck, through all the vicissitudes of war and reconstruction, through four hard years of tragedy and triumph; for decades it was the foundation of the Italian Republic. So these wartime intrigues did matter. They set up a claim to the Fascist succession, indeed helped to determine that succession. But they did not bring Fascism down. Only the king and the army could do that, and even they needed help.

Finally, a word on the Church in these years. Vatican City was, of course, neutral territory. Yet the Vatican was deeply involved in the war – organizing exchanges of disabled prisoners, providing relief for refugees and orphans, trying desperately to prevent the bombing of Rome, negotiating constantly with all sides. As John Lukacs has remarked, the Vatican's influence during the Second World War 'was very great, far greater than during the First World War; indeed, greater than at any time in the modern history of Europe'.[18] Above all, there was the Church's persuasive role within Italy. Vatican Radio and the *Osservatore Romano* provided alternative sources of information; they, and parishes throughout the country, also diffused alternative values to those of Fascist militarism. In 1917 Benedict XV had called the First World War a 'useless slaughter'. The words were just as applicable to Italy's war twenty-five years later, and although Pius XII was far too fastidious a diplomat to use such a phrase, his Christmas address in 1942 came fairly close, condemning both 'State-worship' and racialism. The Church's attitude was clear. The war had to be endured, but it could not be welcomed. It was, in all probability, a punishment sent by God. This resigned view, much denounced by Fascists and policemen – pastoral letters were often sequestered for 'defeatism' – accorded perfectly with the sentiments of most Italians. It was not defeatism exactly, just scepticism: *pazienza*, soon the war would be over, and then things could return to normal. The Church was speaking for the 'real country' at last. If her voice was muted, that too was a welcome change from the strident tones of militant Fascism.

14.7 THE JULY PLOT

In the winter of 1942–43, as the war was being lost and the Fascist regime was collapsing, the political and diplomatic manoeuvres naturally became more intense. In the background were heard the distant rumble of guns in Libya and bombs on Milan, of strikes in Turin and food riots in Matera, of runs on banks and anti-Fascist congresses; in the foreground, in Rome itself, shadowy figures – some resolute, many fearful – held worried conversations, and sent out oblique signals to friend and foe alike. Another Caesar was about to fall in the Capitol; but how? And should no man else be touched, but only Caesar? How would the Germans, and the Allies, and the Fascists, and the Italian people react? Who would replace the *Duce*? Above all, how would Italy get out of the war? Nothing, in those months, was clear; nothing was inevitable. Italian politics suddenly reverted to its familiar stereotype. It became a vast Renaissance drama, with plots and counterplots around the Court, with passionate loyalties and filial betrayals. The leading actors wore impressive costumes and bore resplendent titles – King, Pope, Marshal, *Duce*, Grand Council – but they all improvised their parts, and they all covered their tracks.

The leading role, as always in a crisis, was that of king. Victor Emmanuel III had been on the throne for nearly forty-three years, and had learned to be sceptical of politicians. He was an intelligent man, but unimaginative, timorous and remote. He was not likely to take any initiative if he could avoid it, let alone one that would risk his Crown. He wrung his hands, and hesitated: perhaps something would turn up. His chief adviser, the Minister of the Royal Household, Duke Acquarone, was far more busy. Acquarone talked to everybody who mattered, put people in contact with each other, and transmitted messages to the king.

If the king were to act, he would need the army. Fortunately the army was still available. It had not been Fascistized, and it remained loyal to its king. It might have lost the war, but it knew its duty – to maintain order at home. Back in May 1940 General Soddu, as Under-secretary for War, had told the king's aide-de-camp that the king should not assume supreme command of the war 'so that the Crown can save the Country if the regime becomes decrepit or even threatens to collapse'.[19] In October 1941 General Hazon, commander of the *carabinieri*, told him that 'everyone is looking to the Crown to be a sheet-anchor if the war ends in defeat', and reassured him that the *carabinieri* and public security forces were 'anti-Fascist in tendency'.[20] General Hazon was obviously 'reliable'; so was the chief of police, Senise (unfortunately he was sacked in April 1943); so was the new Under-secretary of the Interior, Albini; and so was General Ambrosio, who took over from Cavallero as Chief of the General Staff in February 1943. All these men sent messages of devotion to the king, and the implied message was obvious. They would all accept whatever the king decided. They assumed that the king would call on one of his marshals to head a military government; their job would be to preserve public order thereafter.

The king, too, thought that the post-Fascist transition could best be tackled by a military government, although he toyed with various other possibilities (e.g. Bonomi, or Orlando). But he could not carry out a *coup* on his own, or even with the army. That would have exposed the Crown. What if the new government failed? What if there were an unexpected Fascist backlash in the country? What if the Germans moved in? From the king's viewpoint, it was wise to wait until the military situation became absolutely desperate, i.e. until everyone could see that there was no alternative. And it would be even better if some other group took the initiative and overthrew Mussolini first.

There were, in fact, several possible ways in which that might happen, none of them pleasant. The Germans might engineer an 'ultra-Fascist' *coup*, replacing Mussolini by some real hardliner like Farinacci. That would get rid of Mussolini, but would solve no other problems, and it would force Italy to continue her hopeless war. Alternatively, there might be a popular revolt, led by Communists or Republican anti-Fascists – not a likely prospect, admittedly, but a very unwelcome one to conservative monarchists. Far more probable was Allied intervention: after further defeats, Italy would have to offer 'unconditional surrender', and the Allies would impose some political solution of their own. That might not be too bad if the Allies installed Bonomi, but unfortunately the Americans seemed keen on a Sforza government and on a republic. Finally, a group of 'moderate Fascists' – men like Dino Grandi, Giuseppe Bottai, and Luigi Federzoni – might overthrow the *Duce* and negotiate an armistice with the Allies. But these men were not trusted by Allies, Germans or king, and in the unlikely event of them succeeding they might well expect a reward – themselves in government, and a moderate Fascist regime continuing. No wonder the king hesitated. The least bad outcome would be a 'limited' moderate Fascist move against the *Duce*, enabling the king to install a reliable marshal in government before anyone had time to react. But how was this to be managed? And how were the Allies to be squared?

Fortune intervened. On 5 February 1943 Mussolini made the king's task easier by sacking half his Cabinet. Grandi ceased to be Minister of Justice, Ciano to be Foreign Minister, Bottai to be Minister of Education. They now had all the more reason for disaffection, and all the more time to conspire. In March came the Northern industrial strikes. They brought about a strong Fascist reaction and a tough new party secretary, so the dissidents had to act quickly before worse befell them. The strikes also led Farinacci to propose that the Grand Council should be convened, to restore morale. And the war, too, came closer. On 13 May the Axis troops in North Africa finally surrendered. On 9 July British, Commonwealth and American troops landed in Sicily, and met little resistance. Within a week the Western half of the island was in Allied hands, and the Chief of the General Staff was recommending surrender. Finally, Mussolini's rather feeble efforts to persuade Hitler to switch men and arms from Russia to the Mediterranean failed. When he came back empty-handed from his final meeting with the *Führer* at Feltre in mid-July, it was obvious that mainland Italy was completely exposed. In these circumstances Mussolini could not refuse the call for a Grand Council meeting, supported as it was both by the 'moderate' Fascists and by hardliners like Farinacci. So here was a chance for the dissidents to unseat Mussolini by 'constitutional' means.

As for the Allies, the king's task was to persuade them that he, not they, should install the next government; and that they should offer an acceptable peace, preferably in secret. These two points were connected. The Allies would not offer peace as long as Mussolini remained in power; and any new government had to be acceptable to them, or they might not offer peace at all. There was, therefore, much secret Italian diplomacy in 1942–43, sounding out Allied intentions and seeking to discredit *emigré* politicians – especially Sforza – whom the king disliked. Ciano approached the British Foreign Office in November 1942; the heir apparent's wife, the Princess of Piedmont, passed messages from Lisbon; the new Duke of Aosta promised to overthrow Fascism. Nothing much came of these efforts: Churchill was sympathetic but Eden was not. The Vatican, with its international links, was far more useful. In December 1942 the Apostolic Delegate in Washington was instructed to make it quite clear to the US government that Count Sforza

is not thought, by informed people, to be a suitable person for the circumstances mentioned above, if only by reason of his age. He is thought by some to be motivated by anticlerical ideas and sentiments, which cannot fail to arouse anxiety among Catholics . . . in general the Italian *emigrés*, either because of their political outlook which would lead them to repeat the errors and weaknesses of the past, or because of the spirit of revenge and vendetta which it would be difficult for them to avoid, or – especially – because of their inadequate knowledge of the present circumstances and needs of Italy, which have greatly changed in recent years, do not seem capable of the tact necessary to meet the difficulties which would face any successor government.[21]

Thus did the Vatican 'interfere' in Italian politics; and successfully. By February 1943 the Americans were asking Vatican advice on the next government and on the monarchy question. On 22 May the Vatican replied that 'the Italian people is in general attached to the monarchy'; the king should be allowed to choose his Prime Minister – 'governments imposed by other people would certainly not be welcome to the Italian people'.[22] On 29 May Roosevelt's negotiator in Washington told the Apostolic Delegate that the USA accepted the idea of a military government, and promised to negotiate a separate peace – or rather, to accept a separate surrender; the king should be told. At last the way was clear.

Not only clear, but compulsory. If Fascism were not overthrown, the Americans would bomb Rome, thousands of people would be killed, and Italy would suffer the fate of the defeated. These were no vain threats. On 19 July Allied planes did bomb Rome for two hours, killing 1,500 people – including General Hazon, commander of the *carabinieri* – and wrecking the Basilica of San Lorenzo. It was, possibly, a political air raid: if so, it achieved its aim. In the next few days the Minister of the Royal Household made careful arrangements with the army and the various police forces: all was made ready for the royal *coup*.

On the evening of 24 July the Grand Council met at last. Grandi had drawn up a masterly resolution, vague and superficially unexceptionable. It urged that the various State institutions – government, parliament, and corporations – should resume their proper functions. The Fascist regime might continue, but the one-man dictatorship must end. The resolution also called upon the *Duce* to ask the king to resume effective command of the Armed Forces, and with it 'that supreme initiative of decision-making which our institutions attribute to him'. This was the real point. It was a virtual invitation to the king to overthrow Mussolini. The debate was acrimonious and confused, and went on until the early hours of the morning. Many of the Fascist leaders present clearly did not grasp the implications of what they were discussing. In the end Grandi's resolution was carried by 19 votes to 7 (or 19–8 including Farinacci, who voted for a separate motion of his own). Even the *Duce*'s son-in-law, Galeazzo Ciano, voted in favour. The Fascist *gerarchi* had thrown in the sponge. Why? The extreme circumstances of July 1943, with Sicily invaded and Rome bombed, were mainly responsible; but it needed also Dino Grandi's brave initiative among the weary *gerarchi*, and the king's known attitude, to pull it off.

The next afternoon Mussolini visited the king, and was not only dismissed, but arrested. Meanwhile the *carabinieri* took over the radio stations, the post offices and the telephone exchanges; the Ministry of the Interior was occupied, and so was the Fascist Party headquarters. A few leading *gerarchi* were also arrested. A tank division moved into central Rome. It all passed off very quickly and successfully – but then a *coup d'état* is not all that difficult if king, army, police, populace and even most governing politicians are all on the side of the rebels. Later that evening the king appointed Marshal Badoglio to be the new Prime Minister. His government was to be 'technical', i.e. to consist of civil servants and generals, not politicians. The State radio broadcast the news at 10.45 p.m.: Fascism had fallen, but the war continued.

It was a fitting end. The Fascist regime had fallen, as it had arisen, because of war. It had glorified High Politics; and it was overthrown by the monarch, and replaced by a marshal. The new government dissolved party, Grand Council, Special Tribunal and Chamber; the Militia, being armed, was merged into the army. Hardly a Fascist stirred. In Rome, it was as if Fascism had never been. The years of rhetoric and posturing, the Battles for Wheat and Births, the Empire and the Pact of Steel, had left, it seemed, no legacy at all. They had been a bad dream, best forgotten: a mere 'parenthesis', in Croce's phrase. Yet Fascism was not dead yet. It took two more years of war and civil war before the regime finally disappeared. And Fascism did leave a legacy. Post-Fascist Italy was set up as the regime's inverted image: a peace-loving, democratic, decentralized republic, guaranteeing civil liberties and run by men with impeccable anti-Fascist credentials.

REFERENCES

1. *Ciano's Diary 1937–38*, London 1952, p. 32 (entry for 13 Nov. 1937).
2. *Ciano's Diary 1939–43*, London 1947, p. 125 (entry for 13 Aug. 1939).
3. *Ciano's Diary 1937–38*, London 1952, p. 33 (entry for 14 Nov. 1937).
4. For this letter see C. J. Lowe and F. Marzari, *Italian Foreign Policy 1870–1940*, London 1975, pp. 350–52; and E. Faldella, *L'Italia nella Seconda Guerra Mondiale*, Bologna 1959, pp. 16–17.

5. The speech is given in full in R. De Felice, *Mussolini il Duce*, ii, Turin 1981, pp. 841–42.

6. Report dated 27 Jan. 1941, in L. Ceva, *La Condotta Italiana della Guerra*, Milan 1975, pp. 191–92. On the poor training of Italian troops, see also Faldella, *L'Italia nella Seconda Guerra . . .*, pp. 51–52.

7. F. Minniti, 'Il Problema degli armamenti nella preparazione militare italiana dal 1935 al 1943', *SC*, ix (1978), 24; cf. C. Favagrossa, *Perché Perdemmo la Guerra*, Milan 1946, p. 14.

8. Memorandum of Cavallero 19 Jan. 1942, quoted in Ceva, *La Condotta Italiana . . .*, p. 199. Cf. P. Puntoni, *Parla Vittorio Emanuele III*, Milan 1958, p. 94 and p. 98; F. W. Deakin, *The Brutal Friendship*, Harmondsworth 1966, p. 237 and p. 293.

9. A. S. Milward, *War, Economy and Society, 1939–45*, London 1977, p. 97.

10. G. Gorla, *L'Italia nella Seconda Guerra Mondiale*, Milan 1958, p. 242.

11. Report dated 9 Dec. 1940, in P. Melograni (ed.), *Rapporti Segreti della Polizia Fascista 1938–40*, Bari 1979, pp. 128–29.

12. Puntoni, *Parla . . .*, p. 34.

13. Gorla, *L'Italia nella Seconda Guerra Mondiale*, p. 250.

14. G. B. Guerri, *Rapporto al Duce*, Milan 1978, pp. 330–31.

15. Gorla, *L'Italia nella Seconda Guerra Mondiale*, p. 288.

16. A. Rhodes, *The Vatican in the Age of the Dictators*, London 1973, p. 246.

17. Deakin, *The Brutal Friendship*, p. 254.

18. J. Lukacs, *The Last European War*, London 1976, p. 367. This judgment is confirmed by the published Vatican documents: *Actes et Documents du Saint Siège relatifs à la Seconde Guerre Mondiale* (11 vols), Rome 1965–81.

19. Puntoni, *Parla . . .*, p. 12.

20. *ibid.*, p. 77.

21. Mgr Tardini to Mgr Cicognani, 7 Dec. 1942, in *Actes et Documents du Saint Siège*, vii, p. 131.

22. Card. Maglione to Mgr Cicognani, 22 May 1943, *ibid.*, p. 362.

PART FOUR

1943–95

CHAPTER FIFTEEN

Resistance and renewal: Italy from 1943 to 1948

In July 1943 a 'regime of popular unity founded on war' collapsed; it was soon replaced by another regime of popular unity, founded this time on anti-Fascism. This was surprising, considering how tender a plant anti-Fascism was in 1943. Yet there were good reasons for its sudden success. The fall of Fascism left a political vacuum, and Italians abhorred that; the king had less influence on events after 8 September 1943, and could not block the anti-Fascists; the Communist leaders were moderate, and anxious for alliances; clerical politicians joined the other anti-Fascists, rather than setting up as rivals; the Americans were sympathetic and supportive. By June 1944 the anti-Fascist parties controlled the government in Rome, despite the king. By June 1946 they had established a Republic, and were drafting a new Constitution. So a new 'regime' emerged. It looked remarkably like the old pre-Fascist one, especially that of the Giolittian era – but without the king, without the Nationalists, without the militarism and without the High Politics.

15.1 THE FORTY-FIVE DAYS

'The war continues.' That was Marshal Badoglio's message to the Italian people as he took over power on 25 July 1943; but few believed him. Most Italians rejoiced that Fascism had fallen, and thought peace was imminent. Nor did Badoglio himself mean what he said. The war had to continue for a time, it was true, so as to deceive the Germans while an armistice was negotiated with the Allies; but it would only be for a few days, or at most weeks.

Yet the new government failed in its main task. It did not make peace quickly enough, or secretly enough, to get Italy out of the war. It was not altogether Badoglio's fault. The Allies proved reluctant to 'negotiate'; they wanted 'unconditional surrender', although they were not sure themselves what that meant. By mid-August the slogan had become 'honourable capitulation', not much clearer. The Badoglio government sent envoys to Lisbon, Tangiers, and Madrid. They explained that Italy wanted to surrender, indeed wanted to change sides, but could not do so yet. The Germans were pouring divisions over the Brenner and clearly intended to take over the fight within Italy. If the Italians surrendered immediately, the Germans would seize Rome. So Badoglio could do nothing, not even surrender, unless and until the Allies sent parachutists to the Rome area; in that case the Italians would hold the airfields and start fighting the Germans.

Here was a promising basis for negotiations, but there were unforeseen delays. General Castellano, Badoglio's envoy in Lisbon, talked there with British and American generals, but forgot to take a radio with him. So the Italian government knew nothing of the talks' progress until a week later, when Castellano arrived back in Rome (by this time another general had been sent to Lisbon to find out what was happening). Meanwhile Churchill was out of Britain from 6 August to 19 September, conferring at Quebec and visiting Washington. Eventually an agreement was patched up. General Eisenhower consented, not very enthusiastically, to send airborne troops to the Rome area. On 3 September General Castellano signed a secret 'short armistice' (i.e. military only, without political or economic clauses) at Cassibile, near Syracuse in Sicily. The landings near Rome, and the major Allied thrust at Salerno, were to be six days later, and the armistice would be announced then.

The plan misfired. The Germans suspected what was going on, and by 7 September they controlled the airfields. So Eisenhower did not send his parachutists. But he carried on with his Salerno plans, and – despite all Badoglio's pleas – he announced the armistice, at 6.00 p.m. on 8 September. The consequences were as foreseen. In the next three days the Germans took over Rome. Badoglio gave the Italian army no clear orders to prevent this takeover, or indeed to do anything at all. There was some confused resistance by infantry units, and some street-fighting in the city itself, but on the whole Rome was simply left to its fate. Moreover, on news of the armistice Italian troops throughout the country dispersed in confusion, or were taken prisoner by the Germans. The next day Allied troops landed near Salerno and faced a long and bitter battle against the Germans, with negligible Italian support. In North-East Italy, in Venezia Giulia and the South Tyrol, and in Fiume, the Germans took over formal control of their 'new provinces'. On 12 September a daring German commando raid 'rescued' Mussolini from his enforced retreat in the Abruzzi mountains, at Gran Sasso, and took him off to Germany. So the haggling over the armistice provisions – ·over the release of British prisoners-of-war, the handover of airfields, the passing-on of information about German supplies – had come to naught; with one important exception. The Italian navy sailed to Malta, more or less intact, and thereby freed many Allied ships for the Atlantic or Far East. The whole balance of naval power was changed – a fact appreciated by Churchill, if by few others at the time.

But that was the only ray of light. Rome had been lost, the army had disintegrated, the country had become a battlefield for Allies and Germans.

'The war continued', with a vengeance. It not only continued, but devastated the Italian mainland for the next twenty months. Italy was no longer allied to Germany; she was occupied by her instead. Badoglio had failed not only diplomatically, but strategically. He had failed to mine the Alpine passes and tunnels – and thus prevent German troops entering Italy – he had failed to hold the airfields near Rome, he had failed even to organize the city's defences. The Allies found themselves not with one opponent less, but with one campaign more: a long, hard slog up the peninsula, fought by tired troops for doubtful military objectives. Perhaps the botched armistice had even more serious consequences. If the Allies had landed successfully north of Rome, Central and Northern Italy might have been taken quite quickly. By 1944 Anglo-American troops might have swung round into the Balkans, and reached Eastern Europe before the Red Army. This argument, although speculative, gives some measure of Badoglio's (and the Allied) failure.

In the restricted perspective of Italian politics, the most important event of 8–9 September was the king's action. In the early morning of 9 September he, the royal family, Badoglio, the government and the general staff fled Rome to avoid capture. By the next day they were safely installed in Brindisi, on the South-East coast. The king had abandoned not only his army, but his capital. It was an ignominious royal betrayal, and it was never to be forgiven or forgotten. On 9 September Victor Emmanuel III threw away what goodwill he had won on 25 July. His flight was to mean the end of his dynasty three years later, and even before then it greatly reduced royal influence on affairs, amid all the crises and horrors of war. And yet . . . the king's flight was not merely a *débâcle*. Despite everything, he still symbolized the State. He was alive and well, and living in the South. It was not only the war which was to continue.

15.2 THE ALLIES AND THE 'KINGDOM OF THE SOUTH'

Yet the king's Italy had evidently shrunk. Rome and the ministries were in German hands; Sicily already, and most of Southern Italy soon, came under direct Allied rule by the Allied Military Government (AMG); Central and Northern Italy were run by the Germans, or by Mussolini's puppet-regime that the Germans had installed on Lake Garda (see below, §15.3). The Badoglio government 'controlled' only Sardinia and four provinces on the South-East Italian mainland, and even these were only allowed it 'in order to preserve such remnants of dignity for the new regime as had survived the ignominious (though necessary) flight from Rome'.[1] Moreover, an 'Allied Control Commission' was soon set up to 'supervise' the government and the provincial Prefects; the Badoglio administration had minimal independence even in its 'own' areas. Badoglio sought desperately for status. He and the king pleaded to be allowed to join the war as an Ally. Churchill refused – allies have claims to equal status. Even so, on 13 October Badoglio declared war on Germany. Italy became not an ally but a 'co-belligerent' – an ambiguous status, but better than being a defeated ex-enemy. Badoglio's strongest card was that his government had signed the 'military' armistice. In late September he went on to sign the political and financial 'long' armistice. These armistices gave the Allies control over Italian economic and military resources, and great influence over Italy's whole political future. Thereafter it was in their interests to preserve the government that had signed such terms. But in every other respect the Badoglio government was weak. It was supposed to be a military government, but there was virtually no army left – twenty-one poorly-equipped divisions at most, out of the sixty-two that had existed on 8 September. No army, no marshal; perhaps no army, no king.

The Allies – especially the Americans – soon realized the need for a 'broader-based' government, more able to rally Italians to the cause. Even Churchill recognized this, though he insisted that Badoglio must remain in office, and that the armistice terms must be observed. But the king had no particular wish to see the government broadened, and hardly anybody else was willing to broaden it. Anti-Fascist leaders detested the king and the marshal, saw no reason to support the royal military government, and suspected it had signed dishonourable armistice terms. Most anti-Fascists naturally wanted to take over power themselves. In Rome, Bonomi's United Freedom Front changed its name to the 'Committee of National Liberation' (CLN), deplored the king's 'dereliction', and went underground. In Naples, which Allied troops took on 1 October, both Benedetto Croce and the returned exile Carlo Sforza refused posts in a reshuffled Badoglio government; they insisted on the king abdicating and on a new, anti-Fascist government being formed. In January 1944 the anti-Fascist parties held a congress at Bari. They resolved that a 'Constituent Assembly' should be elected after the war to settle the 'institutional question' – i.e. whether Italy was to continue to be a monarchy – and to draw up a new Constitution. The congress also proclaimed the need for the king to abdicate immediately: this was necessary, in Sforza's view, so that a new regime might more credibly 'defend the sacred borders of the fatherland and our old and honoured colonies'.[2] Here was a powerful argument. The king was portrayed as the major obstacle not only to an 'anti-Fascist' government but to the very preservation of the country. Although Victor Emmanuel refused to abdicate, he eventually agreed to allow his son Humbert to become 'Lieutenant-General of the Realm', once Rome was taken. This did not satisfy the anti-Fascists, who still refused to join Badoglio's government. Indeed, at Bari they had elected a *Giunta*, or executive, to act as an alternative and more legitimate government.

By this time the anti-Fascists' 'traditional' supports were gradually coming back to them. As the Allied armies advanced, so more territory was handed over to the Badoglio government – in February 1944 it was 'given' Sicily and most of the South, and the government moved camp to Salerno. These zones now enjoyed a more or less free press, often run by anti-Fascist intellectuals. Local government, too, was coming into different hands. The Allies replaced most Prefects and police chiefs by colourless junior officials. They also appointed 'sound' or 'anti-Fascist' local notables as mayors, a policy which was particularly disastrous in Western Sicily as it handed back local power to the Mafia bosses. The new mayors were often assisted by committees – the doctor, the priest, the schoolteacher, a token peasant; in them the parties could find a platform. Local 'Committees of National Liberation' sprang up in the major cities; and there was ample opportunity everywhere for acquiring weapons and ammunition. In short, the anti-Fascists' position was stronger than it seemed. Time was on their side. The Allies would not rule Italy for ever; and the king's flight had discredited the major obstacle to their ambitions.

The political *impasse* between the Italians reflected divisions between the Allies. Britain had been fighting Italy for three years in the Western Desert, and wanted her armistice reward. Eden detested the Italians so much that even his own officials were said to call him 'almost psychopathic'.[3] Churchill had no love for the anti-Fascists in general or for Sforza in particular: his *Memoirs* describe Italian politics in 1943–44 as 'an endless series of intrigues among the six or seven Leftish parties . . . to get rid of the King and Badoglio and take the power themselves',[4] and he called Sforza 'a useless, gaga, conceited politician', who was probably aiming to become king himself.[5] From his perspective Badoglio was the best bet. Roosevelt, on the other hand, had 600,000 Italo-American voters to worry about, and a Presidential election coming up. The US army had not been fighting the Italians for long, and the State Department had little interest (then) in the future balance of power in the Mediterranean. The anti-Fascists could count on sympathy in Washington, and could play the Allies off against each other.

Eventually Stalin resolved the issue. In March 1944 the USSR officially recognized the Badoglio government. Two weeks later the Communist leader Palmiro Togliatti arrived in Naples from Moscow and announced that the Communists were willing to join the royal government. Most Communists were dismayed to hear it, but Togliatti's new policy – known ever afterwards as the '*svolta* of Salerno' – worked. If the Communists joined the government, the other parties had to join as well, or risk a huge increase in Communist influence. So Togliatti, Croce and Sforza all became 'Ministers without Portfolio', as did Socialist and Liberal representatives. 'Broadening' was at last achieved, mainly by the Russians, or by Togliatti.

The new government was, in fact, broader than it was long. Seven weeks later, on 4 June, the Allies entered Rome, and Crown Prince Humbert took over officially as Lieutenant-General. More significantly, the anti-Fascist leaders in Rome – Bonomi, Nenni, Ruini, De Gasperi, Cianca – emerged blinking from the catacombs. They demanded a new government, led by a civilian; indeed, they demanded to be the new government. The Americans supported this claim; Togliatti and the Communists could hardly oppose it, any more than could Humbert. So Badoglio had to resign. A new government was hastily cobbled together in the Grand Hotel. It was led by Bonomi, and it consisted mainly of leaders of the six parties in the Committee of National Liberation. The Rome CLN had taken over, in a bloodless *coup* against a phantom monarch and against the British. Churchill, who had been away watching the Normandy embarkation, was furious: 'I am not aware, at this present time, that we have conceded to the Italians, who have cost us so dear in life and materials, the power to form any Government they choose without reference to the victorious Powers and without the slightest pretence of a popular mandate.'[6] But there was nothing he could do. It was true that the central CLN represented nobody in particular; but it did represent an idea, the idea of 'national unity founded on anti-Fascism'. That was a powerful formula. It offered a real prospect of 'making Italians' on a new basis, even of overcoming the old divide between 'legal Italy' and the 'real country'.

After June 1944 a 'normal' routine of politics was gradually established in Rome. Everyone agreed that the 'institutional question' could wait. Meanwhile Bonomi, like Badoglio, sought to make his government more credible. He was fortunate in that the Allies were concentrating their resources on Normandy, and so needed more Italian support. The Italians managed to put three divisions in the field by November, although in Sicily 80 per cent of potential conscripts dodged the draft. Moreover, the American elections were approaching, and Roosevelt needed to be seen to be treating Italy well. Accordingly the Allied Control Commission dropped the word 'control' from its title, although not from its activities. In September the Allies announced a huge economic and medical relief programme. In October the USA resumed full diplomatic relations with Italy. The British, too, eventually came round. Bonomi had accepted the armistice terms. Besides, the Communists were looking quite powerful, especially in the North. It might be better to back a reliable old war-horse like Bonomi than risk facing a Communist takeover. On one point the British remained adamant: Sforza was not to be Foreign Minister. Bonomi did not mind. His government pursued reassuringly conservative policies at home, and although it passed tough legislation to punish Fascists and 'purge' the administration, it showed little sign of fanaticism in implementing it.

In November 1944 came another political crisis. The Party of Action and the Socialists were unhappy about the slowness of the 'purge' – only about 500 officials had been dismissed by this time. They were also worried, as always, about appointments. The government insisted on its right to appoint Prefects and other officials in newly-liberated areas, e.g. Florence in September 1944: Rome's writ, not that of the local CLN, should run even in the radical North. The Socialists and Actionists found this doctrine strange. Where did the government's legitimacy come from, if not the CLN? The obvious answer was 'the Crown', but that was not acceptable to them. So they left the government. Bonomi carried on much as before, with Liberal, Christian Democrat and Communist support. The Christian Democrat leader De Gasperi became Foreign Minister, a vital post at that time. The episode showed that the CLN's claim to be the fount of post-Fascist legitimacy could and would be resisted. It also showed that parliamentary politics could be conducted even without a parliament; that temporary majorities could be constructed even without deputies; that Socialists and Communists could split apart even while formally allied. Things were clearly getting back to normal.

15.3 THE REPUBLIC OF SALÒ

But not in the North. There, in September 1943, the Germans had restored Mussolini as head of a new Fascist regime, the 'Italian Social Republic'. Mussolini agreed rather reluctantly to this turn of events. He did not want to be an Italian Quisling, and told Hitler so – an unfortunate *gaffe*, for the *Führer* apparently admired the Norwegian puppet. But the *Duce* soon changed his mind. A Fascist restoration gave him the chance to strut once more upon the stage; and it might prevent direct German rule in Northern and Central Italy. The new government was based, not in Rome which the Allies might take within weeks, but in various Northern cities – the Ministry of Finance was at Brescia, that of Public Works was at Venice, etc. Mussolini himself was at the Villa Feltrinelli in Gargnano, but the regime soon became known as the 'Republic of Salò', for it was in that small town on Lake Garda that the Ministry of Popular Culture was set up; and propaganda was the Republic's chief function.

Fascism, proclaimed the *Duce*, had been betrayed by the king and the Establishment, indeed by some of its own leaders. All those who had voted for Grandi's motion on 25 July were condemned to death. Most had fled, but Marshal De Bono, Galeazzo Ciano and three others were shot in January 1944. Ciano was the *Duce*'s son-in-law, but Mussolini rejected pleas from his favourite daughter to spare her husband's life: treason could not be tolerated, and Fascism could not be sentimental. However, the king was the main target of Mussolini's scorn. It was he who was really to blame for Italy's failures and defeats. Henceforth, said the *Duce*, Fascism would be republican and radical, as well as loyal to its wartime ally.

These were brave words, and Mussolini made some effort to live up to them. The reconstituted party – the Fascist Republican Party – attracted 487,000 members by March 1944, a surprisingly high figure given the circumstances. In November 1943 it held a congress at Verona, and approved an eighteen-point programme, including the promise to convene a Constituent Assembly. In 1944 the government went further. It declared that all large firms were to be 'socialized' – run by a management board on which half the members would be elected by the workers. Basic industries would be run by the State. The new system would replace the defunct corporatism of the 1930s.

The 'socialization' law annoyed Northern industrialists; it disturbed the Swiss, who owned much of Italian industry, and the Germans, who hoped to; and it failed to impress the workers. Indeed, the Communists organized a successful general strike in March 1944, with up to 500,000 taking part, just after the measures were announced. In practice, hardly any firms were 'socialized' – just the newspapers and publishing houses, and they only nominally. Few people believed in the new radical Fascism. Nor were the leaders of Salò new radical Fascists. They were either the same old conformists and careerists as before – Buffarini Guidi at the Interior, Marshal

Graziani at Defence, Tarchi at the Ministry of Industry – or else fanatics like party secretary Alessandro Pavolini and 'Racial Inspector' Giovanni Preziosi. The civil servants and judges were also the same officials as before: most of them avoided taking the oath of loyalty to the new Republic, but they kept their jobs.

The government's real problem was that it had responsibility without power. All the old colonies had gone, as had Slovenia, Dalmatia, and the Southern third of Italy. Venezia Giulia and the South Tyrol were separate regions, run by *Gauleiters* with no allegiance to Salò. Even in the Republic, the Germans ran practically everything. They controlled the government's telephones, and censored the government's letters. Hitler's ambassador, Rudolf von Rahm, and Himmler's man, SS General Karl Wolff, had far more power than any Fascist. The Germans kept 600,000 former Italian soldiers in internment camps in Germany, and used them as cheap industrial labour. They tried to transfer machinery, indeed whole firms, to Germany – many units of Innocenti were in fact moved from Milan in 1944. They insisted on calling up youths for military or 'industrial service', i.e. forced deportation to Germany. And they deported at least 7,500 Italian Jews to German concentration camps; 6,885 of them died there, mostly in the gas chambers.

The Germans also gave orders to the Republic's army and police. Not that the Republic had much of either. Marshal Graziani, as army commander, had 45,000 reliable men at most, plus a varying number of ill-armed conscripts – perhaps 80,000 early in 1944 – liable to desert at any moment. There were also 40,000–50,000 men in coastal battalions or anti-aircraft units, and various semi-private armies, e.g. Prince Valerio Borghese's *'Decima Mas'* (Tenth Torpedo-boat Squadron). These forces were quite inadequate for war, but like the party membership figures they show that Mussolini's Republic had some support; desertion was easy, after all. As for the Republic's policing, it was a tragic farce. The *carabinieri* were dissolved as being too monarchist – it was they who had arrested Mussolini on 25 July – and a 'Republican National Guard' was set up to replace them as the main police force in the countryside. The GNR, with a nominal 100,000–150,000 men, was basically a mixture of the old royal *carabinieri* and the old Fascist Militia; but it was ill-trained and inexperienced, except for the *carabinieri* within it. The ex-*carabinieri* squabbled with the ex-Militiamen, and were reluctant to hunt down anti-Fascists; they frequently deserted. The GNR soon had to withdraw from most rural areas, literally leaving the field free for anti-Fascist partisans.

But the GNR was not the only police force. The Ministry of the Interior had its own Republican Police – the old 'public security' forces – in the cities. These were professional policemen, suspected by the Germans of being too soft on anti-Fascists and Jews. The party ran its own 'Black Brigades' – *squadristi*, in short, for fighting anti-Fascists. Giovanni Preziosi had his own special force for hunting Jews; the Germans had the SS. Furthermore, most prominent Fascists retained their own private police forces, which robbed and murdered the citizenry at will, quarrelled fiercely among themselves, denounced rivals to the Germans, and carried out 'dirty tricks' for other police units. Almost anybody could run a 'special police force'. All you needed was a handful of criminal thugs and a political protector. Buffarini Guidi, the Minister of the Interior, backed the 'Koch band', run by a sadistic cocaine addict named Pietro Koch. Roberto Farinacci supported the 'Muti', a mercenary company of 2,300 men, much used against partisans in the hills. These and other 'police groups' spent much of their time on private enterprise – bank-robbing, industrial espionage, kidnapping and political blackmail.

Mussolini looked on helplessly. Occasionally he sent a vain protest to Hitler; once, in December 1944, he went to Milan – in an open car! – and roused the Fascist faithful with a stirring speech. But he knew he had lost, and lost ignominiously. The Republic of Salò was a grisly parody of the old Fascist regime. It failed to protect Northern Italy from German savagery, and it finally destroyed the myth of Mussolini as all-powerful *Duce*. He was revealed as an impotent *poseur*, mouthing futile slogans. It is difficult not to feel some sympathy for him. He was an old man, defeated in life, wasted by sickness, abandoned by his daughter, surrounded by a squabbling family, bullied by the Germans, without friends and without hope. Still, he deserved his fate. He was an arrogant bully, and he had miscalculated. As the war crept nearer, he attempted to negotiate with the Allies. But so did General Wolff; and the eventual German surrender made no provision for the Fascist leaders. On 25 April 1945 Mussolini fled with his mistress Claretta Petacci for a romantic last stand in some Alpine redoubt. Even this was denied him. Communist partisans caught up with him at Dongo, on Lake Como. On 28 April he was shot in the back, and his body was brought back the next day to Milan to be hung up, face downwards, for public execration in piazzale Loreto. The other leading *gerarchi* – Farinacci, Arpinati, Starace, Buffarini Guidi – were shot too; Preziosi killed himself. Many lesser figures escaped, sheltered by friends or business contacts, but no matter: the anti-Fascists had killed the *Duce*, and had dramatically demonstrated their vast new power.

15.4 THE RESISTANCE

The Salò Republic's most spectacular failure was in maintaining public order. This was not just because of inadequate policing. Right from the start, in September 1943, there were huge numbers of ex-soldiers, without orders but often still armed. There were also escaped British, Greek and Slav prisoners-of-war (50,000, according to some estimates); and there were urban evacuees of all kinds wandering through the countryside, many of them very anxious to avoid German and Italian officialdom. Half the population of Tuscany is said to have moved during the year after September 1943, usually from town to country.[7] Such men formed the first 'armed bands', living in the hills and woods of Central and Northern Italy. Sometimes they were outsiders terrorizing the local peasants, more often they were local men – e.g. returned soldiers – helped and fed by them. In either case they were real outlaws. In some rural areas they became a virtual mass insurrection, especially in the spring of 1944 when Mussolini's government called up three more age-groups, and when the Germans stepped up their deportations of workers to Germany. The young men took to the hills to avoid this fate. By June 1944 the army High Command estimated there were 82,000 'rebels', and Marshal Graziani told the *Duce* 'call-up to the army is practically void. The mass of young people prefer to take to the *maquis* . . . rather than go to Germany . . . In practice the government of the Italian Social Republic controls, and that only up to a point, the stretch of plain astride both banks of the Po. All the rest is virtually in the hands of the so-called rebels, who are supported by large sections of the population.'[8]

It was not surprising that most peasants supported them. They had sons of call-up age too. Moreover, the 'rebels', or rather the 'partisans', gave 'help' in wage negotiations with landowners, and helped the peasants to fiddle their grain quota allocations. The partisans seized part of the grain that the peasant was supposed to deliver to the authorities, and gave him a 'receipt' for double the amount they took. The Fascists accepted this receipt at face value. The peasant could then sell the other half of the grain on the black market, at ten times the price the State would have paid him. He made a lot of money, and the partisans obtained peasant goodwill as well as free food. The system depended, of course, on collusion, or fear, on the part of the local Fascists, but there was usually no problem about that.

The partisans specialized in surprise attacks, in sabotage and blowing up bridges, in seizure of booty and political assassination. This was a real guerrilla war – rural, small-scale, improvised, mobile, a war of fierce hatreds and cruel local vendettas, with plenty of scope for individual heroism and cunning. And it was savage, on both sides. Anti-Fascist sources later claimed that 35,000–40,000 partisans and around 10,000 'civilians' were killed in Central and Northern Italy from the autumn of 1943 to the end of the war. Some whole villages were massacred. Here was a new kind of anti-Fascism. It was not the squabbling, self-important exile politics of pre-war years, nor the jockeying for position of Bari and Rome, nor even the disciplined, tenacious underground organizing and pamphleteering of Communist tradition. It was a spontaneous popular rising, local rather than national, military rather than political, often anti-city and anti-State rather than specifically anti-Fascist. It was very unexpected, caused by the sudden collapse of the old order and by the sudden German occupation; yet it was very 'traditional' too – a primitive war of rebels and bandits, fighting against the hated 'authorities', often to avoid conscription.

Here was a marvellous opportunity for the anti-Fascist parties in the North. Their leaders had some money, some organization, and some experience of fighting; and their colleagues in the South had contacts with the Allies, who could supply guns, ammunition and food. Thus the party leaders had a lot to offer; in return, they acquired more or less reliable militias – a wonderful asset in an uncertain world. Some bands were founded by parties directly, especially by the Communists and the Party of Action. By 1944 most of the other bands had become party-affiliated. Communist partisans ran the 'Garibaldi brigades'; the Socialists controlled the 'Matteotti bands'; the Actionists manned 'GL'. They all had 'political commissars', charged with propaganda and with ensuring loyalty. This development permitted some tenuous regional and national co-ordination, although it also encouraged rivalries – occasionally Communist and Actionist bands took to fighting each other, and the Christian Democrat 'Green Flame' bands were regarded with much suspicion by the others. But the parties did not really control the partisans. One 'Garibaldi brigade' in Val d'Ossola had a priest as political commissar. Many people simply joined the nearest band, irrespective of ideological colour; others followed a local hard man or ex-army officer into the hills, and he chose his party later, according to circumstances, or chose no party at all.

The parties were not alone in seeking to channel the partisan movement. Some bands consisted mainly of workers from particular firms; many were financed and armed by industrialists, anxious to grant favours that would become repayable later. The owners of Fiat probably gave over 100 million lire in cash to the partisan bands, quite apart from vehicles, petrol, etc. Nor was 'resistance' confined to the countryside. The Communists had their urban guerrillas too, the GAP – *Gruppi di Azione Patriottica* – which were extremely effective, both in killing prominent Fascists and in provoking fierce German reprisals, thus alienating ordinary Italians even further from the regime. There were also factory committees of agitation, sabotaging war production and smuggling out arms and supplies. Many industrial firms helped the slow-down of output, by hiding machinery in Alpine valleys or by obstructing German plans for a transfer to the *Reich*. Above all, there were strikes, repeated, public and defiant – in Turin in November 1943, throughout Northern Italy in March 1944, by Fiat in June, in Milan in September, in Turin in November, in Turin and Milan in March and April 1945. Admittedly they were for higher wages rather than for liberty, but they were effective: production at Fiat was about 10 per cent of normal by late 1944.

Inasmuch as the Resistance was organized at all, the Communists were the major organizers and beneficiaries. In September 1943 the Italian Communist Party (PCI) was still very small, with perhaps 5,000 members, few of them industrial workers. But the party had capable '*cadres*' – dour, tough-minded organizers, experienced in underground work; men, in short, like the party's Resistance leader, Luigi Longo ('Gallo'). Three thousand of them, including Longo, Secchia and Scoccimarro, had just been released from prison by Badoglio, in August 1943. The party also had money, and it had friends over the border in Yugoslavia. So the 'Garibaldi brigades' were soon the most widespread of the partisan bands: they included perhaps 50,000 men, around 60 per cent of all active participants. Moreover, the low living standards of 1944–45 were a marvellous opportunity for propaganda: average daily wages, at constant 1938 prices, fell from 13.91 lire in 1943 to 5.16 in 1944, 40 per cent of their 1913 level. In the chaos and disruption of 1943–45, a well-led party could achieve miracles. The PCI encouraged strikes, campaigned for higher wages, and threatened employers. By January 1945 it had 12,000 members in Turin, and over 70,000 in German-occupied Italy; most of them were factory workers.

In short, the Resistance was a Communist success story. Many Communists wanted to go further. They thought that the armed Resistance was a marvellous opportunity for revolution. Togliatti, in government, was more cautious. He knew the Western Allies were the real power in Italy, and he could not afford to alienate them: American economic aid would be essential for years to come. He also knew that British troops were busy crushing Communist partisans in Greece; he wanted nothing similar in Italy. He was not going to risk all the real Communist gains on one hazardous throw. The PCI in 1943–45 became a major force in the emerging anti-Fascist Establishment – an example, as one British officer put it, 'of dedication to the State and to the interests of the nation rather than the proletariat'.[9] That was enough, at least for the time being.

The 'Party of Action' formed the second largest number of partisan units. There were about 28,000 members of the 'GL' bands by March 1945, about a quarter of the total number of partisans. But most of them were not members of the party, which remained the classic 'professors' party', the party of students and journalists, of men who were zealous, righteous, and not much afflicted by doubt. Yet it was extremely influential. It was the Actionist leader, Ferruccio Parri, who first urged that the partisans must be a people's army rather than just a number of small intelligence-gathering groups. It was the Party of Action which insisted on 'purging' the administration, on setting up a republic, and on radical political change. The Actionists envisaged a second *Risorgimento*, a national uprising that would cleanse away the stain of Fascism and establish a new Jerusalem, lay, radical and democratic. They helped to win the war; but they always had unrealistic hopes of the peace. When the war ended, the 'GL' bands were dissolved. The party, as such, had put down few roots.

The Christian Democrats had less need to build up an organization, for parishes existed already, and so did Catholic Action. Indeed, in Northern Italy the party organization was only formed in March 1944. Many Churchmen were still not convinced that it was a good idea to have a single Catholic party. The Christian Democrat partisans, the 'Green Flames', emerged therefore from Catholic Action (especially the youth movements) rather than from the party. Most priests in Northern Italy were sympathetic to the cause, many taking an active part in the fighting. In Udine, for example, the provincial clergy formally decided that the Germans were 'unjust invaders' whom it was lawful to oppose. The bishops were normally more cautious, but the Cardinal Archbishop of Turin visited partisan units in the hills, heard confessions and celebrated Mass with the guerrillas. Convents and hospitals provided food and refuge, and sometimes stored arms. How many divisions had the Pope? None, but in 1944 he had around 20,000 partisans.

This policy made sense for the Church. She wanted a quick end to the war and a peaceful transfer of power; but she could hardly stand out against popular passions, and it was not prudent to let the Communists, Socialists and Actionists monopolize the Resistance. Fascism was obviously doomed; the Catholics, too, had to establish their credentials for the post-war world. The armed struggle provided these. It also furnished a veto on excessive political or social change, and on any suggestion of anticlericalism. The Resistance was a popular insurrection; it must not become a Communist revolution.

The other two major Resistance parties were the Socialists and the Liberals. The Socialists were allied to the Communists, but were much weaker in organization, and in strategy were often closer to the Actionists: they stressed *political* change (especially the abolition of the monarchy), were horrified by Togliatti's *svolta* in March 1944, were suspicious of the Church, and pressed for a thorough-going 'purge' of officials. The Liberals were fewer, and some of them were suspect as royalist or '*Badogliani*', but they enjoyed much financial support from industrialists and others.

There were, therefore, five main anti-Fascist parties in the North, as in Rome and the South (not counting Bonomi's Democratic Labour Party, which was almost entirely a Southern creation). As in the South, these parties set up local and regional Committees of National Liberation (CLNs), although the parties included were different in each province, and although other people – Republicans, Trotskyists, anarchists, and free-lancers – sat on them as well. CLNs were also set up in factories, offices, transport services, etc., for the task was not just to co-ordinate military operations: 'every liberation committee that arises is another blow struck against Fascism, and is another stone laid to help build the new democratic State'.[10] The CLNs had real power, especially in liberated zones; they ran the fifteen 'partisan republics' which sprang up temporarily in 1944. The Actionists, in particular, hoped that they would continue after the war as the tutors of democracy, purging and uprooting 'the profound roots of Fascism, not just the Fascists'.[11] In Piedmont, the regional CLN founded its own purge commission, which investigated private firms as well as State officials: it condemned the managing director of Fiat to death, although the Allies rescued him just in time.

In January 1944 a supreme politico-military authority, the Committee of National Liberation for Upper Italy (CLNAI), was formed to co-ordinate the activities of both CLNs and partisans. This body soon asserted its claims to power, not only against Germans and Fascists in the North but also against the official government and against the Allies. In August the Allies sent General Raffaele Cadorna, the son of the First World War commander, to the North to 'control' the partisan units. Eventually the Allies agreed to recognize the CLNAI as the legitimate political representative of the Resistance forces, and to entrust it with maintaining public order in liberated zones until an Allied Military Government could be set up; but it was to ensure that all arms were handed over immediately at the end of the war, and meantime the supreme military commander was to be Cadorna. Longo and Parri were made 'vice-commanders'; in practice both of them took more decisions than did Cadorna.

So did the CLNAI, which in the last months of the war burgeoned into a virtual provisional government. Individual parties sometimes acted on their own initiative, but on the whole the party leaders learned to collaborate with each other. In particular, they agreed to proclaim a general insurrection throughout Northern Italy in mid-April 1945, to liberate the Northern cities before the Allied troops arrived; they even agreed on sharing out the official jobs afterwards. The Communists would have acted alone if necessary, but the other parties could not allow that. They, too, realized it was vital to salve Italian honour and secure some political strongholds; so they joined in, however reluctantly in some cases. So did thousands of 'last-minute partisans'. There had been 80,000 partisans in March 1945; there were 130,000 by mid-April, and 250,000 by the end of the month. In the second half of April 1945 the North Italian cities fell to the anti-Fascists. It was the CLNAI which temporarily ran the liberated areas; it was the CLNAI, or the local CLNs, which purged the old officials and appointed new mayors, police chiefs and Prefects; it was the CLNAI which co-ordinated relief work and emergency supplies. And it was the CLNAI which handed over Milan to the Allies, with most public services working.

What was the significance of the partisans' efforts? Militarily, they undoubtedly contributed much to the Allied cause. They deprived Germany of manpower, and helped to tie down German soldiers – twenty-six divisions – and policemen in Italy. Their guerrilla activities were far from negligible. Marshal Kesselring estimated that in just three months, June–August 1944, they killed some 5,000 Germans and put a further 25,000–30,000 out of action.[12] They also helped thousands of escaped Allied prisoners, acquired and passed on information, and disrupted war production, transport of war material, and Fascist morale. However, one should not exaggerate all this. The 80,000-odd partisans did not liberate whole regions by themselves, nor form a people's army, nor hold a front line: Italy was not Yugoslavia.

The real effects were political. The Resistance not only aborted Fascist attempts to restore 'national unity' after September 1943; its leaders could reasonably claim to have achieved a new 'national unity', on anti-Fascist terms. The peasants were 'involved' in the national struggle; the major cities of Northern Italy were liberated by Italians, not Allies. The new political system would not be merely an Allied imposition. The Communist Party benefited most, appropriately since it made the main contribution to the fighting. The Resistance 'legitimized' the PCI, and made it an indispensable pillar of the new 'national unity'. The Communists gained both democratic credentials ('we joined with everyone else in the struggle against Fascism') and revolutionary ones: an ideal combination. But the other parties benefited too. Actionists, Socialists, Christian Democrats and Liberals could all point with pride to dead heroes and to living legends (e.g. Parri or Pertini) as proof of their anti-Fascist credentials. Moreover, for the Northern party leaders the Resistance meant the CLNs – inter-party bargaining arenas, where men had learned to compromise for the common good. This experience had a profound impact on Italy's post-war Constitution-makers, and on the tacit conventions of the post-Fascist political game. Thus an unexpected, rather 'primitive' popular rebellion, with no united social or political programme, with no outstanding military or political leader – there was no Mao, no Tito, in Italy – achieved some surprising results. Post-Fascist Italy was to be a 'party-system', some would say 'partyocracy', legitimized by the overriding ideology of anti-Fascism and national unity.

Just as the First World War had provided political myths and political leaders for a whole generation, so too did the closing stages of the Second World War. The 'values of the Resistance' became sacrosanct. Even thirty years later a major law on public order laid down stiff penalties for any group who dared to criticize them.[13] This ideology was certainly glamorous and in many ways admirable, but it had, and has, unfortunate implications. The Resistance was usually portrayed in subsequent rhetoric as far more 'revolutionary' and far more united than it had been in reality. Post-war Italians looked back with pride to what had in fact been a chaotic period of national defeat, civil war and popular vendetta. The 'values of the Resistance' were vague: they might include romanticizing violence and taking a generously extensive view about who was a Fascist. They might also 'legitimize' not only anti-Fascism, but guerrilla warfare, political assassination, and urban terrorism. If the post-war political regime proclaimed these values too loudly and too carelessly, it was going to lay up trouble for itself later on.

That was one snag. There was another. The Resistance had been restricted to Northern and Central Italy. There had been no popular insurrections in the South, apart from the 'four days' of Naples in September 1943 before the Allies arrived. The old Southern political and economic system remained intact, and the Left parties were very weak. Even in Rome itself there had been no insurrection against the Germans. It was the Vatican, not the anti-Fascist parties, that in 1943–44 had provided an alternative focus of loyalty, had protected the city from bombing, and had sheltered thousands of Jews; and it was the Vatican that in 1944–45, after the city's liberation, continued to provide food and shelter for the city's starving poor and for thousands of refugees, and to maintain close contacts with the government ministries. The Vatican's prestige in Rome had never been higher: even the Chief Rabbi became a Catholic convert in February 1945. Thus the anti-Fascist Liberation of Northern Italy in April 1945 posed the same question as had the Fascist March on Rome in October 1922. Would a new Northern-based élite, with a title to rule based on Northern fighting experience and with Northern ideas and institutions, conquer Rome and the South? Would it take over the State, or would it be absorbed by the system?

15.5 THE WIND FROM THE NORTH

In May 1945 a CLNAI delegation went to Rome. It demanded a new government, more representative of the Northern Resistance. The CLNs in the North should continue running local government, public services and industrial firms. The civil service should be immediately 'purged' and decentralized. There should be jobs for the partisans. The Romans had to agree, at least verbally. Bonomi resigned, and the Resistance leaders were brought into the government. The new Prime Minister was Ferruccio Parri himself, the Action Party leader who symbolized 'the values of the Resistance'. His government was another 'CLN' six-party coalition, but fourteen of its twenty members were Northerners. In Northern Italy, the local CLNs remained in being, and the Prefects and police chiefs they had appointed remained in office. CLN commissars managed the major industrial firms. CLN 'purge commissions' and local partisan groups took their revenge on Fascist officials, managers and landowners: at least 12,000–15,000 people were murdered in April–June 1945, 3,000 of them in Milan alone. It was a passionate wave of collective hysteria and private vengeance, horrible in its impact but understandable in its context, and mercifully brief – although in the 'triangle of death' in Emilia the killings went on for several years.

Yet the Resistance leaders' victory was only apparent. The CLNAI had agreed that all partisans would lay down their arms at the end of the war. Most of them seem to have done so eventually, although rumours of a 50,000-strong Communist military organization circulated for years to come. So Parri had no anti-Fascist militia at his disposal. He could not use a body of armed partisans as a political bargaining counter in Rome, as Mussolini had done twenty years earlier. Worse, not all the partisans became peaceable citizens. Bandits and armed bands flourished in 1945–46, and although many of them were in the South and had nothing to do with the partisans, they all served to alienate public opinion and to discredit anti-Fascism. Thus Parri not only failed to maintain an armed militia, the first task of any revolutionary government; he also failed to maintain order, the first task of any government.

The government also had to cope with the disastrous economic legacy of war. Hundreds of thousands of ex-soldiers and former prisoners-of-war clamoured for jobs. Inflation reached record levels. Prices in 1945 were 24 times the 1938 level, even after a freeze on gas, electricity and rents. The government had no revenue, for the tax system had virtually collapsed. Over 3 million houses had been destroyed or badly damaged, as had most of the country's railway stock, lorries, bridges and ports. Industrial output in 1945 was about a quarter of the 1941 figure, and indeed was about the same as in 1884; the gross national product was about that of 1911, and income per head was lower than in 1861. One survey found that the average Italian took in only 1,650 calories a day in July 1946, compared with 2,650 pre-war.[14] These matters could not be put right quickly, and the government took the blame for disappointed hopes. Again, the comparison with Mussolini is instructive. The Fascists had been able to exploit post-war economic distress. They had come to power only in 1922, four years after the war, when things were getting back to normal and when, indeed, the economy was starting an impressive upswing. Parri had no such luck.

Above all, the government aroused hostility by its efforts at a 'purge'. It was not just public officials who worried about dismissal. Tough decrees had been passed, laying down criminal sanctions against those who had 'collaborated' with the Nazis or with the Salò regime. They could be applied to virtually anyone in Northern Italy who had not actually been a partisan – i.e. to 30 million people. So millions of ordinary Italians began complaining about the injustice of retrospective legislation, and fearing denunciation by personal enemies. The courts often refused to convict, for judges and juries had held Fascist party cards themselves. The Liberals, swamped by protests, withdrew their support from the government. By the end of November 1945 Parri was forced to resign, protesting furiously that his efforts to create a new moral Italy had been sabotaged. Mussolini had conciliated the Establishment; Parri had alienated it. And so the 'wind from the North' blew itself out, after a mere six months.

Parri's government of 1945 was the most 'radical' that Italy had ever had, yet it achieved very little. It did not restore public order, nor 'purge' the administration; nor did it introduce long-term economic or social changes. There were no post-war nationalizations, no Health Service, no Welfare State, no seizing the 'commanding heights' of the economy. Why not? The answer is simply that hardly anybody in power, even among the Communists or Socialists, thought in such terms. The Left-wing parties were, in fact, very suspicious of the public economic agencies (IRI, etc.), and regarded them as a Fascist legacy. They preferred 'hiving-off' to extensive State control; and they preached 'reconstruction' and 'national unity' like the others. The Communist leader proclaimed, in the party newspaper, that even if the Communists were in government by themselves they would still rely on private initiative to rebuild the economy.[15] The Communists insisted that there should be no dismissals, but neither they nor the Christian Democrats had any alternative economic strategy. There was no ready-made blueprint for change à la Beveridge. Politicians wanted merely to end the old 'autarchic' restrictions, to dismantle the corporate State, and to get back to pre-war production levels. In any case, in a six-party government the Liberals and Christian Democrats had to agree to every measure, which in itself precluded radical change; and the Allied Military Government was still formally in charge of most of Northern Italy until December 1945. What the Parri government did achieve, however, was to discredit the Northern Resistance leaders, and the Party of Action in particular. Future governments would still be anti-Fascist party coalitions, but their base would be in Rome, not the Northern hills; and their leaders would be cautious professional politicians, most of whom had been in Rome or the South in 1943–45 and had taken little if any part in the fighting.

The new government formed in December 1945 was led by Alcide De Gasperi, the first Catholic politician to become Prime Minister of united Italy. He was to remain leader of successive governments until August 1953. He led a no-nonsense, 'law-and-order' government, anxious to show that anti-Fascism could be responsible. It abolished the 'Purge Commission', and tacitly abandoned the 'purge'. It sacked the CLN 'commissars' running the big firms, which were returned to their owners. Above all, it replaced virtually all the CLN-appointed Prefects and police chiefs in the North. By January 1946 the State machinery was back in the hands of career officials, who served De Gasperi as they had once served Mussolini. Five months later Togliatti, as Minister of Justice, issued a general amnesty, and most 'purge' cases were immediately dropped. The 'State' had, apparently, triumphed over the 'Resistance'; and it was still recognizably the same State, with the same officials and the same institutions.

15.6 THE 'INSTITUTIONAL QUESTIONS'

Yet that was soon to change. The anti-Fascist parties had agreed back in 1944 that after the war a 'Constituent Assembly' would be elected, and that 'the institutional question' – i.e. whether Italy was to remain a monarchy or become a republic – would be settled either by that Assembly or by referendum. Eventually it was decided to hold a referendum, on the same day as the elections to the Constituent Assembly: 2 June 1946. A month earlier Victor Emmanuel III had finally abdicated, and so the referendum decided the fate of his son, King Humbert II, who had been acting as 'Lieutenant-General' since June 1944. The anti-Fascist parties were fairly solidly Republican, except for the majority of the Liberals and about a quarter of the Christian Democrats. The referendum produced a Republican majority, but only by 12.7 million votes (54.3 per cent) to 10.7 million; there were 1½ million blank or disqualified ballot-papers. All Northern and Central regions, except Latium, voted for the Republic; Rome and all the South voted monarchist, with a peak of 79 per cent in Naples. Italy was still divided into two halves, as it had been in 1943–45; 'the values of the Resistance' flourished only where the Resistance had flourished. This has remained true ever since. The 1946 referendum, highlighting the split between a conservative, monarchist South and a radical, Republican North, proved an excellent guide to subsequent voting patterns: much the same split was still evident in the next popular referendum twenty-eight years later, on divorce. After a few days Humbert II left Italian soil, not without protesting at alleged electoral irregularities. The 'institutional question' was settled. Henceforth the monarchy lived on only in the glossy weekly magazines.

It was the anti-Fascist parties' greatest victory. But what if the departure of the House of Savoy meant that Italy would revert to the Papacy? That was what the Constituent Assembly elections seemed to indicate. The Christian Democrats won 35.2 per cent of the vote and 207 seats out of 556. They were the largest single party, and might reasonably expect to dominate the new Republic. The Communists won 104 seats, their Socialist allies 115; they too were mass parties, and would remain so. Between them, these three parties won 75 per cent of the vote. The other three CLN parties stood revealed as electorally negligible. The Party of Action won only 7 seats, and dissolved itself the following year. Bonomi's Democratic Labour Party had 9 deputies; even the Liberals were reduced to 41. And 30 seats were won by a new 'Party of the Average Man', representing the resentful white-collar workers of Rome and the South, who had little sympathy for anti-Fascism and were still worried about being purged. So the elections of 2 June 1946 abolished CLN government, as well as the monarchy. De Gasperi formed a new government of the three main parties plus the Republicans, who had won 23 seats. He established a pattern for the future. Henceforth the Italian Republic would have three major parties. It would be governed by the Christian Democrats, but always in alliance with other groups. The CLNs were dead; long live the anti-Fascist alliances.

The Constituent Assembly's main task, of course, was not to reveal party strengths but to draft a new Constitution. The task was not too difficult. Neither Catholics nor Marxists had any blueprint for a new State. The Constitution, therefore, enshrined the values of the constitutional lawyers, most of whom were Liberals, although there were occasional concessions to the other parties' particular hobby-horses. The Republic was to be anti-Fascist by definition; anything that smacked of a strong State, of High Politics, was suspect. The Constitution carefully listed, and guaranteed, civil and political liberties. There was to be no one-man government, as in 'Presidential' systems. The President would be a largely symbolic figure, elected mainly by parliament, and influential mainly when a government had fallen: he would then nominate a Prime Minister-designate, whose new government had to seek parliamentary confidence within ten days. Governments were to be Cabinets responsible to parliament, as in Britain. However, it had already been decided to elect parliaments by proportional representation, so no one party was likely to have a parliamentary majority. The Senate was henceforth to be elected, apart from a few life Senators (ex-Presidents of the Republic, etc.). Various 'social rights' – e.g. the right to own property, or to join trade unions – were inserted. Citizens could insist that parliament should debate particular issues, and could challenge most legislation by popular referendum. A Constitutional Court would be set up, with powers to strike out legislation that infringed the Constitution. Judges were to be freed from government control, and regulated by a Supreme Council of the Judiciary consisting of judges and lawyers. The bureaucracy was to be decentralized, and regional governments were to be established throughout the country.

Here was a charter for weak government, unable to dominate parliament or people; a charter for liberty. Yet many of the provisions were too abstract to give much effective protection. A whole series of rights was proclaimed – to freedom from house searches, to free movement within Italy or abroad, to meet in public places, to form associations – but in each case the 'right' might be restricted by particular laws. Article 15, for example, laid down that: 'the freedom and secrecy of correspondence and all other forms of communication are inviolable. They may be limited only by a warrant issued by a magistrate according to the procedures laid down by law.' So telephone-tapping could continue as usual, quite legally. Similarly, the right to strike was to be exercised 'within the framework of the laws that regulate it' (article 40); to this day no such laws have been passed, so the Constitutional clause has remained meaningless. Furthermore, the existing laws were mainly those in Rocco's penal code and the public security law of 1931, and the Constitution-makers omitted to repeal these texts. They therefore remained in force, even though they prohibited precisely the kind of political or trade union activity that the Constitution protected. Moreover, some essential institutions established by the Constitution, e.g. the Supreme Council of the Judiciary and even the Constitutional Court itself, were not set up until the late 1950s. In short, the Constitution was unenforceable, or at least unenforced. Italians soon began joking that the only clause which was actually applied was article 12, laying down the colours of the national flag. The joke was unfair. The powers of Head of State, of government and of parliament in the new Republic were very different from those in the old regimes; and new legislation was bound to be passed eventually. Meantime, Italy had a Liberal Constitution, a Catholic government, and Fascist laws.

On one point the new Constitution was specific, or seemed to be. Article 7 stated firmly that

the State and the Catholic Church are, each in its own sphere, independent and sovereign. Their relations are regulated by the Lateran Pacts. Modifications of the Pacts, accepted by the two parties, do not require the procedure for Constitutional amendments.

Many lay Italians were horrified by this article, and it was only approved with the help of Communist votes – Togliatti being anxious as ever to conciliate the Church. The Church's position was, therefore, guaranteed in the very Constitution of the new Republic. Yet even that was to prove ambiguous. Many Catholics supposed that the *content* of the Lateran Pacts of 1929 had been 'written into' the Constitution; but lay lawyers always argued that article 7 merely stated what was the basis of Church–State relations, and how that basis might be changed in future. Even so, article 7 was a real victory for the Church. And many of the Constitution's other clauses reflected traditional 'social–Catholic' ideals of a weak State, political liberties and small-scale property.

That was particularly true of the Constitution's one extraordinary innovation, regionalism. Christian Democrats from Sturzo onwards had been regionalists; their leader in 1946, De Gasperi, himself came from the Trentino and before 1918 had been a deputy in the Vienna parliament. Moreover, both the Party of Action and the Republicans stood for decentralized government as an essential feature of the new participatory Republic. These arguments seemed persuasive to most Northerners, particularly as the centralized machinery of State in Rome had not been 'purged'. The Communists could hardly oppose regionalism without rousing suspicions about their dictatorial aims; and besides, they might come to power in the Central regions. Furthermore, the professor of constitutional law at Rome University, Gaspare Ambrosini, was a Sicilian who had been a convinced regionalist for years.

Constitutional lawyers have always been taken too seriously in Italy, particularly during a Constituent Assembly when they were drafting the texts.

Above all, regionalism was introduced because it had to be. The strong State had collapsed in 1943. Thereafter there were real threats of revolt or secession in the outlying regions, especially where there were ethnic or linguistic differences from mainland Italy. This was true in Sicily and Sardinia, in French-speaking Valle d'Aosta, in German-speaking South Tyrol, and in the Slav-speaking parts of Venezia Giulia. Foreign powers – France, Austria and Yugoslavia – encouraged the secessionists in all three Northern regions. In Sicily, 'traditional' forms of banditry flourished in 1943–47, provoked mainly by foolish government attempts to reintroduce conscription; many outlaws were enrolled in an independent army led by conservative landowners. The Sicilian élite had little desire to be ruled from Rome at all, and even less to be governed by Northern Resistance partisans.

Italian politicians, faced with powerful groups demanding concessions, acted true to type. They bought them off. 'Separatism' could not be countenanced; but 'regional autonomy' was all right. Sicily, Sardinia, the Valle d'Aosta and 'Trentino-Alto Adige' (see below) became 'regions of special statute'. They were allowed to elect their own assemblies, and were given certain legislative and administrative powers. The local élites could thus preserve their own languages and cultures, their own economies and welfare systems, and their own jobs. Regional agitations died down, so much so that in January 1948 the grateful President of the Südtiroler Volkspartei told De Gasperi 'no one better than you, born in the Trentino, can understand that the desire for autonomous government, rooted in our people for centuries, is not a threat to national unity but the finest way of capturing the hearts of our people'.[16] Even so, De Gasperi took no chances. The German-speaking South Tyrol did not become a region on its own, but was lumped together with the Italian-speaking Trentino: the 'Germans', although allowed back home and guaranteed their language, would always be a minority in the regional assembly of 'Trentino-Alto Adige'. And regional government was laid down not just for the outlying 'ethnic' areas, but for the whole country. It had to look like a constitutional principle, not a desperate political device. Admittedly only the four 'special' regions were actually set up, for the time being, but the Constitution made it clear that the new Republic would not be over-centralized. That was an astonishing departure from the traditions and institutions of united Italy.

The new Constitution, approved in 1946–47, came into force on 1 January 1948. In the meantime the Constituent Assembly had had to accept several unwelcome reminders of the real world outside Rome. The peace treaty, drafted by the victorious Allies and signed in Paris in February 1947, deprived Italy of all her colonies except Somalia, which she retained on a ten-year trusteeship. Eritrea was handed back to Ethiopia; Libya, occupied by the British, became independent in 1952. The treaty also gave France various Alpine territories, including the Mont Cenis plateau and the Tenda and Brig valleys, where the Italians had built reservoirs and hydro-electric stations. Italy retained the German-speaking South Tyrol, but Dalmatia, Istria and Fiume were handed over to Yugoslavia. Italy also had to pay reparations, especially to Greece, Yugoslavia and the USSR. Worst of all, the treaty refused to recognize Italy's contribution to her own liberation. Many prominent Italians were furious. Orlando accused the government of 'lust for servility', and Nitti called the treaty 'a humiliating and odious *diktat*'.[17] Sforza, by now Foreign Minister at last, appealed for 'revision' on the day it was signed. But the Constituent Assembly had to ratify it, under protest. It all showed that being anti-Fascist was not enough. High Politics was unlikely to go away, and Italy had been left defenceless.

The peace treaty did not settle the future of the Trieste area. Most of Venezia Giulia had been occupied by Yugoslav partisans at the end of the war, as had Trieste itself. In June 1945 Tito agreed to withdraw east of the 'Morgan line', so that an Allied Military Government could be set up in Trieste and in the Western rump of Venezia Giulia. The Yugoslavs took over the rest. Negotiations dragged on, inconclusively. The USSR supported Tito; Britain and the USA wanted to show Italian voters the benefits of Western support. Each major Power drew its own line on its own map. Eventually the French line was agreed on for the Northern part. It ran well to the west of the Morgan line, and gave Yugoslavia most of the Isonzo valley and – an important symbol – Caporetto. Italy retained Gorizia, Gradisca and Monfalcone in Venezia Giulia, and Tarvisio in Friuli; but she lost the rest of her First World War gains. No agreement was reached for the areas south of the Duino River. The French line there would have given Trieste and Capodistria to the Italians, but Capodistria was on the other side of the Morgan line and was occupied by Yugoslav troops. So the peace treaty simply termed the whole disputed area in the South 'the Free Territory of Trieste', and it remained divided *de facto* into two zones: Zone A (Trieste), occupied by Anglo-American troops, and Zone B (Capodistria), by the Yugoslavs. Over the next few years Capodistria became incorporated into Yugoslavia. In 1954 the Western Allies handed over Trieste to Italy, after complicated negotiations in London. Relations with Yugoslavia rapidly improved, to the great benefit of both sides.

15.7 THE EXCLUSION CRISIS

In the meantime Italian politics had been transformed yet again. The 'wind from the North' had died down; the problems now came from East and West. An Iron Curtain divided Europe; its shadow fell across Italy. The anti-Fascist alliance of Christian Democrats and Communists was becoming anachronistic. The Communist leader Togliatti began denouncing the government and threatening revolution – extraordinary behaviour for a coalition partner, and explicable only in terms of having to please the Russians, or keep control of his followers. The Church, too, had long been worried about the alliance. Pius XII told Truman's special envoy in June 1946 that his 'main aim has been and is to fight Communism'.[18] In November a Vatican dignitary, possibly the Under-secretary of State Mgr Montini, visited De Gasperi and told him that 'any kind of collaboration with the anticlerical parties, not only in the municipality of Rome but in the government, is no longer admissible. If the Christian Democrats were to continue with such collaboration, they would be considered a party favouring the enemy. The Christian Democrats would no longer have our support or our sympathy.'[19] De Gasperi persuaded his adviser that it was best to wait until the Constitution had been drawn up and the peace treaty signed, but clearly the Church had spoken: no Christian party could ignore her views.

Moreover, the USA was still providing much-needed aid and investment, and was beginning to wonder – rather tardily – whether the money was being well spent. Bankers, at home and abroad, argued that the currency would collapse unless deflationary monetarist measures were taken; but these would increase unemployment, and the Communists could hardly agree to that. Above all, De Gasperi had to worry about the South. It had voted monarchist in 1946, and the 'Party of the Average Man' was strong there. The Southerners wanted the PCI out of government, they wanted American aid to continue, and they wanted jobs. They had to be conciliated. The new Republic was fragile, and the Christian Democrats could not risk the South becoming a focus for Right-wing disaffection.

In May 1947, therefore, De Gasperi excluded the Communists and their Socialist allies from his coalition. But that did not solve all his problems. The Communists might well cause more trouble in the unions and on the shopfloor, now that they were out of office. They might even start an insurrection – the American National Security Council reported in February 1948 that they were 'believed to have the military capability of gaining initial control of Northern Italy'.[20] Or they might win an election, especially if their alliance with the Socialists survived. The obvious tactic, therefore, was to woo the Socialists; but the Socialist leader Nenni chose Togliatti rather than De Gasperi. If the Socialists could not be won over, they could at least be split. In January 1947 Giuseppe Saragat had founded the 'Socialist Party of Italian Workers' (PSLI; later called 'Social Democrats'), an anti-Communist rival to Nenni's party; 52 of the 115 Socialist deputies joined him.

The anti-Fascist parties divided, therefore: Left v. Right, East v. West, Communists v. Christian Democrats. True, there were several other pro-Western parties, e.g. the Republicans, the Liberals and the new PSLI, but the Christian Democrats were the only mass party on the 'Western' side. As the elections to Italy's first post-war parliament grew nearer, the USA increased its anti-Communist investment: shiploads of food, promises of Marshall Aid, pledges on Trieste, guns and ammunition for the police, even posters and leaflets. Thus the Christian Democrats had both America and the Church behind them. Priests and bishops threatened excommunication for anyone who voted Communist; parish halls became electoral headquarters. The Pope himself, in his Christmas message of 1947, warned that 'he who gives his support, his services and his talents to those parties and forces that deny God is a deserter and a traitor'.[21] The Christian Democrats also had a huge organizational advantage over the other parties: Catholic Action. Early in 1948 Luigi Gedda, its president, founded 'civic committees' in each parish, to arouse the hesitant and mobilize the vote. Catholic Action's 1.8 million members became an unpaid army of election workers.

Thus the parliamentary election of 18 April 1948 was held in a fervent, passionate atmosphere of crusading zeal and 'Red Threat', heightened by the Communist seizure of power in Czechoslovakia only two months previously. The Christian Democrats' manifesto was entitled 'Save Liberty'; the party symbol on the ballot-papers was a shield inscribed with the single word *Libertas*. Virtually overnight the party became the Defender of Western Civilization. In the South, the middle classes abandoned the 'Party of the Average Man' and rallied to the Church; even in the North, 15–20 per cent of the Left's 1946 votes switched to the Christian Democrats, and the party defeated the combined Communist–Socialist list in all Northern regions (although not in the Left-wing strongholds of Central Italy). Overall, the 'Popular Democratic Front' of Communists and Socialists won 31.0 per cent of the vote, compared with 39.8 per cent for the two parties in 1946; the Christian Democrats secured 48.5 per cent, compared with 35.2 per cent in 1946, and won over half the seats in the Chamber of Deputies. The Church had, unexpectedly, provided mass backing for democracy.

15.8 CONCLUSION

The election of 1948 established a new 'regime' – perhaps not the rule of the Saints, but the rule of the Clericals. It was a far cry from the days of the CLNs, of inter-party agreements and anti-Fascist unity; a far cry too from the liberal pluralism proclaimed by the new Constitution. Only the Church could protect Italy from Communism, and the Church was not liberal. Moreover, the Christian Democrats necessarily relied on the old unpurged Roman institutions – police, judiciary, Prefects, civil service; and these were not liberal either. All this was much resented by Left-wing Northerners. Their revolution had been betrayed, their claims to rule had been ignored, the State they had created had been snatched from them. They had defeated Fascism after years of hard fighting; they had founded the Republic. Yet within two years another 'one-party regime' had been established, led yet again by a single dominant leader, and excluding them yet again from influence or reward. No wonder they felt bitter. Ever since 1947–48 radical Northerners have seen the Rome Establishment as illegitimate, indeed as 'Fascist'; their resentment has proved a constant source of weakness to the Republic.

And yet the 'anti-Fascist' theme survived, precariously. The Resistance partisans and the Constituent Assembly deputies had not fought and laboured in vain. The Christian Democrat Party may have been clerical, but it was anti-Fascist too; it may have been backed by conservative Southerners, but it was usually led by reforming Northerners. De Gasperi was cautious in victory. His governments, even after April 1948, were coalitions: they included Liberals, Republicans and Saragat's Social Democrats. He governed with the Centre, not the Right, and he was unwilling to be too dominated by Pius XII's Vatican. Moreover, there was room for dissent and opposition in the new Republic. The Communists may have been excluded from government, but they were never outlawed from the system. As for the undeniable social and economic conservatism of the new Republic, that too was 'anti-Fascist' in a way – the Fascists had run a 'planned economy' and a 'Welfare State', and had all but discredited both. Italy by 1948 had turned her back on Fascism, on nationalism, and on High Politics. Imperial Italy had reverted, thankfully, to *Italietta*.

REFERENCES

1. C. R. S. Harris, *Allied Military Administration of Italy 1943–5*, London 1957, p. 74.
2. E. L. Woodward, *British Foreign Policy in the Second World War*, London 1971, ii, 518–19.
3. US Ambassador Kirk to State Dept. 15 July 1945, reporting views of senior Foreign Office officials; quoted in D. Ellwood, *L'Alleato Nemico*, Milan 1977, p. 159.
4. W. S. Churchill, *The Second World War:* v, *Closing the Ring*, London 1952, p. 167.
5. Woodward, *British Foreign Policy . . .* , ii, p. 512.
6. *ibid.*, p. 543 (Churchill to Roosevelt 10 June 1944).
7. G. Bertolo *et al., Operai e Contadini nella Crisi Italiana 1943–4*, Milan 1974, p. 326.
8. F. W. Deakin, *The Last Days of Mussolini*, Harmondsworth 1966, p. 202.
9. R. Faenza and M. Fini, *Gli Americani in Italia*, Milan 1976, p. 112.
10. *L'Italia Libera*, iii, no. 1 (Jan. 1945).
11. 'Stato e Governo', *L'Italia Libera*, ii, no. 5 (Oct. 1944).
12. P. Spriano, *Storia del Partito Comunista Italiano*, v, Turin 1975, p. 365.
13. Law of 22 May 1975 no. 152 ('legge Reale'), art. 7.
14. A. Giovagnoli, 'La Pontificia Commissione Assistenza e gli aiuti americani (1945–48)', in *SC*, ix (1978), 1090.
15. *L'Unità* 28 Aug. 1945; quoted in G. Bocca, *Palmiro Togliatti*, Bari 1973, p. 463.
16. Ammon to De Gasperi 31 Jan. 1948, quoted in M. Toscano, *Alto Adige, South Tyrol*, Baltimore 1975, p. 134.
17. N. Kogan, *Italy and the Allies*, Harvard University Press 1956, p. 170.
18. Myron Taylor to Pres. Truman and Byrnes 3 June 1946, quoted in E. Di Nolfo, *Vaticano e Stati Uniti 1939–52*, Milan 1978, p. 491.
19. G. Andreotti, *Intervista su De Gasperi*, Bari 1977, pp. 72–73.
20. National Security Council 10 Feb. 1948, in US State Department, *Foreign Relations of the USA, 1948*, iii, Washington 1974, p. 767.
21. R. Faenza and M. Fini, *Gli Americani . . .* , p. 273.

CHAPTER SIXTEEN

The triumph of 'Low Politics'

This chapter is about the political system of Republican Italy after 1948. I have already discussed the Constitution adopted in that year, and how it provided for weak government (§15.6); and I have also described how the 'Red Threat' came to dominate domestic and international politics in 1947–48 (§15.7). Thereafter the Communists were excluded from government, despite their anti-Fascist record; the Christian Democrats, permanently in power from December 1945, set up a new conservative regime, respectable and quietist. It was a regime of 'Low Politics', like that of parliament and local government in the nineteenth century: it practised the politics of compromise and patronage, of temporary deals and temporary governments, of granting favours and buying support, and of political 'interference' in administration. Many Italians, therefore, regarded it as inherently corrupt, just as their nineteenth-century predecessors had done.

16.1 PARLIAMENT AND THE PARTIES

The Chamber of Deputies was elected in large multi-member constituencies, using a list system of proportional representation which ensured that the parties held roughly the same proportion of seats as they won votes. Hence small parties could and did win seats: there were rarely less than nine or ten parties represented in the Chamber. The system also ensured, normally, that no one party won an overall majority. The Christian Democrats did so once, in the exceptional 'Cold War' election of 1948, but after 1953 their vote hovered around 40 per cent. They were 'the party of relative majority', but they could not govern alone. The other parties also retained a remarkably stable vote between 1953 and 1972. The Left-wing vote (Communists and Socialists) remained between 35 per cent and 40 per cent; and the Right-wing (Liberals, Monarchists and neo-Fascists) regularly secured between 12 per cent and 15 per cent (see Table 2).

So Italian government was coalition government, and there was only a

Table 2 Votes (%) and Deputies in the Chamber of Deputies 1948–79

	1948 %	1948 D	1953 %	1953 D	1958 %	1958 D	1963 %	1963 D	1968 %	1968 D	1972 %	1972 D	1976 %	1976 D	1979 %	1979 D
Radicals (PR)	—	—	—	—	—	—	—	—	—	—	—	—	1.1	4	3.4	18
Social Proletarians (PSIUP) (Democratic Proletarians, DP, in 1976; United Proletarians, PDUP, in 1979)	—	—	—	—	—	—	—	—	4.5	23	1.9	—	1.5	6	2.2	6
Communists (PCI)	31.0 [bracket]	183 [bracket]	22.6	143	22.7	140	25.3	166	26.9	177	27.2	179	34.4	227	30.4	201
Socialists (PSI)	[bracket]	[bracket]	12.7	75	14.2	84	13.8	87	14.5 [bracket]	91 [bracket]	9.6	61	9.6	57	9.8	62
Social Democrats (PSDI)	7.1	33	4.5	19	4.5	23	6.1	33	[bracket]	[bracket]	5.1	29	3.4	15	3.8	20
Republicans (PRI)	2.5	9	1.6	5	1.4	6	1.1	6	2.0	9	2.9	15	3.1	14	3.0	16
Christian Democrats (DC)	48.4	304	40.1	263	42.3	273	38.3	260	39.1	266	38.8	267	38.7	263	38.3	262
Liberals (PLI)	3.8	19	3.0	13	3.5	14	7.0	39	5.8	31	3.9	20	1.3	5	1.9	9
Monarchists (PNM, later PDIUM) (National Right, DN, in 1979)	2.8	14	6.9	40	4.8	25	1.7	8	1.3	6	8.7 [bracket]	56 [bracket]	6.1 [bracket]	35 [bracket]	0.6	—
Neo-Fascists (MSI)	2.0	6	5.8	29	4.8	25	5.1	27	4.5	23	[bracket]	[bracket]	[bracket]	[bracket]	5.3	30
Others	2.4	6	2.8	3	1.8	6	1.6	4	1.4	4	1.5	3	0.8	4	1.3	6
		574		590		596		630		630		630		630		630

limited number of possible coalitions. There were three main types: 'Centrist' or 'Centre-Right' governments, consisting of Christian Democrats, Republicans, Social Democrats and (sometimes) the Liberals; 'Centre-Left' governments, excluding the Liberals but including the Socialists; and 'governments of national unity', backed by all the main anti-Fascist parties, including the Communists. These three types are in loose chronological order for the thirty years after 1948. 'Centrist' coalitions normally governed the country from 1948 to 1962; 'Centre-Left' ones did so from 1963 to 1972; and thereafter there were serious, if unsuccessful, attempts to bring the Communists fully back into the political fold.

One way of interpreting this story is to see post-1948 politics as a gradual process of 'reconciliation' among the anti-Fascist parties. First the Socialists returned into the system, in the late 1950s and early 1960s; and then, a decade later, so did the Communists. 'Reconciliation' is the polite term for this process; those who dislike it speak of 'absorption', or *trasformismo*. Alternatively, it can be seen as a gradual shift to the Left. The Christian Democrats, bereft of enough support on their Right, were forced to turn to the two mass Left-wing parties (Socialists and Communists) in order to maintain their parliamentary majority. At any rate, the 'Christian Democrat regime' was never wholly Christian Democrat: coalition and compromise were constant necessities.

The major parties were the Christian Democrats (*Democrazia Cristiana*, DC), the Communists (*Partito Comunista Italiano*, PCI), and the Socialists (*Partito Socialista Italiano*, PSI). These three parties normally won between 75 per cent and 80 per cent of the vote. The Christian Democrats were, originally, hardly a party at all, merely a coalition of laymen from Catholic Action, from the pre-Fascist Catholic unions and co-operatives, or from the old Popular Party. Their leader, De Gasperi, tried to win greater autonomy from the Church, and after his death Amintore Fanfani tried to build them up as a nationwide organization; but they were always a heterogeneous, ramshackle party, and their vote remained predominantly 'religious' – even in the 1970s Church attendance was still the most significant correlation with Christian Democrat voting, and at least two-thirds of their voters claimed to have gone to mass the previous week. Not that the DC was simply a 'confessional' party. Anti-Communism brought it much support, even from non-Catholics. It appealed particularly to women (who provided 60 per cent of its votes), to the elderly, to small landowners, and to rural or small-town dwellers, especially in the 'White Belt' of Northern Italy. It stood for anti-Communism, for religion and the family, for peasant landownership and small-scale local enterprise, for co-operatives, profit-sharing and *voluntary* welfare. The DC was a complex, ill-disciplined body with many different local bases and bosses, some of them of dubious origins and talents. Still, it was an inter-class party, as it claimed; it was 'populist', sometimes even progressive; and its support (though not members) remained essentially 'Northern'. In 1963, for example, the DC won over 50 per cent of the vote in only ten provinces: eight of them were in the North, and in the province of Vicenza the party won 64 per cent.

The Communists, on the other hand, began as a well-organized party, indeed as the victorious party of the Resistance. They inherited, or took over, many of the traditional areas of Socialist strength in pre-Fascist times – the rural labourers of Emilia, the share-croppers of Tuscany, the industrial workers of the Northern cities. They soon dominated the 'Red Belt' of Central Italy: their highest vote was in the share-cropping province of Siena, where a quarter of the electorate were party *members*. Organization and discipline were their great strengths. The party built up a network of workplace cells and local 'sections' throughout the land; it had hundreds of full-time officials, organizing not only the party but trade unions and other flanking bodies, running local government, publishing a host of newspapers and local weeklies; and it had ample funds, allegedly seized from Mussolini at the end of the war.

As for strategy, the party proclaimed an 'Italian Road to Socialism', a long-term policy reminiscent of that of the 'intransigent' Catholics in the nineteenth century. Communists were to infiltrate all corners of society, and be 'present' and active in every social gathering. The ultimate aim was to establish Communist 'hegemony', to use Gramsci's term: automatic acceptance of Communist values and leadership. It was a peaceful strategy, with little talk of revolution or bloodshed; but it was uncompromising for all that. These were the years of the 'Cold War' and of ideological struggle. The party preached a rival Gospel to that of the Church, celebrated rival martyrs, and proferred a rival Heaven. Above all, it built up a rival hierarchy.

The Socialist Party was very different. It was badly divided, and it lacked effective organization or leadership. In 1947 the PSI's Right wing split away to form a new 'Social Democrat' Party. The remaining Socialists maintained their alliance with the Communists. They even fought the vital 'cold war' election of 1948 on a joint PCI – PSI slate, thus obscuring the difference between the two parties. In 1946 the PSI had won 20.7 per cent of the vote, the PCI 18.9 per cent; the next time the two parties fought separately was in 1953, when the Socialists won 12.7 per cent and the Communists 22.6 per cent. The Socialists remained largely a Northern party in the 1950s. In 1953, for example, they won 15.4 per cent of the vote in Northern Italy, but only 8.4 per cent in the mainland South and 7.5 per cent in Sicily – where the Communists had already managed to spread their influence and organization.

So had the minor parties of the Right, i.e. the Monarchists and neo-Fascists. In 1953 the Monarchists picked up 15.4 per cent of the vote in the mainland South, and the neo-Fascists won 11.8 per cent in Sicily. Southern conservatives were clearly angry at the Christian Democrats, because of the land reform (see §17.2). As monarchist memories faded, the neo-Fascists were left as the main party of Southern protest. They also won many votes from 'nostalgic' civil servants in Rome. Indeed, by the early 1970s the neo-Fascists had become the fourth largest party in the country. The other three parties – Liberals, Republicans and Social Democrats – were lucky to pick up 10 per cent of the vote between them. The Liberals claimed to be the party of the Northern entrepreneurs, the Republicans that of 'managed' capitalism, and the Social Democrats that of democratic labour – though their critics called them the 'Voice of America', in an unkind reference to their sources of finance.

These political parties were huge organizations, bigger than any other parties in Western Europe. The PCI had over 2 million members every year from 1946 to 1956, and retained at least 1½ million thereafter; the Christian Democrats had over 1 million by 1948, reached 1.6 million in 1963, and peaked at almost 1.9 million in 1973. The Socialists claimed 700,000 members between 1947 and the late 1950s. Why were the parties so big? Giorgio Galli has suggested that Italians had become used to joining a party under Fascism, and carried the habit over into post-war life.[1] This seems unlikely, if only because it persisted for so long.

There were two other plausible explanations, the 'ideological' and the 'materialist'. In the 'ideological' view, the parties were the secular arms of rival Churches and rival sub-cultures. Political rhetoric, therefore, revolved around the great ideological divides: Church–State conflict, East–West relations, capitalism or Socialism. Each speaker appealed to a known, reliable audience, rightly confident that his listeners were even more 'partisan' than he was. Deputies regarded themselves as being responsible to their own parties, or at most to their own voters, rather than to the electorate as a whole. And the parties recruited mainly from huge rival networks of 'flanking organizations' – Catholic Action, trade unions, youth clubs, peasants' co-operatives, tenants' unions, ex-partisan associations, even cinemas and sports clubs – in which the right values were transmitted and the right loyalties rewarded. In short, the parties were not mere electoral bodies, appealing for votes at election time and then vanishing from sight. They were permanent social networks, and mutually exclusive. The Catholic and Marxist 'sub-cultures' were realities, at least in certain regions, and had been so since the late nineteenth century. The electoral system helped perpetuate them, for proportional representation does not much penalize ideological intransigence, and may even encourage it. The parties did not need to court the 'floating voter'; they needed only to rouse their own faithful. Elections did not decide who was to form the next government. They simply gave the voter an opportunity to affirm his beliefs. Italian politics became cast in an ideological mould. It accurately reflected the 'little world of Don Camillo', but it ignored much else, and it was slow to adapt to changing values.

However, the 'ideological' interpretation of Italian parties was not the only one. The parties could, equally plausibly, be seen as huge political 'machines', distributing benefits to members and voters. These benefits were nothing if not material: jobs, pensions, increased pay, cheap seeds, crop insurance and so forth. The voter, in this view, did not express an ideological commitment when he went to the polls. He simply engaged in trade. He sold his vote for cash, or for payment in kind. Italian politics was not about ideology at all; it was about favours, patronage, jobs. That was why parties had huge memberships: it paid to join. The 'flanking organizations' were not so much 'embodiments of social values' as dispensers of material gratifications. However, the two rival interpretations were not really incompatible. Parties could provide both ideological and material resources. A party card could proclaim both a set of beliefs, and a willingness to be helped find a job. And, of course, the parties could base their appeal on different grounds in different regions, or among different classes.

Indeed, the parties were not homogeneous. Most of them were divided into factions ('*correnti*'), each with its own finances, its own journals, and its own organization throughout the country. These factions were sometimes 'ideological' in nature, but usually they were regional, or linked to some pressure-group, or simply the supporters of some leading politician ('friends of the Honourable Moro'), clustering round their man in hope of jobs and reward. They were numerous – the Christian Democrats usually had between six and nine, the Socialists four or five – and they were, arguably, the real parties in Italy.

Furthermore, they too were perpetuated by the electoral system. Most electors voted only for a party, but they could also, if they wished, express a 'preference' for particular *candidates* of that party: almost 40 per cent of Christian Democrat voters did so in 1972. The party's seats in parliament were allocated to the candidates with the most 'preferences'. Hence each candidate had to beware of rivals within his own party, normally much more of a threat than the candidates of other parties. Factions and preference votes were interlinked. The factions helped to group the rival candidates within each party, and channel the preference votes. They gave electors a choice between candidates on different wings; and they limited the personal rivalries and animosities between politicians. They were the real heirs of the shifting parliamentary groupings of pre-Fascist Italy. Only the Communists, true to the Leninist tradition of democratic centralism, had no organized factions; but their voters used the preference vote system to excellent effect in 1948, when 132 'Communist' deputies were elected from the joint list with the PSI, compared to only 51 'Socialists'.

It was factionalism, rather than multi-party coalition government, which was responsible for the instability of Italian politics. From June 1945 to December 1970 there were 28 governments, with an average life of 11 months; they were led by 12 Prime Ministers. Governments rarely fell because of a parliamentary vote or a major policy dispute; but they often fell because some faction leader was discontented. Perhaps his followers had done well in a local or regional election, and felt they deserved better jobs at national level; perhaps government policy was hitting particular groups of a faction's supporters, or failing to reward them adequately; or perhaps he was simply jealous of his rivals. Whatever the reason, his faction would withdraw its backing; and that meant government legislation might be lost, for the deputies' voting in the Chamber was usually secret. Prime Ministers had constantly to reassure and reward everybody; and so did the party secretaries, whose task it was to conciliate the various faction bosses and persuade them to compromise. Indeed, arguably the most important post in the country was not Prime Minister, nor President of the Republic, but secretary of the Christian Democrat Party.

Thus Italian politics was, superficially, complex; but underlying it there was stability, even monotony. Every eleven months the pack was reshuffled; but the same cards kept coming out on top. Some ministers remained in their posts for years, and the key jobs – Interior, Foreign Affairs, Treasury – rarely changed hands. Elections came and went, but the Christian Democrats always ruled. Many of the party leaders in the mid-1970s – Andreotti, Moro, Fanfani, La Malfa, Pertini – had been prominent thirty years earlier, in the age of Truman and Stalin.

Parliament, then, was where the parties and factions competed for jobs and favours. And the individual deputy competed too. He could not rely solely on his party, or his faction; he had to win his own preference votes if possible. He had to find people jobs, he had to arrange for soldiers and officials to be transferred nearer home, he had to write 'recommendations' and give advice on land deals, wills, even marriages. He was the poor man's friend, the advocate in Rome through whom all things were possible. Often he *was* an advocate: lawyers retained, at least in the early years, much of their traditional dominance of parliament, together with journalists and teachers. Another traditional feature was the link with local government: 70 per cent of the deputies up to 1963 had been, or still were, mayors or local councillors.

One of the deputy's main tasks was to push through legislation on his clients' behalf. The Italian parliament approved about 400 laws a year, compared with less than 100 in Britain. Most of them were '*leggine*', little laws, granting favours to small groups of people – raising the pensions of prison warders, say, or subsidizing orphans' homes. Passing such laws was made easier by the fact that Chamber and Senate were divided up into parliamentary committees, or 'Commissions', each covering a major area (Defence, Agriculture, etc.). These 'Commissions' could discuss and amend all bills, but above all they could and did act as 'mini-parliaments', approving over three-quarters of all legislation without any general debate by other members, and usually without press publicity. Deputies could, therefore, push their pet ideas through, or reward their supporters, if they sat on the right 'Commission'; in that way they could build up support and keep their seats.

Even the Communists worked the system, although in their case it was the party machine, not the individual deputy, which dealt with constituents' affairs. The Communists had no factions, nor were their deputies reliant on preference votes. Almost two-thirds of them had been full-time party or trade union officials. They sat for two terms in parliament as part of their bureaucratic careers, and paid back more than half their parliamentary salary to the party. Here was a very different kind of deputy. But the rest of the Chamber conformed surprisingly closely to the pre-1914 pattern. In the 1958–63 Chamber, for example, out of 596 deputies there were 124 advocates, 75 teachers, 36 university professors and 24 journalists, as well as the (mainly Communist) 177 trade union or party officials.[2] Party officials were much more likely to sit for Northern or Central Italian constituencies. Generalizing grossly, the 'typical' Southern deputy was a lawyer, of middle or upper-middle-class background, still practising his profession and resentful of party discipline; the Northern–Central deputy was a Communist organizer, of lower-middle or skilled working-class origins, who had worked long years in local government or the trade unions, and who owed everything to the party.

'Preference' votes at elections, and the 'Commission' system in parliament, had further consequences. Outside pressure-groups like farmers' associations and industrialists' federations needed only to lobby 50-odd deputies instead of 600; the system greatly encouraged their influence on legislation. Furthermore, each deputy had an interest in supporting the schemes of the others; tomorrow it would be his turn to need their votes. So there was no real opposition. The deputies of opposition parties voted for most bills, including those brought in by government supporters. In 1968–72, for example, neo-Fascist, Liberal and Communist spokesmen all declared that their deputies were backing most of the laws going through parliament, and even at the height of the 'Cold War' the Communist deputies voted for almost two-thirds of all laws. Similarly, there was no real government party. Governments could not control the agenda, nor push their own unpopular bills through, nor prevent unwelcome legislation being passed. That was true even for major bills, discussed in plenary session of parliament: in the 1970s laws were passed legalizing divorce and abortion, both strongly opposed by the 'majority party'.

The Italian parliament, in short, was 'scrambled' – government and opposition deputies were all mixed up together. The system gave real influence to minority groups outside parliament, and to factions and 'opposition' parties within. In that way it helped to integrate or 'absorb' them into the general political system. However, there were snags. The economic cost was considerable. And such a parliament was no good at 'controlling' public spending, or at watching over the government or civil service: deputies' questions were usually ignored. Above all, there were always more people wanting favours than could possibly be satisfied. The individual deputy might win popularity, but parliament as a whole lost respect, especially among the high-minded.

16.2 GOVERNMENT, SUBTERRANEAN AND LOCAL

So did the dominant party. From the early 1950s onwards the Italian press was full of tales of scandal and corruption. The Christian Democrats were always in office; and permanent power corrupts permanently. The Christian Democrats, like the Fascists before them, attracted place-seekers. They, too, had to reward or placate these supporters; and they, too, aspired to run a modern industrial State. Moreover, they too had inherited an old-fashioned and unwieldy civil service, slow-moving, legalistic and overmanned. Yet for them it was more difficult than for the Fascists. They could not set up a single-party system, nor after De Gasperi's death in 1954 did they have a single undisputed leader who could control their own intra-party conflicts, nor could they muzzle the press. So what could they do?

The answer was '*sottogoverno*', 'subterranean government': a term that meant much more than the good old nineteenth-century 'interference' in administration. '*Sottogoverno*' implied a consistent, organized effort to bring key ministries under political control. It implied political appointments. Above all, it implied the 'colonization', or creation, of special agencies to run welfare services and huge sectors of the economy – the formation of a 'parallel administration', in short, bypassing the normal civil service. These agencies would employ the party's supporters; and they might also be used to finance the party's activities, both at national and at local level.

Here was 'Low Politics', with a vengeance. It was also a logical continuation of traditional Catholic social doctrine: the numerous associations of civil society were to be taken over and run by the godly. Indeed, the President of Catholic Action had kindly offered to do so back in August 1943, when he suggested to Marshal Badoglio that Catholic laymen – 'morally sound, of proven loyalty to the country and totally free of any partisan passions' – might assume control of the ex-Fascist youth organizations, radio stations, *Dopolavoro* and welfare bodies.[3] After 1945 they did so. They 'inherited' thousands of local or provincial charities (orphanages, etc.), many of them already run by the Church, subsidized by public funds, and regulated still by Crispi's law of 1890 (see §5.6). They also took over 118 major national welfare agencies (the National Agency for Motherhood and Infancy, the National Association for Industrial Accident Victims, etc.), and founded 75 new ones in the twenty years after 1948; and they ran much of State-owned industry as well. Or rather, the State industries and welfare bodies became immersed in Christian Democrat faction politics. A faction leader might reasonably hope to control some agencies; but if the agency was large enough and rich enough, as the State-owned National Hydrocarbons Agency (ENI) was in the 1950s, it might control its own unofficial 'faction' and dominate party policy on energy. Thus was the 'colonizer' colonized.

'*Sottogoverno*' was not, therefore, a simple or direct matter. It was not exactly 'corruption', nor even party control of economic and social resources, nor a genuine 'spoils system'. It was a curious mixture of faction networks and a quest for efficiency, of financing party politics and genuine concern for welfare, of jobs for supporters and moral crusade. It was linked to the 'Commission' system in parliament, to factionalism in the major governing parties, to 'preference' voting and to outside pressure-groups. A huge number of agencies – perhaps 40,000 – were involved. Most of them were local welfare bodies: for example, each of the 8,000 municipalities in Italy had its own sickness insurance fund for peasant landowners. But even these were vital politically, and some – e.g. the provincial Savings Banks and the Industrial or Agricultural Development Agencies – were vital economically. They all provided jobs, and some even provided services.

The Christian Democrats were not alone. Key appointments to major agencies were shared out not only among the DC factions, but also among the various coalition parties. Soon over half the presidents of provincial Tourist Boards were Social Democrats, a surprisingly high proportion for such a small party. When the Socialist Party joined the government after 1963 it rapidly became known as 'the party of vice-presidents'. In one famous scandal, a major tax-collecting agency INGIC was found to have contributed vast sums to Christian Democrats and Communists alike. But the Christian Democrats did best. They had a traditional interest in charities, in local enterprise, and in helping peasants and artisans. As majority party, they retained control of the big national agencies and banks. Many lower party officials were on agency pay-rolls, and even the DC leaders held, or had held, jobs in welfare or banking. Those who lost their seats in parliament were compensated elsewhere: in 1974 the president of the National Association for the Protection of Youth, the president of the National Insurance Institute (INA), the president of the Paper and Cellulose Agency and the vice-president of the *Credito Fondiario* bank were all former Christian Democrat deputies. Thus the Christian Democrats sought to fuse State and society, 'legal Italy' and the 'real country'. The party acquired wealth and power, and eventually it could afford to ignore clerical promptings. But the agencies were too numerous for any central co-ordination or control, and the jobs were too numerous to be filled by *reliable* party men. The Catholics infiltrated Italian society, but as they did so they became less Catholic. They may have gained a whole world, but what of their souls?

Still, there were compensations. The welfare services may have been fragmented, but at least they were not run by the State bureaucracy. And the economic agencies, especially ENI, had some dramatic successes. They pioneered new ideas of management and labour relations, and they modernized the whole Italian infrastructure (see §17.1). In any case, the Christian Democrats had no choice. It was '*sottogoverno*' or nothing. If they were to achieve anything at all, they had to bypass the traditional civil servants.

They also had to squeeze the traditional 'notables' out of control of local government, for after 1950 the Southern landowners and gentry deserted the Christian Democrat Party, in protest at the party's land reform measures (see §17.2). Control of public agencies enabled the Christian Democrats to fight back, and to retain their Southern vote. Vast new central agencies arose, under tight political control. The Fund for the South and the Land Reform Boards were richer and more powerful than any Southern *comune*. They distributed land, housing, credit and jobs on a huge scale, and in the Christian Democrat interest. Local landowners and 'notables' could not compete, even if they still ran the local council.

Thus the traditional power structure of the rural South was transformed, almost overnight. No longer did Prefects court the 'Great Electors'; no longer did political stability rest upon the landlords. The agencies had themselves become the new patrons, with all the wealth of the State at their disposal. Other social and economic changes, e.g. emigration, also undermined 'notable' influence. Landowners had far less influence over their tenants once the tenants knew they could earn good money in West Germany. But it was the agencies which dominated the fate of those who remained, building and distributing houses even in areas where the major economic agencies were absent. Moreover, a special law in 1953 allowed provinces and municipalities to set up agencies to deal with health, welfare, training and agricultural improvements; but they could only do this if they had the funds, and it was the central State machinery that provided the cash. State-financed local government boards ran public transport and refuse services: the tram-drivers of Catania, the dustmen of Palermo, became bywords for idleness and affluence. Hospital managers provided hundreds of astonishingly highly paid jobs for surplus medical professionals and unskilled porters alike. In Catania, again, the local hospital was 'the third largest industry in the province', with 1,200 employees.[4] It also had 1,500 patients, so neglected that in 1972 the army was moved in to rescue them. He who controlled the local hospital controlled local government. The point is not that local government was run any better or worse than before, nor that there were fewer local power-struggles; it is that the landowners lost control. In the provinces of Bari and Brindisi, for example, only 4.6 per cent of the mayors were landowners or rentiers by 1965 (it had been 10.6 per cent in 1952, and 43.1 per cent in 1926); the new mayors were teachers (29.2 per cent in 1965, 19.7 per cent in 1952) or public employees (23.1 per cent in 1965, 15.2 per cent in 1952). By 1970, indeed, over one-third of all Italian mayors were public employees. A 'new class' of teachers and public employees dominated the local councils, and fought for the favour of national public agencies.

In other respects local government remained unchanged until 1970, except that after the war councils and mayors were elected once again. The municipalities were kept permanently poor, and could hardly afford any capital investment without government approval and government funds. They needed friends in Rome – deputies, ministers, party officials at headquarters, cardinals. It was the mayor's job to attract central resources and central agencies, and a good mayor would always bypass official channels if he could. The provincial Prefect continued to exercise strict 'control', especially over Left-wing town councils and mayors. In the big cities, it made little difference in practice who was in charge. The municipal budget was raised the same way and spent on the same mundane things – street lighting, local charities and the drains. Local government was not wealthy, nor glamorous, nor powerful. But it did provide jobs. Local elections were therefore fought hard, and government ministers were often candidates. The campaign rhetoric was always about 'national' or international issues. In 1951, at the height of the Korean crisis, it was about peace or war, religion or atheism; in 1956 it was dominated by the recent twentieth Congress of the Soviet Communist Party. Only in the outlying 'special regions' were local issues significant, but even there government control of finance usually ensured government control of policy. Thus the centralist tradition of Italian public administration survived largely intact, despite some Christian Democrat misgivings.

16.3 THE CIVIL SERVICE

The Italian civil service had, in fact, recovered rapidly from the nervous shocks of 1943–47. Indeed it flourished, in true Parkinsonian style. In 1948 there were around 150,000 civil servants proper (excluding manual workers); by 1969 there were 280,000. This was not, of course, the total number of public employees. The number of local government employees, for example, more than doubled between 1951 and 1975, from 271,000 to 576,000. One recent estimate is that *total* public employment rose from 1,932,000 in 1951 to 3,599,000 in 1971, the biggest increase being in the public agencies (*'sottogoverno'*).[5] And there had already been a big increase in the early post-war years. The Ministry of Defence, for example, somehow employed 76,000 more people in 1949 than it had done in the bad old days of Fascist imperialism.[6]

Many of the new recruits were reliable Southerners recommended by priest or bishop, or brought in by Allied administrators unwilling to rely on Left-wing partisans. The 'wind from the North' may have blown a few Northerners into government in 1945, but the South wind proved stronger. The machinery of State was 'meridionalized', particularly at the top. Since 1948 over half of Italy's senior civil servants have been Southerners, and the proportion shown up in surveys increased steadily: 56 per cent in 1954, 63 per cent in 1961, perhaps even 76 per cent in 1965. It was a far cry from the days when Nitti, in 1900, could complain that only a quarter of the top State jobs were held by men born in the South.

Thus the civil service, which in pre-Fascist times had been small and Northern, became big and Southern. This was a real transformation. It further alienated Northerners, including many Christian Democrats, from the post-war State. Worse, it created a gulf of mutual suspicion and hostility between the ruling politicians, who were predominantly Northerners appealing to anti-Fascist values, and the permanent administrators, who were predominantly Southerners with no experience of the Resistance. The great majority of senior civil servants had joined the service under Fascism, and had bitter memories of the attempted 'purge' after the war. One political scientist, probing the attitudes of the Italian administrative élite, found to his dismay that they were 'illiberal, élitist, hostile to the usages and practices of pluralist politics, fundamentally undemocratic'.[7] No longer could sound Establishment men flit comfortably from politics to administration, as in Liberal times; nor could the civil servants be easily bullied or threatened, as under the Fascists. Instead, politicians and administrators lived side by side, resenting each other's presence. The resentment must often have had class overtones: senior civil servants were not only Southerners, they had far more lowly origins than did most ministers, lower even than those of the bishops. And it became institutionalized. Each minister had his own private 'Cabinet' of political advisers and party functionaries, who not only helped draw up policy but helped run the ministry, i.e. gave orders to the civil servants and influenced their promotions. No wonder the civil servants complained.

In other ways the civil service remained formally unchanged. It was still

ill-paid, cumbersome, and suspicious; it still operated under the same archaic legalistic rules; half its top administrators were still lawyers; and it was still subject to the same complicated checks and double-checks. 'Interference' by deputies and pressure-groups was another traditional feature. In the 1950s the civil service's inefficiency, although much lamented, did not matter too much: it could always be bypassed by the agencies. In the 1960s it began to matter rather more. The civil service, or somebody, had to cope with huge problems, but it did so extraordinarily slowly, if at all. In 1976 the Treasury Minister revealed that 740,000 claims for compensation for war-damaged housing were still being considered.[8] Pensions were a national scandal, and it might take years of badgering and political pressure before they were finally paid to some destitute old woman. On the other hand, Italy could not afford to carry on founding special agencies, just because the civil service was inefficient. Moreover, after 1963 the Socialist Party was in government, and would insist on its share of jobs and influence in any new agencies that were set up.

So people began to worry more about the civil service itself, and seek ways of reforming it. Everyone agreed on what was wrong; nobody could agree on the cause or the cure. Was the civil service inefficient because of its formal procedures, or because of the lack of co-ordination between the different ministries, or because of all those Southerners? Was it because it had not been 'purged' after the war? Or was it simply too full of lawyers rather than technocrats, 'generalists' rather than specialists? Was the civil servants' lack of any experience outside their own ministries to blame? Was lack of specialized managerial training the problem? Was civil service pay too low to attract talented people? – it was certainly much lower than in the public agencies or nationalized industries, and lower in real terms than in 1861! Was it, perhaps, that Italians in general and Southerners in particular saw no harm in favouring their friends and relations, and indeed sometimes felt obliged to do so? Or had public administration simply become 'overloaded' by too many new functions, both at the 'policy-making centre' and at the 'implementing periphery'? Was lack of 'informed feedback' the major problem? Would administrative decentralization improve matters, or make them even worse? 'Ministers for Civil Service Reform' were appointed, to discuss these questions. They discussed them for twenty years, but nothing happened.

In 1948 the Italian civil service had been still unpurged; in 1970 it was still unreformed. In its senior ranks, it had turned into an immobile closed caste of Southern lawyers, defensive and resentful, quite ignorant of the modern industrial society of Northern Italy. It was no longer part of the élite, merely of the provincial – especially Sicilian and Neapolitan – middle classes. There was no Oxbridge, no *Ecole Nationale d'Administration,* no *Grands Corps* of prestigious administrators to carry on the glorious Piedmontese tradition of selfless State service. Much of its work was bypassed, by agencies or by party. Its main achievements were negative ones, but important for all that. It slowed down unwelcome change; it ensured the spread of '*sottogoverno*'; and, by its very existence, it prevented the Christian Democrats from taking over the machinery of State.

16.4 THE JUDICIARY

After 1945 most of the judges, too, were conservative Southerners. They, too, were a closed caste, recruited in their mid-twenties straight out of law school, with no legal or other worldly experience. They, too, were ill-paid, so that few talented or energetic people joined them. And they, too, resented the new Northern cult of anti-Fascism. They clung obstinately to their old familiar ways, arguing that existing laws had to be applied until parliament passed new ones. The highest court, the Court of Cassation, distinguished itself in the early post-war years by upholding the existing (Fascist) penal and civil codes. Even the Fascist laws against moving to the cities remained in being, and were occasionally enforced during the massive rural exodus of the late 1950s. Crimes like 'defamation of the State institutions' became surprisingly common – there were 550 cases in 1957 – and obviously limited press freedom. Above all, the courts often acquitted prominent former Fascists, but convicted ex-partisans for robberies of arms and food during the Resistance.

Only in 1956, when the Constitutional Court promised in the Constitution was finally set up, did matters begin to change. Thenceforth *any* judge could refer a law to the Constitutional Court if he suspected it might be unconstitutional. It was the lower ones, not the judges of Appeal or Cassation, who did so. The Constitutional Court slowly struck out most of the obviously Fascist legislation, much to the annoyance of many senior judges. For some years the Constitutional Court and the Court of Cassation glowered at each other, each side defending its own sacred texts.

Despite these squabbles, judges had one common interest, in enhancing their independence as a separate branch of government. In this, at least, they succeeded triumphantly. In 1958 the Minister of Justice lost some of his traditional ways of influencing judges. Control over discipline and promotions was entrusted to a 'Supreme Council of the Judiciary', a body consisting of, and mainly elected by, the judges themselves. This was a real innovation in Italian legal history. Hitherto judges had been faithful servants of the executive; they had to be. After 1958 judges could ignore the government's wishes with relative impunity. On the other hand, it was vital to be on good terms with the top men in the Supreme Council. So elections to the Council were bitterly contested. Judges formed rival factions, Left v. Right, progressive v. conservative, young v. old. The new system had many advantages. Henceforth an accused citizen could easily find out his judge's allegiance, and pitch his defence accordingly. If convicted, it was always worth an appeal: the appeal judge might belong to a different faction.

Judicial disputes were made more acute by the existence of the Constitutional Court. Young anti-Fascist judges might refer laws to the Constitutional Court, their natural ally, but they knew that their superiors would disapprove; and their superiors controlled the Supreme Council, which decided on promotions. So they demanded that promotion should be based on seniority. The quarrel between ancients and moderns continued for some years. Eventually the older men lost, partly through natural wastage, partly through calculations of interest. After all, even the most conservative judges would benefit if promotions became virtually automatic: they could no longer be made to do any work. In 1966 it was laid down that Tribunal judges would move up to the Appeal Court after eleven years; in 1973 this system was applied to promotions to the Court of Cassation. Judges would rise in twenty-three effortless years, from junior *pretore* to the Court of Cassation. As a former Minister of Justice remarked in parliament: 'We are creating thousands of new Cassation judges, and hundreds of section presidents of Cassation, i.e. people who once had to be appointed by a specific decree of the Council of Ministers. It is a revolution.'[9]

But, even so, the judiciary remained politicized. The years of agitation had left their mark. The fact that they all now enjoyed independence for life freed the judges from unnecessary inhibitions. They began using their investigatory powers to the full. Left-wing judges pursued Christian Democrat politicians and senior businessmen; Right-wing ones delved into trade union affairs. Moreover, many new laws – e.g. on divorce, or labour disputes – gave wide discretion to quite junior judges. People soon began complaining of 'judge power', of 'judicial interference' in normal administration, of 'judicial harassment' and 'judicial prejudice'; but there was nothing anybody could do about it. A judge's decision could only be altered by another judge. A powerful 'corporation', over 6,000 strong, had discovered its strength, and it was quite uncontrollable by parliament or government. Who would judge the judges themselves?

16.5 THE POLICE

The police forces underwent no such dramatic changes, at least after the early years. In 1943 the Badoglio government had hastily 'militarized' the public security (civilian) branch, i.e. subjected it to military discipline and courts; and in 1944–46 special riot police units, the *reparti celeri*, were founded to ensure crowd control. These innovations were thought necessary because there was no longer a reliable army. Otherwise the main change was in numbers. The 'public security' force had had 17,500 members in the pre-war police State; in the new democratic Republic of 1946 it had 51,000, and by 1949 it had 75,000. Thousands of ex-partisans were recruited in 1945–46, as a reward for their efforts; but many of them were soon purged. The *carabinieri* (the military police, formally part of the army) increased less rapidly, but still increased – from 65,000 in October 1945 to 75,000 a year later. To these forces should be added the 40,000 Finance Guards, dealing with fraud, excise and customs offences, and the 60,000 urban or rural '*vigili*' (traffic police, etc.). Some commentators thought that Italy in the 1950s had the highest number of policemen in the world, per head of population. Most of them were Southerners, ill-trained and poorly educated.

In other respects policing remained fairly traditional. The *carabinieri* controlled the countryside and guarded the more sensitive official institutions (courtrooms, airports, Presidential palaces); the public security maintained urban order. Each police force was, as always, jealous of its rivals and of outsiders, especially if politicians or judges. Only around 10 per cent of the policemen spent their time investigating crime, a job which in any case was formally reserved to judges and supposedly carried out by the police, if at all, only under the judges' instructions. The main task was to 'maintain public order'. Policemen 'admonished' vagabonds and 'suspected persons', and sent them back to their municipality of origin. They issued annual licences to restaurant owners and newspaper vendors, to carpark attendants and taxi-drivers, and relied heavily on these 'informing classes' for the 'evidence' they needed in court. In Northern and Central Italy the police coped with Communist demonstrators, and kept industrialists informed about their workers. In the South, the police contained the post-war land occupations and the occasional urban riot. Riots were not, by historic standards, frequent after 1948 – only sixty-eight people were killed in public demonstrations between 1949 and 1968 – and political terrorism was virtually non-existent until 1969 except in the German-speaking South Tyrol. So the police could claim reasonable success.

Even so, they had few friends, and no glamour. Detective novels were few, and there was no Italian Simenon or Agatha Christie. Even in films the courtroom drama was a rarity, and policemen rarely appeared. 'Community policing' remained an aspiration, often not even that; recruitment, training, pay, morale and equipment, particularly of the public security forces in the cities, were all inadequate. Moreover, in 1958 a zealous lady senator named Merlin pushed through a law closing down the licensed brothels, a traditional source of police information, gossip and funds. Arguably police work in Italy has never recovered from this blow. Another well-meaning law with disastrous consequences was the anti-Mafia law of 1965, which enabled the courts to order suspected *Mafiosi* to stay outside Sicily. Soon Lombardy, rather than Sicily or Sardinia, became the kidnapping centre of Italy; the police in the North proved as helpless as their Southern counterparts before a new, or rather displaced, wave of 'Mediterranean crime'. Altogether, it was an inadequate and unmodernized police that faced the student rioters and incipient terrorists of 1968–69; its luck had held for twenty years, but it was to hold no longer.

The *carabinieri* perhaps deserve a special word. They remained the best-equipped and best-trained of the various police forces, but even they declined sadly until the early 1960s, when an energetic new commander, General De Lorenzo, took them over. Unfortunately, in July 1964 he seems to have contemplated taking over the government as well, admittedly on behalf of the President of the Republic. In the event, nothing much happened: the other *carabinieri* generals ignored De Lorenzo's instructions, the *carabinieri* troops remained in their barracks, and Aldo Moro put together a new 'Centre-Left' government in some haste. As news of this obscure affair leaked out, suspicions focused not on the *carabinieri* themselves, who had obviously remained loyal, but on the *carabinieri*-dominated military intelligence and counter-espionage service, SIFAR (later renamed SID), which De Lorenzo had also run for some years. SIFAR, it emerged, spied on everybody. It had 157,000 dossiers on leading Italians, even the most respectable; it tapped telephones, it opened letters, it infiltrated unions and parties, it sold information to industrialists. All this was hardly novel in Italy, and indeed it was what anybody would expect counter-espionage services to do, but in the heady atmosphere of the late 1960s SIFAR's activities seemed certainly offensive, probably disloyal, and possibly Fascist – an impression strengthened when De Lorenzo later became a neo-Fascist deputy.

16.6 THE ARMY

Still, at least the police forces had a real job to do. That could not be said of the army. It had, under the Fascists, lost its traditional nineteenth-century role of maintaining internal order; after the *débâcle* of September 1943 its claims to be the country's defender against external attack also became less credible. The army derived little prestige from the Resistance, even though hundreds of ex-officers had fought in it, and even though some Italian troops had given valuable support to the Allies in 1944–45. Upstaged by the partisans, discredited by defeat, distrusted by the politicians, the army seemed a pointless organization. It seemed even more pointless when the peace treaty deprived Italy of her colonies, and when people began to think that future European wars would probably be nuclear.

Yet the army survived. People also remembered how dangerous the ex-officers had been in 1919–20; better to keep them in the army, out of harm's way. This argument served also against any talk of a 'purge'. Politicians of both Right and Left supported conscription: the Right wanted lots of soldiers, the Left, echoing Engels, somehow thought that conscripts would be less likely to fire on demonstrators. By 1948, with the advent of the 'Cold War', the army came to seem a good deal less pointless. Troops might be needed to help Allied forces in the Balkans, or to suppress a Communist rising at home. For these purposes a disciplined 'professional' force was essential: any nonsense about a 'nation in arms' or a 'partisan army' would simply play into Communist hands. Some 3,700 ex-partisans were, in fact, allowed into the army after the war, but they included only 125 officers (one lieutenant-colonel and thirteen captains; the rest were lieutenants). So the army was rebuilt more or less on the old structure. By 1952–53 almost 17 per cent of the budget was going on defence, quite like old times.

Nationalist feeling was not quite dead. Trieste remained a powerful symbol, and Tito's attempt to take it over in 1953 almost provoked an Italo-Yugoslav war. Several divisions were rushed to the frontier, and the army seemed useful again. However, the dispute was soon settled, and in 1954 Trieste became part of Italy. One further show of military muscle followed in 1957, when Italy massed *carabinieri* along the San Marino frontier in order to dissuade the *Sanmarinesi* from allowing their Communists into government. But the thaw in East–West relations soon reduced military influence once again. The Italian army settled down to a comfortable routine, enlivened only by earthquake relief and by anti-terrorist activity in the South Tyrol.

It remained, however, fairly large. In 1967 it had 267,000 men, not including the 78,000 *carabinieri*, and it employed a further 40,000 civilians directly. The navy contained some 39,000 men, and the air force had 64,000. Sceptical observers noted that most 'defence spending' went on pay and pensions, that one serviceman in every seventeen was an officer, and that there was a remarkable number of generals and admirals – 822 in 1967. The navy had two admirals for each ship, and the army was even more fortunate: along the Yugoslav border, where the main potential threat lay, it could station one general every 200 metres. Officers, like civil servants, tended increasingly to come from the South, and from lower-class backgrounds.

There was little, if any, parliamentary control. Policy was made, officially, by the new Supreme Council of Defence, consisting of the President of the Republic, the Prime Minister, five top ministers, and the Chief of the General Staff. Unofficially, the services ran themselves as usual, although their insertion in Nato meant that overall policy was rarely in Italian hands, and that most of the weaponry came from the USA. Nor was there any significant army influence in politics. The army asked only for a quiet life, and its request was granted.

But one should never underestimate military factors. By their very existence, the Armed Forces demonstrated Italy's pro-Nato policy. They were Italy's pledge to the West. Moreover, the army had a real impact on the economy and on 'Low Politics'. It conscripted almost 200,000 young men each year, about half the age-group. In the 1950s many of them still learned basic literacy and numeracy during their military service, and many more learned mechanical and electronic skills for later civilian use. But they had to put up with fifteen months' military discipline and unpaid discomfort, for no very obvious reason. They often disliked it intensely, particularly in the late 1960s when the Vietnam War had a disastrous impact on educated conscript morale. In post-Fascist Italy, national defence had been entrusted to more legitimate hands across the sea. But what if America herself were acting illegitimately?

16.7 FOREIGN POLICY

If the Italian military seemed pointless after the collapse of Fascist High Politics, so too did Italian diplomacy. There were, fortunately, fewer diplomats than soldiers – the Foreign Service was the one lightly staffed section of the bureaucracy, perhaps because it consisted largely of Roman aristocrats; but there seemed equally little for them to do. The peace treaty of 1947 (see §15.6) was imposed on Italy, not negotiated by her; so, too, was the Trieste settlement of 1954. Informed observers noted that Italy always seemed to toe the American line, and questioned whether she had a foreign policy at all. This was unfair. She had lost her always dubious Great Power status, as well as all her colonies, but she remained in a key strategic position, and she remained economically weak. She was vulnerable, and needed allies. So she was, naturally, willing to join alliances. Italy accepted Marshall Aid, membership of Nato, and the EEC. They all helped to 'rehabilitate' her in the eyes of the democratic world. They also secured American economic and military support, weakened both Communism and nostalgic nationalism at home, and helped Italy to escape from the British yoke in the Mediterranean. Italy did have a foreign policy after all. It may have been subservient, but it worked. It provided guarantees of security, without Italy having to do much herself. It was an ideal policy for the post-Fascist era.

Most Italians cheerfully ignored foreign policy. Opinion polls regularly revealed an astonishing lack of knowledge of the outside world. Half of them did not know, in 1958, what Nato was; three-quarters of them had no idea, in 1962, that reducing tariffs was one of the aims of the European Community. Newspapers provided little foreign coverage. Debates in parliament were rare and ill-attended. Events abroad mattered only when they had repercussions at home. If Russia suppressed the Hungarians or the Czechs, that proved the *Italian* Communists were bloodthirsty tyrants; if the Americans fought an unpopular war in Vietnam, it showed that the *Italian* government leaders were Fascist imperialists at heart. Parliament had a long and passionate debate about joining Nato, but only because doing so implied permanent exclusion of the PCI from government. Hardly anybody thought another world war was likely. Indeed, ministers in favour of Nato had to play down the defence angle and stress the economic advantages, much to American annoyance. Secretary of State Acheson complained to his ambassador in Rome that 'it is disconcerting to read . . . that majority Ital Cabinet appraising Italy's commitments in light two premises: a) disbelief in likelihood of war; b) necessity subordinating rearmament expenditures to stability of lira'. (He, therefore, suggested inviting the Italian Treasury Minister to Washington, 'during which every effort would be made to reorient his thinking'.)[10]

As for the European Community, few people cared one way or the other about joining it, because there were no obvious domestic implications. Italy did not send her best men to Brussels; she did not renew her representatives at the European parliament after 1959, as the old ones retired or died; and she did not fight her corner when the Common Agricultural Policy was being drawn up. Consequently she remained a net contributor to EEC funds for many years until, luckily, the British joined. But the Italians did not mind. Foreign policy did not matter any more; America would always provide. Only in the Middle East was there any independent Italian initiative, and even there it was mainly by businessmen for commercial reasons.

Italy was, indeed, extraordinarily fortunate. For many years America did provide. Italy had no Great Power ambitions, no colonial worries, and few security problems. Her political system, weak and unstable though it appeared, survived intact, whereas the very similar Fourth Republic in France soon collapsed. High Politics, it seemed, had been successfully banished at last. Politicians could concern themselves with Low Politics alone, as was proper.

16.8 SUMMARY

Post-war Italians were, therefore, left in peace to practise the 'politics of accommodation'. The politicians bargained constantly among themselves. They made concessions to outside groups, and filled State and agency jobs with their supporters, sometimes on a huge scale. In this way they succeeded in containing popular disaffection. Labour unrest was rare, trade unionists grumbled about the workers' *embourgeoisement*, and university teachers complained about how docile and conventional their students were. No Italian deputy questioned in 1967 thought crime was a serious problem, and hardly any of them thought Church–State relations were; most of them looked forward to a future of peace and stability.[11] They were wrong about the future, but they were right about the immediate past. Italy's political stability was a remarkable achievement.

Yet the reasons for it were fairly obvious. The 'economic miracle' of the 1950s and early 1960s had made most Italians unexpectedly prosperous. Furthermore, the Fascists' failure had discredited nationalism, and there were few divisive strategic or foreign policy issues, at least to the Right of the Communists. The overriding 'anti-Fascist' ideology, derived from the Resistance, helped the parties to collaborate together. The Church's ample influence helped make the Republic respectable. There was no Strong Man waiting in the wings, and no important group or interest really wanted a different system. The Communists, excluded from government though they were, were allowed a share of local government and union power, and so working-class leaders became accustomed to democratic politics. As usual, participation bred responsibility. Above all, both Communists and clericals kept control of their own followers. Decorous bargaining could proceed, unimpeded by the shouts of the vulgar.

Even so, the politicians' task was made harder by the fact that much of the machinery of State was in Southern hands, and was neither respected nor effective. Nor did it necessarily share the politicians' values. There was no Christian Democrat 'Establishment', any more than there had been a Fascist one. The Southern élite had voted Monarchist in 1946, but had lost; the radical Northerners had tried to take over the State in 1945, but had also lost. The Christian Democrats ruled Italy instead, but they enjoyed little 'legitimacy' among the influential.

Nor were the masses noticeably enthusiastic. High-minded American political scientists lamented the fact that Italians were 'overwhelmingly ignorant about political affairs, basically uninterested in the political process ... their identification with the political system is minimal and their attitudes towards it startlingly negative'.[12] Half of them never read a newspaper at all, and very few read the political pages – only 1,500 people in all Italy, according to one journalist.[13] Almost two-fifths of the adult population had no idea who was Prime Minister, and two-thirds never discussed political issues with others.

The political system clearly rested on indifference, and on the Italians' liking for unofficial improvisation (*l'arrangiarsi*). The Republic had few symbols of its own, and noticeably lacked a glorious or successful history. Even anti-Fascism was, according to some polls, not all that ingrained: only just over one-third of young people agreed in 1958 that 'Fascism was a regime that brought the country to ruin'.[14] The 'clerical' party was respectable, but no more; and even that became dubious as scandal succeeded scandal, and as public sector inefficiency discredited '*sottogoverno*'. Indifference is not, perhaps, too bad a basis for a regime, and it was a big advance on the traditional hostility, but it was not enough. In any case, it did not last. By the late 1960s fundamental social and economic changes had occurred, exacerbating all kinds of tensions and loosening the hold of the existing élites. Italians were suddenly plunged into an unexpected 'legitimacy crisis'.

REFERENCES

1. G. Galli, *Il Bipartitismo Imperfetto*, Bologna 1966, p. 149.
2. G. Sartori *et al., Il Parlamento Italiano*, Naples 1963, p. 25 and p. 89.
3. T. Sala, 'Una Offerta di collaborazione dell' ACI al governo Badoglio (agosto 1943)', *RSC*, i (1972), 517–33.
4. M. Caciagli, *Democrazia Cristiana e Potere nel Mezzogiorno*, Rimini 1977, p. 323 ff.
5. A. Pignatelli, *The State as Paymaster*, Strathclyde University 1980, p. 11.
6. Camera dei Deputati, *Inchiesta sulla Disoccupazione in Italia*, iv, pt iii, Rome 1953, p. 380.
7. R. D. Putnam, 'The political attitudes of senior civil servants in Western Europe', *British Journal of Political Science*, iii (1973), 278.
8. L. Lettieri, *La Pratica può Attendere*, Turin 1978, p. 119.
9. E. Reale, speech to Justice Commission of Chamber of Deputies, 27 Nov. 1973.
10. Acheson to Dunn 2 Dec. 1950, in US State Department, *Foreign Relations of the United States, 1950*, iii, Washington 1977, p. 1502.
11. R. D. Putnam, *The Beliefs of Politicians*, Yale University Press 1973, pp. 119, 135, 146.
12. J. La Palombara, in L. Pye and S. Verba (eds), *Political Culture and Political Development*, Princeton University Press 1965, p. 286.
13. E. Forcella, '1500 Lettori', in *Tempo Presente*, June 1959, p. 451.
14. J. La Palombara and J. B. Waters, 'Values, expectations and political predispositions of Italian youth', in *Midwest Journal of Political Science*, v (1961), 49.

CHAPTER SEVENTEEN

The economy and society under the Republic

17.1 RECONSTRUCTION AND THE 'ECONOMIC MIRACLE'

As we have seen (§15.5), the Italian economy was in a dreadful mess at the end of the war. There was only one thing to be said in its favour: things were almost bound to get better. And so they did, more rapidly than anyone expected. By the autumn of 1945 most of the main-line railway tracks and bridges were restored, and trains were moving regularly again. Moreover, it turned out that the wartime destruction could have been a lot worse. Iron, steel and shipbuilding had been badly hit, but most hydro-electric plants were intact, and so was most industrial machinery. Factories were soon able to resume production, if they could acquire fuel and raw materials, and here American aid proved invaluable. Italy received $2,200 million of aid, cheap loans, etc., between 1943 and 1948, mainly in the form of food and fuel; and Marshall Aid contributed another $1,500 million in the following four years. The State-owned banks, the State itself, and the relief organizations were all able to grant credit cheaply and readily in 1946–47, and there was no lack of borrowers. Those who owned land or machinery were anxious to expand their businesses, for they knew that there would be no problem in selling goods – any goods were better than cash, in those days of shortages, political uncertainty and high inflation. So the 'real economy' revived quickly. By 1948 manufacturing industry was back to pre-war levels of production. By 1950 the same was true of agriculture, and of income per head – admittedly at only $290.

But there was a major snag in this recovery programme. Cheap State-backed credit boosted the money supply, and boosted inflation. The wholesale price index rose from 2,600 in June 1946 (1938 = 100) to 5,100 in May 1947, and to 6,200 in September; the unofficial 'trading' lira fell from 346 to the dollar in May 1946 to 906 a year later. All this worried bankers, but it worried industrialists and politicians too. De Gasperi could not afford to bankrupt middle-class savers and public servants. Moreover, inflation meant constant labour agitations, which the Communists could not control for ever.

And after May 1947 the Communists were excluded from government, so they were not likely to try.

Thus in autumn 1947 economic policy was reversed. The Budget Minister, Luigi Einaudi, imposed a monetarist squeeze. Banks' liquidity was reduced in order to stop them lending, and they were forced to hold reserves equal to a quarter of their deposits. Interest rates were raised sharply. That soon stopped inflation. By early 1948 a dollar could be had for 575 lire, and the rate remained fairly stable at about 625 lire for the next twenty-five years. But the squeeze also stopped, or at least slowed down, the recovery boom, although arguably the slow-down was bound to occur anyway once pre-war levels had been reached.

'Reconstruction', then, was achieved quickly and with remarkably little political dispute, at least until mid-1947. But Italy was still a backward and poverty-stricken country. She had few natural resources; 44 per cent of her labour force was in agriculture; most of her industrial firms were tiny (90 per cent of them employed five people or less), and those that were not were overprotected; and the official figures in 1950 showed over 2 million unemployed, which was certainly an underestimate. In the next thirteen years, however, all was changed. The gross domestic product more than doubled, growing twice as quickly as it had even during the 'take-off' period between 1896 and 1913. Industrial production rose by an average 8.1 per cent p.a., faster than anywhere in the world except Japan and perhaps West Germany: by 1966 it was treble the 1951 level. Whole new industries – motor-scooters, washing-machines, refrigerators – emerged from nowhere, and soon dominated world markets. The car industry competed successfully in Europe: in 1967 Fiat sold more cars in the Common Market than any other firm, even Volkswagen. Olivetti made almost 1 million typewriters a year, and pioneered office calculators; Necchi produced 500,000 sewing machines. The chemical industry grew fastest of all, producing not only fertilizers but oil-based plastics and fibres on a huge scale. By 1969 the leading firm, Montecatini–Edison, was the largest business in the country by sales and asset value, although Fiat just led it in number of employees. By the late 1960s Italy, or at least Northern Italy, had become a modern industrial country, with a GNP per head of almost $1,500. Millions of people had moved from country to town: in 1971 only 18.8 per cent of the active population was still in agriculture. It was, to all appearances, an 'economic miracle'.

But it is the historian's mundane task to explain miracles; and there is no lack of plausible explanations. The monetary policies of 1947–49 may have slowed down recovery, but they increased confidence in the lira. People began to save again, and their savings were often channelled (via banks or State credit institutions) into new industrial investment. American aid helped not only to rebuild damaged plant in the immediate post-war period, but to 'restructure' basic industries like steel and cement. Italy acquired a modern, fairly efficient steel industry, for the first time in her history. It was based on 'integrated' coastal plants, using high-quality imported ore rather than scrap. Steel became plentiful and cheap: by 1962 the Italian price was well below

349

that of France or West Germany. Here was one of the bases for an engineering boom. More generally, Italy made up for lost time. She had been cut off from world trade for at least one decade, possibly two; now she could purchase up-to-date technology from abroad, without all the risks and costs of research.

Labour costs, too, were low in post-war Italy. Unemployment remained at over 2 million until the late 1950s, and the millions of rural emigrants moving to the towns kept wages low and discipline fairly tight. Trade unions were feeble, even non-existent in many industries. In any case, they were split along political lines. Strikes may sometimes have been nasty and brutish, but they were always short. Fiat had no strikes at all between 1954 and 1962 – a real economic miracle if ever there was one.

Above all, there was energy. In the age of steam, Italy had lacked coal; but now it was the age of oil. Italy lacked that too, but so did her European competitors, and Italy was nearer to the Middle East. Furthermore, the State-owned AGIP firm had discovered natural gas in the Po valley in 1944, and after the war the gas deposits were rapidly developed. The biggest field was a mere forty kilometres from Milan, and pipelines soon carried abundant cheap energy throughout the Northern industrial triangle. This was a startling change for Italy. She now had her own energy supplies – hydro-electricity from the Alps, natural gas from the Po valley. In 1953 AGIP was regrouped into a new State holding company, the National Agency for Hydrocarbons (*Ente Nazionale Idrocarburi*, ENI), run by a dynamic entrepreneur named Enrico Mattei. The new energy company discovered oil at Gela and Ragusa, in Sicily, explored for oil in the Middle East, signed long-term contracts to import oil from the Soviet Union, and built huge refineries in the main ports. ENI had the sense to sell its gas and oil cheaply. It thus undercut the international oil cartel, and gave Italian industry the cheapest energy in Western Europe.

Altogether, industrialists could hardly go wrong. Steel and energy costs were low, labour costs were low, trade unions were powerless, money was sound. All they needed was a market – preferably protected at home, open abroad. That is exactly what they got. In May 1950 Italy introduced a new '*ad valorem*' tariff, not quite as protectionist as the 1921 tariff but still giving an 'average' protection, according to GATT, of around 24 per cent, the highest in any of the countries it analysed (and even that did not include an extra 10 per cent or so for special trading taxes).[1] Sugar had a tariff of 105 per cent, wines and liqueurs between 28 per cent and 50 per cent, cars and tractors from 20 per cent to 45 per cent; even wheat was still protected by a 27 per cent tariff, despite pre-war memories. This tariff was lowered gradually, especially once Italy joined the EEC, but for a few vital years it effectively protected domestic markets. As for sales abroad, there too Italy was fortunate. The Korean War boom in 1951–52 came just at the right time to lift her out of her deflationary trough. Thereafter cheap Italian goods could easily be sold in a reviving West European market. There were few balance of payments worries before 1963, and no need, therefore, for governments to restrain economic growth. Tourists flocked in, spending their cash; Southern emigrants found labouring jobs all over Europe, sending their foreign earnings back home to their families. Italy enjoyed a famous 'export-led boom'. Among her chief exports, admittedly, were suntan and people, but shoes, cars and refrigerators were even more remunerative.

Finally, there was the State's contribution. Overall economic policy was made largely by a handful of academic economists and bankers like Luigi Einaudi, who believed in the classical free-market economics of the Liberal tradition. These men ended wartime controls, ruled out rationing post-war, and opened up Italy to foreign trade. In so doing they transformed the economy. Einaudi has some claims to be the father of the 'economic miracle', just as Sonnino has of the 'take-off' in the 1890s. Arguably monetarism suited Italy. High interest rates did not hit business too badly, for industrialists could always borrow fairly cheaply from special credit institutes. In any case, 'there was no alternative'. Fiscal policy was not an option, if only because the tax-gathering machinery was so feeble. In effect, the State permitted businessmen to avoid taxes, and that naturally encouraged reinvestment.

In other ways, too, the State proved helpful. The Great Inflation had reduced its own debts and thus its interest payments. It also thoughtfully lost its colonies, which greatly cut down spending and, as ex-colonists returned home, helped swell the labour reserve. After 1948 only about a quarter of the budget went on interest payments, defence and colonies, compared with about two-thirds in the late 1930s (and also between 1861 and 1914). More positively, the State provided cheap energy and cheap steel, as described above, and it provided much else. The largest State economic agency, IRI (Institute for Industrial Reconstruction), managed many important and glamorous enterprises. It ran airlines (Alitalia) and the telephone network, built motorways, ships, cars (Alfa Romeo) and machine tools, and provided a quarter of the electricity supply. By 1971 over 350 firms were at least partly State-owned and State-controlled; they employed over 400,000 people, and dominated the economy.

The various State firms – or rather, the Christian Democrats – recruited and trained a new entrepreneurial class, more open to new business methods and more sympathetic to the social–Catholic version of managed capitalism. They also recognized unions, or at least Catholic unions, and willingly negotiated with them. Indeed, in 1957–58 the State firms left the employers' organization, *Confindustria*, and founded their own new body, named *Intersind*, to represent their collective interests. For many years the State firms were run as businesses, and flourished. Most of them made profits, and borrowed much of their investment requirements from private investors. They seemed to embody the progressive ideals of the mixed economy.

Conversely, the State-owned banks and credit institutes controlled the cash flow and credit facilities of most private firms. State credit to industry was cheap, perhaps too cheap: many firms borrowed too much. Partly for this reason the State's role in the economy gradually increased. Private firms in trouble were rescued with public cash, and the State holding companies

351

usually picked up some of the shares in return. In 1963 Italian private firms accounted for 66.4 per cent of the turnover of the top 194 firms in Italy (Fiat, Montecatini and Edison alone had 28.7 per cent); by 1971 they had only 42.3 per cent, and by then Montecatini–Edison itself had had to be rescued, with a fifth of its shares in public ownership.[2] In other words, by 1971 nearly 60 per cent of the large firms' turnover was in State or foreign hands – and one firm, Fiat, accounted for one-third of the rest. This was a unique situation for an advanced 'Western' economy.

It was also a vulnerable one. The State sector was often well managed, but it was not 'planned', nor even co-ordinated. It was 'protected' from market forces, and 'guaranteed' by State cash. It might easily become a drain on the Exchequer, especially if its managers became overtly political appointees, or if its unions began securing unjustified pay rises. During the late 1960s that is exactly what happened. The unions – especially the largest confederation, the CGIL, which was linked to the Communist and Socialist Parties – enjoyed greater influence after 1963, because the Socialists were normally in government. The first major strikes since 1948 took place in 1962–63, just as the first 'Centre-Left' government was being formed and as electricity was being nationalized. *Intersind* began to bargain independently of the private employers, and more generously: wages in the State firms became much higher than those in private industry, often nearly double for the same job. Private firms had to follow suit to some extent, and so wages rose sharply overall – official figures for manufacturing industry show industrial wages rising by 77 per cent between 1964 and 1971, labour costs by 90 per cent, and productivity by 42 per cent. These trends were clearly leading to trouble: Italian workers were pricing themselves out of the market.

Of course, it was not merely the unions and the 'Centre-Left' governments that were responsible. The 'labour reserve' had grown smaller: unemployment had fallen from 1,500,000 in 1957 to 500,000 in 1963, remaining thereafter at between 500,000 and 750,000 (admittedly these official figures took no account of emigrants). But governments were responsible for a good deal. They greatly extended the system of welfare benefits, paid for by employers' contributions. By 1970 employers' social security contributions were over half the average wage, and were the highest in the EEC. And the public sector firms could not have raised wages so cheerfully if governments had refused to borrow more money to pay them; nor could private firms, if governments had refused to bale them out.

By 1969 Italy had become enmeshed in a vicious circle of rapid labour cost increases, low productivity rises, higher inflation, low investment, State rescue bids, bigger budget deficits and political instability. After 1963 rich Italians exported their capital in suitcases to Switzerland, rather than invest it at home. Indeed, private investment never recovered after 1963 – share prices halved between 1961 and 1972 – and that, too, brought more firms into the State's rescuing arms. The most convincing economic explanation for these ills seems to me the higher labour costs, which snuffed out the export-led boom, and induced both a flight of capital and chronic balance of payments deficits. The fundamental reason, however, was political. It became obvious that no major firm, and few medium ones, would be allowed to go bankrupt. The Christian Democrats were increasingly using the State firms as sources of funding and patronage. Fuller employment led to greater self-confidence among workers, especially young workers who had not known anything else; and Socialists in government meant that workers could not be pushed around so easily. Even so, one should not exaggerate the post-1963 problems. Exports doubled in volume between 1963 and 1968; income per head went up 20 per cent. The 'economic miracle' may have been over, but few people in 1969 foresaw that it would turn into an economic nightmare.

The public sector and the big private firms like Fiat were not the whole of the Italian economy. In the 1960s Italians noticed that they had developed a new kind of 'dual economy', overlapping the traditional North–South dualism. On the one hand, there were the State-financed, capital-intensive, unionized, 'technocratic' large firms; on the other, a competitive, export-oriented private sector, often consisting of small non-unionized businesses, or family concerns with small workshops. In 1971 81.8 per cent of manufacturing firms had less than five workers, and around one-fifth of all industrial workers worked in firms with less than ten employees. Furthermore, over one-quarter of the labour force in 1971 was self-employed. Thus the artisan tradition survived in the age of State enterprise and multinational cartels.

Semi-legal or clandestine activities – second jobs and the like – also appeared to be remarkably widespread. Indeed, Italy had acquired a real 'subterranean' economy, as well as subterranean politics. Informed observers estimated that there were about 2½ million 'unofficial' workers, mainly the young, the elderly or the female.[3] They worked at home (e.g. dress-making) or in small workshops (e.g. mechanical repairs); they were non-unionized; they paid no taxes; and they were outside the social security system or, rather, parasitic upon it. Many of them received sick pay from other jobs, or long-term 'disability pensions' that could be claimed after five years' contributions elsewhere. In 1977 5¼ million people claimed such pensions, 1 million more than were claiming old-age pension; 85 per cent of the people of working age in the province of Avellino were said to receive one. The unofficial economy was much deplored by public men, and it sometimes meant real sweated labour; but it was, undeniably, the 'real Italy', the competitive workshops where the clothes were made that were later sold in the fashionable boutiques of New York or Paris. Textile employers reverted, after a century of factory production, to the old 'putting-out' system: they may have lost some economies of scale, but they saved on social security contributions. Nor was the phenomenon restricted to industry. In commerce, the 1960s may have seen the first Italian supermarkets, but they also saw a 16,000 increase in the number of small shopkeepers, a class apparently threatened with extinction elsewhere in Europe. And life in Italy was enriched by a host of activities – music-teaching, taxi-driving, child-minding – that were often done as a relief from the dreary bureaucratic routine.

17.2 AGRICULTURE

But it was in agriculture that small enterprises were most common. Despite the flight from the land in the late 1950s and 1960s (see §17.4 below), rural Italy remained, indeed in some areas became, a peasant society. There were still at least 1½ million peasant-owner families in 1970, together with almost 250,000 share-cropping ones: i.e. at least 5 million people. However, three-quarters of the farm holdings had less than five hectares, and almost one-third had less than one hectare. In other words, many of the family farms were not big enough to support a family. So some families had several holdings: there were 3½ million peasant-owned holdings in the country. Other families – perhaps half the total – were not full-time peasants.

How had this situation come about? Mostly it had been inherited. Small, fragmented plots were common long before the Second World War. In 1946 there were 9½ million farm properties, 93 per cent of them less than five hectares in size. Local studies sometimes tell an even more dramatic story. At Castelluccio Inferiore, in Potenza province, there were 3,409 'properties' on the 2,791 hectares of land, i.e. 0.8 hectares each, and even these were further split up into strips. Furthermore, these were the years of huge inflation. It was sensible to borrow money to buy land, and almost 1 million hectares were bought by small peasants just after the war.

Sometimes there was no need to buy. In Central Italy, share-croppers organized by Socialist and Communist unions secured permanent tenure, and then gradually squeezed out landlords from their share of the produce. In 1951 the share-croppers were 10 per cent of the active population, a huge group of crucial political importance; by 1971 they were below 2 per cent, and even these were soon given their land in law as well as in practice. In Southern Italy, where after the war there were still over 2 million landless labourers lucky to pick up an annual income of 60,000 lire (£35), many of the *latifundia* were taken over by force from 1943 onwards, just as they had been after the First World War. This time, however, the peasants were led, not by ex-servicemen's organizations or priests, but by militant Communist organizers anxious to establish a rural base. Governments were faced by rural revolt and, as usual, bought it off.

The result was a major land reform, the only serious attempt in South Italian history to set up a rural society of peasant farmers. A series of laws in 1950 provided that large uncultivated, or badly cultivated, estates in huge areas of Sicily, Sardinia, and the mainland South, and also large tracts in the Po Delta and the *Maremma* of Latium and Tuscany, might be expropriated by State land reform agencies. These agencies would improve the land and then sell it to peasants, preferably landless peasants, at low cost and on long mortgages. They would also provide essential services (irrigation, agricultural advisers, houses, roads, livestock, electricity, etc.) at public expense. This latter aspect was no innovation, for Fascist and pre-Fascist governments had done the same. Indeed, the Christian Democrat land reform was very similar to the Fascist 'reclamation' (*bonifica*) of the Pontine Marshes, and often employed the same administrators and technicians. But taking over land compulsorily and then redistributing it was new; and so was the daring idea of settling local, Southern, peasants on it instead of Northerners. It naturally infuriated the big landowners, although they could usually keep one-third of their land if they developed it, and they received compensation for the rest.

The land reform had major political consequences. It broke the political power of the big landowners, both at local and national level (see §16.2). And it created a 'client class' in the countryside, dependent on the agencies. The new peasant-owners grew what the agency told them to grow, lived where the agency told them to live (often in houses built by the agency), and sold their produce through agency-run co-operatives. They also voted for the party that ran the agency. Did land reform defuse revolutionary fervour? It was certainly intended to do so, and perhaps it did in some areas, e.g. the Sila mountains where two-thirds of the peasant applicants acquired land; but in most places less than 5 per cent of the peasants got anything, and it is difficult to see why the rest should have been satisfied. Certainly rural unrest became less evident after 1950, but the reason is probably that landless peasants could find better jobs more easily in towns, and moved there instead (see §17.4).

Economically, too, the land reform did not have all the consequences sometimes claimed for it. The end of the *latifundium*, after more than 2,000 years, sounds a dramatic story; but many big estates were already split up into peasant-leased properties long before 1950, and these were usually left alone. In any case the big owners kept one-third, often developing it with land reform grants; and the sharper ones had split up their estates among their family before the law was applied. Middling landowners, the 'rural bourgeoisie', were not affected by the new laws. Altogether, about 700,000 hectares were allocated to peasant-owners by the end of 1962: 113,000 peasant families acquired land, but that was only 1 per cent of the rural population. Most of the new owners had been landless peasants. They were inexperienced in farming techniques. Their holdings were normally on poor land, and were usually too small to support a family. In later years, with the increasing use of tractors and specialized machinery, and with increased competition from the North and from Common Market farming, these failings became more evident. Most of the landless labourers got no land, and got nothing else either: Russell King rightly remarks that changes in the labour laws or tenancy agreements would have done far more good to far more people at far less cost than the land reform did.[4] In short, the land reform was too little, and too late. Far from solving the 'land question', it simply increased the number of poor peasants. However, this harsh overall judgement must be tempered by local successes, e.g. at Castiadas in South-East Sardinia, around Metaponto on the Ionian coast, and above all in the *Maremma* – a suitable showpiece near Rome, as the Pontine Marshes had been.

In 1970 perhaps half the peasant landowners of Italy were not full-time farmers. Some sociologists, therefore, began writing of 'post-peasants':

picturesque rural figures who owned and tilled the land, but drew much of their income from other sources – industry, commerce or welfare. Attention focused, in particular, on the rural welfare agencies, which seemed extraordinarily generous. Net welfare payments (receipts less contributions) to small landowners rose from 50 billion lire in 1954 to 245 billion lire in 1960, to 909 billion lire in 1968 and to 1,412 billion lire in 1971. By then about one-third of the value of all agricultural production was going in welfare payments to small landowners, and this figure excludes other agricultural subsidies. It was, literally, a system of outdoor relief, producing votes for politicians rather than food for consumers.

The votes were channelled by two major organizations, both dominated by the Christian Democrats. The 'union' for small landowners, the 'Confederation of Direct Cultivators' (*Coldiretti*), had nearly 1¾ million *families* as members in the late 1950s. It was a huge reserve of local and national power: between eighty and ninety deputies were members, as were over a quarter of Christian Democrat local councillors. The other body was the Federation of Agricultural Consortia (*Federconsorzi*). This had been founded originally as a grouping of producer co-operatives, but in the 1920s had become the Fascists' national organization to carry out grain purchases and stockpiling. After 1948 it simply continued its operations much as before, acting as a compulsory Grain Marketing Board supporting the price of wheat. It also provided fertilizers, seeds, tractors, cheap loans and insurance, and ran its own marketing and processing firms. These were usually a local monopoly in *Federconsorzi* hands, so the peasants had no option but to buy. The *Federconsorzi* soon acquired immense funds ('*mille miliardi*', 1,000 billion lire, to use the famous slogan of the early 1960s); and, together with the *Coldiretti*, it controlled most of the Italian countryside, at least outside the 'Red Belt' of Central Italy where Communist-run co-operatives provided similar services at a similar political price. The two bodies also ran the peasants' health and old-age insurance schemes (*Casse Mutue*), a further fruitful source of votes and fiddles; and they dominated other agencies, e.g. local Land Reclamation or Irrigation Boards, which were busy distributing jobs or land. Altogether, Italian agriculture was run on political, not economic lines, long before the EEC's Common Agricultural Policy came into operation.

Still, in one obvious sense Italian agriculture was successful. Food production doubled between 1950 and 1970 – perhaps the finest achievement ever in Italian agricultural history. Yields per hectare increased sharply, because of better seeds, more fertilizers, and a needlessly high grain price. So although the area under cereals declined, far more wheat was produced: just under 7 million tonnes p.a. in 1948–51, 8.9 million tonnes in 1957–59, 9.6 million tonnes in 1967–69. The 'problem of wheat' became one of over-production and under-consumption. People ate less bread and less pasta, but they ate more dairy produce: in 1958 imports of cheese exceeded exports, for the first time ever. They also ate twice as much meat – 38 kilograms per head in 1967–68, compared with 19 kilograms in 1952–53 – and drank considerably more wine. By the late 1960s Italy was producing about a quarter of all the wine in the world. She also introduced effective quality controls, and doubled her wine exports.

Most people in the country were eating better, and more, than ever before; especially more. Calabria, as usual, was the gloomy exception. The *average* Calabrian was still severely malnourished in 1963–64; but elsewhere there was surprisingly little difference between the diet of rich and poor, except that the poor ate more bread. Food was more likely to be canned, and by the 1970s frozen, but there were few changes of taste. Italians may have succumbed to Coca-Cola, but they rejected the fish finger. Strawberries were the biggest post-war novelty – they had always been picked wild, of course, but had hardly been grown commercially before 1945. As the strawberry came in, the dried fig went out. Other fruit, especially apples and oranges, became far more commonly grown and eaten, although bananas, being a State monopoly, stagnated.

Not everything in the kitchen was lovely. Half the beef and veal had to be imported, and the shortages grew worse as young people left the land: the cattle population fell from almost 10 million in 1960 to 8.7 million in 1971. Furthermore, Italy notably failed to corner the Common Market in citrus fruit or tomatoes. Sugar, too, was a national scandal, with inefficient beet-producers securing a high tariff and excluding imports. In general, Italy still had to import much of her food; but now the imports were not wheat, but beef. That was, presumably, progress. It was also a drain on resources. Almost a quarter of all imports were food; it was the second biggest item, after oil. Still, Italian agriculture could have done a lot worse, and in the past always had. And some of the foods in short supply, e.g. butter and sugar, were precisely the ones suspected elsewhere of being long-term health risks.

17.3 THE BATTLE FOR THE SOUTH

The biggest economic problem, or series of problems, lay south of Rome. In 1951 Southern income per head, at £90 per year, was less than half that of the rest of Italy; one in four Southerners was illiterate; well over half the labour force was in agriculture. Unemployment was high – between 33 per cent and 50 per cent in the rural areas – and underemployment widespread. Industry, where it existed at all, usually meant artisans and tiny workshops. The South, in short, had most of the features of an underdeveloped country; but, with 17.4 million people and almost 40 per cent of the national territory, it was larger than many underdeveloped countries. What, if anything, could be done?

Initially, governments responded in fairly traditional ways, stressing the need for agricultural improvements and public works. The land reform laws of 1950 applied mainly to the South; and, to supplement them, a special Fund for the South (*Cassa per il Mezzogiorno*) was set up. The Fund, in its early years, was essentially a rural spending agency, providing 'infrastructure' – roads, houses, electricity, water – in rural areas. In its first decade it spent 1,214 billion lire (£700 million). It soon became a major patronage body, firmly in Christian Democrat hands, and was used, like the land reform boards, to undermine the power of local landlords, and to bypass local government. The Fund's operations, together with the land reform effort, created a group of 'development experts' whose careers depended on developing the South. These men soon spread a 'development agency mentality' into key factions of the ruling party. In many ways it was a repeat performance of what had happened in Libya and Ethiopia, and often the same men were in charge. The Fund for the South was a 'Ministry of Modernization', pouring capital into the South as if it were a prestigious colony, and always wary of the local chiefs.

In 1957 came its first real success. The then Minister for the South, Giulio Pastore, accepted the economists' argument that agriculture and public works were not enough. Industrial investment was needed as well, if the South were ever to 'catch up', and the government would have to provide incentives. Indeed, given the State-controlled nature of Italian industry, the government would itself have to provide much of the capital investment, by placing its factories in the South. It would also have to switch its public works programme towards industrial rather than agricultural 'infrastructures'. Thus Christian Democrat Italy, with its free-market economy, its short-lived governments and its incompetent bureaucracy, embarked on one of the most ambitious and most centralized industrial development programmes in the world – a State-financed programme, run by technocrats and experts, immensely expensive, bitterly opposed by Northern industrialists, and with no guarantee of immediate or even long-term success. It was an extraordinary decision; but it probably seemed at the time simply a logical development of existing policies.

In fact, it reversed many of them. Henceforth Southern Italy enjoyed, in effect, industrial protection. There may have been no tariffs round her frontiers, but Southern industry had cheaper credit, higher investment grants, and lower taxes than industry elsewhere, as well as numerous special favours from government agencies. The government selected promising large 'industrial development areas', as well as smaller 'nuclei of industrialization', and concentrated the Fund's and the State firms' resources there. By 1975 there were twenty-five 'development areas' and eighteen 'nuclei', mainly in Apulia and Sardinia. Even more important, State-owned firms were directed to put 60 per cent of their new manufacturing investment, and 40 per cent of their total investment, in the South (as compared with the 20 per cent already there in 1957). Soon a huge new steel plant arose at Taranto; petrochemical refineries started up at Brindisi and at Porto Torres, in Sardinia; Alfa Romeo built a car factory near Naples.

And the cost of all this? Between 1957 and 1975 the Fund for the South spent 8,433 billion lire (at constant 1975 prices) on its various activities, which after 1960 were mainly infrastructure and industrial incentives. But other development agencies were busy in the South too, both Italian (*Isveimer, Irfis,*

Cis, etc.) and international (e.g. the European Investment Bank, which had put in 3,300 billion lire by 1978); and so were the State industries and holding companies – IRI alone invested 649 billion lire in the South in one year, 1971. Cao-Pinna has estimated that between 1964 and 1975 it all added up to 11,865 billion lire, at constant 1970 prices, invested in *industrial* activities in the South: i.e. some £8,000 million, or $19,000 million, again at 1970 prices.[5]

Throwing money at selected parts of the South was not necessarily wise. The incentives to private firms were given to capital, not labour; they made capital artificially cheap. They therefore led to capital-intensive projects, providing few jobs. Similarly, the State steelworks and refineries were modern plants, using the latest technology. They employed few people, and those few tended to be engineers or skilled craftsmen, often brought down from the North. Such plants had little to offer the local labourers, at least once the initial building work was finished. They became known as 'cathedrals in the desert', a curious term as they were all along the coast. It was hoped that they would eventually trigger a 'take-off' of other local industries; but by 1970 there were few signs of that happening. The small local firms, which might have provided more jobs, received very little State support, and indeed declined in the face of better communications and increased Northern competition. And some of the poorest Southern regions, e.g. Calabria, Basilicata and Molise, were given no industrial development areas at all.

In 1971, therefore, development policy was modified. Agriculture and lesser public works were entrusted to the new regional governments; promises were made to inland areas; more tax and credit concessions were made to small firms; and big private firms like Fiat and Olivetti were 'encouraged' to move South, or prevented from expanding in the North. The Fund's major task henceforth was defined as administering 'special projects', i.e. big infrastructural works, like de-polluting the bay of Naples or building an industrial port at Cagliari. It was still investing in physical assets, rather than people; and it was still substituting for central and local bureaucrats. As for the State firms, they were instructed to step up their investments in the South to 80 per cent of their new, and 60 per cent of their total, investment. This policy had a considerable impact in the next few years. It gave the South a great deal of refining capacity, just when oil became impossibly expensive; and a great deal of steel, just when the world market collapsed.

Altogether, the industrialization drive was not an immediate success. In 1973 it was still confined to coastal enclaves in Apulia, Sardinia and Sicily. It provided, at most, 150,000 new jobs in 'modern' industries like engineering and petrochemicals. But they were 'subordinate' jobs in branch factories. Top management stayed in the North, as did research and development. Construction and public works had 350,000 extra jobs in 1975 compared with 1951, but even this could do little to absorb the 2.1 million who left agriculture. The total number of jobs in the South actually went down by over 500,000 in this period, while the population rose by 1.5 million. Unemployment in the mid-1970s was three times the Northern rate, and the 'activity rate' – the proportion of the population with jobs – had declined steadily since 1951. In 1971 income per head was still half that of the rest of the country. So in 1976 Southern employers were exempted from social security contributions for newly-engaged workers – a real shift towards subsidizing labour as well as capital. It was also decreed that cheap credit would not be given to projects costing over 15 billion lire (£10 million). These measures had a considerable effect, at least in some areas. But certainly the benefits of the top-heavy capital investment programme of 1957–75 were meagre, and the costs were huge, especially the unquantifiable 'opportunity costs', i.e. what the same money might have achieved if spent in other ways. The 'Southern problem' had perhaps been contained, but it had certainly not been solved.

However, the South did change in these years, and quite dramatically. It was not the industrialization drive that did it so much as better health – malaria was virtually eradicated in the late 1940s – better education, better roads, mass emigration and massive welfare. The *relative* gap may have remained as wide as ever, but income per head tripled in twenty-five years, thanks mainly to emigrants' remittances, welfare payments and patronage politics. The South had indeed acquired a modern economy, more modern than anything the planners had envisaged. Her industries consisted of State-owned high technology; her agriculture survived on State subsidies; her rulers were State bureaucrats and economists; her people were State-educated and jobless. In 1950 the South had been poor and relatively self-sufficient. In 1975 she was better off and utterly dependent. She had gone straight from an agrarian to a 'post-industrial' society, without the intervening stage of industrialisation.

17.4 EMIGRATION

The most visible changes in the South came through emigration. After 1945 it became possible to move overseas, especially to Argentina. In the 1950s prosperous West European countries like France and Switzerland became magnets for unskilled labourers. In the 1960s it was the Northern Italian cities whose streets seemed paved with gold. About 1.75 million people left the South between 1951 and 1961, i.e. almost 10 per cent of the 1951 population. A further 2.3 million left in the following ten years. These net figures do not include seasonal workers – another 250,000 Southerners worked away from home all summer in the mid-1960s – nor do they take account of other migratory flows. Southern peasants did not necessarily leave the South: many moved to Southern cities like Naples, Catania or Syracuse. They did not even necessarily leave the countryside: in the land reform areas of Metaponto and Southern Calabria, for example, men moved *down* from the hills to settle on the plains for the first time in 1,500 years, and Russell King remarked that 'the coastal plains of Southern Italy are about to replay their classical role'.[6] Nor were all emigrants from the South. The 'flight from the land' was even more marked in the Northern and Central regions than in the South. So migration may be viewed in various ways. It may be seen as an abandonment of agricultural jobs, which went down from 8.6 million in 1951 to just under 3 million in 1975 (in the Northern and Central regions, from 4.9 million to 1.5 million); as urbanization, the movement from country to town; or, validly but more partially, as a transfer of people from South to North. However it is seen, it was on a vast scale.

As for the reasons, men were pushed out of the countryside by poverty, and/or pulled to the cities by prospects of wealth. The migrants were young, and they departed with few apparent regrets. They themselves often regarded the old rural way of life as obsolete. Behind them they left deserted villages, or rather Southern towns inhabited only by the women, the children, the old, and the dead – for burial plots back home remained popular even with long-term emigrants, and in some places grave-digging was the only flourishing local industry. Such towns came alive, so to speak, only at Christmas or during the summer holidays. Most of the time they survived on remittances. In the late 1950s an emigrant could send around 500,000 lire (£300) a year back to his family, twice what he would earn in total at home.

In that sense emigration obviously worked. It produced the cash, and it relieved rural overcrowding. This in turn reduced the economic and political power of the landowners, though not of the new public agencies, which had to help subsidize the families left behind. Emigration was, as usual, a political safety-valve. The huge disaffected rural proletariat, the '*braccianti*', could find work at last. The poor became upwardly, or at least outwardly, mobile; the middle classes found bureaucratic posts. Perhaps nobody was too unhappy with this process. Despite the often appalling conditions of emigrants' life and work, it was better than staying at home. And there were some ecological benefits. The abandoned hills began reverting to pasture and forest, just what Italy needed. Even so, it was not an altogether healthy development. Rural Italy was becoming parasitic on the industrial societies of Western Europe and of the Northern cities. It was already an old people's home; and it seemed to have no future, except as a tourist zone or a nature reserve.

The impact of migration was even more apparent in the towns than in the country. The cities became hopelessly overcrowded. The eleven largest ones grew from 6.9 million inhabitants in 1951 to 10.2 million in 1971. Turin had to cope with 700,000 immigrants in fifteen years, and by 1970 had more Southerners than any other Italian city except Naples. Rome, with 1.1 million inhabitants in 1936 and 1.6 million in 1951, passed the 2 million mark in 1960 and had over 2.75 million by 1971. Dreary housing estates arose all round city outskirts, most of them put up without benefit of planning permission and often without roads, schools, lighting or even sewage. Parks and open spaces were destroyed. The hapless immigrants were often put into huge blocks of flats, with densities of 500 people per hectare in some parts of Rome. Even worse were the hideous shanty-towns, providing shelter but little else for thousands of newcomers. In short, Italian cities became 'Americanized'. The Northern ones became North American: commercial complexes surrounded by industrial estates. The Southern ones became South American: administrative centres surrounded by shanty-towns.

Since many of the immigrants to Northern cities were Southerners, they aroused much resentment and even 'racial' hostility among the natives. The immigrants were, as usual, blamed for crime, illiteracy, sponging on the welfare, and overloading the available public services – transport, public housing, schools, etc. They also tended to vote Communist, which worried many respectable Northerners. Yet all this was part of the cost of 'making Italians'. Millions of Southerners were being assimilated into 'Northern' cultural values at last, although the process must often have seemed to be working the other way round.

17.5 POPULATION, HEALTH AND THE FAMILY

Migration and urbanization were by far the most dramatic features of post-war population history. Births and deaths were more mundane: they simply became rarer. In the post-war years Italy was completing the 'normal' demographic cycle. She was already a low mortality country, and she became a low fertility country too. The main change was among the Southerners, who gradually adopted Northern habits. By 1950–51 the South was as healthy as the North, at least judging by the crude death-rates. The Southern birth-rate also fell steadily towards 'Western European' levels, although Northerners were and remained even less prolific. Women born between 1926 and 1930, for example, produced over 3 children each on average in Calabria and Sardinia; meanwhile their Piedmontese and Ligurian counterparts had 1.5 and 1.4 respectively. Thus several Northern regions went below replacement levels. In the country as a whole, the crude birth-rate was 17.8 (live births p.a. per 1,000 population) in the 1950s, and 18.0 in the 1960s; it had been 23.2 in the late 1930s.

This decline is a little mysterious. Marriage was more popular than ever, and women were marrying at much the same age (24.3) as previously. And yet they had fewer children. The obvious reason is contraception, but most devices were distrusted or disliked, and few Italians used them – indeed, selling or distributing them was illegal until 1971. Most couples relied on *coitus interruptus*, known as 'being careful' (*'stare attenti'*). Such was normal sex in the age of the *Dolce Vita*. When things went wrong, there was always abortion. That was illegal too until 1978, but it was apparently widely practised, usually by doctors or midwives.

Fortunately, more of the infants who were born managed to survive their first few years, so there were still some children around. Before the Second World War 1 child in 10 had died in his first year; by 1954–57 that was down to 1 in 20, and by 1971 to 1 in 35. That was still dreadful by North European standards, but it was a great deal better than before. Italians in general were more healthy than at any previous time. They ate better; they were more hygienic; and they were covered by health insurance schemes. Malaria had been virtually wiped out in 1945–46. All this had measurable effects. By the late 1960s the average Italian was almost as tall as the average Frenchman. Conscripts in 1947, i.e. those born in 1927, had been 166.95 centimetres tall; in 1969 they were 169.69 centimetres tall, and six years later the figure had gone up to 171.48 centimetres. The literal gap between Northerners and Southerners was also diminishing. People were not only longer, they lived longer: life expectancy at birth rose by fourteen years between 1946 and 1971. And they died of the respectable diseases of affluence and old age. However, it all meant that the population was steadily ageing: pensions – usually payable at 60 to men, at 55 to women – became an increasing burden on a faltering economy.

Good health depends on good housing. The post-war years saw a frenetic building boom, not just in the cities. The new houses were normally built by co-operatives or by public agencies like *INA-Casa*, with public subsidy; and they were built for sale, not rent. By 1979 55 per cent of houses were owner-occupied. Italy gradually became a 'property-owning democracy', or rather a nation of mortgagees borrowing from the banks and relying on inflation to reduce their debt. Rented housing in the cities, although much needed by immigrants and others, remained scarce. Another problem was that many of the new buildings were aesthetically displeasing or even, as in Naples and Agrigento, structurally dangerous. Even so, most Italians were far better housed, despite the shanty-towns, the urban slums, and the occasional earthquake. In 1951, over half Italy's dwellings had no drinking water supply and no internal toilet. By 1971 86 per cent of the houses had piped water, and 96 per cent an indoor toilet.

These changes in fecundity, housing and health obviously had a big impact on Italian families. The 'extended family' – including grandparents, cousins and all – survived as a network for mutual support in times of crisis, or for job-seeking, but declined as a residential unit: from 22.4 per cent of all families in 1951 to 16.9 per cent in 1971. Most people lived in the standard 'nuclear family' (husband, wife, and children), although couples on their own became more common as time went on (from 11.3 per cent of families in 1951 to 15.5 per cent in 1971). Young adults, unless emigrants, continued to live with their parents until marriage, i.e. until around age 27 for men. No wonder so many of them were discontented. But as time went on far more people lived alone. By 1971 there were over 2 million of them, twice as many as twenty years previously. Many of them were elderly. A quite new figure had appeared on the Italian scene, the old-age pensioner. He, or more probably she, lived alone or with his/her spouse, and depended on State welfare.

Why did these changes occur? Part of the explanation, clearly, is that the 'extended family' is a life-support system. It was less needed when families received State health, education and pensions. Old people could survive alone, for once. In any case, the new urban housing was built for small families, not 'extended' ones. Young single people, on the other hand, could not easily find bedsitters or cheap flats – they did not qualify for public housing, and in the private market rents were frozen, so hardly anybody let out property, at least officially. But more deep-rooted economic and ideological forces were also at work. The share-cropping system in Central Italy had depended on 'extended' families; as the one declined, so did the other. In land reform areas, creating small family farms meant creating small families. And then there were the strange new doctrines of female education and emancipation, being brought in by government edict, tourism and Hollywood. Country girls were moving to the towns because they were unwilling to marry a peasant; they were even more unwilling to live with the peasant's mother.

Thus Italian families slowly changed, not only in size but in nature. Generalizing wildly, one might say they were becoming less authoritarian and more 'co-operative'; less a grim inflexible structure designed for economic survival, more a voluntary association aiming at humanizing life in an impersonal society. This transition was, inevitably, far from painless; the new role was just as difficult as the old. And it was not sudden. Indeed, the transition was not easily apparent in the 1960s, even in the cities. It was only in the 1970s that the 'crisis of the family' joined the other, manifold, crises of authority in Italian society.

17.6 EDUCATION AND ITS USES

Italian schools in the post-war period continued in their traditional ways – assessing, testing, selecting: overproducing useless graduates, classifying everyone else as a failure. Fact-laden syllabuses, drawn up by the ministry in Rome, were set to be memorized; pupils were constantly tested, in front of the whole class, on what they could repeat from the textbooks. Those who failed the annual examinations were held back to repeat the year, even in primary school, so only about half the children 'graduated' from primary school at the 'right' age.[7] There was no attempt to link the separate subjects, let alone to link school with the outside world. Teachers in Rome who taught ancient history were not allowed to take their pupils to see the Colosseum. This frightful, rigid, unreal, enclosed, boring and profoundly stupid system did its best to anaesthetize successive generations of pupils. One wonders who suffered most from it: the 'failures', who left school as early as possible, stigmatized and barely literate; or the 'successes', arrogantly convinced that what they had learned at school was worthwhile knowledge. Probably the latter, for their taught lack of common sense and ignorance of the real world would often prove a terrible handicap in later life.

Readers may think this judgement is too harsh. There were no doubt some exceptions, especially at primary level. None the less, the Italians were, in Sylos Labini's words, 'a people of semi-illiterates'.[8] In 1951, 12.9 per cent of the population aged over six was officially classified as 'illiterate'; by 1971 only 5.2 per cent were. That does not sound too bad, but in 1971 at least a quarter of the adults had not passed the elementary school-leavers' certificate, testifying to basic literacy and numeracy; and half of them had got no further. In the early 1950s less than a quarter of eleven to thirteen-year-olds attended a secondary school (the rest were still in primary school, or had left altogether). In 1962 a new law merged the lower age range of the various existing secondary schools into one 'lower middle school', or junior comprehensive. It was supposed to be compulsory, but for some years only about a quarter of the age-group passed successfully through this school. However, the proportion was up to 60 per cent by 1971. The bulk of them were girls, and mass secondary education for girls was perhaps the major innovation in post-war Italian education.

The new secondary schools, like the primaries, essentially taught rhetoric and mathematics. Hardly any of them had science laboratories, or taught more than three hours' science a week (the norm was two hours a week during the first two years, compared with six hours and nine hours of Italian). Even fewer recognized, let alone encouraged, imaginative or 'lateral' thinking. The same was true of the higher reaches of secondary education, which remained unchanged except that they attracted more pupils – 500,000 in 1954–55, 1.1 million ten years later, 1.6 million in 1969–70. At age 14 those still at school passed into *licei classici* or *licei scientifici* for the academic élite, technical institutes or professional institutes (*istituti tecnici o professionali*) for the others, teacher-training schools (*istituti magistrali*) for aspiring primary teachers. There was not much difference between the two *licei*, except that the 'classical' ones taught Greek. In the so-called 'scientific' *licei* fifth-year pupils were taught seventeen hours of humanities subjects per week, but only eight hours of science, even including maths and geography as sciences. Most pupils went to the technical or professional institutes, for vocational training – as always, the most successful sector of Italian education. But the technical institutes themselves became more academic, their courses dominated by languages and history. Incidentally, there was practically no teacher-training for secondary-school teachers, except on voluntary courses; and two-thirds of the teachers were employed on a casual basis, often part-time.

Most of the élite went on to university, to study the traditional subjects. In 1951 almost a quarter of the graduates were lawyers, and a similar number had read literature. These two subjects, together with medicine, continued to predominate in the next few years, although from the mid-1960s they were challenged by an even less useful subject, sociology. Italy had never been able to find jobs for all her graduates; nor could she do so in the post-war years, despite valiant efforts to expand the bureaucracy. But a bad situation became far worse in the late 1960s. More people were going through the secondary schools; economic slow-down meant fewer jobs for young people, and hence more of them went on to university; and in 1969 access to universities was opened up to anyone with a diploma from *any* senior secondary school. The number of students rose rapidly; from 176,000 in 1959–60 to almost 500,000 ten years later. They could not be taught properly, for libraries, laboratories and professors remained as few as ever. The universities had been 'élite factories'; now they became 'parking lots', somewhere to put young age pensioners for a few idle years. They had boasted of being places of exciting intellectual challenge; the reality was bureaucratic tedium and autocratic absentee professors.

And so a huge 'intellectual proletariat' appeared. Most students rarely attended classes, and half of them never graduated. A little learning proved to be a dangerous thing. In the late 1960s student riots flared up in most major Italian cities. In Rome, students battled ritually with the police in March 1968, two months before the famous outbreaks in Paris; in Turin, the student 'Committee on University and Society' solemnly banned the use of books, perhaps making a virtue of necessity. The Italian riots hardly need explaining, given the nature of Italian universities, although other factors – disillusionment with the Centre-Left governments, or hostility to the Vietnam War – no doubt contributed. At any rate, the years of routine neglect suddenly caught up with the academic Establishment.

Finally, how did education fulfil its primary task, of guarding the gateways to top jobs and thus maintaining social stability? Pretty well, apparently. In the mid-1960s only about 15 per cent of university students came from manual working-class backgrounds (including artisans and peasant farmers), and these students were more likely to drop out. And although many more clerical workers and managers were needed in the post-war boom, very few of them – perhaps only 5 per cent – came from the working class. The élite's position was no longer based on property, as in pre-1914 days; two world wars and two huge inflations had seen to that. By the 1960s it rested firmly upon the rock of State employment. The richest men in the country were members of the 'State bourgeoisie', managers of State industries and agencies – secure in their jobs and guaranteed in their pensions. Even many 'professional' workers like doctors, architects and teachers, were employed by the State in all but name – in 1975, for example, only one-fifth of Italy's engineers were self-employed. And where did a State job come from? Political connections, of course; but also from education. The new class – or 'New Class' – structure of post-war Italy had little obvious justification, but what little it had came from the formal titles of higher education. Fiat was managed for years by a '*professore*'; successive governors of the Bank of Italy, or chairmen of nationalized industries, were also '*professori*', or at least '*dottori*'; even Gianni Agnelli was known as 'the advocate'. These titles were often the only claim men had to their income, status and power. No wonder they insisted on using them. They furnished the essential social distance between the élite and the vulgar throng.

17.7 CULTURE, HIGH AND LOW

What were the Italian newspapers and the media doing in these years? Was it not their task to win popular support, to transmit the values of the dominant classes, and to provide a harmless outlet for disaffection? Did they succeed in the 1950s, but fail in the late 1960s? If so, why? Or did they have little influence at either time? This second view seems true for the press, for only half the adult Italians read newspapers anyway (see §16.8). There were, in the 1960s, about eighty daily newspapers in the country, most of them fairly provincial; they had a total circulation of 6 million at most. Most of them were written in an esoteric, over-literary style, full of allusions; written to be decoded by the élite, not absorbed by the public.

Journalists were themselves an élite. They were a formal profession, with rigorous entrance standards and the highest pay in the world. Political careers were still founded on journalism, as in the days of Mussolini and Gramsci. Leading politicians, when asked to state their profession, proudly answered 'journalist' – in 1976 the Chamber of Deputies contained fifty-six 'journalists', including the Prime Minister, the secretary of the Communist Party and the next President of the Republic.[9] Furthermore, they practised their calling while in office. Most newspapers lost money. They were owned by industrialists, who thought them useful as mouthpieces or as business props. Enrico Mattei, boss of the State oil company ENI, found it advantageous to start his own newspaper, *Il Giorno*, which he subsidized with public money. Some papers were run by the political parties, although only the Communists, with *L'Unità* and their daily newspaper in Rome, *Paese Sera*, had much success. Italy conspicuously lacked a popular press, except for the three or four 'sports dailies' devoted entirely to sporting news. She also lacked a serious journal of record, like *Le Monde*. What she soon acquired, instead, were the 'political glossies' – weekly news magazines like *L'Espresso, Panorama, L'Europeo*, etc., full of marvellous photography and wonderfully melodramatic scandals. Here was the true, vivid face of Italian journalism, with its predictable villains and its utter innocents.

So radio and television were all the more important. A regular TV service began in 1954, produced by the State broadcasting monopoly RAI, and tightly controlled by the Christian Democrats. It was dull but novel, and so people watched it. By 1963 there were 4¼ million licence-holders, and most people had access to a set. For many years the political programmes were grindingly official, with obsequious interviewers, set-piece lectures by ministers, and no mention of unwelcome news. Nevertheless, TV had an immense impact. Possibly it was the real 'School of the Nation'. It depicted 'modern' ways of life – the tolerant family man, the compulsive consumer, the hygienic housewife. And it showed, reluctantly, some of what was happening in the rest of the world. It 'deprovincialized' Italy; it helped to spread 'secular' values; it held up a 'superior' model of industrial civilization. It was a medium with a message: the message being, to Southern peasants and Northern intellectuals alike, that their world was archaic.

This message was reinforced by films, especially those from Hollywood, and by travel and migration. But some Italian films were quite different. The 'anti-Fascist generation' of post-war directors made marvellously sensitive films, usually about the poor, with a social or political theme – Rossellini's *Roma Città Aperta*, De Sica's *Umberto D* and *Bicycle Thieves*, Visconti's *La*

Terra Trema and Fellini's *La Strada*. Most of them were enormous successes abroad, and commercial failures at home. Italian intellectuals had, for once, turned to the people for inspiration; but the people had turned to Hollywood. Film-makers like Sergio Leone soon followed them: by the mid-1960s the most common type of film being made in Italy was the 'spaghetti Western'. There were also lots of 'sword and sandal' epics, and fifty-odd 'Giacomo Bonds'. Other directors retreated hastily back into their ivory towers, and made tedious intellectual films about tedious intellectuals. Even so, genius still flourished. The true poets and interpreters of their age were film directors like Antonioni, Rosi, Olmi and Pasolini, as well as the great names already mentioned. Their audience may have been relatively small, but it was larger than most poets and playwrights ever reach.

What was true of films was true also of books. After 1945 new novels appeared, much concerned with social issues. Many of them took the Resistance as their theme. Moreover, Left-wing intellectuals were reading the writings of Antonio Gramsci, the Communist leader whom Mussolini had imprisoned in 1926, and who had died in 1937. Gramsci had been an exceptionally intelligent and sensitive reader. He had noted, rightly, that Italian intellectuals wrote only for their own kind. That must stop. Literature should be 'national–popular', and should reflect the 'values of the people'. Unfortunately, only one post-war writer lived up to Gramsci's ideals, and he was a Catholic. Giovanni Guareschi's *Don Camillo* books were certainly popular, indeed populist both in style and content, but they were naturally derided by the intelligentsia. Other authors, like Pasolini and Sciascia, depicted low life realistically enough, but omitted the right kind of moral and political uplift; they, too, were unsuitable as 'national–popular' writers. The *avant-garde* writers, like the film directors, soon abandoned the kailyard and resumed their normal cerebral joylessness; just as well, for their claim to be depicting 'popular' values had always been bogus. *Fumetti* – filmstrip comics – remained the most popular 'reading' in Italy. And the most popular novel in post-war Italy – indeed, in Italian history – was the aristocratic, aloof, unsentimental *The Leopard (Il Gattopardo)*. Published in 1958, it sold over 1 million copies. That was what the public wanted.

Altogether, the culture industry was too diverse and too intellectual to have much impact; the only exception, television, had huge but totally unexpected effects. A 'mass', 'lay' society was gradually forming; no one had anticipated it, and few intellectuals welcomed it. The growth of industry and cities, the mass transfer from country to town, the provision of roads, electricity and water, the opportunity to have jobs, money, pensions, schooling, scooters – all these changed the values and living patterns of the Italian people far more than any writers could. It is difficult, in fact, to grasp the extent and speed of this 'modernization', but perhaps transport will make the point. Italy in 1950 was a country of bicycles; in 1960, of motor-scooters; in 1970, of cars. The car was probably the greatest agent of social change. Its success was sudden and overwhelming: 1.6 million vehicles on the road in 1960, 11.3 million in 1971.

In some ways Italy became a 'leisured society'. Men worked more regularly, but for fewer hours. The family seaside holiday only became common in the 1960s. By then most prosperous families had second homes in the countryside, as did many ex-peasant families settled in the towns: the 1971 census found 1½ million such second houses in the country, almost half of them newly built (or newly abandoned) in the 1960s. In some areas, e.g. the Adriatic coast of Romagna, parts of the South Tyrol, above all North-East Sardinia, tourism had a sudden and overwhelming impact on the local economy and society. In the 1930s fewer than 300 tourists a year had visited Sardinia; in 1966 there were 300,000. But what is most striking about post-war Italian leisure is the lack of innovation, certainly compared with Fascist times. The '*Dopolavoro*' system survived, suitably renamed; city children continued to go to 'holiday colonies' by the sea; the cinema was still the place for urban evenings. Even the popular sports remained the same – football, cycling, motor racing. The main change was that sport became a consumer good rather than a patriotic duty. Football, for example, was said to be the Italians' favourite sport, but few of them actually played it. They watched it, or rather they watched the official Football League games on Sunday afternoons. They were passive consumers, whose only role was to pay and to applaud. Occasionally they arose from their torpor – at Caserta in 1969 rioters burned down the post office and the railway station after the Football League had cancelled the local team's promotion. But usually they remained apparently content with their allotted role.

Similarly, less organizable leisure pursuits than football seemed to be in danger of dying out. *La Strada* was a lament for the vanishing world of strong men and sword-swallowers, of country fairs and urban festivals. The 1961 census (admittedly a dubious source) found 1,678 professional singers, less than half the number of 1911. Was Italy still the land of *bel canto*? There was a similar sad decline among violinists, painters, sculptors, clowns and ballad-singers (*cantastorie*). Seven out of eight Italians played no musical instrument. The one agreeable and active leisure pursuit that not only survived but flourished was 'hunting', or rather shooting. Every autumn millions of Italians took to the fields and shot at everything in sight, including each other. It meant an annual massacre of wildlife, especially migratory birds; and it also meant that Italians had, in practice, the 'right to bear arms' – almost 2½ million gun licences were issued in 1974, and not all the guns were to be used for sport.

As Italians became more prosperous, they became more uniform. In the 1960s it was sometimes difficult for a foreigner to tell them apart. They all seemed to eat the same food, to wear the same readymade clothes, to speak in standard urban accents, and to drive standard Fiat cars. That was, of course, an illusion (dialect was still spoken by three-quarters of the population, even in 1974), but even so the old diversities and symbols were slowly declining. In the 1950s, for example, men still went to the barber to be shaved, twice a week at most: only the really prosperous could afford to appear always clean-shaven. The spread of the safety-razor and of piped water in the 1960s destroyed a reliable indicator of social class. It would be foolish to complain about this. For most Italians the new patterns of life were immensely

369

welcome. Anthropologists reported a new optimism in rural areas. Feliks Gross, for example, had found at Bonagente in 1957 that people were still looking nostalgically back to the past (*'c'era più lavoro, più ordine'*); by 1969, however, things were much better, people had TVs, cars, electricity, water, and they thought things would get even better in the future.[10]

17.8 SECULARIZATION

These changes may be seen as part of an all-embracing process of 'secularization' of Italian society. In this view, prosperity, towns and education undermined belief, or rather undermined the Church's traditional hold over welfare, schools and propaganda. In 1976 the Jesuit father Bartolomeo Sorge wrote of a 'transformation of the scale of values that used to unite us, for better or worse; man's whole outlook is altering. We are living through a change of culture and a change of civilization.'[11]

But he surely exaggerated. The nineteenth-century Church had no monopoly of social life, indeed saw herself as a beleaguered fortress; and in the 1930s the Fascists had greatly extended *State* welfare and *State* secondary education. Italy was hardly a monolithic Catholic country even in 1948, when the Christian Democrats won their greatest electoral victory. Church attendance may have been high in the post-war years (in 1956 69 per cent of adult Italians claimed to have been to mass in the previous week, although counts at the church door usually produced markedly lower figures), but religious observance reflected social pressure at least as much as personal belief. Another Jesuit found that over half the Italians were 'indifferent believers', who may have attended church, but ignored her teachings. A further 20 per cent, according to him, were simply superstitious, believing in the evil eye, or the powers of the local saint, or witches – a view confirmed by the many observers of Southern ritualism, and expressed perhaps most forcibly by Liliano Faenza in a study of share-croppers near Rimini in the early 1950s: 'the religious beliefs of the masses are the absolute negation of any intimate experience of the divine'.[12]

In short, those who were practising Catholics were practising quite different things. None the less, Italy in the 1950s seemed a Catholic country, for the same reason that the Middle Ages seem an Age of Faith: the clergy were politically powerful, or were thought to be. These were the Marian years. In 1949 Pius XII proclaimed the Madonna as patron saint of the *carabinieri.* A year later the Christian Democrat mayor of Padua dedicated the city to her, a scene repeated in countless villages. The dogma of the Assumption was officially promulgated in November 1950. The wireless provided regular homilies by the famous Father Riccardo Lombardi, the 'microphone of God', a figure who symbolized the new regime's mastery of the media. Rome herself was a 'sacred city': special regulations governed which books and films might be on view there. Catholics were the insiders, sharing out the jobs among the reliable, and it was prudent to show a decent conformity. Civil weddings were rare: they were an open challenge to authority, and might well jeopardize a man's career. In 1956 the bishop of Prato denounced a couple who had had a civil wedding as 'public concubines'. They sued him for slander and unexpectedly won, whereupon Cardinal Lercaro of Bologna ordered his cathedral to be dressed in mourning for a month, and church bells tolled throughout the land. That was exceptional, but it was quite normal for the clergy to pronounce on every political issue, and for their views to be heard with outward deference. Above all, the Church maintained her 'flanking organizations' – Catholic Action with its 2½ million members, the Christian Association of Italian Workers with over 1 million, the unions, the co-operatives, the savings banks – under hierarchical control. Here was a real 'reserve clergy', influential throughout Italian society.

This rigid, closed world did not survive the years of social and cultural transformation unchanged. In 1958, when Angelo Roncalli became Pope John XXIII, the overdue *aggiornamento* began. Roncalli was himself an elderly conservative, but he allowed the Christian Democrats to move cautiously towards alliance with the Socialists, and above all he summoned the Ecumenical Council that was eventually to remodel the Italian (and not only the Italian) Church. The results included the mass in Italian, more power for lay deacons, in general a more 'open', 'collegiate' Church. The Italian Bishops' Conference, founded in 1971, was the first body in Italian history to provide the bishops with a collective voice. Thus the Church, after a century of tight-lipped defensiveness, began to relax.

But as the ancient public façade of Italian Catholicism crumbled, the edifice behind it was revealed to be weaker than expected. Self-reported weekly church attendance fell sharply – 69 per cent of adults in 1956, 53 per cent in 1961, 48 per cent in 1968, 35.5 per cent by 1972. These figures presumably bore some relationship, however hazy, to actual observance, and perhaps even to belief. Priests began leaving their parishes, bemused about their vocations and their usefulness; far fewer young men applied for the priesthood. Catholic Action almost withered away – 2.6 million members in 1966, half that number four years later, half again by 1978, with the bulk of defections in the youth movement. The Association of Christian Workers left the Catholic fold altogether, and proclaimed itself to be Socialist. 'Dissenting' Catholic groups sprang up, denouncing the official Church as the ally of the rich. Just as the laymen were being given more say in the Church, they were saying the Church was not for them.

Altogether, the Church should have been strengthened by the Council, but she seemed much weaker. People began to talk of 'the eclipse of the sacred', and to wonder whether religious perspectives were possible within industrial society. The Church, as an institution, retained control of the 'rites of passage' – baptisms, weddings, funerals – but she retained little else. Pope Paul VI gloomily told seminary pupils in 1968 that 'the Church is going through a time of disquiet, of self-criticism, one might even say self-destruction'.[13] He, too, exaggerated; but clearly the Church could no longer provide stability in an unstable world.

17.9 SUMMARY

It is difficult to suggest a framework within which all the various changes discussed in this chapter may be seen coherently. Obviously they were all interconnected. A 'materialist' historian might emphasize electricity, or safe water, or the eradication of malaria, as the key factors. In 1950 most rural hamlets did not have electricity; in 1970 they did, and so a more homogeneous TV-watching consumer society had become possible. An 'idealist', on the other hand, would stress the diffusion of secular ideas from across the Alps and across the Atlantic: the Church may have worried about Communism, but the biggest threat to her influence came from the West, not the East.

Both, however, would recognize two main features. Firstly, there was an unusual gap between wealth, status and power in post-war Italy. Industrialists felt surrounded by hostile forces, and prudently stored their wealth abroad. Bureaucrats in agencies and party political functionaries took most decisions, but had little status. And the traditionally dominant class, the landowners, lost their status, their local power, and even some of their land. In short, Italy still had no unifying 'Establishment' worth the name. Catholic Action and the various Christian Democrat factions came closest, but they were far from dominant in many key areas – industry, the military and police, the civil service. Secondly, these post-war changes, confusing as they were, contributed greatly to the process of 'making Italians'. The rural exodus, the South–North migrations, and the advent of mass literacy *in Italian*, all ensured more homogeneity, even though there may have been little loyalty to the Italian State.

But the social and economic changes of the 1950s and 1960s were too rapid and overwhelming for stability. In the cities, transport, hospitals, schools, housing, and welfare simply could not cope with the new demands; by 1969 they had virtually collapsed. The less evident effects were just as important. The modern world, with its material wealth and its claims to individual rights, had suddenly arrived. It could not easily be absorbed within the old hierarchical institutions. A 'crisis of authority' affected every institution – the factories and unions, the schools and universities, the family, the Church, the State. Italy was about to undergo a difficult and violent upheaval.

REFERENCES

1.   GATT, *Le Commerce International en 1952*, Geneva 1953, quoted in A. Pedone, 'Il Bilancio dello Stato', in G. Fuà (ed.), *Lo Sviluppo Economico in Italia*, Milan 1969, ii, p. 257.

2. R. Prodi, *Sistema Industriale e Sviluppo Economico in Italia*, Bologna 1973, p. 11.

3. G. Fuà, *Occupazione e Capacità Produttiva*, Bologna 1976, pp. 29–36.

4. Russell King, *Land Reform: the Italian Experience*, London 1973, p. 225.

5. V. Cao-Pinna, *Le Regioni del Mezzogiorno*, Bologna 1979, p. 87.

6. Russell King, *Land Reform* . . . , pp. 206–7.

7. School of Barbiana, *Letter to a Teacher*, Harmondsworth 1970, Table E, pp. 130–31.

8. P. Sylos Labini, *Saggio sulle Classi Sociali*, Bari 1975, pp. 125–29.

9. F. Simoncini, 'La composizione sociale del Parlamento italiano', *Rassegna Parlamentare*, xix (1977), 94.

10. F. Gross, *Il Paese*, New York 1973, p. 140.

11. B. Sorge, 'La chiesa accetti la sfida marxista', *Il Mondo*, 19 Feb. 1976.

12. L. Faenza, *Il Comunismo e il Cattolicesimo in una Parrocchia*, Milan 1959, p. 79. The Jesuit quoted is S. Burgalassi, in *Le Cristianità Nascoste*, Bologna 1970, esp. pp. 164–81.

13. *L'Osservatore Romano*, 8 Dec. 1968, quoted in A. Parisi, 'Per una interpretazione delle trasformazioni in atto nella chiesa cattolica italiana', *Rassegna Italiana di Sociologia*, x (1969), 378.

CHAPTER EIGHTEEN

The Great Cultural Revolution: Italy in the 1970s

In May 1968 France experienced a totally unexpected social upheaval. Students rioted, factories were occupied, workers went on general strike. De Gaulle's regime seemed on the point of collapse. Yet within a month it was all over. The Gaullists were confirmed in power with a huge parliamentary majority, and the economy soon recovered. In Italy events went very differently. There, too, workers joined a huge protest movement of strikes and occupations, culminating in the 'Hot Autumn' of 1969. But the struggle continued for years. Student riots became an everyday occurrence scarcely noticed by the media. Industrial militancy also became routine. The economy staggered from recession to stagflation. Protest spread to the schools, to the welfare services, to the police and army, to all the political parties, to the Church, even to the family. Most startling of all was the outbreak of urban terrorism in 1969. Italy had been fairly free of political violence for two decades, except in Sicily and the South Tyrol; but in the next few years she reverted to her earlier traditions. Bombings and assassinations became a normal part of the Italian drama. The crisis obviously had deep social and cultural causes, absent elsewhere – the legacy of rapid industrial growth, of migration into the cities, of inadequate schools and public services, of 'secularization' and of excessive expectations. These issues could not easily be tackled by the existing political system, constructed as it was for weak government and constant compromises.

18.1 THE UNIVERSITIES

The universities were a particularly striking example, both of social conflict and of political inertia. Their problems were not new: libraries and laboratories had been overcrowded long before 1968. But in 1969 admission to university became a great deal easier (see §17.6). In 1968–69 there were 416,000 students attending courses; three years later there were 631,000, and the number of law and medical students had doubled. By 1978–79 the total had increased to 778,000 – over a quarter of the age-group. The number of graduates rose from 40,000 in 1968 to 77,000 ten years later. Only about 15 per cent of them were in science or mathematics, most of these being girls – a curious Italian tradition. Industry employed 2,391 new graduates in 1969, but that was the peak year; by 1976 it was taking 1,278, about 2 per cent of the country's graduate output. The reluctance of Italian firms to employ graduates was understandable. By law, graduates had to be paid more than other people, yet there was no guarantee they would know anything, and a fair possibility they might turn out to be revolutionaries. As for the professions, they were all in much the same state as medicine. In 1978 almost 15,000 new doctors qualified (compared to 3,800 in Britain); and 35,000 medical students began their training. Yet already there were 30,000 unemployed doctors. Italian universities had always produced too many unemployable intellectuals, but never on such a scale as this. There seemed to be a whole generation of perpetual students, born around 1950, too highly educated to stoop to manual labour, too numerous for bureaucratic posts, bitterly resentful of the system that had reared them, and hopeful only of overthrowing it.

Successive governments did little to mitigate these problems. Italy did not found new universities, nor did she expand her few polytechnics. She simply pushed more students into the existing universities, and provided some extra Chairs. Thousands of temporary 'assistants' were hastily recruited, to do the actual teaching. The policy was not a success, but the only ones that might have worked – restricting university entrance again, or raising the fees – were politically unthinkable. The universities were left to fester. Most students never saw their professor, except at examination time when he might fail them. Ill-taught students began, not surprisingly, to riot; many of the 'assistants', desperate for permanent jobs, began to join in. So the new 'mass university' generated new mass movements. The best-known was the *Movimento Studentesco* – a spontaneous, radical 'Maoist–Catholic' body, demanding an end to capitalism, bureaucracy and the academic Establishment. Student demonstrations were lively and exhilarating, but they did not achieve Utopia. Indeed, the various student organizations soon burned out; their members joined Left-wing 'extra-parliamentary' parties. Student rioting continued, but by the late 1970s it seemed a fairly trivial concern. By then the universities had evidently become one of the main breeding grounds for terrorists. Even some of the professors were arrested for organizing terrorist gangs.

18.2 THE ECONOMY

The crisis was no less evident in the factories. In November 1967 shipyard workers in Genoa and Trieste went on strike, protesting against 'rationalization' plans already accepted by their unions. It was the first of a vast series of unofficial 'wildcat' stoppages, street demonstrations, protest marches and factory occupations, spreading throughout Northern Italy in 1968–69. These events were totally unexpected – they happened suddenly, after two decades of fairly peaceful labour relations – and they had huge economic and political consequences.

Why did they occur? There were, obviously, economic reasons. Despite the increases in 1962–64, wages in Italy were still lower than elsewhere in Western Europe. Jobs were fairly secure, and there were few unemployed: people expected to be able to find new jobs easily. Furthermore, the workers in Northern Italy were changing. In the car industry, for example, new technology and work methods meant that unskilled men – often young Southern immigrants – replaced skilled craftsmen. The newcomers often detested industrial discipline, and were suspicious of the old trade unions. In any case, the existing unions were weak, absent from the shop-floor, and divided on political lines into three major confederations. Only about a quarter of Italy's engineering workers belonged to any of these unions in 1968, and they tended to be the skilled workers jealous of their now outmoded craft status and privileges. In short, the unions were out of touch. They had no real contact with most workers, and were unable to negotiate on 'factory' issues – hours, working conditions, etc.

Thus one explanation for the clashes of 1968–69 is that the unions could not channel grievances effectively. Other factors also played a part. Students in France and Italy were busy showing the way, and radical 'gruppuscoli' helped found many workers' committees and liaison groups (e.g. at Pirelli). In those heady days, it seemed essential to avoid the routine bureaucratic channels, and to rely instead on mass meetings and mass participation. Moreover, workers in the crowded Northern cities had many grievances *outside* the factory: housing, public transport and health services were all inadequate. 'Centre-Left' coalition governments (Christian Democrat and Socialist) had been in office since 1963, yet little had been done for ordinary workers. In these circumstances the Italian tradition is to riot; and that is what people did. The only difference from usual was that in 1968–69 many of the riots took place inside factories.

The agitations were not confined to young unskilled immigrants. Many of the older, skilled, unionized workers joined in too, and sometimes provided the initial impetus, as at the Innocenti works in Milan. Some of these men had a Resistance past, and the 'Hot Autumn' of 1969, although it involved millions of people, was reminiscent of the Resistance. It, too, was a largely spontaneous revolt against harsh industrial discipline, a celebration of solidarity against the 'Fascist' oppressors, a strike wave without parallel elsewhere in Europe. It, too, saw new institutions arise, to lead the host of local movements. In the factories, the workers elected 'delegates' to 'Factory Councils', and demanded workers' control over factory conditions, the end of skilled workers' differentials, and equal pay rises for all. They denounced not only the bosses, but also the 'complicity' of the official unions and parties, and even the irrationality and inhumanity of the industrial process itself.

Employers and unions naturally tried to regain control of events. One way was to 'buy off' unrest. They negotiated big rises in the basic wage – over 15 per cent on average, a huge increase in those days of low inflation. Hourly wages in industry almost doubled between 1969 and 1973, from 489 to 957 lire. More importantly, the militant 'delegates' and 'Factory Councils' were absorbed into the official union structure. Employers negotiated with them on local issues like piece-rates and working conditions. The union branches helped in these negotiations, co-ordinated the various factories' efforts, and often signed the eventual agreements. So the 'delegates' became, in effect, shop stewards: elected by the workers, but usually loyal trade unionists themselves, and co-operating closely with local union officials. Indeed, in 1972 the unions defined the 'Factory Councils' as the 'primary trade union body, with powers of negotiation at the workplace'.[1] The 'delegates' often won real benefits, especially on bonuses, hours and job-enrichment schemes; but they had also become more responsible and respectable.

Thus the 'Hot Autumn' agitations strengthened the trade unions. They put down roots into the factories, and they attracted more workers. By 1976 over half the workers in the country were union members, about the same as in Britain. The unions also began to co-operate much more among themselves, and the three leading engineering unions actually merged into one. Similarly, in June 1972 the three major confederations signed a 'Pact of Federation', supposedly the first step on the road to eventual unity. Little came of this, but for some years relations between Communist, Socialist and Catholic trade unionists remained cordial, and party politicians had less say in union affairs. In 1970 a new law, rather grandiosely entitled the *Statute of the Workers*, made many of the unions' conquests – including the 'right of assembly' within the factory – legally binding.

The trade unions sometimes took other political initiatives. There were repeated short 'general strikes' in favour of better pensions, social security, health services, public transport, housing, or investment in the South. Such campaigns were designed to demonstrate to local members that factory extremism was not enough: permanent national organizations were needed for any real, lasting improvement in living conditions. They also showed that the various union confederations were active, and could join together on a common platform. And they won some successes. Regional differences in wage-scales were abolished in 1968–69. A new pension law was passed, providing around two-thirds of a worker's final wage at age 60, with some indexing for inflation. A housing law in 1971 provided for compulsory land purchase, and was thought likely to increase the stock of public housing. In 1972 most workers won the right to 150 hours of paid education or training each year – a great opportunity to contact radical students. There was a big increase in Southern investment. Above all, in 1975 the existing limited system of index-linked pay rises was greatly extended. Henceforth the 'mobile scale' gave automatic protection against inflation, the same increases for everybody.

These provisions were a triumph for the unions. They had clearly done a marvellous job in protecting their members' interests. Yet the snags soon became clear too. Since inflation was over 20 per cent p.a., the index-linked portion of pay soon grew larger than the union-negotiated basic wage. That left the unions without much to do, especially since any extra pay rises, over and above the automatic ones, were only likely to come from increased productivity – and 'productivity' had become synonymous with 'exploitation'. In practice, the Communist-led unions in the 1970s followed the party line of responsible, co-operative behaviour, preaching 'austerity' and wage restraint. They were much abused for their pains. The major union confederations had undoubtedly helped to 'absorb' working-class militancy after 1968, and had been co-opted on to a host of government agencies and regional planning boards, but by the late 1970s they were becoming irrelevant. The leaders could neither control their own members nor provide them with significant benefits. Membership began to fall: by 1978 a quarter of the CGIL's members were in fact retired.

Indexing posed other problems too. Since the inflation-proofing was equal for all, skilled workers soon began complaining that they were paid little more than labourers. In the late 1970s working-class militancy increasingly reflected the frustration of skilled or 'professional' workers (e.g. air traffic controllers) anxious to preserve their status and differentials. This kind of militancy was usually in State-owned enterprises (Alfa Romeo, railways) or services (hospitals, courts). It was usually either unofficial, or led by small 'autonomous' unions whose leaders had nothing but contempt for the major union confederations and for the major political parties. It could not be bought off, without annoying the unskilled majority; yet, as it persisted, it led to a virtual collapse of some public services and discredited all the unions together.

The large pay rises of 1969–70 had obviously raised industrial costs. Inflation-proofing of wages simply froze this situation for the indefinite future: real wages could not fall without everybody noticing. The result was that many firms were priced out of the market. They could not lower wages, nor did they dare to dismiss anybody; all they could do was to lay people off 'temporarily'. That did not worry workers too much, for in 1975 the State insurance fund (*Cassa Integrazione Guadagni*) had also been greatly extended. Henceforth people continued to receive at least 80 per cent of their pay if laid off, and this happy arrangement could continue for a year. But it did not solve employers' problems. Industrial labour costs rose by 90 per cent in three years after October 1975; by 1980 the Dresdner Bank estimated wage costs per unit of production were 39 per cent higher in Italy than in West Germany or Britain.[2] Profits suddenly disappeared. Fiat, faced with constant stoppages and high absenteeism, responded to indexing (and to the 'revolt against the assembly-line') by installing robots. Many firms could not adapt so readily, and went bankrupt; the larger ones invited takeover bids, either by the State or by foreign competitors.

Other firms, especially in textiles and light engineering, simply carried on decentralizing and sub-contracting their operations (see §17.1). Factories had become uneconomic. Henceforth individual workers, or tiny firms, received the raw materials and worked on them at home, being paid at piece-rates for the product. Employers thus avoided paying index-linked wages, avoided unions, avoided safety regulations, avoided taxes and avoided social security contributions; the costs of unofficial 'cottage industries' were reckoned to be about one-third of those in a factory. There was nothing primitive or backward about this small-firm, clandestine sector. It thrived in vital export industries like fashion and shoes, it could 'mass-produce' millions of goods (e.g. jeans), it was most widespread in the prosperous Northern regions, and it obviously employed millions of people – many of them absentees from 'official' jobs in factories. It was a great economic success story. But it did little for the State's revenues, and even less for the unions.

Moreover, index-linking made it almost impossible for young people to find a 'regular' job. Who would employ a fifteen-year-old, if it meant giving him a guaranteed real income for life? By 1977 there were almost 1 million unemployed young people (aged 14–24) in Italy; they were the bulk of the officially unemployed, and the number would have been much greater without the 750,000 students and the 250,000 conscripts, to say nothing of the 2 million emigrants abroad. This was a horrifying outcome. The cities were full of disgruntled young people, existing precariously off 'black' labour or off their families. What was worse, these young people knew that their elder brothers and sisters, who had jobs, were doing extremely well, indeed were the most affluent age-group in the country. No wonder the under-thirties seemed a real threat to public order. In 1977 the government set up a Youth Opportunity Scheme, subsidizing employers to take on young people; in the first 2½ years 898,000 people applied, but only 59,000 were found jobs, and 44,000 of these were in central or local government.

Indeed, the 'official' economy was in real trouble. It was not merely a matter of low investment and high unemployment. Inflation remained high, at least 15 per cent p.a.: since wages were indexed, industrial costs were bound to keep rising. And the five-fold increase in oil prices at the end of 1973 hit Italy particularly badly. She had virtually no coal, oil or nuclear power, and her natural gas supplies, vital to her growth in the 1950s, were quite inadequate to her needs in the 1970s. So she had to import oil, at huge cost (almost $20 billion in 1980). It all contributed to semi-permanent 'recession'. In 1975 the gross national product fell by 3.7 per cent – the first time it had fallen since 1945. Public spending, too, seemed out of control. The State spent huge sums on Southern development, on its attempts at social welfare, and on industrial subsidies. By 1979 the budget deficit was over 30,000 billion lire. Here was a real 'fiscal crisis', which would have been even worse if government agencies had spent the money allocated to them. As for the lira, it had to be 'floated' in February 1973, and thereafter fell steadily against other European currencies and the American dollar. The average exchange-rate in 1972 was 183 lire to the Deutschmark; by 1976 it was 330 lire, and by December 1979 468. For years the country lived off foreign loans. Governments also, of course, increased taxes – most Italians began paying income tax, for example, only in the mid-1970s – and raised interest rates, but just when these policies started having some effect the renewed oil price rises of 1979 brought in another recession. By 1980 Italy had had ten years of virtually unrelieved 'crisis', mitigated only by the unofficial economy. Admittedly the Italian GDP *had* grown, by about 3 per cent p.a.; but that was about half the rate of the 1960s. Italy's lack of energy, and her growing backwardness in research and technology, were ominous signs for the future.

So, too, were the problems of the major State-owned firms (see §17.1). IRI broke even in 1973, but lost 500 billion lire in 1975, 900 billion lire in 1977, 1,346 billion lire in 1979, and around 2,200 billion lire – 6 per cent of gross domestic product – in 1980. Steelmaking was the major culprit, but the new Alfa Romeo car plant near Naples allegedly made greater losses than any other car factory in the world, and there was close competition from the petrochemical group Montedison, from the State shipbuilding firms, from the State mining and minerals agency, and even from telecommunications. It was not necessarily the managers' fault. Governments forced them to charge low prices, to invest in the South, to employ redundant workers and to accept 'political' appointments.

The disasters of the official economy were accompanied by a series of financial scandals, spectacular even by Italian standards. In 1976 it emerged that several international oil companies had paid large sums to Italian parties, probably in return for tax concessions. The Lockheed aircraft company was also revealed to have bribed leading politicians, in order to sell its Hercules C 130 planes to the Italian air force. Throughout the 1970s the Italian press was full of such rumours. Parliamentary committees of inquiry sat regularly; investigating magistrates questioned Prime Ministers; two former Cabinet ministers were imprisoned. It all contributed to an atmosphere of suspicion and distrust, of accusations and counter-accusations, of scapegoats and villainy – a crisis of ethics as much as of economics.

18.3 DIVORCE AND THE FAMILY

Indeed, cultural changes were even more striking than economic decline. By the 1970s only just over one-third of the people went to mass weekly; over half declared that they were 'indifferent to religion'.[3] Vocations to the priesthood fell away sharply, and the average age of priests and nuns became ever higher. Church-run institutions, whether schools, co-operatives, or trade unions, appealed only to a minority. Religious practice had ceased to be a social habit and had become a minority sub-culture, or even a matter of private belief.

Most churchgoers had been women, and 'secularization' made its major impact on them. A survey of Italian women in 1972 produced some startling responses. Twenty or thirty years previously, these women thought, most of them would have wanted a husband, children, a well-equipped home, and someone to protect them; by 1972 the four main priorities were education, a job away from the house, freedom to think and act as they liked, and prosperity. Not that these women were particularly liberated, by most Western standards. Of the married ones, only 10 per cent reported that their husband 'helped regularly' with the housework, and only 16 per cent thought he should do so; 93 per cent would disapprove of their daughter living with a boy-friend; over two-thirds of them had never heard of 'feminism'.[4] Still, it was clear that migration, urbanization and secondary education for girls had done their work. Moreover, by 1972 there were already over 250,000 female graduates. For the first time in Italian history there were substantial numbers of educated young women. Naturally there was also a great deal of male prejudice against them, except in some traditional women's jobs like teaching – and even these jobs were becoming rarer. By the mid-1970s Italy had a vociferous 'women's movement', agitating for at least equal rights and opportunities. Most of the active women were young and educated. They greatly embarrassed the existing political parties by their demands. These demands were much the same as those of their sisters elsewhere, except for one – divorce.

Until 1970 there was no divorce in Italy. Church marriages could be 'annulled' (i.e. declared invalid) by the Vatican on certain grounds, and in fact over 800 annulments were granted in 1970. Alternatively, the State's tribunals could grant a 'legal separation', which might include maintenance orders and decisions on the custody of children (normally granted to the father). These 'legal separations', some 9,000 p.a. in the late 1960s, were tantamount to divorce, except that the ex-partners could not remarry. Many people, therefore, contracted 'illicit' unions, with illegitimate offspring – as did many of those who separated unofficially. Emigration and urbanization helped to break up marriages, and led to new partnerships. The whole issue could not be ignored for ever, for huge numbers of people were affected.

In 1965, therefore, a Socialist deputy, Loris Fortuna, put forward a bill introducing divorce after five years' legal separation. The next year a new pressure-group was founded, the *Lega per l'Istituzione del Divorzio* (LID). This was a rare type of organization in Italy, for it grouped together people from all parties and from none, although it was necessarily anti-Church and anti-government. Its main appeal was to the radical middle classes, especially journalists and lawyers, and its first secretary was Marco Pannella, who was also secretary of the tiny Radical Party. Italian Radicalism, dormant since the 1940s, suddenly revived. The divorce campaign provided the Radicals with their first real opportunity for years, and they made the most of it. Pannella, for example, became a national figure by staging a successful hunger strike outside parliament to protest against filibustering on the bill. The constant pressure was, eventually, successful. By December 1970 Italy had her first divorce law, allowing divorce in certain restricted circumstances.

Many Catholics were horrified by this law. Pope Paul VI argued that it was a breach of the 1929 Concordat, by which the State had agreed to 'recognize the civil effects of the sacrament of marriage' (article 34). Catholic lawyers argued that it was unconstitutional, but to no avail. However, the Italian Constitution includes provision for a referendum, if 500,000 electors request it; the referendum can 'abrogate', i.e. repeal, all or part of most laws. In other words, there is a potential popular veto on legislation, although no referendum had actually been held since the 1946 one on the monarchy. Here was a marvellous opportunity. Catholic laymen founded a National Committee for a Referendum on Divorce on the very day the law was passed. It soon collected the necessary signatures, and it expected to win.

But it was 3½ years before the referendum was eventually held. By this time about 90,000 divorces had been granted. Public opinion, as measured by the polls, had swung round. All the political parties except the Christian Democrats and the neo-Fascists spoke out in favour of divorce, and even these two were divided. By 1974 there was a 'Committee of Democratic Catholics' campaigning for the divorce law; it claimed that over 20 per cent of the priests it had contacted supported its views, and polls showed that many practising Catholics did accept the new law. In the event, 19 million voters (59.1 per cent) opted in May 1974 to retain the divorce law, with 13 million against. Anti-divorce sentiment prevailed only in the Catholic North-East (Veneto and Trentino-Alto Adige) and in the mainland South, although in all areas the countryside was more traditional than the towns. The result was a great victory for the Radicals and for the lay Left generally, and a crushing defeat for the Church and for the Christian Democrats. It symbolized the triumph of lay, 'progressive', 'Enlightenment' values in Italy.

Divorce was the most spectacular aspect of the 'crisis of the family', but it was not the only one. In 1975 parliament hastily updated its family legislation. Dowries were abolished, wives were allowed to keep their maiden name, and it was solemnly laid down that wives and husbands should jointly agree on where (and how) to live. Meanwhile civil marriages had become more common, partly because divorced people could not remarry in church: from 1.2 per cent of all marriages in 1967, they had risen to 8 per cent in 1972, and to 11.9 per cent in 1979. In the big cities, one marriage in three took place outside church. But many couples did not bother to get married at all. In 1973 there were 418,979 weddings; by 1979 there were only 325,598. Ironically, divorce also became rarer: what was the point, unless you wanted to remarry? People preferred to 'separate' instead, just as they had done before 1970. In 1979 there were 10,800 divorces, but 25,900 separations (8 per cent of the marriages in that year). And 'living together' (*convivenza*) became socially acceptable, even to many parents. It replaced the former period of 'engagement', and some people thought it would replace marriage itself.

Others began worrying about the next generation. Would there be one? The birth-rate had been declining for years from its 1964 peak, but from 1974 onwards the fall became acute: 868,882 live births in 1974, 670,078 in 1979. Furthermore, almost half of them were in the South, which stimulated Northern fears of 'meridionalization'. In the North-West and in the 'Red Belt' of Central Italy there were more deaths than births by 1979. Part of the explanation is that reliable contraceptives, such as the Pill, were freely available; and economic hardships no doubt played their usual role. But the real reason seems to me more fundamental. Younger people, especially women, had changed. They were now urban and literate. They wanted satisfying jobs, not domestic chores.

They also wanted, and secured, legal abortions. After 1974, when divorce had been won, abortion on demand became the great battlecry of Italian feminists. It was not easily granted. Illegal abortions were apparently fairly common, but that was no reason, in Catholic eyes, for legalizing them. Many doctors, too, had conscientious scruples, and many of the others did not want to lose a lucrative sideline. And in many hospitals most of the nurses were nuns. Altogether, it needed very determined pressure by the various women's movements and by the Radicals and Socialists before the 'lay' majority in parliament could finally be persuaded to approve an abortion law – unthinkable just a few years previously, and still surprising in a country with a Christian Democrat-dominated government. But there was to be no abortion on demand, at least in principle. The decision was formally left to the doctors, but they were only supposed to carry out abortions in public hospitals, on women over eighteen, and during the first three months of pregnancy. Once the law was passed, two-thirds of Italy's doctors refused to perform them; but there were so many other doctors left that 200,000 legal abortions took place each year, more than a quarter of the figure for live births.

There was naturally a great deal of controversy about abortion. As in the case of divorce, committed Catholics soon began petitioning for a referendum. Anticlerical Radicals and feminists also wanted one, in order to secure 'the woman's right to choose'. As previously, most political parties were embarrassed and anxious not to become involved. Nearly all Christian Democrats were hostile in principle to abortion, but hesitated to ally yet again with the neo-Fascists, fighting another losing crusade on an issue calculated to alienate women and young people. Even the Church was perplexed, for the eventual 'Catholic' proposal at the referendum was not that abortion should be banned altogether, but that it should be limited to cases of real danger to the woman's life or health. So the bishops proclaimed that the 'Catholic' proposal 'should not lead anyone to think that the remaining provisions on abortion may be considered morally permissible and practicable'.[5] In the event, the two referenda on abortion in May 1981 confirmed the 1978 law: 88.5 per cent voted against the Radical proposal for abortion on demand; more significantly, 67.9 per cent voted against the 'Catholic' proposals. Only in one region, Trentino-Alto Adige, was there a popular majority for them; in Rome itself only 27.2 per cent of the voters supported them. The anti-abortionists of 1981 secured a smaller vote than the anti-divorce campaigners of 1974, and smaller even than the Christian Democrat vote in 1976 and 1979. It was an extraordinary indication of how deep-rooted 'secularization' had become.

It all posed an enormous challenge to the Christian Democrat 'regime', a challenge personified by the anticlerical Radical Party. This tiny group of journalists and mavericks won a series of astonishing victories – not just on the 'anticlerical' issues of divorce and abortion, but on conscientious objection, prison reform and admissions to State-run mental hospitals. The referendum became a favourite Radical device. The trick was to collect 500,000 signatures; even if no referendum were held, parliament might well be frightened into changing the existing law. In 1978 the Radicals collected the signatures for eight referenda, although the Constitutional Court ruled out six as unconstitutional. In 1981, in addition to the call for free abortion on demand, referenda were held on three other 'Radical' issues – the new anti-terrorist laws, life imprisonment, and the right to own guns (the Radicals were against all of them). Again, six other referenda had been ruled out, on such diverse topics as legalizing marijuana, hunting, courts martial in peacetime, the libel laws and nuclear power. These issues all expressed a 'libertarian' or 'environmental', even 'post-materialist' approach to politics, and they all appealed to young, educated, affluent urban voters. The Radicals were accused of being 'irresponsible', but that was their whole point. They set out to shock the bourgeoisie, and they delighted in making both the Christian Democrats and the Communists seem terribly staid and old-fashioned. Soon they elected their first deputies – four in 1976, eighteen in 1979 – who had an enjoyable time in parliament, publicizing other politicians' shady deals and filibustering energetically against laws they disliked. Admittedly the Radicals always lost their referenda, but they kept Italian politics on the boil. They symbolized the values of a new generation, perhaps of a new way of life.

Perhaps the biggest 'Radical' achievement was in helping to dismantle the State's broadcasting monopoly. In 1976, after years of agitation, the Constitutional Court ruled that RAI's monopoly infringed the citizen's right to freedom of speech. Hundreds of local radio and TV stations sprang up immediately, many of them very tedious but some (e.g. 'Radio Radicale') a constant source of embarrassment to the Establishment. Broadcasting, like the economy, had acquired a local, cheap, unorganized and lively sector, quite outside State control. No longer could governments dictate the issues of political debate; no longer could political parties dream of establishing a cultural 'hegemony'. Even the official TV became less reverent, and actually began discussing live issues. Italy had become a multi-media society, with no control over nor consensus about news, values, or morality. Hard-core pornography, for example, could henceforth be seen on TV: it was already available, from the mid-1970s onwards, in freely-sold magazines and in many cinemas. It all confirmed the Great Cultural Revolution of the previous few years; a revolution, moreover, from below.

18.4 TERRORISM

The most disturbing and dramatic aspect of all this social and political ferment was the growth of violent crime, including political terrorism. The student and workers' demonstrations of 1968–69 really frightened many respectable bourgeois. Like their counterparts fifty years earlier, some of them turned to the Fascists to deal with the 'Red Threat'. In 1972 the neo-Fascist vote went up to 8.7 per cent nationally. But it was not just Fascism of the ballot. Fascist 'squads' revived too, bent on 'restoring order' and repressing the Left. The various groups – *Ordine Nuovo, Squadre di Azione Mussolini, Avanguardia Nazionale, Rosa dei Venti*, etc. – were ill-co-ordinated and ill-led, but they had plenty of money, they had (rarely acknowledged) links with the official neo-Fascist party, the *Movimento Sociale Italiano*, and they obviously had some influential sympathizers within the police and security services. Apart from beating up student leaders or Communists, the Fascists apparently adopted a 'strategy of tension', i.e. they aimed at causing chaos. This would, they hoped, force the army to step in, impose martial law and overthrow parliamentary democracy. The Fascists were generally believed to be responsible for the first major terrorist act of the decade, the bomb in piazza Fontana, Milan, in December 1969, when 16 people were killed and 90 injured; they killed 7 Left-wing demonstrators at Brescia in May 1974; they derailed the Rome–Munich express in August 1974, with 12 dead; and in August 1980, after some years of relative inactivity, they blew up the restaurant at Bologna station, killing 84 people and injuring 200 more.

Fascist violence was at its peak in the early 1970s. Rumours of plots and army *coups* abounded. Communist leaders, surrounded by armed bodyguards, slept in different houses each night. Prince Valerio Borghese, former commander of the 'Tenth Torpedo-boat Squadron' in the war, actually occupied the Ministry of the Interior for a few hours in December 1970. One former head of the Secret Intelligence Service was arrested for treason (he later became a neo-Fascist deputy); another was imprisoned for procuring a false passport for a Fascist squad leader. Perhaps the Republic was in serious danger – Greece, after all, was run by its Colonels from 1967 to 1974 – but somehow it survived; 1972 was not 1922 all over again. The Fascists lacked an effective leader, and labour militancy was less threatening after 1970 – indeed, the Communists firmly restrained their own militants. The Christian Democrats wooed the respectable Right, i.e. the Liberals, but ignored the neo-Fascists; and they retained the support of Church, Europe and Washington. Furthermore, after Franco's death Spain was no longer available to the Fascists as a refuge and source of arms. So Fascist violence died down. The 'strategy of tension' had failed.

Right-wing terrorism had been, essentially, a response to student demonstrations and to the 'Hot Autumn' of 1969. So, too, was Left-wing terrorism. It emerged from the semi-revolutionary ferment of the late 1960s – from hopes of Utopia, from outrage at slum housing and injustice continuing under Centre-Left governments, and from disillusionment with the Communist Party's 'reformist betrayals'. The 'generation of 1968' rejected 'the system', deeming it Fascist. Moralistic, uncompromising, and blindly convinced of their own righteousness, small groups of students and intellectuals set out to overthrow the State. Many of them were young, affluent, urban, self-confident and as well educated as Italy's universities permitted. But there were other kinds of terrorist too. Many young unemployed were recruited, for example, as were immigrant workers horrified by factory conditions. Some Northern factories – e.g. Magneti Morelli, Alfa Romeo at Varese, Sit Siemens – became virtual terrorist enclaves. So did some of the prisons, where captured terrorists mixed freely with ordinary criminals. Some terrorists, like Alberto Franceschini, emerged from the Communist sub-culture of Emilia-Romagna; others, like Renato Curcio and Margherita Cagol, from Catholic backgrounds;

many others from the desperate, violent world of the urban poor. Some aimed simply at 'fighting Fascism'; others at overthrowing the 'imperialist State of the multinationals'. Some were cool, clever intellectuals; others were impulsive *enragés*. By 1976, indeed, there were 140 separate Left-wing terrorist groups active in the country; it was not surprising that they differed from each other. But what they had in common was perhaps more significant. They all shared a fierce hatred of the 'regime', a hatred that had its roots in Italian history. Some were the sons of Resistance fighters. Their fathers had risked all in the struggle against Fascism; now it was their turn. The leaders of the Italian Republic had spent thirty years lauding the legitimacy of revolt against tyranny; they could hardly complain now if young men took to guerrilla warfare against the new Fascists.

The other common features, at least until 1978, were plenty of money, and some public sympathy. Terrorism was partly self-financing through bank robberies, kidnappings, etc., but that did not account for all the costly exploits of the mid-1970s. The first Left-wing groups, the *Gruppi di Azione Partigiana* (GAP), were founded by a guilt-ridden millionaire, Giangiacomo Feltrinelli, who later blew himself up planting a bomb at Segrate, near Milan. Left-wing terrorism might never have become a serious threat without his money and his organizing drive. Later on, international links became more important, particularly in providing advanced weaponry training. The terrorists learned their trade in Czechoslovakia, Cuba or South Yemen. Feltrinelli himself had been inspired by the Tupamaros in Uruguay, as well as by Castro and Mao.

As for public support, this was evident enough on the Left. To use Mao's image, the terrorist fish were swimming in a warm, sheltered sea. Many Communists felt a sneaking sympathy for the terrorist 'comrades': their methods might be 'mistaken', but clearly their hearts were in the right place. Certainly they should not be denounced to the police, nor to the bosses. Many young people felt the same. The 'extra-parliamentary Left' was more actively involved. After 1969 there were several small political movements on the Left – e.g. *Lotta Continua* and *Potere Operaio* – which sometimes had their own military units, whose journals spread much the same message as the terrorist groups, and whose members often joined them. Above all, there were the autonomous groups – unofficial, militant, powerful in the factories, dockyards and universities, and thoroughly contemptuous of capitalists and Communists alike. Here terrorists could acquire weapons, recruits and information: where the money was kept, and which managers deserved a taste of 'proletarian justice'.

By the late 1970s terrorist acts had become fairly commonplace – over 2,000 a year, according to official figures, including about 40 murders. The favourite targets for the bullets were industrial managers, journalists, prison warders, judges, policemen, and Christian Democrat politicians; but threats could be made against anyone, and bombs could easily kill passers-by. Some cities, notably Bologna and Padua, lived through periods of virtual guerrilla war. Captured terrorists could not be tried, for nobody would serve on the jury. Kidnapping, too, could be used against anyone thought rich enough to pay the ransom. Italy enjoyed world leadership of this industry – about 300 *reported* cases a year – although most kidnappings had financial rather than (or as well as) political motives. Newspapers were filled with accounts of terrorist exploits, of police *coups* and failures, of irreproachable heroes and degenerate villains. Terrorist communiqués, drivelling on about imperialist hegemony, were treated as tablets of stone; private radio stations played tapes of kidnap victims' 'confessions'. It was a national melodrama, difficult to take too seriously unless you knew someone personally affected. There were, in fact, probably never more than a few hundred professional terrorists active at any one time, although there were thousands of part-timers, free-lancers and sympathizers.

The most famous group was the Red Brigades, founded by Renato Curcio and others in Milan in 1970. It had, like the other groups, a complex and unstable history, beginning in romantic, even quixotic style – e.g. short-term kidnappings with the victim released unharmed without needing to pay a ransom. Indeed, the Red Brigades did not murder anyone until 1974. By 1976, however, Curcio was in prison, his wife Margherita Cagol had been killed, and the Brigades were led by tougher men. In March 1978 came their most famous exploit. They kidnapped Aldo Moro, President of the Christian Democrat Party and former Prime Minister. Here was real 'propaganda by the deed', especially when Moro was 'persuaded' to write incriminatory letters against his former colleagues. For two months the politicians agonized over their choice. Should they release a number of imprisoned terrorists, as the Red Brigades demanded, and hope for Moro's safe return? Or should they refuse to negotiate with terrorists, and risk Moro being killed? The hardline argument, backed by Christian Democrats and Communists and opposed by Socialists, prevailed. The Red Brigades then killed Moro. They had proved their own efficiency and ruthlessness; they had shown up the incompetence of Italy's various police forces; and they thought they had delegitimized the Christian Democrat 'regime'.

18.5 THE POLITICAL RESPONSE: THE 'HISTORIC COMPROMISE'

How did the ruling politicians react to all this social upheaval? As usual, they sought to 'absorb' potential troublemakers into the existing political system. This process of 'absorption' took several forms. I have discussed the new role of the trade unions already; the other outstanding example was the 'historic compromise'.

The 'historic compromise' was a 'flirtation of convenience' between the Christian Democrats and the second largest party in the country, the Communists. It may seem surprising that Christian Democrat politicians should woo their Communist rivals, but they had little choice. Their 'regime' was collapsing around them, amid economic crisis, financial scandal, incipient terrorism and rampant 'secularization'. Drastic economic and security measures seemed necessary, and these presupposed agreements – on the shop-floor, between the major trade union confederations, in parliament, and between the major parties. In any case, by the mid-1970s the Christian Democrats had no alternative allies. The Socialists were refusing to join any more 'Centre-Left' coalitions, having lost too many members and voters to the Communists and Radicals. They would not enter another government unless the Communists were in it too: let them share the blame in future for things going wrong. So moderate Christian Democrat leaders like Andreotti and Moro began making approaches to the PCI.

The Communist Party secretary, Enrico Berlinguer, was happy to accept these advances. Communist strategy had been based for years on the need for popular, 'anti-Fascist' alliances. In particular, the party had been visibly helping the Church ever since the Constituent Assembly in 1947, when it voted in favour of recognizing the 1929 Concordat; and it had occasionally been able to mediate in favour of Catholics in Vietnam and Eastern Europe. The party leaders welcomed a further opportunity to make themselves useful, to pursue their strategy of *'presenza'* (see §16.1), of being 'present' everywhere in Italian society, organizing and influencing, providing order and leadership for popular agitations.

Moreover, Berlinguer was also deeply worried by the national crisis. He believed that many key institutions – the police, the army, the judiciary, the senior civil service – were under Fascist influence. He also knew what had happened in 1922. Labour militancy and Communist success at the polls might frighten the middle classes into the Fascist arms. Alternatively, the Communists might find themselves in government without any real control over the 'State': the fate of Allende in Chile was a dreadful warning of what might happen next. The party was not respectable enough, and Italy's economy was not strong enough, to make any *sole* exercise of power a feasible proposition. Nor would Italy's allies have tolerated a Communist government. Power-sharing with some respectable party like the Christian Democrats was the most that the Communists could hope for; indeed, power-sharing was essential, for fear of what worse might befall.

In September 1973, therefore, Berlinguer put forward his famous proposal for a 'historic compromise' with the other political parties, especially the Christian Democrats. The Communists, he proclaimed, were available as partners. They would act responsibly, they would help to restore the economy and maintain public order, they would respect the Church and civil liberties; in return, they would expect to secure some social reforms and to influence general policy. And he was as good as his word. In the next few years the Communists discouraged labour militancy, and they arranged profitable trade with the Soviet Union and Eastern Europe. The party even endorsed Italy's membership of Nato, on the grounds that it had no wish to endanger *détente*. Just before the 1976 elections Berlinguer stated, no doubt truthfully, that he felt 'more secure' in the West.[6] And in December 1977 the Communist deputies formally voted in favour of Italy's foreign and defence policies.

All this was meant to be reassuring; and for a time it worked. After 1975 the Communists not only ran six regions and most of the big cities, but their deputies in the Chamber rose from 179 in 1972 to 227 in 1976, only 36 fewer than the Christian Democrats, Parliament could not function without them, and did not try. In August 1976 Giulio Andreotti formed a new Christian Democrat government, which could count on PCI abstention on votes of confidence; in 1977 the Communists helped to draw up the government programme; by March 1978 the PCI was part of the government's parliamentary majority, and so voted *for* the government. Only the final step, Communist ministers in the Cabinet, remained to be taken.

However, the 'historic compromise' failed at the final fence. There were many reasons. Most Christian Democrats remained implacably hostile to Communism, and Moro's death removed the most persuasive advocate of an 'understanding'. International tensions also grew worse in 1978–79, and this naturally affected inter-party relations in Italy: the Italian Communists could not hope to share power overtly after the Russian invasion of Afghanistan. The election of Cardinal Wojtyla as Pope John Paul II in October 1978 undoubtedly strengthened the Vatican's resolve to struggle against Communist doctrines. Relations between the Church and the Communists were much worsened by the 1977 regional laws (see below, §18.6), which for a time brought thousands of Church-run charities under political control. There were also furious squabbles among the politicians over jobs. The PCI claimed its share in State industries, banks and broadcasting; thousands of ordinary Christian Democrats held grimly on to their own.

Many Communists disliked the 'historic compromise' too, and refused to co-operate. Most of them detested the Christian Democrats, and had little sympathy for the Church. Berlinguer's supporters began drifting away. Party membership fell, for the first time in years, and the Communist vote declined (down at the 1979 general election from 34.4 per cent to 30.4 per cent). Communist trade unionists found that their pleas for wage restraint were spurned; worse, that workers were turning to the unofficial 'autonomous' unions. So the Communists had to become militant again, to win back the rank and file. Certainly they could no longer guarantee peaceful labour relations, a fact which removed much of their usefulness in Christian Democrat eyes. In any case, the economic crisis appeared less acute in 1978–79: there was even a brief surplus on the balance of payments. Perhaps Communist backing was not necessary after all. The Communists were not, therefore, fully 'absorbed' into the government. By 1979 they had returned formally to opposition, and Berlinguer was praising Lenin.

Even so, an enormous change had occurred. Thousands of party members held posts in regional and local government, in advisory bodies, on schools or health councils. There was *de facto* co-operation with other parties in parliament and unions, and throughout the country. The party *was* 'absorbed into the system' at all levels except the very top. Moreover, it was distancing itself ever more from its international affiliations. The Communist leadership was extremely sympathetic to the Solidarity movement in Poland, and shared most of its aims. So the military takeover in Warsaw at the end of 1981 appalled the party leaders in Rome. Berlinguer wondered aloud whether the Soviet experience still had any relevance for Western Europeans; Moscow replied by branding the PCI as 'anti-Soviet' and accusing it of giving 'direct aid to imperialism and anti-Communism'.[7] The dispute caused some unrest among the party faithful, but in the long run it helped the PCI. It reduced the influence of the remaining pro-Soviet 'Stalinists' within the party's ranks; above all, it diminished the 'international' reasons why it should not be allowed to join an Italian government.

18.6 THE REBIRTH OF REGIONALISM

In one sense the Communists were already in Italian government – in six regional governments, that is. The regions were another fine example of 'co-involvement', and not just of the Communists. The principle of regionalism had been included in the Italian Constitution in 1947–48 (see §15.6), but in practice regional governments existed before 1970 only in the outlying fringe areas – Sicily, Sardinia, Trentino-Alto Adige, the Valle d'Aosta and (since 1963) Friuli-Venezia Giulia. None of them was a great success, nor did regional government in Trentino-Alto Adige prevent terrorism by disaffected German-speakers. The rest of the country was governed from Rome, with weak local government at municipal (*comune*) level. The Christian Democrats, firmly entrenched in central government, were not anxious to hand over any power, especially if it meant allowing the Communists to run the 'Red Belt' regions of Central Italy. By the late 1960s, however, the old centralized system was visibly breaking down. It was clearly not providing welfare, housing and schools, let alone urban renewal. A new breed of technocratic planner urged the need for greater co-ordination with local government and for decentralizing the civil service. These planners were prominent in the Socialist Party, and most governments were then 'Centre-Left' coalitions between Christian Democrats and Socialists. Above all, the Communist Party appeared less of a menace than it had at the height of the 'Cold War'. Other politicians saw that it might be useful to give it some experience of governing, and to make it 'co-responsible' for Italy's intractable problems.

Thus the long-term arguments for 'efficiency' were boosted by a favourable short-term political situation. In 1968–70 the Centre-Left governments carried through an astonishing transformation. After a century of centralized government, Italy became a 'regional State'. Henceforth, in addition to the five existing 'special regions', there were to be fifteen 'ordinary regions' throughout the land, each with its own elected council and its own powers to pass laws 'within the framework of national legislation' on agriculture, town-planning, public works, health services, social welfare and many other matters. The regions would also have their own officials, responsible for the same topics, and their own sources of finance. Few people took much notice.

There was little or no popular agitation for regionalism in 1968–70; indeed, it was about the only issue over which people were not rioting at that time (except in Reggio Calabria). The change was pushed through by a coalition of party élites – Left-wing Christian Democrats devoted to 'participation', Socialist technocrats anxious for efficient planning, and Communist politicians wanting to run Central Italy and prove the party's fitness to govern.

The first councils in the 'ordinary regions' were elected in June 1970, but throughout the 1970s disputes continued about their powers. The regions might pass laws on certain topics, but in each region there was a 'Government Commissioner' with a temporary delaying veto. If the dispute continued, the regional law might be overruled by parliament, or it might be deemed unlawful by the Constitutional Court if, for example, it conflicted with the Constitution or with Italy's international and EEC obligations, or with 'the fundamental principles established by the laws of the State'.[8] In practice, the regions usually accepted the Government Commissioner's directives, although the Constitutional Court did overrule many regional laws, especially in the early 1970s. As for regional administration, it was the same story. The central State – i.e. the Government Commissioner, or the 'regional department' of the Prime Minister's Office – retained a general power of 'direction and co-ordination' of administration; and regional 'control commissions' or the Council of State itself could overrule regional officials on points of law. Further-more, central civil servants were reluctant to let any power slip out of their hands, and even more reluctant to be transferred from Rome to the regional centres. For some years, therefore, administration in the regions was restricted and hesitant. The regions had little money of their own, and certainly not enough to carry through independent policies. They were usually 'delegated' specific tasks by the ministries: Rome provided the instructions and the cash, regional administrators did the work under Rome's supervision.

However, in the mid-1970s this picture began to change. The Christian Democrat Party was under siege. Socialists and Communists insisted on 'real' regionalism as the price of their support. So in 1975–77 parliament passed another series of regional laws, transferring more powers and far more civil servants to the regions, and – much more significantly – abolishing or 'handing over' most of the national or local agencies (*enti pubblici*) on which Italian public administration had come to depend. Fifteen 'general directorates' in the central ministries were abolished; thousands of quangos were suppressed, including such venerable institutions as the National Agency for Assistance to Workers (the former *Dopolavoro* of Fascist memory), the Italian Hunting Federation and the Italian Fashion Agency. Henceforth the regions, or the municipalities under regional supervision, could found and staff their own specialist agencies for welfare, run their own subsidy schemes for farmers and artisans, and organize their own co-operatives and nursery schools. They could draw up regional development and land use plans; they could take over the Chambers of Commerce. For a time they could even close down, or take over, most of the Church-run, publicly subsidized charities, some of which had been operating ambulances or welfare schemes for centuries; but the Constitutional Court eventually ruled this out, after much clerical protest. Even so, the regions' new powers were huge, and expanded constantly as they were 'brought into' new legislation. The Southern ones, for example, acquired a role in industrial planning for the South in 1976; all of them were expected to run the youth employment scheme in 1978. By 1980 the regions were spending 18 per cent of the national budget, and had become the main bodies responsible for health and social services. Perhaps most startling of all was the handing over of the vital task of 'safeguarding public morals' – i.e. the power to issue licences to restaurant-owners, shopkeepers, taxi-drivers, gun-owners and the like. These were real powers of patronage and policing. Here, at last, was a revolution in government.

For all these tasks, the regions needed people. Most of the regional officials were former central civil servants, many transferred against their will, but the top jobs were naturally kept for local men. In the Marches, for example, only one 'director' (*dirigente*) came from Rome, and 'very few' did in Piedmont.[9] They were political appointments, so it obviously mattered which parties were in control. In fact, the regions were a mixed bag politically. In 1975–80 the Communists helped run six of the twenty regions (Piedmont, Liguria and Latium, as well as their three Central Italian strongholds of Emilia-Romagna, Tuscany and Umbria). The Socialists shared power with the Communists in these six, and with the Christian Democrats in six others. The Christian Democrats ran two by themselves, and shared control of eleven others with various parties. The minor parties also retained considerable influence – the Social Democrats were present in twelve regional governments, the Republicans in seven. After the 1980 elections the Communists lost their power in Liguria, but joined the coalition in Sardinia; the Christian Democrats were still in thirteen regional governments, as were the Socialists and Social Democrats.

This diversity was important. As the regions acquired more powers, *regional* élites were forming and governing on regional lines, not just in the regional governments themselves but in the host of specialist agencies that they created or absorbed. It all helped to make regional politicians ever more independent of their central party leaders. In the 1950s the Christian Democrats had used their control of central agencies to break the power of the (then) local élites. Now the boot was on the other foot. The regions – six of them run by Communists – had acquired the bulk of this vital patronage. The Christian Democrats fragmented even further into local baronies; even the Communists showed similar tendencies. The local politicians naturally enlisted the advice and help of local pressure-groups. Trade unionists, businessmen, amenity campaigners, self-appointed experts and spokesmen, all found that their voices were listened to respectfully at long last. Building speculators flourished as never before; so did the Calabrian 'Mafia' (*'ndrangheta*) and the Neapolitan *camorra*. That, too, was important. There may have been little popular enthusiasm for the regions, but many of the organized interest-groups thought they were splendid. By the late 1970s 'co-involvement' was clearly well advanced. Everybody who mattered had been brought into the system.

Local councillors sat on the new health boards, which had huge resources at their disposal. Voluntary bodies became included in regional and national legislation, e.g. on family counselling or drug abuse. And there were plenty of other efforts at inducing 'participation', e.g. in the new 'schools' councils' and the 'district councils' set up within big cities in 1976. No longer did all roads lead to Rome.

Was Italy simply reverting to type? Had United Italy been merely a temporary interlude in the long history of Italian city-states? It is, perhaps, still too early to be sure. However, the regions' essential task was to reconcile people to the State, not to supersede it; to help the central State become more efficient, not to dismantle it. Italy was not a federal State like Switzerland or West Germany: the regions had limited powers, subordinate to central government, in certain specified spheres only. Admittedly these spheres were important, but they were not the central ones of High Politics. The old unitary State remained in being, and remained, too, in control of much of the cash. It was simply being updated, that was all. But it was an unusual achievement to update it – to disperse the old elephantine bureaucracy, to abolish or transfer many of the key resources of political patronage, to abandon any hope of centralized, one-party control. Only an exceptional political crisis could have forced the politicians to act so resolutely.

REFERENCES

1. *Rassegna Sindacale*, 30 July 1972.
2. Survey by Dresdner Bank, quoted in *Financial Times*, 22 Oct. 1980; also Eurostat (Luxemburg), *Wages and Incomes*, 5 March 1980.
3. D. Wertman, 'The Catholic Church and Italian politics: the impact of secularisation', *West European Politics*, v (1982), 99–100; S. Burgalassi, *Le Cristianità Nascoste*, Bologna 1970, pp. 164 ff; E. Pin, *La Religiosità dei Romani*, Bologna 1975, p. 342.
4. *Bollettino della Doxa*, xxvii, 20 June, 1 and 30 July 1973, pp. 69–134.
5. Declarations of the Italian Bishops' Conference, 9 Feb. and 17 March 1981.
6. *Corriere della Sera*, 15 June 1976.
7. 'Vopreki Interesam Mira i Sotsializma', *Pravda*, 24 Jan. 1982.
8. Article 117 of the Italian Constitution.
9. F. Sidoti (ed.), *L'Organizzazione e il Personale delle Regioni*, Milan 1979, p. 24 and p. 104.

CHAPTER NINETEEN

The economy and society, 1980–95

19.1 THE YEARS OF 'THOUGHTLESS PROSPERITY'

By 1980 there were signs that the long years of economic and social crisis would soon come to an end. Pirelli, for example, made a small profit that year, the first for ten years; Olivetti turned, just in time, to computers and word-processors. As the European recession ended in 1983–84, Northern Italy embarked on a period of rapid growth and very considerable prosperity. The Italian economy imported raw materials and exported much of its manufactures. Cheaper commodity prices – especially the falling oil price after 1986, a 1970s-style 'oil shock' in reverse – were therefore a huge stimulus. Manufacturing increased by 7.5 per cent p.a. between 1986 and 1991; inflation, over 20 per cent in 1980, still 14.6 per cent in 1983, after 1986 was at a mere 5–6 per cent p.a.; balance of payments problems disappeared; even the lira was fairly steady, having joined the European Monetary System in 1979. It was Italy's traditional areas of strength – engineering, furniture, ceramics, footwear and clothing, office machinery – that flourished most, helped by more clandestine and even more profitable activities like arms sales to the Middle East, and a virtual Sicilian monopoly of the heroin trade. Even on official figures, Italy had become the world's fifth industrial power. Her GDP exceeded Britain's by 1987; per capita income was $15,120 by 1989, compared with Britain's $14,610 (and the USA's $20,630). And there was a real consumer boom at home. Economists wrote of Italy's 'second economic miracle' – achieved, moreover, without any indigenous coal or oil.

Labour costs and labour agitations, perhaps the major economic issue of the 1970s, were far less evident in the 1980s. In October 1979 Fiat actually fired 61 of its most troublesome workers, alleging that they had sabotaged production and threatened other workers with violence. A year later the management went further. It announced plans to lay off 23,000 workers. The unions naturally called a protest strike. After several weeks the unthinkable happened: 40,000 Fiat workers marched through Turin, defying their leaders and demanding a return to work. The strike collapsed. Tough management had reasserted its authority at Fiat, for the first time since 1968, and the precedent was noted all over Italy. Industrial tribunals began upholding the dismissals of employees who rarely turned up for work.

The trade unions never recovered from this defeat. In 1982 the employers' federation formally challenged the system of automatic indexed wage rises applied since 1975, and managed to get the indexed part of wages reduced by 15 per cent; further reductions followed later. Craxi's Socialist-led government, faced with soaring public sector deficits, used the issue to tackle the Communist unions in the public sector. The 'federation' between Communist, Socialist and Christian Democrat-led trade union confederations fell apart in 1984. The following year, after much agitation, a national referendum confirmed the wage-index reductions. The economic effects were not significant, at least in the short run. By 1984 only just over half the average wage had been indexed anyway, and price-driven wage rises would have slowed after 1986 in any case. In the longer term, however, it meant that skilled workers could now expect to be paid significantly more than their unskilled counterparts. The real effects were political. It was a historic defeat for the Communist unions and the Communist Party, comparable to the defeat of the miners in Britain, and furthermore ratified by popular vote.

The trade unions were also hit by the shake-out of 'traditional' industrial and agricultural jobs in the early 1980s: over a million industrial jobs were lost between 1981 and 1991 (from 7.4 million to 6.4 million, according to the Census). Henceforth jobs were to be found, if at all, in commerce, transport and services; above all, in small firms (firms with less than 50 employees employed 37.4 per cent of Italy's industrial workforce by the 1990s) and among the self-employed artisans and the 'white-collar' middle classes. These were not fertile areas for union recruitment, except among health workers and teachers. By 1986 the three major union confederations represented only 5.4 million 'active' (i.e. not retired or unemployed) workers, 1.5 million fewer than ten years earlier, and most of these were in the public sector. Nearly a third of all trade unionists were pensioners; only 27.9 per cent of industrial workers were union members. The unions had no real shop-floor presence, and little influence over the Factory Councils. Fiat ignored the unions altogether for eight years after 1980, and even in 1988 only summoned them in order to 'dictate' a three-year wage agreement. There was some union recovery in the boom years of the late 1980s, but eventually, in the budget crisis of 1992, wage indexation was abolished altogether and wages frozen for a year. In July 1993 it was agreed that national minimum wages should be negotiated for each industry, so the unions regained a significant role. But by this time they had become orphans, as the major political parties were discredited. The Italian trade unions – which had always been highly political bodies – survived the political storm of 1992–93, but were left facing, on their own, a hostile, market-oriented environment and another big labour shake-out.

The restructuring of industry did lead to big productivity gains. In Northern and Central Italy, a host of small businessmen flourished as never before. Lombardy alone had 350,000 companies, two-fifths of them in manufacturing

– often flexible, family-run 'cottage industries', sometimes *de facto* decentralized outposts of major corporations, and nearly always specialized, dynamic and export-oriented. They tended to be found in geographic clusters – Sassuolo for ceramic tiles, Arezzo for jewellery – where specialized skills were common, local government supportive and inter-family rivalry intense. In short, a 'Renaissance model' of industrial development predominated. The most successful *condottieri* – Luciano Benetton in textiles, Silvio Berlusconi in the media – built up huge family-owned businesses, unconstrained by professional managers or institutional shareholders.

The gap between dynamic export-oriented family firms and the slothful 'guaranteed' sector of State firms and major corporations became ever more significant politically during the 1980s, but probably diminished economically. The big firms (e.g. Fiat) became more efficient too, although admittedly Fiat was much helped by governments keeping Japanese cars down to 1.4 per cent of the Italian car market. State holding companies like IRI regained some of their 1950s *élan*. And of course the relationship between big and small, between 'market' and 'State', was often symbiotic. The small firms often relied on big ones for contracts; there were plenty of public subsidies for 'artisans' and small entrepreneurs; many workers in the 'market economy' also held undemanding and generously paid jobs in local government or public sector agencies, with long holidays and early pensions. Indeed, it was thought that 15–30 per cent of employed Italians had second jobs: the first job provided security, the second ready cash. Less obvious forms of State subsidy came through the tax system and social security. Tax inspectors were not noted for excessive zeal, and tax evasion among small businessmen was on a heroic scale. As for welfare, 8.1 million people were drawing invalidity benefit in 1988.

The 'years of prosperity' were real. Northern Italy by 1990 was one of the richest regions in the world, even on official figures. But Italy had several major weaknesses. Much of the public sector was still notoriously inefficient. It provided much patronage and subsidy, but lousy services (incompetent health care, long-delayed pensions, hopelessly malfunctioning postal and telephone communications) to an increasingly sophisticated and impatient public. Its members had minimal job satisfaction; its top posts, and many of its middle and junior ones too, were political appointments distributed among the leading parties. Above all, it was expensive. Government spending was 33 per cent of GDP in 1980, but by 1989 had reached 41.1 per cent. The annual budget deficit, 71,000 billion lire in 1982, had doubled by 1990, and exceeded 10 per cent of GDP. Each year the accumulated National Debt rose accordingly, reaching 1,487,986 billion lire by 1992, well over 100 per cent of GDP. In the boom years of the middle and late 1980s this issue – a debt of Third World proportions – was largely ignored, but in 1990 a European recession began after German unification, and real interest rates rose sharply. Treasury bonds paid over 14 per cent in December 1990, and rates stayed high for years. So Italian governments found themselves paying out huge sums – 125,700 billion lire in 1990, virtually the entire deficit – just to service the public debt. Every time interest rates went up, the debt increased. Here was a real vicious circle, or rather spiral, that threatened to bring down the whole financial system.

By 1992 the party was over. Italy found herself at the wrong end of International Monetary Fund (IMF) advice: cut spending, freeze wages, impose higher taxes. European Community pressure was applied to the same purpose, for Italy could not hope to meet the Maastricht monetary criteria for a single currency, yet was reluctant to be left out of the European mainstream. Italian governments had to be led by a former Treasury Minister like Giuliano Amato in 1992–93 and by the former Governor of the Bank of Italy, Carlo Ciampi, in 1993–94. They did what they were told and raised taxes very sharply. In the summer of 1992 the situation was eased by leaving the European Monetary System; the lira was allowed to 'float', but promptly sank by around 20 per cent. This was a boost to exporters and to the real economy, which thereafter recovered rapidly from the 1990–92 recession, but even the recovery did little to resolve the inexorable rise in debt. The collapse of the currency, with attendant hyper-inflation, had become an ominous possibility.

Much political debate therefore centred around public spending, and how to cut it. Pensions were a particular problem, costing 194,000 billion lire in 1991, more than the entire budget deficit; they had gone up by 50 per cent in the previous four years. There were simply too many pensioners – over 20 million of them, in fact. The population was ageing, and people were retiring earlier. But they all had votes. The Ciampi government in 1993–94 tried to cut entitlements, and to remove the more obviously bogus 'disability' pensions, largely in vain. In October 1994 similar proposals by the Berlusconi government provoked the largest demonstrations seen on Italy's streets since 1945.

The other major proposal, to 'privatize' State-owned firms, was hardly less contentious. 'Privatization' had, of course, always been part of the 'IRI formula' (see §13.1): private firms in trouble were supposed to be taken over *temporarily* by the State holding companies, given some restructuring and new investment, and then sold off again in a healthier state. In the 1970s rescuing had been very common but there had been little sign of 'rationalization' and few resales. In 1981 IRI had shares in over a thousand companies, with over half a million employees; it produced half Italy's steel, owned many of the banks and even made a quarter of Italy's ice cream. It also made huge losses – 3,000 billion lire in 1983 – and almost collapsed. However, from October 1982 until 1988 a dynamic and effective economics professor, Romano Prodi, took over, and the old formula was re-applied. Four or five major firms a year were sold off, usually to other companies (e.g. Alfa Romeo to Fiat in 1986). IRI also sold off minority stakes in other firms, while retaining overall control (e.g. Alitalia, Banca Commerciale). All this raised about 1,500 billion lire a year; by 1986 IRI was almost breaking even, and by 1990 it made a net 1,100 billion lire profit. The point, however, is that 'privatization' in the 1980s still meant essentially what it had meant in the 1930s or 1950s: rationalizing production, boosting productivity, and selling off slowly. Italy had, as yet, no 'Reaganite' or 'Thatcherite' revolt against State industries or State welfare.

By 1992–93, as IRI's deficit soared again in the recession, and as public protests about corruption and '*sottogoverno*' became more strident, the long-delayed reaction occurred. A different model of 'privatization' was advocated as the remedy for both political and economic ills. The need now was to bring in the money as quickly as possible, and to 'depoliticize' much of the economy. In 1992 the leading State holding companies – still publicly owned – were turned into joint stock companies, and told to become more market-oriented; the Ministry of State Participations was suppressed in 1993, after a referendum; at ENI, the second largest holding company, there was a wholesale clear-out of the old directors and managers, and the company disposed of 60-odd medium firms. The leading banks were sold off – Banca Commerciale to a host of small shareholders – and plans were made to sell the State telecommunications and electricity supply businesses. Then the problems began. One was that there was no effective regulatory agency, apart from a weak 'anti-trust' authority hastily set up in 1990 with a remit over both private and public firms. A public monopoly was therefore likely to be replaced by a private one, admittedly subject to less political interference, but even less accountable to the public interest. Another problem was that privatizing utilities often meant big price rises for consumers, for previous prices had been held low for political reasons. Above all, it would mean job losses – a real threat to millions, particularly in the subsidized South.

By 1993–94 the whole issue had become enmeshed in political bargaining. As in Eastern Europe or East Germany, many of the old firms were simply too inefficient to compete in a fair market. As for the rest, how should they be sold: *en bloc*, or split up? Selling them *en bloc* would mean making existing firms even bigger, as had happened when Fiat swallowed Alfa Romeo; and there were not many potential cash-rich purchasers within Italy. Most of IRI's holdings were simply too big; where would the money come from, to buy them? So privatization might simply mean foreigners taking over Italian industry very cheaply, with little benefit to State coffers. Or it might mean management buy-outs – i.e. the old gang of political appointees continuing to run things as previously. It was difficult, in these circumstances, to see how privatizing firms would boost competition, the great justification for privatiz-ations elsewhere. And the political will to push through privatization was not overwhelming, even on the Right. Berlusconi's government, the most ideol-ogically committed of all to the programme, managed in seven months to sell off half of the State insurance fund INA, but nothing else. Certainly by 1993–94 the economic structure bequeathed by Fascism was being challenged for the first time, and most of the more prominent political appointees had lost their posts, but change was slow by the standards of Britain, France or Germany.

Italy's most serious economic problem remained the condition of the South. The successive oil price rises and steel gluts of the 1970s had devastated the South's most modern industries, and they never recovered. Even in the boom years of the late 1980s unemployment in the South was around 20 per cent, and far higher among young people (44.1 per cent in 1990). Moreover, young Southerners could no longer emigrate, for there were few jobs available in France or Germany, and the car factories of Northern Italy were now manned by robots. The South, with 36 per cent of Italy's population, produced about 24 per cent of its output, much the same as in the 1950s. Disposable income per head was around 65 per cent of that in the Centre–North, and even that figure was only reached because of transfer payments from the North, through the social security system.[1] The production gap between North and South grew after 1983, despite the efforts of myriad Italian and European agencies. The whole 'development model' of the 1950s–70s was long discredited, a fact symbolized by the abandonment of the Gioia Tauro steelworks in 1979. But it had left behind a network of inefficient, loss-making big State corporations, usually in declining industries and certainly unlikely to employ more people.

In 1984 the much-criticized Fund for the South, perhaps the most expensive regional development programme in the world, was finally abolished. Thereafter investment decisions were taken by a complex series of institutions, including Cabinet committees, a new Department for the South, a central financial agency, a parliamentary commission and a committee of representatives from the Southern regions. The aim was that the regions should make the initial proposals; the others should co-ordinate and distribute resources. In practice, the old 'infrastructure and incentives' system continued; 5,000 billion lire p.a. was spent in 1986–93 on 'extraordinary intervention' in the South. Texas Instruments was given huge subsidies to produce there; Fiat opened new plants (e.g. at Melfi), to attendant fanfares of publicity and much self-congratulation by local notables, just as in the old days. But these were exceptions. Most international corporations gave Southern Italy a wide berth, and there was a net outflow of industrial firms in the 1980s.

As the Southern regions took more decisions, subsidies went to job-creation rather than to capital, and were often selective – given to favoured entrepreneurs, not to all. Similarly, incentives and public works contracts tended to go to smaller, local firms; and the grants were handled by Southern banks, dominated by local politicians. The pre-1984 Fund for the South had been a real source of centralized, Christian Democrat patronage and power in the South. The new system boosted regional élites and local – especially Socialist – politicians. It soon proved even more obviously corrupt than the old one, and in some regions organized crime moved in for the pickings. Public contracts, jobs, subsidies, incentives, State-owned firms: these became the familiar themes of political debate and, by the early 1990s, of judicial investigation. To Northerners, it seemed a hugely expensive system of patronage and clientelism, failing to 'develop' or industrialize the South but all too successful in transferring wealth away from the North, and in keeping corrupt politicians in office. And, of course, this argument applied not just to 'extraordinary interventions' in the economy, but even more forcibly to the routine spending of the social security system, through which far greater resources were transferred.

These arguments were persuasive, but one-sided. The transferred money was not useless. It certainly improved Southern education, transport, housing and health; it also enabled Southerners to buy Northern goods, and gave some Northern industries a cheap supply of processed materials. Moreover, quite large parts of the South did prosper. Textile and furniture firms in Abruzzi and Molise, light engineering in Apulia, electronics near Caserta – these sectors all flourished, as did Northern Sardinia and much of Sicily, the latter for less reputable reasons. Indeed, by most international (as opposed to Italian) standards Southern growth rates were impressive: the North–South gap did not widen much in the 1980s, even though the North was becoming one of the richest regions in the world. And State spending in the South was not actually all that high: per capita, it was less than in the Centre–North, although the Northerners paid far more in taxes.[2]

However, in December 1992 Northern resentment and the State's need to cut spending ensured that the 'extraordinary' incentive system for Southern development was finally abolished, together with the associated agencies. Incentives might still be given by the Ministry of the Budget in Rome, which would also supervise the regions' policies, both in the South and the North. Many Southerners were horrified. The Southern regions lost their institutional input into central funding decisions – just at a time when the chemical industry was in recession, tourism had collapsed, welfare spending was being curtailed, agriculture was being hit by European Community quotas and competition from Greece and Spain, and State industries were being sold off. In 1993 Southern unemployment rose 57 per cent in one year, to three times the Northern rate. The South was being abandoned to its fate. Hit by recession, bereft of its traditional political patrons and threatened by militant Northerners, the mainland South turned resentfully to its traditional post-1950 protest party, the neo-Fascist MSI.

19.2 SOCIAL CHANGE AND THE FAMILY

The 1980s' prosperity ensured material gratifications of all kinds. Car ownership reached saturation point: by 1990 there were 27.4 million cars on the road, one for every two inhabitants. Most families had colour TV and washing-machines, and nearly everybody had a refrigerator and a telephone. Nearly two-thirds of Italian families owned their own houses; over 5 million had holiday homes as well. Homelessness was rare, even among immigrants. And people moved out of the big cities into smaller towns: Milan's population fell by 16 per cent in the 1980s.

The new 'post-industrial' jobs were more likely to go to women than to men. Some ancient discriminations were removed: after 1977 women could even become judges. The number of working women increased by 50 per cent from 1970 to 1985, and by the latter date 60 per cent of married women, of child-bearing age, had jobs. This was a real shift in the nature of marriage and in cultural values, as well as the economy. Since married women earned their own income, they became less dependent on their husbands. By 1991 half the couples in Italy's Northern cities were opting, on marriage, for each individual to keep his/her own income and property legally separate from that of the spouse.[3] Women with jobs spent less time at home, had wider social contacts and, above all, fewer children.

In the 1980s the Italians, long renowned for their love of children and their family-centredness, had probably the lowest birth-rate in the world (with the possible exception of China). By 1991 each female gave birth, on average, to 1.3 children, a rate which, if sustained, and in the absence of net immigration, would lower the population by 40 per cent every generation. Between 1980 and 1989 there were 588,712 births p.a., down 288,202 on the previous decade. The difference may be partly accounted for by legal abortions of around 150,000 p.a. However, until 1993 births still just exceeeded deaths, so the overall population did grow in the 1980s, albeit slowly, from around 56.5 million to 57.2 million. It also became more 'Southern' – the birth-rate in the South was twice that of the North – and grew older. Life expectancy, indeed, was very high – 73.5 for males, over 80 for females by 1990 – and rose by about 2½ years in the 1980s. Here, perhaps, was a demographic time-bomb. Few were being born, but the old were living longer. Who would pay their pensions, and look after them in old age? It was unlikely, on existing trends, to be 'the family'. Already old people were expected to live separately, or in care. And 'social' old age, i.e. retirement, might occur long before biological old age: civil servants could retire at 35, and draw their pensions for another forty years. D'Azeglio's famous dictum 'now we must make Italians' had acquired a new significance.

Over much of the country the one-child family became the norm, with the mother returning to work as soon as possible after the birth, helped by plentiful crèches and nursery schools. By 1991 37 per cent of all Italians lived alone, or in couples; another third lived with one child only. No longer could young Italians count on a vast support network of brothers, sisters, aunts and cousins. This was an astonishing transformation. Arguably the true foundations of Italian society were being rapidly eroded.

Or were they? Certainly, the innovations of the 1970s and 1980s – civil marriage, divorce, legal abortion, reliable contraception, equality within marriage, fewer children – were all huge social changes. But family life remained important. Over 300,000 couples married each year, and since most people lived longer, most marriages lasted longer too: orphans were fewer, and widows were older. Furthermore, the 'unofficial' economy, with its range of part-time jobs done at home, greatly helped domestic stability. Since young people could not find jobs, parents were needed for longer; they provided the cash, as well as a 'refuge of affection' at home, and some of them provided separate housing as well. Arguably, too, some of the other changes were more apparent than real. Abortion, contraception and premarital sex were not invented in the 1970s. Divorce was rare by international standards – 15,650 in 1985 – and although the number rose after 1987 when the 'waiting period' after the initial grant of legal separation was reduced from five years to three, it was only 17,890 in 1991. Most divorced people were in their forties, affluent, educated and Northern. The new 'living together' was often just the old 'marriage', though unblessed by Church or State. But few children were born outside marriage (only 6.7 per cent in 1992). Unmarried mothers still suffered social stigma, and most one-parent families were headed by widows. The Italian family, in short, was not dying out. It had become smaller and older, but also richer and more tranquil. It had adapted, painfully but surprisingly quickly, to the modern urban world, to the age of the microchip, of working at home and increased leisure.

As Italy produced fewer people of her own, she began to import them. In the 1980s Italy became a country of immigrants – a total transformation from the 1960s or early 1970s. The incomers were predominantly from Somalia, Senegal, Eritrea or North Africa; after 1989 further waves came from Eastern Europe, particularly Albania. They took ill-paid and often clandestine jobs on building sites, in agriculture, fishing or domestic service, or (a Senegalese speciality) worked as street pedlars. They arrived, of course, in a country with increasing unemployment and a declining need for unskilled labour. Many arrived 'illegally', coming ashore at night on Italy's vast coastline; the coastguards reckoned to catch one in ten. In 1986 and again in 1990 amnesties were granted to illegal immigrants, amid much controversy. No one knew how many immigrants there were: the official figure, based on residence registrations, showed a net immigration of 110,765 (including 62,000 from Africa) in 1990, and a total settled immigrant population of around a million (excluding European Community nationals); but these figures omit most of the 'illegal' immigrants, as well as the more transitory ones. To many Africans – especially North Africans, where population pressure was intense – Italy, even Southern Italy, was a prosperous, peaceful and nearby country, a land of opportunity and a refuge from persecution. Many had a Catholic or kinship network in Italy, to help them on arrival. So Italy at last became, like other European countries, a mixed multi-racial society. Resentment and occasional racial violence soon appeared in the cities, but immigration never became a really contentious political issue, and it was noticeable that even the neo-Fascists (unlike their counterparts elsewhere) were reluctant to play the racist card.

19.3 HEALTH AND WELFARE

The longevity of Italians clearly owed much to plentiful supplies of good food. The Fascists had boasted of growing 2 tonnes of wheat per hectare, but by the early 1990s the yield was around 10 tonnes, produced by a far smaller labour force. By this time the average Italian ate 76 kilograms of meat a year, twice as much as in the late 1960s. Conscripts into the army grew taller each year: by 1992 the average recruit was 173.6 centimetres tall, 1.16 centimetres more than in 1981, and the gap between Northerners and Southerners, at 2.6 centimetres, was half what it had been thirty years earlier.

Another reason, presumably, why people lived so long was better health care. But the 'National Health Service', founded on the British model in 1978 when the Left was influential, was always highly controversial. It was much criticized for overstaffing, for being run by politically-appointed managers, and for being grossly inefficient and expensive. Nor was it free to the user. Patients were expected to pay a bewildering set of constantly changing fees, unless they could secure one of an equally bewildering set of exemptions. The system ignored mental illness and failed to adapt to new health needs, such as drug addiction and AIDS-related illnesses. However, the service did provide lots of jobs for medical staff – Italy had more than twice as many doctors as Britain, for a very similar population. It also ensured lots of benefits for political parties (who ran the health boards and made the appointments), and lots of money (over half of NHS spending) for private health providers – specialists, private hospitals, old people's homes, etc. – contracted to provide services. Spending on drugs doubled, in real terms, in the 1980s. By the early 1990s 63 per cent of Italians thought the quality of health care provided was 'bad', and 10 per cent relied entirely on private health insurance. Indeed, the health service had become one of the great 'delegitimating' institutions of the country, and in 1992 the Northern League began collecting signatures for a referendum to abolish it altogether. Everyone knew of at least one case of harrowing incompetence or neglect, and blamed the politicians, often rightly: the 1992–93 corruption investigations began in the health sector, and led to many charges against managers and politicians. At the end of 1992 the system was therefore recast. The local health boards became much larger, and run by a professional manager; policy-making, finance and supervision were to be provided by the regions, not the communes; specialized hospitals were allowed to opt out of regional control and become '*aziende*' (independent trusts). But this reform, also influenced by British precedents, was not likely to make the service any more popular, especially as it was accompanied by a marked increase in prescription charges. In effect, the 1970s' aspiration to create a universal health service, with similar provision throughout the country, was no more. It had been brought down by, and by its weaknesses had greatly contributed to, popular resentment against the established parties.

The major health issue of the 1980s was linked to the sudden spread of drug usage, from the late 1970s onwards. The first official death from heroin overdose occurred in 1973; by 1989 there were over a thousand. By then estimates of intravenous drug users varied from 100,000 to 250,000, and of course there were far larger numbers using cocaine and cannabis. Until 1990 it was not illegal to possess a 'small quantity' of drugs for personal use, although trafficking was a criminal offence, and users were expected to undergo treatment – which brought about an astonishing growth in private residential 'therapeutic communities', run by Catholic charities or lay volunteers, both of them totally contemptuous of the State's efforts at regulation. However, in 1990 a tough new law inspired by Craxi's Socialists, bowing to the usual American pressure, imposed automatic jail sentences for possession of more than a 'daily dose', even of soft drugs. The result was predictable. Within a couple of years there were 14,000 drug users in prison, about a third of all convicted criminals. They cost the Italian taxpayer 400,000 lire a day each, and brought the penal system close to collapse. The Amato government of 1992–93 had to revoke the law, amid much controversy, and in 1993 an unlikely alliance of libertarian Radicals and 'therapeutic' Christian Democrats secured a referendum victory (by 55 per cent of voters) de-criminalizing the 'personal use' of all drugs. The issue remained contentious, the more so as two-thirds of Italy's AIDS cases were reckoned to be drugs-related, and by 1992 over 7,000 people were dying of AIDS-related illness each year. And, of course, the drug trade was dominated by organized crime.

One striking feature of 1980s Italy was a big expansion of voluntary work. By 1990 over five million people gave their time freely to such activities. Innovative, non-profit-making 'associations' and 'communities' became respon-sible for running much of the welfare and health-related services, especially for the mentally ill and handicapped, drug addicts, ex-prisoners, immigrants and the old. Most welfare had been decentralized to the regions in the 1970s, and many regions were anxious to encourage 'participation' and often to subsidize volunteer groups – Lombardy spent one-third of its social assistance budget this way. More leisure, education and prosperity also no doubt contributed, as did youth unemployment. At any rate, the corrupt, inefficient and profligate 'welfare state' was increasingly replaced by a host of 'welfare associations'. The State, or the region, provided much of the cash, but the volunteers provided the services. This rosy picture needs some qualification. Dubious 'welfare' associations could and did attract politically motivated funding; even genuine ones could easily become simply 'arms-length' regional bodies, run by a handful of paid professional managers rather than by the original volunteers. Even so, such cases seemed relatively rare. Most of the voluntary sector was flexible, committed and performed immensely valuable work, if only in 'humanizing' social relations in an impersonal society.

19.4 THE CHURCH

About two-thirds of the 'volunteers' were practising Catholics, and volunteer work became the most prominent activity of the Church, or rather of lay bodies associated with the Church. The parish was often the organizing centre of local voluntary bodies. The Church, threatened by secularization and consumerism as she still was, had rediscovered a mission. Local churches were admirably suited to a 'post-materialist' world in which people distrusted State institutions, political parties and professional management alike, and sought instead satisfaction and identity in 'face-to-face' associations and civil solidarity. Many Catholics, too had lost interest in older, more formal bodies – including the Christian Democrat Party, which had let them down badly on divorce and abortion – and turned instead to social welfare and above all to religious associations, which by 1990 had an astonishing 4 million members. 'Comunione e Liberazione', founded in 1969 as an association for pious laymen, had 60,000 members in 1979, became very influential in universities, and in the late 1980s became active in local politics.

But the more formal aspects of organized religion revived too. Karol Wojtyla proved an extremely popular choice as Pope. Church attendance ceased to decline in the 1980s, and even rose slightly: around 30 per cent of Italians claimed to attend Mass regularly. Among the young, Marxism was no longer fashionable, and sex was no longer a novelty. Attention turned in the early 1980s to anti-nuclear protest, in which Catholics were very prominent, in Italy as elsewhere. Surveys found that three-quarters of the population regarded themselves as 'religious'; priests enjoyed high social prestige, and fewer of them left their ministry; over 80 per cent of marriages were in church. Of course, most Italians ignored the Church's teachings on sexual matters, but they used the Church's 'rites of passage', and respected her new role in society. In short, they were not anticlerical, nor materialist; and arguably they were more charitable than ever before.

In February 1984 a new Concordat revised formal Church–State relations for the first time since 1929. Catholicism ceased to be the official religion of the Italian State (although it was stated that 'the principles of Catholicism are part of the historical patrimony of the Italian people'), and religious teaching ceased to be compulsory in State schools. But in practice between 90 and 95 per cent of pupils opted for it anyway. Church property became fully taxable, and the Vatican bank came under Italian legal regulation. State stipends for priests were phased out, replaced by tax-deductible contributions by the faithful and by a voluntary 0.8 per cent supplement to income tax, which almost half Italian taxpayers paid in 1992.

The Church, in 1960, had seemed hopelessly old-fashioned and cumbersome; but by the 1980s she had transformed her structure, her activities, her liturgy and her whole mentality. There were still, in 1989, 38,854 diocesan priests and over 20,000 ordained monks and friars, as well as another 140,000 full-time employees – non-ordained friars, nuns, etc. – throughout the land. But she had lost many of her pretensions to power. She had become, once again, a sanctuary from a heartless world.

19.5 THE PRESS AND MEDIA

By the 1980s the media apparently dominated Italian society. The average Italian watched 25 hours of TV a week, and Italian TV was one of the least regulated in the world. It was also arguably one of the worst, a relentless diet of old films, soaps, chat shows and sport. In 1976 the Constitutional Court had ended RAI's monopoly of local broadcasting (see §18.3), but upheld it at national level. RAI's three national TV channels were in practice shared out among the major parties, including the Communists after 1978. However, private (local) TV broadcasters soon realized that there was nothing to stop them using videotapes and relay stations to transmit their programmes nationwide at virtually the same time; and this device led to the rise of *de facto* 'national' channels (four by 1983, nine by 1990) owned by private entrepreneurs. Silvio Berlusconi, originally a builder in Milan, created a huge media empire in this way. He operated three channels that could reach 70 per cent of the population, were virtually unregulated, had no restrictions on advertising, obscenity or violence, had no obligations to be politically impartial, and certainly none to provide programmes with any educational or cultural content. His programmes were hugely successful. By the mid-1980s 44 per cent of prime-time viewers were watching Berlusconi's channels, compared with 40 per cent watching RAI's. RAI soon adapted to the competition, as did the genuinely local stations.

But Berlusconi's operations were legally somewhat dubious: they soon attracted judicial investigations and temporary bans. He therefore turned to his political protector, the Socialist Prime Minister Craxi, who in October 1984 issued a special decree legitimating Berlusconi's stations. In 1990 a further made-to-measure law permitted a single owner to control 25 per cent of the 'national' networks: Berlusconi had three out of twelve channels (but nearly half the audience). Moreover, Berlusconi also owned a Milan daily newspaper and many periodicals, a leading publisher, a chain of cinemas and a hugely profitable TV advertising agency. All this triggered a long resentful debate. How should the media be regulated? Which anti-monopoly methods would be effective? Could one man be allowed to control private TV, and thus dominate access to information, including political information? Might he not abuse this power for his own ends?

The press remained more diverse, and also more critical. Indeed, by the late 1980s there was a marked contrast between the bland, consumerist ethos of TV, and the strident denunciations of political and financial scandal that filled much of the press. Eugenio Scalfari's *La Repubblica*, with a circulation of 375,000 in 1985 and almost double that in 1992, was perhaps the most prominent critic of the Establishment, but it had many rivals. However, the press was also subject to take-over bids and political pressure. By 1989 four industrialists controlled over half the national newspapers. *La Repubblica*, together with the weekly *L'Espresso*, ended up partly owned by Carlo De Benedetti, boss of Olivetti. Far fewer people read daily newspapers (5.3 million copies in the early 1980s, 6.7 million by 1988) than watched TV, but newspapers were still hugely influential, and their ownership raised the same issues as did that of TV.

REFERENCES

1.   Svimez, *Rapporto 1991 sull' economia del Mezzogiorno*, Bologna 1991, p. 49.

2. C. Trigilia, *Sviluppo senza Autonomia*, Bologna 1992, p. 56, quoting F. Padua Schioppa, *L'Economia sotto Tutela*, Bologna 1991, pp. 93 ff.
3. M. Barbagli, 'Communione o separazione dei beni?', in *Polis*, vii, 1 (1993), 143–60, at p. 149.

CHAPTER TWENTY

The collapse of the 'First Republic'?

The huge budget deficits of the late 1980s, and the need to compete in wider markets, had dramatic political consequences. Italy's post-war political system, based on constant concessions and on patronage, could no longer be funded. And the end of the 'Cold War' deprived Italy's post-war rulers of vital foreign support. In 1992–93 the old parties collapsed, leaving much political uncertainty and threatening even the unity of the country.

20.1 THE ESTABLISHED PARTIES

Throughout the 1980s Italian politics remained set in its 'Cold War' mould. However, signs of instability soon became apparent. The 'historic compromise' of the 1970s was over, and the Communists were trying to 'oppose' and reassure simultaneously. The Christian Democrats (DC) were in their usual faction-ridden disarray. The parliamentary election of 1979 showed large swings between the major parties, higher abstention rates, a considerable protest vote and greater popularity of regional parties; and all these trends continued in later years. The general 'collapse of legitimacy' of the 1970s had clearly undermined traditional voting behaviour. Soon there were even more dramatic blows to the Christian Democrat 'regime'. Several leading party members were found to be members of a dubious Masonic lodge, the 'P2', together with notorious neo-Facists. Government efforts at providing relief for earthquake victims in Basilicata and Campania in 1980–81 were generally regarded as derisory, and corrupt local officials and criminals were alleged to have pocketed most of the relief funds. The Vatican bank was deeply involved in the 'Sindona affair', involving corruption and links to organized crime. In 1981 came the abortion referendum, when only 32.1 per cent of the voters approved the 'Catholic' proposals. In that year the Christian Democrats temporarily lost their greatest political prize, when the other parties refused to serve under a DC Prime Minister. Giovanni Spadolini, a Republican, became Prime Minister, the first non-Christian Democrat to hold the office since 1945. The long period of Christian Democrat dominance of Italian government was clearly coming to an end. In the 1983 general election the party received almost 2 million fewer votes, dropping dramatically from 38.3 per cent in 1979 to 32.9 per cent, and lost the Prime Ministership again, together with other major government posts.

The DC never really recovered from this defeat. It remained a loose alliance of squabbling factions without an acknowledged leader; and because of the real clashes of interest between different social groups and regions, it was simply unable to formulate coherent policies on major issues. The party secretary from 1982 to 1989 was Ciriaco De Mita, a Southern Left-winger who failed to modernize the party and who alienated many of its Northern supporters, particularly in the Veneto. The end of the 'Cold War' after 1989 was another real blow. Anti-Communism had been one of the Christian Democrats' major sources of appeal, and it had guaranteed American and European support. Suddenly, in 1991–93, the Communists were no longer a threat. Moreover, in 1991 the Pope, and many Catholics, opposed the Gulf War. Giulio Andreotti's government ensured that Italy's military commitment to it was little more than symbolic. The USA's backing for the Christian Democrats became distinctly lukewarm thereafter.

By 1992, when the DC secured only 29.7 per cent of the vote nationally, it won 39 per cent in the South, and only 25 per cent in the Centre–North. The party's traditional 'sub-cultural' bastions had been clearly eroded. The Church, and many Catholics, were distancing themselves from party politics: in the mid-1980s only 63 per cent of practising Catholics voted DC. Instead, the party now relied even more on patronage politics to win the Southern vote. Yet throughout the 1980s it had had to make desperate efforts to retain key public sector posts. Accusations of corruption, of improper appointments and of illicit party financing, had become endemic. And by 1992 the money had run out. Huge budget deficits (see §19.1) ensured that distributing patronage and rewarding supporters was no longer a sustainable strategy. The Christian Democrats had run out of both friends and funds. Just as the Fascists had glorified war and been brought down by it, so the Christian Democrats had coveted money; and money was the cause of their downfall.

So had the other major parties. In the 1980s Craxi's Socialist Party (PSI) had become far more influential, as a result of Christian Democrat disarray. Craxi himself was Prime Minister from August 1983 to March 1987, Sandro Pertini was President of the Republic until 1985, and the party often held a third of the Cabinet seats and top government agencies. However, the party failed to take advantage of its position. The Socialist vote at a general election never exceeded 14.3 per cent (in 1987), the party never overtook its Communist rival, and Craxi never became Italy's Mitterrand. Above all, Craxi's proclaimed 'ability to take decisions' in government was always far more apparent than real. In truth the Socialists outdid even the Christian Democrats in their eagerness for spoils at all levels. Soon they had become a national joke, although of a somewhat bitter kind. Not surprisingly, their vote, too, had become 'meridionalized': in 1992 the PSI won almost 17 per cent of the

Southern vote, 12 per cent elsewhere, a reversal of the situation twenty years earlier.

Nor were their main rivals an appealing alternative. Throughout the 1980s the Communists (PCI) remained outside national government, isolated and helpless. The vote declined steadily from its 1976 peak, and was down to 26.6 per cent by 1987. By 1985 the party had lost control of many of the city administrations won in the mid-1970s, and the 1985 referendum on index-linking of wages (see §19.1) was a very serious defeat. Trade union weakness contributed to low party morale, already worsened by long-term social changes, notably the loss of industrial and (especially) agricultural labouring/share-cropping jobs, and by the shift to non-union employment. And the party seemed stuffy and outmoded in other ways too. New issues – feminism, environmentalism, civil liberties – were taken up by other groups, not by the PCI. The party even managed to reaffirm its support for nuclear power in April 1986, a few days before Chernobyl.

Despite all the Italian Communists' efforts, over many years, to distance themselves from the East European regimes, the collapse of those regimes in 1989 was still a huge blow to an already demoralized party. If Communism had so visibly failed, what was the point of the PCI? In February 1991 the party leader Achille Occhetto pushed through a change of name: the PCI became the Democratic Party of the Left (*Partito Democratico della Sinistra*, PDS), but in so doing it suffered a significant split away on the Left – 150,000 members joined 'Communist Refoundation' – and it alienated many of its traditional supporters. By the end of 1991 the new PDS had around 400,000 members, compared with the old PCI's 1.3 million a year earlier, and in the 1992 general election it secured only 16.1 per cent of the vote. It retained its strongholds in Central Italy, but it had lost most of its members, it had lost its organizational discipline, and it had lost any claim to represent progress.

In short, the three major parties were in difficulties throughout the 1980s, and in real trouble by 1990. Governments in the 1980s were normally five-party coalitions – DC, PSI, PSDI, PRI, and PLI – and were brittle, turbulent groupings, squabbling for temporary privileges. The Socialists failed, in their years of maximum influence from 1983 to 1987, to tackle the public sector deficit; they also engaged in rows with the judges, and protected Berlusconi's media empire. From 1987 to 1992 it was the Christian Democrats' turn to hold the Prime Ministership again, but it was an unreformed and 'Southernized' DC whose activities were unacceptable to many erstwhile Northern supporters.

All this mattered more than usual, because Italy was essentially ruled by a 'partyocracy'. Few businesses, trade unions, TV channels, newspapers, football teams or opera houses were without political protectors; up to a million jobs in the public sector were said to be in the direct gift of the parties. If the parties failed, everything might fail. And the parties did fail. They became ever more fragmented, more localist and more concerned with appointments and patronage. The serious political issues were constantly sidestepped, not resolved. Italian government became paralysed by permanent inter-party and intra-party negotiations; there was always some

410

lobby that had to be appeased. Clear decisions could not be taken, except by referendum. That was the only way the voters could affect the outcome; they could certainly not do so by voting for a party. At each election, fewer people voted for the two major parties – 72 per cent had done so in 1976, but only 61 per cent in 1987, and 46 per cent in 1992. By then only 28 per cent of voters were reckoned to be committed supporters of a particular party.[1] The sub-cultures were vanishing, taking the mass parties' vote with them.

In short, the existing parties had entered a classic 'legitimacy crisis'. Their ideologies were seen as outmoded and absurd, their activities as corrupt and parasitic, their capacity to reform themselves or anything else as negligible. Governments could not govern; the opposition could not replace them. To the North, the model of competitive, progressive 'Europe' (approved by 96 per cent of Italian voters in 1990) was a constant reproach. How could Italy enter fully into the new Europe?

20.2 REFORM BY REFERENDUM

From the late 1970s, at least, there had been insistent calls for political and institutional reform. How could party control be diminished? Or was the *weakness* of the major parties the real problem? Should governments be made stronger, so as to be able to get their bills through parliament (instead of having to issue decrees, valid for sixty days, as a substitute for legislation)? Should proportional representation be abandoned in favour of single-member constituencies, which (it was believed by some) would turn elections into a straight contest between 'government' and 'opposition', and give future governments a real mandate? Or should Italy adopt a 'Presidential' system of government, like France? In 1983 a parliamentary commission under the Liberal Senator Bozzi was set up to discuss these issues, but it was split on party lines and produced no real proposals. However, one change was eventually introduced. The Craxi governments of 1983–87 had been defeated 155 times in parliament, largely because deputies usually voted in secret except on formal votes of confidence. In 1988 secret voting by deputies was abolished, with various exceptions, such as issues of conscience. The aim was to enable governments to legislate, and also to make deputies more 'responsible', more subject to party discipline. This latter aim, at least, was not attained: since they had less influence on decisions, deputies simply stopped bothering to attend parliament.

This was the only concrete result after years of debate, apart from a cosmetic increase in the role of the Prime Minister's office. In 1991 a Ministry for Institutional Reform was set up, although the new minister said he did not believe in reforms at all. But somebody did – the President of the Republic, Francesco Cossiga, who in his last two years in office (1990–92) issued a series of *'esternazioni'* (proclamations) denouncing the abuses of his fellow-politicians.

411

One mechanism did exist to 'unblock' the system. Between 1981 and 1990 fourteen national referenda had been held, usually on issues unwelcome to the major parties. In 1989–90 a maverick Christian Democrat from Sardinia, Mario Segni (son of a former President of the Republic) founded a Committee for Electoral Reform and began collecting signatures to promote reform from below, by popular vote. Segni favoured direct election of mayors, and single-member constituencies in parliament, but such themes were ruled out initially by the Constitutional Court. However, the Court accepted the validity of a more modest proposal – to reduce the number of 'preference votes', which voters could give to particular candidates of their chosen party (see §16.1), from three or four to just one. This, in Segni's view, would prevent candidates being elected on the coat tails of some eminent politician, and thus reduce factionalism within the parties. The major parties – except the PDS, which after some hesitation backed Segni – were not best pleased: Craxi called the referendum 'unconstitutional, polluting, unjust and antisocial',[2] and advised voters to go to the seaside instead of voting. However, 95.6 per cent of the voters, on a 62.5 per cent turnout, approved the change at the referendum in June 1991; the general election of April 1992 was held under the new system. The 'single preference' made little difference in itself, but it was a huge symbolic blow to the old parties and their regime. 'Partyocracy' had been successfully challenged, for the first time.

20.3 THE NORTHERN LEAGUES

Over the next two years the regime virtually collapsed, because of two more factors. The first was the rise of regional 'leagues', a delayed consequence of introducing regional government in the 1970s. The first league was founded in the Veneto in 1979, as much to preserve local dialects and culture as to press for greater regional autonomy, but by the late 1980s these folkorist, linguistic origins had been forgotten. The leagues became populist, political bodies and spread very rapidly throughout much of Northern Italy, as protest movements for small businessmen, skilled workers and the urban self-employed. They were hostile to taxes, to immigration and to crime, above all hostile to the corrupt, arrogant State run by Rome-based parties and incompetent Southern bureaucrats. Why, asked the leagues, should the regions not have far greater powers? Why should the hard-working, honest people of Lombardy pay 23 per cent of Italy's taxes, and receive 13 per cent of the public spending? Why should they pay anything to idle, bloodsucking Rome at all, when public services were dreadful, Southern 'development' schemes were a device for subsidizing organized crime, and when business and politics were centred on Europe or on international trade? The State was simply a brake on progress. The leagues believed in privatization and in Europe – 'with us in Europe, or with Ruanda Burundi', as their leader graphically put it.

The crisis of the other parties had left a host of disillusioned voters, and the leagues proceeded to attract them. In 1983 the Venetian League won 4.3 per cent of the vote at a general election. In 1984 the 'Lombard League' was founded and in 1987 it won 3 per cent of the vote in Lombardy, electing one deputy and one Senator, Umberto Bossi, its charismatic and highly unpredictable leader. In May 1990 came a huge breakthrough: the Lombard League won 16.4 per cent at the Lombardy regional elections, and 12.9 per cent in Milan itself, electing eleven councillors in the home fief of Socialist leader Craxi. In 1991 Bossi managed to ally the various regional leagues – including those from Emilia-Romagna and Tuscany – into a 'Northern League', with a common programme: Italy was to become a federation of three autonomous republics – North, Centre and South – each responsible for education, justice, commerce, welfare, industry and fiscal policy. An 'Italian' government would remain in being, to deal with foreign policy, defence, higher justice and policing, and monetary issues, although it was hoped that all these would soon be settled at European level; a Senate would represent the federal units.

By this time the Northern League was not just a spokesman for popular rancour. It controlled, or strongly influenced, local government in much of Northern Italy; and localism was, as ever, the key to political success. The leagues argued that local communities were under threat, from immigrants, crime, corruption and political placemen. The argument was plausible. Local communities were indeed threatened in this way. But localism was not the only factor, nor was hostility to the old parties, nor the decline of the old sub-cultures. Bossi caught on quickly to the full implications of the collapse of Communism and of class-based politics, and to which ideas were likely to replace them – including ideas about 'Europe' and about the decentralized nature of international trading economies. He linked the demand for federalism to a Thatcherite insistence on market forces and State frugality. Above all, he spread his views throughout Northern Italy, and created a 'Northern party' capable of tackling Rome. Indeed, by 1991–92 the leagues seemed a threat to the whole legacy of Cavour and the Risorgimento, to the whole project of 'making Italians'.

20.4 CORRUPTION, 'TANGENTOPOLI' AND ORGANIZED CRIME

The other major factor in the collapse of the old parties was criminality and public order. This may seem surprising, for the great public order issue of the 1970s had long ceased to be a problem. Moro's murder in 1978 (see §18.4) had demonstrated not the triumph but the futility of terrorism. The Red Brigades had thought to 'strike at the heart of the State'; they discovered there wasn't one. Many of their former sympathizers were shocked by the Moro affair. Many more were shocked a few months later, when the Red Brigades killed a Communist worker in Genoa who had informed against them. The Red Brigades became an isolated and demoralized sect. Tough new anti-terrorist laws were passed, strengthening police powers; and a new anti-terrorist squad was formed, led by General Dalla Chiesa. Information began to flow in, especially from captured terrorists. In 1979–80 the police broke up most of the Red Brigade 'columns', and arrested many apologists. Their greatest success was in December 1981, when they freed the kidnapped American General Dozier, but that episode confirmed what was already evident. Italian terrorism had failed to 'destabilize' the country, and it had failed to make the State too authoritarian, or to provoke a *coup*. It remained for some years an occasional nuisance, but it was no longer a political threat. In the short term it probably strengthened the democratic State, and rallied Italians behind their crumbling institutions.

Yet the police and judiciary were not rewarded for their efforts. Indeed, the defeat of terrorism made the politicians complacent once again. Throughout the 1980s relations between the judiciary and politicians – especially the Socialist politicians who controlled the Ministry of Justice – were remarkably cool. The reason was that many examining magistrates were anxious to probe political corruption, and on occasion (e.g. the Banco Ambrosiano case in the early 1980s) even did so. In 1987 the Socialist Party backed a successful referendum making judges personally liable in civil law for damages caused by 'negligent' detention on remand – the damages were knocked off the judge's salary. It was a clear warning to the judges, to lay off corruption cases. Moreover, in 1989 a new code of criminal procedure was pushed through, giving greater rights to defendants and ending secrecy during the preliminary investigations. The 1987–92 parliament went on to pass over fifty laws on the administration of justice, most of them imposing restrictions on the judiciary. These innovations were much resisted by the judges, who even went on strike for two days. By 1991 most of the Supreme Council of the Judiciary was at loggerheads with the Minister of Justice and the President of the Republic, over alleged interference in the Council's activities, and there was another one-day strike.

It was the electoral success of the Northern leagues that gave examining magistrates in the North a chance to hit back: any move to prevent them investigating corruption would be a propaganda gift to Bossi. So the corruption scandals started in the North, not in the even more suspect South. Indeed, they started in Milan, the 'moral capital' of Italy, a city whose mayor was Craxi's brother-in-law and where the Socialist Party secretary was Craxi's 28-year-old son. In February 1992 Mario Chiesa, the Socialist director of a council-subsidized old people's home, was indicted for accepting a 7 million lire bribe. His arrest led to further investigations, known as 'Operation Clean Hands'. Soon the Milanese judges had uncovered a vast web of corruption throughout Milan (renamed 'Tangentopoli', or Bribesville) and Lombardy. The most prominent magistrate, Antonio Di Pietro – a Southerner, from Molise – became a heroic symbol of judicial rectitude. Judges elsewhere joined in. Craxi himself was indicted on numerous counts, resigned as Socialist leader and, when his parliamentary immunity expired, fled to Tunisia. Other Socialist ministers were also indicted, including De Michelis at the Foreign Ministry and – sweet revenge for the judges – Martelli, Minister of Justice. So, too, were leading figures from most other parties, including virtually the entire Christian Democrat leadership in Naples. By mid-1993 prosecutors had requested the lifting of parliamentary immunity of 395 deputies and senators, almost a third of the total; 18 per cent of all local councillors were under investigation; top civil servants and businessmen – including past presidents of both IRI and ENI – disappeared into prison, or killed themselves. By 1994 the net had caught over 3,000 top people. A political and economic class had been brought down. It was a 'legal revolution' in every sense, and one quite unique in world history.

However, 'political corruption' had many shades of meaning. It might mean little more than 'clientelism', the traditional exchange of votes for favours (jobs, houses, etc.). There was nothing new in this, indeed in many regions it was the traditional basis of politics, although limited resources had made it increasingly difficult by the early 1990s to satisfy all the voters. Or 'corruption' might mean citizens encouraging officials to deal with their cases more favourably, or more quickly. Again, this was a traditional practice, carried out by millions of Italians every day and seen by them as no more reprehensible than, for example, trying to avoid taxes. Or 'corruption' might mean simply a 'commission' paid to intermediaries – 10 per cent to local politicians, say, in return for a public works contract: an equally time-honoured and generally accepted custom, and the basis of most business deals. Often it meant a transaction between public institutions: most 'bribes' were paid by public agencies, with public money, to political parties or their factions.

All this was basically 'honest graft', common for decades if not centuries. It became slightly less honest as more and more public works schemes were ordered, not for any conceivable public good, but merely for the pay-off. And where licenses were needed to ply a trade, the politicians' demands on small businessmen could become tantamount to extortion: pay up, or close down. But the real novelty in the 1980s was the amount of money involved, and the flagrant shamelessness of many leading politicians. Italians were not surprised to learn, officially, that their politicians were corrupt: *La Repubblica* and *L'Espresso* had been telling them that for years. But they were surprised by the extent of the corruption. Estimates of amounts paid each year in extortion rackets and pay-offs to politicians varied from 2,500 billion to 30,000 billion lire, with between 200,000 and 350,000 'victims'. Bribes of around a billion lire seemed to be normal; it was embezzlement on a huge scale. Moreover, politicians' collusion with organized crime, with threats of violence and arson, began to be evident. At the 1990 local elections 400 candidates had been indicted for racketeering; the criminals were moving directly into government.

It was these aspects that alarmed the public most; and the public, too, had changed. Most educated Northerners had become all too aware of the costs of the existing system – poor job prospects, inadequate welfare services, environmental degradation. For example, Northern and Central Italy had acquired a reasonably active Green movement in the 1980s – thirteen deputies were elected in 1987 – and these young activists, agitating for better parks or public transport, often came up sharply against the harsh reality of corrupt local decision-making. Northerners knew, too, that Italian business would not be able to compete in the single European market, if it had to keep paying for millions of political hangers-on back home. The corruption scandals of 1992–94 may thus be seen as yet another example of the clash of two cultures that is endemic in Italian history and society: an austere, high-minded 'legal-rational' perspective, facing the confused reality of everyday Italian life and politics. Or, more cynically, it may be seen as a brief 'periodic fit of morality', hugely enjoyable while it lasted but unlikely to undermine deep-seated social and political practices.

It was corruption in the North that brought the old regime down in 1992–93; but it was awareness of organized crime in the South that had fatally undermined it. In the late 1970s and early 1980s 'Mafia'-type organizations flourished in Sicily, Calabria and Campania as rarely before, boosted by Middle Eastern arms deals, by regional government contracts and above all by enjoying a virtual monopoly, from the late 1970s to the late 1980s, of the European heroin trade. Heroin was processed in laboratories near Palermo, and for some years Sicily also supplied a third of the heroin entering the USA. Profits were reckoned to be at least $600 million p.a. by 1989. They were soon recycled into private banks, construction, tourism and other legitimate businesses (most of them subsidized by regional, national or European bodies). The Sicilian economy came to depend on this new source of huge wealth.

So did the Italian Treasury: it was estimated that 30 per cent of Treasury bond (gilt-edged) purchases were bought with drug money. The State needed these sales to finance its constant budget deficits. On the other hand, it could hardly allow whole regions of the country to slip out of official control. In 1991 the Ministry of the Interior estimated there were about 450 organized gangs operating in Italy, with 15,000 members; up to a million people were involved in extortion, drug traffic and smuggling. The constant 'Mafia' killings – about 300 a year in each of the three worst-affected regions, throughout the 1980s – could not be ignored, particularly as they included the murder of nine judges in Sicily alone, as well as scores of policemen, politicians and journalists. Nor could the State ignore overseas – especially American – pressure to clamp down hard on the drugs trade.

In 1982, after a particularly bloody internecine 'Mafia war' in Sicily during which both the President of the Sicilian region and the leader of the Communist Party in Sicily had been killed, General Dalla Chiesa, having smashed the Red Brigades, was sent to Palermo as 'Superprefect' to crush the Mafia. He lasted five months before being assassinated. A new law was hastily passed, for the first time making membership of 'mafia-type associations' a criminal offence in itself, and permitting the seizure of members' assets. At the general election the following year the Christian Democrat vote dropped very sharply indeed in Palermo, a clear sign of *Mafioso* disapproval of central interference. Even so, the crack-down continued. A 'pool' of investigating magistrates in Palermo took up the challenge. They were helped by the new law and, above all, by the testimony of 'repentant' ex-*Mafiosi*, 'supergrasses' who had lost out in the 'Mafia war' and who decided to seek revenge by telling all to the authorities. Tommaso Buscetta, in particular, soon became a real source of information, as did Antonino Calderone of Catania. In 1986 nearly 500 suspected *Mafiosi* were put on trial together at a vast, highly publicized 'maxi-trial' in Palermo; 344 were found guilty. This was the most sustained campaign against 'the Mafia' since the days of Prefect Mori in the 1920s. By this time, too, Leoluca Orlando had become the city's mayor, leading an unusual anti-Mafia coalition and trying to clean up the city's administration; Enzo Bianco was attempting the same task in Catania.

But 'the Mafia' – or rather, the hundreds of criminal gangs competing for control of territory – had deep roots. By this time the gang bosses controlled, indeed, more resources than the politicians, providing many jobs and even the security that the State could not guarantee. Indeed, many of their activities were legitimate. They often enjoyed considerable authority and prestige locally, and could influence large numbers of voters. Moreover, the national anti-judge sentiment during and after the 1987 referendum hampered the prosecutors, and the new criminal code made it more difficult to arrest suspects without solid proof. In short, the anti-Mafia impetus died down in 1988–89. However, it revived in 1991 when the Minister of Justice appointed Giovanni Falcone, the most prominent of the Palermo investigators, to be Director of Penal Affairs at the Ministry in Rome. Falcone proposed sweeping changes: new centralized police and judicial agencies were to be set up to combat organized crime, as was an American-style Drug Enforcement Agency and a witness protection programme. House arrest for convicted criminals awaiting appeal court verdicts was abolished. Above all, in January 1992 the Supreme Court of Cassation confirmed many of the maxi-trial convictions, to the surprise and dismay of the convicted. Retaliation soon followed. In May 1992 Falcone was assassinated outside Palermo, as was his colleague Paolo Borsellino two months later.

These murders provoked a national outcry. So had many before them, but this time was different. The outcry over Falcone's murder was a huge blow to 'the Mafia'. It led to much new legislation on the lines proposed by Falcone before his death, and to a very intensive anti-Mafia drive in 1992–93 which resulted in the arrest of over seventy leading *Mafiosi* – including Salvatore Riina himself, alleged head of Cosa Nostra, after no less than 23 years on the run (most of them spent at home living with his family). Buscetta claimed that the Mafia was on its last legs. Certainly, by murdering Falcone, the 'Mafia' had overreached itself, just as the Red Brigades had done fourteen years earlier by murdering Moro.

The Falcone murder was also a blow to the political regime. It was already very weak by the summer of 1992, and the judiciary was, for once, extremely popular. Although, as I have argued, the State had pursued the *Mafiosi* vigorously since 1982, the accusation that the leading politicians had 'colluded' for years with organized criminals, and had reduced much of Southern Italy to violent lawlessness, appeared all too credible. In 1993 Giulio Andreotti himself, seven times Prime Minister and the incarnation of the old

Table 3 Votes (%) and Deputies in the Chamber of Deputies 1983–94

	1983		1987		1992		1994				
	%	D	%	D	%	D	% (PR)	D (PR)	D (SMC)	D (total)	
Democratic Proletarians (PDUP); from 1992 Communist Refoundation	1.5	7	1.7	8	5.6	35	6.0	11	29	40	
Communists (PCI); from 1992 Democratic Party of the Left (PDS)	29.9	198	26.6	177	16.1	107	20.4	38	77	115	Progressive Alliance 34.4 per cent 213 D
Socialists (PSI)	11.4	73	14.3	94	13.6	92	2.2	0	15	15	
Social Democrats (PSDI)	4.1	23	3.0	17	2.7	16	—	—	—	—	
Republicans (PRI)	5.1	29	3.7	21	4.4	27	—	—	—	—	
Democratic Alliance	—	—	—	—	—	—	1.2	0	17	17	
Green List	—	—	2.5	13	2.8	16	2.7	0	11	11	
Social Christians	—	—	—	—	—	—	—	—	6	6	
Network	—	—	—	—	1.9	12	1.9	0	9	9	
Pact for Italy	—	—	—	—	—	—	4.7	13	0	13	
Christian Democrats (DC); from 1994 Popular Party (PPI)	32.9	225	34.3	234	29.7	206	11.1	29	4	33	
Christian Democrat Centre							—	—	32	32	Pole of Liberty, Pole of Good Government. 46.4 per cent 366 D
Liberals (PLI)	2.9	16	2.1	11	2.8	17	—	—	—	—	
Radicals (PR); from 1994 Pannella List	2.2	11	2.6	13	1.3	7	3.5	0	6	6	
Forza Italia	—	—	—	—	—	—	21.0	30	67	97	
Neo-Fascists (MSI-DN); from 1994 National Alliance	6.8	42	5.9	35	5.4	34	13.5	23	86	109	
Northern League	—	—	—	—	8.7	55	8.4	11	111	122	
Others (regional parties)	3.2	6	3.3	7	5.0	6	3.4	0	5	5	
		630		630		630		155	475	630	

Notes 1994 abbreviations   % (PR) percentage of national vote in proportional ballot   D (PR) deputies elected in proportional ballot
D (SMC) deputies elected in single-member constituencies   D (total) total of deputies elected for each party

Christian Democrat regime, was indicted on charges of collusion with organized crime.

Andreotti's indictment symbolized the fall of an entire political system. Within Italy, it showed that 'Operation Clean Hands' was not just directed against individuals. Both the campaign against 'the Mafia' in the South, and the anti-corruption drive in the North, were part of a larger struggle against 'partyocracy'. Andreotti's indictment also signified, to Italian eyes at least, that the old order's international friends had abandoned it. With the 'Cold War' over, the USA had lost interest in protecting the Christian Democrats; perhaps was even anxious to punish them for disloyalty during the Gulf War.

20.5 ELECTIONS, REFERENDA AND PARTIES, 1992–94

In April 1992 Italian voters went to the polls, for what turned out to be the last parliamentary election of the old regime. Although the League was already a major threat in Northern Italy, and although voters now had only one preference vote (see §20.2), the election was still largely of the traditional kind, fought by much the same parties as usual. Indeed, the campaign was fought largely on familiar 'historic' issues: the plots of the P2 Masonic lodge, the activities of Nato's 'stay-behind' network '*Gladio*', the role of former Communist leader Togliatti in Russia in 1943. And, despite the huge public debt, there was the usual pre-election spending spree. In just one month, January 1992, new laws and decrees approved 80,000 billion lire more spending, mostly on agriculture and construction; conspicuous amounts were also allocated to 'research institutes' and to the commendable goal of 'collaboration with Eastern Europe', dear to the heart of Foreign Minister De Michelis.

The results, however, were a shock. At least a quarter of the electorate changed its vote from the previous election. The Christian Democrat vote, at 29.7 per cent, went below 30 per cent for the first time; on the Left, the PDS vote collapsed to 16.1 per cent, yet the Socialists failed to make gains. The League took 17.3 per cent of the vote in Northern Italy as a whole (20.5 per cent in Lombardy) and elected 55 deputies and 25 Senators. In the Centre–North, the voters had turned against all the major parties. Of the League's voters, over a quarter had voted DC in 1987, 18.5 per cent for the PCI, 12.5 per cent for the PSI[3]. The 'blocked' political system, essentially unchanged since 1947, had suddenly been unblocked, indeed destabilized. It made forming an effective government even more difficult than usual; nor was there an effective opposition. The four parties of Andreotti's pre-election coalition – DC, PSI, PSDI, PLI – won only 48.8 per cent of the vote for the Chamber (although they had 331 of the 630 seats). Andreotti therefore had to resign, and until the next election in 1994 governments were led by semi-outsiders: firstly the Socialist constitutional lawyer Giulio Amato (1992–93) and then the former Governor of the Bank of Italy, Carlo Ciampi (1993–94). Most of the ministers were non-political 'technocrats'.

Moreover, Mario Segni's Committee for Electoral Reform was as active as ever. It had organized a cross-party 'Pact', whereby 152 candidates had pledged themselves to vote for change to the electoral law in the next parliament. It had also promoted a referendum on electoral change to the Senate, where the existing region-based system could be altered to one based largely on single-member constituencies simply by 'abrogating' some clauses in the existing law, thus meeting the Constitutional Court's requirements.[4] In practice, any change in the Senate was bound to lead to change in the Chamber of Deputies as well. For Segni's supporters, 'electoral reform' was the people's answer to 'partyocracy'. This was mostly rhetoric, but in the climate of 1993 anything opposed by the existing politicians looked desirable.

In April 1993 came Segni's moment of glory: 82.7 per cent of the voters, on a turn-out of over 60 per cent of the electorate, voted for change. The North was markedly more enthusiastic than the South: 76 per cent of voters in Veneto voted 'yes', but only 36 per cent in Calabria. Seven other referenda were held on the same day, abolishing the Ministries of State Participations, Tourism and Agriculture (founts of corruption), prohibiting State appointments to boards of savings banks (henceforth regionalized), ending the State financing of political parties (previously 83 billion lire p.a.), ending the environmental policing role of local health boards (ineffective), and decriminalizing the possession of drugs (impossible to enforce). But the real question was not any of these, nor even electoral reform, which few people understood or cared about. Essentially the Italian voter was being asked one simple question: 'do you want to kick out the corrupt old gang?'. The answer was an overwhelming 'yes'.

The corrupt old gang, which had been discussing electoral reform for a decade, and which was still dominant in parliament, was thus forced to accept a new electoral law. It provided for 'first-past-the-post' single-member constituencies for 75 per cent of the seats, both in the Senate and the Chamber of Deputies. In the Chamber, the remaining 25 per cent were allocated on the old party-list proportional system, but only to parties that achieved a national threshold of 4 per cent of the votes.[5] In the Senate, a quarter of the seats were also allocated by proportional representation, but on a regional basis that in practice required a party to win at least 10 per cent of the regional vote to qualify. The new system was largely dictated by the question posed at the referendum, which itself was determined by Segni's need to meet legal requirements and win the Constitutional Court's approval. But it was also a compromise between the parties. It was designed to produce stable, polarized Right v. Left contests in the single-member constituencies, and also to allow the smaller parties some representation via the proportional seats. It was, nonetheless, a real leap in the dark. Italy was adopting an electoral system geared to two-party conflict, just as the existing parties were collapsing. No one, in the summer of 1993, had much idea who would benefit from the new rules, although many people assumed that the League would win the North, the PDS would hold on to the Centre and the Christian Democrats would survive in the South.

The first real indication came in autumn, when local elections were held in the larger towns, also under new rules that provided for directly elected mayors whose supporters would receive 60 per cent of the seats on the council. These elections showed that the individual candidate's personality was likely to be all-important in future; party allegiance was irrelevant or even a handicap. Gianfranco Fini, leader of the neo-Fascist MSI, almost became mayor of Rome; Alessandra Mussolini, the *Duce*'s grand-daughter, nearly won Naples. Above all, the local elections showed that there was no longer a respectable Centre–Right party. The DC were not helped by their one popular figure, Segni, for he had formally left the party before the referendum (a fact which left him isolated in the post-referendum manoeuvring). Indeed, quarrels and recriminations within the DC continued to the point that in January 1994 the party split, the centre and left wings resuming the old name of Popular Party, the right breaking away to form the Christian Democrat Centre. In any case, the DC as a centre party was squeezed by the new electoral system's 'bipolar' (Right v. Left) logic. The old system's dominant party was dominant no longer. On the Right, there remained only the Northern League and the neo-Fascists, and even the League seemed unable to form alliances and thus win mayoral contests – it won Milan, but failed in Venice and Trieste. The Socialists, by this time little more than a patronage distribution network, no longer had any patronage to distribute and collapsed completely; most of the other parties of the Centre followed suit. The Left-wing coalition – i.e. the PDS and its various allies, including the Greens and Orlando's anti-Mafia 'Network' – did remarkably well. The PDS won 103 out of 218 mayoral posts; the Left looked set to win any new parliamentary elections.

At this point a new and totally unexpected political movement erupted on to the scene. Italy's most prominent media boss, Silvio Berlusconi, had always enjoyed very close support from powerful politicians, particularly Craxi; he had even had a special media law passed for his benefit in 1990. But now the Socialist ship had sunk. Berlusconi did not relish a PDS-led Left-wing government, which would certainly have curtailed his Fininvest media empire. He therefore founded '*Forza Italia*' ('Go Italy!') as an *ad hoc* political movement, or rather as a series of supporters' clubs throughout the country, that soon attracted thousands of members but had no role in policy-making. '*Forza Italia*' (FI) certainly represented a new style of politics. It was entirely a media creation, based on and financed by Berlusconi's three national TV channels and other assets; it was run by Berlusconi's media managers, especially the advertising executives of Publitalia, who selected the parliamentary candidates (nearly always local businessmen, and often employees of Fininvest); and it relied on marketing techniques. 'Focus groups' – representative samples of voters – were gathered together in eight different regions, to discuss political issues and give an idea of what the voters wanted. They wanted lower taxes, less regulation and bureaucracy, better public services, a sound lira and a million new jobs. And that is what they were promised.

Berlusconi looked competent, talked smoothly, appealed to women voters, and could be marketed as a political outsider. He had one indisputable virtue: he was committed to the great cause of cheering everybody up. He promised an end to all the gloomy talk of corruption and pursuing the guilty men – a promise that went down very well by this time with many small businessmen and officials, who were beginning to worry as the over-zealous corruption investigators probed ever deeper. Above all, he was a more attractive prospect than anyone else on the Right. A self-made Milanese businessman, he was the archetype of a successful Northerner, more prominent than anyone in the League; he was just as market-oriented and anti-bureaucratic but, arguably, less vulgar than the unstable and ill-educated Bossi; and he was not tainted with neo-Fascism, unlike Fini. He was clean but not moralistic, and he might save Italy from the Left.

But to do so, given the new electoral system, he would need to form an electoral pact with the political pariahs, the League in the North and the neo-Fascists – now claiming to be 'post-Fascist', and renamed as the 'National Alliance', AN – in Rome and the South. These two groups detested each other and pursued completely different policies on basic economic and constitutional issues. They refused, in fact, to ally with each other, and their candidates stood against each other in many constituencies; but Berlusconi allied with each, separately. This was a real political achievement. The pact gave the League and AN much free media publicity, and some respectability. Moreover, Bossi stipulated that 70 per cent of the candidates in the Northern single-member constituencies should be *leghisti*, thus ensuring League over-representation in the new parliament. The Right-wing ex-Christian Democrats and the supporters of former Radical Marco Pannella also joined the alliance, and were also allocated more than their fair share of seats.

At the general election of March 1994 this extremely loose coalition won 46.4 per cent of the 'proportional' vote, and 366 seats in the Chamber of Deputies (but only 155 seats in the Senate, less than a majority). It was an extraordinary transformation: 70 per cent of the deputies and Senators won seats for the first time. The corrupt old parties were replaced by a 'new Right': 97 businessmen and media executives of FI, 122 small businessmen and artisans of the League, bent on a Sack of Rome, and 109 'post-Fascists', advocates prominent among them, desperate to preserve 'Italy' from the League and social spending from the free marketeers. Berlusconi himself was a political unknown, or rather known politically only as a *protégé* of Craxi and as a former member of the P2 lodge. He had risen from nowhere, in three short months, and had won a parliamentary election. His party was no more than the offshoot of a business corporation. He proclaimed the virtues of consumerism and professed a vague patriotism based largely on football, but in reality he represented little except fear of Communism – and Communism had collapsed already. He won because he filled a political vacuum, at least in Northern and Central Italy.

But he was not the biggest winner of the election. In the mainland South, the political vacuum was filled by Fini, not by Berlusconi: AN picked up 23 per cent of the vote there, and 94 of AN's 109 deputies were elected in Latium and the South. The 'post-Fascists' could claim to have been right all along – not only about Communism, but also about the corrupt nature of the DC regime. After the election they entered government for the first time since 1945, the most potent symbol yet of the end of a republic founded on anti-Fascism.

This new coalition of the Right was not an obvious recipe for stability, but it did defeat the Left. There, too, there was an electoral pact in March 1994, between the PDS and at least six other parties across a wide spectrum. The Left was no more coherent than the Right. It had no common programme and not even an agreed Prime Minister candidate (except the incumbent Ciampi, a Christian Democrat banker pushing through an austerity programme). The PDS was successful in the proportional part of the ballot, its vote going up to 20.4 per cent from 16.1 per cent in 1992, but most of its allies failed the 4 per cent hurdle and won seats only in the single-member constituencies. Conversely, Mario Segni's centre grouping 'Pact for Italy' failed to win any direct seats at all, but won thirteen in the proportional ballot, much to Segni's embarrassment. The biggest losers were the ex-DC in the new Popular Party. Their 'proportional' vote was halved, and in the single-member constituencies their candidates were squeezed out between Left and Right, although 32 Right-wing ex-Christian Democrats were elected as part of Berlusconi's coalition.

The new electoral system had manifestly failed to deliver. There were no coherent policies on offer, and no realistic chance of stable parliamentary government, either on Right or Left. Instead, after March 1994 there were fourteen parties in parliament. It took six weeks of haggling before Berlusconi could form a government. Thereafter both government and opposition were loose, faction-ridden coalitions, which spent most of their time squabbling over appointments to quangos, as in the bad old days. Admittedly Berlusconi's position was extremely difficult. He had to reconcile the conflicting demands of Bossi and the North – for spending cuts, privatization, lower taxes and federalism – with those of Fini and the South – more welfare, more subsidized State industries and a strong Italy. Bossi, not in government himself and worried by Berlusconi's inroads into the League's vote, soon realized that the government was not going to deliver federalism or even decentralization, and became a vocal critic.

The government's main immediate concern was to dismiss the existing board of the State broadcasting company RAI, replacing it by four businessmen and a conservative historian. Three more national TV channels thus came under Berlusconi's influence. The other major issues concerned Berlusconi's media empire, pensions, and the corruption investigations. Berlusconi's promises to relinquish control of Fininvest temporarily, while Prime Minister, were not generally believed; it proved impossible to agree to legislation on this matter, or on rules guaranteeing equal access to the media to opposition parties, or on limits to one man's media ownership. Even a general anti-trust law was lacking, which made the government's privatization programme much less acceptable. The Berlusconi government did make some effort to alter Italy's complex and overgenerous pension provisions, but in so doing alienated all State employees and many of its own supporters. The real blow to the government came from the judges. A government decree in July limiting pre-trial custody for corruption suspects infuriated the judiciary, and had to be withdrawn within a week. Soon Berlusconi's brother was being investigated, and in December Berlusconi himself was interrogated for seven hours on his own business dealings. The Constitutional Court ruled that no individual should be allowed to control a quarter of national TV channels. The final blow for the government was when the judicial hero Antonio Di Pietro suddenly resigned his post in Milan, alleging improper political pressures. Bossi seized his chance, the League proposed a vote of no confidence, and Berlusconi had to resign, yet another victim of the judiciary. His government had lasted seven months. It had been unable to pass contentious legislation; its main preoccupations were over public appointments; it fell, without a parliamentary vote, when a coalition partner withdrew support. All this had a distinctly familiar ring, and rather belied premature talk of a 'Second Republic'.

Berlusconi was succeeded by his former Treasury Minister, Lamberto Dini, a former chief executive of the Bank of Italy who had been an IMF official for many years. His government was initially designed to be a stopgap, to avoid the immediate new elections called for by Berlusconi. It had a limited programme: budget cuts, pensions reform and a law on the media. It consisted of experts and 'technocrats', contained no parliamentarians at all and, in order to win parliamentary votes of confidence, relied on support from the Left – the losers in the 1994 election – and from the League. The League and the new Popular Party soon split on the issue of whether to support Dini or Berlusconi. The new parties were thus just as fissiparous as the old. However, the Left coalition did anoint a potential leader and Prime Minister candidate, the ex-president of IRI Romano Prodi, and in spring 1995 it won control of nine of the fifteen 'ordinary' regions, as well as many local councils. Meanwhile Dini and the non-elected bankers and 'technocrats' ruled, appointed by an old-fashioned Christian Democrat President of the Republic, Scalfaro, and pledged essentially to sound finance; the Constitution remained as yet unchanged.

20.6 CONCLUSION

In 1992–93 a regime based on Christian Democrat practices and values, run by an élite educated in the traditional humanities, collapsed together with the party. The successor rulers were secular, indeed often Masonic. Governments were now led by businessmen or bankers, who took a hard-nosed view of the Christian Democrats' (or Fascists') efforts at 'social protection', and of the old-school intellectuals and professors. They operated under the eye of a far more independent-minded judiciary, which had temporarily acquired real political power and could bring down governments and commercial empires.

'Representative government' and legitimacy remained extremely problematic. At the local level, from 1993 onwards mayors were directly elected by the voters in communes of 15,000 or more, which seemed to make them better known and more effective. Many argued that, in the absence of well-rooted parties, Prime Ministers (or Presidents) should be directly elected too, especially as this might encourage 'alternation' in government. Meanwhile party squabbles and manoeuvres continued in parliament, but parties could no longer provide jobs, and parliament had lost so much legitimacy as to appear almost insignificant. Even its role in legislation was often bypassed, sometimes by direct negotiations between government and particular interests. The Dini government, for example, succeeded in reaching an agreement on pension reform in 1995, but not in parliament: it was the major trade union confederations who agreed, and parliament which had to ratify later. Alternatively, parliament was bypassed by referenda, which provided a populist mitigation of technocratic rule. They were now held almost annually on a whole range of highly detailed topics: in June 1995 there were twelve, three of them giving an unexpected boost to Berlusconi's efforts to keep control of his TV channels, and one calling successfully for the privatization of RAI. Signatures were being collected for eighteen more.

One major challenge to the old system seemed to have died down by 1995, at least temporarily. The League had helped to bring down the old parties, but had failed to mobilize the Northern middle classes. Bossi, like other Northern leaders before him, had made little impression on the permanent power structures in Rome, and the threat of federalism – the 'revolt against the Risorgimento' – had receded. The institutions of united Italy had little prestige, but they remained intact for the time being. Yet the 'anti-Fascist' foundations of the post-war system had been undermined. Fini, unlike Bossi, had succeeded in gaining middle-class support. The 'National Alliance' had held key government posts – environment, heritage, transport – under Berlusconi, and in 1995 could claim to be the last custodians of the ideals and myths of 'united Italy'.

Above all, the 'Cold War' was over. Italians now had to face up to the loss of the many benefits it had brought, particularly American support and a divided Germany. Italy could not hope to mediate any longer between East and West, or even North and South. Instead, she had to adjust to the traditional discomforts of her minor European status. If bankers ruled, that was partly due to 'European' – i.e. German – pressure. In short, the end of the 'Cold War' posed, yet again, the Italians' age-old dilemma. Should they aspire to become 'modern', 'progressive', market-oriented 'Europeans', as most Northerners and businessmen demanded? This option, however economically attractive, might well mean loss of effective independence – Italy as the 'Southern region of a new German Europe', in the words of Gianfranco Miglio (who welcomed the prospect).[6] It would certainly mean a strong German influence on Italian policies, as in the days of the Triple Alliance before 1914 or of the Axis before 1939. Or should Italians rather seek a 'Mediterranean', 'Southern' role, trading with the Middle East and North Africa, and necessarily pursuing their own geographic and strategic interests? Might not such a role be forced on them in any case, given that by 2020 65 per cent of the Mediterranean population would be living on its Southern and Eastern shores? This was the view of Rome, of the South and of the National Alliance. Could the interests of Northern and Southern Italians – to say nothing of myriad other local complexities – be reconciled, and if so through which institutions? Essentially, both the Christian Democrat regime and the Berlusconi government fell because they failed to mediate effectively between these interests. Could any parties, or institutions, do so in future?

In the nineteenth century 'Italy', i.e. the Italian State, had been 'made'; the problem, as D'Azeglio remarked, was to 'make Italians'. By the late twentieth century things were not so clear. The meaningful survival of 'Italy' could no longer be taken for granted. Many key issues – agriculture, migration, customs and excise duties, defence, environmental protection, even the currency – were now decided by European or international bodies, where the Italian input was not conspicuous. 'Italy' was, to all appearances, being absorbed into a European State and an unregulated global economy. Conversely, universal education and welfare, together with mass communications, sport, and supermarkets (Berlusconi prominent in all three), had at last 'made Italians', i.e. given them a common cultural background. Yet people were less mobile within Italy in the 1980s than in many previous decades, African immigrants had become numerous, and regional identities had revived strongly. The 'Italians' might have to be remade all over again.

REFERENCES

1. R. Mannheimer, 'Mercato elettorale e competizione fra i partiti', in *Quaderni di Sociologia*, xxxvi, 3 (1992), 91–114, at p. 96.
2. *La Repubblica*, 14 May 1991; quoted in P. McCarthy, 'The referendum of 9 June', in *Italian Politics*, vii (London 1992), 11–28, at p. 17.
3. P. Corbetta, 'La Lega e lo sfaldamento del sistema', in *Polis*, vii, 2 (1993), 229–52, at p. 241.
4. Referenda in Italy may not propose new legislation, but only 'abrogate' the old (see §18.3). The previous electoral rules for the Senate had permitted direct election of candidates who secured 65 per cent of the vote, a threshold so high it was rarely attained.
5. To be more exact, the 'proportional' results were adjusted by deducting (normally) 25 per cent from the 'proportional' vote of candidates who had been successful in the single-member constituencies; thus some allowance was made for the seats won there, and more 'proportional' seats were allocated to the losing parties.
6. G. Miglio, *Io, Bossi e la Lega*, Milan 1994, p. 93. Miglio was here writing of Northern Italy.

Bibliography

For reasons of space I have restricted this bibliography essentially to works in English, except for a few general histories and the occasional outstanding book in Italian. Readers needing more detailed information might consult one of the excellent bibliographical guides available in G. Candeloro, *Storia dell' Italia Moderna* (vi–xi), Milan 1970–86, or in several multi-volume series: *Storia d'Italia*, edited by Giuseppe Galasso, published by UTET in Turin, 23 vols, 1979– (vols 20–23 are relevant to post-1870 period); *Storia dell' Italia Contemporanea*, published by Edizioni Scientifiche Italiane in Naples and edited by Renzo De Felice, 7 vols, 1976–83; *Storia d'Italia dall' Unità alla Repubblica*, published by Il Mulino, 6 vols, Bologna 1979–85; *Storia d'Italia*, edited by G. Sabbatucci and V. Vidotto, published by Laterza, Bari and Rome, 1994– . Other bibliographies are mentioned in the various sections below, for each period.

The main journals covering post-Unification history are (in English) *Modern Italy* (1995–); on contemporary events, see the annual *Italian Politics* (1986–). In Italian, the leading journals are *Rivista Storica Italiana*, *Nuova Rivista Storica* and *Clio* (all more or less 'Liberal'); *Storia Contemporanea* (ed. R. De Felice); *Nuova Antologia*; *Italia Contemporanea*, *Studi Storici*, *Movimento Operaio e Socialista* (renamed *Ventesimo Secolo* 1991–), *Società e Storia*, *Rivista di Storia Contemporanea*, and *Annali dell' Istituto Giangiacomo Feltrinelli* (all more or less 'Left-wing'). The leading Catholic journal is the *Ricerche di Storia Sociale e Religiosa*; for strictly ecclesiastical history see also *Rivista di Storia della Chiesa in Italia*. And, of course, there is *Quaderni Storici* (see this volume §1.2) and *Passato e Presente*. On general southern history, see *Meridiana*; virtually every region has its own specialist historical journals.

On the archives, see above all P. D'Angiolini and C. Pavone (eds), *Guida Generale degli Archivi di Stato Italiani* (4 vols), Rome 1982–94. The first volume covers the central State archive in Rome where most of the modern State papers are housed. See also R.J. Lewanski, *Guide to Italian Libraries and Archives*, New York 1979 and F. della Peruta (ed.), *Biblioteche ed Archivi: Guida alla Consultazione*, Milan 1985. Basic statistical information is available in Istat, *Sommario di Statistiche Storiche d'Italia 1861–1975*, Rome 1976, in *Sommario di Statistiche Storiche 1926–85*, Rome 1986, and in L. Bergonzini, *Il Volto Statistico dell' Italia 1861–1981*, Rome 1984. For more detail, see the annual *Annuario Statistico Italiano* and the various series of the *Annali di Statistica.*

Finally, for some recent surveys of history-writing in Italy see F. J. Coppa and W. Roberts, *Modern Italian History, An Annotated Bibliography*, Westport, Conn. 1990; M. J. Bull, *Contemporary Italy. A Research Guide,* Westport 1996; L. Valiani, *L'Historiographie de l'Italie Contemporaine*, Geneva 1968; R. Romano, *La Storiografia Italiana Oggi*, Rome 1978; N. Tranfaglia (ed.), *L'Italia Unita nella Storiografia del Secondo Dopoguerra*, Milan 1980; L. De Rosa (ed.), *La Storiografia Italiano degli Ultimi 20 Anni* vol. iii, Bari 1989; and G. Galasso, 'L'Italia unita nella storiografia del secondo dopoguerra', in *Rivista Storica Italiana*, xci (1979), 617–40.

A. GENERAL WORKS

In English

P. Arlacchi, *Mafia, Peasants and Great Estates*, Cambridge 1983

R. M. Bell, *Fate and Honor, Family and Village*, Chicago 1979

A. Blok, *The Mafia of a Sicilian Village 1860–1960*, Oxford 1974

S. B. Clough, *The Economic History of Modern Italy*, New York 1964

S. B. Clough and S. Saladino, *A History of Modern Italy: Documents, Readings and Commentary*, New York 1968

F. J. Coppa (ed.), *A Dictionary of Modern Italian History*, Westport, Conn. 1985

F. J. Coppa (ed.), *Studies in Modern Italian History*, New York 1986.

P. Corner, *From Peasant to Entrepreneur*, Oxford 1993

A. De Grand, *The Italian Left in the Twentieth Century*, Bloomington 1989

C. Duggan, *A Concise History of Italy*, Cambridge 1994

D. Forgacs, *Italian Culture in the Industrial Era*, Manchester 1990

H. S. Hughes, *The U.S. and Italy* (3rd edn), Cambridge, Mass. 1980

A. C. Jemolo, *Church and State in Italy 1850–1950*, Oxford 1960

M. Livi Bacci, *A History of Italian Fertility During the Last Two Centuries*, Princeton 1977

C. J. Lowe and F. Marzari, *Italian Foreign Policy 1870–1940*, London 1975

D. Mack Smith, *Italy: A Modern History* (2nd edn), Ann Arbor 1969; *Modern Sicily*, London 1968; *Italy and its Monarchy*, New Haven 1989

A. W. Salomone (ed.), *Italy from Risorgimento to Fascism*, Newton Abbot 1971

J. and P. Schneider, *Culture and Political Economy in Western Sicily*, New York 1976

C. Seton-Watson, *Italy from Liberalism to Fascism*, London 1967

E. R. Tannenbaum and E. P. Noether (eds), *Modern Italy*, New York 1974

R. Webster, *Christian Democracy in Italy 1860–1960*, London 1961

V. Zamagni, *The Economic History of Italy 1860–1990*, Oxford 1993

In Italian

I have already mentioned several multi-volume series on the post-1870 period for their bibliographies. In addition, there is the *Storia d'Italia*, published by Einaudi, Turin, in 6 vols with a companion series of '*Annali*' in 9 vols, 1972–86; and a separate Einaudi series on each region: *Storia d'Italia. Le Regioni dall' Unità ad Oggi*, Turin 1984– (11 published by 1994). Other general works of interest are:

M. Barbagli, *Disoccupazione Intellettuale e Sistema Scolastico in Italia*, Bologna 1974

R. J. Bosworth and S. Romano (eds), *La Politica Estera Italiana 1860–1985*, Bologna 1991

M. De Giorgio, *Le Italiane dall' Unità ad Oggi*, Bari 1992

T. De Mauro, *Storia Linguistica dell' Italia Unita*, Bari 1963

G. De Rosa, *Storia del Movimento Cattolico in Italia* (2 vols), Bari 1966

G. Fuà (ed.), *Lo Sviluppo Economico in Italia* (3 vols), Milan 1969–81

A. Gramsci, *Quaderni del Carcere* (4 vols), Rome 1975

R. Romeo, *Breve Storia della Grande Industria in Italia*, Bologna 1961

E. Serra, *La Diplomazia in Italia*, Milan 1984

E. Sori, *L'Emigrazione Italiana dall' Unità alla Seconda Guerra Mondiale*, Bologna 1979

P. Sylos Labini, *Saggio sulle Classi Sociali*, Bari 1974

G. Toniolo (ed.), *Lo Sviluppo Economico Italiano 1861–1940*, Bari 1973

N. Tranfaglia, *Dallo Stato Liberale al Regime Fascista*, Milan 1973

O. Vitali, *Aspetti dello Sviluppo Economico Italiano*, Rome 1970

B. 1871–1914

—, *Chiesa e Religiosità in Italia dopo l'Unità (1861– 78)* (4 vols), Milan 1973

L. Albertini, *The Origins of the War of 1914* (3 vols), Oxford 1952–57

A. Aquarone, *Alla Ricerca dell' Italia Liberale*, Naples 1972; *L'Italia Giolittiana* (2 vols), Bologna 1981–88

P. L. Ballini, *Le Elezioni nella Storia d'Italia dall' Unità al Fascismo*, Bologna 1988

D. H. Bell, *Sesto San Giovanni*, New Brunswick 1986; 'Worker culture and worker politics: the experience of an Italian hill town 1880–1915', *Social History*, iii (1978), 1–21

R. J. Bosworth, *Italy, the Least of the Great Powers*, Cambridge 1980; *Italy and the Approach of the First World War*, London 1982

L. Cafagna, 'Italy 1830–1914', in C. Cipolla (ed.), *The Fontana Economic History of Europe*, iv, pt. 1, London 1973, pp. 279–328

A. Caracciolo, *Stato e Società Civile*, Turin 1960

F. Chabod, *Storia della Politica Estera Italiana dal 1870 al 1896* (2 vols), Bari 1951, reissued 1971

M. N. Clark, 'La storia politica e sociale 1847–1914', in M. Guidetti (ed.), *Storia dei Sardi e della Sardegna*, iv, Milan 1990, pp. 243–85

J. Cohen, 'Financing industrialisation in Italy 1894–1914', *Journal of Economic History*, xxvii (1967), 363–82

F. Crispi, *The memoirs of Francesco Crispi* (3 vols), London 1912–14

B. Croce, *A History of Italy 1871–1915*, Oxford 1929

J. A. Davis, *Conflict and Control. Law and Order in Nineteenth-Century Italy*, London 1988; (ed.), *Gramsci and Italy's Passive Revolution*, London 1979

J. Davis, *Land and Family in Pisticci*, London 1973

N. Douglas, *Old Calabria*, London 1915

R. Eckaus, 'The North-South differential in Italian economic development', *Journal of Economic History*, xxi (1961), 285–317

D. Farini, *Diario di Fine Secolo* (2 vols), Rome 1961

P. Farneti, *Sistema Politico e Società Civile*, Turin 1971

R. Foerster, *The Italian Emigration of our Times*, Cambridge, Mass. 1919

R. C. Fried, *The Italian Prefects*, New Haven 1963

A. Gerschenkron, *Economic Backwardness in Historical Perspective*, Cambridge, Mass. 1962

M. Gibson, *Prostitution and the State in Italy*, New Brunswick 1986

G. Giolitti, *Memoirs of My Life*, London 1923; *Quarant'anni di Politica Italiana* (3 vols), P. D'Angiolini, G. Carocci and C. Pavone (eds), Milan 1962

J. Gooch, *Army, State and Society in Italy 1870–1915*, London 1989

G. A. Harrison, *Mosquitoes, Malaria and Man*, New York 1978

E. J. Hobsbawm, *Primitive Rebels*, Manchester 1959

R. Hostetter, *The Italian Socialist Movement. Origins, 1860–82*, Princeton 1958

H. S. Hughes, *Consciousness and Society*, London 1959

E. Jacobitti, *Revolutionary Humanism and Historicism in Modern Italy*, New Haven 1981

J. Joll, *The Anarchists*, London 1964

D. Kertzer, *Family Life in Central Italy 1880–1910*, New Brunswick 1983

B. King and T. Okey, *Italy Today*, London 1901

A. L. Lowell, *Government and Parties in Continental Europe*, i, London 1896

J. S. Macdonald, 'Agricultural organisation, migration and labour militancy', *Economic History Review*, xvi (1963), 61–75

H. G. Marcus, *The Life and Times of Menelik II*, Oxford 1975

S. Merlino, 'Camorra, Maffia and Brigandage', *Political Science Quarterly*, ix (1894), 466–85

J. Morris, *The Political Economy of Shopkeeping in Milan 1886–1922*, Cambridge 1993

V. Pareto, 'The parliamentary regime in Italy', *Political Science Quarterly*, viii (1893), 677–721

E. Ragionieri, *Un Comune Socialista: Sesto Fiorentino*, Rome 1953

J. Ridley, *Garibaldi*, London 1973

D. A. Roe, *A Plague of Corn – the Social History of Pellagra*, Ithaca 1973

R. Romanelli, *L'Italia Liberale*, Bologna 1979; *Il Comando Impossibile*, Bologna 1988; 'Political debate, social history and the Italian bourgeoisie', *Journal of Modern History*, lxiii (1991), 717–39

R. Romeo, *Risorgimento e Capitalismo*, Bari 1959

M. Rossi-Doria, 'The land-tenure system and class in Southern Italy', *American Historical Review*, lxiv (1958), 46–53

A. W. Salomone, *Italy in the Giolittian Era* (2nd edn), Pennsylvania 1960

F. M. Snowden, *Violence and Great Estates in Southern Italy*, Cambridge 1986

S. J. Surace, *Ideology, Economic Change and the Working Class*, Berkeley 1966

G. Thayer, *Italy and the Great War*, Wisconsin 1964

C. Tilly *et al.*, *The Rebellious Century 1830–1930*, London 1975

L. Tilly, *Politics and Class in Milan 1881–1901*, Oxford 1992; 'I Fatti di Maggio: the working class of Milan and the rebellion of 1898', in R. J. Bezucha (ed.), *Modern European Social History*, Lexington, Mass. 1972, pp. 124–58

G. Toniolo, *An Economic History of Liberal Italy 1850–1918*, London 1990

N. Valeri, *Giovanni Giolitti*, Turin 1972

P. Villani, 'Gruppi sociali e classe dirigente all' indomani dell' Unità', in the Einaudi *Storia d'Italia*, *Annali* i, Turin 1978, pp. 881–978

G. Volpe, *Italia Moderna 1815–1915* (3 vols), Florence 1943–52

R. Webster, *Industrial Imperialism in Italy 1908–15*, Berkeley 1975

J. Whittam, *The Politics of the Italian Army*, London 1976

G. Woodcock, *Anarchism*, London 1963

For a full bibliography, see the *Bibliografia dell' Età del Risorgimento in onore di A. M. Ghisalberti* (4 vols), Florence 1971–77. For labour history, see 'Ente per la Storia del Socialismo e del Movimento Operaio Italiano', *Bibliografia del Socialismo e del Movimento Operaio Italiano* (2 vols, in 6 parts), Rome and Turin 1956–68; F. Andreucci and T. Detti (eds), *Il Movimento Operaio Italiano: Dizionario Biografico 1853–1943* (5 vols), Rome 1975–78; and A. T. Lane (ed.), *Biographical Dictionary of European Labor Leaders*, Westport 1995. For 'Social Catholicism', see F. Traniello and G. Campanini (eds), *Dizionario Storico del Movimento Cattolico in Italia 1860–1980* (3 vols), Casale Monferrato 1981–82.

C. 1914–43

—, *Actes et Documents du Saint Siège relatifs à la Seconde Guerre Mondiale* (11 vols), Rome 1965–81

R. Albrecht–Carrié, *Italy at the Paris Peace Conference*, New York 1938

A. E. Alcock, *History of the South Tyrol Question*, London 1970

A. Aquarone, *L'Organizzazione dello Stato Totalitario*, Turin 1965

A. Aquarone and M. Vernassa (eds), *Il Regime Fascista*, Bologna 1974

G. Baer, *The Coming of the Italo-Ethiopian War*, Cambridge, Mass. 1967

D. Binchy, *Church and State in Fascist Italy*, London 1941

M. Blinkhorn, *Mussolini and Fascist Italy*, London 1984

P. V. Cannistraro (ed.), *Historical Dictionary of Fascist Italy*, Westport, Conn. 1995; *La Fabbrica del Consenso*, Bari 1975

A. L. Cardoza, *Agrarian Elites and Italian Fascism*, Princeton 1982

A. Cassels, *Mussolini's Early Diplomacy*, Princeton 1970

O. Chadwick, *Britain and the Vatican during the Second World War*, Cambridge 1986

G. Ciano, *Ciano's Diary 1937–8*, London 1952; *Ciano's Diary 1939–43*, London 1947; *Ciano's Diplomatic Papers*, London 1948

P. Ciocca and G. Toniolo (eds), *L'Economia Italiana durante il Fascismo*, Bologna 1976

M. N. Clark, *Antonio Gramsci and the Revolution that Failed*, New Haven 1977; 'Italian squadrismo and contemporary vigilantism', *European History Quarterly*, xviii (1988), 33–49

J. Cohen, 'Fascism and agriculture in Italy: policies and consequences', *Economic History Review*, xxxii (1979), 70–87

S. Colarizi, *L'Italia Antifascista dal 1922 al 1940* (2 vols), Bari 1976

J. W. Cole and E. R. Wolf, *The Hidden Frontier*, New York 1974

P. Corner, *Fascism in Ferrara*, Oxford 1974

J. F. Coverdale, *Italian Intervention in the Spanish Civil War*, Princeton 1975

A. Dal Pont and S. Carolini, *L'Italia Dissidente e Antifascista* (3 vols), Milan 1980

F. W. Deakin, *The Brutal Friendship*, London 1962

R. De Felice, *Mussolini il Rivoluzionario*, Turin 1965; *Mussolini il Fascista* (2 vols), Turin 1966–68; *Mussolini il Duce* (2 vols), Turin 1974–81; *Mussolini l'Alleato* (2 vols to date), 1990– ; *Fascism: an Informal Introduction to its Theory and Practice*, New Brunswick 1976; *Interpretations of Fascism*, Cambridge, Mass. 1977

A. H. De Grand, *The Italian Nationalist Association and the Rise of Fascism in Italy*, Lincoln, Nebraska 1978

V. de Grazia, *The Culture of Consent*, Cambridge 1981; *How Fascism Ruled Women*, Berkeley 1992

A. Del Boca, *The Ethiopian War*, Chicago 1969

C. Delzell, *Mussolini's Enemies*, Princeton 1961

E. Di Nolfo *et al.*, *L'Italia e la Politica di Potenza in Europa 1938–40*, Milan 1985

C. Duggan, *Fascism and the Mafia*, New Haven 1988

C. Falls, *Caporetto*, London 1966

D. Forgacs (ed.), *Rethinking Italian Fascism*, London 1986

H. Finer, *Mussolini's Italy*, London 1935, reissued 1964

D. J. Forsyth, *The Crisis of Liberal Italy 1914–22*, Cambridge 1993

C. Haider, *Capital and Labor under Fascism*, New York 1930

S. W. Halperin (ed.), *Mussolini and Italian Fascism*, New York 1964

A. Hamilton, *The Appeal of Fascism*, London 1971

C. Hibbert, *Benito Mussolini*, London 1962

H. S. Hughes, *Prisoners of Hope*, Cambridge, Mass. 1983

A. Kelikian, *Town and Country under Fascism*, Oxford 1986

P. Kent, *The Pope and the Duce*, London 1981

I. Kirkpatrick, *Mussolini: a Study of a Demagogue*, London 1964

M. Knox, *Mussolini Unleashed*, Cambridge 1982

T. H. Koon, *Believe Obey Fight*, Chapel Hill 1985

E. Ludwig, *Talks with Mussolini*, London 1932

J. Lukacs, *The Last European War*, London 1976

A. Lyttelton, *The Seizure of Power*, London 1973; (ed.), *Italian Fascisms*, London 1973; 'Italian Fascism', in W. Laqueur (ed.), *Fascism: a Reader's Guide*, London 1976, pp. 125–50

D. Mack Smith, *Mussolini*, London 1981; *Mussolini's Roman Empire*, London 1976

C. S. Maier, *Recasting Bourgeois Europe*, Princeton 1975

O. Malagodi, *Conversazioni di Guerra 1914–19* (2 vols), Milan 1960

F. Martini, *Il Diario 1914–18*, Milan 1966

G. Megaro, *Mussolini in the Making*, London 1938

M. Michaelis, *Mussolini and the Jews*, Oxford 1978

E. Millar (ed.), *The Legacy of Fascism*, Glasgow 1989

P. Morgan, *Italian Fascism*, London 1995

L. Minio-Paluello, *Education in Fascist Italy*, Oxford 1946

L. Passerini, *Fascism and Popular Memory*, Cambridge 1986

P. Pecorari (ed.), *Chiesa, Azione Cattolica e Fascismo nell' Italia Settentrionale durante il Pontificato di Pio XI (1922–39)*, Milan 1979

F. Perfetti and G. Parlato, *Il Sindacalismo Fascista* (2 vols), Rome 1988–89

J. F. Pollard, *The Vatican and Italian Fascism*, Cambridge 1985

W. A. Renzi, 'Italy's neutrality and intervention into the Great War: a re-examination', *American Historical Review*, lxxiii (1968), 1414–32; 'The Entente and the Vatican during the period of Italian Neutrality, August 1914–May 1915', *Historical Journal*, xiii (1979), 491–508

A. Rhodes, *The Vatican in the Age of the Dictators*, London 1973

S. Ricossa, 'Italy 1920–70', in C. M. Cipolla (ed.), *The Fontana Economic History of Europe* (vi, pt. 1), London 1973, 266–322

D. D. Roberts, *The Syndical Tradition and Italian Fascism*, Manchester 1979

E. Robertson, *Mussolini as Empire-Builder*, London 1977

F. Rosengarten, *The Italian Anti-Fascist Press*, Cleveland, Ohio 1968

L. Rosenstock-Franck, *L'Economie Corporative Fasciste en Doctrine et en Fait*, Paris 1934; *Les Etapes de l'Economie Fasciste Italienne*, Paris 1939

A. Rossi (i.e. A. Tasca), *The Rise of Italian Fascism*, London 1938

D. Rusinow, *Italy's Austrian Heritage*, Oxford 1969

G. Salvemini, *Under the Axe of Fascism*, London 1936

R. Sarti, *Fascism and the Industrial Leadership in Italy*, Berkeley 1971; 'Fascist modernisation in Italy: traditional or revolutionary?', *American Historical Review*, lxxv (1970), 1029–45; (ed.), *The Ax Within*, New York 1974

C. Schmidt, *The Plough and the Sword*, New York 1938

H. W. Schneider, *Making the Fascist State*, New York 1928

H. W. Schneider and S. B. Clough, *Making Fascists*, Chicago 1929

P. Secchia (ed.), *Enciclopedia dell' Antifascismo e della Resistenza* (6 vols), Milan 1968–89

C. Segre, *Fourth Shore*, Chicago 1974; *Italo Balbo*, Berkeley 1987

F. Snowden, *The Fascist Revolution in Tuscany*, Cambridge 1989; 'On the social origins of agrarian Fascism in Italy', *Archives Européennes de Sociologie*, xiii (1972), 268–95

P. Spriano, *Storia del Partito Comunista Italiano* (5 vols), Turin 1967–75

J. Steinberg, *All or Nothing*, London 1990

Z. Sternhall *et al.*, *The Birth of Fascist Ideology*, Princeton 1993

A. Stille, *Benevolence and Betrayal*, London 1992

E. R. Tannenbaum, *Fascism in Italy*, London 1973

D. Thompson, *State Control in Fascist Italy*, Manchester 1991

G. Toniolo, *L'Economia dell' Italia Fascista*, Bari 1968

M. Toscano, *The Origins of the Pact of Steel*, Baltimore 1968

A. Treves, *Le Migrazioni Interne dell' Italia Fascista*, Turin 1976

D. Veneruso, *L'Italia Fascista*, Bologna 1981

R. Vivarelli, 'Revolution and reaction in Italy', *Journal of Italian History*, i (1978), 235–63

W. G. Welk, *Fascist Economic Policy*, Cambridge, Mass. 1938

P. Willson, *The Clockwork Factory*, Oxford 1993

E. Wiskemann, *The Rome-Berlin Axis*, London 1949

S. J. Woolf (ed.), *European Fascism*, London 1968

More detailed bibliographies may be found in R. De Felice, *Bibliografia Orientativa del Fascismo*, Rome 1991; in G. Quazza, *Storiografia e Fascismo*, Milan 1985; in Lyttelton, *The Seizure of Power, op. cit.*; in Mack Smith, *Mussolini, op. cit.*; in Veneruso, *L'Italia Fascista, op. cit.*; and in G. Candeloro, *Storia dell' Italia Moderna, op. cit.*, viii and ix. On the First World War, see G. Rochat's discussion of the literature in *L'Italia nella Prima Guerra Mondiale*, Milan 1976. On Fascist foreign policy, see A. Cassels (ed.), *Italian Foreign Policy 1918–45. A Guide to Research Materials and Research*, Wilmington, Delaware 1981.

D. 1943–95

K. Allen and A. Stevenson, *An Introduction to the Italian Economy*, London 1974

P. Allum, *Italy – Republic without Government?*, London 1973; 'Italy', in S.

Henig (ed.), *Political Parties in the European Community* (2nd edn), London 1979; *Politics and Society in Post-War Naples*, Cambridge 1973

S. Aquaviva, *The Eclipse of the Sacred*, Oxford 1979

U. Ascoli and R. Catanzaro (eds), *La Società Italiana degli Anni Ottanta*, Bari 1987

Z. Baranski and R. Lumley (eds), *Culture and Conflict in Post-War Italy*, London 1990

M. Barbagli *et al.*, *Dentro il PCI*, Bologna 1979

S. H. Barnes, *Representation in Italy*, Chicago 1977; *Party Democracy*, New Haven 1968

J. Barth Urban, *Moscow and the Italian Communist Party*, Ithaca 1986

L. Barzini, *The Italians*, New York 1964

R. Battaglia, *The Story of the Italian Resistance*, London 1957

S. Berger (ed.), *Organising Interests in Western Europe*, Cambridge 1981

S. Berger and M. Piore, *Dualism and Discontinuity in Industrial Societies*, Cambridge 1980

D. Blackmer, *Unity in Diversity*, Cambridge, Mass. 1968

D. Blackmer and S. Tarrow (eds), *Communism in Italy and France*, Princeton 1975

M. Bull and J. Newell, 'Italy, elections and victory of the Right', *Parliamentary Affairs*, xlviii (1995), 72–99

M. Calise, 'The Italian partyocracy', in *Political Science Quarterly*, cix (1994), 441–66

J. C. Campbell (ed.), *Successful Negotiations: Trieste 1954*, Princeton 1976

S. Cassese (ed.), *L'Amministrazione Pubblica in Italia*, Bologna 1974

R. Catanzaro, *Men of Respect*, New York 1992; (ed.), *The Red Brigades and Left-Wing Terrorism in Italy*, London 1991

J. Chubb, *Patronage, Power and Poverty in Southern Italy*, Cambridge 1982

J. Chubb and M. Vannicelli, 'Italy – a web of scandals in a flawed democracy', in A. Markovits and M. Silverstein (eds), *The Politics of Scandals*, New York 1988, pp. 122–50

B. Clark, *Academic Power in Italy*, Chicago 1977

M. N. Clark, 'Italy: regionalism and bureaucratic reform', in J. Cornford (ed.), *The Failure of the State*, London 1975, pp. 44–81; 'La Storia Politica e Sociale 1914–75', in M. Guidetti (ed.), *Storia dei Sardi e della Sardegna*, iv, Milan 1990, pp. 389–456

M. N. Clark and D. Hine, 'The Italian Communist Party: between Leninism and social democracy?', in D. Childs (ed.), *The Changing Face of Western Communism*, London 1980, pp. 112–46

S. Colarizi, *La Seconda Guerra Mondiale e la Repubblica*, Turin 1984

R. Collin, *The De Lorenzo Gambit*, London 1976

M. Cotta, 'The rise and fall of the "centrality" of the Italian Parliament', in G. Copeland and S. Patterson (eds), *Parliaments in the Modern World*, Ann Arbor 1994

F. W. Deakin, *The Last Days of Mussolini*, Harmondsworth 1966, i.e. Part Two of *The Brutal Friendship*, London 1962

D. Della Porta (ed.), *Terrorismi in Italia*, Bologna 1985; (ed.), *Lo Scambio Occulto*, Bologna 1992

C. Delzell, *Mussolini's Enemies*, Princeton 1961; 'The Italian Anti-Fascist Resistance in retrospect', *Journal of Modern History*, xlvii (1975), 66–96

B. Dente, 'Centre-local relations in Italy', in Y. Mény and V. Wright (eds), *Centre-Periphery Relations in Europe*, London 1985, pp. 125–48

M. Diani, *Green Networks*, Edinburgh 1994

G. di Palma, *Surviving without Governing*, Berkeley 1977

D. Dolci, *To Feed the Hungry*, London 1959; *Waste*, London 1963

J. B. Duroselle, *Le Conflit de Trieste 1943–54*, Brussels 1966

D. W. Ellwood, *Italy 1943–45*, Leicester 1985; *Rebuilding Europe*, London 1992

R. H. Evans, *Co-existence: Communism and its Practice in Bologna*, Notre Dame 1967

G. Falcone, *Men of Honour*, London 1992

P. Farneti, *The Italian Party System*, London 1985

F. Francioni, *Italy and E.C. Membership Evaluated*, London 1992

H. Frankel, *Mattei: Oil and Politics*, London 1966

C. Frayling, *Spaghetti Westerns*, London 1981

G. Freddi, 'Regional development, administrative decentralisation, and bureaucratic performance in Italy', *Policy and Politics*, viii (1980), 383–98

A. Friedman, *Agnelli and the Network of Italian Power*, London 1988

P. Furlong, *Modern Italy*, London 1994; 'Political terrorism in Italy', in J. Lodge (ed.), *Terrorism: a Challenge to the State*, Oxford 1981, pp. 57–90

T. Gallagher, 'The regional dimension in Italy's political upheaval', *Parliamentary Affairs*, xlvii (1994), 456–68

G. Galli and A. Prandi, *Patterns of Political Development in Italy*, New Haven 1970

D. Gambetta, *The Sicilian Mafia*, Cambridge, Mass. 1993

J. Gatt-Rutter, *Writers and Politics in Modern Italy*, London 1978

P. Ginsborg, *A History of Contemporary Italy*, London 1990

M. Grindrod, *The Rebuilding of Italy*, Oxford 1955

J. Harper, *America and the Reconstruction of Italy*, Cambridge 1986

C. R. S. Harris, *The Allied Military Administration of Italy 1943–45*, London 1957

J. Haycraft, *The Italian Labyrinth*, London 1985

P. Hebblethwaite, *In The Vatican*, London 1986

S. Hellman, *Italian Communism in Transition*, Oxford 1988

H. Hess, *Mafia and Mafiosi*, London 1973

G. H. Hildebrand, *Growth and Structure in the Economy of Modern Italy*, Cambridge, Mass. 1965

J. Hilowitz, *Economic Development and Social Change in Sicily*, Cambridge, Mass. 1965

D. Hine, *Governing Italy*, Oxford 1993; 'Italy', in F. F. Ridley (ed.), *Government and Administration in Western Europe*, Oxford 1979, pp. 156–203

D. Horowitz, *The Italian Labor Movement*, Cambridge, Mass. 1963

A. Jamieson, *The Heart Attacked: Terrorism in Italy*, London 1989

D. Kertzer, *Comrades and Christians*, Cambridge 1980

R. King, *Land Reform – the Italian Experience*, London 1973; *Italy*, London 1987; 'Italy', in H. Clout (ed.), *Regional Development in Western Europe* (2nd edn), London 1981, pp. 119–49

N. Kogan, *A Political History of Post-War Italy*, New York 1981; *The Politics of Italian Foreign Policy*, New York 1963

R. Lamb, *War in Italy 1943–45*, London 1993

P. Lange and M. Regini (eds), *State, Market and Social Regulation*, Cambridge 1989

P. Lange and S. Tarrow (eds), *Italy in Transition*, London 1980

J. La Palombara, *Interest Groups in Italian Politics*, Princeton 1964; *Democracy – Italian Style*, New Haven 1987; 'Italy – fragmentation, isolation and alienation', in L. Pye and S. Verba (eds), *Political Culture and Political Development*, Princeton 1965, pp. 282–329

R. Leonardi and R. Nanetti, *Regional Development in a Modern European Economy; the Case of Tuscany*, London 1994

R. Leonardi and D. Wertman, *Italian Christian Democracy*, London 1989

P. Leprohon, *The Italian Cinema*, London 1972

J. Low-Beer, *Protest and Participation*, Cambridge 1978

R. Lumley, *States of Emergency*, London 1990

V. Lutz, *Italy – a Study in Economic Development*, Oxford 1962

P. Luzzatto-Fegis, *Volto Sconosciuto dell' Italia* (2 vols), Milan 1956–66

G. Mammarella, *Italy after Fascism*, Notre Dame 1966

J. E. Miller, *The United States and Italy*, Chapel Hill 1986; 'Taking off the gloves: the U.S. and the Italian elections of 1948', *Diplomatic History*, vii (1983), 35–55

D. Moss, *The Politics of Left-Wing Violence in Italy 1969–84*, London 1989; 'The kidnapping and murder of Aldo Moro', *European Journal of Sociology*, xxii (1981), 265–95

S. Negrelli and C. Santi, 'Industrial relations in Italy', in G. Baglioni and C. Crouch, *European Industrial Relations*, London 1990, pp. 154–98

R. Nanetti, *Growth and Territorial Politics*, London 1988

P. Nichols, *Italia, Italia*, London 1973

B. Novak, *Trieste 1941–54*, Chicago 1970

I. Origo, *War in Val d'Orcia*, London 1947, reissued 1985

G. Palazzoli, *Les Régions Italiennes*, Paris 1966

M. Pantaleone, *Mafia and Politics*, London 1966

A. Parisi (ed.), *Democristiani*, Bologna 1979

G. Pasquino (ed.), *Il Sistema Politico Italiano*, Bari 1985

D. Pinto (ed.), *Contemporary Italian Sociology*, Cambridge 1981

A. Pizzorno and C. Crouch (eds), *The Resurgence of Class Conflict in Western Europe since 1968* (2 vols), London 1978

G. Podbielski, *Italy: Development and Crisis in the Post-War Economy*, Oxford 1974

G. Poggi, *Catholic Action in Italy*, Stanford 1966

M. Posner and S. J. Woolf, *Italian Public Enterprise*, London 1967

R. Putnam, *The Beliefs of Politicians*, New Haven 1973; 'The political attitudes of senior civil servants in Western Europe', *British Journal of Political Science*, iii (1973), 257–90

R. Putnam, R. Leonardi and R. Nanetti, *Making Democracy Work*, Princeton 1993

C. Richards, *The New Italians*, London 1994

D. Rusinow, *Italy's Austrian Heritage*, Oxford 1969

G. Sani, 'Determinants of party preference in Italy', *American Journal of Political Science*, xviii (1974), 315–29

D. Sassoon, *Contemporary Italy*, London 1986, 2nd edn 1996; 'Italy – The advent of private broadcasting', in R. Kuhn (ed.), *The Politics of Broadcasting*, London 1985, pp. 119–57

School of Barbiana, *Letter to a Teacher*, Harmondsworth 1970

G. Servadio, *Mafioso*, London 1976

A. Silj, *Never Again Without a Rifle*, New York 1979

S. Silverman, *Three Bells of Civilisation*, New York 1975

B. E. Smith and E. Aga Rossi, *Operation Sunrise*, London 1979

F. Spotts and T. Wieser, *Italy: a Difficult Democracy*, Cambridge 1986

G. Statera, *Death of a Utopia*, New York 1975

A. Stille, *Excellent Cadavers*, London 1995

P. Sylos Labini, *Le Classi Sociali negli Anni 80*, Bari 1986

S. Tarrow, *Between Centre and Periphery*, New Haven 1977

M. Toscano, *Alto Adige, South Tyrol*, Baltimore 1975

C. Trigilia, *Sviluppo Senza Autonomia*, Bologna 1992

US State Dept, *Foreign Relations of the United States 1943–* , Washington 1963–

P. Vannicelli, *Italy, Nato and the EEC*, Cambridge, Mass. 1974

R. Wade, 'Fast growth and slow development in Southern Italy', in D. Seers (ed.), *Underdeveloped Europe*, Brighton 1979, pp. 197–221

J. Walston, *Mafia and Clientelism*, London 1988

A. Weingrod and E. Morin, 'Post-peasants: the character of contemporary Sardinian society', *Comparative Studies in Society and History*, xiii (1971), 301–24

D. Wertman, 'The Catholic Church and Italian politics: the impact of secularisation', *West European Politics*, v (1982), 87–107

R. Willis, *Italy Chooses Europe*, Oxford 1971

S. J. Woolf (ed.), *The Rebirth of Italy 1943–50*, London 1972

R. Zariski, *Italy: the Politics of Uneven Development*, Hinsdale, Ill. 1972

For more detailed bibliographies see S. Colarizi, *La Seconda Guerra Mondiale e la Repubblica, op. cit.*; P. Ginsborg, *A History of Contemporary Italy, op.cit.*; P. Furlong, *Modern Italy, op. cit.*; and D. Hine, *Governing Italy, op. cit.* Many important articles on contemporary issues are to be found in English in *West European Politics* and other leading political science journals, as well as in the annual publication *Italian Politics* (London 1986–). In Italian, see especially *Il Mulino, Polis, Quaderni di Sociologia* and the *Rivista Italiana di Scienza Politica*.

Maps

1. Modern Italy

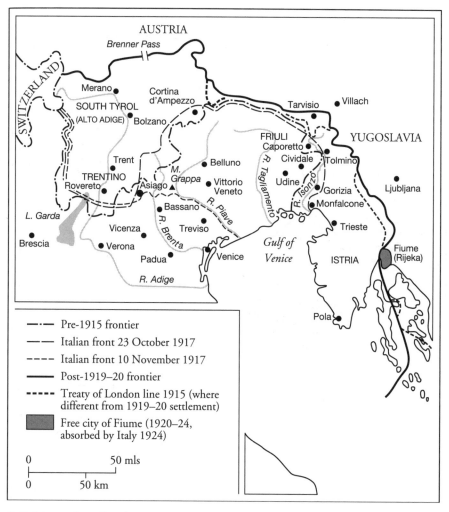

2. Italy's northern frontiers

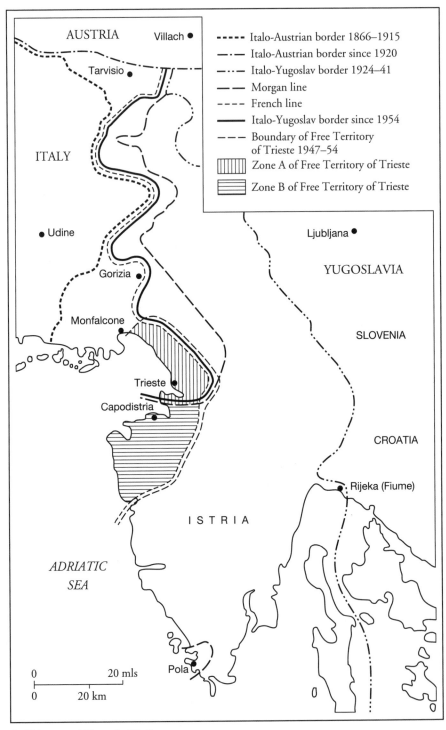

AUSTRIA   Villach ●

Tarvisio ●

- - - - Italo-Austrian border 1866–1915
— · — Italo-Austrian border since 1920
— · · — Italo-Yugoslav border 1924–41
— — Morgan line
- - - - French line
—— Italo-Yugoslav border since 1954
— — Boundary of Free Territory
of Trieste 1947–54
||||| Zone A of Free Territory of Trieste
≡ Zone B of Free Territory of Trieste

ITALY

● Udine

Ljubljana ●

YUGOSLAVIA

Gorizia ●

SLOVENIA

Monfalcone ●

Trieste ●

Capodistria
●

CROATIA

Rijeka (Fiume)
●

I S T R I A

ADRIATIC
SEA

Pola ●

0   20 mls

0   20 km

3. Trieste and Venezia Giulia

Index

Abba, Giuseppe, 167
abortion, 164, 362, 382–3, 401
  legalisation of, 334, 382–3, 405, 408
Abruzzi, 15, 20, 52, 69, 303, 400
  Duke of (Luigi Amedeo di Savoia), 125
  emigration from, 32, 166
Abyssinia, *see* Ethiopia
Academy, Royal Italian, 243
Acheson, Dean, 345
ACLI (*Associazione Cristiana dei Lavoratori Italiani*), workers' association, 371
Acquarone, Pietro, 296
Action, Party of, 294, 295, 307, 308, 317, 318, 319, 321
  and Resistance, 312, 313, 314, 315, 317, 318
Acton, William, 34
Adda, River, 165
Addis Ababa, 100
  Treaty of (1896), 100
Adowa, battle of (1896), 100, 103, 114, 151, 152, 154, 281, 282
Adriatica (shipping line), 265
Adriatic coast, 14, 27, 369
Adriatic sea, 181, 182, 203, 204
Aegean Sea, 154
Afghanistan, 389
Africa,
  colonies in, 46–8, 49, 81, 99–101, 112, 153–5, 167, 199, 204, 243, 266, 267, 268, 281–2, 284, 285, 286, 322
  see also North Africa
Afrika Korps, 286
Agadir crisis (1911), 152, 153
agencies, public, 133, 234–5, 265–6, 267, 271, 318, 335–7, 338, 339, 354–6, 357–9, 361, 366, 372, 379, 391–3, 399, 409, 423
  see also ENI; Institute for Industrial
  Reconstruction; land reform; '*sottogoverno*'
AGIP (*Azienda Generale Italiana dei Petroli*), State oil company, 266, 350
Agnelli, Gianni, 366
Agnelli, Giovanni, 125, 192, 208
Agrarian Defence League, 94
agriculture, 12–21, 25–6, 47, 67, 72, 94–6, 101, 120, 127–31, 142–3, 166, 193–4, 198, 209–210, 215, 249, 268–71, 278, 311, 336–7, 349, 354–7, 359, 360, 361, 390, 391, 402, 419, 426
  Minister of, 102, 151, 210, 213
  Ministry of, 133, 138, 420
  production, 18, 127–8, 194, 210, 269, 290, 348, 356–7, 400, 402
  see also food; labourers; landowners; peasant landowners; share-croppers; wheat
'agricultural quadrilateral', 127–8, 131
Agrigento, 21, 33, 363
Agro Romano, 14, 17, 20, 30, 70, 82–3, 129
AIDS (acquired immuno-deficiency syndrome), 403, 404
aircraft, 233, 252, 283, 288, 298, 380
  industry, 125, 190, 206, 266, 267
air force, 233, 282, 286, 288, 380
Air, Minister of, 233, 286
Alamein, El, 286
Albania, 181, 207, 280, 283, 286, 402
Albanian language, 34
Alberini & Santoni (film company), 168
Albertario, Davide, 104, 107, 108
Albertini, Luigi, 172, 183, 187, 196, 216, 225, 231
Albini, Umberto, 296
Aleramo, Sibilla, 164
Alessandria, 109

Alessio (coachwork firm), 125
Alexandria (Egypt), 286
Alfa Romeo (car firm), 288, 351, 358, 378, 380, 385, 397, 398
Alitalia (airline), 351, 397
Allende, Salvador, 388
Alliance of Labour, 220
Allies (against Italy in Second World War), 296, 297–8, 302–4, 305–7, 308, 310, 313, 314, 315, 316, 322, 323, 343
Allied Control Commission, 304, 307, 338
Allied Military Government (AMG), 304, 314, 318, 323, 338
Alpine Club, Italian, 167
Alpine regiments, 49, 167
Alpine zones, 13, 14, 86, 120, 185, 187, 244, 285, 304, 310, 312, 322, 350
Alvisi, Giacomo, 98
Amato, Giuliano, 397, 404, 419
Ambrosini, Gaspare, 321
Ambrosio, Vittorio, 296
Amendola, Giovanni, 175, 185, 212, 216, 223, 224, 225, 231, 294
America, continent of, 109
emigration to, 32–3, 122, 165–7, 169, 272–3, 360
grain from, 14, 19, 72, 94, 104
America, United States of (USA), see United States of America
AMG (Allied Military Government), see Allies
Amharic language, 100
anarchists, 73–5, 76, 77, 78, 79, 86, 87, 88, 100, 101, 103, 109–10, 180, 204, 206, 208, 220, 314
assassinations by, 75, 117, 231
insurrections of, 74–5, 77, 79, 103, 180
see also syndicalists, anarcho-
Ancona, 180
Andreotti, Giulio, 256, 333, 367, 388, 389, 409, 417, 419
Annales, 6
Ansaldo (steel firm), 191, 192, 206, 263, 265
anticlericalism, 4, 63, 81, 82, 87, 89, 102, 108, 140, 142, 146, 158, 214, 381–3, 389
anti-Communism, 220, 242, 283, 323, 325, 329, 345, 384–5, 389, 390, 409
anti-Fascism, 3, 246, 251–3, 259, 289, 299, 302, 307, 311, 315, 316, 317, 318, 320, 323, 325–6, 338, 340, 346, 347, 385–7, 388, 423, 425
anti-Fascists, 218, 220, 225–7, 230–2
during Fascist regime, 230–2, 240, 241, 246, 247, 251–3, 259, 293–5, 298, 299
in Resistance (1943–45), 302, 305, 306–7, 309, 310, 311–17

after Second World War, 317–19, 320, 324–5, 329, 385–7
Bari Congress of (1944), 305, 311
Pan-American Congress of (1942), 293
see also partisans; Resistance
anti-nuclear protest, 405
anti-Semitism, 246, 257–8, 261, 295, 309, 310
Antonelli, Pietro, 99
Antonioni, Michelangelo, 244, 274, 368
Aosta, Duke of,
Emanuele Filiberto di Savoia, 221
Amedeo di Savoia, 286
Aimone di Savoia, formerly Duke of Spoleto, 292, 298
Aosta, Valle d', 34, 322, 390
Appelius, Mario, 291
Apulia, 9, 37, 110, 132, 157, 161, 273
agriculture in, 17, 19, 74, 96, 130, 166, 193
industry in, 272, 358, 359, 400
Archives, Central State, 7
Arditi, 190, 214, 215, 218
Arditi del Popolo, 220
Arezzo, 396
Argentina, 32, 122, 166, 360
aristocrats, 29–30, 85, 87, 125, 235–6, 257, 344
armistice (1943), 302–3, 304, 305, 306, 307
arms, 60, 70, 75, 79, 99, 169, 208, 220, 226, 253, 310–11, 315, 317, 369, 384, 385, 386, 394, 416
arms industry, 26–7, 51, 122, 123–4, 134, 152, 190–3, 198, 206, 264, 266, 267, 278, 287–9, 315
Arms and Munitions, Under-secretariat of, 191, 197
army, 44, 47, 48–51, 63, 78, 92, 113, 114, 152, 182, 184, 204, 205, 209, 215, 221, 227, 239, 304, 305, 337, 341, 343–4, 351, 372, 374, 385, 388, 409, 413, 426
colonial campaigns of, 49, 51, 99–100, 153–5, 181, 281–3, 286
in First World War, 185–90, 193, 197
in Fascist regime, 221, 227, 233–4, 238, 239, 257, 258, 261, 278, 343
in Second World War, 284, 285–8, 291, 303, 304, 305, 307
and fall of Fascism (1943), 295, 296, 298–9
of Salò Republic (1943–45), 309, 311
Chief of Staff (army), 48, 186–90, 204; (joint), 233, 286, 296, 297, 344
officers, 50, 186, 200, 204, 214, 215–16, 218, 221, 226, 233–4, 235, 238, 261, 287, 291, 343–4
and public order, 49–50, 51, 69, 71, 74, 75, 88, 103–4, 180, 207, 208, 219, 221, 227, 234, 341, 343

as school of nation, 36, 49, 51, 177, 200
structure of, 49–50, 69, 233
see also carabinieri; conscripts; martial law; nation in arms
Arpinati, Leandro, 216, 240, 244, 250, 310
Arrivabene, Silvio, 151
artisans, 21–3, 24, 29, 88, 126, 133, 166, 170, 272, 273, 278, 336, 353, 357, 366, 391, 395, 396, 412
political activities of, 73, 77, 79, 81, 101, 114, 142, 145, 216, 422
Artom, Isacco, 46
Artusi, Pellegrino, 163
Ascension day, Mussolini's speech on (1927), 275
Asia, 19, 94, 199
Asor Rosa, Alberto, 42
Assab, 47, 100
assassinations, 75, 117, 136, 146, 156, 181, 224, 231, 253, 280, 311, 316, 317, 374, 385–7, 413, 416, 417
Assumption, dogma of, 370
Asti, 235
Atlantic, 33, 165, 166, 244, 303, 372
Austria (after 1919), 281, 283, 285, 322
Austria–Hungary, 32, 75, 79, 95, 120, 174, 183, 186, 198, 203
and irredentism, 79, 153, 174, 181–2, 183, 184–5
and Triple Alliance, 46, 79, 150, 153, 181–2, 184–5
war against, 185–6, 188–90, 195, 196, 209, 261
autarchy, 266, 267, 268, 275, 318
'autonomous' movement, see trade unions
Avanti!, 111, 117, 144, 156, 183, 199, 211, 212, 214, 231
Avellino, 131, 353
Aventine hill (Rome), opposition parties 1924–26, 225, 226–7, 230, 231–2, 240
Average Man, Party of (Uomo Qualunque), 319–20, 324, 325
Axis, Rome–Berlin (Italo-German alliance), 282, 284, 426

Badoglio, Pietro, 233, 282, 286, 299, 302, 306
governments of, 299, 302–6, 307, 312, 341
Bagnoli, 124, 132
Bainsizza, 187
Bakunin, Mikhail, 73, 74, 75, 85, 86
Balbo, Italo, 216, 217, 226, 227, 233, 240, 244
Baldesi, Gino, 222
Balearic islands, 282
Balilla, Fascist youth organisation, 245, 246, 255, 261

Balkans, 153, 154, 181, 281, 282, 285, 292, 304, 343
Banca Cattolica Vicentina, 147
Banca Commerciale Italiana (Comit), 120, 121–2, 123, 124, 129, 172, 192, 206, 265, 397, 398
Banca Generale, 97
Banca Romana, 97–9, 102
Banco di Roma, 120–1, 153, 172, 254, 263, 265
Banca di Sconto, 120, 192, 206
Banco Ambrosiano, 414
Bank of Italy, 122, 124, 265, 366, 397, 419, 424
banks, 76, 97, 132, 133, 158, 165, 172, 191, 192, 242, 264, 266, 295, 324, 336, 348, 349, 351, 363, 389, 397, 399, 408, 416, 420, 424, 425
crises of, (1893), 97, 120; (1920) 206; (1929–33) 264–5
'German', 97, 120, 121–2
'mixed', 120–1, 265
rural, 76, 87, 107, 128, 131, 146, 147, 148, 198, 271
savings, 97, 121, 165, 194, 265, 335
scandal (1890s), 97–9, 101, 102, 114
Baratieri, Oreste, 45, 100
Barbagli, Marzio, 39, 171
Barbapedanna, 41
Barbato, Nicola, 102, 103
Barcelona, 259
Bari, 33, 337
anti-Fascist Congress at (1944), 305
Barletta, 16
Barsanti, Pietro, 78
Bartolomasi, Angelo, 187
Barzilai, Salvatore, 194
Basati, 149
Basilicata, 20, 37, 126, 132, 170, 359, 408
agriculture in, 15, 132, 133
emigration from, 32, 130, 166
population in, 161, 162, 275
Bassano, 139
Basso, Lelio, 294
Bastogi (finance house), 192
Bava Beccaris, Fiorenzo, 51
BBC (British Broadcasting Corporation), 291
Beckx, Pietro, 82
Bedaux system, 249
Belgium, 123, 284
Benedict XV, Pope (1914–22), 149, 183, 188, 197, 295
Benedictines (religious order), 82
Beneduce, Alberto, 266
Benetton, Luciano, 396
Benevento, 74
Benghazi, 286

Bergamini, Alberto, 172
Bergamo, 146, 148
Berlin, Congress of (1878), 47
Berlinguer, Enrico, 367, 388–90
Berlusconi, Paolo, 424
Berlusconi, Silvio, 396, 406, 410, 421, 422, 423, 424, 425, 426
  government of, 397, 398, 423–4, 426
Bertozzi, G. C., 17
Bessemer converter, 23
Best, Geoffrey, 41
Beveridge, William, 318
Biagini, Gustavo, 98
Bianco, Enzo, 417
Bible, the, 149, 256
Bignami, Enrico, 76
Binchy, Daniel, 84
birth-rate, (1871, 1881) 31; (1900–1) 161; (1911) 161, 164; (1930s) 275, 362; (1970s) 382, 383; (1980s) 401
births, battle for, 240, 274–6, 278, 299
Biscaretti di Ruffia, Roberto, 125
bishops, 3, 83–4, 85, 86, 87, 105, 117, 147–8, 149, 197, 255, 313, 324, 338
  Conference of Italian, 371, 383
Bismarck, Otto von, 92, 95, 97, 145
Bissolati, Leonida, 81, 145, 154, 155, 156, 183, 194, 195, 196, 199, 204
Bizerta, 46
Black Brigades, 309
'black economy', 268, 290, 311, 353, 378–9, 394, 396, 401
Blackpool, 41
Blasetti, Alessandro, 244
Blum, Léon, 282
Bocchini, Arturo, 232, 233, 253
Boccioni, Umberto, 174
Bologna, 89, 130, 131, 151, 161, 180, 210, 219, 244, 371, 385, 386
  political activities in, 89, 143, 147, 151, 180, 183, 210, 215, 216, 217, 219, 231, 385, 386
  rising (1874), 74, 79
  University of, 39, 80, 216
Bolsheviks, 196, 199, 242
Bolzano (Bozen), 253
Bombacci, Nicola, 213
Boncompagni Ludovisi family, 30, 236
Bondi, Max, 192, 206
Bonghi, Ruggiero, 65, 114
bonifica, see land reclamation
Bonnefon Craponne, Luigi, 158
Bonomelli, Geremia, 167
Bonomi, Ivanoe, 145, 154, 156, 219, 224, 319
  as anti-Fascist organiser, 294, 295, 296, 297, 305, 306, 314

government of (1921–22), 219, 266
governments of (1944–45), 306–7, 317
Borghese family, 236
Borghese, Valerio, 309, 385
Borgo (Rome), 274
Borsellino, Paolo, 417
Bosco, Rosario Garibaldi, 102
Boselli, Paolo, 195, 197
Bosnian crisis (1908), 152
Bossi, Umberto, 413, 414, 422, 423, 424, 425
Bottai, Giuseppe, 223, 240, 249, 278, 297
Bourbons, 85, 103
Bovio, Giovanni, 81
Boy Scouts, 245, 255
Bozzi, Aldo, 411
braccianti, see labourers, agricultural
Brazil, 32
Breda, Vincenzo, 24
Breda (engineering firm), 28, 191
Brenner Pass, 203, 283, 303
Bresci, Gaetano, 117
Brescia, 308, 385
brigandage, 49, 53, 69–70, 73, 74, 88, 311
Brig valley, 322
Brin, Benedetto, 26, 62
Brindisi, 304, 337, 358
Britain, 18, 29, 39, 41, 124, 125, 127, 128, 190, 267, 269, 278, 288, 298, 320, 322, 323, 333, 345, 375, 377, 378, 394, 395, 398, 403
  and First World War, 181, 182, 183, 191
  and Second World War (1940–43), 285–8, 291, 297, 303, 306, 310
  and Resistance period (1943–45), 306–7, 313
  colonial rivalry with, 204, 281, 282, 283, 285, 345
  navy of, 181, 281, 282, 284
British Commonwealth, 297
brothels, 34, 41, 53, 164, 187, 254, 342
Bruno, Giordano, 105
Brussels, 345
budget, State, 25–8, 40, 48–9, 59–60, 63, 122, 134, 191, 266, 343, 351, 352, 379, 392, 396–7, 408, 409, 416, 419
  Minister of, 349, 400
Buffarini Guidi, Guido, 240, 308, 310
Buggerú, 144
building boom (1880s), 21, 30, 89, 97
building trades, 21, 22, 72, 88, 126, 127, 138, 165, 193, 214, 272, 274, 359, 406, 416, 419
Buitoni, Giovanni, 126
Bulgaria, 154
Burgalassi, Silvano, 149, 370
Buscetta, Tommaso, 417

Cabrini, Angelo, 156
Cacherano di Bricherasio, Emanuele, 125
Cadorna, Luigi, 186, 188, 189, 190, 195, 197
Cadorna, Raffaele, 314
Caesar, Julius, 274, 287, 296
Cafagna, Luciano, 27
cafés, 40, 42, 52, 168, 243
Cafiero, Carlo, 74
Cagliari, 359
Cagol, Margherita, 385, 387
Cairo, 42
Cairoli, Benedetto, 75, 80, 89
Calabria, 9, 31, 37, 38, 52, 69, 132, 170, 362, 392, 416, 420
  agriculture in, 31, 52, 128, 132, 133, 357, 360
  emigration from, 32, 130, 166
  industry in, 24, 359
Calamandrei, Piero, 294
Calatabiano, 71
Calderone, Antonino, 417
California, 128
Caltagirone, 148
Caltanissetta, 60
camorra, 392
Campagna Romana, 14, 33, 270, 272
Campanella, Federigo, 80
Campania, 15, 31, 272, 408, 416
Campo de'Fiori (Rome), 105
Canevari, Emilio, 258
Cannistraro, Philip, 244
Cantieri Riuniti (shipbuilders), 265
Cao-Pinna, Vera, 359
Capitol (Rome), 273, 296
Capodistria, 323
Caporetto, 323
  battle of (1917), 185, 186, 188–9, 190, 195, 197, 198, 199
carabinieri, 51, 52, 177, 296, 298, 299, 309, 341–3, 344, 370
  and public order, 51, 53, 60, 70, 71, 219, 299, 342
Caracciolo, Alberto, 6
Carducci, Giosuè, 80, 89
car industry, 120, 125–6, 190, 191–2, 206, 264, 267, 268, 273, 349, 350, 351, 358, 376, 380, 396, 397, 399
  labour disputes in, 158, 193, 207–9, 212, 220, 289, 308, 312, 350, 376–8, 385, 394
cars, 125, 126, 264, 268, 349, 350, 351, 368, 369, 370, 400
Carnera, Primo, 244
Carocci, Giampiero, 72
Caroncini, Alberto, 153
Carpi, Leone, 30, 33, 34, 37
Carrà, Carlo, 174

Carso, 187
Casalini, Armando, 226
Casati, Alessandro, 227, 228, 230, 294
Casati Law (on education, 1859), 37
Caserta, 369, 400
Cassa Integrazione Guadagni, workers' insurance fund, 378
Cassa per il Mezzogiorno, see Fund for the South
Cassibile, 303
Castelgandolfo, 84
Castellano, Giuseppe, 303
Castellini, Gualtiero, 155
Castelluccio Inferiore, 354
Castel San Pietro, 74
Castel Sant' Angelo (Rome), 163–4
Castiadas, 355
castor-oil, 205, 216
Castro, Fidel, 75, 386
Catania, 31, 102, 103, 165, 337, 360, 417
Catholic Action (1905–), 147, 183, 198, 252, 253, 255–6, 260, 294, 313, 324–5, 329, 331, 335, 371, 372
  for detailed activities, *see* Catholic movement; for period before 1905, *see also Opera dei Congressi e dei Comitati Cattolici*
Catholic movement,
  co-operatives, 76, 87, 106, 107, 146, 147, 148, 198, 209, 210, 254, 329, 331, 371, 380
  economic and social, 76, 86–7, 89, 104, 105–8, 138, 141, 142, 146–50, 167, 198, 331, 335–6, 370–1, 380, 402, 403, 404–5
  Electoral Union, 147, 157
  mutual-aid societies, 76, 106, 107
  pious, 86, 147, 148
  political, 2, 3, 37, 57, 65, 85, 87, 93, 94, 104, 105–8, 115, 136, 142, 146–7, 148–9, 150, 155, 157, 158, 159, 169–70, 177, 195, 197, 200, 211, 213, 214, 224, 236, 239, 294, 295, 302, 313, 319, 320, 324–5, 330, 331, 335–6, 346, 351, 370–1, 385, 409
  reorganisation of (1892–94), 107; (1905) 147; (1915) 198
  student (FUCI), 255–6
  sub-culture, 147, 149–50, 331, 335, 382–3
  trade unions, 106, 107, 138, 141, 147, 148, 150, 158, 198, 207, 209, 210, 213, 218, 247–8, 250, 254, 255, 331, 351, 371, 377, 380, 395
  women, 86, 147, 150, 163, 164, 198
  youth, 107, 108, 147, 150, 168, 245, 255–6, 313, 331
  see also Christian Democrat Party; 'clerico-moderates'; Popular Party

Cavallero, Ugo, 286, 287, 296

Cavallotti, Felice, 51, 81, 112, 113, 114

Cavour, Camillo di, 255, 413

cemeteries, 20, 138, 361

Censuses, 9
 census: (1871) 9, 22, 31, 32, 35, 36, 132; (1881) 9, 14, 24, 34, 36; (1901) 9, 24, 36, 149, 163, 169; (1911) 9, 36, 126, 127, 132, 149, 192; (1921) 9, 192; (1936) 9; (1961) 369

Central Italy, 87, 107, 111, 149, 180, 207, 256, 308, 310, 311, 316, 342, 395–6, 399
 agriculture in, 14, 17, 19, 25, 127, 128, 137, 162, 193, 209, 210, 215–16, 269, 354, 356, 364
 emigration from, 32, 361
 politics in, 64, 74, 75, 87, 107, 109, 111, 138, 139, 144, 180, 207, 210, 212, 215–16, 217, 224, 304, 308, 310, 316, 319, 321, 325, 330, 334, 390, 391, 392, 410, 413, 420, 422
 population in, 161, 275, 382

CGIL (*Confederazione Generale Italiana del Lavoro*), Communist–Socialist trade union confederation, 352, 375–8

CGL (*Confederazione Generale del Lavoro*), Socialist trade union confederation, 141, 143, 145, 180, 198, 207, 220, 222, 224

Chabod, Federico, 5

Chamber of Deputies, 48, 60, 61–6, 98, 139–40, 148, 157, 194–5, 212–13, 219, 222, 227, 231–2, 254
 activities of, 45, 61–2, 115–16, 184–5, 225–7, 232, 239
 in Fascist regime, 224–8, 231–2, 234, 236, 239, 248, 299
 President of, 98, 140, 238
 since 1948, 325, 327, 328, 332–4, 367, 389, 418, 419, 420, 422
 see also Aventine; deputies

Chambers of Commerce, 391

Chambers of Labour, 111–12, 141–2, 144, 145, 170, 207, 210

charities, 69, 82–3, 86, 167, 198, 254, 335, 336, 389, 391–2, 403–5
 Crispi's law on (1890), 65, 105, 137, 335
 see also local government; mutual-aid societies; welfare

Charles Albert, King (1831–49), 44

Charter of Labour (1927), 249

'Cheka', 224, 225

chemical industry, 23, 25, 119, 121, 126, 128, 133–4, 191, 264, 266, 272, 349, 358, 359, 380, 400

Chernobyl, 410

Chessa, Francesco, 165

Chiesa, Mario, 414

children, 81, 142, 245–6, 252, 258, 275, 276, 277, 278, 361, 362, 380, 381, 401
 in industry, 22, 71, 94, 113, 137

Chile, 388

China, 22, 45, 49, 401

cholera, 20, 162

Christian Democracy, movement for, 106, 148, 150; *see also* Catholic movement, political

Christian Democrat Centre (1994–), 418, 421, 422, 423

Christian Democrat Party (DC), 256, 294, 307, 412, 418, 423, 424
 activities since Second World War, 5, 318, 319, 320, 321, 323–4, 325, 327, 329, 330, 332, 333, 335–6, 337, 338, 339, 346, 347, 351, 356, 358, 367, 371, 372, 376, 381–4, 385, 386, 387–90, 391, 392, 404, 405, 408, 409, 410, 415, 419, 421, 423, 426
 and 'family' issues, 382, 383, 404–5
 founding of, 294, 329
 membership of, 329, 331
 in Resistance (1943–45), 312, 313–14, 315
 and '*sottogoverno*', 334–7, 339, 341, 347, 352, 353, 358, 372, 399, 409–10, 415, 419, 423
 votes for, 319, 325, 327, 328, 329, 332, 336, 356, 370, 383, 409, 416, 418, 421
 see also Popular Party

Christie, Agatha, 342

Church, Catholic, 3, 30, 46, 72, 81–8, 146–50, 155, 213, 239, 242, 254–6, 258, 261, 293, 294, 295, 313, 321, 324, 325, 329, 330, 370–2, 374, 388, 402, 404–5, 409
 Law of Guarantees (1871), 46, 80, 83–4
 relations with State, 80, 81–5, 87–8, 89, 105, 140, 146, 150, 159, 164, 177, 197–8, 208, 211, 239, 253, 254–6, 258, 293, 295, 298, 313–14, 321, 323–4, 331, 346, 370, 381, 389, 405
 religious observance, 85–6, 149, 167, 197, 256, 275, 329, 370, 371, 380, 404, 405
 religious orders, 82–3, 85, 86, 105, 163, 256, 380, 383, 405
 role in society, 46, 81–3, 85–7, 105–6, 142, 146–50, 197, 198, 254–6, 274, 294, 295, 321, 323–5, 335, 336, 346, 370–2, 381–3, 385, 389, 404–5
 see also anticlericalism; bishops; Catholic movement; clergy; Lateran Pacts; Papacy; religious beliefs; Roman question; Vatican

Church estates, 14, 215, 254
 sale of, 16–17, 18, 25, 29, 30, 69, 82, 85, 86, 101

Churchill, Winston, 280, 291, 298, 303, 304, 305, 306–7

Ciampi, Carlo, 397, 419, 423

Cianca, Alberto, 306

Ciano, Edda, 308, 310

Ciano, Galeazzo, 8, 240, 244, 257, 283, 284, 285, 290, 297, 298, 299, 308

Cincinnatus, 72

Cinecittà, 244

cinemas, 168, 187, 244, 247, 331, 369, 384, 406; *see also* films

circus, 41, 168

citrus fruit, 128, 269, 357

civil service, 55–7, 92–3, 97, 137, 171, 199, 206, 214, 218, 222, 223, 256, 277, 294, 299, 341, 348, 359, 360, 365, 379, 401, 412, 421

   decentralisation of, 57, 65, 80, 113, 317, 320, 321–2, 339, 390–3

   in Fascist period, 222, 234–5, 240, 248, 257, 258, 271, 275, 290, 309, 338

   Northern dominance of, 55, 171, 338

   political interference in, 57, 65, 66, 115, 327, 335, 339

   purge of (1943–47), 307, 313, 314, 315, 317–18, 319, 320, 321, 338, 339

   since Second World War, 325, 330, 334–5, 336, 337, 338–9, 358, 372, 388, 390–3, 415

   Southern dominance of, 338, 339, 344, 346, 412

   see also '*sottogoverno*'; regional autonomy

Clemenceau, Georges, 186

clergy, 37, 41, 75, 81–4, 85, 86, 87, 107, 146, 147, 149–50, 162, 164, 187–8, 197, 209, 253–6, 269, 275, 312, 313, 354, 370–1, 380, 382, 405

   political influence of, 30, 39, 83–4, 86, 107, 147, 148–50, 155, 164, 197, 209, 253, 255–6, 269, 291, 306, 312, 313, 324, 370–1

clerical workers, 29, 97, 165, 218, 237, 273, 320, 366

Clerici, Ambrogio, 225

'clerico-moderates', 37, 106, 108, 146–7, 148, 149, 150, 154, 155, 156

clientele, see patronage

CLN, *see* Committee of National Liberation

CLNAI, *see* Committee of National Liberation for Upper Italy

coal, 23, 26, 120, 123, 181, 190–1, 204, 264, 284, 288, 350, 379

Cogne (mines), 192

Cogni, Giulio, 258

Colajanni, Napoleone, 98, 102

Coldiretti (Confederation of Direct Cultivators), peasant farmers' association, 356

'Cold War', 327, 330, 334, 343, 390, 408, 409, 419, 425

Coletti, Francesco, 32

Colombo, Emilio, 256

Colonial Ministry, 171

colonial wars, 49, 51, 63, 81, 261, 264, 266, 267, 345

   in Ethiopia, (1890s) 99–101; (1935–36) 266, 281–2

   in Libya (1911–12), 153–4

colonies, 46, 47–8, 100, 104, 112, 114, 134, 150, 153–5, 167, 175, 199, 204, 243, 258, 266, 267, 268, 275, 276, 282, 285, 286, 299, 305, 309, 338, 343

   loss of, 286, 309, 322, 343, 345, 351

Colonna family, 236

Colosseum (Rome), 80, 254, 273, 364

Columbus, Christopher, 32, 109

Comintern, *see* International, Communist

Committee of Action for the Union of the Italian People, 293

Committee of National Liberation (CLN), 305, 306–7, 319, 320

   in factories, 314, 316

   local and regional, 306, 307, 314–17, 318, 320, 325

   for Upper Italy (CLNAI), 314–17

Commonwealth, British, 297

Communism, 246, 250, 256, 261, 283, 323, 325, 345, 372, 389, 413, 422, 423

Communist Manifesto, 78

Communist Party (PCI), 3, 8, 171, 220, 226, 231, 233, 251–2, 253, 259, 293, 297, 306, 307, 311

   deputies of, 213, 231, 319, 328, 332, 333–4, 388, 389

   founding of, 220, 251

   in Resistance (1943–45), 4, 289, 293, 294, 295, 306, 307, 308, 310, 312–13, 314, 315, 317

   membership of, 252, 253, 313, 317, 324, 331, 346, 389, 410

   organisation of, 312, 317, 330, 332, 333–4

   since Second World War, 317, 321, 323–4, 326, 329, 330, 336, 342, 343, 345, 346, 348–9, 356, 367, 376, 384, 385, 386, 387–90, 391, 392, 395, 406, 408, 409, 410, 416, 418, 419

   strategy of, 226, 302, 306, 318, 321, 330, 385, 387–90

   trade unions, 330, 333–4, 346, 354, 376, 377, 378, 389, 395, 410

   votes for, 224, 319, 325, 327, 328, 330, 362, 388, 389, 410, 418, 419

   see also Democratic Party of the Left

Communist Refoundation Party, 410, 418

Como, 22, 88

Como, Lake, 310

comuni, see local government

'Comunione e Liberazione', 405

Concordat (1929), *see* Lateran Pacts; (1984),
    405; *see also* Church, relations with State

Confindustria (employers' confederation),
    248, 334, 351, 395; *see also* industrialists

'confino', 232, 233, 253; *see also* enforced
    domicile

conscripts, 9, 49, 50, 69, 70, 156, 186–7, 193,
    197, 209, 287, 290, 307, 309, 310–11, 322,
    343, 344, 379, 383
  clergy as, 82, 86, 187, 197, 255
  height of, 20, 51, 268, 363, 402–3
  literacy of, 35, 36, 49, 156, 187, 344

Constituent Assembly (1946–47), 319, 322,
    323, 325, 388
  agitation for (1870s), 78; (1918–19) 211, 212,
    215; (1942–46) 293, 294, 305, 308

Constitution of Italian Republic (1948–), 302,
    305, 320–2, 325, 327, 340, 381, 390, 391, 424
  drafting of, 315, 320–2, 324

Constitution of Kingdom of Italy (1861–1946),
    see Statuto

Constitutional Court, 320, 321, 340, 383, 384,
    391, 392, 405, 412, 420, 423

Contarini, Salvatore, 280

Conti, Ettore, 263

contraception, 164, 275, 362, 382, 394, 401

co-operatives, 76, 79, 87, 106, 107, 109, 111,
    121, 142, 144, 145, 146, 147, 198, 210, 212,
    247, 254, 329, 371, 380, 391
  agricultural, 76, 111, 129, 131, 132, 143, 148,
    194, 209, 331, 355, 356
  building, 138, 142, 210, 363
  National League of, 138
  retail, 76, 79, 142, 198, 272
  see also Catholic movement; Socialist Party

Coppino, Michele, 37

Corfu, 168, 281

Corleone, 102

corporations, 234, 240, 248, 249–50, 265, 267,
    268, 298, 318
  Ministry of, 234, 249, 264
  National Council of, 249–50, 268
  see also syndicates, Fascist

corporatism, 3, 106, 124, 140, 152, 159, 177,
    205, 242, 248, 249, 250, 260, 308, 341

Corradini, Camillo, 169, 195

Corradini, Enrico, 151, 155, 173, 175

Corridoni, Filippo, 183

Corriere della Sera, Il, 151, 172, 183, 196, 225,
    231, 243

Corriere d'Italia, Il, 153, 172

corruption, 16, 17–18, 53, 54, 56–7, 59–61,
    65–6, 85, 92, 93, 98–9, 101, 112–14, 115,

129, 133, 139, 151, 172, 223, 237–8, 268,
    327, 331–2, 333–7, 339, 356, 380, 384,
    392–3, 408, 409–11, 413–16, 417, 419, 420,
    422, 423
  judicial investigations 1992– , 403, 413–16,
    419, 422, 424
  see also parties, financing of; 'partyocracy';
    patronage; *'sottogoverno'*

Corsica, 79, 284, 291

Cosa Nostra, see Mafia

Cosenza province, 170

Cossiga, Francesco, 256, 411

Costa, Andrea, 74, 75, 77–8, 88, 110

cotton, 22, 23, 96, 119, 122, 124, 126, 173,
    266, 287

Council of State, 57, 84, 93

coup (d'état), 50, 51, 204, 221, 296–7, 298,
    299, 306, 342, 385, 387, 414

Court of Accounts, 55, 136

courts, 54–5, 56, 66, 75, 93, 113, 164, 233, 239,
    318, 340–1, 378, 404, 413, 414, 417
  of Appeal, 54, 55, 59, 340, 341
  of Cassation, 54, 72, 116, 164, 340, 341, 417
  martial, 49, 103, 104, 188, 384
  Tribunals, 54
  see also Constitutional Court; Council of
    State; judges; labour tribunals; Special
    Tribunal for the Defence of the State

Craxi, Bettino, 403, 406, 409, 412, 413, 414,
    421, 422
  governments of, 395, 411

Credaro, Luigi, 140

Credito Fondiario, 336

Credito Italiano, 120, 124, 192, 265

Credito Mobiliare, 97, 121

cremation, 89

Cremona, 167, 216, 217, 236, 237

Crespi, 165

cricket, 168

criminology, 53

Crispi, Francesco, 40, 89, 92, 94, 98, 109, 112
  ecclesiastical policy of, 65, 87–8, 102, 105,
    137, 255, 335
  foreign policy of, 47, 92, 95, 97, 99–100, 102
  governments of, 57, 92–3, 98, 100, 102–3,
    110, 112, 113

Crispo Moncada, Francesco, 225

Critica, La, 173, 246

Critica Sociale, La, 109, 176

Croatia, 203, 204, 252, 292–3

Croce, Benedetto, 4–5, 136, 172, 173, 231,
    246, 252, 253, 299, 305, 306

Cronaca Bizantina, 40

Cuba, 75, 386

Culture, National Fascist Institute of, 243

Cuneo, 18, 62
Cuore e Critica, 109
Curcio, Renato, 385, 387
Curiel, Eugenio, 251
cycling, 167–8, 244, 289, 369
Cyrenaica, 154
  see also Libya
Czechoslovakia, 196, 283, 325, 345, 386

Dachau, 292
dairy produce, 18, 94, 96, 127, 128, 269, 356
Dalla Chiesa, Carlo Alberto, 414, 416
Dalla Torre, Giuseppe, 198
Dallolio, Alfredo, 191, 197
Dalmatia, 182, 196, 199, 203, 204, 205, 293, 309, 323
Dalmine (steel firm), 265
Daneo-Credaro law (on primary education, 1911), 169
D'Annunzio, Gabriele, 150, 175–6, 183, 184, 185, 187, 225
  and Fascist movement, 214, 215, 217, 218, 220, 225
  and Fiume, 204–5, 248
Dante Alighieri Society, 243
d'Azeglio, Massimo, 2, 30, 31, 34, 401, 426
DC (*Democrazia Cristiana*), see Christian Democrat Party
De Ambris, Alceste, 183, 205, 248
Dè Amicis, Edmondo, 38, 49, 150, 167
death-rate (1871, 1891–1900), 31; (1900), 161; (1909–13), 161; (1950–51), 362
De Benedetti, Carlo, 406
Dè Bono, Emilio, 226, 308
De Felice, Renzo, 218, 232, 257, 260
De Felice Giuffrida, Giuseppe, 102, 103
Defence,
  Minister of, 259, 309
  Ministry of, 338
  parliamentary Commission on, 333
deflation, 251, 264, 270–1, 324, 349
deforestation, 15, 16, 21, 28, 30
De Gasperi, Alcide, 294, 295, 306, 307, 321, 322, 324, 326, 329, 334, 348
  governments of, 318–19, 320, 324, 325–6
De Gaulle, Charles, 374
Delegation for Repatriation (in South Tyrol), 292
De Lorenzo, Giovanni, 342–3
De Mauro, Tullio, 35
demesne land, sale of, 15–18, 25, 29, 69, 101
De Michelis, Gianni, 414, 419
De Mita, Ciriaco, 409
Democratic Alliance, 418
Democratic Party of Labour, 294, 314, 319

Democratic Party of the Left (PDS), 410, 412, 418, 419, 420, 421, 423; see also Communist Party
Democratic Proletarians (DP, later PDUP), 328, 418
De Nicola, Enrico, 224
Denmark, 284
Depression (of 1930s), 249, 250, 251, 257, 264–5, 266, 268, 270, 271, 273
Depretis, Agostino, 45, 60, 61, 67, 72, 92
  governments of, 62, 99
deputies, 54, 60, 61, 62–3, 65, 66, 98, 113, 139–40, 146, 157, 182, 184, 213, 231–2, 236, 307, 328, 331, 332, 333–4, 356, 415, 418, 419, 420, 422, 423
  and civil service, 57, 65, 66, 67, 333, 339
  and local elites, 58–9, 60, 61, 62–3, 65–6, 67, 236, 333, 337, 356
  see also Chamber of Deputies; parliament
De Rosa, Gabriele, 4
De Ruggiero, Guido, 294
De Sica, Vittorio, 367
De' Stefani, Alberto, 234, 263, 264
De Vecchi, Cesare, 223, 257
De Viti De Marco, Antonio, 140
dialects, 34–5, 74, 369
Diaz, Armando, 189, 190, 204, 221, 222
Dieppe, 125
Difesa della Razza, La, 258
Di Giorgio, Antonino, 230
Dini, Lamberto, 424, 425
Di Pietro, Antonio, 414, 424
diplomats, 30, 45, 46, 50, 280, 281, 344; see also foreign policy; Foreign Affairs, Ministry of
di Robilant, Carlo, 45, 48
di Rudiní, Antonio, 100, 103, 108, 114, 116
  governments of, 104, 107–8, 112, 115
divorce, 82, 146, 164, 334, 381, 401–2
  agitation against, 87, 157, 164, 211, 334, 381–2, 383
  agitation for, 81–2, 334, 381–2, 383
  law on (1970), 341, 381–2, 383, 405
  National Committee for Referendum on, 381–2
  referendum on (1974), 319, 382, 383
Djibouti, 100, 281, 284
DN (*Destra Nazionale*), see National Right
dockworkers' union, 141, 220
doctors, 21, 39–40, 79, 144, 164, 171, 240, 277, 306, 337, 362, 366, 374–5, 383, 403
Dodecanese (islands), 154
Dogali, 87, 99
Domenica del Corriere, 172
'Don Camillo', 331, 368

Dongo, 310
Dopolavoro, 240, 245, 251, 335, 369, 391
Doria, Francesco, 16
Dozier, James, 414
Dresdner Bank, 378
Dronero, 62
drugs, 393, 394, 403, 404, 416, 417, 420
  enforcement agency, 417
Duce, see Mussolini, Benito
Duino, River, 323
Dumini, Amerigo, 225

Eastern Europe, 304, 388, 398, 402, 410, 419
Eboli, 16
Eckaus, Richard, 18
Ecole Nationale d' Administration, 339
'economic miracle' (after 1945), 348–52, 353
Eden, Anthony, 298, 306
Edinburgh, University of, 80
Edison (electricity company), 120, 206, 267, 352
education, *see* schools
  Minister of, 277, 278, 297
  Ministry of, 37, 39, 222, 364
EEC (European Economic Community), *see* European Community
Egypt, 284, 288
Einaudi, Giulio, 6, 246
Einaudi, Luigi, 349, 351
Eisenhower, Dwight, 303
Elba, 23, 123, 124, 132, 133
elections, municipal, *see* local government
elections, parliamentary, 62, 64–5, 67, 74, 87, 99, 230, 324, 328, 331, 333, 411; (1874) 62, 64, 85; (1876) 62; (1882) 77; (1886) 81; (1900) 111, 113, 114, 116, 136, 146; (1904) 139, 140, 143, 146, 149; (1909) 143, 146; (1913) 140, 155, 157; (1919) 212, 215; (1921) 213; (1924) 224, 226; (1946) 319–20; (1948) 324–5, 327, 328, 330, 370; (1953), 327, 328; (1958) 328; (1963) 328; (1968) 328; (1972) 328; (1976) 328, 388; (1979) 328, 389, 408; (1983) 409, 413, 418; (1987) 413, 418; (1992) 412, 418, 419; (1994) 418, 420–3, 424
  abstention at, 64, 74, 85, 107, 108, 146, 408, 411
  fixing of, 60–1, 62–3, 99, 139, 157, 213, 235
elections, regional, *see* regional autonomy
electoral reforms, proposed (1923–5), 223–4, 226, 227; (1983–93), 411, 412, 420, 423, 425, 426 n5; *see also* proportional representation
electorate, parliamentary, 64, 156, 212; *see also* suffrage

local, *see* local government
electricity, 120, 266, 272, 354, 358, 370, 372
electricity industry, 120, 121, 206, 265, 267, 272, 351, 398
  nationalisation of (1962), 352
Elena, Queen (1900–46), 282
Ellena, Vittorio, 22, 23, 24, 34
emigration, 2, 16, 32–3, 35, 67, 96, 103, 106, 120, 122, 130–1, 150, 165–7, 169, 175, 272–3, 275, 336–7, 350–1, 360–1, 363, 367, 379, 381, 399
  agents, 33, 166
  anti-Fascist, 222, 252, 259, 293, 298
  General Commission for, 166
  remittances, 122, 193, 350–1, 360, 361
  as 'safety-valve', 70, 88–9, 166, 273, 361
  see also America; Europe; immigration; migration; urbanisation
Emilia,
  agriculture in, 127–8, 129, 130, 131, 137, 142–3, 166, 194, 210, 215–17
  industry in, 129, 289
  politics in, 74, 80, 111, 130, 137, 142–3, 166, 168, 210, 215–17, 218, 317, 330, 385, 392, 413
Emilia-Romagna, 80, 128, 143, 385, 392, 413; *see also* Central Italy
Empire, *see* colonial wars; colonies
Enciclopedia Italiana, 246
encyclicals, Papal, 84, 106, 107, 146, 147, 255
'enforced domicile', 53, 88; *see also* 'confino'
Engels, Friedrich, 74, 112, 343
engineering industry, 23, 25, 26, 27–8, 96, 119, 120, 123, 124–6, 127, 130, 134, 190–3, 264, 267, 272, 273, 288–9, 309, 348, 349–50, 358–9, 376–8, 380, 400
  labour disputes in, 71–2, 158, 192–3, 207–8, 212, 247, 264, 289, 308, 375–8, 385, 394
England, 35, 163; *see also* Britain
ENI (*Ente Nazionale Idrocarburi*), State oil and gas agency, 8, 335, 336, 350, 358–9, 367, 398, 415
Eritrea, 100, 281, 286, 322, 402
Espresso, L', 367, 406, 415
Ethiopia, 51, 99–101, 122, 151, 154, 257, 266, 267, 281–2, 286, 322, 358
EUR (*Esposizione Universale Romana*), 83, 274
Europe, emigration to, 32, 166, 273, 336–7, 351
European Community, 345, 349, 350, 352, 355, 357, 391, 399, 402, 409, 411, 412, 413, 416, 425, 426
  agricultural policy of, 2, 355, 356, 357, 400
European federalism, 293, 412–13, 425, 426
European Investment Bank, 359
European Monetary System, 397

Europeo, L', 367
ex-servicemen's associations, 190, 209, 210, 354
'extra-parliamentary' movements, 375, 385–7

Faccio, Rina, 164
Facta, Luigi, 219, 221
factions, 332–3, 334, 335, 336, 412, 423
factories, 22–3, 24, 34, 71, 125–7, 162, 164, 192–3, 206–9, 249, 257, 261, 288–9, 312, 317, 318, 348, 353, 372, 374, 375–7, 378–9, 380, 385, 386, 388, 394, 399
  councils (of workers), 207, 212, 376–7, 395
  occupation of the (1920), 207–9, 212, 215
  occupations of (1968–), 374, 375–7
  see also engineering; industrial workers; industry; strikes; trade unions
Faenza, Liliano, 370
Falck, Giorgio, 24
Falcone, Giovanni, 417
family, 33–4, 142, 162–4, 193, 243, 247, 274–6, 329, 353, 354, 355, 361, 362–4, 369, 372, 374, 379, 380–3, 393, 400–2
  agricultural, 33–4, 163, 193, 274–5, 354–5, 364
  allowances, 251, 275, 289
  National Agency for the Protection of Motherhood and Infancy, 275, 335
Fanfani, Amintore, 246, 329, 333
Farina (coachwork firm), 125
Farinacci, Roberto, 216, 217, 218, 232, 236–7, 239, 240, 250, 257, 260, 292, 297, 299, 310
Farini, Domenico, 8, 44, 50, 66, 100, 114, 115, 116
Fasci di Combattimento, see Fascist movement
Fascio of National Defence, 195–6, 199, 214
Fasci Siciliani, see Sicilian *Fasci*
Fascist movement, 203, 213, 214–21, 224–8, 236–8, 257–9, 260–1, 317–18, 325
  ideology of, 185, 200, 242–3, 244–7, 250, 254, 257–9, 260–1, 285, 295, 326, 409
  origins of, 185, 196, 215–16, 272
  taming of, 222–3, 236–8, 239
  women's associations, 237, 276
  youth organisations, 237, 240, 243, 245, 255, 335
  see also Dopolavoro; syndicates, Fascist
Fascist National Party (PNF), 217, 219, 223, 234, 235, 236–9, 240, 245, 257–9, 260, 290, 291–2, 297, 299, 311, 314, 317, 318, 340, 402
  deputies, 213, 219, 226, 232, 236
  membership, 217, 218–19, 223, 236–9, 258, 260, 291, 317, 318, 331, 334
  organisation of, 235, 236–9, 271, 291

votes for, 224
  see also neo-Fascists
Fascist regime, 5, 104, 205, 222, 230, 239–41, 242–61, 263–78, 280, 285, 289, 310, 338, 346, 347, 398, 409, 424
  collapse of (1943), 290–3, 295–9, 302, 314
  and existing institutions, 230, 232–6, 238–41, 254–6, 257–9, 259–61, 277–8, 280, 343
Fascist Republican Party (1943–45), 308
federalism, *see* regional autonomy
Federconsorzi (Federation of Agricultural Consortia), 356
Federterra (agricultural labourers' union), 142–3, 210
Federzoni, Luigi, 195, 199, 222, 225, 230, 232, 237, 240, 297
Fellini, Federico, 368
Feltre, 297
Feltrinelli, Giangiacomo, 386
Fenoaltea, Sergio, 294
Fenoaltea, Stefano, 26, 120, 123
Fermi, Enrico, 258
Fermo Proposito, Il, 146
Ferrara province, 129, 130, 210, 216, 217
Ferraris, Dante, 158
Ferrero di Ventimiglia, Alfonso, 125
Ferruzzano, 16
'feudal' rights, 15–16, 70
Fiat (car firm), 125–6, 133, 190, 191, 192, 193, 266, 294, 314, 352, 353, 359, 366, 369, 395, 396, 397, 398, 399
  labour disputes at, 158, 193, 207–9, 212, 220, 312, 350, 378, 394
  production at, 126, 133, 190, 206, 267, 268, 288, 349
Figaro, Le, 174
films, 168, 244, 342, 367–8, 405; *see also* cinemas
Finance,
  Minister of, 197, 208, 257
  Ministry of, 92, 308
Finance Guards, 341
Fini, Gianfranco, 421, 422, 423, 425
Fininvest, 421, 423
FIOM (*Federazione Italiana Operai Metallurgici*), Metal-workers' union, 141, 158
First World War, 95, 119, 133, 137, 162, 170, 256, 276, 287, 290, 291, 295, 314, 323, 354
  campaigns of, 185–6, 188–90
  economic change during, 190–4, 289
  Italian entry into, 181–5
  political developments during, 194–200, 239, 242, 257, 260, 261, 316

Fiume (Rijeka), 203, 204–5, 206, 214, 215, 248, 250, 260, 281, 303, 323
Fiume League, 205
Fiume Legionaries, National Federation of, 214
Florence, 59, 62, 75, 147, 161, 174, 175, 307
  Fascism in, 227, 237
Fogar, Luigi, 253
Foggia, 33
Fondo per il Culto, 197
food, 19–20, 163, 192–3, 268, 289–90, 324, 340, 356–7, 369, 402
  shortages of, 19–20, 71, 74, 103–4, 193, 289–90, 295, 317, 348, 357
  taxes on, 24, 59, 69, 71, 101, 104, 113
  see also riots; tariffs; wheat
food-processing industries, 23, 119, 126, 129, 130, 131, 165, 271, 272, 356
football, 168, 244, 369, 410, 422
Forche Caudine, Le, 41
Ford (car firm), 125
Foreign Affairs,
  Minister of, 8, 45, 46, 184, 195, 196, 197, 240, 280, 283, 293, 297, 307, 323, 333, 414, 419
  Ministry of, 46, 182, 226, 280, 344; *see also* diplomats
foreign policy, 45, 46–8, 65, 89, 92, 95–6, 99–101, 153–4, 159, 181–2, 184, 195, 196, 199, 203–5, 258, 280–5, 298, 302–4, 323, 343–6, 388, 409, 413, 425–6
  public debate about, 47, 79, 81, 89, 145, 150–1, 152–6, 173, 175, 182–5, 196, 199, 204, 258–9, 261, 305, 345, 388, 389–90, 409
  see also irredentism; London, Treaty of; Nato; Triple Alliance; Versailles, Treaty of
Forges Davanzati, Roberto, 244, 245
Forlì, 214
Formia, 139
Fortuna, Loris, 381
Fortunato, Giustino, 16, 66
Forum (Roman), 273
Forza Italia, 418, 421
France, 57, 81, 112, 125, 141, 168, 172, 181, 243, 269, 278, 290, 345–6, 363, 374, 376, 398, 411
  emigration to, 32, 75, 77, 293, 360, 399
  finance by, 97, 102, 120, 183
  rivalry with, 46–8, 95–6, 99, 100, 102, 153, 154, 204, 253, 281, 282, 283, 284–5, 322–3
  trade with, 14, 19, 22, 24, 94–6, 101, 122, 123, 350
Franceschini, Alberto, 385
Franchetti, Leopoldo, 59, 60
franchise, *see* suffrage

Franco, Francisco, 259, 261, 282–3, 385
Franco-Prussian War (1870–71), 27, 46
Francis Joseph, Emperor of Austria, (1848–1916), 79
Francis Ferdinand, Archduke of Austria, 181
Frassati, Alfredo, 231
Freemasons, 56, 80, 89, 140, 155, 157, 183, 196, 198, 223, 256, 408, 419, 422, 424
  and Fascist movement, 223, 231, 232, 233, 234, 236, 237, 238, 240, 242, 254, 256
free trade, 28, 63, 94, 107, 113, 172, 173; *see also* tariffs
French language, 34, 322
'French line', 323
French Revolution, principles of, 155
Freud, Sigmund, 246
Friuli, 34, 323
Friuli-Venezia Giulia, region of, 390
Fuà, Giorgio, 119
FUCI (*Federazione Universitaria Cattolica Italiana*), *see* Catholic movement, student
Fund for the South, 336, 357–9, 399
Futurists, 174, 176, 183, 204, 214, 215, 242
Futurist Political Party, 214

Galbiati, Enzo, 236
Galli, Giorgio, 331
Gallipoli, 256
Gandolfo, Asclepia, 226, 228
GAP (*Gruppi di Azione Partigiana*), 386
GAP (*Gruppi di Azione Patriottica*), urban guerrillas, 312
Garda, Lake, 304, 308
Gardone, 217
Gargnano, 308
Garibaldi, Giuseppe, 50, 72, 74, 75, 80, 89, 185
Garibaldi battalion, 259
Garibaldi brigades, 186, 312
gas, natural, 350, 379
Gasparri, Pietro, 254
Gasteiner, E, 258
GATT (General Agreement on Tariffs and Trade), 350
Gazzetta dello Sport, La, 167, 172
GDP (Gross Domestic Product), 349, 379, 380, 394, 396
Gedda, Luigi, 325
Gela, 350
General Confederation of Labour, *see* CGL
Genina, Augusto, 244
Genoa, 126, 141, 168, 172, 375, 413
  Socialist Congress of (1892), 109–10, 112
Gentile, Giovanni, 222, 243, 277, 278
Gentiloni, Vincenzo, 157, 158
Gentiloni Pact (1913), 2, 157, 211

German (language), 252, 253, 281, 283, 322, 323, 342, 390; *see also* South Tyrol
Germany, 148, 190, 244, 258, 260, 266, 271, 281, 282, 283–5, 398, 399
  finance by, 97, 120–1
  and First World War, 122, 181, 188
  and Second World War, 266, 283–5, 286, 287, 288, 290, 292, 296, 297, 302–4, 305, 308–11, 312, 313–15, 316
  Social Democrat party in, 76, 106, 109
  trade with, 24, 123, 124, 128, 266
  in Triple Alliance, 46, 48, 79, 150, 181, 182
  United (1990–), 396, 425–6
  see also Axis; Nazis; Pact of Steel
Germany, East, 398
Germany, West (1949–90), 337, 349, 350, 378, 393
Gerschenkron, Alexander, 18, 25, 26, 96, 119, 120, 121, 123, 134
Ghia (coachwork firm), 125
Giardino, Gaetano, 190
Gibraltar, 286, 288
GIL (*Gioventù Italiana del Littorio*), Fascist youth organisation, 245, 255
ginnasio, see schools, secondary
Gioia Tauro, 399
Giolitti, Giovanni, 45, 55, 65, 98, 116, 136, 169, 189, 195, 196, 198, 214, 219, 221, 222, 225, 226, 294
  governments of, 98, 102, 122, 136–59, 204, 205, 206, 208, 210, 213, 215
  and Catholics, 146–50, 153–4, 155, 157–8, 169–70, 210, 213, 219
  and elections, 62–3, 139, 213
  and intervention crisis (1914–15), 184–5, 195, 199
  political 'system' of, 111, 121, 136–41, 143–4, 145, 150–1, 154–9, 172–3, 176, 180, 185, 194, 222, 239, 302
  and social issues, 102, 136–9, 141, 143, 145, 158, 173, 177, 207–8, 210, 215
  and Socialist Party, 141–5, 146, 152, 156, 158, 175, 180–1, 208, 212, 213, 215
Giolittians, 116, 156–7, 184, 195, 196, 200, 211, 212, 219, 224, 226, 261, 294
Giornale d'Italia, Il, 172
Giorno, Il, 367
Gioventù Cattolica Italiana (Catholic youth movement), 147, 255–6, 313
'Giovinezza' ('Youth'), 245, 257
Giro d'Italia (cycle race), 244
Giuriati, Giovanni, 237
GL (*Giustizia e Libertà*, Justice and Liberty), anti-Fascist movement, 252, 253, 259, 293, 294

partisan bands (1943–45), 312, 313
'Gladio', Nato body, 419
Gnocchi-Viani, Osvaldo, 76, 77
GNP (Gross National Product), 265, 317, 349, 379
GNR, *see* Republican National Guard
Gobetti, Piero, 5
Gogol, Nikolai, 16
gold, convertibility of lira to, 19, 26, 94
Gonzaga, Maurizio, 238
Gorizia, 185, 188, 323
Gospels, the, 148, 149
Government Commissioner (in regions), 391
GPA (*giunta provinciale amministrativa*), 93
Gradisca, 323
Gramsci, Antonio,
  as literary critic, 42, 368
  as political thinker, 1, 5, 6, 7, 42, 94, 212, 330
  as politician, 173, 212, 233, 367
Grand Council, Fascist, 223, 237, 238–9, 292, 296, 297, 299
  meeting of 24–25 July 1943, 297, 298–9, 308
Grand Hotel (Rome), 306
Grande Italia, La, 152
Grandi, Dino, 217, 240, 257, 297, 298–9, 308
Grands Corps, 339
Gran Sasso, 303
Graziani, Rodolfo, 286, 309, 311
Great War, *see* First World War
Greece, 154, 280–1, 313, 323, 385, 400
  war on (1940–43), 285–6, 287, 290, 291, 292
Greek language, 34, 170, 365
'Green Flame' (partisan bands), 312, 313
Green movement, 3, 415, 418, 421
Grimaldi family, 41
grist-tax (*macinato*), 24, 53, 63, 71, 73, 78, 80, 89
Gronchi, Giovanni, 294
Grosoli, Giovanni, 147
Gross, Feliks, 370
gross domestic product, *see* GDP
gross national product, *see* GNP
Guadalajara, battle of (1937), 259, 283
Guareschi, Giovanni, 368
GUF (*Gioventù Universitaria Fascista*), Fascist student organisation, 246–7
Gulf War (1991), 409, 419
Guttuso, Renato, 246

Hazon, Azzolino, 296, 298
health, 19–21, 50, 133, 161–2, 201, 268, 269, 270, 360, 362–3, 372, 400, 402–4
  administration of, 58, 105, 318, 337, 376, 377, 389, 390, 393, 395, 396, 403–4, 420

hegemony, 1, 4, 5, 6, 42, 76, 89, 177, 247, 330, 384

heroin, *see* drugs

'High Politics', 44, 46, 47, 48, 50, 57, 65, 66, 92, 99, 115, 152, 159, 182, 203, 230, 232, 259, 299, 302, 320, 323, 326, 344, 346, 393, 425–6

Himmler, Heinrich, 309

'historic compromise', 387–90, 408

history-writing, 4–7, 218–19, 259–61, 316

Hitler, Adolf, 281, 282, 283, 284, 285, 286, 291, 297, 308, 309, 310

Hollywood, 244, 364, 367, 368

hospitals, 7, 21, 58, 82, 83, 105, 256, 313, 337, 372, 378, 383, 403

'Hot Autumn' (1969), 374, 375–7, 385

housing, 20, 21, 162, 163, 165, 174, 192, 289, 317, 336, 337, 339, 354–5, 358, 361, 362, 363, 372, 376, 377, 385, 390, 400, 401

Humbert I, King (1878–1900), 45, 46, 48, 49, 50, 51, 75, 76, 98, 100, 102, 104, 112, 115

assassination of, 75, 117, 136

Humbert II, King (1946), 239, 319

as Lieutenant-General (1944–46), 305, 306, 319

Hungary, 345; *see also* Austria–Hungary

hydro-electricity, 24, 120, 121, 191, 206, 266, 272, 288, 322, 348, 350

Idea Nazionale, L', 152, 158

illiteracy, 29, 35–7, 40, 41, 49, 64, 156, 163, 169, 172, 177, 187, 278, 344, 357, 362, 364–5, 372, 382

Illustrazione Italiana, L', 9

Ilva (steel firm), 124, 172, 191, 192, 206, 265

Imbriani, Matteo, 79, 81

IMI (*Istituto Mobiliare Italiano*), State industrial finance house, 265

immigration, 400, 401, 402, 404, 412, 413, 426

Imola, 74

'*imponibile di mano d'opera*', 210

INA (*Istituto Nazionale Assicurazioni*), State insurance fund, 336, 363, 398

industrialists, 18, 24, 29, 125, 126, 172, 181, 191–2, 193, 206, 207–8, 288–9, 341, 342, 343, 348, 350, 351–3, 360, 367, 372, 376–9, 386, 394–5

Confederation of, 248, 334, 351, 395

and Fascism, 183, 215, 226, 231, 247–50, 251, 258, 263–4, 266, 288–9, 308

political activities of, 123–4, 129–30, 134, 152, 158, 172, 183, 204, 206, 208, 215, 226, 231, 263–4, 331, 351–3, 358, 367, 392, 414–15, 421–4

and Resistance, 312, 313, 314, 318

and tariff agitation, 23, 94, 123–4, 129–30

Industrial League, 158

industrial mobilisation (1915–18), 191, 192, 198, 199–200, 261

'industrial triangle', 126, 131, 165, 191, 272, 349, 350

industrial workers, 3, 22–4, 71, 88, 107, 126–7, 137–8, 162, 166, 239, 247, 249, 253, 267, 272, 273, 276, 294, 330, 342, 346, 350, 352–3, 366, 376, 379, 385, 395, 410

during wars, 186–7, 192–3, 198, 206, 288–9, 308–9, 311, 312–13

labour agitations of, 71, 88, 138, 141, 158, 206–9, 212, 247–9, 250–1, 264, 289, 308, 312, 350, 352, 374, 375–9, 384, 385, 389, 394–5

see also factories; industry; strikes; trade unions

industry,

domestic, 13, 21, 23, 126, 350, 353, 378–9

factory, 22–3, 24, 34, 125–7, 162, 164, 192–3, 206–9, 249, 288–9, 312, 348, 353, 374, 375–8, 380, 394–6, 400, 423

finance of, 97, 120–1, 124, 191–2, 265–6, 348–9, 351–3, 358–60, 379

growth of (1880s), 24, 25–6, 28, 124

'take-off' (after 1896), 95, 119–27, 134

under Fascism, 263–8, 272, 273, 276, 308–9, 317

after Second World War, 317, 348–53, 375–80, 394, 400, 413

privatisation of, 397–8, 423–4; *see also* Institute for Industrial Reconstruction

Infallibility, Papal, 86

infant mortality, 31, 162–3, 275, 362; *see also* death-rate; family

inflation, 191, 193, 194, 206, 207, 218, 264, 271, 272, 290, 317, 348–9, 351, 352, 354, 363, 366, 376, 377–8, 379, 394, 397, 421

influenza, 201

Innocenti (car firm), 309, 376

Institute for Industrial Reconstruction (IRI), State holding company, 265–6, 267–8, 318, 351–2, 358–9, 380, 396, 397–8, 415, 424

'institutional question', *see* Republic, agitation for

Institutional Reforms, Ministry for, 411

intellectuals, 4, 6, 7, 162, 172, 173–6, 232, 305, 367–8, 424

and Fascist regime, 243, 246, 252, 257, 277, 290

political activities of, 3, 73, 81, 101–2, 109, 111, 112, 144, 148, 151, 171, 173–6, 185, 212, 214, 249, 252, 313, 375, 381, 384, 385, 386, 406, 424 unemployable, 40, 171, 214, 234, 257, 277, 365, 375

Interior,
Minister of, 87, 93, 186, 199, 219, 225, 230, 232, 237, 240, 308, 310, 333
Ministry of, 52, 55, 60, 172, 199, 226, 233, 236, 299, 309, 385, 416
and elections, 61, 62
Under-secretary of, 93, 195, 244, 296
see also Prefects

International, Communist (Third), 212, 253

International Monetary Fund (IMF), 397, 424

International Working Men's Association (First International), 73, 74, 75
Upper Italian Federation of, 76

Intersind (State? firms' negotiating body), 351–2

intervention crisis, 181–5, 200

interventionists, 183, 185, 186, 193, 194, 195, 196, 197, 200, 204, 211, 214–16

Ionian coast, 355

Ireland, 17, 60, 204

IRI (Istituto per la Ricostruzione Industriale), see Institute for Industrial Reconstruction

iron industry, 23, 25, 27, 119, 123, 124, 132, 192, 264, 266, 267, 288, 348; see also steel

irredentism, 47, 79, 80, 89, 153, 174, 175, 181–2, 183, 184–5, 186, 218

irrigation, 129, 132, 162, 270, 272, 354, 356, 358

Isnenghi, Mario, 244

Isonzo, River, 182, 323

Istituto Cotoniero Italiano, 126

Istituto Tecnico Superiore (Milan), 40

Istria, 182, 203, 204, 205, 323

Italia, L' (shipping line), 265

Italia Irredenta, L', 79

Italia Libera, L', 230, 294

Italian Fashion Agency, 391

Italian Hunting Federation, 391

Italian language, 34–5, 36, 41, 169, 177, 200, 244, 252, 276, 369, 371, 372

Italian Revolutionary Socialist Party (PSRI), 72, 78

Italian Social Republic, see Salò, Republic of

Ivrea, 126

Jacini, Stefano, 12, 13, 14, 18, 20, 131

Jacobins, 65, 67

James, Henry, 30

Japan, 349, 396

Java, 291

Jesus, Society of, 82, 370

Jews, 121, 257–8, 266, 309, 316

John IV, Emperor of Ethiopia (1872–89), 99

John XXIII, Pope (1958–63), 371; see also Roncalli, Angelo

John Paul II, Pope (1978–), 389, 405, 409

journalists, 40–1, 80, 98–9, 172–3, 174–5, 214–15, 230–1, 246, 253, 347, 367, 381, 416
political importance of, 40, 98–9, 111, 113–14, 140, 153–5, 156, 172–3, 174–5, 183, 185, 214–15, 230–1, 252, 313, 333, 367, 381, 383

judges, 52, 53, 54–5, 56, 72, 81, 219, 256, 309, 318, 325, 340–1, 342, 380, 386, 388, 399, 400, 406, 410, 414–19, 424–5
political dependence of, 54, 72, 113, 233, 320, 340–1
see also courts; Supreme Council of the Judiciary

juries, 55, 72, 318, 387

Justice, Minister of, 54, 72, 81, 108, 225, 232, 248, 297, 319, 340, 341, 414, 417

Kesselring, Albert, 315

Keynes, John Maynard, 264

kidnapping, 70, 272, 310, 342, 386, 387

king, powers of, 44–5, 61, 65, 83, 100, 114–15, 116, 159, 221, 225, 227–8, 231, 238–9, 242, 293, 296–9, 302, 304, 305, 306, 308, 319
appointment of Prime Minister, 45, 221, 225, 226, 227–8, 239, 241, 252, 260, 293, 296, 299, 306, 307
influence on army, 45, 48, 100, 113, 221, 225, 227–8, 230, 240–1, 260, 296, 299, 304, 305
influence on foreign policy, 45, 89, 100, 113, 182, 184, 258, 280, 298
see also Humbert I; Humbert II; Victor Emmanuel II; Victor Emmanuel III

King, Russell, 355, 360

Koch, Pietro, 310

Korean War (1950–53), 337, 350

Kristallnacht (1938), 258

Krupp (armaments firm), 123

Kuliscioff, Anna, 112, 222

Labour, Minister of, 208, 266

labour movement, see Communist Party; Socialist Party; strikes; trade unions

labour tribunals, 137–8, 240, 248, 249, 395

labourers, agricultural (day-), 13, 15, 70, 107, 130, 166, 268, 270, 271, 273, 330, 354, 355, 359, 402, 410
agitations of, 71–2, 75, 130, 142–3, 151, 210
emigration of, 15, 32, 166, 273, 361
leagues of, 76, 77, 86, 101, 109, 111, 112,

130, 137, 142, 144, 145, 149, 166, 210, 215–16, 217, 218, 239, 330
Labriola, Arturo, 208
Labriola, Teresa, 163
La Malfa, Ugo, 333
Lancia (car firm), 288
land, occupations of, 194, 209, 210, 342, 354
landowners, 13–19, 29, 30, 33, 67, 88, 102, 103, 129, 130, 167, 194, 209–10, 218, 268–9, 270–1, 272, 290, 311, 348, 354–5, 356, 372
and local government, 16, 33, 59–60, 210, 215–16, 235, 322, 336–7, 361, 372
and national politics, 12, 17–18, 19, 67, 94, 102–3, 139, 140, 158, 196, 209–10, 215–16, 223, 238, 258, 268–70, 294, 317, 329, 356, 358, 361
see also peasant landowners
land reclamation (bonifica), 80, 127, 129, 130, 131, 132, 142, 268, 270, 272, 274, 275, 278, 354–5, 356
land reform, 17, 103, 194, 210, 215, 268, 270, 274, 330, 336, 354–5, 357, 364
agencies, 17, 274, 336–7, 354–5, 356, 358
Lanital, 266
Lanza, Giovanni, 45, 83
Lateran Pacts (1929), 2, 239, 254–5, 258, 321, 381, 388
Lateran Palace (Rome), 84
Laterza, Giovanni, 173, 246
latifundium, 13, 15, 20, 21, 60, 102, 103, 194, 209, 354, 355
Latin (language), 35, 276, 277, 278
Latium, 9, 50, 157, 212, 319, 392, 423
agriculture in, 14, 30, 193, 194, 209, 354
Laval, Pierre, 281
lawyers, 29, 33, 39–40, 54, 163, 171, 272, 277, 320, 321–2, 340, 365, 374, 381
in administration, 56, 171, 339, 365
in politics, 16, 54, 60, 63, 111, 140, 144, 218, 235, 322, 333, 381
see also courts; judges
Lazzaretti, Davide, 70
Lazzari, Costantino, 143, 198
League for the Defence of Liberty, 112
League of Democracy (1879), 80
League of Nations, 205, 230, 266, 281, 282
leaseholders, 13, 17, 103, 130, 132, 215, 216, 218, 271
Lega per l'Istituzione del Divorzio (LID), 381
legal separation, 81, 381, 382, 402
Leghorn, see Livorno
leisure, 41–2, 167–9, 243, 244–5, 251, 369
Lenin, Vladimir, 199, 332, 389
Leo XIII, Pope (1878–1903), 64, 85, 87–8, 106, 108, 147

Leonardo, 174
Leone, Sergio, 368
Lercaro, Giacomo, 371
Letino, 75
Liberal Party, 28, 30, 37, 39, 56, 62–3, 64–5, 66, 89, 137, 139, 146, 149, 150, 155, 157, 159, 211, 213, 216, 219, 222, 223, 225, 226, 230, 238, 240, 263, 294
Left-wing, 62, 63, 64–5, 66, 67, 81, 83, 89, 108, 112, 115–16, 137, 156, 157, 184, 195, 196, 200, 211, 212, 223, 224, 226, 294
Right-wing, 59, 62, 63, 65, 67, 82, 83, 108, 114–15, 152, 180, 194, 196, 211, 212, 223, 224, 225, 231
in Resistance period (1943–45), 294, 306, 307, 314, 315
after Second World War (PLI), 318, 319, 320, 324, 326, 327, 328, 329, 330, 334, 385, 410, 418, 419
Liberal regime (1861–1922), 1–2, 4–5, 44–68, 69, 85, 87, 88–9, 92–117, 136–59, 176, 177, 184–5, 200, 203–21, 239–41, 257, 259–60, 281, 291, 302, 338
collapse of, 203–28, 230–41
Liberation Front (in Yugoslavia), 293
Libya, 153, 154, 181, 233, 240, 257, 281, 286, 287, 288, 322, 358
campaigns in (1940–43), 286–8, 295, 297, 306
Libyan War (1911–12), 145, 153–6, 157, 158, 168, 172, 173, 175, 176, 183, 184, 187
liceo, see schools, secondary
life insurance, 137, 158, 189, 263
Liguria, 50, 55, 70
agriculture in, 13, 17
industry in, 22, 23, 24, 126, 129, 191, 207, 272
politics in, 79, 80, 156, 392
population in, 32, 161, 165, 275, 362
Lingotto factory (of Fiat), 206
Lisbon, 298, 303
Littoria, 235, 270
Littoriali, 247
Livi, Rodolfo, 50
Livorno, 24, 62, 133
Llandudno, 41
Lloyd George, David, 186
Lloyd Mediterraneo, 206
Lloyd Transatlantico, 192
Lloyd Triestino, 265
local government, 30, 33, 56, 144, 147, 211, 237, 239, 248, 305–6, 316, 327, 330, 333, 334, 336–7, 338, 346, 389, 390–3, 410, 413, 415
activities of, 16, 55, 58–61, 138–9, 142, 146, 210, 215–16, 231, 245, 335, 336–7, 358, 379, 391, 415

and education, 37, 169–70
elections, 85, 102, 112, 114, 139, 146, 155,
    210, 211, 213, 231, 239, 276, 332, 337,
    410, 413, 421, 424, 425
electorate, 16, 59–60, 85, 93, 103, 114, 276
independence of, 58, 59–61, 93, 113, 133,
    139, 235–6, 333, 336–7, 358, 359
and policing, 52, 59, 101, 392
and local taxes, 59, 101, 104, 210
and welfare, 59, 69, 105–6, 138, 146, 198,
    335, 337, 389, 403, 404
see also mayors; regional autonomy
Locarno, Treaty of (1925), 281
Lockheed (aircraft firm), 380
Lombardi, Riccardo, 370
Lombard league, 413
Lombardy, 29, 36, 37, 55, 87, 107, 148, 149,
    167, 342, 404, 414
  agriculture in, 13, 14, 18, 19, 22, 127–8, 130,
    131, 269, 271
  industry in, 22, 23, 24, 126, 191, 272, 395–6
  labour agitations in, 71–2, 76, 77, 137, 247,
    289, 294
  political activity in, 72, 76, 77, 80, 87, 89,
    107, 109, 110, 146, 147, 148, 168, 412–13
  population in, 32, 161, 165
Lombroso, Cesare, 53, 163
London, 74, 323
  Radio, 290, 291
  Treaty of (1915), 182, 184, 196, 203–4
Longo, Luigi, 259, 312, 314
Los Angeles, 244
Lotta Continua, 386
Lotta di Classe, 214
lottery, State, 42, 79
'Low Politics', 44, 57, 63, 65, 99, 230, 327, 335,
    344, 346, 392–3, 408–11, 413–19, 422–4
Lucania, see Basilicata
Lucca province, 85, 149
Lucidi, Giuseppe, 258
Lukacs, John, 295
Lunigiana, 103
Luzzatti, Luigi, 76
Luzzatto, Gino, 25

Maastricht, Treaty of (1991), 397
Macerata, 32, 39
macinato, see grist-tax
Mack Smith, Denis, 5
Madrid, 259, 303
Maffi, Antonio, 81
Mafia, 399, 404, 408, 412, 413, 415, 416–19
  Sicilian, 60, 88, 101, 272, 306, 342, 416–17
  Calabrian, 392, 416
magistrates, see judges

Magliani, Agostino, 63
Magneti Morelli (engineering firm), 385
maize, 19, 128, 162, 269, 289
Malagodi, Olindo, 184, 199, 213
Malaparte, Curzio, 260
malaria, 14, 15, 21, 33, 162, 270, 360, 363, 372
Malatesta, Errico, 74, 75
Malon, Benoît, 73
Malta, 284, 286, 303
Mancini, Pasquale, 47–8
Manifesto of Racial Scholars, 258
Mantua, 72
Mantua province, 72, 76, 88
Mao Tse-Tung, 316, 386
Marches, the, 17, 20, 79, 180, 392
Marconi, Guglielmo, 177, 246
Marcora, Giuseppe, 140
Mareb, River, 100
Maremma, 129, 270, 272, 354, 355
Marinetti, Filippo, 173, 174, 214
Mario, Jessie White, 102
Marne, battle of (1914), 181
marriage,
  age at, 162, 275, 362, 363
  civil, 81, 254, 255, 371, 382, 401
  see also family
Marshall Aid, 324, 345, 348
Martelli, Claudio, 414, 417
martial law, 49, 51, 69, 103, 104, 115, 188,
    221, 385
Martini, Ferdinando, 8, 182, 195
Marx, Karl, 73–4, 75
Marxist ideas, 5–6, 74, 78, 109, 110, 112, 142,
    145, 176, 246, 320, 405
Masons, see Freemasons
Massawa, 47, 48, 99, 100
Massola, Umberto, 294
Matapan, battle of Cape (1941), 286
Matera, 295
Matese rising, 74–5, 77
Mattei, Enrico, 350, 367
Matteotti bands, 312
Matteotti crisis, 224–8, 230, 231, 247, 253, 260,
    263
Matteotti, Giacomo, 224, 225, 226, 227, 236,
    237
Mattino, Il, 172, 231
Mayhew, Henry, 22
mayors, 16, 54, 58, 59, 60, 81, 93, 101, 117,
    131, 139, 144, 169, 207, 306, 315, 333, 337,
    370, 412, 417, 421, 425
  government appointment of, 58, 59, 60–1,
    93, 231, 235–6
  see also local government; podestà
Mazzini, Giuseppe, 46, 73, 78, 79, 80, 113, 142

meat, 19, 187, 192, 289, 356, 357, 402
Meda, Filippo, 149, 173, 195, 197
Mediterranean, 27, 46, 47–8, 175, 242–3, 281,
 282, 284, 285, 286, 287, 297, 306, 345, 426
 First Mediterranean Agreement (1887), 48
'Mediterranean crime', 70, 342
Melfi, 399
Melograni, Piero, 274
Menelik II, Emperor of Ethiopia (1889–1913),
 99–100
Meridiana, 7
Merlin, Angelina, 342
Merlino, Francesco, 75
Messina, 132, 165
Metaponto, 355, 360
Mezzogiorno, see Southern Italy
Micheli, Giuseppe, 210
Michels, Robert, 144
Middle Ages, 370
Middle East, 266, 282, 345, 350, 394, 416, 426
Miglio, Gianfranco, 425
migration,
 within Italy, 97, 127, 130, 163, 164–5, 192,
  271, 273–4, 340, 349, 360–2, 364, 367,
  374, 376, 381, 399, 412, 426
 seasonal, 13, 15, 21, 32, 168–9
 see also emigration; urbanisation
Milan, 33, 40, 41, 50, 113, 120, 152, 167, 168,
 172, 184, 221, 254, 263, 295, 317, 385, 406,
 422, 423
 industry in, 120, 126, 127, 165, 263, 289,
  309, 350, 376
 labour agitations in, 71, 72, 81, 144, 207–8,
  247, 251, 289, 312, 376
 local government in, 106, 112, 138, 211, 315,
  413, 421
 political activities in, 75, 77, 78, 81, 89, 109,
  112, 114, 152, 184, 215, 216, 272, 290,
  310, 312, 315, 317, 385, 386, 387, 421–2
 population of, 31, 127, 162, 163, 164, 165,
  192, 273, 400
 riots in (1898), 51, 71, 101, 103–4, 115
'Milan Programme' (1894), 106
Milanese Socialist League, 109
Militia, Fascist (MVSN), 205, 222, 223, 225,
 226, 227, 228, 232, 233, 234, 236, 238, 239,
 243, 253, 257, 258, 259, 260, 271, 299, 309
Mille Miglia (car race), 244
Minculpop, *see* Popular Culture, Ministry of
Minghetti, Marco, 57, 63, 83
ministers, 45, 61, 66, 92, 115, 183, 225, 234,
 238, 240, 306, 333, 337, 338, 340, 367, 380,
 389, 409, 411, 414–15, 419, 424
ministries, 56–7, 92–3, 234, 248, 304, 339, 398,
 417, 420

Minniti, Fortunato, 287
Minozzi, Giovanni, 187
Missiroli, Mario, 216
Mitterrand, François, 409
Modena, 24, 232
modernism, 148
Molinelli, Raffaele, 79
Molise, 15, 34, 359, 400, 414
 emigration from, 32, 166
Monarchists, since 1946 (PNM, later PDIUM),
 327, 328, 330, 346
Monde, Le, 367
Mondo, Il, 225
Monfalcone, 323
Montale, Eugenio, 246
Montalto, Giacomo, 102, 103
Mont Cenis, 322
Monte Cassino, abbey of, 82, 87
Montecatini (chemical firm), 191, 266, 267, 352
Montecatini-Edison (Montedison),
 electro-chemical firm, 349, 352, 380
Monte Grappa, 190
Montenegro, 154, 204
Monterchi, 9
Montevideo, 293
Montgomery, Bernard, 286
Monti, Carlo, 197
Monticone, Alberto, 188
Montini, Giovanni Battista, 256, 324; *see also*
 Paul VI, Pope
Monza, 117, 141
Morandi, Rodolfo, 246
Moravia, Alberto, 246
Mordini, Antonio, 98
Morello, Vincenzo, 1
Morgan line, 323
Mori, Cesare, 219, 272, 417
Moro, Aldo, 256, 332, 333, 342, 388
 assassination of, 387, 389, 413, 417
Morocco, 48, 152, 153, 154
Morpurgo, Emilio, 18
Morra di Lavriano, Roberto, 103
Mosca, Gaetano, 176
Moscow, 212, 306, 390
motor-scooters, 349, 368
motor vehicles, *see* car industry
Movimento Studentesco, 375
Movimento di Unità Proletaria, 294
MSI (*Movimento Sociale Italiano*), *see*
 neo-Fascists
municipalities (*comuni*), *see* local government
'municipal Socialism', 138–9, 142, 210
murders, 70, 142, 156, 220, 224, 225, 226,
 227, 272, 310, 311, 317, 386–7, 413, 416,
 417

Muro, 20

Murri, Romolo, 148, 175

Mussolini, Alessandra, 421

Mussolini, Arnaldo, 240

Mussolini, Benito, 143, 180, 187, 197
  as journalist, 156, 173, 183, 214–15, 230–2, 291, 367
  and intervention crisis (1914–15), 183, 184, 185, 214–15
  as leader of Fascist movement (1919–22), 185, 213, 214–15, 216–17, 218, 219–21
  as Prime Minister (1922–25), 203, 222–8, 263–4, 317, 318
  as *Duce* of Fascist regime (1926–40), 205, 230–2, 232–9, 239–41, 243–7, 247–50, 253, 254–6, 257–61, 263–71, 272, 274, 275, 280–5, 319, 368
  as war leader (1940–43), 261, 285–99
  fall of (1943), 8, 293, 295–9, 309
  and Salò Republic (1943–45), 303, 304, 308–10, 311, 330

'Mussolini law' (on land reclamation), 270

Mussolini, Bruno, 244

Mussolini, Edda, *see* Ciano, Edda

Mussolini, Rachele, 254

Mussolini, Vittorio, 244

mustard gas, 282

Muti, Ettore, 244

Muti band, 310

mutual-aid societies, 72, 76–7, 78, 88, 94, 101, 109, 111, 137
  Italian Federation of, 138

MVSN (*Milizia Volontaria per la Sicurezza Nazionale*), *see* Militia, Fascist

Naldi, Filippo, 183

Namier, Lewis, 66, 139

Naples, 20, 29, 30, 31–2, 34, 41, 50, 58, 172, 231, 305, 306, 339, 363, 392, 415
  Bay of, 15, 359
  industry in, 124, 132, 133, 272, 358, 380
  political activity in, 53, 73, 74, 75, 152, 163, 171, 172, 220, 223, 305, 316, 319, 392, 415, 421
  population of, 20, 31–2, 164, 165, 360, 361
  University of, 39, 73, 171

'nation in arms', 49, 50, 80, 113, 187, 315, 343

National Agency for Assistance to Workers, 391

National Alliance (*Alleanza Nazionale*), *see* neo-Fascists

National Debt, 191, 396–7

National Hydrocarbons Agency, *see* ENI

National Institute, Washington, 8

National Library, Florence, 8

National Right (DN), 328

Nationalists, 1, 136, 150–3, 167, 171, 173, 174–5, 180, 242, 302
  Congresses of, 152, 155
  and Fascist movement, 196, 215, 222, 223, 224, 225, 226, 231, 232, 242
  and First World War, 183, 195, 196, 197, 199–200
  and foreign policy, 150–1, 152–3, 154, 155, 175, 183, 204, 215
  and productivism, 151–2, 199–200, 206, 211, 242

Nato (North Atlantic Treaty Organisation), 344, 345, 388, 419

Nava, Cesare, 197

Nave, La, 152

Navigazione Generale Italiana (shipping line), 124

navy, 26, 47, 48, 63, 94, 121, 123, 124, 278, 282, 344
  Minister of, 26, 45, 48, 204, 222, 228, 233, 286
  Ministry of, 123
  and Second World War, 286, 287, 303
  and steel industry, 26–7, 94, 123

Nazis, 244, 257, 258, 260, 284, 292, 318

Nazi–Soviet Pact (1939), 259

Nazzaro, Felice, 125

Necchi (sewing machine firm), 349

Nenni, Pietro, 173, 183, 259, 306, 324

neo-Fascists (MSI, later National Alliance), 3, 327, 328, 330, 334, 343, 382, 383, 384–5, 400, 402, 408, 418, 421, 422–3, 425, 426
  and terrorism, 384–5

Netherlands, 284

Network party (*La Rete*), 418, 421

neutralists (in First World War), 183, 184, 185, 195, 196, 198, 200, 211, 261, 284

newspapers, 35, 40, 42, 99, 104, 107, 108, 111, 153, 158, 172–3, 177, 187, 189, 198, 199, 204, 214–15, 216, 226, 227, 240, 261, 291, 308, 318, 330, 345, 347, 366, 367, 387, 406, 410
  see also Avanti!; journalists; periodicals; *Popolo d'Italia;* press

New York, 353

Nice, 46, 79, 291

Nitti, Francesco, 55, 140, 152, 166, 171, 194, 195, 197, 200, 204, 212, 213, 214, 223, 323, 338
  government of, 204–5, 206, 207, 212, 213

non abbiamo bisogno, 255

non expedit, 85, 108, 146

Normandy, 307

North Africa, 47, 48, 153–5, 243, 285, 286, 297, 402, 426
  see also Libya; Morocco; Tunisia

Northern Italy, 24–5, 29, 47, 50, 69, 101, 111, 174, 177, 256, 304, 399, 419, 423
  agriculture in, 13–14, 19, 25, 127, 128–9, 131, 162, 166, 193, 209, 269, 311, 355, 361
  Church in, 86, 87, 256, 313
  education in, 36, 38, 170, 171, 245
  emigration from, 32, 166, 360–1
  industry in, 22, 23, 24–5, 114, 120, 126, 137, 140, 174, 186, 187, 191–3, 206–9, 247, 272, 275, 289, 308, 312, 339, 342, 349, 350, 353, 358, 359, 362, 375–6, 379, 385, 394, 395–6, 399, 400
  local government in, 106, 112, 138–9, 144, 146, 169–70, 210, 211, 215–17, 220, 235, 314–17
  political activity in, 2, 64, 87, 111, 112, 114, 116, 137, 140, 142, 144, 146, 149, 150, 157, 172, 193, 207–9, 211, 212–13, 214–15, 216, 217, 220, 224, 232, 245, 272, 304, 307, 308–18, 319, 321, 322, 324, 325, 329, 330, 334, 338, 340, 342, 346, 362, 375–8, 385–7, 394, 409, 412–13, 414–16, 419, 420–2, 423
  population in, 31, 161–2, 165, 187, 192, 275, 276, 289, 310, 311, 360–1, 362–3, 382, 401, 402
Northern leagues (from 1991 Northern League), 3, 403, 412–13, 414, 418, 419, 420, 421, 422, 423, 424, 425
North Tyrol, 292
Norway, 284, 308
notables, local, 17, 57, 58, 62, 65, 66, 67, 159, 187, 237, 306, 336, 337, 399
  see also landowners; local government
Novara province, 13
nuclear power, 379, 384, 405, 410
Nuvolari, Tazio, 244

Oberdank, Guglielmo, 79, 117
Occhetto, Achille, 410
occupations, of factories, see factories; of land, see land
Odero, Attilio, 124
oil, 123, 266, 282, 287, 288, 348, 349, 350, 357, 359, 379, 380, 394
olive oil, 14, 19, 96, 128, 269
Olivetti, Camillo, 126
  typewriter firm, 126, 267, 349, 359, 394, 406
Olmi, Ermanno, 368
OND (*Opera Nazionale Dopolavoro*), see Dopolavoro
opera, 42, 410
Opera Assistenza agli Operai Italiani, 167
Opera dei Congressi e dei Comitati Cattolici, 87, 106–7, 108, 147
  see also Catholic movement; Christian Democracy
Opera Nazionale Balilla, see Balilla
Opera Nazionale Combattenti, 190
Opinione, L', 40
Oppressed Nationalities, Congress of (1918), 196, 199
organised crime, see Mafia
Oriani, Afredo, 175
Orlando, Giuseppe (economist), 18
Orlando, Giuseppe (shipbuilder), 124
Orlando, Leoluca, 417, 421
Orlando, Vittorio Emanuele, 65, 186, 195, 196, 199, 203, 204, 213, 219, 224, 225, 226, 296, 323
  government of, 186, 189, 195, 196, 204, 212, 213
orphanages, 105, 138, 162–3, 275, 333, 335
Orsini, Felice, 117
Osservatore Cattolico, L', 107, 149
Osservatore Romano, L', 146, 291, 295
Ostia, 42
'OVRA' (Fascist secret police), 232–3
Oxbridge, 339

Pacciardi, Randolfo, 259
Pacelli, Ernesto, 153
'Pact for Italy', 418, 420, 423
'Pact of Brotherhood' (1864), 78, 113
'pact of pacification' (1921), 217, 219, 220
'Pact of Steel' (1939), 283, 284, 299
Padovani, Aurelio, 223
Padua, 370, 386
Paese Sera, 367
Paganuzzi, Giambattista, 108
Palazzo Venezia (Rome), 261, 282, 285, 292
Palermo, 15, 71, 102, 168, 272, 337, 416–17
Pani Rossi, Enrico, 20
Pannella, Marco, 381, 418, 422
Panorama, 367
Pantano, Edoardo, 140
Paolucci, Raffaele, 226
Papacy, 46, 83, 84–5, 86–7, 147, 148, 255, 313, 316, 319
  see also Church, Catholic; Lateran Pacts; Roman question; Vatican
Paper and Cellulose Agency, 336
Papini, Giovanni, 173, 174
'*parecchio*', 184, 185, 195
Pareto, Vilfredo, 99, 176
Paris, 40, 172, 204, 252, 353, 366
  Commune of (1871), 73, 78
  Treaty of (1947), 322–3, 343, 344
Parkinson, Northcote, 338

parliament,
before First World War, 44, 48, 56, 57, 61–6,
78, 80, 93, 94, 98–9, 102, 113, 114–16, 136,
139–40, 143, 145, 152, 157–9, 173, 176
and First World War, 182, 184–5, 194–6,
199–200
before Fascist regime (1919–25), 214, 219,
220–1, 224–8, 231, 261
in Fascist regime (1925–43), 234, 236, 239,
242, 254, 298
since Second World War, 307, 320, 321,
327–34, 340, 344, 345, 380, 384, 385, 388,
391, 411, 414, 418, 419–24, 425
commission of inquiry into agriculture
(Jacini), 12–15, 16, 20
commission of inquiry into conditions of
peasantry in South (Faina), 17, 132
commission of inquiry into hygienic
conditions, 20
commission of inquiry into reform of State
(Bozzi), 411
commission of inquiry into navy, 123
legislative commissions, 333, 334, 335, 399
see also Chamber of Deputies; deputies;
elections, parliamentary; Senate; Senators
'parliamentary revolution' (1876), 27, 59, 62
'Parliamentary Union', 195, 196
Parma, 110
Parri, Ferruccio, 313, 314, 315, 317, 318
government of, 317–18
parties, financing of, 40, 98–9, 183, 210, 215,
217, 231, 311, 312, 324–5, 332, 409
see also corruption; 'partyocracy';
'sottogoverno'
partisans, in Resistance, 309, 310, 311–16,
317, 318, 322, 325, 338, 340, 341, 343
see also Resistance
'partyocracy', 2, 237, 294–5, 302, 306–7,
314–16, 317, 326, 329, 334–7, 380, 408–11,
412, 414–15, 419, 420, 423; see also
'sottogoverno'
Party of the Workers, 109–10; see also
Socialist Party; Workers' Party (POI)
Pascoli, Giovanni, 154
Pasolini, Pier Paolo, 274, 368
Passanante, Giovanni, 75
Passato e Presente, 7
'passo romano', 257
Past and Present, 6
Pastore, Giulio, 358
patronage, 3, 56, 60, 61–2, 66, 133, 159, 171,
234–5, 237–8, 267–8, 314–15, 317–18, 327,
331–2, 333–4, 335–7, 338, 346, 347, 351–3,
356, 358, 360, 366, 380, 389, 392–3, 399,
408, 409, 410, 414–16, 421

Paul III, Pope (1534–49), Tower of, 105
Paul VI, Pope (1963–78), 256, 323–4, 371–2,
381; see also Montini, Giovanni Battista
Pavese, Cesare, 246
Pavia, 78
Pavolini, Alessandro, 244, 309
PCI (Partito Comunista Italiano), see
Communist Party
PDIUM (Partito Democratico Italiano di Unità
Monarchica), see Monarchists
PDS (Partito Democratico della Sinistra), see
Democratic Party of the Left
PDUP (Partito Democratico dell' Unità
Proletaria), see Democratic Proletarians
peasant landowners, 3, 13–20, 25, 32, 86, 111,
129, 130, 132, 193, 198, 209, 211, 216, 218,
268, 270–1, 290, 329, 335, 336, 354, 355,
356, 366
see also agriculture; landowners
pellagra, 19, 162, 269
Pelloux, Luigi, 45, 50, 62, 115, 136, 237
governments of, 108, 112, 115–16
pensioners, 60, 353, 363, 378, 395, 396, 397,
401
pensions, 76, 79, 137, 206, 339, 353, 396, 397,
401, 424, 425
Pentecostalists, 70, 167, 256
periodicals, 35, 40–1, 107, 108, 152, 172,
174–5, 176, 232, 252, 330, 332, 367, 384,
386
Perrone, Mario and Pio, 192, 206, 263
Perseveranza, La, 40
Pertini, Sandro, 315, 333, 367, 409
Perugia, 221
Petacci, Claretta, 292, 310
Pétain, Henri, 285
Petersen, Jens, 219
Peveragno, 62
phylloxera, 96, 101
Piana dei Greci, 102
Piave, River, 185, 189, 190
piazza Fontana (Milan), 385
piazza Montanara (Rome), 67
piazza San Sepolcro (Milan), 215
piazzale Loreto (Milan), 310
Piedmont, 29, 32, 35, 36, 37, 50, 55, 57, 97,
107, 149, 207, 221, 256
agriculture in, 13, 17, 19, 34, 127, 128, 131
industry in, 22, 23, 24, 125–6, 191–3, 272,
289, 294, 314, 394–5
political activities in, 107, 109, 207, 212, 289,
294, 314, 362, 392
population of, 32, 161, 165, 289
Princess of (Maria José), 298
see also Northern Italy; Turin

Piedmontese, 55–6, 57, 58, 66, 67, 184, 186, 213, 339
Pietralata (Rome), 274
Piombino, 123
Pirandello, Luigi, 246
Pirelli, Giovanni Battista, 24
    tyre firm, 165, 191, 267, 376, 394
Pisa, University of, 106
Pitré, Giuseppe, 33
Pius IX, Pope (1846–78), 82, 84
Pius X, Pope (1903–14), 146, 147, 148, 155
Pius XI, Pope (1922–39), 250, 254–5, 256, 258
Pius XII, Pope (1939–58), 153, 295, 296, 323, 324, 326, 370
PLI (*Partito Liberale Italiano*), *see* Liberal Party
PNF (*Partito Nazionale Fascista*), *see* Fascist Party
PNM (*Partito Nazionale Monarchico*), *see* Monarchists
podestà, 231, 235–6
POI (*Partito Operaio Italiano*), *see* Workers' Party
Poland, 196, 283, 284, 389–90
'Pole of Good Government', 418
'Pole of Liberty', 418
Polesine, 75, 129
police, 51–4, 60, 66, 74, 137, 138, 151, 199, 219, 225, 232, 238, 239, 240, 255, 256, 292, 294, 295, 296, 298, 299, 305, 309–10, 315, 317, 318, 324, 325, 341–3, 372, 374, 385, 386, 387, 388, 413, 414, 416, 417
    and public order, 52, 75–6, 78, 79, 104, 144, 145, 151, 193, 216, 219, 227, 309–10, 342, 366, 385–7, 392, 414
    riot- (*celeri*), 341
    secret, 7, 232–3, 237, 253, 290, 294, 342–3, 385, 414
    and strikes, 137, 143–4, 145, 158, 219
Polis, 7
'political provisions', 115–16
Pontine marshes, 270, 355
Popolari, see Popular Party
Popolo, Il, 294
Popolo d'Italia, Il, 183, 214, 215, 243
Popular Culture, Ministry of, 243, 258
    of Salò Republic, 308
'Popular Democratic Front', 325
Popular Party (PPI) in 1919–26, 210, 211, 212, 213, 216, 219, 221, 252, 294, 329
    and agriculture, 210, 211, 216
    and Fascism, 222, 223–4, 225, 231, 236, 254
    and the Vatican, 211, 223–4, 225, 231, 254
    votes for, 210, 212, 213, 224
    1994– , 418, 421, 423, 424

see also Catholic movement, political; Christian Democrat Party
population, 31, 161–2, 164–5, 273–6, 278, 359, 360–1, 362–3, 382, 383, 397, 401–2, 403
Portoferraio, 123
Porto Torres, 358
positivism, 53–4, 89, 109, 110, 143, 170, 173, 176
Posts and Telegraphs, Ministry of, 92
Potenza, 354
Potere Operaio, 386
Po valley,
    agriculture in, 20, 94, 127, 129, 130, 215–16, 270, 354
    industry in, 126, 266, 350
    political activities in, 72, 77, 88, 94, 110, 111, 130, 142–4, 210, 215–16, 272, 311
PPI (*Partito Popolare Italiano*), *see* Popular Party
PR (*Partito Radicale*), *see* Radicals
Prague, 283
Prato, bishop of, 371
Prefects, 18, 33, 54, 58, 66, 117, 210, 222, 235, 239, 304, 305, 307, 325
    administrative tasks of, 16, 18, 57, 93, 133
    appointments of (1943–47), 305, 307, 315, 317, 318–19
    and elections, 60–2, 139, 159, 235, 336
    and local government, 58–61, 93, 131, 138, 139, 147, 235–6, 237, 337
    and policing, 52, 58, 102, 107, 131, 137, 139, 144, 158, 207, 216, 219, 225, 227, 232, 235, 272, 274, 304
    political tasks of, 7, 58, 60–1, 102, 107, 108, 131, 133, 137, 138, 139, 146–7, 159, 183, 198, 210, 219, 222, 227, 232, 235, 268, 304, 319, 325, 336
preference votes, 332, 333, 334, 335, 412, 419
President, of Italian Republic, 320, 321, 333, 342, 344, 367, 409, 411, 412, 414, 424, 425
press, 4, 40, 98, 115, 116, 145, 152, 171, 172–3, 177, 196, 225, 230–2, 233, 234, 238, 240, 243, 249, 254, 258, 305, 334–5, 367, 380, 386, 410, 422
    law on (1925), 231
    political influence of, 40, 42, 99, 111, 144, 153–6, 158, 172–3, 183, 185, 199, 211, 214–15, 216, 224–8, 230–1, 240, 243, 252, 291, 333, 334, 340, 347, 366–7, 381, 383, 406
Preziosi, Giovanni, 257, 309, 310
Prezzolini, Giuseppe, 173, 174, 175, 176, 260
PRI (*Partito Repubblicano Italiano*), *see* Republican Party
priests, *see* clergy

Primavalle (Rome), 274
Prime Minister, 45, 48, 61, 92, 98, 121, 132,
    136, 146, 184, 186, 294, 317, 318, 344, 347,
    367, 380, 387, 391, 406, 408–9, 410, 411,
    417, 423, 425
  appointment of, 45, 61, 115, 184, 221, 239,
    241, 298, 299, 320
  and parliament, 61–2, 65, 67, 93, 98, 132,
    136, 140, 184, 225–7, 332–3, 408, 409,
    411
printers, 73, 88, 127, 141, 165, 273
privatisation, see industry
Procacci, Giuliano, 5
procurators, 54, 72
Prodi, Romano, 397, 424
productivism, 151–2, 199–200, 206, 242, 248
Progressive Alliance, 418, 423, 424
proportional representation, 212, 221, 223,
    320, 327, 331, 411, 418, 420, 423
prostitutes, 34, 52; see also brothels
protectionism, see tariffs
provinces, 58, 93, 137, 159, 169, 216, 221, 235,
    237, 238, 248, 270, 274, 337
  see also Prefects
PSDI (Partito Socialista Democratico Italiano),
    see Social Democrat Party
PSI (Partito Socialista Italiano), see Socialist
    Party
PSIUP (Partito Socialista Italiano di Unità
    Proletaria), see Social Proletarians
PSLI (Partito Socialista dei Lavoratori
    Italiani), see Social Democrat Party
PSRI (Partito Socialista Rivoluzionario
    Italiano), see Italian Revolutionary Socialist
    Party
PSRR (Partito Socialista Rivoluzionario di
    Romagna), see Romagna Revolutionary
    Socialist Party
public security guards, see police
Public Works, 415
  Minister of, 291
  Ministry of, 133, 308
Publitalia, advertising agency, 421
Punta Stilo, battle of (1940), 286
purge, see civil service

Quaderni Storici, 6–7
Qualunquista, see Average Man, Party of
Quasimodo, Salvatore, 246
Quebec, 303
quinine, 162
Quirinal palace (Rome), 146
Quisling, Vidkun, 308

Radicals, 3, 77, 78, 80–1, 87, 89

  in 1890s, 98, 99, 101, 102, 103, 105, 108, 109,
    110, 112–14, 115, 116,
  1900–14, 132, 136, 140–1, 143, 145, 146, 148,
    152, 154, 157, 158, 163, 164, 171, 180
  and First World War, 183, 194, 195, 196
  1919–25, 212, 213, 223
  as anti-Fascists (1925–45), 231, 252, 294
  since 1966 (PR), 328, 381, 382, 383–4, 388,
    404, 418
  Radio Radicale, 384
  see also Action, Party of; GL
Radini Tedeschi, Giacomo, 148
radio, 243–4, 245, 290, 291, 299, 303, 335,
    367, 370, 384, 387, 389
Ragionieri, Ernesto, 5, 8
Ragusa, 350
Rahm, Rudolf von, 309
RAI (Radio Audizioni Italiane), State
    broadcasting corporation, 8, 291, 299, 367,
    384, 405–6, 423, 425
railways, 25, 27, 29, 48, 51, 88, 97, 109, 124–5,
    132, 148, 151, 171, 177, 218, 234, 276, 317,
    348, 369
  labour disputes on, 71, 115, 137, 141, 180,
    207, 217–18, 220, 378
  nationalisation of (1905), 62, 63, 120, 124
  railway-building, 21, 25, 26, 27–8, 55
Rapallo, Treaty of (1920), 205, 215
Rapisardi, Mario, 81
'ras', Fascist squad leaders, 216, 218, 220,
    222–3, 226, 227, 235, 236, 237, 238, 239
Rattazzi, Urbano, 45
Ravenna, 76, 78, 180
Reagan, Ronald, 398
Reconciliation, see Church, relations with
    State; Lateran Pacts
Red Army, 304
'Red Belt', 330, 356, 382, 390
Red Brigades, 387, 413–14, 416, 417
Red Sea, 47–8, 99, 100
'Red Week' (1914), 180, 181
referendum, 320, 381, 383–4, 395, 403, 404,
    410, 411, 412, 414, 417, 425
  on abortion (1981), 383, 408
  on divorce (1974), 319, 381–2, 383
  on electoral reform (1993), 420, 421
  on monarchy (1946), 319, 346
'reform of customs', 240, 257, 258
reformists, see Socialist Party
Reformist Socialist Party, 156, 183, 194, 195,
    211, 212, 213, 219
refrigerators, 349, 351, 400
Reggio Calabria, 170, 269, 391
regions, 30, 100, 322, 389, 390–3, 399, 418,
    424, 426

regional autonomy, 57, 58, 69, 320, 321–3, 337, 359, 389, 390–3, 403, 404, 412–13, 416, 420, 425
agitation for, 3, 57, 113, 149, 292–3, 294, 321–2, 339, 390, 412, 423
Regno, Il, 174–5
Reichstag, 106, 109
religious beliefs, 33, 42, 70, 75, 85–6, 149, 167, 247, 256, 367, 370, 371, 380, 405
see also Church, religious observance
Repubblica, La, 406, 415
Republic, Italian (1946–), 259, 260, 295, 297, 299, 302, 319–26, 327–47, 384–93, 408–26
agitation for (1942–46), 293, 297, 305, 307, 313, 314, 319
Republican National Guard (GNR), 309
Republican Party and Republicans,
before 1895, 57, 64, 73, 78–80, 88, 89, 104, 105, 109, 110, 113, 115, 117
1895–1914, 113, 115, 116, 117, 143, 154, 170, 180
1914–25, 180, 183, 186, 194, 195, 196, 211, 220, 224, 252
as anti-Fascists (1925–43), 231, 252, 259, 294, 295, 297
in Resistance (1943–45), 294, 295, 297, 314
since Second World War (PRI), 320, 321, 324, 326, 328, 329, 330, 331, 392, 408, 410, 418
mutual-aid societies, 76, 78, 177
Republican Police, 309
Rerum Novarum, 106, 147
Resistance, the anti-Fascist (1943–45), 2, 4, 200, 293, 310–16, 317–19, 322, 325, 330, 338, 340, 343, 368, 376, 386
values of, 316, 317, 319, 346, 386
Resto del Carlino, Il, 130, 183
Rhineland, 282
Rhodes, 154
Ribbentrop, Joachim von, 284
Riccione, 245
rice, 13, 19, 34, 94, 96, 127, 128
Ricotti, Cesare, 48, 50
Rieti, 9
Riforma, La, 40, 102
Righetti, Igino, 256
Riina, Salvatore, 417
Rimini, 41, 74, 77, 370
riots, 49, 54, 60, 67, 71, 74, 86, 88, 97, 101, 102–3, 117, 174, 180, 207, 234, 342, 369, 376, 391
bread, 71, 74, 116, 193, 207, 295
Fascist, 227, 237
grist-tax, 53, 71, 73, 78
student, 171, 183, 342, 366, 374–5

in Turin (1917), 193, 195, 197, 199
in 1898, 44, 51, 71, 103–4, 108, 112, 115, 116
Ripacandida, 20
Risorgimento, 38, 44, 47, 63, 65, 92, 115, 168, 175, 176, 187, 259, 413, 425
Rivista Internazionale di Scienze Sociali, 106
Rocco, Alfredo, 152, 225, 232, 233, 240, 248, 260, 321
Rochat, Giorgio, 48
Rochdale, 76
Romagna, 50, 70, 71, 214, 369
political activities in, 71, 74, 77–8, 79, 110, 113, 148, 156, 180, 218
see also Emilia-Romagna
Romagna Revolutionary Socialist Party (PSRR), 77–8
Roman question, 46, 82, 84–5, 87, 107, 147, 150, 211, 239, 254–5
see also Church, relations with State; Lateran Pacts; Vatican
Roman salute, 205, 257
Romani, Mario, 18
Rome, 7, 8, 21, 24, 40, 47, 50, 54, 82, 84, 100, 108, 114, 168, 172, 183, 214, 223, 226, 239, 240, 242, 281, 282, 283, 284, 285, 286, 290, 298, 299, 303, 304, 306, 308, 318, 322, 344, 345, 364, 367, 370, 390, 400, 412, 417, 426
agriculture near, 14, 17, 20, 21, 30, 33, 82–3, 129, 272, 355
ancient, 67, 101, 152, 168, 176, 225, 240, 243, 254, 273–4, 292, 364
local government of, 30, 58, 155, 236, 324, 421
March on (1922), 220, 222, 274, 285, 316
new buildings in, 30, 97, 105, 273–4, 361
Pact of (1890), 113
political activities in, 78–9, 80, 85, 113, 172, 184, 196, 199, 212, 221, 237, 294–6, 298–9, 302, 304, 305, 306–7, 311, 314, 316, 318, 319, 320, 321, 325, 330, 333, 383, 421, 422
population of, 31, 35, 162, 164, 165, 273–4, 361
and rest of country, 7, 56–8, 60–1, 65, 67, 131, 133, 138, 139, 186, 222, 238, 307, 321–2, 333, 337, 390–2, 400, 412–13, 425
University of, 163, 258, 321, 366
Romeo, Rosario, 5, 18, 25, 120
Romita, Giuseppe, 295
Rommel, Erwin, 286
Roncalli, Angelo, 148, 371
Roosevelt, Franklin, 298, 306, 307
Rosi, Francesco, 368
Rosminians (religious order), 82
Ross, Ronald, 162
Rosselli, Carlo and Nello, 252, 253, 259, 294

Rossellini, Roberto, 367
Rossi, Alessandro, 23, 24, 94
Rossi, Cesare, 225, 226, 227
Rossi, Ernesto, 252
Rossoni, Edmondo, 218, 240, 248, 249, 260
Rovigo, 72
Royal Household, Minister of, 226, 296, 298
Ruanda Burundi, 412
Rubattino (shipping line), 47
Rudiní, see di Rudiní
Ruini, Meuccio, 306
Rumania, 196, 288
Rumor, Giacomo, 147
'rural theft', 70
Russia, 46, 73, 252, 253, 265, 288, 323, 337,
    345, 389, 419
  Bolshevik Revolution in (1917), 196, 199, 207
  and First World War, 181, 183, 188, 196
  and Italian Communist Party, 220, 323, 388,
    389–90, 410, 419
  and Second World War, 284, 285, 286, 287,
    297, 304, 306, 323, 419
  trade with, 18, 350, 388
Russolo, Luigi, 174

Sacchi, Ettore, 140
Saffi, Aurelio, 79–80, 89
Salandra, Antonio, 152, 159, 195, 211, 213, 285
  and Fascist movement, 219, 221, 224, 225,
    226, 228, 230
  and First World War, 182, 183, 184–5, 194,
    285
  government of, 180, 185, 195, 213
Salerno, 32, 69, 303, 305, 306
Salesians (religious order), 82
Salò, Republic of (1943–45), 308–10, 311, 315,
    318
Salvatorelli, Luigi, 223, 294
Salvemini, Gaetano, 3, 5, 63, 175, 185, 222,
    250, 252
Salzburg, 284
San Basilio (Rome), 274
San Giuliano, Antonio di, 153, 181, 182
San Lorenzo, Basilica of (Rome), 298
Sanluri, 71
San Marino, Republic of, 343–4
Sant'Elia, Antonio, 174
Sanusi, 281
Saraceno, Pasquale, 133
Saragat, Giuseppe, 324, 326
Sarajevo, 181
Sardinia, 64, 70, 71, 87, 144, 162, 212, 304,
    342, 369, 400, 412
  agriculture in, 14, 128, 193, 354–5
  industry in, 358, 359

population of, 33, 162, 362
regional government, 322, 390, 392
Sarrocchi, Gino, 227, 228, 230
Sassari, 39
Sassuolo, 396
Savona, 123–4
Savoy, 46, 79
  House of, 49, 50, 51, 62, 79, 84, 86, 99, 125,
    186, 304, 319
  see also king, powers of
Scalfari, Eugenio, 406
Scalfaro, Oscar, 424
Scarfoglio, Carlo and Paolo, 231
Scelba, Mario, 256, 294
Schio, 23
schools, 35–9, 51, 76, 79, 80, 81, 82, 86, 113,
    129, 132, 163, 165, 167, 169–71, 177, 194,
    223, 245–6, 252–3, 254, 256, 258, 263, 272,
    276–8, 292, 293, 360, 361, 362, 363, 364,
    368, 370, 372, 374, 380, 389, 390, 393, 413,
    426
  primary, 36–8, 40, 64, 138, 169–70, 245–6,
    252–3, 277, 278, 364, 365
  take-over by State, 131, 139, 169–70
  private (clerical), 36, 38, 39, 83, 170, 254,
    256, 278, 380
  religious instruction in, 37, 82, 157, 223, 255,
    405
  secondary, 38–9, 40, 170–1, 246, 256, 276–7,
    278, 365, 381
    complementare, 277, 278
    ginnasio, 38, 39, 170, 276–7, 278
    istituti magistrali, 277, 278, 365
    junior, 278, 365
    liceo, 38, 39, 170, 171, 246, 276–7, 278, 365
    scuola normale, 38, 170
    seminaries, 39, 148, 149, 254, 371
    technical institute, 38, 39, 170, 171, 276–7,
      278, 365
    technical school, 38, 39, 170, 171, 276–7,
      278
Sciascia, Leonardo, 368
Scoccimarro, Mauro, 312
Scorza, Carlo, 292
Scotland, 35, 125
scuola normale, see schools, secondary
Secchia, Pietro, 312
Secolo, Il, 40, 80, 113
Second World War, 9, 94, 244, 273, 274,
    284–8, 288–99, 302–5, 306, 308–16, 317,
    323, 362, 385
Secret Intelligence Service, 385
Segni, Mario, 412, 420, 421, 423
Segrate, 386
Sella, Quintino, 61, 63

Semeria, Giovanni, 197

'*Sempre Pronti!*', 233

Senate,
  in Liberal period (1871–1922), 65, 98, 99
  in Fascist regime (1922–43), 215, 225, 226, 231, 239, 264
  since Second World War, 320, 333, 420, 422, 426n4
  President of, 44, 100, 116

Senators, 60, 65, 197, 231, 239, 277, 320, 415, 419

Senegal, 402

Senise, Carmine, 232, 296

Serbia, 154, 181

Sereni, Emilio, 16

Serpieri, Arrigo, 128

Serrati, Giacinto, 173, 199, 212, 213

servants, domestic, 22, 34, 83, 127, 162, 163, 165, 258, 272, 276, 402

Sesto Fiorentino, 8

Sesto San Giovanni, 142

Sforza, Carlo, 252, 293, 297, 298, 305, 306, 307, 323

share-croppers, 13, 14, 15, 19, 33–4, 129, 130, 209, 216, 271, 330, 354, 370, 410
  families of, 13, 33–4, 161, 162, 193, 354, 364

Shaw, Bernard, 246

shipbuilding industry, 24, 25, 26, 49, 51, 93, 94, 95, 121, 122, 124, 133, 172, 183, 192, 206, 207, 215, 264, 265, 266, 267, 272, 348, 351, 375, 380

shipping lines, 47, 122, 124, 133, 153, 192, 265

Shoa, king of, 99

shopkeepers, 9, 22, 29, 60, 163, 193, 207, 218, 272, 276, 353, 392

Sicilian *Fasci*, 71, 101–3, 110, 214

Sicily, 9, 29, 30, 33, 83, 87, 107, 132, 290–1, 297, 299, 303, 305, 307, 339, 350, 359, 394, 400
  agriculture in, 14, 15, 17, 30, 94–5, 101, 103, 128, 129, 130, 272, 290, 354–5
  crime in, 70, 71, 88, 272, 306, 322, 342, 374, 394, 416–17
  emigration from, 103, 130, 166, 339
  local government in, 59, 60, 101, 102, 148–9, 306, 337
  political activity in, 64, 74, 87, 107, 149, 290–1, 292, 304, 330, 416
  regional autonomy of, 149, 292, 322, 390

SID (*Servizio Informazioni Difesa*), military intelligence service, 343, 385

Siemens, Martin (furnace), 23

Siena, 41, 330

SIFAR (*Servizio Informazioni Forze Armate*), military intelligence service, 343

Sighele, Scipio, 153

Signorie, 260

Sila, 355

silk industry, 13, 22–3, 24, 88, 94, 95, 96, 126, 128, 133, 267

Simenon, Georges, 342

Sindona, Michele, 408

Sinigaglia, Oscar, 206

Sit Siemens, 385

skiing, 244

Slav (languages), 34, 252–3, 293, 322

Slovenia, 252–3, 293, 309

Snia Viscosa (artificial fibres firm), 267

Social Christians, party, 418

Social Democrat Party (PSDI), 324, 326, 328, 329, 330, 331, 336, 392, 410, 418, 419

Social Democrat Party (SPD), of Germany, 76, 106, 109

'Social-Fascism', 252

Socialist Party (PSI) and Socialists,
  activities before 1892, 66, 72, 73, 76–8, 86, 88, 100
  foundation of (1892), 77, 106, 109–10
  1892–1900, 2, 101–3, 104, 105, 110–12, 115, 116, 117
  1900–14, 117, 136, 137–8, 141–5, 146, 148, 152, 154, 155–6, 157, 158, 159, 164, 170, 171, 175, 176, 177, 180
  and First World War, 183, 188, 195, 196, 197, 198–9, 200, 214
  1919–25, 3, 206–8, 210, 211–12, 213, 214, 215, 216, 217, 218, 219, 220, 221, 223, 224, 231, 245, 254, 261, 271
  and anti-Fascism (1926–43), 251–2, 259, 271, 293, 294, 295
  in Resistance period (1943–45), 294, 295, 306, 307, 312, 314, 315, 318
  since Second World War, 318, 319, 324, 325, 327, 328, 329, 330, 331, 332, 336, 339, 352, 353, 371, 376, 383, 387, 388, 390, 391, 392, 395, 399, 403, 409, 414, 418, 419, 421
  co-operatives of, 111, 129, 138, 142–3, 145, 198, 210
  deputies of, 78, 88, 103, 111, 112, 116, 136, 140, 141, 143, 144, 145, 155–6, 157, 198, 199, 212, 213, 319, 324, 328, 332, 381, 383, 418
  ideas of, 75–8, 89, 102, 104, 108, 110, 112, 140, 142, 143, 146–7, 150, 151, 158, 168, 175, 176, 214, 219, 246, 271, 283, 314, 318, 331, 387, 390, 391
  in local government, 93, 103, 111, 112, 138–9, 142, 144, 198, 199, 210, 211, 212, 213, 215–16, 399
  membership, 110–11, 144, 253, 331, 388

organisation of, 110–11, 144, 145, 199, 314, 330–1, 332

reformists, 111–12, 138, 143, 145, 154–6, 158, 176, 198, 199, 206–7, 211–12, 220, 221, 224, 251–2

revolutionaries, 143, 144, 145, 155–6, 180, 183, 199, 211–12, 214, 220, 251

sub-culture, 142, 144, 145, 150, 331

trade unions, 3, 72, 73, 76–7, 88, 111, 137, 138, 141–4, 145, 148, 149, 151, 152, 158, 159, 180, 198–9, 206–9, 210, 211–12, 213, 216, 217, 218, 220, 221, 231, 248, 250, 352, 354, 376, 377, 395

votes for, 111, 116, 143, 144, 157, 212, 213, 224, 325, 327, 328, 330, 388, 409–10, 418, 419

see also Avanti!; Reformist Socialist Party

Socialist Party of Italian Workers (PSLI, later PSDI), see Social Democrat Party

Social Proletarians (PSIUP), 328

Società Bancaria Italiana, 120

Soddu, Ubaldo, 296

Solidarity (in Poland), 389–90

Somalia, 100, 223, 281, 286, 322, 402

Sommaruga, Angelo, 40–1

Sondrio, 18

Sonnino, Sidney, 64, 114–15, 116, 166

as Foreign Minister (1914–19), 182, 184, 195, 196, 197, 203, 204

governments of, 132, 140

on Sicily, 17, 59, 60, 132

as Treasury Minister (1894–96), 122, 351

Sorel, Georges, 176

Sorge, Bartolomeo, 370

'sottogoverno', 133, 142–3, 318, 327, 331–2, 333, 334–7, 338–9, 347, 351–3, 356, 358, 389, 392–3, 396, 398, 403, 406, 409, 413–16, 420, 423; see also 'partyocracy'

Southern Italy, 2, 3, 20, 21, 29, 30, 69–70, 87, 107, 112, 172, 177, 186, 191, 232, 293, 317, 344, 357–60, 398–400, 402, 413, 417, 419, 426

agriculture in, 2, 14–18, 21, 25, 30, 94, 96, 128, 129, 131–3, 137, 162, 209, 210–11, 269, 270, 272, 273, 294, 336–7, 342, 354–5, 357–8, 360–1

Church in, 85, 149, 256, 370

deputies from, 60, 63, 64–5, 66, 67, 139, 140, 212, 224, 226, 320, 330, 334, 336

education in, 36–7, 39, 64, 169, 171, 278, 360, 400

emigration from, 2, 16, 32, 33, 47, 130–1, 165–7, 169, 272–3, 336–7, 340, 350–1, 360–1, 399

industry in, 2, 23–5, 28, 131–3, 137, 141,

272, 353, 357–60, 377, 379, 380, 392, 398–400, 412

local government in, 16, 33, 59–60, 65, 67, 131, 133, 149, 169, 235, 272, 305–6, 336–7, 355, 358, 360

migration northwards from, 165, 273, 360–2, 372, 376, 399, 412

Minister for, 358, 399

political activities,

in Liberal period (1871–1922), 2–3, 15–18, 47, 49, 60, 64–5, 66, 67, 71, 74–5, 80–1, 87, 101–4, 107, 131, 132, 139, 140, 148–9, 156, 197, 212, 256, 294

in Fascist period (1922–43), 218, 223, 224, 226, 237–8, 272, 292, 293, 304

since 1943, 2–3, 304, 305, 309, 311, 314, 316, 318, 319, 320, 324, 325, 330, 336–7, 338, 339, 342, 346, 360, 361, 382, 399–400, 409–10, 419, 420, 422–3, 426

population in, 20–1, 31–3, 34, 130–1, 161–2, 165–6, 167, 272–3, 275, 359, 360–1, 362–3, 382, 399, 401

'Southern question', the, 2, 17, 62, 131, 149, 232, 243, 272, 357–60, 398–400

South Tyrol, 182, 196, 203, 252–3, 281, 283, 285, 292, 303, 309, 323, 369

'Option' in, 283, 292

regional government in, 322, 390

terrorism in, 342, 344, 374, 390

see also Trentino-Alto Adige

South Yemen, 386

Soviet Union, see Russia

Spa (car firm), 288

Spadolini, Giovanni, 4, 408

Spain, 74, 75, 261, 269, 385, 400

Spanish-American War (1898), 104

Spanish Civil War (1936–39), 259, 267, 280, 282–3, 291

Spalletti Rasponi, Gabriella, 163

Spataro, Giuseppe, 294

SPD (Sozialdemokratische Partei Deutschlands), see Social Democrat Party, of Germany

Special Tribunal for the Defence of the State, 232, 233, 253, 293, 299

Spoleto, Duke of (Aimone di Savoia, later Duke of Aosta), 292, 298

sport, 41–2, 150, 167–8, 172, 243, 244, 245, 255, 276, 331, 369, 405, 426

Spriano, Paolo, 4

squads, Fascist, 215–17, 218, 219, 220, 221, 222–3, 226, 227, 230, 235, 236–7, 238, 245, 247, 254, 255, 257, 260, 263, 292, 309, 384–5

SS (*Schutzstaffel*), 232, 309
Stakhanovite movement, 269
Stalin, Josif, 290, 306, 333
Stampa, La, 154, 172, 231
St Antony's College, Oxford, 8
Starace, Achille, 238, 240, 310
State intervention in industry, 25–8, 63, 93, 120, 124, 132, 133–4, 151–2, 183, 191–3, 199–200, 242, 250, 261, 265, 267–8, 289, 326, 348, 349–53, 358–9, 379, 396, 397–8
State Participations, Ministry of, 398, 420
Statistical Office, 30
Statute of the Workers, 377
Statuto, 44–5, 113, 114–15, 116, 246
steel industry, 23, 25, 26, 27, 48, 51, 96, 119, 122–5, 129, 130, 132, 177, 183, 190–1, 192, 207, 267, 272, 282, 288, 348, 349–50, 351, 358, 359, 380, 397, 398, 399
  and Fascist movement, 183, 206, 215, 264, 266, 272, 288
  political influence of, 26, 93, 123–4, 132, 133, 177, 191–2, 206, 266
  and tariffs, 94–6, 122–3, 129, 130, 133, 206, 358
Stevens, Harold, 291
St Imier, 74
St Paul's Without-the-Walls (Rome), 82
Strada, La (film), 368, 369
Stresa, agreement of (1935), 281
strikes, 49, 54, 71–3, 78, 79, 86, 88, 89, 94, 111–12, 115, 138, 141, 143, 148, 151, 176, 207, 209, 212, 217, 234, 248–9, 251, 350, 394, 414
  agricultural, 71, 72, 74, 102, 137, 151, 210, 212
  general, 137, 145, 180, 207, 220, 225, 308, 377
  of 1904, 49, 144, 146
  of Piedmont (1920), 207
  of August 1922, 220, 221
  and 'Hot Autumn' (1969), 374, 375–7, 378
  industrial, 71, 72–3, 141, 192, 198, 207–9, 212, 217, 247, 249, 251, 264, 289, 292, 294, 295, 297, 312, 313, 350, 374, 375–7, 378, 394
  law on, 72, 102, 138, 143, 248, 320–1, 341
  and Resistance (1943–45), 292, 294, 295, 297, 308, 312, 313
students, 39–40, 170–1, 246–7, 272, 276, 277, 290, 346, 365–6, 374–5, 379
  political activities of, 73, 80, 102, 153, 183, 214, 216, 219, 246–7, 252, 255–6, 313, 366, 374–5, 376, 377, 384, 385, 386
  see also riots; universities
Studi Storici, 5–6

Sturzo, Luigi, 129, 148–9, 173, 183, 198, 211, 213, 219, 224, 225, 321
Sudan, 99, 281
Sudetenland, 283
Südtiroler Volkspartei, 322
suffrage, 63, 169, 276
  agitation for extension of, 63, 65–6, 77, 78, 79, 80, 81, 112, 143, 163, 198, 276
  reform of local (1890), 93, 106, 114
  reform of parliamentary (1882), 63, 64–5, 81, 88; (1912), 140, 156–7, 159, 169; (1918–19), 212
  see also electoral reforms; electorate; local government; proportional representation
sugar, 95, 128, 129–30, 133, 172, 192, 215, 289, 350, 357
sulphur, 2, 101, 132
Supreme Council of Defence, 344
Supreme Council of the Judiciary, 320, 321, 340, 414
Supreme Council of Labour, 138, 158
Supreme Inter-Allied Council, 189
Switzerland, 79, 281, 393
  capital exports to, 266, 352
  capital from, 24, 120, 308
  emigration to, 32, 214, 252, 360
  trade with, 22, 24
Syllabus of Errors, 82, 87
Sylos Labini, Paolo, 6, 29, 364
syndicalists,
  anarcho-, 141, 145, 154, 156, 158, 171, 180, 207, 208, 209, 212, 220
  pro-war, 183, 204, 205, 211, 214, 215, 216, 217, 242
Syndical Union, Italian (USI), 207, 220
syndicates,
  Fascist, 217–18, 222, 225, 234, 239, 242, 243, 245, 247–50, 251, 260, 263, 264, 268, 271, 289
  National Confederation of, 218, 248, 249
  see also corporations; syndicalists, pro-war

'*Tangentopoli*'(Bribesville), 414; *see* corruption
Tangiers, 303
tanks, 286, 287, 288, 299
Tanlongo, Bernardo, 98, 99
Tarabella, Aldo, 236
Taranto, 165, 272, 358
Tarchi, Angelo, 309
tariffs, 2, 24, 28, 107, 113, 121, 133, 151–2, 173, 208, 264, 345, 350, 357, 358
  of 1878, 26, 93
  of 1887, 95–6, 104, 113, 120, 121, 122–3, 124, 126, 127, 128, 129, 133

agitation for, 19, 23, 28, 94, 151
on wheat, 2, 127, 128, 269, 350
'tariff war' (1888–92), 93–6, 97, 101, 166
Tarvisio, 323
taxes, 24, 25, 32, 48–9, 64, 71, 84, 113, 131,
  166, 180, 208, 215, 218, 254, 263, 266, 267,
  268, 275, 291, 317, 351, 353, 358, 359, 360,
  378, 379, 380, 396–7, 400, 404, 405, 412,
  413, 415, 421, 423
land-, 71, 75, 94, 129, 131, 132, 133, 180, 210
local, 59, 64, 101, 210, 267
see also grist-tax; tariffs
teachers, 29, 34, 36–7, 162, 169, 170, 214, 245,
  246, 252–3, 258, 276, 277, 364, 365, 366,
  381, 395
political activities of, 60, 140, 142, 144, 214,
  218, 253, 306, 333, 337
Teatro Argentina (Rome), 80
technical schools and institutes, see schools,
  secondary
television, 367, 368, 369, 372, 384, 389, 396,
  400, 405–6, 410, 421, 423, 424, 425, 426
tenant-farmers, 13, 19, 72, 102, 128, 129, 130,
  132, 194, 209, 210, 211, 270, 271, 337
Tenda valley, 322
Teramo province, 16, 183
Terni steelworks, 26, 48, 96, 121, 123, 124, 265
terrorism, 75, 176, 233, 253, 293, 310, 311,
  316, 317, 342, 344, 374, 375, 384–7, 388,
  390, 413–14
see also squads, Fascist
Testaccio (Rome), 168
Texas Instruments, 399
textile industries, 22–3, 72, 93, 94, 95, 119,
  123, 124, 126, 127, 141, 148, 207, 264, 267,
  276, 353, 378–9, 396, 400
Thaon di Revel, Paolo, 222, 230
Thatcher, Margaret, 398, 413
Theology, Faculties of, 40
Third World, 396
Ticino, 79
Tigré, 100
Timor, 291
Tirrenia (shipping line), 265
Tito, Josip, 316, 323, 343
Tittoni, Romolo, 153
Tittoni, Tommaso, 153, 204
Tobruk, 286
Togliatti, Palmiro, 259, 306, 313, 314, 318,
  319, 321, 323, 324, 419
Toniolo, Gianni, 18
Toniolo, Giuseppe, 106
Topolino (Fiat car), 268
Torlonia, Leopoldo, 30
Tornielli, Giuseppe, 46

Tosi (firm), 28
Tosti, Luigi, 87
Toulouse, 293
Touring Club Italiano, 167
Tourism, Ministry of, 420
tourists, 122, 237, 268, 274, 350, 361, 364, 400,
  416
tourist boards, 336
trade unions,
before First World War, 71, 73, 76–7, 78, 88,
  107, 111, 137, 138, 140, 141, 145, 147,
  148, 149, 150, 151, 152, 158, 159, 163,
  165, 177
1914–25, 180, 198–9, 206–9, 210, 211–12,
  213, 216, 217, 218, 220, 221, 231, 239,
  247, 248, 250, 254
in Fascist period (1925–43), 251, 255
since Second World War, 268, 294, 320, 321,
  330, 331, 333–4, 341, 343, 346, 350, 351,
  352, 353, 354, 371, 372, 375–9, 380, 387,
  388, 389, 392, 394–5, 410, 425
'autonomous', 378, 386, 389
Catholic, 106, 107, 141, 147, 148, 150, 158,
  163, 198, 207, 209, 210, 213, 216, 218,
  247–8, 250, 254, 255, 331, 351, 371, 377,
  380, 388, 395
Communists and, 330, 333–4, 346, 352, 354,
  376, 377, 378, 388, 389, 395, 410
Socialist, 3, 72, 73, 76–7, 88, 111, 137, 138,
  141–4, 145, 148, 149, 151, 152, 158, 159,
  180, 198–9, 206–9, 210, 211–12, 213, 215,
  216, 217, 218, 220, 221, 231, 248, 250,
  352, 354, 376, 377, 395
see also labourers' leagues; strikes;
  syndicates, Fascist
trams, 120, 125, 138, 289, 337
Tranfaglia, Nicola, 260
Trapani, 102
Trappists (religious order), 82–3
'trasformismo', 62, 63, 92, 329
Treasury,
Minister of, 63, 122, 136, 192, 195, 213, 263,
  333, 339, 345, 397, 424
Ministry of, 92, 98, 122, 396, 416
Trede, Thomas, 86
Trent, 79, 182, 186, 190, 203, 204, 291
agitation for, 79, 153, 181, 182, 183, 186,
  187, 189, 196, 291
Trent and Trieste, National Association for, 153
Trentin, Silvio, 293
Trentino, 182, 186, 195, 218, 285, 321, 322,
  382, 383
Trentino-Alto Adige, 382, 383
regional government in, 322, 390
see also South Tyrol

Treviso province, 13
Tribuna, La, 154, 158, 172, 184
Tribunals, *see* courts
Tricolore, Il, 152
Trieste, 79, 174, 182, 190, 203, 204, 205, 253, 285, 323, 324, 343, 344, 375, 421
  agitation for, 79, 153, 174, 181, 182, 183, 187, 189, 196, 291
  Fascism in, 215, 253, 272
  Free Territory of, 323
Triple Alliance (1882), 46, 48, 79, 81, 95, 104, 112, 114, 150, 153, 181, 182, 184, 425
Tripoli, 47, 48, 153, 154
Tripolitania, 153, 154
Trotskyists, 314
Truman, Harry, 323, 333
Tunis, 46
Tunisia, 282, 284, 291, 414
Tupamaros, 386
Turati, Augusto, 237, 240, 250
Turati, Filippo, 81, 104, 112, 138, 143, 144, 145, 156, 158, 176, 198, 224
  and founding of Socialist Party, 109–10
Turiello, Pasquale, 70
Turin, 24, 38, 50, 53, 94, 131, 168, 232, 313, 366
  industry in, 125, 126, 158, 163, 190, 192–3, 251, 289, 294, 295, 394
  labour agitations in, 71, 158, 192–3, 207–9, 212, 289, 295, 312, 350, 378, 394
  local government in, 138, 144, 147
  political activity in, 94, 152, 172, 193, 207–8, 212, 223, 289, 294, 295, 312, 313, 366
  population of, 31, 161, 162, 163, 165, 192, 273, 289, 361
  riots in (1917), 193, 195, 197, 199
Turkey, 18, 153, 154, 155
Tuscany, 7, 9, 29, 35, 50, 70, 85, 87, 219
  agriculture in, 14, 129, 209, 215, 216, 270, 272, 354
  local government in, 59, 62, 215–16, 219, 235
  political activity in, 59, 62, 79, 87, 103, 110, 215–16, 219, 330, 392, 413
  population of, 161, 310
TV, *see* television
Tyrrhenian coast, 15, 27

Uccialli, *see* Wichale
Udine, 186, 313
Umbria, 9, 14, 209, 392
under-secretaries, 92–3, 191, 195, 197, 225, 233, 243, 249, 296
unemployment, 14–15, 32, 53, 72, 97, 166, 206, 207, 220, 250–1, 264, 268, 270, 271, 274, 324, 349, 350, 352, 353, 357, 359, 375, 376, 379, 385, 395, 400, 402, 404

see also intellectuals
Ungaretti, Giuseppe, 246
Union of Popular Education, 170
Union for Social Studies, 106
Unione Democratica Nazionale, 231, 294
Unione Zucchieri, 129
Unità, L', 231, 294, 318, 367
Unità Cattolica, L', 87
'United Freedom Front', 295, 305
United States of America (USA), 191, 394, 404, 416, 417
  economic aid from, 307, 313, 324, 345, 348, 349
  emigration to, 122, 166, 272–3, 291, 293
  foreign policy of, 196, 203, 204, 293, 297, 298, 302, 305, 306, 307, 323, 324, 331, 344, 345, 385, 409, 419, 425
  industry in, 125–6
  National Security Council, 324
  and Second World War, 284, 291, 293, 297, 298, 302–3, 304–7, 315, 318
  State Department, 293, 306
  trade with, 128, 244, 416
  see also America, continent of
universities, 38, 39–40, 80, 129, 143, 170–1, 173, 177, 182, 214, 246, 254, 272, 276, 277, 365–6, 372, 374–5, 385, 386, 405
  teachers in, 39, 45, 80, 143, 144, 171, 246, 258, 275, 333, 346, 365, 366, 375
  see also students
University of the Sacred Heart (Milan), 254
unofficial economy, *see* 'black economy'
urbanisation, 21, 31, 97, 127, 149, 163, 164–5, 192, 263, 271, 273–4, 340, 349, 360–2, 364, 374
  effects of, 149, 169, 177, 200, 274, 350, 355, 361–2, 364, 367, 368, 370, 372, 374, 381–2, 385
  see also emigration; immigration; migration
Urbino, University of, 39
Uruguay, 386
USA, *see* United States of America
USI (*Unione Sindacale Italiana*), *see* Syndical Union
USSR (Union of Soviet Socialist Republics), *see* Russia

Val d'Ossola, 312
Valle, Ondina, 276
Valle d'Aosta, 34, 322, 390
Vannutelli, Cesare, 251
Varese, 385
Vatican, 30, 150, 197, 239, 274, 291, 295, 298, 316, 381, 389
  and banks, 120–1, 153, 172, 254–5, 405, 408

and Fascist movement, 223–4, 225, 239, 241, 254–5, 258, 274, 291, 295, 298

influence since 1943, 294, 295, 298, 316, 323–4, 326, 371, 381–2, 383, 389

and Liberal State (1871–1922), 46, 66, 67, 84, 87, 100, 102, 105, 108, 115, 147, 150, 155, 208

newspaper, 146, 155, 291, 295

and Popular Party, 211, 223–4, 225, 231, 254

Radio, 291, 295

see also Church, relations with State; Lateran Pacts; Papacy; Roman Question

Vatican City, State of, 254–5, 295

Vatican Council,

First (1869–70), 86

Second (1962–65), 371

Vecchi, Ferruccio, 215

vendetta, 69, 70, 311, 316

Venetian league, 413

Veneto, 19, 20, 29, 55, 86, 87, 107, 148, 189, 289, 382

agriculture in, 13, 18, 19, 20, 76, 127, 128, 131, 166, 209

emigration from, 32, 166, 168

industry in, 23

local government in, 147, 170

political activity in, 86, 87, 107, 146, 147, 148, 209, 289, 382, 409, 412, 413, 420

population of, 161, 273

Venezia Giulia, 188, 205, 252–3, 292–3, 303, 309, 323

regional autonomy in, 322, 390

see also Trieste

Venezia Tridentina, *see* South Tyrol; Trentino

Venice, 147, 174, 175, 308, 421

Vercelli, 13

Verdi, Giuseppe, 42

Verga, Giovanni, 33

Verona, 71, 147, 197, 237, 308

Verro, Bernardino, 102

Versailles, Treaty of (1919), 204, 219, 221, 260, 280, 281

negotiations for, 203–4, 211, 219

Via della Conciliazione (Rome), 274

Via dei Fori Imperiali (Rome), 273

Via Veneto (Rome), 30

Vicenza, 13, 147, 209, 329

Victor Emmanuel II, King (1849–78), 35, 38, 45, 46, 48, 49, 87, 105

Victor Emmanuel III, King (1900–46), 49, 136, 140, 146, 156, 257

and First World War, 182, 184, 189

and March on Rome (1922), 221, 260

and Matteotti crisis (1924–25), 225–8, 230

and Fascist regime (1925–43), 230, 239, 240–1, 252, 257, 280, 281, 282, 285, 308

and fall of Mussolini (1943), 293, 294, 296–9, 304, 308

after 8 September 1943, 302, 304, 305, 306, 319

Vidussoni, Aldo, 291–2

Vienna, 184, 321

Vietnam War, 344, 345, 366, 388

Villa, Tommaso, 81, 164

Villa Boncompagni Ludovisi (Rome), 30

Villa Borghese (Rome), 67

Villa Feltrinelli (Gargnano), 308

Villani, Pasquale, 6

Villari, Pasquale, 37, 60, 114

Villari, Rosario, 5

vineyards, 13, 14, 18–19, 96, 269

Virgil, 72

Visconti, Luchino, 367

Visconti Venosta, Emilio, 46, 83

Vitali, Ornello, 9, 271

Vitrotti, Giovanni, 168

Vittorini, Elio, 246

Vittorio Veneto, 190, 200, 261

Voce, La, 175

Volksverein, 148

Volkswagen (car firm), 349

Volpe, Gioacchino, 5

Volpi di Misurata, Giuseppe, 264

Vorwärts, 111

wages, 37, 56, 71–2, 106, 151, 206, 220, 248, 249, 250–1, 264, 271, 289, 313, 339, 350, 389, 395, 397

agricultural, 19, 71, 72, 102, 130–1, 142, 166, 210, 273, 311

during Fascist regime, 248, 249, 250–1, 264, 271, 273, 289, 311, 313

index-linking of, 377–9, 395, 410

industrial, 71, 141, 149, 165, 187, 193, 198, 208, 289, 352, 376–9, 394–5

see also industrial workers; labourers; strikes; trade unions

Wales, 35

War,

Minister of, 45, 48, 187, 222, 228, 233, 286

Ministry of, 51, 233

Under-secretary of, 225, 233, 296

War Production, Ministry of, 288

Warsaw, 390

Washington, 8, 298, 303, 306, 345, 385

water, drinking, 19, 20, 129, 132, 138, 162, 165, 358, 363, 368, 369, 370, 372

Watergate, 224, 225, 227

welfare,
   in Liberal period (1871–1922), 59, 76, 82,
      86–7, 105, 113, 137–8, 140, 147, 158, 177,
      198, 200, 207
   in Fascist period (1922–43), 234, 240, 245,
      251–2, 254, 264, 272, 275, 289
   since Second World War, 2, 289, 315, 316,
      318, 322, 326, 329, 335, 336, 337, 352,
      353, 356, 360, 361, 362, 363, 370, 372,
      374, 378, 379, 390, 391, 392, 396, 399,
      400, 403–4, 405, 413, 415, 423, 424,
      426
   see also charities; local government;
      mutual-aid societies; pensions
wheat,
   battle for, 240, 269–70, 272, 275, 299, 356
   price of, 19, 96, 101, 104, 127, 269, 356
   production of, 18, 103, 127–8, 210, 269, 290,
      356, 402
   tariff on, 2, 94–5, 127, 269, 350
   see also agriculture; food; grist-tax
'White Belt', 329
Whitehall, 282
Wichale, Treaty of (1889), 99, 100
Wilson, Woodrow, 196, 199, 203, 204, 211
wine, 350
   consumption, 19, 41, 142, 162, 168–9, 187,
      356
   production, 14, 96, 128, 269, 271, 357
wine shops, 41, 42, 52, 163, 168
Wojtyla, Karol, 389, 405; *see also* John Paul II,
   Pope
Wolff, Karl, 309, 310
women, 33–4, 142, 163–4, 172, 207, 256, 276,
   329, 361, 362, 365, 375, 400–1, 422
   in agriculture, 34, 193

Catholic organisations, 86, 147, 150, 163,
   164, 198
emancipation of, 79, 80, 112, 163, 198, 276,
   364, 365, 380–1, 382, 383, 400–1, 410
Fascist organisations, 237, 276
illiteracy of, 36, 169, 278
in industry, 22, 34, 71, 113, 126–7, 137, 141,
   162, 163, 192, 276, 353
National Council of Italian, 163
wool, 22, 23, 126, 191, 266, 287
workers, *see* artisans; industrial workers;
   labourers
Workers' Party (POI), 72, 77, 78, 81, 88, 109,
   110, 112

youth,
   Catholic organisations, 107, 108, 147, 150,
      168, 245, 255–6, 313, 331, 335
   Fascist organisations, 237, 240, 243, 245,
      255, 335
   job opportunity scheme, 379, 392
   National Association for the Protection of,
      336
   Socialist organisations, 110–111, 142, 144–5
Yugoslavia, 196, 312, 315, 323
   rivalry with, 196, 204, 205, 281, 292, 322,
      323, 343, 344

Zaccagnini, Benigno, 256
Zamboni, Anteo, 231
Zanardelli, Giuseppe, 75, 108, 114, 116,
   131–2, 164
   government of, 140
Zaniboni, Tito, 231
Zara, 205
Zimmerwald, conference at (1915), 199